Personality

Harold W. Bernard
Oregon State System of Higher Education

Personality / Applying Theory

HOLBROOK PRESS, INC.   BOSTON

Photo Credits

From *Stock, Boston*

Owen Franklin, p. 2, 415; Norman Hurst, p. 19, 212, 422; Anna Kaufman Moon, p. 26, 254, 282, 308; Patricia Hollander Gross, p. 48, 228; C. Wolinsky, p. 74, 436; John Running, p. 98; Frank Siteman, p. 122; D. Patterson Jr., p. 148, 200; Franklin Wing, p. 278; Philip Jon Bailey, p. 332; Christopher Morrow, p. 350; Jeff Albertson, p. 376; Nicholas Sapieha, p. 400; Peter Vandermark, p. 166; Julia Green, p. 176.

Other

Mike Philips, p. 399

Cover design: Jeff Albertson, *Stock, Boston*

Library of Congress Catalogue Card Number: 73-93284

Contents /

Preface

The meaning of personality has been a matter of concern at least since the time of the Greek philosophers. The study of psychology, however, has a history of less than one century. Of these years, the last decade has seen psychological insights progressing by great flashes. Early psychologists (even though they lived in the twentieth century) had little accumulated knowledge with which to work. Their contributions consisted largely of raising questions and initiating further study. These early leaders were noteworthy partly because of their fruitful hypotheses and partly because the competition was limited. The authorities of today are less prominent because so many insightful scholars are capitalizing on readily available, expanding knowledge. They often arrive at much the same conclusions at about the same time.

In this book, the contributions of some of the pioneers are presented when their postulations seem to be pertinent to the contemporary scene. However, history is not enough; attention is also devoted to personality theories that are now in the active process of formulation. This presentation is not confined to an examination of psychological theories. Sociologists, anthropologists, historians, and statesmen also have perceptions worthy of examination. The maturing personality is a concern of men and women in all walks of life. Hence, the book, in considering many views, must be characterized as being interdisciplinary.

The study of personality shares with other academic disciplines the legacy of "knowledge explosion." One way of indicating the phenomenon of knowledge explosion is the statement that ninety percent of the scientists the world has ever known are alive today. This places the study of personality in an extremely dynamic perspective. It might be that some of the prominent personality theorists were prominent because there were so few of them. Today, with so many scientists alive, it is difficult to discern who will continue to be outstanding when today becomes history. With so many hypotheses with which to work, with the *zeitgeist* of the time open to new insights, it may be that the prominent theorists in the next few years will be some of those who were initiated through the classes in which this book is used. In short, personality theory is not complete; it is still evolving.

The author's orientation is humanistic, or proactive, *when and if* the humanistic view is regarded as being one which recognizes: 1) the potential of the biological organism, 2) the dynamics of past experiences (or conditioning), *and* 3) the causal power of one's perception of goals for the future. Personality is caused by the push of the past *and* by the pull of the future. It is shaped by the reality of experience *and* by the accuracy, or distortions, of one's perceptions of the past, present, and prospective.

As a counselor, counselor educator, and teacher, the author's orientation also leans toward the practical. Sound theory is deemed to be highly practical because it can be translated into application to the varied life situations of unique readers. It was only in my earlier years that I would offer specifics, or panaceas, for dealing with difficult babies, introverted children, delinquent youth, and discouraged adults. Now, and herein, *approaches* to the enhancement of ego, *principles* of problem solving, *interpretations* of responsibility and freedom are offered for the reader's consideration. It is the readers who must bring the meaning to the printed page. It is they who can make personality theory applicable to their daily lives.

Personality: Applying Theory is arranged around three major themes. The first six chapters deal with basic considerations, beginning with a discussion of what it is all about and what will follow. Other chapters in Part One deal with genetic, socioeconomic, and family influences on personality, and then with cross-cultural influences. The first part ends with a perspective on what is hoped will be the practical, applied outcome—a self-actualizing person.

Part Two deals with some of the prominent theories of personality. Limitations of space prevent the presentation of other theories that would be familiar to other authors and professors. At the same time that I profess humanistic leanings, I think that contrasting views have merit. At the same time that I have taken a position, I feel that the dynamic theoretical state which we must now be in will lead to new theories in keeping with the continuing knowledge explosion.

Part Three considers personality theories in terms of their application to human relations and communications, occupations, conformity and divergency, problems of adjustment and maladjustment. The latter leads to the discussion of treatment of nonadjustive behaviors. This part, and the book, concludes with an emphasis on how one can move toward a maturity of personality. Ways in which maturing can be promoted are not so much matters of *How to do it* as they are of challenging the reader to make the theory contribute to his *way of doing it.*

This book is addressed to the undergraduate college student, one not familiar with "psychologese." However, when technical vocabulary does serve to emphasize distinction and nuances of meaning, it is used. When used, it often is immediately explained and then used in context. At other times, a glossary lightens the vocabulary load. There has been an attempt to use the new vocabulary item again as soon as possible. In short, I have chosen not to talk down to the reader but to treat the student as a student.

It has been challenging to try to collate my experience in teaching, consulting, counseling, and writing into one book. Typist Sandi Dietrichs has been my prompt, productive, and critical helper once more as she has been in several similar endeavors. Dr. Richard Huston graciously read each chapter as it "came off the pen," offered suggestions, and tried to keep me on the track. Publishers who permitted quotations are cited, and their contribution acknowledged in footnotes.

Harold W. Bernard

Notes to the Reader /

Applying personality theory must be done by the reader. Theory cannot be applied by the author—except to and for himself. In order to encourage application of theory, I have used an unusual book format.

Each chapter is preceded by a number of learning activities. The purposes of these "pre-reading" activities are to: 1) seek the involvement of the student, 2) get him or her to take a position, 3) set a focus for the reader's deriving personal meaning from the chapter, and 4) give some idea of what is to come. The responses to these pre-reading items are neither right nor wrong. Their function is to initiate student reaction and proaction (see Glossary).

At the end of each chapter, there is a page of "follow-up" learning activities. To an extent, these will serve as a check on comprehension. To an extent, they will provide a review of important points. To an extent, they will help expand and apply the chapter. These activities will have degrees of correctness. Correctness can be checked by referring back to the chapter. It can be checked by comparing with fellow students.

The pre-reading and follow-up learning activities have another major purpose besides application. In recent years, I have been greatly impressed by the varied learning styles of quite able students, at least some of whom were not eager or able readers. I have also been impressed that for about thirty years I have not done very much about these learning styles. Each of you is asked to think about your own learning style. If you are a reader, pay attention to the "Suggested Readings." If you learn by talking, give major attention to the items: "Compare and discuss. . . ." If you learn best by doing, reflect on some of your past behaviors. If you learn best by observing, make major use of the observation activities. Hopefully, providing for the exercise of varied learning styles may make the important study of personality interesting to others besides those who read eagerly.

I have tried, in the learning activities, to keep the amount of writing to a minimum, though some students report that their learning style is writing. Many times all that is necessary is to mark your X. However, the X or the writing does commit you. Research shows, that those few minutes spent in previewing and in reviewing the chapter do more to promote lasting learning than more lengthy time periods spent in passive reading. Hopefully, the activities will bring enough satisfaction that you will be lured back for a reexamination next year—or even five years from now.

H. W. B.

/one/
Basic Considerations

1
Personality Theory and the Person

Personality is formed by culture.

LEARNING ACTIVITIES

Studies show that learning is easier and more effective when the student is involved. Recording your position on the following items will give you a better "set" for learning than if you enter "cold." It will cause you to have to defend your stance or will confirm the position you have marked.

I believe that man is basically
   good _____ bad _____ neutral _____ other _____

I believe that my personality is mostly determined by
   heredity _____ family _____ culture _____ education _____
   my own choice _____ physical structure _____ health _____
   other, or comments:_____
   _____
   _____
   _____
   _____

I think mankind's greatest asset is his ability to
   grasp and use tools _____ ability to talk _____
   ability to think _____ to record past events _____
   walk upright _____ other _____
   _____
   _____
   _____

I am taking this course because
   it is required _____ it was recommended _____
   I needed to fill my schedule _____
   I thought it would yield personal benefits _____
   Other _____
   _____

Of what significance is the reason you checked in the above
item? _____
   _____
   _____
   _____
   _____

Students often remark that they hope that a certain course will be practical; educational critics and campus protestors refer to a "relevant" curriculum. These references seem to mean, "We want someone to tell us how to resolve some of the dilemmas that we face in life and work." The professor is caught in the double bind. He knows that presenting theory is the most practical approach he could use, but he knows that pleasing his students means using a "how to do it yourself" (often called the "cook book") approach.

An attempt is made in this chapter to show that personality *theory is* the best approach to understanding self and others that can be used. Individual case studies of success or failure in life, love, or work—the areas of personality concern that will be the foci of this book—are interesting and informative; but, a case is not directly applicable to the needs of Tom and Dick and the reader. Theory is the really practical approach because it is the **construct*** that is most likely to embrace the multitude of factors that relate to the time, place, and circumstance in which personality functions. The "how to do it" may have much practicality if we are concerned with making a Sioux Indian an effective person in the Sioux culture of 1850; or with producing an effective person in the business world of the United States in the 1970's. However, not all persons want to, or need to, become proficient Sioux or businessmen. For example, some readers study this text because it is required. Others hope to gain insights into the dynamics of their own personalities. Some study this text because they want to understand and live more effectively with others. Hopefully, the theories presented here will be inclusive enough to encompass the time, place, and circumstance of many lives.

BASIC CONSIDERATIONS

Concepts of personality

Definitions often result in misleading simplification. For this reason some authorities believe that a definition of personality should appear at the end, rather than at the beginning, of one's study of it (Bischof, 1964, p. 9). On the other hand, this cautious scientific approach would leave the question of just what one is studying so open that it could be bewildering.

To the man-on-the-street, personality means **"it"**—the characteristics of an individual that make him or her easy to know and worth knowing. One who has **"it"** possesses **charismatic** qualities and

*Words appearing in bold face type are defined or discussed in the glossary.

talents. Such a person does, indeed, have personality. So too does the withdrawn, seclusive person. So too does the vicious, antisocial inmate of a prison or mental hospital. In a sense, personality is everything a person is, has, and does. A textbook in educational psychology or principles of sociology, or one dealing with historical characters is about personality. One's personal philosophy of life considers what one is and what he might become. According to Karl Menninger, personality:

> . . . has been used to describe almost anything from the attributes of the soul to those of a new talcum powder. As I shall use it, it means the individual as a whole, his height and weight and loves and hates and blood pressure and reflexes; his smiles and hopes and bowed legs and enlarged tonsils. It means all that anyone is and all that he is trying to become.[1]

Although the foregoing appears to be inclusive, a vital factor is omitted. That factor is the view of the person that is taken by others. The aggressive, combative, authority-challenging, *and effective* personality of the leader of a ghetto gang is not favorably viewed by a teacher attempting to conduct a classroom. (A moral is involved here: One who defines the personality of another is, in fact, revealing a part of himself.) Benedict (1934) and Mead (1935) revealed clearly, through anthropological studies, that the kind of personality prized in one culture may be quite different from that admired, and hence fostered, in another. The Zuni Indians of New Mexico, at least prior to "contamination" by dominant American culture, admired the sober, moderate, self-effacing individual. The Kwakiutls of Canada respected the individual who was competitive, pretentious, and bold. It takes a different kind of personality to survive and to belong in the lower-lower class of unemployed and unemployable in the United States than is demanded by the upper-upper class of landed aristocrats—"the Four Hundred." Hence, in addition to defining personality as the sum total of one's behaviors, attitudes, intelligences, physical characteristics and his loves, hopes, and hates in terms of what one is, has been, and will be, one must add: ". . . *as he is viewed by* fellowmen in his culture."

From an unabridged dictionary theorists have selected 18,000 words that could be used to analyze and discuss personality. This list was combined and reduced to 4,500 trait names, that were further reduced to 171 clusters of synonyms. Finally the synonyms were condensed into five major factors—extroversion, agreeableness, conscientiousness, emotional stability, and culture (Janis *et al.*, 1969, p. 660).

The problem of defining personality is no less difficult than is the

---

[1]Karl A. Menninger, *The Human Mind*, 3d ed. (New York: Alfred A. Knopf, Inc., 1953), p. 23.

classification of words used to describe its aspects. There are at least 50 definitions (Guilford, 1959) and some of those would probably be modified in terms of recent discoveries about *DNA*, *RNA*, brain chemistry, and processes of enculturation. Stagner (1961) states that personality is defined in terms of two broad categories; i.e., in terms of the stimulus value a person has on others and in terms of response or behavior. He does not, however, believe that these two orientations are contradictory.

An aspect of personality that is implicit in the varied definitions is the matter of individual uniqueness. Because uniqueness is a pervasive theme in this book, the definition used is: Personality is the unique and rather predictable patterns of orientation and response to biological, psychological, and social factors that influence one's impact on others. Hence, the study of personality must include heredity and prenatal factors. It includes physical and social environmental influences as they are seen by the individual and give direction to his life, love, and work.

The place of theory

Humans have an inclination to group and to classify. For example, they speak of animals, fowls, and reptiles; blacks, whites, and others. This concern for cataloging is seen in all scientific fields. Classifications systems or categorizations for personality will appear occasionally throughout this book. Some examples are introverts, extroverts, and ambiverts; convergent, divergent, and dormant personalities; esthenic, pyknic, athletic, and dysplastic types. A major **concomitant** problem is the matter of how to get away from the generalizations of classification and back to the unique case of the individual.

Theory is man's attempt to reduce the complexities of many related phenomena in a given area to a grouping that is small enough in size or numbers to be handled conceptually. Thus, theory in personality attempts to cut down to size the 18,000 words descriptive of personality. Theory condenses the 171 clusters into an understanding of personality that is explicable to others. Theories in the physical and social sciences are designed:

> . . . to reduce the overwhelming diversity and complexity of reality to simple theoretical regularities so that events can be understood, and, if possible, the future predicted on the basis of the laws discovered. Two steps are generally considered necessary in the evolution of a theory. First, observations of the facts or phenomena to be described, and, second, the formulation of a theory that will cover all the observed facts. It can then be tested by using it for the purposes of prediction: as long as it gives valid results, it remains useful. However, if exceptions are found, it should be modified so that it will cover all the observed facts.[2]

---

[2]Robert Theobald, *The Challenge of Abundance* (New York: Mentor Books, New American Library of World Literature, Inc., 1961), p. 40.

Theory, like a seacoast chart in sailing, tells one what to look for, conditions to expect, and how to get to a destination via the shortest course. Those students who call for the practical instead of the "merely" theoretical are acting on a premise, or theory, of behavior that is intuitive and implicit; for example, "Don't cross your bridges until you come to them," or "We'll just play it by ear."

Theories have value, even when they are not valid, because they stimulate investigation and attempts to verify or repudiate. Thus, Cesare Lombroso (1836–1909), who is credited with being the founder of early criminology, postulated that criminals could be identified by means of facial characteristics—low forehead and protruding brows, thick lips, and large ears. He believed that such a person was atavistic—reverting to an earlier type of primitive man. He believed, too, that genius was a type of degeneracy. His theoretical postulations have stimulated much research; and the contemporary theories of Sheldon and others (1942, 1954) that relate personality to body build are still contending for respectful consideration. Some people still cling to the notion of genius as degeneracy, and can, of course, point out some bizarre examples of the twisted lives of geniuses.

Theory has practical value because it serves to harmonize and direct the various forces that influence one's life. The theory that one formulates, or accepts, of life and learning helps to shape his daily behavior. If, for instance, one theorizes that he is what he is because of childhood experiences, he then needs to take no responsibility for his choices and decisions today. Skinner (1971), as will be shown later in some detail, theorizes that man really has no freedom of choice. Freud (1943) gave much weight to the idea that one could either credit or discredit his mother for his current life style.

Because the reader will be evaluating various personality theories, deciding which is relatively more respectable or acceptable, the following description of "good" theory is pertinent. A good theory may be said to have five formal attributes:

A good theory is clear in that there is agreement among its general principles (philosophy), and agreement of its consequences with observation (science). It is clear in that it is communicable, and those who read it will understand what is meant. It is an easily read map.

A good theory is comprehensive in that it has scope and accounts for much behavior. It will explain what happens to many people in many situations. It approaches all-purpose utility.

A good theory is explicit, that is, it has precision. While it may make use of evocative statements such as "psychological warmth," and "fully functioning," these concepts will be translatable into **denotative** statements so that they can be checked against clear referents in the real world (Frank, 1949, p. 27). It is not the mystical or obscure talk of the theorist that spoils his theory, but it is his failure to translate his poetry into science.

A good theory is parsimonious and does not overexplain phenomena. A theory that explains a given event five different ways is likely not to explain it at all.

Finally, *a good theory generates useful research*. Some theories may stand for decades untested because they lack this formal attribute. Other theories more **heuristic** may be excellent theories simply because they stimulate much research which itself proves them false.[3]

There are five ways of testing personality theories and their assumptions:

- *Cross cultural.* Traits or behaviors that are thought to be universal may, through studying another human community, be found to be weak or absent; for example, in Mangaia sexual intercourse begins at age 12 to 14, and with careful instruction and supervised practice (Marshall, 1971). In contrast, in an island community in Ireland women marry at an average age of 25 and men at an average age of 36 and are celibate and uninstructed (Messenger, 1971). Freudian assumptions relating to sex anxiety, developed in upper class European culture, do not survive cross-cultural testing, although parts of Freudian theory relating to **polarity** and conflict remain as fruitful hypotheses.

- *Developmental.* Personality is viewed as being a function of heredity, environment, and growth processes. One is born with predispositions (*e.g.*, thick- or thin-skinned) and learns his behavior from the environment in which he lives. Case studies, experimental procedures, or cross-cultural comparisons may be used to test the theory.

- *Clinical.* Formulation or testing of theory is accomplished from the study of clients in a **therapeutic** setting. Many of the data on personality in the early 1900's (*e.g.*, Freud's psychoanalysis) were clinically derived. Much of personality study has been based on abnormality but recently clinical data have been buttressed by the emphasis that Maslow (1954, 1972) placed on the study of the unusually healthy person.

- *Experimental.* Matched subjects (having similar measured characteristics) are placed in a controlled situation to see which variable conditions (drugs, hormones, or methods of treatment) result in changed behaviors. An example, so frequently cited that it might be called a classical study, is that of the effect of democratic, autocratic, or laissez-faire leaders on the aggressive behaviors of 12-year-old boys (Lewin, *et al.*, 1939).

- *Quantitative.* Quantitative studies of personality are of questionable merit. Unlike the natural sciences, measurement of physical properties in the behavioral sciences has vague and tenuous value. The brain can be weighed but intelligence cannot

[3]Buford Stefflre, *Theories of Counseling* (New York: McGraw-Hill Book Company, 1965), pp. 9–10.

be—at least not in the same exacting terms. Adrenalin can be measured. Determination or hostility cannot be measured. Quantitative measures, such as data from personality inventories, are used to provide supplementary evidence to clinical, developmental, cross-cultural, or experimental data. Hence, "questionable merit" does not mean without merit.

The ultimate aim of good personality theory is to predict and control behavior prior to its happening. To some, this means directing, or programing, the lives of children, students, and adults. To others, prediction and control mean being able to foresee, in general terms, the probable consequences of (1) various kinds of human potentials, (2) functioning in debilitating or envigorating environments, and (3) the **idiosyncratic** perceptions of a responsive, sentient, and unique person.

CONCEPTIONS OF MAN

Man, as a biological organism, is not particularly strong or speedy. He is not equipped with claws or fangs that would seem to fit him for the so-called battle for survival. Yet his survival is indisputable. From wherever the cradle of humanity might have been, mankind has spread to the highest peaks and is now exploring the possibility of living under the sea. Man lives and thrives in the tropics and in the frigid zones. He can eat a wide range of organic materials. He can live in crowded cities or in isolated mountains. Huxley (1956) says that man is the toughest of all mammalian creatures. In addition to living everywhere and eating omnivorously, he can tolerate frustration, excitement, and terror in amounts that would drive other animals into frenzy or collapse.

Uniqueness of man

Quite another view of man is taken by Eiseley (1971). He thinks that man's survival capacity resides in his tenderness. Human babies, having no ready-made instinctual responses, are born weak and helpless. They remain completely helpless for about a year (the period of infancy). Then for another 12 to 20 years (childhood and adolescence) they progress slowly to strength and independence. Furthermore, the period of dependence steadily grows longer as technology progresses. If it were not for tenderness—other-concern, protection, and love—during this developing period, mankind would not survive.

Some species survive (flies, rats, lemmings) because of their prolific rate of reproduction. The lower a creature is on the phylogenetic scale the more abundantly it must reproduce in order to survive. Mankind survives,[4] say some demographic authorities, because of the

---

[4]In 1650, about 300 years ago, world population was calculated to be about 500,000,000. Currently world population is in excess of 3,400,000,000. Robert Bierstedt, *The Social Order*, 3d ed. (New York: McGraw-Hill Book Company, 1970), p. 105.

continuousness and efficiency of reproductive processes. Other high-level animals have a mating season and females have a period of **estrus**. Lest Women's Liberation proponents become concerned about blame placing, let it be said that male mammals have a parallel season of **rut**. In normal human animals the sexual season is continuous. Females, from the time of first menstruation to beyond the time of menopause, are continuously sexually receptive. Human males are continuously responsive to or aggressive about sexual urges. Because of tenderness toward, and protection of, babies and because one disease after another is controlled, thus lengthening the life span, population is increasing at an accelerating rate. Hence, overbreeding and over-population have come to be man's greatest threat to survival (Asimov, 1972). And, at this point, one faces a question of personality theory that can be adapted to numerous contexts: Will or can man choose *to control* or *be controlled* by _____ (love-hostility, others-self, past events-dreams of the future), and in this context, sex or logic?

Man's uniqueness may be attributed to 1) his anatomical ability to oppose thumb and fingers, 2) his capacity for the development of language, and 3) his ability to think abstractly.

Opposition of thumb and fingers has allowed and prompted man to be a tool-using creature. With tools he has increased his speed, strength, and scope. From a simple club or cutting stone he has evolved the power to leap to the moon and return.

The development of language has enabled man to share ideas with his contemporaries. He is able to profit from the ideas of his ancestors. Through linguistic manipulations he can solve problems before they become acute. In the context of personality, some authorities postulate that personality deviation is largely an inability to communicate clearly.

The ability to think about things in their absence—to remember the past and postulate the future—is the human attribute most frequently and enthusiastically eulogized. The ability to use symbols to condense ideas has solved many problems, but it seems that current problems are so great that nothing parallel could have happened previously. The pervasive question in personality theory is whether man is just a high-level animal responsive to conditioning or whether he is a thinking person.

Reactive man   The prevailing psychological orientation in our culture is the stimulus-response (*S–R*) emphasis. Many repeats, variations, and extrapolations of Pavlov's conditioned response experiments on salivation in dogs have been made on human subjects. These human and animal subjects can be made to salivate, perspire, blink, jump, experience internal changes, and have emotions as the result of simultaneously presenting an adequate stimulus and a neutral one. For example, one can be made to blink at the sound of a tuning fork or be made to experience fear at the sight of purple. People sometimes remark, "I wonder what made me do that." They are searching for some past event that has conditioned them to respond in a **stereotyped** manner.

The prevailing psychology of learning in our schools is connectionism—a behavioristically oriented explanation expressed in three major and five minor "laws of learning." Briefly, the major laws are: 1) *Exercise:* The more frequently a modifiable connection is made between a situation and a response the stronger the connection will be. 2) *Effect:* A modifiable connection between a stimulus and a response is strengthened if it results in satisfaction, and it is weakened if it results in annoyance (this law later was modified by its originator). 3) *Readiness:* When a modifiable connection is ready to act, to do so is satisfying; when it is not ready to act, to do so is dissatisfying (Thorndike, 1924, 1932). Thus, learning is viewed as the formation of bonds between stimuli and responses. Physiologically, these bonds are the synapses between nerves in the organic system. Character and personality are built into the individual in accordance with the conditions he has experienced and the connections that have been formed: for example, "Bring up a child in the way you would have him become and even when he is a man he will not depart therefrom."

Burrus F. Skinner is the current popular and persuasive proponent of behaviorism. He has described a Utopian community in which children are carefully and systematically rewarded for approved behavior. Punishment is unnecessary because experimental thrusts of behavior are dropped when they are not reinforced by being noticed, by scolding, or spanking. Punishment is positive, reinforcing feedback that one is not being ignored (Skinner, 1948). It is his belief that man brings misery and frustration to himself as the result of believing that he has choice and freedom (Skinner, 1971). When we accept the fact that one can and must be conditioned to behave in certain ways, then we can get on with the job of establishing those conditioning circumstances that lead to approved and effective behavior. Then we can concentrate on rewarding those behaviors that we wish to have continued. When inappropriate circumstances have resulted in maladjustive behavior, the promise of relief to the individual and to society resides in behavioral counseling. This is a procedure that involves rewarding—by praise, a glance, a touch—the small steps that are taken in the direction of improved behavior (Krumboltz, 1972).

Proactive man

At the other end from the behavioristic conceptual scheme is a polar opposite view of man, in which man himself is a part of the interactional milieu. Man is *not*, in the proactive view, a sort of machine, or automaton, that reacts in a predictable and specific manner to internal and external environment; rather, by virtue of his unique perceptions and considered reactions, he can choose, and dream, and aspire, and set his own goals of behavior. Thus, the future, as well as the past, become a part of the influences that shape present behavior. Proactive psychology—drawing upon the prefix, pro, meaning forward—may be said to be propelling, progressing, provocative.

> The concept of being-in-becoming lends to proactive psychology its dynamic character. In Freudian psychodynamics, man "grows" only in the very restricted sense that his present self is but a repetition of what he has been. Proactive psychology affirms that man changes as he moves in the direction of what he intends to become. It further holds that, although man is a part-product of his past, he is also an expanding self modified by his future. From this point of view, the true mark of the healthy man is a high degree of self-inductiveness. He does not linger in the past but dwells firmly in a foreworld. The ideals and values which have no acceptable place in conventional psychology, are the life and substance of the healthy individual. Through ideals and values we can observe the individual in the process of becoming a person. Without ideals man is not fully human, for the essence of humanness is the capacity to envision and actualize ideal ends. Proactive psychology asserts that each individual, in the light of his own experience and knowledge chooses to create the life that he aspires to achieve. His personality is described in his self-affirmation: "I am what I will do."[5]

The proactive conception of man places much emphasis on choice. One can, for instance, decide not to allow the horn-honking, tail-gating car driver to evoke an angry response. One does not *have* to respond in kind to offensive personalities; he does not *have* to let others control him.

Philosophers and psychologists have long recognized the forward-looking role and uniqueness of man; for instance, Goethe, "He who strives ever forward, Him can we save." Woodworth (1918) was among the first specifically to seek recognition of the organism as an interacting variable to be added to the S—R symbolization. His conception was S—O—$R:$ stimulus acting on organism, to produce a response. Here the organism mediates the stimulus and produces a response. The proactive view would add to this the idea that the future (F) represents a pull (goal attraction), in addition to the push or thrust of the individual:

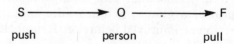

Now, with the future as an attraction, the individual is changed into a seeking rather than a merely submissive organism, and the arrows become reversible or two-way:

[5]Hubert Bonner, *On Being Mindful of Man* (Boston: Houghton Mifflin Company, 1965), p. 7.

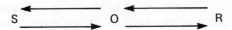

One cannot react to everything in the world, so the matter of perception, what one will give attention to, is also a concern. A young person with impaired vision can focus on his handicap. He can look forward to his disability payments, or, he can develop his remaining talents and find some way to be self-sufficient, proud, and to create for himself. He does this through mastery of the inescapable obstacles, a mastery of life. The symbol becomes:

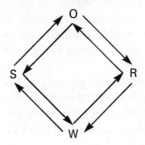

The arrows are all two-way. One can start where he wishes. For example, the organism selects from the total world those stimuli that have relevance for him. The stimuli produce, through the organism, certain kinds of responses. Once those responses have been made, the world and the organism have altered a little, and the person's selections of, and responses to, stimuli are changed. The shift has been made from a mechanistic conception of personality to a dynamic, ever-changing postulation. "Dynamic psychology" was the name given to the psychology promulgated by Woodworth.

There were other psychologists who sought to highlight the dynamic role of the individual. James (1899, pp. 77–78) referring to the drunken Rip Van Winkle, the legendary long-sleeper, said that Rip might not count the next drink; but it was being counted nonetheless; down among the nerve cells and fibres the moral lapse was being counted, to be stored up and used against the next temptation. James said that *each of us is spinning his own fate*, good or evil, and never to be undone. Kelly states the issue in equally colorful words:

> . . . We take the stand that there are always some alternative constructions available to choose among in dealing with the world. No one needs to paint himself into a corner; no one needs to be completely hemmed in by circumstances; no one needs to be the victim of his biography. We call this philosophical position *constructive alternativism*.[6]

[6]George A. Kelly, *The Psychology of Personal Constructs, I. A Theory of Personality* (New York: W. W. Norton & Company, Inc., 1955), p. 15.

There are many varieties of behaviorism, of psychoanalytic theories, and of proactive orientations. Other names for what has been called proactive in the foregoing discussion are phenomenology (Combs and Snygg, 1959), humanistic psychology (Maslow, 1972), existentialism (May, 1969), and third-force (Bruce, 1966). In discussing "directional growth," Rogers (1961) and Menninger (*et al.*, 1963) in speaking of **heterostasis,** are giving the human organism credit for an *en*active role (organism initiated) in contrast to a *re*active role in behavior.

In this introductory treatment only two of the more divergent views of the nature of human personality have been presented. More details are supplied in subsequent chapters. Basically, the contention of proactive psychology is that man should be viewed in terms of not only what he now is, but also in terms of what he can become.

Reconciliation of conceptions of man

It is not necessary for one to accept one point of view and repudiate the others. Various viewpoints regarding the causes and study of behavior have been enthusiastically, and even zealously, presented. Each viewpoint has left its impact as a facet of light being thrown on the total field of psychology.

Bradford Titchener left the legacy of introspection—looking at what happens within oneself—as a method of study. This is what one is asked to do in **basic encounter** and **inter-personal process** groups. William James formulated hypotheses on how the nervous system works and emphasized psychology in everyday life. He finally condemned psychology as a "nasty little science" because it examined details of psychology too minutely. Psychology failed to embrace the complexity and totality of behavior. He finally turned to philosophy, as did John Dewey, and to some extent E. L. Thorndike and Abraham Maslow.

James A. Angell and John Dewey were proponents of functionalism—psychology applied to education, child growth, animal behavior, individual differences, and mental development. Robert S. Woodworth may be identified as a proponent of dynamic psychology—in which the organism selectively perceives and behaves both reactively and enactively.

John B. Watson believed that psychology could be reduced to a study of conditioning and wanted no part of such abstractions as will, desire, and ambition. B. F. Skinner is currently making such an emphasis with regard to the "myths" of freedom and choice.

Gestalt psychology (capitalized because it is a German noun) was formulated by Max Wertheimer, Wolfgang Kohler, and Kurt Koffka, and emphasized that it was the totality of figure-ground plus perceptual insight that gave psychological phenomena significance. Time, place, circumstances, persons, purpose, and past must be evaluated if behavior is to be understood.

Psychoanalysis had several proponents, the outstanding ones being Sigmund Freud, Carl Jung, and Alfred Adler. All of them emphasized the polar nature of behavior, with one tendency striving for first place in personality against another. Freud stressed love-hate, Ego-Id, self-other. The importance of childhood and infancy in forming adult personality constitutes a major contribution. Jung stressed such polarities as the conscious versus the unconscious, introversion versus extroversion, sublimation versus suppression. All these concepts are part of today's explanations of personality. Adler, known as the founder of individual psychology, perceived the individual as "instinctively" striving for power. He left some concepts that are current: feelings of inferiority or superiority, style of life, compensation, and creative self.

Humanistic psychology seems to have appeared as the result of a converging of thought by many persons at about the same time. In some words or another, the proponents are saying that man has an inborn urge to grow and become. In the process, man is responsible for making the choices that will be maximally productive for both self and society.

No viewpoint is right or wrong, or correct or incorrect. The error, if any, seems to occur when an enthusiast becomes so insistent on a particular phenomenon that he develops tunnel vision and cannot see the merit of other considerations. There are more than 25,000 members in the American Psychological Association. Many are qualified but are not members. The great majority would not identify themselves as being adherents to any one point of view. Indeed, much of the wisdom of the first generations of psychologists has been incorporated into the main body of psychological terminology (introspection, feelings of inferiority, ego, Id, heterostasis, etc.). The source of the wisdom has lost its initial identity. The enthusiastic endorsement of a given orientation (*e.g.*, proactive psychology with its emphasis on responsibility and choice vs. behavioristic psychology and the outer-directed nature of personality) may lead to neglect of other views. As we think of the power of empathic mothering to mold personality trends we must not forget that, as one achieves **maturity** and the potential for logical and creative thinking, he need not continue to be the "victim of his biography." He need not carry the emotional overburdens of disadvantaged living throughout his life.

There is a place for behavioristic-connectionistic theory in the explanation of learning. Multiplication tables will not be ready references through insight into how they come to be; they must be memorized and the law of use (Thorndike) seems apropos. Drill in spelling is necessary because so much of our spelling is not phonetic or consistent—it is conventional. These facts should not blind us to the importance of the ego concept in the disposition to learn; that is, he who thinks well of himself can best utilize whatever talent and capacity he has for being an able student. If a golfer thinks he cannot drive the ball across the water hazard hole, he is quite likely to see it make a splash. However, it is practice, not faith, that causes one to "groove" his golf swing.

There is a place, too, for various methods of psychological study. The experimental, factually based data are helpful in understanding personality—adrenalin in the blood, IQ of pupils, scores on a personality inventory. The "armchair philosophers" also have their honored place. Freud, for example, combined a vivid imagination and creative intuition with laboratory and clinical data. How one views man (be he student, professor, or writer) makes a difference in how he behaves and thinks.

> The diverse views of human nature as neutral, evil, or good have important ethical and educational implications. Whichever view one accepts, it is apparent that man is a highly educable creature and that his development for good or evil can be greatly influenced by environmental conditions. But here agreement ends. If man is by nature hostile and aggressive, society through the school must shape him by exerting stringent controls; if, on the other hand, man's natural tendencies are for good, society through the school can best achieve its purposes by structuring the environment in such a way as to allow the child considerable freedom for creativity and self-development.[7]

Varied views of the nature of personality do not have equal merit. The merit, indeed, may be a very personal thing. The readers are asked to be open-minded about the theories presented here; but not so open-minded that the theories go in one ear and out the other. The student is asked to engage actively in choosing.

McDonald (1964, pp. 24–25) made some observations about the relative worth of psychological viewpoints that are pertinent to evaluating ideas about personality. Personality theory 1) should be based on scientific data, 2) must deal with social problems, 3) must account for developmental processes, 4) should lead to the practical result of controlling or influencing behavior, and 5) must have persistent concern for the uniqueness of the individual.

DIRECTING THE COURSE OF PERSONALITY
DEVELOPMENT

Views of the nature of man were considered in the first part of this chapter. In the discussion a prominent issue was that of determinism as opposed to the possibility of personal choice. This theme is now dealt with in more detail.

---

[7]Paul Bruce, "Three Forces in Psychology and Their Ethical and Educational Implications," *Educational Forum*, Vol. 30, 1966, 285.

The philosophical issue of determinism vs. choice or free will is a verbal abstraction. However, the ideas in back of the issue have significant impact on personality in daily life. The determinist believes that his personality is created by forces external to himself. He believes that for every behavior there is a cause that can be identified; and, if given enough data, that the outcome of a given situation can be predicted. Nothing, according to the determinist, happens by chance.

Primitive man, according to legend, would have adhered to a deterministic orientation—that which happened was the result of supernatural forces—spirits, demons, fate, or a god who demanded obedience and obeisance. Remnants of such views are much in evidence. Some people believe strongly in astrology—others really do not believe that their fate is written in the stars. Some say, "Astrology is an interesting parlor game, but there is no use in tempting fate." Many people speak of the will of God as though He had a predetermined plan for each of us. Others think of their "Heavenly Father" as one who (like the wise father of the adolescent) provides guidance, gives encouragement, is ever present in a time of trouble, but provides his children with freedom of choice and the autonomy to build their own life structures.

Determinism is not fatalism—the belief that one has no ability whatsoever to control his life. Fatalism implies that one's destiny was irrevocably decided at the moment of conception, or birth, or perhaps even when one's mother was fated to respond to the gleam in the eye of his father.

The natural causes of a healthy or unhealthy personality are (1) organic causes, endocrine glands, heredity, bodily constitution, and especially the structure and chemical composition of the brain; (2) psychological forces—conflict, conditioning, learning, childhood experiences, **traumatic** events, formal education, etc.;* and (3) social and cultural dynamics, such as socioeconomic class, ethnic contrasts, customs, and social conventions.

The idea of causality serves as an impetus to continued scientific investigation and data analysis. Some of the behaviors we have called lack of determination have been found to have at least some organic basis. Determination may be caused by calcium assimilation or adrenalin flow. Anxiety neuroses have been found to be at least partially attributable to amount and production of lactate (Pitts, 1969). Brain chemistry (*RNA*, enzymes, oxygen, proteins) may account for much of what we have called intelligence and deliberative functions (Krech, 1972). At the present time such things as conscience and conscious choice seem to be uniquely initiated by external causes. However, the external event or teaching *is interpreted by the individual.*

---

*"Etc." is appropriate because the listing could be continued *ad nauseam.*

The deterministic orientation is a stimulus to critical thinking. It has, for example, caused psychologists to discard, or at least minimize, the use of some vaguely defined words; for example, "instinct," "mind," "will," "soul," and other words are becoming suspect because they lack clear meaning. Current examples are "intelligence" and "neurosis." There are many kinds of intelligences and many kinds of neuroses and when each of them can be identified the generic term can be discarded. Psychology was at one time a part of philosophy. Later, the search for natural causes, rather than arguing points of view led to psychologists' breaking away from the parent discipline, philosophy. In the process it was remarked, "Psychology first lost its soul, then its consciousness, and now it is losing its mind." The words "soul" and "instinct" are now rarely found in psychological writing. Mind and consciousness are sparingly used—and more knowledge about the causes of behavior is steadily accumulating. However, some of these causes seem to be internal and individually generated.

Choice and freedom

Psychologists do not readily give up the ideas of choice, freedom, and responsibility. Current literature contains many references to these and such things as "building one's life," and the need to escape being encapsulated by technology and its demands for conformity. Adherents of the "choice" orientation believe that after one has matured to the level of being able to do **cognitive** thinking, it is possible to escape the pressures of determinism by permitting inner resources to influence behavior and personality. Rational analyses, creative and divergent thinking, feelings, and ambitions are not concrete, material things but they are forces that can be made to shape personality. The ability to think makes the difference between purely physical causation and internal influencing of future life and current behavior. There is a place for setting goals, for swimming against the current. There is a time for choosing not to let the physical circumstances of life dictate one's style of life.

The exercise of choice, the assuming of responsibility, is not a popular or easy pattern of behavior. Some wag has said, "Five per cent of the people think, ten per cent think they think, and the rest would rather die than think." Frankel (1971) refers to "the awful idea of being an individual." He says that freedom, choice, and responsibility are inseparably bound up with the matter of becoming an individual. Surely, he maintains, each of us is an individual statistic. *Real* individuality comes from one's breaking away from conventional molds and questioning whether one wants to stay with the crowd. Some will choose to establish and maintain the security of membership and fit the roles. If one breaks away and makes a great discovery or creative contribution to society he is applauded. If he merely breaks away he is condemned. ". . . there is no getting around the fact that the

In schools—or slums—one chooses what kind of person to become.

thought of being an individual, when its full force dawns on one, is a rather formidable and frightening thought" (Frankel, 1971, p. 87).

The adherents of each point of view, determinism vs. choice, are typically emphatic about the correctness of their own conviction.

> It is a dangerous act of self-delusion if one attempts to get rid of an unpleasant moral obligation by claiming that human action is the inevitable result of an inexorable law of nature. The human being who looks upon his future as already determined by fate, or the nation that believes in a prophecy which states that its decline is inexorably decreed by a law of nature, only acknowledges a lack of will power to struggle and win through.[8]

An issue parallel to choice in terms of its potential for disturbing psychological equilibrium is the matter of control (Miller, 1972). If psychology does reach its goal of scientific determinism, then it will be possible to control behavior by controlling the causes. It would be

Control

[8]M. Planck, *The New Science* (Cleveland: World Publishing Company [Meridian Books], 1959), p. 63.

possible for some monster of encompassing intellect (a là science fiction) to create and rear a race of biologically alive robots who would take satisfaction in obeying the will of their master. Proactive psychologists believe that the creative and aspiring aspects of being humanly human have been vastly underestimated. It is time to begin choosing the course of personality development and the destiny of mankind. Things do not need to just happen; they can be made to happen.

Pierson (1965), in studying the field of counseling, found that there were some professionals who professed to be determinists and some who were existentialists. Determinists insist that they are "thinkers" who, as scientists, gather causal data to solve problems. Existentialists admit that data are necessary but that some of those data must come from feelings and beliefs. Let the determinists be tough-minded; the humanists will be human-minded.

A place for values   The foregoing discussion is related to the matter of values. What does one hold to be worth pursuing? What is most worth preserving? One of the criticisms of science is that the matter of values has been neglected. Scientists have, it is claimed, created atomic power but are unconcerned about how it is used and they leave the concern of use to others. Bonner (1965, p. 126) claims that psychologists, who have greater stake in the problem of values, have barred them from systematic consideration. If values have been neglected by psychologists, the same cannot be said of our nation's founding fathers. "We hold these truths to be self-evident, that all men are created equal, that they are endowed by their Creator with certain inalienable Rights, that among these are Life, Liberty, and the pursuit of Happiness." It was "self-evident," not worth arguing, that values have a place in life.

The whole course of man's history has been concerned with values. Enjoyment of life, responsibility for the welfare of one's fellow beings, the right to have a voice in one's own affairs, love, loyalty, bravery, patriotism are all examples of the pervasiveness of values. Values are a part of the definition and development of personality.

Responsibility and autonomy are values that have been touched in the preceding materials. Other values that have intimate bearing on personality relate to matters of pleasure, satisfaction, tolerance for stress, and work and drudgery. There are some persons who lead sober, hard-working lives and, in the eyes of others, have lived a day-to-day existence that adds up to nothing. Others seem to have enjoyed life, have seen places, have been in contact with people, have lived a day-to-day existence and that, finally, seems to add up to nothing.

One of the things that concerns personality theorists is that youth of today* seem to be so pleasure oriented that they have little tolerance

---

*The adjustive technique called projection is at work in this discussion. One who finds conditions unpleasant or intolerable blames them on other people, external events, or, in this case, another generation.

for arduous work, doing something one does not want to do, or delaying immediate satisfaction for possibly greater satisfaction at a later time. Such things have been said of the younger generation for centuries—Socrates, over 2000 years ago, referred to the decline of youth morality and the lack of respect for elders and convention. Today the adult accusations refer to youth's lack of sexual restraint, avoiding difficult courses in high school and college, preference for play over work, and resort to drugs as a way to instant pleasure. Meyer (1972), in a survey of opinions about youth, found that they are accused of being characterized by rapacious **hedonism** and reluctance to assume responsibility. They are said to be materialistic and selfish. Pileggi (1969) cites *some* youth as saying "We want the world and we want it now."

The choice of values relating to pleasure, immediate satisfaction of desires, individual rights and privileges, as contrasted to accountability, are a pivotal concern in personality orientation. A few theorists seem to believe that children should study just those things that interest them (Goodman, 1968; Dennison, 1969); and a few child-rearing specialists give the impression that permissive child rearing should be practiced. Other theorists are reluctant to give youth much responsibility in inventing new social and governmental mores, because they lack experience and wisdom. Many adults are not ready to condemn the world totally just because failure has attended some efforts to implement humanitarian ideals. There is some consensus that:

> One need not be "interested" in all school subjects—interest can be developed as a *result* of study and application. Challenge is an opportunity and, when accepted, is a stimulus to personality development.
>
> One need not enjoy work—although there is a pleasant satisfaction in knowing that one has done his job and exerted an influence.
>
> One is naive about marriage—and creates a burden for himself and spouse—if he believes that there is truth in the legend, "so they were married and lived happily ever afterward." The high frequency of divorce and separation in the United States shows that this fairy-tale concept is not restricted to fairy-tales—happiness is expected.
>
> One is likely to find that an easy life, without obstacles or conflicts, does not challenge one or provide the rigorous exercise needed for optimum growth.
>
> One is suffering from a handicapping **delusion**—if he believes that *others* can reconstruct his personality. It is foolish to believe that there is a short-cut to fame and fortune. It is unwise to blame others for one's own shortcomings.
>
> One is evading reality and responsibility—if he believes that his personality was determined by hereditary structure; or by the

child-rearing practices used by his parents; or that personality is formed by age six, sixteen, or sixty.

There is much reason for believing that the best guarantee of optimum personality development resides not in gaining pleasure but in the *pursuit* of happiness. It is not the achievement of happiness but the process of achieving it that is fundamental.

THE EMPHASES OF THIS BOOK

The theoretical postulations upon which this book is based are:

Personality builds upon heredity and congenital structure *but* this potential is acted upon by the environment as perceived by a unique individual.

Personality is not formed by age two or six, or sixteen or sixty, but is in a constant process (but certainly a continuing process from prior ages) of development throughout life.

Personality has a psycho-neural-bio-chemical basis, but varied perceptions will be taken of these factors; they thus represent probabilities and possibilities rather than determinants.

Choice and responsibility are not universally prized concepts or valued opportunities; but they are essential to a healthy, dynamically adjusting personality.

Personality can best be developed when one has formed a clear idea of what man's nature is. Personality develops best when one sets one's own goals.

The position taken is that personality is the result of a convergence of many influences. Hence, attention is given to morphology and biochemistry. It is assumed that there are inborn, and sometimes rather unique, tendencies toward favored behavior, so added to physiological and mental predispositions are some of the urges emphasized by psychoanalytic theorists. Moreover, an individual's body and mind change as he grows older, so maturational theory has a considered place. There are differences in the perceptions of individuals such that they become a part of their own causal personality influences; and proactive, or humanistic, psychology is important—*especially* important because it is the part most susceptible to individual control and direction. Whatever the equipment with which one begins life it is acted upon by external environment. Thus, behavioristic viewpoints become a part of the data for relevant personality theory. What an individual perceives is influenced by his culture and socioeconomic status. These, too, must be studied as causal influences.

Personality functions in all aspects of one's life but one's life philosophy, his work, and his family life are selected for illustrative purposes. One's challenge and tasks, in this study as well as in others, are expressed in the following:

Greeting his pupils, the master asked:
   What would you learn of me?
And the reply came:
   How shall we care for our bodies?
   How shall we rear our children?
   How shall we work together?
   How shall we live with our fellowmen?
   How shall we play?
   For what ends shall we live? . . .

SUMMARY

Personality is an inclusive concept relating to what a unique individual is, has been, and can become—as viewed by fellow members of his culture. It is in a continuous process of formation and reformation but has a consistency that may be encouraging or discouraging. It is susceptible to genetic influences. It responds to the impact of external physical and internal psychological environment. It is subject to control and direction by the individual himself. Because personality is so inclusive, chaotic thinking would probably result without the formulation and testing of theoretical postulations. The position is taken in this chapter, and in the book, that sound, factually oriented theory is a most practical approach to the study of personality.

Two different conceptions of the nature of man are described. One is that man is the product of those experiences that are successful in that they are reinforced by key people or the wider culture. The contrasting view is that man has the power to think, plan, and choose. He need not be the victim of either his physical or mental constitution nor the passive reactor to environmental conditioning—he can choose to act in the face of negative feedback. These contrasting theories of man, from which personality derives, are not mutually exclusive; neither is right or wrong. Both contribute to understanding the ramifications of personality in action.

The favored viewpoint is that behavior is caused. Hence, determinism has its place in theory. Part of the causes of behavior reside in how man thinks, what he dreams, and what goals he perceives as being relevant. Hence, phenomenology, by whatever name, also has pertinence. The values the reader selects constitute the chart by which his creation of personality may be directed.

SUGGESTED READINGS

ALLPORT, GORDON W., "The Fruits of Eclecticism: Bitter or Sweet?" in *The Person in Psychology: Selected Essays*, pp. 3–27. Boston: Beacon Press, 1968.
   The author takes issue with those who claim that eclecticism is just an

evasion of critical thinking. He indicates that systematic eclecticism can involve rigorous thinking and creative postulations.

BLOS, PETER, "The Child Analyst Looks at the Young Adolescent," *Daedalus,* Vol. 100, No. 4, 961–978, 1971.

The consistency of personality occurs within a context of developmental stages. In dealing with the early adolescent, the author shows that the problems and challenges of life are different at various age levels. The author reveals a psychoanalytic orientation.

FRANKEL, CHARLES, "The Awful Idea of Being an Individual," eds. H. W. Bernard and W. C. Huckins, in *Psychosocial Dynamics of Effective Behavior,* pp. 82–90. Boston: Holbrook Press, Inc., 1971. From: Charles Frankel, *The Love of Anxiety,* New York: Harper and Row, Publishers, 1965.

It is postulated that not all men, in terms of their conditions of life, have freedom to choose; and when they do, it is sometimes a greater responsibility than they wish to assume.

KAUFMAN, WALTER, "Do You Crave a Life Without Choice?" *Psychology Today,* Vol. 6, No. 11, 78–83, 1973.

The difficulty of making a choice is illustrated by the author's list of ten ways people avoid decisions. Kaufman says the autonomous person avoids all ten methods of evasion.

STAGNER, ROSS, *Psychology of Personality,* Third Edition, pp. 3–26. New York: McGraw-Hill Book Company, 1961.

The chapter indicated, "The Scientific Study of Personality," describes the importance of the field, cites some of the numerous definitions, and outlines some of the approaches—together with the limitations—that are used to analyze and understand the subject.

STEFFLRE, BUFORD, "Function and Present Status of Counseling Theory," ed. Buford Stefflre, in *Theories of Counseling,* pp. 1–29. New York: McGraw-Hill Book Company, 1965.

Characteristics of good theory are described and then the author shows how theories are used to provide a framework for one's professional activity—in this case counseling.

FOLLOW-UP LEARNING ACTIVITIES

Why is the study of theory considered to be a practical approach to the study of personality?

_____ It applies directly to each student.

_____ It embraces the variations among individuals.

_____ Basically, everyone is the same.

_____ Theory includes its application.

(Compare your choice with that of a couple of classmates and discuss if there are different answers.)

Name three characteristics of good theory. (Check your answers with the list of the five points cited in the chapter.)

_____

_____

_____

_____

_____

On the following three items compare and discuss with classmates:

Which of the following items is cited in the text as being the focal idea of psychoanalysis?

sex _____ unconscious _____ birth order _____ polarity ____

repression _____ introversion _____

Which of the following is cited as being focal in a behavioristic interpretation of man?

will _____ love _____ reinforcement _____ thinking _____

choice _____ freedom _____

Which of the following is cited as being focal in a humanistic conception of man?

childhood _____ social status _____ extroversion _____

birth order _____ choice _____ heredity _____

List in order of importance, five values which you regard as being factors that influence your life:

1. _____   2. _____

3. _____   4. _____

Date the item above (_____) and check for changes in five years.

198, 235

2
Heredity—Building Blocks of Personality

Are personality similarities outcomes of heredity or of parental teaching?

LEARNING ACTIVITIES

Mark the following from 1 (most influenced by heredity) to 5 (least influenced by heredity):

cheerful or sour disposition _____ intelligence _____
physique and strength _____ knowledge _____
facial characteristics _____

Do you think feeblemindedness could be virtually eliminated if mentally defective persons were sterilized?

Yes _____ No _____ because _____

_____

_____

_____

_____

_____

How much of your intellectual potential would you estimate has been cultivated to its capacity?

10% _____ 25% _____ 50% _____ 75% _____ 90+% _____

(Compare and discuss your answer with that given by one or two classmates.)

Do you believe that medical scientists and/or biologists *should* be allowed to alter our genetic structure?

Yes _____ No _____ because _____

_____

_____

_____

_____

_____

Considering your answer to the above item, do you think taking drugs (vitamins, antibiotics) is basically any different from surgically altering genetic structure?

Yes _____ No _____ because _____

_____

_____

_____

_____

_____

What is the relative importance of your family and of your own choice in what kind of person you will become?

_____

_____

_____

_____

_____

_____

_____

The inheritance of personality traits might be seen in the behaviors of newborn babies. Some come into this world as "easy babies." They suck heartily, hold down their food, cry comparatively little, and sleep soundly. They are easy to handle and a joy to be with. Other infants are "hard babies." They cry much and piercingly, regurgitate their food, have runny and frequent bowel movements, bang their heads against the crib, and are not readily comforted when they are attended. Surrounded by much screaming and demanding, the mother may come to see such an infant as a messy monster. Moreover, these differences are not fully explicable in terms of prenatal care, nutrition, or quality of mothering. There seems to be an hereditary factor at work.

There is little doubt that inheritance is a matter of degree. It functions in a process of interaction with the environment. Eye color is predominantly hereditary. Tooth alignment and jaw formation are somewhat more susceptible to environment (nutrition and orthodontia). There is considerable debate about the relative importance of heredity and environment in intellectual status. It seems that personality traits, such as patriotism or achievement motivation, are predominantly the product of environment.

Personality traits seem to be much more environmental than hereditary. However, it is here postulated that the hazard for personality theory is that hereditary factors might be dismissed too readily. From the standpoint of individual personality there is the hazard that hereditary limitations will not be sufficiently taken into account.

GENERAL CONSIDERATIONS

Histories of groups

Early studies of inheritance were on plants. It was shown that there was a clear pattern of probabilities that certain characteristics would appear in successive generations. Such terms as dominant and recessive traits and unit characteristics appeared in the genetic lexicon. In humans color of eyes, having webbed fingers, hemophilia, or six toes on each foot seemed to have hereditary bases. When it comes to such things as color of hair, tallness, fatness, ambition, sociability, or optimistic or pessimistic mood, the case for heredity becomes more and more tenuous. However, the case cannot be dismissed. Spanish-Americans and Indians do, with high frequency, have brown eyes and skin but otherwise, except for the hereditary transmission of defect, which is universally noted, it becomes hard to say just what personality traits are inherited.

Some evidence indicates that character and personality have strong heritable probabilities. An early report concerned a Martin Kallikak whose union with a feebleminded girl resulted in a lineage of 480 identified persons. Of these, 143 were feebleminded, 36 were illegitimate, 33 were sexually immoral, 24 were drunkards, and three were criminals. In contrast, a study of the descendents of two prominent persons, Richard Edwards and Elizabeth Tuthill, were traced for 200 years. Among the descendants were one of the founders of Yale University, 12 college presidents, 60 professors, 60 physicians, 100 clergymen, 60 noted authors, 75 army officers, 100 lawyers, 30 judges, two senators, and a vice-president of the United States (Carroll, 1940, p. 27).*

Terman (1926) made a landmark study of gifted children—frequency of their occurrence, school records, interests, health, personality, and their ancestry. He found that there is a much greater chance of having an IQ that measures in the top 1 per cent of the population if one's parents are in the professional or semiprofessional and business group. Yet it is the skilled, semi-skilled, and common laborers who constitute the great bulk of the population. Specifically, 30 per cent of gifted children had fathers who were professionals,[1] 50 per cent had fathers who were professionals and businessmen, and 20 per cent had fathers who were in the remaining three occupational categories. Miles (1954, p. 996) reported that the professional group contributed, in terms of "proportional representation," ten times its quota of gifted children. Terman (1926) found 12 children in his study of about 1,000 subjects and their 578 families, who had fathers or grandparents who were in *Who's Who in America*. The statistical chance of a child's having a parent or grandparent in *Who's Who* is one in 2,000. Thus, the data point rather clearly to the conclusion that intellectual giftedness tends to run in families. However, this does not prove the case for inherited intelligence. In addition to having a potential for developing IQ (measured realization of potential) much attention must be given to the environmental conditions that encourage the optimum realization of that potential (Getzels and Jackson, 1963).

The controversy over the relative importance of heredity and

---

*The readers' credulity and mine may be stretched by such data. Actually, only three criminals out of 480 persons seems to be a rather admirable record. And out of all those Edwardses it would seem that there might have been three criminals—even though not indicted. It reminds one of the observation that "There are three kinds of lies: Lies, damn lies, and statistics."

[1]At the time of the study, professionals constituted about three per cent of the total population.

environment was apparently "laid to rest" in 1939. The National Society for the Study of Education published a two-volume report on *Intelligence: Its Nature and Nurture.* The conclusion was that the argument was futile. It takes both nature and nurture to develop IQ and intelligent behavior (the two are not always synonymous).

Jensen (1969), however, convinced by the accumulated evidence on the role of heredity in intelligence, reopened the question. He felt that too little attention was being given to hereditary limitations, in terms of the amount of time and money spent on compensatory education for lower class children. His conclusion, from his own and a survey of numerous other studies, was that heredity accounts for approximately 80 per cent of developed intelligence. He did, however, remark in a footnote (p. 3) that positive claims could be made for other personality characteristics. Compensatory programs of education did have reportedly favorable effects on self-confidence, **achievement motivation,** and attitudes toward school. This raises an issue that will recur throughout this book: It is a matter of what one has (heredity), what one does (response) with his potentials, and what opportunities (environment) one has that shapes one's personality.

Boyer and Walsh (1968), prior to the publication of Jensen's report, challenged the assumption that people were innately unequal in intellectual endowment. As one supporting datum for their challenge they cited the fact that our American progenitors were mainly from the lower, and impotent, classes of western Europe.

> It is very likely that it [competition] is irrelevant to genetic natural selection because of its recent origin. American immigration came largely from the lower classes, a fact which could condemn America to national inferiority if the Darwinian theory were used. In the long span of human history, most societies have relied mainly on cooperative systems or autocratic systems for their survival, and individual competition is an untypical example drawn largely from the unique conditions of Western, particularly American experience.[2]

If intelligence, and hence the capacity for learning, is so largely genetic, then the United States is destined to mediocrity because of ancestral, or hereditary, limitations. Many psychologists and anthropologists would side with Boyer and Walsh in taking hearty opposition to such a conclusion.

Twin studies   The studies of large populations such as those just cited, with their many and inevitable exceptions, provided unsatisfactory data. More exacting studies could be made with monozygotic, or identical, twins. Because the egg splits after fertilization to become separate ova, and

---

[2]William H. Boyer and Paul Walsh, "Are Children Born Unequal?" *Saturday Review,* Vol. 51, No. 42, October 19, 1968, p. 63.

evolves successively to become embryos, fetuses, and infants, the offspring have the same hereditary components. Differences in developed traits can be attributed to environmental differences. When differences do not develop it can be assumed that the trait concerned is hereditary.

Reference has been made to "hard" and "easy" babies, who show personality differences from birth. Twin studies show that smiling and/or fear responses have a high degree of concordance in time and quality in twins and are therefore deemed to be hereditary (Freedman, 1965). Because language is learned, it would seem to be an environmentally induced characteristic; but language disability is in part hereditary (Weiss, 1967). This does not mean that the hereditary potential is unresponsive to teaching and training. Gottesman (1966) produced some evidence that such personality traits as introversion-extroversion, person-thing orientation have strong hereditary tendencies. Investigators have found from their twin studies that some personality traits are relatively more susceptible to hereditary factors and others are more susceptible to learning (Cattell *et al.*, 1955; Scarr, 1965). **Coefficients of correlation** get progressively higher between IQ scores when comparing siblings, fraternal twins, and identical twins. However, a factor that contaminates the data is that environments of twins are typically more alike than is the case with siblings. Moreover, it is probable that the more twins look alike (seeming to be or being identical) the greater is the likelihood that they will be treated alike.

Kallmann and Sander (1963) studied twins who were 60 years old or older and found that traits are remarkably stable. Aged identical twins are as hard to tell apart as when they were children. They are similarly enfeebled, have similar hair patterns and wrinkles. These similarities persist despite different patterns of life (*e.g.*, western rancher and New York state doctor, English speaker vs. foreign language speaker). Twin sisters both developed senile psychoses despite significant differences in social and marital histories. Both became blind and deaf in the same month, and their deaths were five days apart. Mental test data led the investigators to conclude that intellectual potentials depend on genetic factors. The capacity for longevity may be primarily dependent on heredity.[3] The investigators conclude that it is no longer questionable that heredity and constitutional predispositions play a basic role in mental ability and in mental and physical health through the period of senescence.

Studies of twins reared apart show that later intelligence test scores show little difference but that such things as emotional stability, temperament, persistence, effort, and energy are quite different

---

[3]Philosophers are likely to remark that it is not a matter of how long one lives but how well.

(Goodenough and Tyler, 1959, p. 60). It is worth noting, however, that being reared apart does not necessarily mean a markedly different psychocultural environment. It is possible for twins to be reared by different aunts and uncles, living in different cities, but whose occupational, educational, community status, and family milieu are quite similar. It should further be noted, in the marked changes in IQ that were noted at the University of Iowa Child Welfare Research Station, that when marked differences in the environment occurred in the early (*i.e.*, three to five) years the IQ changes were greater (Wellman and Pegram, 1944). Some authorities believe that age three or four may already be too late to effect much lasting change in IQ patterns. Hunt (1968) recommends systematic attempts to stimulate mental development while the child is in the first weeks of his life.

The implications of when and how much heredity limits or prescribes personality development is well expressed in the following:

> . . . No one above the rank of imbecility need be a helpless victim of his hereditary defects, if he has any, nor can he depend on his native gifts to take him on his way unaided by his own efforts or without recourse to the advantages offered by education and training. But people are not alike, and those who wish to make the most of themselves will recognize the fact frankly and try to plan their lives in such a way that their natural abilities will be given the fullest opportunity for expression and the defects or weaknesses from which no one is entirely free will be as little of a handicap as possible. We no longer insist that the man with weak lungs shall try to brave the rigors of a New England winter; we send him to a climate that he can stand. We do not try to make an opera singer from the girl who cannot distinguish one note from another, but instead we try to find out where her talents lie and to direct her training along lines where it seems likely to be most effective. No one need be discouraged because he has weaknesses, nor should he hesitate to look his weak points squarely in the face. Whether they have a hereditary basis or not, they can often be improved if it seems worthwhile to do so; if they cannot, the thing to do is to adjust one's mode of living so that they will interfere with it as little as possible. We cannot change our genes but to a great extent, we can determine for ourselves which of them shall be the governing forces in our lives.[4]

Anastasi (1958) expresses similar thoughts in quite different words and tone. She has suggested that psychologists have been asking the wrong question in the heredity-environment phenomenon. The question that has been asked, typically, is, "How much of a given trait variance is hereditary and how much is environmental?" She asserts that the pertinent question is simply, "How?" The real concern is *how* environment works, be its role major or minor, to produce its impact on inherited potential.

[4]Florence L. Goodenough and Leona E. Tyler, *Developmental Psychology*, third edition. (New York: Appleton-Century-Crofts, Inc., 1959), p. 61.

INHERITANCE OF TRAITS

One conclusion agreed upon by investigators of genetics and personality is that the question is highly complex. Unlike the hereditary transmission of unit characteristics (such as eye color), and even though the dominant-recessive phenomenon is at work, personality traits are difficult to trace. In fact, the scales used to assess personality in various studies often indicate quite different sub-scores in spite of calling the trait by the same words.

Instability of traits

Surprising data are uncovered; for example, the inheritance of a desire to be an osteopath, physicist, or mathematician (the latter holds only for women) (Thompson, 1968). Less surprising is the conclusion that there is a heavy hereditary component in achievement need, self-acceptance, and originality. Although such psychological dimensions as **schizophrenia** and **manic-depressive** states have hereditary factors they are caused by so many genetic factors (polygenes) that prediction in individual cases is dangerous. In fact, the prediction, with the **self-fulfilling prophecy** set in motion, may be as dangerous as the possible genetic predisposition.

> . . . both heredity and environment are important in fixing the expression of traits of personality and intelligence. It is foolish to take sides on the question of which is more important *in general*, though people still do this; but it is important to develop empirical statements as to how the two sets of causes contribute separately and in interaction to the variance of any particular piece of behavior, both between and within individuals. More than just a statistical exercise is involved here. If we can assess the degree of fixity or lability of various traits, we will then have a better idea of the main directions in which we should further explore. Were it to be firmly established, for example, that aggressiveness was a relatively fixed genetic character, there would be little point in devoting much effort to an analysis of how it is affected by such environmental variables as parental discipline, frustration, sociological factors, and the like. It is undoubtedly true that for some traits, genetic influence is trivial, and for other environmental influence is trivial. Which is true in any particular case is a matter for empirical decision.[5]

Some physical characteristics are inherited; behaviors are not inherited. "He's just like his father" is likely to mean that the child has a learning style that is imitative. Perhaps his verbal-linguistic learning style—which would make him heed the wise words of his mother—is comparatively undeveloped. Humans, with learning capacity as a prominent distinguishing characteristic, inherit a potential for the development of behavior. The way that potential, whatever it may be,

Heredity as potential

[5]William R. Thompson, "Genetics and Personality," *The Study of Personality: An Interdisciplinary Appraisal*, eds. E. Norbeck, D. Price-Williams, W. M. McCord. (New York: Holt, Rinehart and Winston, Inc., 1968), p. 167.

is developed is the issue of primary concern. For the great majority of persons the hereditary potential for being much more than they are has been, according to various authorities, virtually undeveloped.

O. Spurgeon English, Lawrence Kubie, Carl Rogers (therapists), Abraham Maslow, Gardner Murphy (psychologists), and Margaret Mead (anthropologist) are among those who estimate that humans really use less than 10 per cent of their intellectual potential (Otto, 1972). Regardless of whether a correct figure is 5 or 10 per cent or 50 or 80, the question asked by Anastasi (see above), "How?" is important. Kubie, a psychiatrist, addresses himself to both "How much" and "Why" in the following:

> It is literally true that no man has ever used more than a small fragment of his brain power. In fact, even the most alert of us are never wholly awake, much less fully in action. If you think that the organ itself is small, I can assure you that you are misled by its appearance. A few years ago the pundits calculated that to duplicate the human brain with existing radio tubes, structure by structure, cell by cell, connecting fibril by connecting fibril, would require for each human being a machine almost as tall as Rockefeller Center and as large in area as the Cow Palace of San Francisco to house the millions of individual units, their cooling and replacement systems, their files, and their message-transmitting components. Another calculated that it would take the power of Niagara Falls to run it and Niagara's rushing waters to keep it from overheating. Although modern transistors and comparable electronic devices would reduce all of these dimensions a hundred-fold what each human head contains, condensed into microscopic units, remains immense. Moreover, the capacity of this machine to store energy and information, to transform information into new questions for which it finds new answers, and to transmit them exceeds the output not only of the best work-producing machines, but even of those fantastic electronic computers which can match in a day the output of many months of man-hours. *This is the brain whose latent capacities we barely use* [italics added].
>
> Why is this? It is because the brain's psychological products are so organized that almost from birth we are continuously blocked by conflicts among internal factions. This has been man's lot from the days of Adam until this moment; yet, it is specifically there that we stand on the threshold of a new kind of life. The future opens up to us the possibility that we may learn to end the waste and destructiveness of this internal impasse, freeing our enormous latent creative powers from the crippling and paralyzing domination of unconscious conflicts.[6]

The almost "continuously blocked" situation, of which Kubie speaks, may begin for an individual during his mother's pregnancy. There is higher incidence of "hard" babies born to mothers who suffered emotional crises and prolonged anxieties during pregnancy.

[6]Lawrence S. Kubie, "Hidden Brain Power," Guest Editorial, *Saturday Review*, Vol. 39, 26, October 13, 1956.

There is a low number of "hard" babies with mothers who eagerly anticipated their baby's birth. Fraiberg (1971) has gathered evidence to the effect that unless the newborn baby is cuddled, talked to, fondled, hugged, and petted—if he is neglected or repudiated—during the critical period from birth to nine months he may lose, permanently, the capacity for becoming fully human. An infant, victim of nonlove, may lose some of his potential for becoming human and is devoid of feeling. Some cases of **autism** have their origin in such neglect. As adults, Fraiberg calls such unfortunates, "hollow persons"—nothing there—no joy, grief, sorrow, guilt, or remorse.

It is herewith surmised that should an individual *healthily* survive the critical prenatal and infant stages, then physical and psychological **trauma** can more readily be assimilated. Parental death, neglect, abuse will be discomforting, but need not permanently impair one's capacity for effective personality development.

BIOCHEMISTRY OF HEREDITY

Thousands of submicroscopic units called genes are present in the fertilized egg cell. They are responsible for carrying hereditary potential from one generation to another.[7] These genes are combined in a random order that has never before occurred. Parents do not provide a new set of genes to their children. They are the carriers from their predecessors of a genetic stream that is shifted to the new individual. It is not accurate to say, "He is a chip off the old block." It is more correct to say, "He and his father are chips off the same block." The mixture of chips in the son are different because the mother, her parents, and her grandparents, have added their ever diminishing share to the genetic predispositions.

Genes

Only four years after Gregor Mendel, about 1865, presented his famous paper on genetic transmissions of traits (and left the terminological legacy of dominant, recessive, and mutant traits), Friedrich Miescher discovered a new chemical in certain cells that was called nuclein. The cellular material is now called deoxyribonucleic acid, or *DNA*. Initially, there was argument between proponents of the gene theory of transmission of traits and those who believed that heredity was the function of the *DNA* substance. Currently it is agreed that *DNA* is the specific chemical substance in the chromosome upon which gene inheritance depends. In 1944 Oswald T. Avery reported that nucleic acids actively determine the biochemical functions of cells. Two decades later, 1964, James Watson and Francis Crick worked out the idea that *DNA* strands are arranged in the form of a double helix.

DNA

[7]Note that it says potential—the potential characteristics are influenced by both intrauterine environment and postnatal environment.

The transformation of thought consists in a shift from perceiving a gene as a living unit to viewing it as part of a living system. Its potential is influenced by intrauterine environment (Stent, 1970).

RNA

There are two nucleic acids in cells, one being *DNA* and the other ribonucleic acid, or *RNA*. Both represent chains of thousands of polynucleotides in continuous linkage. In 1961 Marshall Nirenberg developed a synthetic cell in which it was revealed that RNA was the messenger which carried the code for the development of a monotonous protein (self-replicating) (Stent, 1970). The complete code of instructions for cell development is carried jointly by *DNA* and *RNA*. Together these protein molecules make up the chromosomes that compose the double helix—like two coil springs threaded together. These are located on the nucleus of the reproductive cell. *RNA* are the short extrusions from the main *DNA* thread (Figure 2.1) and are the hereditary messengers. They are bundled together in the shape of flat-topped cones—the chromosomes. There are about a hundred extrusions of *RNA* in each cone-shaped bundle, each cone is about the same length, and they are distributed at regular distances on the *DNA* strand. Different lengths of the *RNA* fibers combine to produce the graduated diameter of the chromosome. In humans there are 23 unpaired chromosomes that reside in the nucleus of the egg and sperm cells, which when united restore the 23 pairs. As the *RNA* extrusions grow, the messenger *RNA* separates from the cone and travels to the nucleus wall (the heavily lined border of Figure 2.1). As it moves, it is chopped into segments by a biological knife—an enzyme. It then passes through the nuclear wall to the cytoplasm and coils into a sphere where it is joined by another piece of *RNA* carrying its hereditary messages. Thus, new living material is formed. The hereditary influence of life depends on the self-replicating and self-varying, or mutating, strings of *DNA*. The *DNA* of a virus, for instance, is capable of reproducing complete copies of itself only when injected into a living bacterial or human cell. The properties of self-variation and self-replication inevitably lead to natural selection.

Implications of breaking the hereditary code

The excitement in the science of biology caused by the identification of *RNA* and *DNA* resides in the possibility that man may be able to control his own evolution. He does not have to wait until natural selection takes its slow course. That slow course has been made still slower by the ability of man to control environment and to make special provisions for the survival of hereditary defect. It may become possible to program evolution with computers. There are several outstanding possibilities:

- Carriers of grossly defective genes (previously known only by results) may be identified and sterilized or institutionalized. However, there are so many carriers of defective genes that this

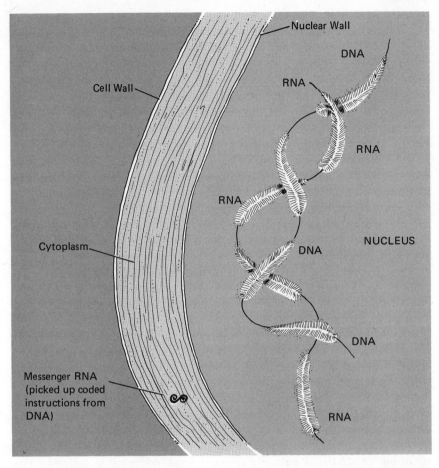

Cell Wall

Nuclear Wall

DNA

RNA

RNA

RNA

Cytoplasm

DNA

NUCLEUS

DNA

Messenger RNA (picked up coded instructions from DNA)

RNA

The code of life.   **Figure 2.1**

would be impractical. It would finally result in but small reduction of defect.

- Genetic surgery (*e.g.*, use of laser rays) may be possible in the future. This would mean reaching into the just fertilized egg and altering the defective gene—a remote possibility.
- There is a possibility of prenatal adoption—implantation of a sound embryo in the uterus of a foster mother. This has already been done in some animals.
- Glass (1969) believes that within 25 years there will be genetic clinics in which prospective marriage partners may be typed for recessive, defective, genes. They can then decide whether they wish to have their own children with high prospect for defect, remain childless, or use adoption—prenatal or postnatal.

- The study of genetics and molecular biology may have implications for learning research as the chemical action of the brain is studied (Rosenzweig and Leiman, 1968).

Lederberg (1972) has observed that although *humanics*, the scientific study of human nature, is not a new word, it is an unfamiliar one. This situation will be changed as knowledge about *DNA* opens the immediate possibility of better tools to control disease, improve agriculture, and to exploit microorganisms in industry. The popular notion of genetic engineering or genetic programming is to produce an evil Frankenstein-like monster who would produce assembly lines of storm-trooper soldiers. It is also possible that parents could be programmed to produce a handsome athlete with an IQ of 350 who had hair that would shear itself at prescribed intervals.

A number of genetic diseases can be detected prenatally. This is accomplished by examination of the amniotic fluid or culture specimens of blood. If incipient disease is discovered the mother may request a therapeutic abortion in order to avoid bearing a severely crippled or severely retarded child. Among such diseases are cystic fibrosis and mongolism, or Down's syndrome. Lederberg suggests that genetic programming may go further by developing in humans the ability to synthesize amino acids internally. This would ease some of the problem of starvation and malnutrition. It might even postpone the gravity of the problem of overpopulation. He says that such a prospect is enhanced by the recent discovery that only Caucasians typically have the genes needed for the formation of lactase, an enzyme for digesting milk sugar. Conversely, many Negroes and Orientals lack this capacity and tend to be intolerant of milk. Such genetic engineering has been, in fact, practiced for some time. Vaccination for smallpox actually consists in introducing a variant virus to compensate for man's normal inherent sluggishness in the production of antibodies against the smallpox virus.

GENETIC ENGINEERING

Prospects of genetic intervention

Scientific knowledge is characterized by its increasing at a geometric rather than an arithmetic rate. Starting at the year one as a base it took 1750 years to double man's knowledge; but it took only 150 years (up to 1900) to double it again; by 1950 it has doubled again, and at the present time it takes only about seven years to double the fund of knowledge. Another way of stating this startling statistic is to say that 90 per cent of all the scientists who ever lived are alive today. Hence, to predict today what will take place in the next 15 years is as hazardous as it was for Nostradamus to predict, in the sixteenth century, what would happen in the next 100 years. Taylor, in 1968, wrote a book, *The Biological Time Bomb*, indicating the speed of recent biological discoveries. He found that before the work could be published some of the possibilities discussed were realities—heart and other organ transplants. This growth of scientific knowledge is fittingly known as the "Knowledge Explosion." This is seen by some scholars to be man's most serious personality problem—adjusting to the rapidity of change (Rogers, 1971; Toffler, 1970).

The range of possibilities for genetic intervention seems limitless. All living things inherit an organic structure and that structure can be altered. The elimination of cystic fibrosis and mongolism have already been indicated as possibilities. Genetic intervention in the size, shape, and complexity of the brain can be used to decrease the incidence of mental handicap. Mental retardation will not be eliminated because there are prenatal developmental sequences not yet understood that permit feeblemindedness to occur in quite normal families. Lederberg (1972) has suggested that our normal body chemical functions can be altered advantageously, (*e.g.*, synthesis of amino acids and the formation of lactase). He also indicates that it might be possible to program genetically for the resistance of disease. Sickle cell anemia and the Rh blood factor are other human hazards that could be diminished through genetic engineering. There is distinctly the prospect that theory ". . . today places in human hands the possibility that henceforth modifying all life, including the nature of our own species." (Glass, 1969, p. 506).

Hazards of genetic intervention

It might appear that geneticists would grasp eagerly the chance to intercede with human evolution. They could improve the lot of mankind in general and of handicapped individuals in particular. Instead, there is a reluctance to proceed without first moving from the science of biology to the philosophy of life. Hitler's endorsement of selective breeding, in which he encouraged selected Aryan maidens to join with brave Aryan youth to produce a super-super race (Aryans were already, in Hitler's opinion, plain super) is viewed with contempt, if not fear. Hitler could eliminate the so-called unfit (the Jews) but such nominations in our culture—or contemporary German culture—would be violently revolutionary.

Scientists such as Lederberg, Glass, and Stent wonder who has the prescience to decide who is fit and who is unfit. Even choice between the obviously unfit and the marginally fit is accompanied by hazards. Glass (1969) reports that while sickle hemoglobin in late stages threatens life, in its early stages it confers protection against malaria. Hence, elimination of sickle cells in Africa might result in racial disaster. Lederberg (1972) believes that attention should be directed to control of cystic fibrosis and Down's syndrome rather than to elimination of the genetic predisposition. There may be unknown concomitant advantages. It seems possible that research devoted to genetic control might result in discoveries that would reduce the threat of malnutrition. However, the elimination of certain genes would constitute an irreversible decision. Attention must be devoted to engineering the environment to ensure optimum development of existing genetic types.

Genetic engineering is, therefore, intimately tied to questions of ethics; and the question of what man is and can be is bound to the question of what man should be. Lederberg says that we must avoid decisions that would reduce flexibility in future generations. Glass reflects much the same emphasis:

> But do men dare assume the cloak of god? It is so frightening a responsibility, like that of the makers of the first nuclear weapons, that we might well draw back in dismay, refusing even to look at the prospect. Yet the consequences of ignorance and of blind laissez-faire are equally appalling. To many geneticists today the only sensible path to pursue is that which requires as careful and dispassionate a study of the possibilities and their eventualities as may be made. It is certainly not for the geneticist to decide what evolutionary goals man should seek. It is, however, his moral and social obligation to inform as wide a public as possible regarding what choices may be made, what pitfalls lurk, what outcomes may be expected from different courses of action or inaction.[8]

SEX CHROMOSOME ABNORMALITY

Chromosomes and crime

The relationship between personality and behavior and biological endowment is clearly illustrated in the composition of the chromosome that determines sex. The normal sex chromosome is *XX*, in which case the offspring is female, or *XY*, in which case the offspring is male. When the sex cell divides the female always contributes an *X* half and the male, on the basis of chance, contributes either *X* or *Y*. Faulty functioning in the ovaries or testes sometimes produces an *XXX* or *XYY* as well as other combinations of supernumerary *Y*'s or *X*'s—for instance, *XXY*, *XXXXY* or *XYYY* (Valenti, 1968). An *XXY* typically becomes a mentally defective male with atrophied testicles, a eunuch-like figure, with female-like breast development. Sex life is possible but often is unsatisfactory and relatively infrequent (Ferguson-Smith, 1966).

Abnormal development often follows abnormal sex chromosome composition. The combinations *XYY* or *XYYY*, or other supernumerary *Y*'s, have been of particular interest because of their relationship to crime (Telfer *et al.*, 1968). Bearers of such chromosomes are characteristically tall, lean, and, as youth, subject to excessive acne.

---

[8]Bentley Glass, "Evolution in Human Hands," *Phi Delta Kappan*, Vol. 50, May, 1969, p. 506.

They sometimes have normal intelligence but usually it is somewhat below average. In some studies it has been found that there is a higher incidence of sex chromosome abnormality in prison populations than in the general public. The incidence of XYY's in prisoners is well above the occurrence of XYY's in the generality (Nash, 1970, p. 41). Tall male prisoners frequently have the abnormal chromosome but scrapings from the mouth (by which the composition of the chromosomes may be determined) of 36 tall college basketball players revealed no such occurrences (Montagu, 1968). Richard Speck, who wrote the notorious message "Born to raise hell," and who was convicted of murdering eight student nurses in Chicago, was found to be of the XYY type. Homosexuality is sometimes accompanied by sex chromosome abnormality but not frequently enough to permit its being regarded as a cause. Most homosexuals have normal sex chromosomes.

Victims of the supernumerary factors are typically unresponsive to psychotherapeutic intervention. This does not mean that they do not express the desire to be helped. It is as though they had suffered minimal brain damage through disease, traumatic birth, or injury with an accompanying loss of behavioral control. Electroencephalographic readings show abnormal brain waves and a high incidence of epileptiform conditions in those with the abnormal sex chromosome (Montagu, 1968).

Predisposition and personality

Studies such as those cited in the foregoing section make it clear—and investigators often repeat the message—that sex chromosome abnormality *does not cause* crime. Not all persons who have the abnormal chromosome are criminals. Genes do not determine anything. They do influence the physical characteristics of an individual and, indirectly at least, the manifestation of behavior. The unsatisfactory sex life of an XXY or XO (second sex chromosome missing) may be due to feelings of inferiority precipitated by atypical physical development (Nash, 1970, p. 39). Hence, the weak ego plus a hostile or unfavorable environment could actualize a predisposition.

It should be noted further that all psychological aberrations need not be considered as being genetically determined (Davis, 1973). This should not imply that some abnormality is not so influenced. There can be no doubt that, in addition to the predisposition, it will sometimes require a contributing environment to shape criminal behavior. On the other hand, XYY's unresponsiveness to psychological therapy cannot be ignored.

Another delicate question is when to intervene—if the decision is made to intervene. How great should the threatened abnormality be? Mongoloid children, for instance, are lovable, congenial, patient persons who, according to some parents who have had one, have much to teach others about optimism, friendliness, and contentment. Siblings have learned, through the Mongoloid member of the family, a respect for differences. They may learn a disrespect for their own conceit and selfishness. There is some consensus that parents should have the chance to choose abortion. If examinations show the presence of abnormality—be it hemophilia, Down's syndrome, *XYY* chromosome abnormality—the mother should have the chance to choose abortion. Valenti (1968) says the practice of compelling a mother to give birth to a baby certain to be severely defective is a cruel and uncivilized custom.

After the baby is born, the challenge is to provide a developmental environment that will be most conducive to developing potential—whatever that potential might be. But this should be the birthright of every child, normal or defective. This, in the final analysis, is what all chapters of this book are about: How to make the best use of whatever predispositions we possess.

IMPLICATIONS FOR ACTION

The principle of multiple causation

In the life of the highly complex human organism there are always multiple factors underlying a particular phenomenon. However, there is another principle relating to behavior that Wheeler (1940, p. 39) called the Law of Least Action: an organism always takes what it perceives to be the shortest route to its goal. This "law" has pertinence here in the notion that if we could blame our genes or chromosomal structure for our deficiencies we could excuse ourselves from the arduous path of assuming responsibility for the direction our life takes. The "organism" does not consistently perceive that often what appears to be the short route to a goal sometimes actually delays the journey. A simple answer (genetic predisposition) prevents one from perceiving that the law of multiple causation also is operative.

In the case of genetic determination of traits, it is necessary to appreciate that genes or chromosomes provide only part of the answer. Referring again, for example, to Terman's studies of gifted children, it was found in a follow-up study that many of the subjects studied did not fulfill the promise of their early intellectual giftedness (Terman, 1947). Personality factors such as faith in oneself, determination of a goal, developing a consuming interest, patience with the foibles of the generality were also factors that must be taken into account in the actual realization of the potential residing in superior mentality. One finds in Terman's data verification for both of two opposed clichés: "Genius will out," and "Genius is 10 per cent inspiration and 90 per cent perspiration."

It has been indicated that one way to influence the development of genetic potential is to use drugs. Eisenberg (1971), after commenting on various ways drugs could be used constructively in child psychiatry, writes:

> Pharmacologic methods provide neither the passport to a brave new world nor the gateway to the inferno. With thoughtful selection, careful regulation of dosage and close scrutiny for toxicity, they [drugs] can add a significant component to total patient care. For all of this, the physician bears a major responsibility as the patient's advocate. To be successful, he will need to enlist the cooperation of teachers, psychologists, parents, and the community as a political body, if he is to create a climate within which each child can attain his human potential.[9]

If Eisenberg had been discussing developmental programs for adults, he might have made an additional observation: The choices one makes, the goals he pursues, and the dedication to one's purposes must also be contributing factors in the multiple processes of personality development.

One of the major problems, and criticisms, of psychology as a scientific study is that of getting away from averages and modes to the case of the individual. It is one thing for an employer to know that young people, by statistical analysis, are better employees if they have been graduated from high school than if they finished only eight grades, and it is something else to select a new worker who will stay on the job and be productive. It is one thing to know that girls who marry prior to age 18 have much greater chances of getting divorced or being deserted than those who marry after age 20. It is another thing if the girl is a college freshman and her sweetheart is going across the country to enter graduate school on a fully-funded fellowship. It is good to know that genes do set some limits on ultimate development but there are several pertinent questions to be asked: What is my basic genetic constitution? What is the way I can best use whatever I have? To what extent, and in what direction, do environmental and personal response factors modify innate genetic endowment?

From the general to the specific

Knotty questions are more abundant than are knowledgeable answers. It has, for instance, been theorized (Jung) that **introvertive** and **extrovertive** tendencies are normal and natural predispositions. Yet parents, teachers, and some clinicians seem to view introversion as some kind of disease or defect. The introvert is urged and bribed and threatened to become something else. He may begin to believe that there is something sick and despicable about his comfortableness with being alone. He may come to think it is odd to be able to work without a steady stream of feedback from his fellows. The situation illustrates

[9]Leon Eisenberg, "Principles of Drug Therapy in Child Psychiatry with Special Reference to Stimulant Drugs," *American Journal of Orthopsychiatry*, Vol. 41, No. 3, 1971, p. 379.

the dilemma of psychology. If the introvertive tendencies are generated by early traumatic experiences, by lack of or insufficiency of adequate mothering, by paucity of experience, then concern may be valid. If the introversion is accompanied by other symptoms of maladjustment, then concern and therapeutic intervention are appropriate. If one is confident, competent, emotionally stable, and still prefers to be alone, then his introversion should be respected as a part of his individuality. From what we know now, it would be best for the introvert not to plan a career as a salesman of electronics equipment or be a "bunny." However, introversion might be no handicap to an Alaskan bush pilot or a research specialist in atomic power. In short, fit the career (or style of life) to the personality rather than undertake molding the personality to some folklore.

Failure to make the transition from the general—and generalities are valuable bits of knowledge—is behind the gross errors made by those teachers and counselors who gravely pronounce that "You are not college material." If it turns out that such is, indeed, the case and the student fails, part of the cause might be the pronouncement itself, rather than being a matter of IQ or work habits. Fortunately, some nonbelievers in the "noncollege material" fantasy have been curious enough to study the matter. Pang (1971) showed that numerous prominent persons—scientists, statesmen, artists, authors—had, as young pupils, been stigmatized as dullards and incompetents. Strauss (1969) made a study of 89 Ph. D.'s in chemistry, physics, and engineering who earned their degrees from Ohio State, Cornell, and the University of California (Berkeley). Records showed that 3 per cent had high school IQ's below 100; 6 per cent had IQ's between 101-110; and 29 percent has IQ's between 111-120. Some IQ devotees (failing to heed the principle of multiple causation) believe that 120 is minimum IQ for *successful* undergraduate work. It is commonly accepted that "average intelligence" is that between IQ 90 and 110. One way of viewing Strauss' data is that, on the basis of IQ, the remark, "You are not college material," must be reserved for about 15.63 per cent of the unselected population.[10] Because there is some selection for intellectual ability in schools, the percentage would be even smaller when referring to school populations.

SUMMARY

Early studies of genetics in human lives depended on family histories. It could be shown that superiority and eminence or dependency and antisocial behavior seemed to "run in families." Today such studies are

---

[10]Consult any text in general or educational psychology or tests and measurements for the meaning and picture of the "normal curve of distribution."

totally discredited because it is realized that children born into either of these varieties of families also "inherit" an environment that may help to bring out the best or worst in a child. Physical features, however, are traceable to strong genetic factors. Intelligence seems to be somewhat less clearly genetic than physical features, but personality factors are most frequently traceable to environmental influences. However, the issue of environment *vs.* heredity in intelligence is far from being settled. Tests are not wholly satisfactory. Determination of what specific environmental factors encourage intellectual growth, and age of subject when environmental impact is most potent are questions that must yet be answered. It is emphasized that for the normal, adult, individual, the really important question is what one does with the potential he has.

Kubie asserts that man's task is to learn how to manipulate the environment so that man's realization of potential will not be blocked—and he believes that the keys to unlocking the potential are near at hand. Meanwhile, geneticists are, with the use of electromicroscopes and refined techniques for testing body fluids, unlocking some of the secrets of heredity. The fact that the chemical bases upon which heredity is based are becoming better known than previously has not yet served to disprove the major thesis and conclusion of geneticists. We do not inherit traits in the form of behaviors but do inherit predispositions to react to stimuli in certain ways. This predisposition is influenced by external factors.

Researchers in various fields have confirmed one another's findings that in some kind of defect the predisposition to react in a certain way is so marked that chances of achieving normal behavior are negligible, if not completely absent. In such cases genetic engineering and genetic surgery present the opportunity and responsibility of choosing whether all children have the right to be born normal. It is possible that we may be able to find infrequently appearing advantageous traits (the ability to synthesize amino acids internally) and program genetically for their more frequent occurrence.

The case for hereditary personality predispositions is well illustrated in chromosomal abnormality. It has been found that those with an *XYY* sex cell do, with more frequent incidence than the generality, contribute to prison populations. Researchers are quick to point out, however, that it takes an environment to activate the predisposition.

Three principles of development derive from the study of genetic predisposition and personality. 1) The principles of multiple causation must be used in understanding personality. 2) Man, as an adult, has the capacity to choose how he will respond to hereditary potential and environmental circumstances. 3) Accurate generalizations and determination of general trends do not provide sufficient data for understanding the uniqueness of individual personality.

SUGGESTED READINGS

KAGAN, JEROME, "Do the First Two Years Matter?" *Saturday Review of Education*, Vol. 1, No. 3, 41–46, April, 1973.

> *Using data from his own studies and from research in Guatemala, Kagan concludes that intellectual deprivation in the first years of life is not irreversible. This view contrasts with that of other authorities.*

LEDERBERG, JOSHUA, "Humanics and Genetic Engineering," eds. H. W. Bernard and W. C. Huckins, in *Exploring Human Development*. Boston: Allyn and Bacon, Inc., 1972. From *1970 Britannica Yearbook of Science and the Future*, Chicago: Encyclopaedia Britannica, Inc.

> *A leader in the field of genetics outlines ways in which genetic engineering may work but he expresses concern about the magnitude of the ethical dilemmas that scientific knowledge creates.*

MONTAGU, ASHLEY, "Chromosomes and Crime," *Psychology Today*, Vol. 2, No. 5, 42–49, October, 1968.

> *The author has surveyed and condensed the reports on crime and chromosomal abnormality up to the date of the article. Illustrations of the abnormal sex chromosome combinations help to clarify his presentation.*

PITTS, FERRIS N., JR., "The Biochemistry of Anxiety," *Scientific American*, Vol. 220, No. 2, 69–75, February, 1969.

> *There are individual differences in the readiness of persons to experience anxiety and show the symptoms of it. In addition, anxiety states and tendencies can be raised or lowered by the use of chemicals.*

THOMPSON, WILLIAM R., "Genetics and Personality," eds. E. Norbeck, D. Price-Williams, and W. M. McCord, *The Study of Personality: An Interdisciplinary Appraisal*. New York: Holt, Rinehart and Winston, Inc., 1968.

> *Perhaps somewhat more than in other readings listed for this chapter, the role of environment in shaping genetic probabilities is emphasized.*

TUNNEY, JOHN V., and MILTON E. LEVINE, "Genetic Engineering," *Saturday Review of Science*, Vol. 55, No. 32, 23–28, August 5, 1972.

> *Genetic counseling, gene therapy, prenatal sampling of amniotic fluid, and fetal transplants are some of the possibilities in man's control over genetic coding. Consideration is devoted to ethical, moral, and legal problems involved in such control.*

FOLLOW-UP LEARNING ACTIVITIES

Talk with some middle-aged person (parent, friend, teacher) about inheritance in the case of personality of an "easy" and "hard" baby. Summarize whether or not that person's view accords with or differs from that presented in the text.

_____
_____
_____
_____
_____

React to the Boyer and Walsh contention that if intelligence is inherited, then the United States is doomed to mediocrity.

_____
_____
_____
_____
_____

Get your instructor to poll the class as to how many have been told by someone, in some words or another, that they were not "college material."
   The proportion was one out of _____
   What is your reaction to the poll?

_____
_____
_____
_____

Some threats to mankind's survival are: overpopulation, knowledge explosion (rapid change), nuclear annihilation, exhaustion of fuel resources.
   Which do you think is the greatest threat?
   _____ because _____
_____
_____
_____

Is one born to become a criminal?
   Yes _____ No _____ because _____
_____
_____
_____

3
Birth and Family Influences

Personality is learned from family dynamics.

LEARNING ACTIVITIES

Talk to a couple of mothers, who have preschool children, about the things they learned regarding the impact of prenatal conditions on the new born. Epitomize their responses.

Mother A _____
_____
_____

Mother B _____
_____
_____

Were you born first _____, last _____, or what place did you have in your family _____?
What effect do you believe your ordinal position in the family has had on your personality?

_____
_____
_____
_____

What effect has the child-rearing practices your father used on you had on your personality?

Practice _____
_____
_____

Effect _____
_____
_____

Do the same regarding your mother's practices:

_____
_____
_____

Do you consider yourself to be motivated to be a high achiever _____, low achiever _____, or indifferent _____?
Describe any family traits that you think contributed to your achievement motivation: _____
_____
_____

In what way, if any, are you a creative person?

_____
_____

Is there anything you might do to become more creative?

_____
_____
_____

Personality consists of predispositions and behaviors that characterize one's unique adjustments to physical and social environments. The way one's predispositions originate and develop are influenced by complicated, interweaving processes that are almost overwhelming. Biological endowment, family and cultural milieu, personal history and experiences, and the aspects of the immediate situation are the major forces that shape personality. In addition to the interaction among these forces, the way an individual responds to them is a focal consideration. A recurrent emphasis throughout this book is that: *One's situation is often no more difficult than the attitude taken toward the situation.*

The concern in this chapter is that of developing some appreciation of the fact that personality is, *in part*, a function of conditions that exist even prior to birth, during birth, and in the first year or two of a baby's life. The message is disastrously misread if the reader comes to believe that prenatal conditions, birth processes, and early family influences *cause* personality to be what it is. It is only for the sake of convenience in academic discussion that various personality influences are discussed in separate chapters. In life, the various influences function together and have various power at different times in life and in dissimilar situations. Personality is influenced by many things but is not caused by anything.

CONGENITAL INFLUENCES ON PERSONALITY

Prenatal conditions
The notion is erroneous that if a pregnant woman is frightened by a dog, her child will have a birthmark resembling the picture of a dog. If she reads good literature her child will not necessarily be a scholar. It is not true that if she listens to good music her child will be musically inclined. These ideas are now classified as fallacies. The idea of prenatal impressions is considered to be a myth. However, there is no doubt that X-rays, poisons, certain trauma, nutrition, and psychological condition of the prospective mother do have some influence on the baby's personality predispositions. What is unknown about these factors is whether the effects are reversible or whether they are permanent (Dayton, 1969).

Sontag (1972) studied a number of pregnant women who suffered severe emotional disturbance during the last trimester (the last three months) of pregnancy. He reported marked increase in fetal movement. After birth these babies showed no congenital defect but were irritable, **hyperactive**, tended to have frequent bowel movements, and three out of ten had marked feeding problems. Sontag thinks that it is possible that these early behaviors predict personality at much later ages. He reported, for instance, using **longitudinal studies**, that unusual activity in the last two months of fetal life was associated with hyperactivity and timidity and anxiety at the age of two and one-half years. At this age babies tended to avoid conflict situations. These same children, in their early twenties, continued to be socially apprehensive. It is tempting to believe that these tendencies are inherited. However, it is possible that nervous, tense mothers provided an interuterine milieu conducive to hyperactivity. Such mothers might continue to supply an anxiety producing environment throughout childhood and adolescence (Mathis, Cotton, and Sechrest, 1970, p. 500).

A number of drugs have harmful effects on the fetus. Some cases of deafness have been traced to the mother's use of quinine for malaria. A fairly recent international scare, focusing largely in Germany, was created by the temporary popularity of thalidomide as a sedative or tranquilizer. It arrested development at a certain critical phase of fetal development and resulted in infant monstrosities or babies without arms, legs, toes, fingers, or whose extremities were shortened in varying degrees up to being mere stubs. Lysergic acid diethylamide (*LSD*) is reported to cause chromosomal damage. Pregnant mothers who used *LSD* seem to have produced a disproportionately large number of defective babies. Although fetal damage from *LSD* is conclusive in rats and mice, the evidence on humans is regarded as inconclusive ("*LSD. . . ,*" 1968). No direct damage is reported to the babies of mothers who are alcoholics. If, however, excessive use of alcohol results in poor diet (which it sometimes does) the baby may suffer from dietary deficiency. The mother's smoking increases cardiovascular activity of the fetus but there is no conclusive evidence that damage is done.

Rubella, or German measles, some forms of influenza, syphilis, and encephalomyelitis are prominent among the diseases that may cause deformity to the fetus, limit or damage brain development, or cause sensory defect. Rh incompatibility was until recently a hazard to normal prenatal development. A number of techniques were developed in the late 1960's that virtually eliminate the Rh danger if the mother takes proper prenatal cautions (Lin-Fu, 1969).

Exposure of the mother to excessive doses of X-ray results in high frequency of abortion and malformation of the fetus. Various studies indicate that about half the babies whose mothers had heavy X-ray treatment during pregnancy were deformed or mentally defective (Montagu, 1954).

The most common factor in abnormal prenatal development is dietary deficiency. In "developing nations" malnutrition reaches an incidence of up to 75 per cent. Marginal diets for prospective mothers may be as high as 30–50 per cent even in the well-fed United States. This is due both to ignorance and poverty. Because the human brain has its greatest spurt of growth in the prenatal period—achieving 70 per cent of adult growth by the time of birth—nutrition must be a serious concern. Poverty increases the probability that organic damage will be done to the brain and that prematurity will result. Fetal mortality is increased by poverty and increases the likelihood that brain damage will occur because of difficult or prolonged birth processes (Hurley, 1969).

Birth processes

The human's powerful brain, focal in personality, is in a sense, quite delicate. It demands a constant and rich supply of oxygen in order to develop and function properly. Anything that interferes with that continual supply of oxygen has some, be it slight or serious, effect on mental growth and activity. Interruption of the supply of oxygen may be slight, as in deprivation coincident with the effect of alcohol on the glutinization of blood cells. Massive brain damage may be caused by oxygen deprivation due to injury, disease, or prolonged and difficult birth processes.

Children who are brought to a pediatric clinic because of **hypo-activity** or hyperactivity, slow learning, unpredictable emotional outbursts, or behavioral disorders cause the physician to ask, "Was his birth normal?"

Many of the conditions cited in the section on prenatal conditions may also contribute to normality or abnormality of birth. If the mother is emotionally upset or anxious about her ability to bear the baby it may cause trouble. If she is the victim of the tradition of pain and travail in childbirth it increases, in varying degrees, her ability to strain and relax alternately. Her muscles are hampered in their performance of requisite reciprocal-alternating activity. In order to obtain the needed release from fear and anxiety, drugs may be used. Too many drugs result in prolonged birth and the chances increase of interrupting the baby's brain oxygen supply. Heavy sedation may cause slowing of the mother's participation in labor and may prompt the use of forceps. Thus drugs may create the hazard of abnormal pressure on, and injury to, the cortex of the neonate.

Both drugs and obstetrical instruments have a valued place in birth. Not to use them in given instances would constitute the hazard. An increasing percentage of prospective mothers in western Europe and the United States are, however, interested in giving their babies as vigorous a start in life as is possible (See Chapter 5).

Babies born under conditions where the mother is "awake and aware" are reported to be, in somewhat larger proportion than otherwise, alert and healthy looking (as contrasted to being bluish and lethargic). Moreover, the mothers themselves are ready to receive, cuddle, and comfort the neonate more quickly than are drugged mothers or ones who have suffered from excessive lacerations. One mother reported to the author, "When I saw the baby come into the world and felt that I did it, I could feel my uterus clamp together as distinctly as closing my fist," and another said, "I was happier than I'd ever been before, and if I'm not that happy again, that's OK because it was enough to last me the rest of my life." And, if these two reports are individualistic, sentimental, and impressionistic, that too is OK by the author because such sentimentality is also part of the story of personality development.

It seems that being the youngest child, oldest child, middle child, or whatever, must surely have some influence on early personality development. Adler (1927) developed some elaborate hypotheses about the oldest child's being displaced in mother's affection by the second child; about the youngest child's struggle to compete with stronger and more mentally mature siblings. Thus, personality traits such as jealousy, aggressiveness, feelings of superiority or inferiority, feelings of power or futility are attributed to birth order.

Birth order

A hazard of the birth order hypothesis is that it seems to function in the lives of some persons; but research fails to confirm the hypothesis in many other instances. No reliable clues are afforded. No sure predictions or confirmations can be made. Clausen (1966), in reviewing many studies, asserts that there are too many contingencies associated with birth order to permit the hypothesis to have much merit. The age of parents, their growing wisdom about child-rearing, number of siblings, differences in mother-father relationships, and varied organic predispositions are among the contingent factors. There would be some differences if the siblings were one year, two years, or ten years apart. The fact of being an only child might be much less important than whether the mother stayed at home or hired a succession of baby sitters so she could be employed.

Even if there were some reliable consistency in probabilities of given kinds of personality deriving from birth order, the hypothesis must be discounted in terms of its practical value. It would indeed make one the victim of fate. It would create a **self-fulfilling prophecy** situation, which it may to some extent do now. For example, in later years it provides an alibi for avoiding responsibility. The adult who was the oldest child can say, "Really, I can't help being jealous. You see, I was the child who felt he had been displaced in my mother's affections." The self-fulfilling hypothesis can also work at a much earlier age. Parents make special efforts to avoid having the oldest child develop into a jealous person. They take special precautions to avoid creating situations that might lead to jealousy, and show fussy concern when they think they see jealousy. The outcome of the latter is that the child is rewarded in terms of receiving attention when he manifests jealousy.

There is also a notion that personality is influenced by being an only child or one with one, two, or a dozen siblings. Again it would seem that there would be some effect but what the effect is is not readily identified. One may be in a family of ten, all of whom are selfish, contentious, vicious persons who turn out to be dropouts, prostitutes, and felonists. One may be one in a family of ten who become studious, socially conscious leaders, and statesmen. Again, maturity of parents, felicity of parents, parental expectations, and how much parents talk person-to-person to babies and children are probably more important factors in shaping personality than is being an only child, one of two, or one of twelve.

CHILD INFLUENCES ON ADULT PERSONALITY

Easy and hard babies

Another important consideration in birth order and number of siblings hypotheses relates to the input of the child. In part, the child's input—his predispositions or life style—may be influenced by heredity or congenital factors such as those described in the previous chapter. Recently child specialists have been emphasizing that babies and children have considerable influence on how they are treated by their caretakers. Korner (1971), for example, reports that she has been impressed in her work (investigating individual differences) with the fact that children have an enduring life style that is distinctive and consistent. This life style may be independent of maternal treatment, conditions of birth, or of nutrition and health. Normal, full-term, well-nourished babies have unique patterns of behavior that elicit differences in maternal behavior. Some babies seem to be, from the time of birth, "sober little judges," others are as consistently happy and easy to satisfy. Still others are, in terms of action, critical and demanding.

Such individual differences should evoke differences in mothering. In addition, the mother has her input, and the quandary deepens. To most mothers smiling, responsive, contented babies are a source of pleasure and they seem to confirm the mother's belief that she is a good mother. They may interpret querulous babies as being evidence of their failure as mothers. There are some mothers, on the other hand, who seem to need difficult babies. An easy baby is no challenge to the skills of mothering. The first mother would tend to reject the complaining child. The second would indulge him because he gives confirmation to the idea that mothering requires stable, respected personality traits.

Boy-girl differences

The obvious difference between boys and girls is that of sex. There are also some differences in intrinsic rates and patterns of growth. *On the average*, boys are somewhat larger at birth than girl babies. However, boys retain this height-weight superiority for only a short time. By the age of puberty, which *on the average* occurs earlier in girls than it does in boys, girls exceed boys in height, weight, and in some measures of strength. After puberty boys regain their height-weight superiority and as adult males are heavier and taller than adult females. More frequently than girls, boys are born with handicaps and defects (sensory impairment and mental deficiency). There is, however, a compensating phenomenon—boys have a greater range of measured characteristics. More boys than girls, according to current evaluative devices, have the potential for becoming intellectually gifted as well as for retardation.

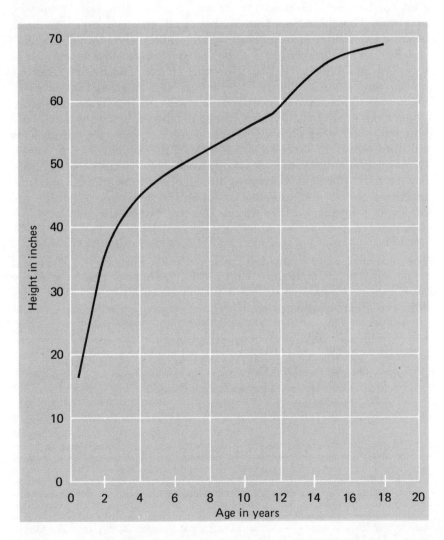

Schematic representation of early rapid growth in height.   **Figure 3.1**

Girls are reported to develop more rapidly than boys in mental and linguistic behaviors. In fact, the phenomenon of girls' rapid mental and verbal development has led to the recommendation that boys be started in school a year later than girls so boys will not develop feelings of inferiority (Peltier, 1972). Considerable doubt can be expressed for such a recommendation. While the growth differences do exist *on the average*, many boys exceed the intellectual and language status of many girls. The words "on the average" do not tell the whole story for individual boys and individual girls. Many boys might be handicapped for a lifetime (in view of graduate school, military service, and taking a job) by being delayed for a year in the early stages of education. Average boy-girl differences must not be allowed to overshadow the fact that: The differences between boys and girls as a group are much less than the differences among individual boys and individual girls.[1]

Boy-girl differences are complicated by role expectations. It is expected, in our culture, that girls will be clean, obedient, tractable, polite, considerate, responsive to emotions. It is expected that boys will be messy, self-assertive, independent, rough, self-centered, and stoic. The awareness of sex differences is sought from infancy on—boys wear blue and girls wear pink, boys wear pants and girls wear dresses (or did until recently). Thus, in terms of the child's influence on personality development, two processes are at work. 1) By virtue of being either boy or girl, different responses are elicited from others—parents, teachers, peers, and friends. 2) Different types of responses get confirming feedback. This accelerates the internalization of those behaviors that are expected by society.

Implications of individual input

The notion of child input and mother-child reciprocity of behavioral responses has an implication that recurs throughout this book. Many things do not "just happen" to a person, something in that person's behavior elicits the response.

> A young woman reported to her counselor with considerable animation, and a smile on her face that denied distress, that she had been raped. And it happened again the following week. She had considerable difficulty coming to the conclusion that she was not a helpless victim of a man's passion but had rather deliberately designed a trap. The trap was no more for the cooperating man than it was a way of denying her own responsibility for sexual relations.

[1]A parallel, current controversy in the psychological community relates to the matter of IQ and race. Incontrovertibly, presently used instruments for evaluating intelligence show that *on the average* whites outscore blacks. However, the fact remains that the differences between white and black scores is much less than the differences among whites or blacks. Differential treatment on the basis of average scores is unwarranted, says Jensen, who is a focal figure in the controversy. He asserts that although differences do not justify differential treatment, scientific investigations of such differences should not be abandoned (Arthur R. Jensen, "IQ and Race: The Ethical Issues," *The Humanist*, Vol. 32, No. 1, January-February, 1971, pp. 5–6). In a parallel manner, boy-girl differences should continue to be investigated. It is not so much to determine differences as to provide clues regarding how better to deal with individuals.

The point of individual input is that birth order, prenatal conditions, unwise parental treatment, or other distressing or handicapping circumstances do not alone produce a personality orientation. There is, in addition, the consideration of the individual's response to those influences. If this aspect of behavior is ignored, the examination of such factors as are discussed in this (and other chapters) may become an excuse for perpetuating self-defeating personality traits.

On the other hand, the study of factors that contribute to personality formation may well constitute a warning against real hazards. Particularly, such study gives notice of definite conditions toward which specific, and small, steps may serve to modify general tendencies. For example, it has been noted that even as babies, some persons are aloof and withdrawn. As an adult, this tendency may be offset by assuming that an open-minded stance may prove that at least some persons are genuinely friendly.

FAMILY INFLUENCES ON PERSONALITY

Along with psychoanalytic theory, biosocial theories, and postulations regarding **morphology**, there is another outlook on personality—learning theory; that is, one "learns" his personality through his experiences. The major sources of such learning are family, the broader culture—including socioeconomic status—and formal education. Socioeconomic status and culture are considered in Chapters 4 and 5.

Child-rearing practices

The description of acceptable child-rearing practices in the United States has undergone a marked change in the last two decades. In place of the "mother knows best," "mind when you are spoken to" orientation there has developed an orientation characterized by permissiveness. This attitude may be the illogical extreme of permitting the child to have his way in all choices—what he will eat, when and where he will sleep, toys he wants. It may mean reciprocal, mutual child-parent relations in which persuasion and **dialogue** are part of an egalitarian atmosphere. It may be a democratic atmosphere in which the voice of all is heard but in which there is a delegation of final authority to those who are most knowledgeable. Whatever the variation, the permissive, egalitarian, or democratic child-rearing stance is in sharp contrast to the authoritarian home of yesteryear.

Those who speak and write about child-rearing methods are not agreed on which is most desirable. They are agreed that the methods used have consequences in terms of adult personality. They agree that child-rearing methods should derive from the kind of adult personality that is sought.

Aldridge (1969) attributes the existence of young people who act as though any exercise of authority—civil or educational—is a violation of their rights as members of some sort of royal, divine family to the fact that parents have avoided exercising authority. He perceives the protesting, rioting college student as using the campus as an arena for acting out the conflict that he never had with parents who would not take a stand. He attributes the hippy's "coital masturbation"—intercourse without obligation or affection—as an outcome of a childhood during which no whims were denied.

Cottle (1969) believes that youth and young adults are lacking a fundamental strength because they have been permitted, if not urged, to assume adult responsibilities too soon. They had exercised adult choice before they had struggled with the developmental tasks of childhood and adolescence. He calls attention to the fact that children and parents are not peers! Certainly, the children do not want it any other way. Children want parents who will provide guidance. They want parents who will help the one who lacks maturity and wisdom with the making of decisions.

Halleck (1971) lists 15 hypotheses concerning student unrest on school and college campuses. He says that the most common explanation is that unrest is the result of too much permissiveness in child-rearing. Parents are so concerned about creating neuroses in children that they have abandoned teaching and disciplinary roles. The result is a generation of greedy, spoiled youngsters who have angry and infantile responses on the slightest provocation. Certainly, not all parents can be so categorized. However, even among well-educated parents, their freedom to criticize, debate, and challenge childish whims results in a contentious personality. Good citizens, of course, do challenge and question so the child-rearing methods are not entirely detrimental. The problem is to distinguish between autocratic, totalitarian, and arbitrary demands and genuine dialogue and adherence to rational standards. It is necessary to scale the approach to the child's level of maturity.

Maslow (1954) provides a psychological rationale for child-rearing practices involving a balance between authority, protectiveness, affection, and acceptance. He postulates a hierarchy of basic human needs that underlie motivation. This hierarchy provides for progressive change throughout a lifetime. There is, in short, no effective child-rearing regime that remains the same from infancy to youth.

The lowest basic needs, according to Maslow, are *physiological*. The child's need for balanced diet, water, warmth, and physiological balance must be met before higher level needs become functional. The next need in the hierarchy is for *safety*. The child prefers an orderly, predictable world upon which he can depend and in which dangerous things do not happen. Routines, regulations, rules, and orderly regimes are needed if the child is not to be overwhelmed by situations his immaturity does not prepare him to cope with successfully. If these two lower level needs are satisfied, or well on the way to being satisfied, the next higher level needs of *belongingness* and *love* begin to be the predominant motivators. When, and if, the child comes to know that he belongs and is loved for his own sake, he outgrows the primacy of love and belongingness and is motivated by *esteem needs.* At this level he seeks a stable, firmly based, positive evaluation of himself and wants both self-respect and the respect of others. After one, typically not until the years of maturity, has had most of his lower level needs at least partially met, his motivation is for **self-actualization.**[2] This means that he functions beyond the level of searching for the esteem of others and seeks to become the most of whatever he can become. "What a man *can* be, he must be" (Maslow, 1970). At the highest level of need one is motivated by *esthetic longings.* A rare person has a truly basic need for beauty; he gets ill in the presence of ugliness and is cured by beauty. Maslow says that this, in the eyes of the scientist, is a difficult area to deal with. He believes the need is present in some individuals in all cultures.

The implications of Maslow's theory for child-rearing are clear. For the sake of mental health and the ultimate goal of self-actualization, the first consideration in child-rearing is providing conditions for a physically healthy baby. Parents are obliged to see that the child receives a balanced diet plus those foods that *he uniquely* needs. Some children, for example, are allergic to milk and suffer long periods of illness and slow development until a diet not containing milk is presented. Rest and activity should be provided on a regular schedule designed for the individual. Again, some children the same age and appearing to have good health need more rest, and some need more activity, than others. Moreover, the amount of sleep needed varies with age. Less and less sleep is required as one reaches adulthood. But the less and less does not mean that the need for sleep fades away completely. Parents may need to exercise adult-parental prerogatives, in terms of physiological needs, and require the adolescent to be in bed at a certain time.

Safety needs suggest that children and adolescents (indeed, some adults) want and must have rules, regulations, and routines (structure) or they feel threatened. Children, many child specialists contend, want to know the limits for their explorative behaviors. Their testing of limits (must one really stay in the yard or must he go to bed at 7 p.m.) does not mean conflict with the stipulation. They merely want to be sure the limit is "for real" and clearly defined. Despite the testing—an inevitable concomitant of the process of *healthy* child growth—children do recognize their lack of experience and knowledge. They are emotionally relieved when they are assured that parents still know who is in charge.

[2]Discussion is omitted here because it has little reference to child-rearing; but the concept will be examined further in Chapter 5.

Adolescents make the parents' job difficult. Parents know there should be a progressive "loosening of the reins." Hence, when the adolescent challenges parental demands about use of the family car, keeping one's room neat, or going to the beach without adult supervision, and the parents finally say, "I give up. Go ahead and do as you _____ please," the adolescent weeps and says, "You don't care what happens to me." At this point it should be noted that what is safety at age eight is not so at 18. Parental protection, "mother knows best" policy, attempting to remove frustrations for the 18-year-old, may threaten the safety that must ultimately come from standing on his own two feet. He must have the chance to take responsibility for his own mistakes. Because the age of the child bears on the different degrees of flexibility and rigidity of rules and regimes, no inclusive prescription can be given. A process can be recommended: Parents and children might engage in dialogue. If dialogue seems frequently to culminate in shouting and recrimination, it may be necessary to seek the help of a "communication facilitator"—counselor, psychologist, or psychiatrist. The presence of a second family can often help to improve parent-child communication (Fullmer and Bernard, 1968).

Love and acceptance are so much a part of salutary child-rearing practices that they might be regarded as techniques. There are some persistent fallacies to the effect that there is a "mother love" that overcomes most hazards. Child abuse, the abandonment of infants, and daily observation of parent-child interaction should be enough to shatter the myth. The mother love idea is, however, deeply engrained in cultural mores. Most mothers do love their babies and some love any and all babies. Others hate the dirty, demanding, doltish little monstrosities; and society will some day have to face the fact that some mothers are incapable of mothering.

Some mothers may have to learn to love—via proximity and contact. One of the advantages thought to derive from the mother's not taking drugs during birth is that she can immediately hold and cuddle the infant. Some mothers, previously undecided, decide at that moment that they want that baby for their very own. We have not yet come to a full appreciation of the implications of studies on the nature of love. If we did it seems that there might be much more casual stroking, petting, squeezing, and cuddling of babies and children. Can mothers learn love through practice? At least tentatively, the answer can be, "Yes." It does take *time* to cuddle, brush, and pat children. The important triumvirate in child rearing is: Love, Time, and Touch.

Acceptance extends the concept of love from the purely affective realm to an inclusion of some aspects of the cognitive realm. Parents can consciously decide that the baby will make a difference in the home regime. It means that rational reasons for valuing him can be determined. It means that he is still loved regardless of being boy or girl, average or slow learning, sensorily normal and sensorily defective. As children they are accepted when they like TV but hate books, like candy but wad up their carrots in a napkin. Acceptance means that the person is getting a healthy start to viewing himself as a different but nevertheless valued person.

Delinquency   The relation of child personality to family structure, stability, and child-rearing atmospheres has been studied most extensively in relation to *delinquency*. The emphases in these studies were on the family as a 1) biological, 2) psychological, and 3) sociological unit. As a biological unit, one's heredity was perceived as a determining factor in delinquency. Some early studies indicated that hereditary **pathology** ran in families. Body build has been studied in relation to delinquency—mesomorphs presumably being more readily susceptible to becoming delinquent (Glueck and Glueck, 1950). The contemporary interpretation of these older and later similar studies are: 1) **correlation** does not mean causation, and 2) behavioral traits are not inherited but are the result of *interaction* (or individual response) to the *environment*.

Adult milieu and child personality

Early studies indicated that harsh and punitive methods prompted the child to develop attitudes of rebelliousness and to seek revenge. Because one's parents and other adults are so comparatively powerful, the child does not fight back directly. He seeks vengeance in sly ways, such as cheating to outwit authority or stealing to compensate for lack of wish fulfillment. He uses drugs to dull the harsh reality of rejection, abandonment, or brutality.

As will be shown in Chapter 6, the notion of the psychological nature of the family in relation to delinquency is supported by psychoanalytic theory. The Gluecks (1950) concluded that delinquents were raised in homes characterized by lack of moral fiber and stability. Delinquents' parents were inadequate guides and protectors. Their parents lacked understanding, affection, and acceptance. Parents, in short, provided inadequate models for children. The McCords (1959) found that overprotective mothers tended to have nondelinquent sons. Rejecting or neglecting mothers, with much higher frequency, had delinquent sons. They found that neglect was more damaging than outright cruelty.

Poverty and unemployment characterize many families in which the rate of delinquency is comparatively high. The term "slum shock" has been used to describe the creeping influence of want, inadequate diet, denial of access to middle class privileges, and contempt that crushes the family of poverty.

> Slum children do not go unprepared when that time comes [leaving home], contrary to the assumptions of some social critics who can only see the life of the poor as aimless, neglected, and always "deprived." Chances are these children receive specific and brutal instruction about the "realities" of life at the age of 2, 3, or 4 so that

when they emerge from the home the police, the hoods, the addicts, the drunks are already familiar, and what happens in the schools or on playgrounds is not disappointing but expected. The mother I have already quoted has also testified to the morality and lawfulness she tries to inspire in her children: "I don't know how to do it. I don't know how to keep my kids from getting stained and ruined by everything outside. I keep them close to me, and sometimes I feel like everything will be O. K., because they know how much I want for it to be, and they'll go make it be, the way I thought I could. But after a while they want to go out. You know how a kid is when he's 3 or 4, he wants to move, no matter where, so long as he keeps going. And where can he move in here? So I let them go, and I stop and say a prayer every morning, and ask for them to be saved, but I have to say it, I'm not expecting my prayers to be answered, not around here, I know.[3]

There is little doubt that family is a contributing factor in delinquency. The consensus of those who have taken a special interest in delinquency, however, is that families do not cause delinquency. There are too many instances in which one boy or girl is delinquent but the siblings are "model citizens" to believe that inadequate families are anything more than contributing influences (Jeffery and Jeffery, 1967). Delinquency prevention must be an individual approach designed to contend with the unique perceptions, predispositions, and personality behaviors functioning within a multitude of influences. The phenomenon of delinquency is a function of the principle of **multiple causation**. The family, religion, schools, recreation, economic status, police, courts, and community all contribute to the personality of the delinquent.

Achievement motivation   In the United States, our culture has been called the achieving society. This is an interesting **stereotype**. However, what evidence we have does not support the stereotype. About half our society is lower class (Havighurst and Neugarten, 1967, p. 19). There are many among them who have ceased the struggle for upward mobility. Others "have got it made" in terms of wages, social security, unemployment compensation, medical care, and so on. Although our culture *as a whole* does not fit the stereotype, there are many in the lower as well as higher classes who do have strong **achievement motivation**. Achievement motivation might possibly stem from glandular activity and constitutional strength and vigor (Williams, 1972). Certain family influences have been found to accompany the relative presence or lack of achievement motivation.

A survey and condensation of many studies reveals that the homes of children who are labeled "Achievers" (*i.e.*, do well in terms of their

[3]Robert Coles, "Violence in Ghetto Children," *Children*, Vol. 14, No. 3, May-June, 1967, p. 102.

measured capacities) are clearly different from those of "under-achievers" (those who perform poorly despite psychometric indications of having ability) (Gilmore, 1969). The underachiever is chronically anxious and hence is handicapped in perceptual processes. His emotional conflict, or ego threat, is such that memory is impaired. The family background that prompts these conditions is characterized by rejection, physical punishment, parental indifference to child performance, apparent lack of affection, and meager communication. Under-achievers tend to have parents who are quick to punish failure or misdeeds but do not comment on accomplishments. The child becomes somewhat confused because he knows what he cannot do but what he should do is not so clear.

> The father is often verbally unrewarding and indifferent. The parental sex roles may be reversed or confused. In a study of private school underachievers, it was found that the father-son relationship was poor, characterized by fear and lack of warmth. It has also been noted that punitive, coercive, repressive, and generally rejecting parents have a damaging effect on the child's intellectual development. Research has indicated that impulsive, acting-out, and punitive behavior in children tends to occur in homes where parents are strict and given to use of physical punishment. The passive, indifferent, and nonempathic family is an important etiological factor in underachievement, especially when parents take no note either of a child's accomplishments or his failures, or when they punish failures without rewarding accomplishments.[4]

In addition to parents who withhold praise, Gilmore's survey showed that underachievers were often victims of the "double bind." The parents utter contradictory messages: Success in life depends on scholastic achievement—don't forget that social life is important. Stand up for your rights—don't talk back to me. Another handicap is the **rationalization** that parents should not help children with homework because the child must do it by himself. This excuse is perceived by investigators as the ploy of parents who are "too busy now." They are preoccupied with their own affairs. The exhortation "do your best" is seen as a factor in contributing to underachievement. The implication is that one has a limited amount of ability and if he works at his level it is enough. The result is satisfaction with mediocrity. The fact is that intelligence tests and academic scores are measures of very much the same thing. One could just as logically say, "your IQ score is low because you do not apply yourself to your studies" (McClelland, 1972). Underachievers, more frequently than achievers, have parents who disguise their indifference with verbalization,

[4]James V. Gilmore, "Parental Influences on Academic Achievement," *Normline*, Vol. 2, No. 2, 1969, p. 3. Published by Test Department, Harcourt, Brace and Jovanovich, Inc.

"you be whatever you want to be." Concerned parents have to be on guard constantly to keep from overemphasizing the uncompromising demands of culture and technology.

The homes of high achievers present a sharp contrast to those of underachievers. In the former, there are warm, strong, and **empathic** relationships between all members—parent-child, child-child, and parent-parent. Parents spend much time talking with children. They praise small accomplishments. They respond to children's questions and their requests for help. Achievers tend to describe their parents as affectionate, trusting, and kind. The parents encourage without seeming to apply pressure. Fathers are perceived as having an important and respected role as leader. Mothers are loving but are neither demanding nor overprotective (Gilmore, 1969).

The foregoing descriptions must be regarded as trends or tendencies, not as inevitabilities. There are several phenomena that might, and do, alter the tendency. Mothers do tend to persist in their approaches and attitudes. There is also evidence that some mothers are attentive and empathic during infancy and early childhood, but as the child grows toward independence and as the tendency to move away emerges (as indicated in the foregoing quotation by Coles) she loses interest. Others prefer the older child and regard the infant as being messy and demanding. Such mothers move from rejection to acceptance and nurturance. Most mothers who are initially affectionate tend to remain so. Those who are permissive with infants may be highly permissive or highly restrictive when the child is ten (Janis *et al.*, 1969).

Parents' orientation toward children and child-rearing practices may be changed by deliberate intent. For example, parents of underachievers have participated in counseling sessions and have changed their behaviors in the space of 15 half-hour sessions. The results were immediately discernable in the improved school marks of some children. A better atmosphere in the home was reported (Gilmore, 1969).

Children have their input into parental behavior. A mother who sees her ten-year-old daughter's shyness and self-doubt may decide to change the methods of strict control she has used for the previous ten years. Another who sees her children becoming demanding and ignoring the feelings of others may decide that a tightening of parental controls is necessary.

A family attending counseling sessions stemming from the 17-year-old girl's staying out all night on various occasions was able to change the home atmosphere abruptly. Father and daughter had not spoken to one another for months. Mother, along with 12-year-old brother, were frequently taking sides. The mother was seeking peace and the boy was hoping to see another battle. During the sixth session the father seemed to wilt. He had previously held up his head, had his shoulders back so his chest was prominent. On this day he dropped his head and sobbed, "When I read and hear about all the things that happen to girls—running away, becoming hippies, going wild at college—it drives me mad with worry. I love Jeanie and I panic." The only way he saw to help her was to be strict and firm, as he consistently had been.

Almost as if stuck with a pin, Jeanie jumped up and went to her father, put her arm around his neck and said, "Gee I thought you were so cranky because you hated me." It turned out that Jeanie, on her nights out, stayed with girl friends, just to make her father worry about her.

Biographies are replete with instances in which the individual's achievement motivation, in school or life, bears no relation to the trends indicated above. Despite either parental indifference or discouragement, the individual achieves. Sometimes it seems that the person acts from spite. He seems to have the urge to show that *he* cannot be licked. He achieves because of the indifference or discouragement. Lest some regard this as an excuse for the use of punitive approaches, it must be said that the probability of achievement's stemming from negative approaches is small. Lest some regard their parents' ineptitude as an excuse for failure, let the variable reaction be noted. Studies of the families of dropouts show that generalizations do hold. The tendencies are not, however, laws. Many things enter the achievement **syndrome**: Tone of the school, intellectual maturity, family income, socioeconomic class, peer pressures, and occupational goals; but the family remains as the critical factor (Cervantes, 1972).

Creativity   Not all parents are content with the fact that their children are achievers of academic status. They genuinely would like their children to be autonomous and self-determining. They seek ways to go beyond the mere satisfaction of cultural expectations and conformity. Child-rearing practices influence personality of children. Parents who would like to have their children develop their creative potential must then become aware of the influences that point toward creativity. Studies of the characteristics of independence and risk-taking are prominent in creative persons (Gallagher, 1964, p. 44). That is, creators must be able to take a stand that is different from the flock. They need the sense of security and independence that allows each to go his own way. Influences that accompany just such development are 1) lack of worry about—or at least absence of discussion about—financial hardship, 2) mothers who work outside the home, and 3) families in which there is an openness to interests and a variety of interests. The child who does not learn that financial security is important can take risks. If his mother works he learns independence. If there is openness to varied interests he can, with parental support, indulge the development of his unique whims. Torrance (1962) reports what may be a surprising point: Families of creative children are often not "well-adjusted." Father and mother have conflicting feelings that are frankly, and sometimes strongly, expressed. Hence, the child's deviations or **regressions** are viewed rather matter-of-factly.

Parnes (1971) characterizes creative processes in terms of sensitivity, synergy, and serendipity. Sensitivity implies awareness and accuracy of all sense. Synergy means the association of elements in a surprising or novel manner (the Gestalt idea that the whole is greater than the sum of its parts). Serendipity refers to the happy quality of discovering one thing when actually engaged in the search for something else. In these terms, children brought up by parents who talk with and show them things, who respond to their questions but who also say, "What do you think?" and who are astonished by the great discoveries of their children are helping youngsters to become sensitively aware. If parts are to work harmoniously together—synergically—then children must learn to live within the framework of society. Hence, freedom is not license; and Parnes emphasizes responsibility. Parents of creative children tend to have the equilibrium with which they can be permissive to an extent and then say, "That's far enough." Parents of creative children tend to have varied interests themselves. Because their interests are alive they avoid smothering the child. They have interests other than the children and are responsive, but not necessarily demonstrative.

The essence of child-rearing and personality

The family has a strong influence on child personality but it is not the only influence. Immature parents who are rejecting and punitive frequently have children who are delinquent, underachievers, or dropouts. Those parents who have achieving and creative children tend to be accepting but not smothering. They use permissiveness within boundaries. They are capable of a progressive untying of the apron strings so that children can progress towards independence. The family that 1) produces a personal relationship, 2) involves some depth in communication, and 3) yields personal satisfactions tends to be the one that develops effective and productive personalities (Cervantes, 1972).

Despite the apparent message of the last 25 years, and depending on what parents want in their children, love is not necessarily enough (Bronfenbrenner, 1972). Love fosters the internalization of adult standards. Too much love may undermine children's capacities for initiative and independence. Time spent with the child—especially if he progressively is treated more like one treats a mature person—is probably a better key to personality symmetry than is love. In addition, parental postures have different influences on boys than on girls. If the family is patriarchal the boy tends to be more responsible, if the home is matriarchal the girl tends to be more responsible.

Either boy or girl can choose to upset the whole theory of

child-rearing methods indicating certain probabilities. A boy may decide, rather early in life, that he is just not going to be like his shiftless, overbearing, selfish father—he repudiates the model. A girl may decide, rather early in life, that she is just not going to be like her peaceful, yielding, patient, resigned mother. She rejects the feminine role she sees portrayed. Extremes seem to beget extremes. The son of a belligerent, pompous con-man may become just like dad. Or, he may become his exact opposite. The girl with a meek, submissive, retiring mother may mirror mother's feelings and actions with discouraging accuracy.

Some fallacies about the father-absent family are extant. It is sometimes believed that absence of the father, occasioned by death, desertion, or divorce, has dire consequences in both boys and girls (Hetherington, 1973). It is hard on boys because of the lack of a male model. Much evidence has been accumulated indicating that father-absent boys will be less masculine than father-present boys (Biller and Borstelmann, 1967). However, the idea becomes fallacious if several other contingent factors are not taken into consideration. Father-absence when the boy is four or five years old is more likely to result in lack of masculinity than when it occurs in the life of a 12- to 14-year-old boy. Father-absence is less serious for boys of the lower class where the chances are larger that the home will be matriarchal anyway. It is more serious in the case of middle and upper class boys. Father-absence in any socioeconomic class may be compensated for by older brothers, uncles, grandfathers, or boarders who live in the home. Finally, much of the boy's reaction to father-absence depends on the mother's emotional stability and her response to father-absence. If she reinforces manifestations of masculinity, the boy will respond differently than he would if the mother were bitter toward males and rejected the show of masculine traits of aggressiveness and impulsiveness. She may, in fact, convey the notion that the boy is now the man in the family. If she can keep from making the burden too heavy, father-absence may constitute a motivation for achieving masculinity (Biller, 1970).

Father-absent family

The matter of parental absence is much more serious as a factor in personality impairment, especially during infancy, if it is the mother who is absent. Numerous studies have followed the report of Spitz and Wolf (1946) to the effect that the separation of six- to nine-month-old infants from the mother caused severe personality damage—including physical and mental regression. Upon separation the infant cried and protested strongly. He withdrew from people. He would remain silent, turn his head toward the wall, and lie motionless. Despair and resignation were reflected in the withdrawn, apathetic behavior. This combination of loss of appetite, loss of weight, susceptibility to

Maternal deprivation

infections and eczema, symptoms of depression, regression in toilet habits, withdrawal from things and people was called anaclitic depression.

The studies that followed those of Spitz and Wolf have confirmed and extended knowledge about the effects of early separation from mother: Any time before the age of two is a dangerous time for mother-child separation. Separation at the age of six to eight months is most consistently correlated with severe personality disturbance. Disaster can be averted by supplying *a* (one!) substitute mother. A succession of baby-sitters, even highly competent ones, is not an effective antidote. Babies who had a close, warm relationship with mother prior to separation were more severely disturbed than those who had less mothering.

Follow-up studies have been made of infants who were traumatized by such early separation. The results range from noticeable to severe damage. On the surface, some seemed to be functioning adequately. On intensive study they showed varying degrees of impairment of impulse control, conceptual thinking, learning ability, and the capacity for close affectional relationships. Fraiberg (1971) asserts that babies who are deprived of human partners in the first two years of life are babies who are in deadly danger of never becoming a human being. When mothers are inadequate, and psychologically set themselves off from the infant, there is a strong possibility that the capacity for love, affiliation, emotional variation, and concern for self and others will be permanently impaired. She calls such victims of mother neglect and separation (psychological) hollow persons.

Surveying numerous studies, Yarrow (1964) identified several influences that condition the impact of mother-child separation: 1) age, 2) quality of mothering prior to separation, 3) quality of maternal care after separation, 4) relationships with others during separation, 5) duration, and 6) experiences that reinforce separation, such as periodic changes in foster homes. In addition, he says that there are apparently different infant constitutional factors in responses. Some babies are **congenitally** sensitive to separation. Others are able to cope. It may also be hypothesized that some babies may have precipitated the desertion. Their constant squalling prompted the mother to abandon the infant or he made her so anxious that she became ill. The child's irascibility may have necessitated a succession of baby-sitters because any one of them could not survive his strident demands.

Parental felicity   Most of the studies on family influences on personality have been on such factors as cited in the foregoing—discipline, socioeconomic status, child-rearing methods, child-parent interaction. The author postulates that more important than those influences listed is how the mother and father get along with each other. There are several arguments to support the hypothesis. 1) If the safety needs of a child have primacy in the early years, then to see icy silence or fiery battle between those two who constitute his world can be a devastating experience for the child. His whole world is threatened.[5] 2) Some parents who cannot get along with one another are simply socially immature (see "hollow persons," p. 68) and may be prone to use the defense mechanism of projection. That is, not daring to fight the bigger and stronger adversary (the spouse), one takes it out on the hapless and helpless child. 3) On the other hand, marital satisfaction helps to produce an aura that pervades one's work, social contacts, and parental responsibility and provides a zest for such functions. 4) Lack of parental felicity may precipitate the phenomena of parent-child separation. The mother or father simply leaves the scene.[6] 5) Children, to a remarkable extent, learn what their parents "are" rather than what they say. Models may be more important than methods. Of course, methods and models are inseparable because one does what one is.

If this thesis is tenable, then an approach (but not a panacea) to generating wholesome family influences is to begin with the question, "What should I be?" rather than with, "What should I do?" Self-examination is a start. It is a difficult course because it is so difficult for one, by himself, to maintain balance between objectivity and being overly critical. Another step would be to join a parental discussion group. There it is often easy to see the effectiveness or errors of other parents; whereas the discrepancy between one's own intent and practice is difficult to discern. A third approach would be to join a basic encounter group (*with a competent facilitator*) where the emphasis is on the "here-and-now" of how one is coming across to others. The focus is on what one is as a person rather than as a parent.

SUMMARY

Predispositions for the development of personality traits such as level of activity, stoicism, or zestfulness, being withdrawn or outgoing are attributed *in part* to congenital conditions. Certain drugs, diseases, X-rays, diet, and emotional trauma of the pregnant woman have influences on personality that exceed the operation of mere chance.

Prolonged birth may injure the cortex of the child. The use of instruments, compression in the birth canal, or temporary oxygen deprivation may result in brain damage. Such prolongation is sometimes attributed to the excessive use of drugs. Many mothers are

[5]The wisdom of incompatible husband and wife staying together "for-the-sake-of-the-children" may be questioned. Either one alone might be an adequate model of mature personality—the constant irritating presence of the other constitutes an unbearable load.

[6]In a recent special training class for paraprofessionals that the author conducted, there were four women, each with from one to five children, whose husbands had just left—three with no announcement of intent.

selecting "natural" or "prepared" childbirth because they believe the infant will get a better start in life.

Birth order or size of family have no consistent relation to personality of the child. Large families among the economically depressed are seen as a source of compounding already heavy burdens.

Babies create, to a degree, the kind of child-rearing milieu they will experience. Hard babies tend to produce irascible caretakers. Easy babies tend to elicit warm mothering. Boys are born being somewhat heavier and taller than girls; but girls grow more rapidly, and by the time of puberty exceed average boys. By the time of adulthood boys have regained height-weight superiority. Average girls grow more rapidly in many mental and in verbal characteristics. Because individual boys may, and sometimes do exceed even superior girls, *no bases* are provided for differential educational treatment.

Babies and children gain in personality maturity when their safety needs are met through order, routine, discipline, and responsible adults. Children profit from contact with adults for satisfaction of love and esteem needs. Hence, important factors in parental behavior are time, touch, and love.

Delinquency, achievement-underachievement, and the manifestation of creative talent were used to illustrate how different family milieus—in terms of maturity of parents, role of parents, child-rearing orientation—bear on the personality development. It was postulated that more important than methods of child rearing was the matter of parental felicity.

SUGGESTED READINGS

CLAUSEN, JOHN A., "Family Structure, Socialization, and Personality," eds. L. W. Hoffman and M. L. Hoffman, *Review of Child Development Research,* Vol. 2. New York: Russell Sage Foundation, 1966.
   Parental personality, older adults and older siblings, number of children, birth order, broken families, and patterns of child-rearing all have influence on child personality—but the intricate interweaving of these influences make prediction of personality a hazardous venture.
FRAIBERG, SELMA, "The Origins of Human Bonds," eds. H. W. Bernard and W. C. Huckins, *Psychosocial Dynamics of Effective Behavior.* Boston: Holbrook Press, Inc., 1971. From *Commentary,* Vol. 44, No. 6, 51–57, December, 1967.
   This might be the "horror story" of the past decade. Mrs. Fraiberg shows how lack of adequate mothering in the first two years of life may prevent the baby from ever becoming a true human being. The personality trends established by cruelty and neglect in the first two years may be irreversible.
HETHERINGTON, E. MAVIS, "Girls Without Fathers," *Psychology Today,* Vol. 6, No. 9, 46–52, 1973.
   The author studied 72 adolescent girls, 13 to 17. She found consistent

differences in girls who had fathers and ones who had lost fathers through death or divorce. Fear of men, sexual aggression, sexual anxiety, response to sex of interviewers were behaviors noted.

RUDIKOFF, SONYA, "Family Fever Chart," *Commentary*, Vol. 52, No. 4, 89–93, October, 1971.

The author caustically reviews some of the pronouncements about the moribund condition of the institution of the family. She challenges the beliefs of some that the family is a decadent and demoralizing anachronism. She asks the question: What will happen to dependent children when adults are all engaged in the self-centered process of becoming "their true selves"?

SONTAG, LESTER W., "Implications of Fetal Behavior and Environment for Adult Personalities," eds. H. W. Bernard and W. C. Huckins, *Exploring Human Development*. Boston: Allyn and Bacon, Inc., 1972. From *Annals of the New York Academy of Science*, Vol. 134, 782–786, 1966.

Emotional trauma of pregnant women result in hyperactive fetuses that, in turn, are predictive of irritability and defensiveness in early childhood; and the tendencies have persisted as personality traits of early adulthood.

FOLLOW-UP LEARNING ACTIVITIES

Examine the responses you made on the pre-reading activities for Chapter 3 (except for the first), and see if you might have "blamed" your family when you might have assumed responsibility. Record your assessment.

_____
_____
_____

Ask your mother if you were a "hard" or "easy" baby. If that is not possible at this time, talk with a classmate who is able to ask the question about himself. What, if anything, seems to be the present impact?

_____
_____
_____
_____

What do you understand to be the **self-fulfilling** prophecy?

_____
_____
_____

(Compare your response with that of a classmate.)
Aside from sex itself, do you think there are any basic boy-girl differences in personality?

_____ Yes. Boys are _____
_____

_____ No. It all depends on what the culture teaches.
(Compare and discuss your response with several classmates.)
At what level of basic need motivation (according to Maslow) do you believe you are now functioning?

In what way have your parents ever placed you in the "double bind?" _____
_____

Talk with a classmate who has experienced father-absence. What is his belief about the result of that experience?

_____
_____
_____

4
Socioeconomic Factors in Personality

Can the imprint of poverty be erased?

LEARNING ACTIVITIES

Using the groups, 1) lower class, 2) lower-middle class, 3) upper-middle class, and 4) upper class, where do you rate yourself?

I am _____

I so rate myself because _____
_____
_____
_____
_____

Describe yourself in terms of your self-concept.
_____
_____
_____
_____
_____

(Compare your response with that of a trusted classmate.)
Check the statement with which you are most in agreement:

_____ Schools tend to make socioeconomic status more rigid.

_____ Schools tend to diminish class differences.

_____ Schools have no real impact on socioeconomic status.

Tell how you feel about the way intelligence tests have been used in your own life. Do you feel good about them? Antagonistic? Other?
_____
_____
_____
_____
_____
_____

What do you think is the difference between compassion and sympathy?
_____
_____
_____
_____

To what extent, if any, has socioeconomic status had an influence on your personality?
_____
_____
_____
_____

If Paiutes are lazy then it follows that Mr. Notales, a Paiute, is lazy. If Mexicans have no visions of tomorrow, then we know that Pete Hurdadez, a Mexican, has no concern about the future.

No one would really accept the logic expressed in the foregoing statements. Nevertheless, much of our thinking about people is expressed in similar stereotypes. It is necessary to be constantly on guard, to avoid the widespread fallacies about: adolescents, old people, Mexicans, blacks, Russians, welfare recipients, Republicans, men teachers, the 400, and the poor.

Man, with his capacity and potential for thinking, is engaged constantly in an attempt to simplify, sort, categorize, and classify. Classes and categories help to reduce complex phenomena into packages that can be handled conceptually. The process has, however, progressed too far when we permit stereotypes to become a substitute for thinking.

In the previous chapter, family influences on personality were discussed. In this chapter some of the factors that influence the nature, composition, and functioning of the family are considered. (In the next chapter culture will be dealt with as a factor in personality.) To the extent that one understands the forces that shape the family, he is better prepared to think and deal with other facets of personality. But, hunters have found, that a mighty poor way to hunt ducks is to shoot at the flock in general. Likewise, a poor way to understand the relationship of socioeconomic class to personality is to stop with the generalizations that exist. For every statement regarding causal relationship between social class and personality, the cautionary principle must be appreciated: *Individual differences within a socioeconomic stratum are greater than those between persons of different strata.*

THE MEANING OF SOCIAL CLASS

Privilege vs. privation

Normally, "birds of a feather flock together" but as a cliché, it is often difficult to separate the bird from the feathers. In the case of man, we are undecided as to whether one's identity derives from his associates or from that vague abstraction called "values." In the western world, the matter of finances is a large factor in socioeconomic status. Socioeconomic status determines one's relative access to social advantages and privileges or the denial of access to developmental opportunities. J. Paul Getty, one of the richest, if not the richest, man in America pays low taxes despite incomes of thousands of dollars per minute. His is the privilege of depreciation allowances, expense deductions, and tax-exempt bonds. The privileges are sustained by the employment of aides who see that legal loopholes are discovered and enlarged. Conversely, the privation of the poor is both consciously and unconsciously perpetuated by the dominant society. This is done through depreciating the egos, by non-sequitur logical deductions, and hidden taxes.

Income is but one of the criteria that define an individual's socioeconomic status. Some authorities list the following as the criteria by which social class status is deduced: amount of income; source of income (rents, royalties, interest, salaries, wages, hourly pay, or charity); education; occupation; kind of residence; place of residence. Social class has received much study in the last two decades. There is currently verbal recognition of the inadequacy of the criteria just cited. The sociologist and cultural anthropologist are faced with the same difficulty that confronts the student of personality: What about the matter of values?

> On graduation from high school, what a boy loves is vastly more important than what he knows. What companions does he choose? What books does he voluntarily read? What ideals does he harbor? These are the really significant characteristics which determine his life's career. Does he chum with wholesome pals, does he read choice literature, does he enjoy good lectures, does he participate in harmless recreation, does he take an interest in civic welfare? Or, does he seek vile companions who tell smutty stories and enter into questionable escapades, does he read trashy and indecent magazines and books, does he sneer at the church, the school, good books, and all serious activities?
>
> His attitude toward society and its problems, his attitude toward religion and morals, his attitude toward duties and obligations, are vastly more important than the few items of intellectual knowledge he has gained. His spontaneous likes and dislikes, his loves and his hates, his longings and aversions, will really determine what manner of man he shall be.[1]

Values are a significant aspect of personality; so too are values a, perhaps *the*, significant aspect of socioeconomic status. Banfield (1970) states that it is not money but perspective that defines one's social class. If one is poor and unschooled, without prestige, but is psychologically capable of envisioning and providing for a distant future he *is* upper class. If one is rich but improvident; if he cannot conceptualize a future or control his impulses—and is therefore obliged to live from moment to moment—he is lower class despite his money.

Values, income, education, or other criteria of social class consti-

---

[1]F. E. Bolton, *Adolescent Education* (New York: The Macmillan Company, 1931), p. 175.

tute continous graded differences, hence the lines between classes are not sharp and clear. In addition, one may be on the vague borderline between classes by having, for example, three criteria (type of residence, education, and occupation) that place him in the upper middle class but four (place of residence, source of income, amount of income, and values) that place him in the lower middle class.

A still further complicating factor in considering social class in relation to personality is that class is clearly distinct from caste. In a caste system one is born into a given stratum; he inherits his position. Intelligence, special talents, behavior, or ability to earn do not alter his rank. In a culture that has a class system—and all societies have some kind of hierarchial ranking—**mobility** is possible. One may move up or down the ladder during his lifetime. He does this by virtue of acquiring, or losing his place on the ranking criteria. One may lose position by use of drugs or becoming alcoholic (and thus lose job, home, and friends). One may lose status by marrying into the next lower class and adopting the values and behaviors of the spouse. Most mobility in the United States is upward. Persons get more education than their parents, they climb higher in occupational ranking, and earn higher and steadier incomes. They adopt the values and behavior of the next higher category.

There is no monopoly on "future orientation" despite general trends within a given social class as was indicated above in reference to Banfield's observation. Another example of overlapping values is that whatever is meant by "honesty" is not easy to place on the social-rank scale. Lower class people are alleged to steal without twinges of conscience from "the haves." They would not, however, cheat their fellows. Upper class people are reputed to be dedicated about keeping their pledged word but consider that cheating on income tax reports is a matter of sound business. *Some* lower class persons will steal from their neighbors and some upper class persons keep their word only when it is convenient in terms of the exigencies of the moment. It is thus being said again, that differences between groups are not so great as the differences within a group.

It may be, some people think, that mass culture has a tendency to obliterate class differences. People of all classes read the same newspapers—although some in the lower classes do very little such reading. All persons are exposed to the same movies and watch the same television programs. However, these are external influences. They are subject to varied interpretations in terms of deep-seated value orientations.

SOCIAL CLASS BEHAVIORAL DIFFERENCES

Differences in status for those on the borderline are hard to discern. There is overlapping in values and behaviors. There are, nevertheless, differences between classes that are, in general terms, internalized. They become a part of individual personality.

The popular stereotype of the *typical* American is that of being middle class. Such typical Americans strive for more education for their children than they have themselves. Lower class persons also verbally espouse education. However, when a child drops out of school the matter is soon forgotten. Educational motivation is strong in the middle class, amounting to what some have called an education compulsion. Pressure is placed on middle class youngsters to achieve in school as early as three years of age (Heffernan, 1966). Lower class youngsters typically are not exposed to books, magazines, and reference volumes. To an extent, they lack both parental models and materials. Middle class people are generally described as being ambitious. Lower class people are described as having been beaten by the press of circumstances—poor health, inadequate income, marginal housing. They may thus become hopeless and shiftless. However, it must be recognized that many—approximately 50 per cent (Havighurst and Neugarten, 1967, pp. 23, 61)—have been upwardly mobile. Consequently the so-called of lack of ambition in the lower class must be used with hesitation. Presumably, those in the middle class are more flexible, tolerant, and nondogmatic than those in the lower class. This is, in part, a function of education and access to education. Those in the middle class are described as being thrifty. They have insurance policies, savings accounts, and own, or are buying, their homes. Those in the lower class are not "thrifty" because they cannot afford insurance. They cannot get far enough ahead to set aside savings. They are unable to accumulate the down payment for a home. Havighurst and Neugarten (1967), p. 21) epitomize the matter of social class personality characteristics in the following words, "While they are only thumbnail sketches and thus cannot do justice to the variety of patterns, they should suffice to point up the most salient differences in life styles. . . ." The classes are more alike than they are different. There is much overlapping of material possessions and philosophical values. Generalizations, by definition, apply to the majority. Generalizations become inaccurate when used as predictions for individuals.

    In terms of personality theory one of the more important concepts is that of power. This means power over the lives of others and power over one's own behavior and future. Those in the upper classes (the top 3 per cent of the total in the upper-upper and lower-upper categories) are self-directing. Autonomy in children is expected and approved, within the limits of upper class social protocol. Although they may not be in visible positions of leadership, they are quite widely the power behind the throne. Upper-middle class persons are in positions of leadership in government, industry, and business. They hire, promote, and fire the minor executives. They own businesses. They tend to be in

Middle class vs. lower class orientation

high executive positions that give them power over the lives of others. Lower-middle class persons are local leaders. They are minor executives for the policies formulated by owners and statesmen. They are in positions of nominal power. They are sometimes frustrated by their being perceived by others as having power but themselves feeling that they are locked into a system from which there is no escape (Schrag, 1969). Lower class people have power neither over the actions of others nor to be self-directing. The "Why don't they . . . ?" syndrome is an almost universal characteristic of these powerless persons. They regard themselves as being pushed by people and circumstances. They feel that they are not really a part of the system. They believe their fate is simply one of enduring their privations and hoping that life will bring a few rewards.

Many authorities regard the self-concept as being the core of mental health. It is a focal concern in personality orientation. If one thinks well of himself, believes that others love him, that he is worthy of being loved, and if he feels responsibility (i.e., can exert some power) for himself and on others, he has the start toward building a life in which he can cope and construct. If, on the other hand, one feels that he is rejected, he also tends to internalize the attitudes and actions of others. He may come to believe he is incapable and that others should rightly exercise power over him. Some become **ambivalent**. They alternately feel the urge to exert the power of self-direction and then to demand that others provide the directions and demands. Some who are rejected come to believe that they really do not deserve decent treatment.

Deirdre was a tall, statuesque, brunette, 24 years old, who was referred for therapy after a feeble attempt at slashing her wrists. Her complexion was clear, her features were such that many would call her beautiful. However, she had a hang-dog expression that seemed almost contagious in the depths of her despair. Her smile, that appeared more frequently in later counseling sessions, was equally as infectious. She was academically brilliant.

On those occasions when she had tried business college or university classes she had earned high grades; several of her instructors had urged her to pursue a professional career.

Deirdre had a severe handicap. She had a self-concept that was composed largely of the feeling that she was not worth much and deserved little better. This concept was generated in large measure by a mother who constantly belittled her. Mistakes were highlighted and achievements were ignored. A stepfather made frequent sexual advances and tried to fondle her during her teen years. The mother, aware of the situation, was jealous rather than being angry with her husband. Deirdre was a thing rather than a person.

Deirdre had had her share of suitors. However, when a worthy man would get serious and begin to talk about marriage she would find flaws in his behavior. She would belittle his worth. On the other hand a sneaky affair with a married man yielded some apparent satisfaction. She finally married a young alcoholic, who could not hold a job, and whose sexual interests focused on other men rather than on Dierdre. Her husband eventually moved out leaving her with no car and a stack of bills. With the help of state rehabilitation funds, she went to business college, quickly acquired needed skills, and took a job as a typist. Shortly she was promoted to being a responsible receptionist and immediately became irascible and undependable. "I was a bitch." After being given indeterminate leave, she took a job as a checker in a grocery store but her back hurt from the hours of standing. Rather then let her go, management promoted her and gave her some office and supervisory responsibilities. She liked the work and was competent but her performance again became careless and her habits were again undependable.

After a short marriage to a competent young engineer, whose work took him to many places and to which he took Dierdre, she became increasingly restless. "He treated me so good and was so forgiving and patient it just made me feel 'Ugh.' He didn't hit me or bawl me out when he found out I had had a date when I said I was going to a movie with a girl friend." She left him to live with another alcoholic—which precipitated the wrist slashing.

Clue after clue and episode after episode indicated that Dierdre had such a low opinion of herself that she did not believe she deserved to have good things (a kind husband or a prestigious job). When she got what she thought she did not deserve, she "messed things up" so that she could then justify her failing to get acceptance and approval.

The lives of many in the lower class seem to show many parallels to Dierdre's life. The press of poverty, the one-parent home, the physical stress of earning a living via hourly pay, inability to pay for dental and medical service, inadequate diet, and the disdain or pity of the "uppers" beats the heterostatic urge down to a state of defensiveness. Good things are perceived as a matter of luck. Good will not last or soon happen again. Social class begins as a congeries of material conditions. It may end by being a part of one's self-concept and personality. However, despite generalities, the hazards of stereotyping must be avoided.

There [in ten black families in the ghettos of Boston] Coles found that the widely held conception of black families as inevitably disorganized simply does not stand up. Among middle class blacks, he reports, the typical family is "much like the Yankee Victorian kind—very strict, very concerned with getting ahead." In his study of Northern blacks, Coles makes other stereotype-breaking observations. He reports, for example, that lower class blacks have family structures similar to prosperous suburbanites; in both cases the father is away from home much of the time, and his absence is not necessarily any more damaging to the black child than to the white.

Black mothers can be as effective at child-rearing as any mothers anywhere. Their youngsters are frequently quite unlike the lost, emotionally sick children described in psychiatric journals; many "have a flesh-and-blood loyalty to one another, a disarming code of honor, a sharp, critical eye for the fake and the pretentious."

Confessed one elementary-school teacher: "That was the hardest thing for me to realize—that a ghetto child isn't a hopeless case or already a delinquent when he comes into the first grade."[2]

Strengths of the lower class

Socioeconomic class does end up being, in part at least, a matter of self-concept. Educators, social workers, employers, and others who come into contact with lower class persons are beginning to perceive the need for a new outlook. Special help in reading or special training to develop job skills has failed to be uniformly helpful. Children and unskilled workers who are treated as though they were a contagious disease find that psychological barriers are as strong as cyclone fences. Working to change the skills of the lower socioeconomic class individual might be questioned. The initial wise effort should be devoted to changing the attitudes of teachers, social workers, and employers who come into contact with the *culturally different* person. This changed attitude is directed toward changing a part of the milieu so that a more robust self-concept may be nourished. The words "economically deprived," "culturally disadvantaged," and "educationally handicapped" are perceived to be ways to initiate or to sustain a burdensome ego concept. Teachers and employers are asked to see some of the differences as strengths. They are asked to begin with analyzing, and considering the implications of those strengths.[3] Some strengths that might be noted are listed below.

Although the stereotype is that lower class people are irresponsible, children ten or 12 years old can capably take care of younger siblings when the mother has to work outside the home (Mc-Creary, 1966).

Branded in school as being obstreperous and unruly in the classroom and on field trips, children from the lower class do not get lost. They have exercised independence on the streets; but the independence is called disobedience.

Pupils are categorized as being slow learners because they have internalized a different culture. That culture calls for adaptive strength and durability. They have, perhaps, learned too much about illegitimacy, unstable marriages, prostitution, unemployment, welfare bureaucracy, and medical neglect.

Pupils are uncooperative with teachers. Their willingness to help a classmate (cheating) or their unwillingness to "rat" on a buddy (lying or sullenness) is an evidence of strong, cooperative in-group solidarity.

Children and adults from the lower class are often described as being linguistically handicapped. Given some respect and a feeling that they can express themselves freely they can utter a

[2]Robert Coles, his life and works described by Ruth Galvin and Virginia Adams, "Breaking the American Stereotypes," *Time*, Vol. 99, No. 7, February 14, 1972, p. 38.

[3]The following statements should be regarded as being prefaced by "In general . . .," "Frequently . . .," "Sometimes . . .," or "On the average . . . ."

stream of verbal content and feeling that is difficult to stem (Riessman, 1972). Their language is *different.* It does communicate with high effectiveness in their own culture.

Both children and adults have a positive attitude toward the value of education; however, taking a long-range view is difficult. Experience has not shown a future perspective to be of great material value. Hence, education must have, even in the upper grades, a specific job and work orientation (Olsen, 1972).

When adults are given a job they will leave it at a moment's notice. They are undependable. From their viewpoint, however, they have found that the pay received is inadequate to cover their basic needs of food, clothing, and shelter. Hence, the rumor of a better job, at higher pay, in another place, is an attractive lure. This is especially true in view of the fact that the present locale is less than satisfactory.

Adults have, on objective analysis, an admirable toughness, resilience, patience, and a compassion for their peers. They teach these same personality traits to their children, nephews, nieces, and foster children by both precept and example.

"If they have these wonderful qualities," the reader may ask, "why are they such a problem?" No simple answer can reasonably be given to such a complicated question. There are many ramifying contingencies. In part, the answer reflects on the definition, given in an earlier chapter, of personality: ". . . as viewed by fellow members of society." The problem is, in part, the fact that lower class people are different in degree from the middle and upper class people who do the stereotyping. It is unrealistically expected that "on the basis of pure logic," lower class people will readily internalize the values of another culture. Relative to the school milieu, Reissman says,

> . . . I emphatically do not mean that a teacher should compromise his standards or that he should condescend to his pupils. I mean that he should recognize that the culture from which these pupils spring has its own standards and its own sense of values and that he must work within these standards, in fact turn them to educational profit.[4]

Contained in the above quotation is a principle of personality development that pervades individual motivation, social competence, and national welfare. It is epitomized in the cliché, "We have met the enemy and he is us." The principle was expressed by Harry Batten, one of the citizens in Philadelphia, who, with some fellow citizens, became disturbed to the point of doing something about crime, fraud in government, snarled transportation, inefficient schools, pollution, and skid row. Batten said, "The trouble with Philadelphia is us."[5]

[4]Frank Reissman, "The Lessons of Poverty," *American Education*, Vol. 1, No. 2, February, 1965, p. 21.
[5]Morris Duane, "Philadelphia: Behind the Renaissance," *Saturday Review*, Vol. 49, No. 2, January 8, 1966, p. 48.

SCHOOLS IN THE STRATIFICATION PROCESS

The stratification of persons into classes with varying degrees of privileges and opportunities versus privations and handicaps is a culture-wide process. Employment, housing, medical service, aid to dependent children, and formal education play a part in the ease or difficulty of access to developmental experience. Some of the processes are designed, with good intent, to enhance opportunity. This does not eliminate the often burdensome outcome in terms of personality formation. The impact of some educational procedures, for example, is as discouraging as if those procedures were maliciously planned. Similar examples might be described in terms of employment training programs (apprenticeship), payment of union dues, or for welfare activities.

Schools as a sorting agency   Education in the United States was initially conceptualized and planned as the agency that would prepare all men to be participating citizens. When population was small, so too, of course, were schools. These schools performed their function well as the new immigrants from various European countries learned some variety of American English. The pupils learned to read, write, and compute and soon became solid citizens of the community. The immigrants from each country quickly acquired the speech and dress of their new country. If there were any **cultural discontinuity** it existed between the parents and children. They spoke different languages and were finding some conflicts in values. Two of the value conflicts concerned woman's place in the family and community and children's prompt obedience to fathers' commands.

Because the schools were small and because there were 30 or 40 pupils of various ages in a one-room school, it was necessary for teachers to plan the work in terms of the developmental level of the pupils. It was clearly not possibly *to teach* geography or arithmetic to beginners who could not read or count in the same "lesson-hearing" session with those who had acquired skills far beyond that of the first graders. While the teacher was working with eighth graders, who might be any age from 12 or 13 to 18, it was necessary for third graders to conduct their own *learning* activities. Perhaps inadvertently, but with some effectiveness, the emphasis—in schools for the Irish, Germans, Swedes, Italians, Polish, Greeks, and French immigrants—was on learning. These schools were much like those currently being endorsed as nongraded and "open" schools (Pavan, 1973). The teacher performed as a consultant, or adviser, or director of the learning process. The pupil whose learning pace permitted was "skipped." His lessons were heard with those a year or so more advanced than his age mates. The pupil who learned at a more deliberate pace was not stigmatized. Ability tests had not been formulated. Brevity of the school year, the necessity of the pupils' working on the farm, in a factory, or serving as domestic help (hired girls) could explain variable achievement. Thus, schools were regarded as the "melting pot" of nationalities. Children and adolescents entered the school as Scotsmen or Bulgarians and came out as Americans. The selecting and segregating function of university education was not of any great import because higher education concerned only a small per cent of the population—only 3 per cent as recently as 1930 in contrast to the 22.8 per cent of the college age group who have degrees today (*Almanac . . .*,1972, p. 322).

With population increase, greater and greater numbers sought the advantages attributed to schooling. The past successes of the schools were such that education was seen to be important. Education became the victim of mass production. The one-room school disappeared. Grade stratification became increasingly rigid. Intelligence and achievement tests received a great boost as instruments for distinguishing between various levels of achievement during World War I (1914–1918).

The function of schooling, despite the best of democratic intentions and respect for human dignity, had been transformed from the melting pot function to an agency for sorting and classification (Havighurst and Neugarten, 1967, pp. 69ff.). Schools initially were designed to prepare children for citizenship and participation in a rural and farm culture. Today, they are serving in an urban and industrial society to emphasize differences. The result is often indoctrination for self- and social-alienation.

Intelligence tests and readiness tests are used to initiate the sorting process. The purpose of testing, in all sincerity, is perceived and planned as a means of individualizing instruction to fit the test-indicated needs of the pupils. In the hands of skilled and sensitive teachers the function is served to the great advantage of individual pupils (Waugh and Waugh, 1972). Many teachers are not skilled. They are not sensitive. The pupils, being held to comparative-competitive grade standards, find themselves strapped to a Promethean bed.

Ability grouping

The evaluation involved in ability grouping is internalized by pupils. Even pupils in the first grade, where tracking is disguised as Bluebirds, Robins, and Cardinals, are quick to learn which are the dummies and which are the brains. They rather readily begin to verify the self-fulfilling hypothesis. Those who are expected to do well, think they can do well. They can accept an occasional failure. Those who receive the disapproval of teachers for poor performance and poor attitudes confirm the expectation. Yet, in fact, their attitudes are psychologically sound. If one cannot have something—a million dollars, a mansion on the hilltop, be president of his corporation, get on the honor roll, or earn high grades—he had better (if he would maintain good mental health) convince himself that he really does not want it. When the child in the Buzzard group does this he is said to be unmotivated, or lazy, or has a negative attitude. He is, in fact, protecting his ego.

In the event that some pupil fails to get the message regarding his superiority or inferiority, the fact of sorting and classification is periodically (each six to nine weeks) brought forcibly to the minds of pupils, parents, and peers by means of report cards. Sometimes the grades are publicly posted. What the practice does to personality is reflected by the boy who took his report card into the lavatory before he could open it. It is hard to ignore the impact when one's friends are crying, "Whajagit?" A practice designed to improve communication between teacher-pupil-parent, it is more than decadent; it induces decay in pupils' self-concepts and blocks teacher-pupil communication.

The rationale of the report card (unnecessary in the day when a teacher could not avoid meeting the parent several times a year) is that it is a means of communication with parents. However, communication is not facilitated by using codes that are not mutually understood. One teacher grades on attitudes, another on comparative status, another on individual progress during the grading period, and still another on who the parents are.[6] Even teachers do not know the code in the same way. The same arithmetic paper, graded by five teachers, may receive grades all the way from *F* to *A*. The self-concepts generated by ability grouping, comparative grading, and report cards would not be so destructive if the personality deterioration were transitory. But the recipients may be handicapped for life. The Brains think of themselves as some kind of royalty who deserve special consideration in business and industry. The Buzzards persistently believe that they must be as dumb in everything as they were in reading or arithmetic. And the self-fulfilling prophecy rides again.

Ability grouping, if it is achieving the results for which it is designed, must be engineered by teachers who keep the ego concept of the pupil in the foreground. Grouping does not eliminate individual differences. It does make it easier to meet those personal needs than was possible in the one-room school. The reason why special classed do result in spectacular achievement gains in many instances is that "special" teachers know a variety of ways to deal with personality differences. Whether there is ability grouping or not, the fact that the teaching-learning process is a human transaction must not be overlooked (Bernard, 1972, pp. 61 ff.).

Intelligence tests   There are as many definitions of intelligence as there are of personality. However, as will be shown in Chapter 15, the variety of instru-

---

[6]This refers to the author, who in his freshman year of teaching had to grade the work of a pupil whose father cashed his warrants and who was a member of the school board.

ments for testing intelligence is smaller than for those used to assess personality. One of the definitions of intelligence is "Intelligence is what intelligence tests measure." This tongue-in-cheek, sarcastic definition nevertheless contains much truth—and the truth is becoming increasingly difficult to manage.

Height, weight, blood composition, blood pressure, lung capacity, and pulse can be measured directly. Different technicians using similar instruments will agree on these measurements. Intelligence, on the other hand, is measured indirectly. The amount or nature of one's intelligence is extrapolated from how much one knows and what he can do at given ages. The score of one subject (person) will vary from one time to another. It varies from one technician to another. Even on equivalent forms of the same test administered at approximately the same time, the results vary. In addition, the tests differ in the kinds of knowledges and behaviors they sample. Each test reflects what the maker of that test conceptualizes intelligence to be. Hence, there is truth in the remark, "Intelligence is what intelligence tests measure."

Currently there is much debate concerning the justice involved in giving intelligence tests. One criticism is that they were designed by psychologists of the middle class. They cannot, therefore, be wisely used on the lower class. They should not be used to classify lower status pupils (McClelland, 1972). It is akin to saying that a white man born and raised in New York City is a moron when he cannot follow a cat track in an African jungle. The opposition argues that moron or not, one's survival in the jungle may reside in his avoiding the cat. One's survival in American life resides in his adaptation to the dominant culture. The matter of justice in intelligence testing seems to reside more in the use of the results than in the instruments and scores themselves. If the scores are used to sort, classify, categorize, and exclude pupils, and thus diminish self-concepts, then the testing process merits condemnation. If the scores are used to detect specific subabilities that merit cultivation and nourishment, then the tests deserve praise.

A prominent psychologist, Arthur Jensen (1969) generated an acrimonious series of arguments: After careful analysis of many data, he declared that compensatory education for lower class children had failed because there was no consistent raising of the IQ. Hunt (1969), and many others, countered his argument. It was claimed that the tests were unfair to those with cultural backgrounds different from those of children who constituted the **standardizing** population. If low scores on intelligence tests cause teachers to abandon hope for, or relax effort in behalf of, the lower class pupil, then the tests are a hazard. This, as a matter of discouraging fact, is what has frequently happened. Furthermore, it is being increasingly appreciated that motivation is probably as important in determining success as is IQ (Bane and Jencks, 1973).

Pupils are classified on the basis of test scores. Those who score low are routed into remedial classes or slow-learning classes. In high school low scorers are guided into vocational rather than college preparatory curricula (Havighurst and Neugarten, 1967; Kemp, 1966; Sexton, 1961). If a mistake is made, and errors do occur, and a bright child is placed in a remedial class, the chances are that he will shortly become a "remedial case." Rosenthal and Jacobson (1968) presented data to show that when teachers were told that certain children (actually chosen at random) were about to "blossom" intellectually, that was actually what happened. Although the handling of the statistical data in this study has been challenged, the hypothesis that pupils will tend to fulfill teacher expectations still is considered to be valid (Thorndike, 1969).

Schools as a developmental agency

Until about 1930 it was believed widely that one was born with a certain amount of intelligence. Barring some shortcomings of testing instruments, it was thought that one's IQ remained the same for life. If such were true, sorting and classifying would have some validity. In the mid-1930's numerous studies indicated that IQ could change considerably, if there were marked changes in the environment. The idea that one was born with a certain amount of intelligence shifted. Today it is believed that one is born with a certain potential for developing intelligence. We believe a salutary environment will develop much of one's potential. A barren environment would permit atrophy of potential. Moreover, research data, from 1930 onward, point to the conclusion that the earlier the intellectually nourishing environment is available the better. The earlier the stimulus the greater is the likelihood that good conditions will have an accelerating effect. Hence, there is a surge of interest in early childhood education. Those children from homes with minimum intellectual and verbal stimulation especially need such opportunity.

Today it is hypothesized that the potential itself may be enlarged or decreased by the experiences one has. If, for example, one's potential for acquiring a second language is not exercised prior to the age of about 12 years, some of the facility for learning a second language is irretrievably lost (Penfield, 1972).

Tests in the early childhood programs are designed to discover talents that might be developed. They should not be used to discover weaknesses that can be used as an excuse for exclusion. This objective tended to become obscure with the advent of mass education. Taylor (1972) recommends that *more* tests be used in programs for the educationally disadvantaged. However, it seems that multiple tests might be used advantageously for the personality development of *all* pupils. Taylor's recommendation is based on Guilford's (1967) theory that intelligence consists of at least 120 different, but interrelated, factors, or subabilities, of intelligence. Most intelligence tests give global scores (see Chapter 15). It is possible, at present, to test for more than 80 of the factors. The more tests that are given to pupils the greater is the chance that a given pupil will be in the top 10 per cent in some factor. His ego concept will be strengthened because he is a top-ranker in something. Thus, instead of 10 per cent., who are top-rankers on the global test, there will be 19 per cent out of the total group who will be in some top 10 per cent with two tests. Twenty-seven per cent will be in some top 10 per cent with three tests. Thirty-five per cent with four tests, etc. There is some "slippage" because one pupil may be a top scorer on two or more tests. Not all will be in a top 10 per cent in something. Taylor's data to date indicate that 99 per cent will be above average in something.

> These calculations yield a beautiful phenomenon and a most promising picture for educators: Not only do new star performers emerge from almost all levels of the previous talent ladder, but those who had not been flourishing in the old talent areas will rise toward the middle of their class in each new talent area in turn. Moreover, nearly all students will have the rewarding experience of being above average in one or another talent area if we cultivate enough different talents in the classroom. In addition, about a third of the students will be found to be highly gifted in at least one major talent area.
>
> This is a very heartening outlook in terms of motivation of students and the potential in our human resources. . . .
>
> The implications of this phenomenon are exciting because, if a variety of talents are tested and trained for, a student can learn a great deal about himself and his abilities and consequently become self-directed. He can steer himself throughout his life into activities that call for his best talents—a course that can well lead to optimum self-actualization and productivity.[7]

Schools that are successful in serving the melting pot function, successful in developing latent talent, successful in promoting self-actualization, are those in which sensitive teachers discern strengths. Strengths can be in art, athletics, leadership. Teachers can deal with individual pupils and concentrate on developing those strengths. Frequently, and fortunately, pride in one's strengths is such that it leads a student to, and gives him confidence that he can, remedy his weaknesses (for example, reading or arithmetic). In schools, the emphasis that continues to shrivel the child's ego will be on weaknesses. They will continue to place the child in a remedial class and magnify the idea that the child is a "remedial case." The child's ego concept will be that he is weak, deficient, not good enough. Personality traits such as tolerance for differences, openmindedness, and breadth of human understanding will develop in those schools that do not have tracking plans or ability grouping. Pupils develop best under the leadership of empathic teachers. Personality traits such as shame, jealousy, egotism, chauvinism, inferiority, superiority, intolerance,

[7]Calvin W. Taylor, "Cultivating New Talents: A Way to Reach the Educationally Deprived," *Journal of Creative Behavior*, Vol. 2, No. 2, Spring, 1968, p. 86.

and suspicion will tend to be generated in schools where Bluebirds, Buzzards, and Buntings roost in separate rooms. Ego deflation stems from teachers who call attention to the deficiencies.

THE PRICE OF STRATIFICATION

The wise student will quite properly question the validity of the sweeping assertions just above. Unfortunately, we do not have instruments (such as intelligence tests, even with their admitted shortcomings) to measure such traits as jealousy, suspicion, and openness. Attempts are being made to devise such instruments but it begins to appear that jealousy is a different thing when it concerns one's spouse and when it concerns one's siblings. Jealousy is different when it concerns one's classmates as contrasted to peers in a neighboring school that is in the same basketball league. (In fact, some authorities are beginning to think that intelligence functions in much the same way—talented mathematicians are not equally gifted in political acumen.) However, one can lay claim to being scientific even without experimental test evidence. It is an intelligible system of events that makes a science (Murphy, 1967). Traits and behaviors have been noted that do point to the conclusion that lack of contact with people of all sorts does tend to limit the total development of individual personality.

The disadvantaged child of suburbia

Two decades ago the schools of suburbia were looked upon as models of sound educational theory and practice. Curricula were relevant and responsive to pupils' needs. Buildings included the latest architectural advantages of function and beauty. Teachers were regarded as being the best obtainable—they had served probationary periods in less desirable schools, earned their master's degrees, and had proven their liking for, and skill with, youngsters. Pay scales and fringe benefits were such as to allay financial discontent. Yet there are numerous observers who note today that there is something seriously awry with the youth of suburbia.

Meyer (1972) calls attention to such disturbing characteristics of suburbia's youth as lacking in sexual restraint, childish tantrums in the face of adult authority, and widespread disposition to follow the crowd and experiment with drugs. These suburban youth share a common background of loving parents, comfortable homes (see Chapter 3), superior health, superior intelligence, and those "good" schools. Yet the youth are pictured as being consumed with self-pity or alienated from society. Some, he says, are so upset that they run away or withdraw through the curtain of drugs.

No one thing can explain the alienation of youth. The fact that there are numerous factors that contribute to the dilemma and discontent of youth should not blind us to the factor of choice. Young people can decide not to use drugs. They can decide not to run away from home. They can decide not to blame their stupid parents. Skinner (1971) denies the reality of choice—man "chooses" this or that because of the experiences he has had. Others (Bonner, 1965; Frankel, 1971; Rogers, 1969) say that the stimulus-response gap, during which man can enact the processes of rational thought, makes the matter of choice an inevitable responsibility. One even chooses not to choose. Choice or not, some factors are thought to contribute to the malaise of suburbia's youth:

The inclination of parents to use permissive approaches in child-rearing results in the youngsters' coming to feel that they should not be subject to adult authority.

Mothers' regulating their lives so that they can transport children to and from their various lessons in art, music, golf, dancing, riding, and baseball games causes youngsters to overrate their own importance. Mother is regarded as a *thing* along with the station wagon (Halleck, 1971).

Cottle (1969) reported that parents, in their attempts to treat children as persons and peers, have placed responsibilities on children before they have enough maturity and experience to make sound decisions. Some parents, on the other hand, tend to hover about children and overprotect them.

Schools are in part responsible for the moral uncertainty (in those cases where it does exist). There are, of course, many suburban youth in whom morality and high ideals are stable and admirable. Choice of courses is desirable but so too is the learning of fundamentals of reading, computing, writing, conversing, and knowing basic principles of science and human behavior—regardless of pupil interest. If interest must be developed, the essentials are nonetheless important. A major defect of the suburban schools is that they are suburban. They are in a new extraordinarily homogeneous strata of society—middle and upper-middle class. Fathers are important, or soon to become important, executives in business and industry. Laborers and part-time workers do not, typically, live in the new and rapidly growing suburbias. Mothers are well educated in colleges where middle class girls are prepared for careers as wives, businesswomen, or artists of varying sorts. Most have had little or no contact with the lower class residents of congested living areas—the slums.

The results of this self-selected segregation, like the tracking and ability grouping practices in schools, is to generate a lack of social perspective. It is one thing to read about the overlapping of differences between groups, to meet an occasional lower class person who displays high intelligence, unusual tolerance, or pervasive honesty. It is quite another thing to come into daily contact with numerous exceptions. Learning from a book about the need for humanity to man, the need for compassion, the need to recognize that we, too, are different is of value but it is only one approach. Living with people who are different does not necessarily increase tolerance and mutual respect. Those who do learn compassion through school or neighborhood associations and where teachers or parents are teaching toward the same ends have such attitudes as a lasting possession.

> . . . Do the hypocrisy and callousness of suburban living really distort the values of modern youth? Unfortunately, it does seem that the tremendous reservoir of young, creative talent located in suburbia is not being cultivated in a manner essential to effective growth of democratic ideals; and there are now some real doubts emerging about the kinds of leadership suburban youth might someday contribute to our society.
>
> Our nation's suburbias are evidently becoming so segregated that children can grow up without genuine contact with others of different racial, religious, or social backgrounds. The result is a growing provincialism in spite of ease of travel and communication. Suburbia's children are living and learning in a land of distorted values and faulty perceptions. They have only the slightest notion of others; they judge them on the basis of suburban standards (such as "cleanliness" and "niceness"), generalize about groups on the basis of the few they might have known, and think in stereotypes. In short, they usually have little association with or knowledge of people who differ in appearance or attitudes.[8]

Compassion—
Self-realization

There is much concern, regret, and even pity for the persons who are victims of class and color discrimination. Compassion, the polar opposite of prejudice, has been called by Jersild (1968, p. 553) the highest and noblest of personality traits. As this is being written, the American reader and televiewer daily is amazed and shocked to see the results of stereotyped thinking regarding Catholics and Protestants in Northern Ireland. It is particularly depressing to listen to Irish children and adolescents so faithfully mirror the prejudices of their parents. It seems that social astigmatism must persist forever. In short, prejudice, discrimination and stereotyped thinking is something that one does to himself. It is a way of stultifying personal and individual growth. Stereotypes block compassion and inhibit the realization of potential for becoming fully functioning human beings.

> The author was raised in the lead-silver mining district of northern Idaho. There the community prejudice was against those "scab" Missourians—Missouri being the only other state doing considerable lead-silver mining. They were a lazy, dirty, lustful, lot whose children were dumb in school and could not even speak acceptable English. They spoke with a Missouri drawl that evoked hilarious and scornful laughter from the sophisticated Idahoan. Many Missourians returned to their familiar and less hostile state.
>
> The irony of this case is that after the author had gone away to

---

[8]James A . Meyer, "Suburbia: A Wasteland of Disadvantaged Youth and Negligent Schools," *Phi Delta Kappan*, Vol. 50, No. 10, June, 1969, p. 575.

college and had taught school for a couple of years, he married the daughter of two Missourians. He has yet to learn, after 37 years of marriage, that Missourians are dirty, dumb, lazy, and lustful; or at least any more so than Idahoans.

Perhaps exposure to a wider range of persons, to teachers who engender self-respect and respect for others, can salvage the would-be Irish bigots. One girl, studying the problem of black-white *de facto* segregation said in her high school class, "I can tolerate my father's attitudes but I swear I'll not share his distorted views, his prejudice, regarding blacks."

Two important issues are related to the bias and bigotry manifested in many places, but illustrated here, in the lives of young people of suburbia. First is the tenuous basis of labeling. My wife's parents were from Missouri but they did not have a Missourian drawl. Catholics and Protestants may be clearly separated in Northern Ireland but the differences did not keep an Irish girl from falling in love with the wrong young man—and having her head shaved in payment for the disgraceful act. Black-white is certainly not a color thing. In the United States over three-quarters of the so-called blacks have "white blood"—whatever that can be when there are A, B, and O types that are transferable within the type. Some blacks "pass" for whites and some have to inform the naive that they are black. One hears about Greek, Jewish, and Arabian noses but wonders where they all went in the Greek, Jewish, or Arabian girls who are beautiful by our provincial standards.

There are differences in behaviors and beliefs that exist in terms of general tendencies between groups of people. If there were not such tendencies, it would be pointless to discuss family, socioeconomic status, and culture as factors contributing to the formation of personality. The challenge is to 1) keep us alert to the potentials for development a given environment most abundantly provides. The challenge is to 2) avoid drawing conclusions about an individual in terms of the stereotype (which may have a basis in its partial truth). For example, suburban children have limited social perspective.

Compassion and empathy may be sought on a selfish rather than altruistic basis. We have not, in fact, gotten very far beyond the medieval notion that one gave alms to the poor in order to save the donor's soul. Often the "in" thing today is to contribute to Community Chest or pay taxes (without excessive grumbling) that go to welfare. The forward step readily available is to be involved in the welfare (access to the advantages of society) of all. This has been said in many ways by mental health authorities, counseling psychologists, and psychiatrists. Man's mental illness is in large part caused by his overconcern about his own gratifications. Man's illness is generated by his detachment from others. Loneliness is generated by one's separation from his fellow beings (Menninger, 1963; Jahoda, 1958; May,

1969). We become concerned about the welfare of others not to save our souls but to save our*selves.*

Menninger (1968) provides an impetus for examining personal input into social conditions. He postulated that we—the good, upright, law-abiding citizens—need crime and evil. We need, furthermore, to punish criminals so that we, says Menninger, can feel more comfortable about the crimes we commit, but for which we are not caught. We need to disdain and despise the criminal personality so that we can tolerate our own rapist, covetous, and violent tendencies. If we can assume some of the responsibility for the mistakes of criminals, then we may take some steps toward moving from punishing criminals and their "paying society for their evil ways" to the matter of rehabilitation.

It is postulated that a similar **defense mechanism** may be at work in our attitudes toward the lower class. We need them to allay the covert suspicion that there was a bit of luck in our rise to status. Perhaps it was not our brilliance, industry, and devotion to task performance that led to socioeconomic position. It may have been the concern, or at least the interest of others that helped us along the way. Or it may have been our wisdom in the parents that we selected.

Einstein was reputed to have said, "I am a pessimistic philosopher but an emotional optimist." The problems of lower status, unemployment, slums, poverty have multitudinous facets. The pessimistic philosopher says these problems will persist. "The poor will be with us always." The emotional optimist says that a journey of a thousand miles begins with the first step. The first step can be taken by the individual. He can study the implications of the words of Jonne Donne, "No man is an Iland, intire of itselfe; every man is a peece of the Continent, a part of the maine." These words—which about one of four readers has posted on a wall, pasted in an album, or underscored in a book—represent a challenge that is difficult to internalize.

SUMMARY

Social class is a phenomenon that, through the family, community, and formal educational processes, has powerful impact on personality. Its effects are felt in income, housing, occupation, education but most tellingly are felt in internalized values. One of the important values is being able to delay immediate gratification in order to obtain a better future. A strong motivating force in personality development is the feeling that one has power—he can in some measure control his own action and is of some moment to others. Generally, lower class persons, with good reasons, feel that they are powerless.

One approach to improving the self-concept of the lower class person and to turning what are often social burdens into social assets is to focus on strengths rather than weaknesses. The lower class has many strengths.

Schools play a part in maintaining class lines by their sorting tactics—tracking, the distribution of grades, and curriculum advisement. It is believed that these techniques were not deliberately designed to perpetuate social status. The result is nonetheless effective in making mobility difficult.

Intelligence tests play a part in selecting pupils and stratifying them in the social hierarchy. In some schools there is a move to stop the use of such tests because of the cultural bias they have. In other schools attempts are made to avoid the bias without discarding the value tests have in providing clues about pupils. The sorting function is particularly culpable as research data show that IQ can be raised through varied and supportive milieus. More tests to find more pupil strengths, giving more pupils a chance to rank high in something, have been recommended to replace the limitations of the one score (global) test.

Sorting and categorization may do harm to those in the higher echelons by limiting their social perspective. Several authorities believe that the super schools of suburbia do harm to balanced personality development. Chauvinism, alienation, provincialism, egotism, pseudo-sophistication, and prejudice are some of the threats that seem to be generated in the isolation of suburbia.

Social class and its granting of privilege to some and its denial of access to the "goodies" of society to others is in part an individual responsibility. To the extent that we help, or at least do not consolidate disadvantage, we build our own more admirable and rewarding personality traits. To the extent that we deny our brotherhood to all men, we shrivel our potential for developing a mature personality.

SUGGESTED READINGS

COLES, ROBERT, his life and works described by Ruth Galvin and Virginia Adams, "Breaking the American Stereotypes," *Time*, Vol. 99, No. 7, 36–42, February 14, 1972.
> *Coles, in his numerous books and articles, may be today's most outstanding personality theorist. Living with people in the slums, ghettos, and rural poverty areas, he finds that privation fosters strength as well as despair and alienation.*

BANE, MARY JO, and CHRISTOPHER JENCKS, "Five Myths About Your IQ," *Harper's Magazine*, Vol. 246, No. 1473, 28–40, February, 1973.
> *Reading about these myths, or fallacies, will help the reader think more wisely about the uses and limitations of intelligence tests.*

HAWK, TRAVIS, "Self-Concepts of the Socially Disadvantaged," *Elementary School Journal*, Vol. 67, 196–206, January, 1967.
> *The author states that the self-concept fell into disrepute under the behaviorism of John B. Watson. It is now perceived as a central factor in*

personality by such theorists as Lecky, Rogers, Snygg, Combs, and Maslow. He shows how the self-concept of lower class children is eroded by certain school practices.

JENSEN, ARTHUR R., "How Much Can We Boost IQ and Scholastic Achievement?" *Harvard Educational Review*, Vol. 39, 1–123, 1969.
   The author has assembled impressive data to show that the role of heredity in determining status cannot summarily be dismissed. He goes against prevailing opinion; and the knowledgeable student should be acquainted with a work that is stirring considerable controversy.

MEYER, JAMES A., "Suburbia: A Wasteland of Disadvantaged Youth and Negligent Schools?" eds. H. W. Bernard and W. C. Huckins, *Exploring Human Development*. Boston: Allyn and Bacon, Inc., 1972. From *Phi Delta Kappan*. Vol. 50, 575–578, 1969.
   The author undertakes the task of showing that, despite their being viewed as an example of the "good life," suburban influences have some detrimental effects on the personality of young people—people who, in large measure, will be tomorrow's leaders.

SCHRAG, PETER, "The Forgotten American," *Harper's Magazine*, Vol. 239, No. 1431, 27–34, 1969.
   Much attention has been given to the sad plight of lower class persons in American society. Schrag reports that those in the lower-middle class are also deeply concerned with status and mobility.

FOLLOW-UP LEARNING ACTIVITIES

Besides those mentioned in the text, list three stereotypes that tend to block thinking. Compare your list with classmates and add three of their best stereotypes.

1 _____

2 _____

3 _____

1c _____

2c _____

3c _____

Evaluate the gist of Banfield's statement, "To envision a future is to be upper class. To live in the present and not work for a better future is lower class."

_____

_____

_____

_____

_____

What are the implications of Banfield's statement, as far as you are concerned personally?

_____

_____

_____

_____

_____

Reread the case of Diedre. Is there anything you do that might be classed as self-defeating behavior?

_____

_____

_____

_____

_____

How do you react to the postulation that motivation, more than intelligence, determines one's status and future?

_____

_____

_____

_____

_____

Some readers have said that the statements about suburbia's children were overdrawn. Do you agree or disagree with the criticism? Why?

_____

_____

_____

5

Personality and Culture

Does art form personality or vice-versa?

LEARNING ACTIVITIES

What are some "strange" behaviors in other people you have experienced, read about, or heard about? (Examples: eating snakes, using a fork upside down, etc.)

_____
_____
_____
_____
_____

(Compare your items with a classmate's list.)
How do you react to eating horse meat or dog meat?

_____
_____
_____
_____

What do your answers to the above two items indicate about yourself? _____

_____
_____
_____
_____

Twenty-five miles from Portland, Oregon, there is a community of Russians who try to maintain their old-country ways. This includes dress, farming methods, and children's education. If you were living in the nearby town, how do you think you would react to them?

_____
_____
_____
_____
_____

Do you think . . .
   it wise for a Catholic and a Protestant to marry?
   Yes _____ No _____ Comment _____
   it wise for a black and a white to marry?
   Yes _____ No _____ Comment _____
   the major purpose of education is economic?
   Yes _____ No _____ Comment _____
   children should have rights equal to parents?
   Yes _____ No _____ Comment _____
   a woman should be head of the household?
   Yes _____ No _____ Comment _____
   technology has an influence on your personality?
   Yes _____ No _____ Comment _____

The interdisciplinary nature of the study of personality is shown in these first chapters. The first chapter dealt with personality in terms of philosophical orientation. The second approached personality from the standpoint of biology and genetics. The third chapter, on the family, viewed personality from the standpoint of the psychology of adjustment and sociology. The fourth chapter used the perspective of the cultural anthropologist. This chapter combines cultural anthropology with sociology and some history. Certainly, it is no surprise that such a pervasive concept as personality would be a concern of many academic disciplines.

It might appear that having dealt with personality in terms of the family and socioeconomic status, the cultural approach would have been discussed in sufficient detail. Socioeconomic status reveals some personality differences within a culture. The cross-cultural approach reveals some even more extensive differences. The major sociological-anthropological similarities are that peoples' needs are much the same. It must be borne in mind that the observations are made by cultural anthropologists and their perspectives have limitations. There are so many anthropologists who have made important contributions to personality theory that only a very small portion of them can be cited.

Not only do anthropologists contribute to the psychology of personality but psychologists make contributions to anthropology. Hence, the reader will find, in this chapter, reference to psychologists, psychoanalysts, and psychiatrists as well as to anthropologists. Ideas and concepts are more difficult to sort and classify than is the academic preparation of authorities on personality. Some authors of personality texts place Horney and Rank with the psychoanalytic theorists. Their contributions, however, fit with some logic into the discussion of cultural impact on personality.

CROSS-CULTURAL DIFFERENCES

Strange people   "The Eskimos are strange people. They seem to put much emphasis on insignificant details. They live in a land of snow and ice, yet they have no word for snow. Instead they have distinct words for fresh snow, packed snow, frozen snow, melting snow, deep snow, blowing snow, snow mixed with rain, and so on. Their language is extremely complex, for instance, they have over 20 words to describe the various parts of one caribou hide."

"The Americans are a strange people. They place much emphasis on insignificant details. A car is not just a car but it is a Ford, a Cadillac, a Buick, a Pontiac, a Chevrolet, a Studebaker, a Plymouth. And as though that were not sufficiently complex, there is a small difference between a coupe, wagon, sedan, sport car, convertible, and a pick-up. Each car has some minor characteristic in terms of head-lights, fenders, folds, creases, and grille that is supposed to make you forget that they are all box-shaped."

What is significant to some cultures, is not to others.

These two paragraphs describe the constant problem of an-thropologists. They attempt the difficult task of laying aside their own cultural biases and viewing another culture with objectivity. They become participant-observers—living with the people of the strange culture. They try to describe it without permitting their feelings to enter the participating and observing. Their occupational hazard is "going native"—liking the culture, or some aspect of it, so much that their personality orientation is altered. Some nonanthropologists, unaware of the hazard, have become strangers in two cultures. The reader may find, in the following pages, some cultural differences that he believes are worth copying.

Personality in primitive cultures

A primitive culture, like strange people, is one in which the functions of life are performed in a manner different from our own. Margaret Mead (1928) made her first contributions, as an anthropologist, to the field of personality by comparing the way one becomes an adult in Samoa and in the United States. In our technological society it takes several years for one to pass from childhood, through adolescence, to adulthood. In Samoa the transition is accomplished with much less time and turmoil. A few dances, some performance tests, some indoctrination lessons and the Samoan child of yesterday becomes a woman ready to marry and rear children. A male is ready to assume his full duties as husband, fisherman, or forest worker. Mead was therefore one of the first to formulate a notion that is now coming to be predominant: *Adolescence is a cultural phenomenon induced by the complexity of technological and urban society.* Puberty is a physiological fact. However, the glandular and morphological changes that precede and accompany adolescence do not explain the American adolescent. Physical changes do not provide a basis for claiming that adolescence is a time of stress and strain, of emotional turmoil, or of identity crisis. Cultural conditions provide more tenable explanations for adolescent turmoil—in those cases where it does exist.[1] Mead (1970), after excursions into the topics of sex, family, and women's liberation, is still trying to get the message across that personality is formed, in some measure, by culture. The differences in customs, stability of a society, and ways of achieving need satisfaction demand varied role performance. Mead, along with Gardner, a statesman (1964), Rogers, a psychologist (1971), and Toffler, a professor and reporter (1970), indicate that the personality trait most needed by modern man is that of flexibility. We need flexibility to cope with the phenomenon of rapid change; and the Samoans are not now exempt.

Mead (1935), perhaps influenced by Freud's concurrent campaign to outgrow the then prevailing, prissy Victorian attitude toward sex, wrote a book called *Sex and Temperament*. She showed that premarital sex, marriage, child-bearing, and sexual deviance are variously viewed in different cultures, circumstances, and historical eras.

> An Arapesh [New Guinea] grows his wife. . . . A little girl is betrothed when she is seven or eight to a boy about six years her senior, and she goes to live in the home of her future husband. Here the

[1]Adolescents have, for generations, indeed eons, been going to the dogs. Socrates noted the decline of youthful personality some 400 years B. C. Today almost any issue of a newpaper or some program on TV will confirm the notion that adolescents are still intent on destroying themselves and society.

Adults, it seems, miraculously appear "out of the blue."

father-in-law, the husband, and all of his brothers combine to grow the little bride. Upon the young adolescent husband particularly falls the onus of growing yams, working sago, hunting for meat, with which to feed his wife. In later years, this is the greatest claim that he has upon her. If she is dilatory or sulky or unwilling, he can invoke this claim: "I worked the sago, I grew the yams, I killed the kangaroo that made your body. Why do you not bring in the firewood?"

. . . to questions of incest I did not receive the answers that I had received in all other native societies in which I had worked, violent condemnation of the practice combined with scandalous revelations of a case of incest in a neighboring house or neighboring village. Instead both the emphatic condemnation and the accusations were lacking: "No, we don't sleep with our sisters. We give our sisters to other men and other men give us their sisters." Obviously. It was as simple as that.[2]

Ruth Benedict (1934) also studied primitive and contrasting cultures. She formulated the hypothesis that individual personality is largely a struggle to fit one's uniqueness into conformance with cultural demands. She perceived that the individual has comparatively little freedom. The behaviorist, Skinner (1971), has also voiced doubt about the concept of freedom. However, Benedict saw "almost limitless" freedom for variety in cultures. Excerpts from her publications give some indication of this variety.

. . . In Dobu [an island of the Trobriands] dourness and prudery go along with prenuptial promiscuity and with a high estimation of sex passion and techniques. Men and women alike rate sex satisfaction high and make achievement of it a matter of great concern. There is no convention of indifference or absorption in a masculine world that supports a man whose wife he suspects of betraying him. The vicissitudes of passion are exploited, whereas in Zuni, for instance, they are moderated by tribal institutions. The stock sex teaching with which women enter marriage is that the way to hold their husbands is to keep them as exhausted as possible. There is no belittling of the physical aspects of sex.

The Dobuan, therefore, is dour, prudish, and passionate, consumed with jealousy and suspicion and resentment. Every moment of prosperity he conceives himself to have wrung from a malicious world by a conflict in which he has worsted his opponent. The good man is the one who has many such conflicts to his credit, as anyone can see from the fact that he has survived with a measure of prosperity. It is taken for granted that he has thrived, killed children and his close associates by sorcery, cheated whenever he dared. As we have seen, theft and adultery are the objects of the valued charms of the valued men of the community.[3]

[2]Margaret Mead, *Sex and Temperament in Three Primitive Societies* (New York: The New American Library, Mentor Books, 1935), pp. 65, 67–68.

[3]Ruth Benedict, *Patterns of Culture* (New York: The New American Library, A Mentor Book, 1934), pp. 155–156.

The Zuni present marked contrasts to the Dobuans. Gentleness prevails and personal power is scorned. If a boy wins too many footraces he is barred from running. The admired Zuni is one who has never tried to be a leader. Theft rarely occurs. Sex is regarded as a private matter. Boys and girls meet, exchange gifts, and then the boy visits the girl's father to ask for her in marriage. The father answers that it is up to the girl. Girls are typically virgins at marriage. If after marriage, the man commits adultery, the wife's reaction is mild. If the misconduct becomes public knowledge, the wife is shamed. She simply stops doing her work, without recrimination, outbursts, or even open recognition. Children are treated mildly and even during boys' initiation ceremonies, each is accompanied by a guardian. Those who whip their children are regarded with horror and contempt. The good Zuni has a yielding disposition and a generous heart. He is polite and should "talk lots" (*i.e.*, he should set people at ease). He readily cooperates with others and should not display arrogance, suspicion, or strong emotion (Benedict, 1934, pp. 91ff.).

Reporting on many cultures, Benedict shows contrasts between frenzy and excess vs. measure and order—to which she gave the names Dionysian and Appolonian personalities. Yet despite the general characteristics of a culture, she insisted that such descriptions do not categorize and interpret the range of individual behavior. It is absurd, she stated, to reduce culture down to the Procrustean bed of generalizations. Generalizations lop off important facts that do not fit the stereotype.

> "No culture yet observed has been able to eradicate the differences in the temperament of persons who compose it. It is always give-and-take" (Benedict, 1934, p. 234).

The self in society

A contemporary of Margaret Mead and Ruth Benedict, George H. Mead (1934) became interested in answering the question, just cited, that Benedict had raised: Despite cultural pressure, why do persons respond differently? His answer was given in terms of self. He was among the first to provide the now accepted view that the self is formed by association with others. Self comes especially from those who, during one's childhood, are closest. The way others behave toward one, and more importantly, the way one thinks others are behaving toward him, influences the way one thinks of himself. Any interpersonal behavior includes an interpretation of what one thinks of himself and what he thinks others think of him.

The self has its origins in communication. Although words in various languages differ, gestures and facial expressions are symbols of communication that are universal. There is language of speech, of the hands, and of the countenance (G. Mead, 1934, pp. 144ff.). He asserts that in some primitive cultures people can conduct elaborate conversations just by expressions of the countenance. The hazard of verbal language is that it may differ in some way in its meaning for the person using it and the meaning it has for the person who is hearing it.

This concern is one that looms large in the thinking of current students of personality and personal adjustment. Basic encounter groups are manifestations of the realization that what one thinks he is saying is not equivalent to what another thinks he is hearing. **Meta communication**, (*i.e.*, discussion about content of communication) is popular in some areas—therapy, for instance. Businessmen are also concerned with meta communication. It is a gigantic problem in international relations.

The self, according to G. Mead, is initially an organization of *particular* and specific attitudes and acts. The self reaches its full stature when it is comprised of *generalized* others—or the perceptions one has of the group as a whole. Selfhood is achieved by progressively moving from subjective and individual perception to the objective. Selfhood is the "generalized other" perceptions of what man and culture are. Step-by-step the partial perspectives are integrated (internalized) into a stable capacity for seeing oneself accurately.

Determinants of personality

Margaret Mead and Benedict periodically remind their readers that, although they focus on culture and personality, they acknowledge the role of constitutional differences. One does not, for instance, expect a cretin in any culture to be able to perform adult functions as well as do normal adults (Benedict, 1934, p. 217). Kluckhohn (1948, 1953), an anthropologist, and his psychologist co-worker, Murray, have stated clearly the multi-faceted and interactionary nature of personality:

1. *Constitutional determinants*. The problem of heredity and environment is meaningless. It takes both a bodily constitution and a culture to develop potential. Excited by discovery of some specified determinant of personality, the unwary student may forget to acknowledge the force of other determinants.

2. *Group membership determinants*. Not a single particle of our religious, governmental, or moral behavior is inherited. "The skills that are acquired, the factual knowledge, the basic assumptions, the values, and the tastes, are largely determined by culture" (Kluckhohn and Murray, 1953, p. 59).

3. *Role determinants*. The culture defines how functions of age, sex, class, caste, or occupations are to be performed. These roles are so distinctive, say Kluckhohn and Murray, that, although they are determined by group membership, it is useful to treat them as separate determinants. The role one performs shields the private aspects of personality (*e.g.*, underlying motivations) from the public personality.

4. *Situational determinants*. In addition to constitutional determinants there are fortuitous events that may shape one's attitudes and behaviors. Physical environment, traumatic

events, accidental encounters, the ordinal position of one's birth are situations that occur in any culture. Kluckhohn and Murray included in this group what others might have made a fifth category; namely, the individual's response. They cite an example of a young man who, undecided about his career, meets an engaging and persuasive advocate of journalism. The young man does not immediately decide to become a journalist but the encounter starts a train of thought that may be decisive in molding his personality (1953, p. 62). The authors, it seems, give some credence to freedom and choice.

Sex behavior   Sexual drive is a constitutional determinant of behavior but the way it is responded to is culturally influenced. Role determinants mold the attitudes of males and females. In addition, there is no doubt that situational factors have pertinence in sex roles. The fleeting allusions to sex in the preceding sketches of the work of M. Mead and Benedict do not indicate how great a portion of their writings deal with sex. Recent studies by anthropologists Messenger (1971) in Ireland, and Marshall (1971) on a Polynesian island, indicate the diversity that "normal" sex behavior may take.

Messenger indicates that the limited sex life of about 400 inhabitants of a community on an Irish island is related to youth's out-migration and to a restricted and unhappy life. Custom and teaching of the priests emphasize that sex is degrading. Any sex activity that is not related to procreation is sinful. Children receive no instruction, infants are kept covered so siblings will not see the naked body. Adults bathe infrequently and wash only part of their bodies at a time. Dressing or undressing is a very private affair and is often done under the bed covers. They sleep in their underwear. Young sailors have never learned to swim because it would mean bodily exposure. Boys play with boys and girls with girls. Young men have so much fun with "the lads" that they delay marriage. They are lads up to the age of 40, with the average age at marriage 36. Women's average age at marriage is 25.

Women are supposed not to enjoy sex. Messenger and his wife report that conversations and questions indicated that female orgasm was rare if not unknown. There is no foreplay in marital sex except some rough slapping or pinching of the buttocks. The sex act is brief. The man attempts to degrade and humiliate his wife. The men soon return to associations with the lads, but homosexuality is unknown. Even babies are not kissed and fondled.

Menstruation and menopause are so distressing that women often become highly neurotic when they occur. Data on frequency of intercourse was evaluated by one woman who reported that men could wait a long time but that women could wait longer. Intercourse is performed without removing underclothing. Deep kissing is unknown. Breast fondling is rare. This would be unenjoyable anyway because the priest emphasizes the sinfulness of it all and the need to control one's animal passions.

Sex is a source of joy, of pervading interest, and varied practice in Mangaia and its delights are mutually shared by males and females. Marshall (1971) reports that it is the society's principal concern—not a morbid preoccupation. Large numbers of children are born to unmarried girls. There is a large number of sexual partners. When married, young couples may have three to five orgasms per night. The orgasm is considered to be a gift to the partner rather than an achievement. The purpose of sex is to delight the partner.

Boys and girls on Mangaia play together for the first three or four years. They then separate into boy and girl groups. This sex separation in public lasts for life. A church deacon will not walk to church with his wife. Such separation does not diminish the intensity of private relationships. A boy's buttocks and penis are rarely covered. Boys begin their sexual activity at about age 13 or 14. Typically, an older woman provides direct sex instruction, using different positions, acts, and instructs him to hold back orgasm until it can be achieved mutually. After being thoroughly initiated the boy seeks nightly copulation. Girls are also taught by older women. From their first male contact they demand virility. Boys are expected to maintain constant in-and-out movements and girls a washing-machine movement for the duration—15 to 30 minutes—of intercourse. The ideal male is one who, like a bull, can perform with woman after woman. The typical Mangaian youth is much more active sexually than the American or European counterpart but may pay a price of earlier impotence. The word for orgasm is the same as that for pleasure, comfort, and perfection.

Childbirth

It would appear from the material above that sex is a psychocultural as well as a constitutional and individual activity. The same seems to be true of childbirth. In some societies **parturition** is a normal, routine, activity that gives the mother little pain or pause in her regular activities. In others, it is a process that is dreaded, if not openly feared. It is accompanied by psychological distress and physiological pain. Some women resume their daily routines immediately after delivery. Others stay abed for days to recover. Sometimes it is the husband who is confined to bed and suffers the labor pains.

Cuna Indian girls of Central America do not learn about intercourse or childbirth until the final stages of marriage (Newton, 1971). Pregnancy is a time of anxiety and fear of the birth process mounts continuously. Children, men, and even the medicine man who provided birth instructions are prohibited from the labor area. Labor is prolonged and so painful that the women sometimes becomes unconscious.

Siriono Indians of Bolivia take a much more relaxed, matter-of-fact point of view. Birth takes place in a communal hut where it may be witnessed by anyone who wishes. No one helps the mother in labor. The mother hangs onto a childbirth rope suspended over a hammock. She drops the infant a few inches into a bed of soft dirt. Labor is extremely short. Seven out of eight labors witnessed by Newton lasted from one to three hours. The eighth took longer because the mother bore twins.

Chabon (1966), Dick-Read (1959, 1962), Vellay (1960), and many others have promoted psychoprophylaxis, or childbirth without fear and pain. They find support for their views in cross-cultural studies of birth and personality. Dick-Read claims that in most instances it is fear and anxiety, and the overuse of drugs, that prevent a woman's having the spasmodic and reciprocal muscular labor movements that result in relaxed childbirth. Anxiety prevents the relaxation of the cervix, which contributes to tearing and pain. There are, of course, he says, cases of structural differences. Small stature or a small birth canal may make the use of drugs and instruments advisable and sometimes indispensable. He does not deny the reality of labor. It is hard work to bear a baby. It merits the grunts, groans, sweating, and exhaustion with which it is performed. However, pain is another matter.

Chabon emphasizes the value of prenatal instruction for both mother-to-be and her husband. This instruction is necessary in order to offset the impact of cultural heritage—born in travail, woman's burden, the curse (menstruation). So deeply are these ideas engrained that some women will not listen to authorities like Dick-Read and Chabon. They contend that "only a man could utter such rubbish. I've been there." The husband is important in terms of creating a psychological climate of mutuality and concern. He can help his wife practice the breathing, tensing, and relaxing that will be used in parturition.

Anthropological studies provide information on the mother's comfort during childbirth. They do not yield data on the impact of childbirth on the personality of children. However, as was seen in Chapter 3, there are empirical data that indicate that prolonged birth processes and maternal anxiety result in a higher than usual incidence of babies who have emotional problems.

Cross-cultural studies do show that what one is led to expect through social conditioning (pain and misery or hard work and satisfaction from task completion) in childbirth is what one gets. The theory of Otto Rank on "birth trauma" may explain how a given idea gets its start. Rank (1924) was a follower of Freud when psychoanalysis was a rather widespread influence in upper-middle class American and European culture. He believed that "birth trauma" affects the life and personality of the individual. The terror and discomfort of leaving the plush, warm, life-giving environment of the mother's womb was deemed to be a legacy for life. Neurotic people are so intimidated by their harsh environment that they subconsciously wish to and seek to return to the peacefulness of the mother's womb. The purpose of therapy is to help the person perceive himself as a separate and independent person without anxiety or guilt.

One does occasionally hear reference, today, to "birth trauma," but it is more likely that he will hear about the normality of birth. After one has lived nine months in a close, dark, humid, restrictive environment and has gained the strength to contend with mild environmental problems, the traumatic thing would be to remain imprisoned in the confines of the womb. Therein space is daily growing tighter and tighter. The kicks and struggles and squirming that precede birth are not a protest against the injustice of exposure to a cold, cruel world. They are expressions of the exuberant anticipation of challenge to test one's capacity to cope.

It would be possible, and interesting to some, to pursue variant cultural influences on such things as:

- What is expected of children
- How should adolescents behave (if the culture permits an adolescent phase)
- How the roles of men and women compare and contrast
- Work expectations in terms of sex and level (laborer, technician, professional).
- How the aged are treated.

The same results would be obtained as from the study of sex behavior and birth: the concept of normality has a wide range. There are *strange* people who are successful in performing certain roles, common in all cultures, in quite different manners. An examination is made of how culture exerts its power in the next section.

AVENUES OF CULTURAL INFLUENCE

As we think so do we speak. As we speak so do we think. Language—man-made audio and visual symbols of communication—is a significant part of culture. Many words are required to describe a caribou hide in a culture where caribou hides are a significant part of life. Many words describe automobiles in our life. Language is constantly changing as patterns of life and values change. In England two centuries ago there were dozens of words to describe how each game bird was cleaned. Today it is sufficient to say, "it is cleaned." Language reflects what is important in a culture. Thus, from early in life, it is interdependent with personality and thought processes. Sapir (1931), another anthropologist contemporary of M. Mead and Benedict, emphasized language as a major means of conducting the child into the ways of his culture. Goldschmidt (1953) has provided an example of

Language

this induction process on a recorded radio broadcast. Johnny, the squalling, red-faced baby, is spoken to by his mother:

> American: "Johnny be good." [He's a bad, naughty youngster].
> German: "Be in line. Get in step." [Stop being an individualist. Be like other Germans].
> French: "Johnny, be wise." [You are capable of being more mature].
> Scandinavian: "Johnny, be friendly." [Crying shows you are selfish and unfriendly. Have concern for others].
> Hopi: "No, no, no. That is not the Hopi way." [It is important to be quiet, serene, gentle as a reasonable Hopi is. We must preserve our proud heritage].

In addition to the words, the tone of the mother's voice, says Goldschmidt, enriches and emphasizes the language. The American mother speaks sharply. The German mother commands. The French and Scandinavian mother state a fact. The Hopi mother expresses wonder that Johnny would thus separate himself from others. In addition to tone, there are gestures and postures that communicate. Today there is much popular literature dealing with gesture and posture, called body language.

Hymes (1967) states the case for language, culture, and personality as follows:

> . . . My premise is that speech is vital to personality, and that it varies significantly from society to society in its role as an oral activity and acquired skill. Differences in this regard seem as important as differences in the use of any other learned mode of behavior or of any other sensory modality. . . .
>
> Speech is but one mode of communication, and its use involves the choice of one sensory modality as opposed to others. Societies and persons differ in the extent to which they choose this modality, the situations in which they choose it, and their evaluation of it. They differ in the ways speech enters into the definition of situations, conceptions of personality types, the socialization of the child. Its universality should not make us forget that speech activity, like sex and weaning, is a variable for the study of personality cross-culturally.[4]

Hymes emphasizes throughout his article that language is a powerful determinant of thinking and personality. It reveals constitutional predisposition, family exigencies, intelligence, and that how one's verbal utterances are received by others are also factors that enter the personality-culture transaction.

Religion and personality

Culture exerts its molding influence on personality in many ways. Family, prevailing occupations, educational practices, and govern-

---

[4]Dell H. Hymes, "The Functions of Speech," ed. John P. DeCecco, *The Psychology of Language, Thought, and Instruction* (New York: Holt, Rinehart, and Winston, Inc., 1967), pp. 79, 83.

mental organization are functions of culture. Religion is another avenue for exerting cultural pressure. Religion is, for some, a way of life and for others a mere matter of some vague concept of social formality. Hence it is not safe to identify religion as a universal factor in personality. It does, in some instances, constitute a pressure point in the external personality mold. It is a determining factor in the lives of some people. In some cultures, religion is a continuously pervading aspect of daily life. In other places it has suffered the fate of so many other man-made institutions. Religion has failed to respond to all the changes man has encountered. Its rigidness and formality have rendered it obsolete. Gardner perceives such rigidity as being the ever present enemy of social and personal health.

> A society whose maturing consists simply of acquiring more firmly established ways of doing things is headed for the graveyard—. . . (Gardner, 1964, p. 5).

He continues by emphasizing that individuals are undergoing a constant process of obsolescence. They can hasten the process by building prisons of habit, stereotype, and routine. An added danger is that the identity of the jailor is not perceived.

Religions, at the present time, show positive, negative, and "no impact" influences. These, furthermore, influence different individuals in different ways. Research data show that inter-religion marriages (*e.g.*, Catholics and Jews) are less stable and satisfactory than intra-religion marriages. Such data simply verify what common sense indicates would occur. Differences in values, beliefs, and behaviors make mutual adjustment more difficult (Konopka, 1973). It should be noted that inter-religion marriages are not doomed to failure. They run the full gamut from highly satisfying to highly dissatisfying. A Catholic and a Jew who are characterized as being "devout," whose whole lives are infused with religious influences, would find mutual adjustment more difficult. A couple whose religion was perfunctory, occasionally practiced, and ritualistic would not feel religion to be a barrier.

The Amish provide an example of the impact of religion on a life style.[5] The Amish have succeeded in achieving some social isolation in communities throughout the United States, where their beliefs pervade the family, vocational, educational, and community life. They believe that education beyond the skills of reading, writing, and computing are superfluous to a life lived close to nature and the land. They read books and magazines. They disdain the technological products of radio and television. They discredit mechanization and technology—or at least yield with deliberate slowness. They value the right to worship as they please—peacefully. They disdain the ostenta-

---

[5]The same rigidity could be indicated in such areas as interdenominational marriage, contraception, secular education, sharing or tithing, and public service.

tion of distinctive clothing, the men wear bib overalls at work and black suits when attending church or going to town for weekly shopping, the women wear bonnets and long black dresses. Boys wear pants and suspenders and round crowned hats. Children go to school only enough to satisfy state law—and the quality and duration of a year's schooling is suspect.

In Harmony, Kansas, considerable community distress was expressed when Sharon, a bright, competent Amish girl, did not attend high school. She could plant, sew, cook, type—skills well adapted to the family life the Amish wished to maintain. The "wider community" and the county school superintendent thought that Amish children should not be handicapped by living such an isolated life. Sharon's case dragged on and finally the family moved to another state to escape further harassment (Erickson, 1969). The case is related to the danger cited by Gardner: The law must be obeyed—a society without law is anarchy, to change is unthinkable.

Two points are pertinent: 1) Religion is a personality factor, expressed when it pervades one's whole way of living. In other cases, where one's religion consists of having his name on a church roster and returning thanks at Christmas dinner, religion is hardly a personality influence of import. 2) People are *strange* when their ideas do not agree with those of the society in which the observer lives.

Describing the rigidity of some religious denominations is not tantamount to criticizing religion. The emphasis on the value of other persons, common in the great religions, relates to a personality trait that is widely appreciated. Jung (1933) has asserted that he had never encountered a person, older than 35 years, whose personality rehabilitation did not consist largely of finding some religious outlook that would focus on others instead of self. The great tasks, as far as personality theory and application are concerned, are to determine which aspects of a religion are pertinent to wider cultural change and which are outdated. For some, religion is a powerful and positive force. But religion *per se* is not the answer. There are those who are fanatics. They pray, and worship, and pronounce blessings but neglect earning their own and their children's bread.

Technology and personality

Periodic and nostalgic references are made to the "good old days" when man lived close to the soil and "mother earth" was the quiet giver of all life. Those, allegedly, were the days of health, serenity, peace, repose, friendliness, and so on. The "good old days" consisted of being able to see clear blue sky, breathe pure air, and drink unprocessed water. Viewed in this perspective, it is easy to see that technology has been a device of destruction—OR HAS IT?

There are those who speak and write about technology as though it were some animate force that is attempting to enslave man and impose indignities upon him. The opposed perspective is that technology is a man-made phenomenon that is amenable to the guiding influence of man and his objectives. Erikson perceives the contrast between these views as a source of youth's confusion. We lack the ability to comprehend the possibility of a humanistic orientation working in a mechanistic society (Evans, 1967). Erikson views the atomic bomb as only a tiny part of technological development. He uses it to show that man can permit technology to pollute and poison the woods, air, and water, in the name of production; on the other hand, man can decide that the major concern is quality of life. Should this decision be made, and he sees youth as having the desire and energy to accomplish it, certain changes will occur:

1. The number of births will be reduced.
2. Men all over the earth will be seen as sharing a common destiny.
3. Awareness of the heritage of the next generation will be an abiding concern.
4. Respect for human potential will replace concern for technological production (Evans, 1967, pp. 34, 108).

Man as the slave of a production compulsion has been a perception for centuries. Whether tending flocks, tilling soil, digging coal, or handcrafting products man must toil to live. Technology and mass production have today so far exceeded *needs* that it is necessary to "stimulate" man's needs to consume with advertising. Advertising convinces people that just a little more of a certain product will bring about the good life. Unless consumer demands can be kept high, the production economy lags. The effect is business recession or financial depression. Thus, man, with all his technological aids, is a slave to production. In order to tie man securely to this notion the ethic of work is incorporated into religion and cultural mores. At the same time greater production efficiency is sought.

The assembly line is perceived as an example of man's enslavement. The work is not so physically exhausting as it is ego-deflating (Bartley, 1971). With an oversupply of workers, the individual employee becomes captive. He cannot strike for the higher pay that would allow the finding and exploitation of alternative avenues. He is a piece of machinery *without power* to exert a force in his own life. Fehr (1963) summarizes the impact of automation as an increasing remoteness of personal control from the locus of decision making. The consequence is a loss of:

- Sense of individual worth
- Personal dignity
- Motivation to achieve
- Faith in established institutions
- Fear of the future
- Disruption of belief patterns

In this "deadly" routine one can shut out reality by day-dreaming, projection, or hallucinations. He can anesthetize his brain by alcohol, drugs, or television.

Childs and Theobald are among those who see technology not as a threat or as a consuming monster, but as an opportunity for the enrichment of life. It is necessary, however, to change our thinking to accord with the changed conditions. Theobald (1965) perceives the necessity of a complete reversal of our view of work. **Cybernation** will increasingly do the goods-producing work of the world. With the help of cybernation, less than 10 per cent of the manpower supply will be needed to produce all the consumer goods of the United States. Moreover, the United States is but a few steps ahead in the course other nations will take. Hence, the urgent priorities are:

- There will be more people engaged in service areas—education, nursing, human welfare.
- Creative and fine arts will be a greater concern of education and a part of the life of all classes of men.
- The aims of education must shift—today's schools and universities are designed for the passing industrial age and the need is to shift to an emphasis on creativity and an emphasis on the individual's uniqueness.
- Everyone must be guaranteed minimum income that assures comfort.

Childs (1971) says that the work ethic must be revised because it is now inappropriate. The challenge is to develop the viewpoint that the aim of education is to develop the capacity to live rich and full lives in which leisure is a predominant factor. Failure to make these shifts in values will be disastrous, say Childs and Theobald. If we succeed in making the value shift, the world can be a truly wonderful place in which to live. In order to make this value shift, personality change is needed.

Education   A criterion of one's social class status is education. One of the more frequently used avenues of upward mobility in social class is education. There is no doubt that education is one of the ways in which culture places its mold on personality. Bierstedt (1970, p. 456) reflects the view of many in stating that a few go to college to improve their minds. Some seek to gain the technical knowledge of professions. Most go because of the status-giving function of a B. A. degree. The son of a laborer in the steel mills of Gary or Pittsburgh is a star football player in high school. He wins an athletic scholarship, he makes a name for himself, and is awarded a job where his name is useful. He marries the boss's daughter. He establishes an upper-middle class home. He must make some changes in personality. He must make changes in language, in manner of dress, in values and objectives, and in his very manner of thinking. Some of these he learns in the common school of experience. Other behaviors are gradually acquired as the direct emphases of formal education.

Even young women raised in upper-middle class homes were, at least until quite recently, sent to elite "finishing" schools to learn how to become ladies. However, fads change. Some observers wryly remark that a purpose of higher education for women today seems to be to teach them how to be men. In any event, there seems to be no doubt that education is not only aimed at forming personality *but* has the reputation for doing so.

The foregoing remarks are probably twentieth century orientation. The historical function of education, from ancient Greece and Alexandria to the beginning of this century, was the cultivation of the mind. Many critics believe that education—at all levels, but especially higher education—is missing the mark with its heavy emphasis on the production of technicians and professionals. The concern is well expressed in the following:

> We know that a shockingly high percentage of college graduates rarely or never read another book after receiving their bachelor's degree. Why should they? Their love now comes from their employer, their wife, their children, not from the approval of parents and teachers. For them, intellectual curiosity never became a motive in its own right. External rewards are appropriate props in early childhood. But we educators, being limited by current inadequate theories of learning, do not know how to help the student free himself from the props of reward and develop a functionally autonomous zeal for learning. With our slavish dependence on reinforcement theory I think it is surprising that we arouse as much internal motivation as we do. In any event, we cannot be proud of the many educational cripples who after graduation, lacking the routine incentive of college, sink into intellectual apathy.[6]

The implications for the student of personality are significant. Is the purpose of education the gaining of external rewards? Is the purpose to gain grades and marks in childhood and jobs and status in adulthood? Or, is the purpose the cultivation of the mind? Is it for laying a base for a lifelong process of learning? The answer is not a matter of generalization. It is inescapably an individual perception. Whatever the person's answer, it is a part of personality.

Man's mind, throughout the ages of history, is what has enabled him to survive when other species have waxed dominant and then become extinct (Highet, 1972). The evolutionary struggle from animalism to humanity is a story of learning, always learning. The ancient Greeks (1000 B. C.), who wrote the first chapters of Western civilization, were dedicated to lifelong enjoyment of learning and

[6]Gordon W. Allport, *The Person in Psychology* (Boston: Beacon Press, 1968), pp. 177–178.

exercising the powers of the mind. Their buildings decayed and were buried under dirt and rubble. Nevertheless, many of their ideas have survived. Today those ideas emerge as the brilliant new discovery in the philosophical or ethical world.

Highet, a teacher, says that one of the great rewards of the profession is to see a boy—excited by a single remark of a teacher, a page from a book, or a new insight into a subject—begin to change and exercise his mind. On the negative side, it is known that man uses but a small part of the functional capacity of his mind. Barriers to the creative path (that Highet, and other teachers, have seen only a few students take) are: 1) There is poverty of intellectual diet (particularly noticeable during the 400 years depression of the Dark Ages when there were no books), sparsity of used and cherished books. 2) There are errors in the educational system. Highet criticizes the encouragement of socialization at the price of neglecting the cultivation of intellectual fields. The author criticizes the misuse of tests and the teachers who deliver the verdict, "Not college caliber." 3) There are deliberate restrictions. Some authorities feel that knowledge should be suppressed. Examples of such, not very successful, attempts today are: Children's study of sex, college students' exposure to Marxism, and nonpsychologists being exposed to "obscene" theories on the hereditary basis of intelligence (Elam, 1972).

Cultivation of the mind is not synonymous with formal education. There have been many famous men, intellectual giants in scientific, governmental, literary, and artistic realms, who were unsuccessful in school. Pang (1971) lists Newton, Churchill, Einstein, Eisenhower, Darwin, Frank Lloyd Wright, and J. Paul Getty as being among those who were distinguished despite having undistinguished academic careers. Pang does not even faintly suggest that poor scholarship caused the success of these persons. Each, in fact, was a scholar but he could not follow a rigid curriculum designed by someone else. There is much evidence that *most* successful people, judged by criteria similar to those used to identify the above, were academically successful (*Manpower Report . . .*, 1970, pp. 162, 185). The above-named were not "self-made" men. Each received help from someone or something— typically books written by "someone." Many other persons have found that helpful "someone" in the school or college milieu. Newton, Churchill, *et al.*, demonstrate that others cannot "make you do it."

William James, one of the first in the then budding field of psychology, said what Highet, Pang, and many others before and after him have said in other words.

> . . . Could the young but realize how soon they will become mere walking bundles of habits, they would give more heed to their conduct while in the plastic state. . . .
>
> . . . As we become permanent drunkards by so many separate drinks,

so we become saints in the moral, and authorities and experts in the practical and scientific spheres, by so many separate acts and hours of work. Let no youth have any anxiety about the upshot of his education, whatever the line of it may be. If he keep faithfully busy each hour of the working day, he may safely leave the final result to itself. He can with perfect certainty count on waking up some fine morning to find himself one of the competent ones of his generation, in whatever pursuit he may have singled out.[7]

Education—either the individually designed course of systematic study or that pursued in educational institutions—inevitably changes personality. There are those who believe that technical and professional educational careers are somewhat less admirable than "cultivation of one's mind." They believe that intellectual excursions into past time and cultures and broad knowledge of the present are not saleable. Fortunately, the two are not necessarily mutually exclusive. In fact, the really prominent surgeons, corporation executives, and statesmen are those who have combined with their technical competence an educational process designed to "free the mind."

It has been claimed that man's knowledge has been accumulating at an increasingly rapid rate throughout the centuries until, at the present time, our fund of information doubles in a decade. Beginning at the time of Christ it took 1750 years to double the information fund; hence, the appropriate current term "knowledge explosion."

Knowledge explosion and rate of change

Humans have an endowment of flexibility. An infant has less equipment than other animals to cope immediately with life. Given time, care, and instruction he can adapt to a range of environments and demands. The capacity for adaptation is unequalled by any other species. But this adaptation does take time; one must learn new methods of behavior when thrust into a strange environment. For example, a man born and reared in Chicago who is thrust into the jungles of Brazil or Borneo or the harshness of the Arctic initially has considerable difficulty.

There are those scholars who perceive the rapidity of change, propelled by the knowledge explosion, as man's greatest present threat and challenge. Horney (1937) wrote a book titled, *The Neurotic Personality of Our Time*. She indicated that although "neurotic" was a cultural and relative term that "our time" did contain threats and difficulties that imposed heavy burdens of adjustment. Freud (1930, 1962), in his book *Civilization and Its Discontents*, hypothesizes that man's instinctual urges for pleasure or libidinal gratification are often in conflict with the restrictions placed by society [civilization]. The consequence is a lifelong struggle. One might infer that the shift from

[7]William James, *Talks to Teachers on Psychology*, New edition (New York: Holt, Rinehart and Winston, Inc., 1939), pp. 77, 78.

primitive to civilized man has been made too rapidly. Freud and Horney may have been more concerned with the form culture has taken rather than with the rapidity of change.

Toffler (1970) has no doubt as to whether the nature of change or the rate of change is the problem—unequivocally the threat to man is the rate of change. He calls it *Future Shock*. He believes that unless the pace of change is consciously slowed down society at large is due for a "massive adaptational breakdown." The accelerating rate of change makes the world today as much different from the world of 30 or 40 years ago as that world was from the world at the time of Christ. The flames of technological change, cultural change, political change all have fuel added to them by the various aspects of the knowledge explosion. Toffler (1970, pp. 371ff.) does, however, offer the hope—especially to young people—of taking personal responsibility for how one responds to change. It is possible that we can gain the knowledge about the basic psychological differences. A person who is resistant to change contrasts with one who is bored by monotonous repetition. There are people who, far from being resistant to new behaviors, actively seek ideas and data to counteract or complement what they already know.

Rapidity of change, either result or concomitant of knowledge explosion, is perceived by Rogers (1971) to be the greatest problem man will face in the coming years. Most people have been concerned with the atomic bomb, population explosion, ecological destruction, and being engulfed with effluent. Rogers believes, however, that the real problem is rate of change. The strain may first be perceived within the family in what has been called the "generation gap." This means that as adolescents and youth move from the home to the out-of-family world, ideas, fashions, values, and behaviors are so much different from the parents' that it becomes virtually impossible to communicate (Konopka, 1973). Rapidity of change is often in terms of technological change. The question, as seen above, is whether man can adapt himself to the new roles forced upon him by technology and cybernation. Rogers says that it is a question of how much humans can "accept, absorb, and assimilate." The task is how rapidly the requisite interpersonal changes can be made. As a successful therapist, Rogers is optimistic about the prospects of man's acquiring the knowledge of the dynamic change that is needed. He has witnessed the glowing effect on the individual to the experience of change, growth, and fulfillment. These feelings of deep personal and social satisfaction are seen frequently in what he calls basic encounter groups. In groups, people seriously consider themselves in relation to the values they are acquiring and have established. He sees this process of studying and discussing oneself and one's life and feelings as a basic transaction. It will become a regular and vital part of the school curriculum by the year 2000.

SUMMARY

The study of personality is cross-disciplinary and one of the contributing disciplines is anthropology. Anthropologists have made it clear that "strange" personalities of various cultures are in part strange because of the input of the perceiver. Mead showed, for instance, that coming of age, or the adolescent personality, is largely a phenomenon of culture. She showed, too, that sexual behavior is a result of cultural expectation and teaching. It is subject to wide variation. Benedict, another anthropologist, postulated that personality is largely a struggle of the individual to conform to cultural demands. George Mead perceived the facts of cultural pressure. He emphasized that people responded differently to such pressures because of individual perceptions and inclinations. Kluckhohn summarized the factors in personality by saying that it is determined by constitutional factors, group memberships, roles, and situations. Sexual behavior and childbirth were cited as examples of how culture shapes personality.

There are numerous specific ways in which culture exerts its influence on personality. Language shapes the ego concepts, values, behavior of the individual. Language is a major medium for gaining feedback on the extent to which the growing individual is being adequately enculturated. Language, in turn, is shaped by cultural values. Religion is a more or less formal institution for teaching the ideologies most prized by a culture. Technology exerts pressure in personality formation. Technology poses hazards for feelings of worth, dignity, motivation, faith, and beliefs. Formal education, especially in a technological society, is an institution designed to compress the learnings that culture places on a high order of priority. A common definition of "disadvantage" is brevity of education that hampers access to the benefits of a culture. The contemporary knowledge explosion is perceived by some as being man's greatest threat to personality stability. Knowledge hastens change and, simultaneously, man's personality stability.

SUGGESTED READINGS

BENEDICT, RUTH, "Continuities and Discontinuities in Cultural Conditioning," *Psychiatry*, Vol. 1, No. 2, 161–167, 1938.
  Using an anthropological study, the author shows how some contrasts and problems of a "primitive" society can illuminate some of the problems within our own society.

HAYAKAWA, S. I., "Who's Bringing Up Your Children?" eds. H. W. Bernard and W. C. Huckins, *Psychosocial Dynamics of Effective Behavior.* Boston: Holbrook Press, Inc., 1971. From *ETC.: A Review of General Semantics*, Vol. 25, 299–308, 1968.
  One of the salient features of our culture is television. The author is

emphatic in stating that something that occupies as much of a child's time as television merits a serious examination in terms of what it does—or does not do—to the personalities of children.

KAGAN, JEROME, "The Concept of Intelligence," *The Humanist*, Vol. 32, No. 1, 7–8, January–February, 1972.

The author, while not denying biological differences—many of them inherited—argues that intelligence is a function of cultural values and cultural milieu.

KONOPKA, GISELA, "Formation of Values in the Developing Person," *American Journal of Orthopsychiatry*, Vol. 43, 86–96, 1973.

The author is an authority on adolescence and youth. She emphasizes the conflicting values present in modern culture in this article. The search for the most helpful values reaches a peak in adolescence and youth.

THEOBALD, ROBERT, "Cybernation, Unemployment, and Freedom," eds. R. M. Hutchins and M. J. Adler, *The Great Ideas Today: Work, Wealth, and Leisure.* Chicago: Encyclopaedia Britannica, Inc., 1965.

Technology has made it possible for a small fraction of the manpower pool to produce the goods needed by all people in our American culture. New orientations on education, work, and values—including the creative use of leisure—are needed to fit the demands of our time. The Puritan ethic of work must be revised.

FOLLOW-UP LEARNING ACTIVITIES

How are "strange" people defined in the text?

_____

_____

_____

_____

Check your responses to the learning activities that precede the reading of Chapter 5. In light of the chapter, what do your responses indicate about your personality?

_____

_____

_____

_____

_____

Find almost any issue of the *National Geographic* magazine. Read about some people in an out-of-the-way culture. What does the article tell you about our own middle-class, American culture?

_____

_____

_____

_____

_____

_____

To avoid the possibility of overgeneralization in the chapters that follow, it will be good to bear in mind the four personality determinants as cited by Kluckhohn. What are they?

1 _____ 2 _____

3 _____ 4 _____

What do the varied culture viewpoints regarding birth processes suggest to you personally (either as woman or man) regarding your role in childbirth?

_____

_____

_____

_____

_____

(Compare your response with that of several classmates.)
What might be the personal implications of the comment, "Language reflects personality?"

_____

_____

_____

_____

_____

_____

6

The Goal of Personality Study: Self-Actualization

What are the essential ingredients of self-actualization?

LEARNING ACTIVITIES

Aside from earning credits and satisfying requirements, what do you hope to gain from your study of applied personality theory?

_____
_____
_____
_____

The chapter presents the idea that it is man's tenderness, rather than his toughness, that makes for survival. Defend the thesis. Man's tenderness enables him to survive because

_____
_____
_____
_____

What *do you do* when someone criticizes you; *e.g.*, says that you interrupt conversations discourteously?

_____
_____
_____

What do you think you should do?

_____
_____
_____
_____

What would be the really healthy thing to do?

_____
_____
_____
_____

Glasser contends that people should not be called mentally ill. Rather we should say, forthrightly, that they are irresponsible. Why do you agree or disagree?

_____
_____
_____
_____

At the end of a year you are bored with your job and you are not really pressed for money. What would you do? Write your response, then discuss with classmates.

_____
_____
_____

Our study of applying personality theory thus far has dealt with various broad considerations of ways in which personality is shaped. Whether personality is determined by heredity and environmental processes or whether one has some choice in how personality determinants shall be perceived was considered. Next, the kinds of influences exerted by birth, family, and by socioeconomic status were presented. Finally, various cultures were studied to see how richly varied—in terms of such facets of personality as values and behaviors—man's responses to his environment and endowment are.

All of these chapters contained the implicit idea that individuals and societies are concerned about how best to make use of human potentialities. Genetics is studied to see if there are ways in which we can enlarge positive personality attributes and limit or control negative ones; family and socioeconomic status are studied to determine what negative personality influences can be controlled and how positive influences can be enhanced. In short, men are universally seeking how to care for their bodies, rear and educate children, and live together. They use their capacities in work and play and determine the goals of living that will be most rewarding. One way of expressing these universal tasks and objectives is the process of self-actualization. This chapter considers the meaning of self-actualization and focuses on ways of embarking on the ever continuing processes of self-actualization.

THE MEANING OF SELF-ACTUALIZATION

Using one's potential

The manner in which people live ranges from those who have been chronically satisfied—but not inertly content—to those who are unhappy, ineffective, and are pests to their fellow beings. The lives of some are creatively productive; the lives of others are so depressing and discouraging that they devise such ingenious ways to avoid reality that they deceive even themselves. The lives of most people place them somewhere between these contrasting polarities.

Anthropologist Margaret Mead agrees with a number of psychologists and psychiatrists who postulate that humans actualize only a small part of the potential with which they are born. These potentials may, through nurture, be brought to more complete functioning (Otto, 1972). The continual lowering of the time in which a mile can be run, raising the height that can be pole-vaulted, shortening the time it takes to swim 200 meters, illustrate the breaking of possibility barriers in the athletic world. The inventions man has recently created illustrate the possibilities in the scientific world. Comparisons are difficult to make with earlier inventors who did not have the fund of background information that is available to today's inventors. Recent advances in the rehabilitation of the mentally ill vividly demonstrate the better use of psychological potential. Four decades ago a psychiatrist who is still famous today summarized the misuse of potential in the following words:

> When a man is promoted to a new job and it worries him so much that he has to quit it; when a woman gets married, finds herself unfitted for married life, and becomes depressed; when a student goes to college with high hopes, but fails in half his subjects; when a soldier goes to war and develops shell-shock at the sound of the first gun; when a lad of promise spurns opportunities of achievement in favor of check-forging or automobile-stealing—then these people are mentally unhealthy; they are unable to adjust themselves to their environment. They are inept and they are unhappy; some of them will end their lives in tragedy.[1]

It is convenient to define self-actualization as though it were an accomplishment—one rarely achieved. It can also be conceptualized, more appropriately, as a process. This puts it at least partially within the range of the normal and typical individual. It is possible to behave in a self-actualizing manner in at least part of one's activities.

> Ida M. was a woman 45 years old, a Mexican-American and former field worker who performed paraprofessional activities (job placement counselor) in a city office of the State Department of Labor. She lacked the formal education that would permit much progress in an office ruled by Civil Service requirements. Although she took advantage of the educational opportunities that were available to her, it is unlikely that she can get enough education, soon enough—even with her obviously superior functional intelligence—to make major contributions to her agency or to society.
>
> Ida faces the fact that "the establishment" imposes burdens on her because of her dark skin, broken English, and shortage of college credits. She has learned that part of one's burdens consist in how one views them. She is happy with her husband and is gratified by the achievements of her sons. She does not, however, try to influence the career goals of her sons, though she shares their confidences and can talk with them as a peer. She is able to accept the feelings of those of her white clients even when they show, and sometimes voice, their prejudices regarding her accent and color. She treats them frankly and says (depending on the circumstances) something to the effect, "I can help you if you'll let me." She does not actually say what quite appropriately could be said, "I know who I, Ida, am. I'm pretty good now and I'm growing better. I'm not going to let you determine what my actions will be. I am in control of myself." Those who can

[1]Karl A. Menninger, *The Human Mind* (New York: Alfred A. Knopf, Inc., 1930), p. 3.

suppress their prejudices find her to be a sensitive human who is genuinely concerned with, and appreciates the weight of the burdens so many persons, of all colors, carry. She has been hungry and knows it is not fatal. She has been alone and knows that a smile and a word of greeting can make a human contact.

Maslow (1970) wrote of "self-actualizing people," those who were fulfilling their functions and making use of their talents and capacities. Perfection was not a criterion of self-actualization, but Maslow did indicate a number of processes—perceiving reality efficiently, accepting oneself and others, refusing to permit convention to hamper spontaneous enjoyment, attacking problems with vigor knowing that there will be more problems tomorrow, and keeping an eye open for those occasions when life is enjoyable and humorous. Ida, in the above case, could not meet all such criteria. She was not "self-actualized" but she was living a self-actualizing life. She was not above anger and disgust at the sight of selfishness and injustice—especially when children were the victims. She was able to talk to herself about the meaning of those feelings and consistently refused to let the actions of others control her responses.

Actualization of potential: Deprivation experiments

A clue to the meaning of self-actualization resides in experiments on sensory deprivation. It appears that sensory mechanisms, at least in part, constitute their own motivation for use. The existence of a capacity, for example, stimulates its possessor to use that capacity. In sensory deprivation experiments the subjects (usually college students) are placed in a cubicle in which normal contacts (by sight, hearing, pressure, and movement) with the environment are denied. In some situations the subjects wear translucent goggles to break up normal light patterns. Their arms are swathed in cotton packing and gauntlets to cut off feelings of pressure, movement, and tactile sensations. The cubicles are soundproof. The subjects only have to lie still but can, when the situation becomes intolerable, press a panic button (Vernon, 1963).

Despite the normality, confidence, and intelligence of the typical subjects, they were unable to tolerate sensory deprivation for more than three or four days. Initially, some welcomed the opportunity to wrestle with problems in quiet and isolation. Within a few hours it became increasingly difficult to concentrate and they drifted into aimless fantasy. It appeared that the subjects created their own sensory world by hallucinating and engaging in incoherent fantasy. Tests given during the isolation and immediately afterward showed marked loss of ability to solve problems and adjust to new conditions. There was a general loss of efficient motor control; reaction time became longer and longer; subjects became restless, bored, and irritable. Hebb (1961) asserts that there is not much doubt that humans cannot function in a normal way without sensory stimulation. Cognitive, perceptual, emotional, and logical processes are disrupted and disorganized in the absence of continuous and varied stimulation. One needs input in order to actualize potential.

Experiments on sensory deprivation are not paralleled by ordinary circumstances in life. Laboratory settings are specifically designed to provide clues for the explanation of behaviors. The experiments indicated that the emotional effects of sensory deprivation were restlessness, irritability, and boredom. They provide a hypothesis for the ennui and disgust that intelligent workmen have for repetitious and monotonous jobs. Sensory deprivation has the effect of increasing the **suggestibility** of the subject. The experiments provide clues for understanding how solitary confinement in war prison camps results in softening-up a victim so that he can be brainwashed more readily. Solitary confinement for criminal acts may not have been devised by a psychologist. Man, however, has intuitively hit upon isolation as one of the cruelest of punishments. Certainly it is designed as a means of retribution rather than actualization. "Solitary" literally drives the prisoner insane—just as the sensory deprivation subject begins to hallucinate. While the prisoner is not *completely* deprived of sensation he does suffer from paucity of stimulation. Driving him mad may take longer than four days.

Denial of the opportunity to exercise any of one's sensory capacities is a laboratory situation. Denial of the opportunity to exploit and develop one's latent talents is, however, an ordinary situation. O'Connor (1941) postulated that lack of opportunity to exercise one's talents is a source of tension and frustration. If an adolescent were deprived of an opportunity to exercise his creative, explorative talents he would be likely to be a behavior problem in school. If an adult were unable to use his manipulative or organizational talents on the job he would be likely to become an unproductive worker. Studies of school age children show that those who are relatively deprived of variety and specificity of environmental stimulation suffer from some retardation of intellectual development (Hunt, 1968; Kagan, 1972). One explanation of bright children's becoming behavior problems and dropouts is that their ability to learn rapidly, independently, and to explore creatively is not recognized in the structured school setting.

Sensory deprivation studies seem to lend credibility to the idea that mature use of one's latent talents is a function of external events. This is, in fact, the theory presented by Skinner (1971). He believes that one is whatever he is because of environmental impact. Behavioral scientists, he says, have been slow to unravel the complexities of human behavior because reliance has been placed on states of mind. These states of mind are: feelings, choice, dignity, and character. He recommends greater reliance on a technology of behavior. This will place responsibility for personality on analysis of the environment (see Chapter 10). Certainly, there is a great deal of emphasis on environmental conditions as behavioral scientists have tried to evolve an understanding of the complexities of personality.

Another group of theorists, while admitting the undeniable existence and role of environment, insist that man is more than a machine responding to power. Man with his brain, ability to conceptualize, and to deal with abstractions does not just yield to forces or respond automatically. He prolongs the stimulus-response gap. He uses the delay to figure out *how* he will use the force, guide its direction, or weaken its power. Planck (1959, p. 63) asserts that it is a dangerous act of self-delusion if one tries to belittle his responsibility and moral obligation by claiming that human action is the result of some law of nature. Allport (1968, p. 104) warns that reducing behavior and personality to conditioning, reinforcement, and statistical analysis is scientific trivialism. He notes, with some hopefulness, the resurgence of the concept of self and emphasis on the virtue of commitment. Bonner (1965) perceives that a too heavy reliance on the past tends to deny the reality of choice, goal direction, and responsibility of individuality.

It is here proposed that use of sensory mechanisms is not merely a matter of fortuitous happenings—of "that's the way life is." The use of senses also includes deliberate planning, selection of, and openness to experience. It is being postulated that talent is more than a unique heredity or congenital gift. Talent is a potential for development that can be cultivated through conscious choice. Self-actualization is both a way of looking at life and of living it.

In a sense, the existence of choice may predate the emergence of logical processes in the life of a child. With millions of genetic variations even newborn babies participate in making their own environment. Some cuddle and coo lat an early age. Another baby, viewing the same mother, is reserved and petulant. Some are aggressively curious and others are indifferent and their explorative tendencies and curiosity are inhibited (Minuchin, 1971). Some of these differences among children are explained in terms of early life experiences—traumatic or salutary. Whatever their response, they elicit some sort of response—indifference or responsiveness—from attending adults. However, as one matures, as the capacity for logical processes evolves (or is cultivated), the burdens and opportunities of choice, freedom, and responsibility begin to appear. The concept of self-actualization does not deny the reality of the past or the presence of the present, but it does emphasize that there is a self.

Social effectiveness   One becomes human through human contact. One *learns* his personality, in part, through his cultural conditioning. Hence, the concept of the socially independent man is a myth. Even the legendary hermit uses tools, food, and ideas that come from various processes of social interaction. As one strives toward self-actualization, he must have taken, or is in the process of taking, the preparatory steps. He must first have his safety, love and acceptance, and esteem needs met. These needs are met through social interaction. Obviously, the needs will be met more readily if one is socially skilled. For instance, the baby who responds warmly and gives positive, smiling feedback to his caretakers tends to find the world kindly and helpful. The adolescent who is friendly, curious, functions within the boundaries of home, school, and wider culture is the one with friends. He has rapport with peers, and is often the leader (Coleman, 1961). Deliberate social planning and better design of adolescent experiences might result in developing a greater portion of the adolescent's full potentialities (Eisenberg, 1969, p. 57). This is especially true in a complex technological society in which the period of adolescence is prolonged.

Can a child be self-actualized?

Darwinian theory has emphasized the idea of survival of the fittest. The strong are the ones who rule and dominate. They seize and hold power—or at least, so goes the argument. There is, however, a little evidence that the doctrine of Christianity, to the effect that "The meek shall inherit the earth," just might be true. Either violence will destroy both strong and weak, or, nations can learn the vital lesson of social cooperation. Social effectiveness means just that—cooperation. Social effectiveness means individual freedom only to the point where it interferes with another's freedom. It means feeling for and with others. Social effectiveness means tenderness instead of violence.

Eiseley (1971) clearly portrays the contrast of Darwinianism and socialization in stating that man was a social animal long before he was man. It is *tenderness*, not toughness, that has made man superior. It is tenderness (care for the young, the infirm, the old, and the foreigner) that will result in survival—if we survive. Our values must shift from the pyramiding of "things" to the enhancement of self-actualization and the cultivation of humanity, says Eiseley. In self-actualization we shall achieve the ultimate victory—"in our individual hearts." The "things" called technology and cybernation were made by man and threaten to steamroller him into personal anonymity. *Tenderness, caring, social regard* can also be man-made if each individual shares responsibility instead of regarding himself and mankind as victims of external forces.

DYNAMICS OF SELF-ACTUALIZING*

There are many kinds of human potentials to be developed. Hence, there are many ways to travel the course of self-actualizing. Maslow (1970) perceives self-actualizing as a possibility—though not an easily achieved or frequent occurrence—for everyone. It is possible for wife and mother, day-laborer, artist, athlete, or statesman. It is a matter of doing one's best with what one has. Some of the steps in the process are described in this section.

Openness to experience

Some persons are curious about, questioning about, observing of, and interested in those things that are strange and new to them. Some are probing ever deeper into the complexities of the subject that is of current interest to them.

> A high school boy took a part-time job as a stock boy in a retail shoe store. He did the best job he could to keep things in order. He warned the owner of approaching shortages. He quickly found stock for the sales force *and the owner took notice.* The boy was soon placed on the floor as an alternate salesman. He began to read about shoes. He found they had an interesting history. He was able to tell his customers about how styles evolved (sandals, high, low, button, lace, moccasin, wooden shoes, boots, and so on) according to need and notion. His interest in his work and people resulted in high sales and customer satisfaction. The owner gave him a full-time position at a good salary when he had completed school.
>
> The young man began to study leathers. He could tell his customers about snake, goat, lizard, alligator, buffalo leather, and cowhide, how it was processed and the comparative advantages of each. He knew the differences between Texas and Argentine cowhide and between Florida and South American alligator leather.
>
> One year the owner was ill during the convention time when shoe dealers met to discuss problems and view new products in Fall

---

*Self-actualization as a source of motivation is discussed in Chapter 9.

River, Masachusetts. He sent the young man in his place. The knowledge of stock, style, and quality that the young man had gained resulted in purchases that moved fast and left small inventory at the end of the year. Thereafter the boss went to Florida for vacation and sent his employee to the particular city where the shoe conventions were currently being held.

At the conventions the young man's expertise came to the attention of manufacturers. He was ultimately hired by a group of them to travel around the world in search of the best buys in leather.

The typical individual has areas in which he is interested. In other areas, however, his reserve is so strong that it may result in active avoidance. This is probably an advantageous tendency. In a society where specialization is a way of life, wide dispersal of energy may lead to superficiality. However, openness to views of how one comes across to others is a characteristic of the self-actualizing person. The confident and purposefully growing individual has no hesitancy about data concerning how he is seen in social transactions with others. The less confident person has a protective shell for defending his ego. Should anyone tell him that he seems impolite, dissembling, or self-centered his vigorous counter-attack would put an immediate stop to the verbal transaction, or the informant would leave the scene.

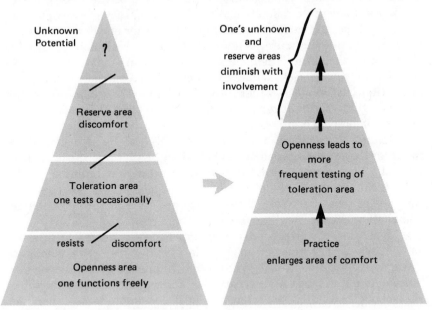

Paradigm of social-personal openness.   **Figure 6.1**

Probing into the area of clearer perception of self is not an easy or comfortable venture. In fact, it is typically a painful experience to realize that one's defenses are so readily seen by others and so hidden from oneself. This painfulness has been called "the trauma of transcendence." It refers to the discomfort that urges one to abandon defeatist patterns and seek a more open stance toward life (Fullmer and Bernard, 1964, p. 18). The magazine *Psychology Today* has published a brief "catalog" of agencies and individuals that are designed to promote self-actualizing processes (Criswell and Peterson, 1972). Some of those listed seem to promise heaven in a few easy lessons while others assert that there will be some temporary agony but a more gratifying future. Some "actualizers" appear to be the advertisements of self-appointed "experts." Others are reputable professionals.

Openness to the clearer perception of self can best be achieved with the help of others. This is partly because the self was initially evolved through feedback from others. Help is needed, also, because it is not easy to be objective when the concern is subjective. One may be either too harsh or too lenient in one's judgments of self. To be too harsh would lead to discouragement. To be too lenient would be conducive to complacency.

Accuracy of perception

The self-actualizing person accepts himself and his limitations as well as accepting others. Hence, he eliminates some of the biases, prejudices, and perceptual distortions that make accuracy of perception so difficult. Money-Kyrle (1944), looking at the other end of the personality continuum—the neurotic—says that the neurotic is not just relatively, but absolutely, inefficient in perception and hence is also cognitively wrong. Self-actualizing people, in contrast, distinguish more clearly than the generality. They sort the actual from the abstract; they distinguish the specific instance from the mass concept, and the objective from belief.

Being self-confident and trusting, self-actualizing persons are consistently not threatened or frightened by change and the unknown. Knowing with certainty that they have coped with tribulations in the past, they are comfortable with change. They know that they will continue to cope effectively. In fact, they are often attracted to change and challenge as a further exercise of their capacities.

Moustakas (1966) provides an example of a self-actualizing person as a teacher. The teacher makes elaborate plans for devising an attractive learning situation but some pupils do not respond. The teacher is not disappointed because he knows that perceptions differ. He accepts the reality that what may be absorbing to himself may not serve as a step toward self-fulfillment for others.

Inner directed

Self-actualized people are consistently those who have a cause and purpose not directed by others. They have aims that extend beyond self-interest. Their purpose is unique but is outside themselves (Maslow, 1967). The same confidence that inhibits apprehension about the future makes it possible to escape the bonds of excessive self-concern.

Rogers (1961, p. 183) reports that he was impressed by the "fluid, relativistic" individuality of the persons who had participated in successful psychotherapy. He refers to such persons as "fully functioning" persons. They are able to participate *and* observe, simultaneously, what is going on in their own lives and the lives of those with whom they function. In contrast, most persons are concerned with their own structure and evaluation of experience. They twist that experience to fit their preconceptions and are annoyed often by events that do not fit their carefully constructed pigeonholes.

Because the individual is free he feels less pressure to behave in a manner expected by others. He is an individualist rather than an abject conformist. Although self-actualizing persons can feel close to, and concerned about others, they are not controlled by them. Their values focus on law, justice, freedom, beauty, and truth. For them the dichotomy between work and joy disappears. Their energy is directed toward the things they love (Maslow, 1967). That which might be an irritation to the typical person is reduced to a process of objective analyzing. The facades and the preconditions that cause his associates to behave aggressively or defensively are analyzed. For example, two men had lunch in a restaurant where possible irritations mounted. The waitress was slow, abrupt, and discourteous. She argued about a mistake in the order and dropped silverware as she jerked plates from the table. The host was queried by his guest about his calm and seemingly indifferent response. He smiled and thanked the waitress for such service as she grudgingly gave. His answer was, "I do not choose to have my manners controlled by another."

It was shown in Chapter 1 that one's concept of the nature of man influences the view that is held of choice, responsibility, and social interaction. Our concept of human nature influences the methods and objectives that prevail in schools. Views of human nature even predetermine the nature of educational research undertaken to define objectives (Strike, 1972). One's view of human nature influences one's regard for the possibilities and processes of self-actualization.

At least from the time of Aristotle, the traditional view of man is that he is a rational, thinking being capable of mediating and influencing the force and direction of physical causes. This conception does not deny the existence of **affective** states or of disruptive emotions; it does, however, assume that man, through logical processes, can understand and control emotions. Logical processes capitalize on past experiences and aim at future goals—as is succinctly stated by the novelist James T. Farrell:

> One of the basic functions of education should be, must be, that of helping the individual student locate himself in life—in the present and for the future—and more, in history. One of our great dangers is that of too many people who may lead directionless lives. Those who lead directionless lives put a direct burden on others and create problems for themselves.

Students have many problems in common. The emotions related to and poured into the problems may be distorted if singled out and blown into special problems. But if students find no way of solving their problems, no help or encouragement, they may become frustrated and their initiative destroyed. Struggle and loneliness are conditions of the life of man—a fact students may be forced to learn too quickly.[2]

Problem solving in the self-actualizing person is a strong focus. However, his concerns are about a mission in life rather than being ego centered. A hazard for youth in the problem-solving orientation is too much self-consciousness and self-awareness and too little selflessness. This means, says Maslow (1970), that talking about values and virtue appears to be "square." The young persons feel they have been thwarted by "dopey" parents. Sometimes there is good cause for the feeling—when the parents are so uncertain themselves that they do not provide a conviction regarding right and wrong. In contrast, the self-actualizing individual is concerned with basic and eternal issues. Racial discrimination, chauvinism, justice for all, and ecological destruction might serve as examples of concern. The consequence of focusing problem-solving energy on basic issues is to lift one above the petty events and irritations of life. This provides a degree of detachment from the trivial occurrences. "Don't sweat the little things," might be the orientation for more successful coping with daily events by the self-actualizing person.

The typical person goes through life feeling that he has meager power to influence daily events and interpersonal transactions, says Perlman (1968). There may be no way to understand these "psychic vitamin deficiencies." There are ways to shore up and compensate for lack of confidence and ego identity. One can take advantage of small opportunities to exercise one's problem-solving ability in daily life. When one helps another to find himself, shows his concern, and speaks kindly and affirmatively to the less fortunate, says Perlman, he is resolving dilemmas both for himself and his fellow men.

Deep interpersonal relations

The accuracy of perception, described above, of the self-actualizing person, extends to the way people are regarded. The consequence is that the self-actualizing person has relatively few personal friendships. Those he does have are deep, confidentially sharing, and lasting. Their circle of friendship is small but healthier, closer, and more productive than is the case of most people (Maslow, 1970, p. 166). This small range of close interpersonal ties is partly explicable in terms of the time required to establish closeness and depth of friendship. Among those Maslow selected as being self-actualizing (about 40 historical and selected contemporary persons) it was found that

[2]James T. Farrell, "A Job That Buys a Dream," *American Education*, Vol. 1, No. 8, October, 1965, p. 3.

exclusiveness of devotion existed alongside a widespread benevolence, affection, and friendliness—especially for children. This ready identification, kindness, and patience, says Maslow, is more akin to love for children than to the general feeling of compassion for all mankind.

Another aspect of interpersonal relations (and one that might be inferred from the preceding paragraph) is that the interpersonal relations of self-actualizers are discriminating. They see the majority of acquaintances for what they are: biased, self-centered, having restricted interests, being pretentious, overly critical, and demanding. They see that most people could, by lowering their facades and practicing the skill of openness, become much more than they presently are. They perceive others as shorting themselves of happiness by making foolish mistakes in intra- and interpersonal relationships. They are more to be pitied than to be condemned. When self-actualizers attack another, and they do, it is on a situational basis rather than on a personal one. It is with the hope that the attack may strengthen the one attacked.

Self-actualizers sometimes attract a few admirers or even worshippers. These are one-sided attachments that more often than not embarrass the actualizer. The admirers demand and expect more than the admired person can, or is willing to devote the time to deliver. He has no need to curry favor. He has his own goals that he pursues because of inner drives, as contrasted to social expectation.

Sharpness of perceptions and range of interests aid the self-actualizer to have a higher than average incidence of **peak experiences.** Otto (1967) refers to this as the Minerva Experience—a consciously recalled incident that resulted in a heightened appreciation of one's self, beauty, awe, or wonder. It is a part of the process in the art of becoming.

Sensory awareness and peak experiences

Peak experiences can occur in many settings. They are most frequently felt in moments of achievement following sustained effort, in the ecstacy of beauty—a sunset, viewing a calm or rough ocean, serene forests, the trust of a child—orgasm in sex relations with one who is deeply loved, childbirth when the mother is fully awake and aware.[3] Although these moments of peak experience occur spontaneously (and with higher frequency in the super healthy individual) they can be magnified by conscious intention. It is not necessary to say to one's loved one, as the couple views Grand Canyon, "This is a great moment." Saying it, however, may add to the feeling's intensity. There is no strict dichotomy between feeling and reason for the self-actualized person. He would make the same selection of work, plea-

[3]Such an experience is described in a mother's letter about childbirth cited in Harold W. Bernard, *Child Development and Learning* (Boston: Allyn and Bacon, Inc., 1973), Chapter 3.

sure, friends, or mate intuitively and impulsively as he could in terms of cold, clinical judgment (Maslow, 1970).

As a laboratory experience, the Minerva Experience is designed to enlarge one's perception of the health-giving aspects of ordinary events (Otto, 1967). The awareness is sought in groups by recalling both the trauma of life (so that conflicts may be resolved) and the triumphs of life (so that one can focus on the uplifting events). Participants in the group experience report recalling the dim memories of enjoyed occurrences. There may be renewed resolve to develop skills and abilities. They may recall upsurges in energy, more accepting attitudes toward parents, siblings, and associates. They may tell how they dealt with unpleasant events so that the pleasant ones were magnified.

Spontaneity, autonomy, and creativity

The self-actualizing subjects in Maslow's studies were described as having a higher degree of spontaneity than most people in both manifest behaviors and in their inner lives. Bonner (1967) and Rogers (1961) are among the many who mention the frequency of creativity among those who reveal the traits and behaviors that are referred to when discussing self-actualizing processes. Having had his more basic needs of safety, love, and esteem met, the self-actualizing person can afford to be spontaneous. The self-actualizer does not feel pressured to make decisions on vital issues that must accord with the hopes of loved ones and the expectations of associates. The self-actualizer can and does make his own choices. He is free. His freedom is a *result* of his release from the pressure of unsatisfied lower level needs. It is a *cause* of further spontaneity, autonomy, and creativity. This free, spontaneous life tends to terrify the less secure and adventuresome individual. ". . . the proactive individual, although facing the same randomness and unpredictability of the future events as the rest of us, can mitigate their effects upon himself through bold imagination, moral courage, and a determined effort to see what lies hidden behind his psychological horizon."[4]

Self-actualizers tend not to allow convention to get in the way of enjoyment or involvement in activities they regard as being vital and basic. They have reached a level of socialization that makes it unnecessary to belittle others in order to achieve status for oneself. Hence, the self-actualizer tolerates ritual and ceremony so that others will not feel diminished. He may, within himself, scorn the pretentions of conventionality, but he accepts convention because others find pleasure in such superficialities. Self-actualizers are somewhat similar to cultural anthropologists, they wish to become "participant-observers" in the society they are studying; they live, dress, work, and communicate with the natives, but they think and observe in terms of

[4]Hubert Bonner, "The Proactive Personality," ed. J. F. T. Bugenthal, *Challenges of Humanistic Psychology* (New York: McGraw-Hill Book Company, 1967), p. 63.

their inner values. They are, like therapists in **client-centered counseling,** nonjudgmental.

Maslow (1954, p. 210) finds that the biggest difference between self-actualizers and others is spontaneity. This difference consists in the fact that self-actualizers are growth motivated. They autonomously seek perfection in terms of their own style of, and purpose in, life. Others are inclined to be deficiency motivated. They struggle to meet basic needs or lacks (*e.g.*, safety, love, esteem). MacKinnon (1971) reports another distinctive trait of creative persons, namely, the ability to achieve a state of passiveness such that unconscious and dimly recalled events can be brought to mind. That is, they can relax and give themselves over to inspiration.

HAZARDS TO SELF-ACTUALIZATION

Honesty demands that the fact of external causality of behavior be recognized. Conditions of birth, diet, medical attention, parental care, nature of schooling, romantic experiences, and work history are all among the important categories that help to shape personality. However, if one believes that proactive psychology possesses some virtue, one also accepts the idea that one has choice and responsibility. One may use the pull of a vision of what might be in the future. The past may explain how one got where he is now but one's visions may dictate where one will go next. The following discussion of hazards to self-actualizing processes presumes both choice and responsibility as conditions of becoming.

Glasser (1970) contends that the historical approach to the resolution of current difficulties is a self-defeating approach. When, as a psychiatrist, he worked with delinquent girls, he let them know that he was not really interested in their history. Explaining how they got to where they were as wards of a custodial institution merely provides excuses. He believed that a girl's recounting the selfishness of her mother, the sexual advances of her father, the unfairness of her teachers, the disdain of school peers, and the lawlessness of her gang companions did less to explain delinquency than it did to justify it. They could thus **rationalize** continuing ineffective and self-defeating behavior. Instead of historical explanations, his emphasis was on: What are you doing? Does it get the results you want? What *can* you do? What are you *going to do*? In short: When are you going to become responsible?

Irresponsibility

History and irresponsibility have merited places in understanding the behavior of an infant, a child, or a moron. A child's misbehavior in school might sensibly be attributed to parental inadequacy. Remediation might best be approached by treating the parents. As one gains in experience, emotional maturity, the ability to use logical processes, and develops perceptual skills, blaming the past becomes futile. Treatment of one's shortcomings through therapy for parents becomes cumbersome, if not abortive.

Objective facts must be acknowledged, of course. One cannot continue in school if he is totally without funds—but some do work, save, and resolve to go at some later time. One cannot change his black skin—but some do say, "I'll use the doors that do not have the letters 'White Only' on them." One may not be a "brain" in school but one high school girl said, "I can't maintain an academic C average; but most of those pictures over there on display are ones I painted."

History may suggest that one has no power and consequently can have no responsibility. To accept this idea as constituting all the truth is to blur reality. Throughout history some men have decided that it was unnecessary for them to be slaves of the past—or even of the present. They have chosen their own goals and, one step at a time, have transformed ambitions into achievement (Pang, 1971). History indicates that one may be victim of the past. He may also be an agent for change, depending on his view of responsibility.

Projection   Projection is a widespread, irradiating device for avoiding the burden of responsibility. It is a major defense mechanism[5] in which blame is placed on another person or some external situation. It does not take into account one's own input. That which might have been done, or could be done, by the person himself is not acknowledged. Self-actualization is the antithesis of projection. It means making the most of whatever input one can marshall.

Projection takes many forms, one of which is the "Why don't they . . . ?" syndrome. This means unrealistically hoping that if others would but do the things *they* should, then the blamer would be able to act effectively. One attempts to avoid responsibility by professing an overload of conflicting duties. One can claim that he never had a chance because of low socioeconomic status, poor school facilities, or non-supportive parents. The projections are plausible because the descriptions are real. However, the self-actualizer, and the realist, pays at least some attention to the future. Banfield (1970) asserts, with considerable pertinency, that it is lack of vision for the future that really constitutes disadvantage.

It may be that everyone uses projection to a certain extent. The burden of seeing all shortcoming and failures as being one's own fault is so heavy that we could be crushed by assuming total responsibility. The relief is temporary at best. The chronic and easy resort to projection is paid for in the distortion of facts and in deluding oneself (Goldenson, 1970, p. 1016). Self-actualization is blocked by forming the attitudes of hostility, intolerance, suspicion, and personal insult that are spawned by projection.

---

[5]Numerous defense mechanisms are described in some detail in Chapter 13.

Because projection is often unconscious, it may require the help of another to detect its functioning in oneself. It may be so deep-seated that getting at the causes through psychotherapy may be necessary before one can deal with the symptom. The boot-strap approach, suggested here, may work effectively for the individual who desires to take, or is taking steps toward becoming a more fully functioning person.

Processes of self-actualizing can be diverted by distortion, or inadequate perception, of reality. Otto (1972) has found that the human's potential for sensory awareness has been submerged by cultural conventions. The sense of smell, acute during childhood, is allowed to atrophy through lack of intentional use. Perfume mixers can, however, detect amazingly small amounts of varied essences. Similarly tea, coffee, and wine tasters use smell and taste with high degrees of accuracy and sensitivity. Potentials are developed and kept alive through practice. Perhaps, Otto believes, this atrophy is actively sought as a defense from the smell of garbage and nauseous gases.

Distortion of reality

Fads in thinking and cultural clichés tend to distort reality. For example, adolescence is viewed by a great many as a time of stress and turmoil. Delinquency, drug usage, alienation, and counter culture are perceived as being almost synonymous with adolescence. Yet cold analysis reveals that despite enormous pressures and the uncertainty that accompanies rapid change, the vast majority of adolescents are behaving and achieving in ways that merit considerable admiration. Far from being destroyed by either deprivation or excessive comfort, the typical young person takes advantage of opportunities and confidently accepts challenge. Assessment of the true nature of reality requires enough thinking to separate canned thinking from balanced evidence.

Failure to face reality evolves from neglecting to check hope against evidence. Such failure begins in childhood when parent-child relations are unsatisfactory and lacking in warmth (Jenkins, 1969). It continues as one engages in reverie and is magnified as the capacity to distinguish fact from fancy deteriorates. Thus, a college student may dream of the day when his talents are appreciated by the public or an employer. He neglects, meanwhile, the onerous tasks of developing the skills that would lead to genuine recognition. This is not just a contemporary dilemma. Accurate perception of reality with emphasis on the assumption of personal responsibility is a major issue in psychotherapy (Erikson, 1964, p. 201).

Probably the great majority of workers, laborers, or professionals, begin their work with the zest of a child when he is being initiated into some novel enterprise. The heterostatic drives make workers productive, at least for a period of time. After varying periods of time the novelty must, of necessity, wane. One learns his job so thoroughly that

Too big for the job

the new learnings become incidental rather than intentional. The laborer may come to feel that he is underpaid and the professional becomes *institutionalized*. This means that he adopts uncritically the attitudes that he hears expressed by his colleagues who have permitted boredom to dominate their work lives. Thus, capable and zestful beginning workers are told not to be so industrious. With such urging the new worker sometimes does begin to view his job with disdain and to treat his associates, particularly subordinates, as things.

It is important to stress that the job itself is not the sole determinant of one's attitude toward it (Herzberg, 1966, p. 59). Often the boredom and routineness that is blamed for lackadaisical performance is really a rationalization. Being bored excuses one's failure to pursue actively psychological growth, or self-actualization. He has little urge to be the best he can. Herzberg suggests that there are three growth orientations that may be taken in one's work life:

- Learning little or nothing on the new job that was not known before.
- Amassing an array of discrete facts about one's job.
- The creative orientation—seeking to find as yet undiscovered relationships between the facts of one's job and possible relations with other jobs. This might include those jobs that currently seem to be not even remotely related.

Being too big for the job is a common disorder in life. It is contributed to by industrialization and automation and by those who have become institutionalized. Bored attitudes and indifferent work are a hazard to self-actualizing. They are not dictated by even the most routine jobs. Boredom is an *internal* state.

Search for safety

A self-actualizing life may be hampered by the fact that lower level needs have not been satisfied. The "too big for the job" stance may be contrasted with the covert belief that one is not big enough for the job. Not "being good enough" may prevent doing school work, being a marriage partner, or having the capacity to meet and mix with people. The hampering need is for safety. One does not dare risk the novel and difficult challenge because of some vague fear of physical danger. Safety may be threatened by apprehension about impending psychological trauma.

The typical reaction is to wait for someone else to pave the way. Safety needs may cause one to wait for someone who will figuratively hold one's hand as the new venture is approached. Even the rather self-confident person may tend to wait for someone "on the other side." We wait for the boss, the minister, the person who is in his familiar setting—to make the first move. Discussion of such situations reveals that both the newcomer and the "at home" person was waiting for the other to make the first move. When neither makes such an approach both begin to attribute to the other attitudes of snobbishness or unfriendliness. Thus the barrier to easy communication is increased. Teachers have described such transactions at the beginning of the school year. At the first staff meeting the new teachers waited for the old ones to make the initial approach. The old ones held back because the newcomer might judge them to be officious.

Actually, in such situations no one is in danger. There is no tangible threat to safety needs. The hazard resides in the imaginative construction of barriers to interpersonal relations. The real peril is holding back and waiting for the other to make an offer of friendship. The danger resides in failure to participate boldly and to exercise the skills that will develop the social arts that will make one feel safe (see Figure 6.1). The whole matter of personality strength sufficient to raise oneself above the safety needs bears considerable relationship to Cohen's (1972) conclusions about the relationship of job success to IQ. His studies demonstrated that it was not IQ that was most important in job success or school achievement. The crucial factors are attitude, motivation, and social behavior. We may admit the possibility that safety needs for babies and children need to be supplied by others; it is probable that adult safety needs must be met by the person himself. Attitudes and motivation for direct attack are the forerunners of skill development that assure safety. Avoidance tendencies result in failure to exercise capacities and keep one from developing strength. True safety, for an adult, resides in his own capacity to deal with, or to tolerate, the "slings and arrows of outrageous fortune." A widespread human dilemma is that faced by Hamlet:

> To be, or not to be: that is the question:
> Whether 'tis nobler in the mind to suffer
> The slings and arrows of outrageous fortune,
> Or take up arms against a sea of troubles . . .

> Shakespeare, *Hamlet*,
> Act 3, Scene 1

Hurry

Hurry has become a cultural characteristic of the typical middle and upper-class American. Those from the lower class who are striving for higher status are likely to find themselves victims of the **compulsion** of hurry. Hurry is a habit tending to produce anxiety and discontent. It contributes to such physical symptoms as ulcers, high blood pressure, heart dysfunction, digestive disorders, and sleeplessness. It is not being suggested that taking the shortest possible time to achieve a goal is always an admirable and productive characteristic. Efficient planning and the scheduling of effort should allow one to do just that—achieve in a minimum of time. The point of distinction is between making maximum use of time and trying to do so much that one's stomach begins to get "tied in knots."

Our powerful automobiles are sometimes blamed for some of the compulsive hurry of Americans. It may be that cars are a contributing factor. But James (1899, p. 212) noted the difference between the deliberate life style of the urban European and the hurried, jerky life style of the American long before the advent of the automobile. He said that hurry was a psychological problem—a bad habit. However, the phenomenon of hurry can be examined by using an automobile as an experimental situation. Let yourself drive in your usual fashion and note the tendency to keep in the traffic stream. Note how you stay at or just a bit above the posted speed. Note how you tap your fingers or scratch your head while waiting for the light to show green. Record the time it took to make the trip. On the next similar trip approach the situation planning not to hurry. Keep the space between you and the preceding car a little longer than usual. When the hurried driver cuts in, drop back again. Determine to see red lights as the time savers they really are. When the traffic jam occurs, think of some unfortunate who recently suffered loss in a fire, flood, tornado, or car wreck and compare your loss of a few seconds. When you finally arrive at your destination, (1) record and compare your time with the previous trip. (2) Compare the mood and feeling of the relaxed trip to the hurried trip.

The "hurry" orientation begins in childhood for the middle class. Children are scheduled for developmental experiences in addition to keeping pace at school: cub scouts, horseback riding lessons, skating lessons, dancing lessons, music lessons, and baseball practice, are "developmental." Of course, one must also watch at least some television in order to get in his average of 22,000 hours of viewing before age 18. Most parents seem to be in such a hurry that they would be pretty well satisfied with their children if they were just about two years older than the date of birth indicates!

It is not realistic to hope that one can rid himself of a lifetime of hurry simply by an act of will. It is possible to begin to cultivate the roots of planned growth. It is possible to choose to review some aspects of one's work. One can plan a deliberate pace instead of continuing one's compulsive, harried, spasmodic haste. At least, the possibility exists for those who share the proactive orientation toward choice and responsibility.

SUMMARY

Making good use of one's potential—self-actualizing—is viewed as a viable goal for the study of personality. Making the best use of one's potentials is postulated as being a way of life, a process, rather than an achievement. The self-actualizing person tends to perceive reality efficiently. He readily accepts himself and others. He refuses to permit convention to hamper spontaneous and respectable enjoyment, and attacks problems with zest. He keeps attuned to the beautiful and humorous aspects of daily life. The self-actualizer controls his own perspective on life—he will not permit others to control his affective life.

Experiments on sensory deprivation indicate the intrinsic motivation man has to adopt the self-actualizing styles of life. Sensory and experiential paucity, for the normal individual, leads to frustration, boredom, and attempts to escape the monotonous. Paucity or richness of chances to use sensory capacities may be viewed either as an external event, or as that, *plus* personal choice and responsibility.

Specific details to be considered in the self-actualizing way of life include being open to experience. It means emphasis on the accuracy of perception (trying to separate the real from the hoped-for). Self-actualizing means developing tolerance for chance. It includes accepting the role of inner-direction as contrasted to overt or covert attempts to please others. It is the capacity to develop deep interpersonal relations with a few selected friends. Peak experiences are felt by the self-actualizing person more frequently than is the case with the generality.

The more common hazards to self-actualization are simply the opposition of the characteristics described in the preceding paragraph: reluctance to assume responsibility, projection onto others for errors and shortcomings, distortion of reality, and feeling that one is too big for the job (or not big enough). The search for safety bestowed by others, and such hurry that one does not tend the roots of growth, are also deterrents to the process of self-actualizing.

SUGGESTED READINGS

BONNER, HUBERT, "The Proactive Personality," ed. J. F. T. Bugenthal, *Challenges of Humanistic Psychology*, pp. 60–66. New York: McGraw-Hill Book Company, 1967.
> *The author places responsibility on the individual for either chronic defense (neuroticism) or for transcendance of his past accomplishments. The proactive man strives to make himself a work of art.*

COHEN, DAVID K., "Does IQ Matter?" *Commentary*, Vol. 53, No. 4, 51–59, April, 1972.
> *Those who feel hampered by what they have been led to believe about the focal role of IQ in achievement may be encouraged to know that some authorities believe that motivation, attitudes, and deportment are powerful determinants of success in life.*

ELLIS, ALBERT, "Humanistic Psychotherapy: A Revolutionary Approach," *The Humanist*, Vol. 32, No. 1, 24–28, January–February, 1972.
> *Man's major ability is that of being able to think and to think about thinking. This concept places man clearly in the center of the universe and gives him "almost full responsibility" for choosing what he will make of himself.*

JOHNSON, DAVID W., "The Affective Side of Schooling Experience," *Elementary School Journal*, Vol. 73, 306–313, 1973.

> *Steps toward self-actualization may be taken in early childhood education. Johnson says that leaving a course of study with at least as much interest in it as one had initially, may be the most important aspect of school. His suggestions for teachers carry implications for everyone.*

LYNN, DAVID B., "Determinants of Intellectual Growth in Women," *School Review*, Vol. 80, 241–257, 1972.

> *Intellectual development in women results from the interaction of biologically rooted potentials, parent-child relations, and cultural forces. The author deals with some of the beliefs and misconceptions held about male-female differences in intelligence, and the discussion should be of interest to readers of both sexes.*

MASLOW, ABRAHAM, "Peak Experiences as Acute Identity Experiences," in *Personality Theory and Counseling Practice*. Conference papers on Personality Theory and Counseling Practice. Gainesville: University of Florida, 1961.

> *Feelings and personal meaning of peak experiences are reported by people who have had them. Maslow interprets these experiences only in part as a discovery of self, but also emphasizes that they are created by the individual.*

SHORE, EUGENE, "Sensory Deprivation, Preconscious Processes and Scientific Thinking," *American Journal of Orthopsychiatry*, Vol. 41, 574–580, 1971.

> *The subjects of Shore's experiments on sensory deprivation revealed the effects reported in other similar experiments; but, in addition, some experienced excitement, alertness, and enthusiasm. Shore believes these may lead to insights on the nature of hunches, intuitions, and creative thought.*

FOLLOW-UP LEARNING ACTIVITIES

List several of the items from the text that hamper self-realization (look back to the section **hazards** if necessary).

1 _____ 2 _____
3 _____ 4 _____
5 _____ 6 _____

See if from your own experience, you can add two more *not* cited in the text:

7 _____ 8 _____

Add two more after discussion with your classmates:

9 _____ 10 _____

Define the term self-actualization or self-actualizing.

_____
_____
_____
_____
_____
_____

List several characteristics of self-actualizing persons:

1 _____ 2 _____
3 _____ 4 _____
5 _____ 6 _____

Can you think of one more that should be added?

7 _____

Add still one more from discussion with your classmates:

8 _____

Which three of these do you think you come closest to having now?

_____
_____
_____

Which do you think are most worthy of striving for next?

_____
_____
_____

Note: It is hoped that such items as the above have enough relevance that the student will refer to them to see if there should be revisions next year, in three years, in five years. Who really defines relevance?

_____
_____
_____
_____

/two/

Personality Theories

7
Psychoanalytic Theories

Love and the capacity to love are cornerstones of personality.

LEARNING ACTIVITIES

If you have heard of Freud's theory, record the highlights of your information. If you have not heard of him, ask a few friends about what they know of his theory. Record what they believe to be his major emphases.

_____

_____

_____

_____

_____

Do you consider yourself to be an introvert _____ or an extrovert _____? List two or three traits that so identify you.

_____

_____

_____

_____

Why do you consider being an extrovert introvert (cross out one) to be an advantage or disadvantage?

_____

_____

_____

_____

What, if any, traits do you think generally describe one's order of birth?

Oldest tends to be _____

_____

"In-betweens" tend to be _____

_____

Youngest tends to be _____

_____

(Compare your notes with those of a classmate.)

Define what you mean when you use the following common terms:

Rationalization _____

_____

Compensation_____

_____

Projection _____

_____

Neurotic _____

_____

No one is really credited with inventing the automobile. It is the culmination of the ideas of many inventors. Each devised a particular part—the self-starter, electric headlights, pneumatic tires, water-cooled engines, air conditioning. The use of culture and family to explain personality formation appear to be theories that evolved much like the automobile. No one individually is credited with having formulated the postulations. This is not the case, however, with psychoanalytic theories of personality.

Sigmund Freud (1856–1939), a Viennese physician, beginning early in the 1900's, was the creative giant who formulated the original psychoanalytic theory. Two of his associates, Alfred Adler and Carl Jung, made some major alterations of Freud's theory and methods. They ultimately disagreed with, or grew away from, Freud. Each promoted his own variation on the psychoanalytic theme. Freud's daughter, Anna, has continued to be a vigorous proponent of psychoanalytic theory. She used it particularly in understanding children. Ernest Jones (1961), himself a prominent English psychoanalyst, served as Freud's biographer and interpreter of his fluidly changing ideas.

Much of what now constitutes accepted ideas about the nature of personality was derived from psychoanalytic theory. Concepts which were initially used to explain varied versions of psychoanalysis are now an integral part of our thinking about personality. Much of current therapeutic practice has psychoanalytic origins. Much psychoanalytic technique and theory are so widespread that the origin is hard to trace.

FREUDIAN EMPHASES

The stimulating value of Freud's prolific writing and theorizing is suggested by the numerous books he wrote. He wrote about childhood, dreams, everyday neuroses, hysteria, anxiety, creativity, civilization's discontents, and, of course, therapy. Even more books were written about him and what his theories really meant. His influence was apparent in the works of later theorists. Not only Jung and Adler but Sullivan, Murray, and Horney are among the notables.

Polarity   Many think of Freud's contribution in terms of his concepts of love and sexuality. Others see approaches to personality therapy as his major significance. Still another interpretation is perceiving man caught between two opposing forces, engaged in a process of persistent **conflict,** and being torn by **ambivalence.** Personality adjustment consists in resolving these conflicts. One must recognize these ambivalences. It is necessary to reduce the tensions generated by these opposing forces, or **polarities.**

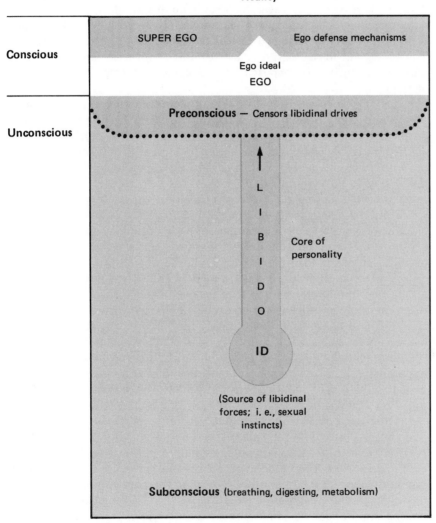

Schematic representation of Freud's concept of personality.   *Figure 7.1*

Polarities may be seen as a matter of the structure of personality. They may be seen as processes that take place between forces. Examples of polarities in daily life are: the drive to be good (be approved) and the urge to be bad (satisfy one's urges on a purely selfish level); the desire to adhere to right (be legal or moral), and the desire to do wrong (to act as, or take what, one wants without regard to the rights of others). Examples of polarities in Freudian literature are: the desire to live—Eros—and the lure of dying—Thanatos. At the same time that one struggles to live, there is a subconscious desire to escape the indignities and pain of life through death. The Thanatos orientation is thought to be unusually strong in persons who risk danger (skydivers, car racers). Those who are accident-prone may be subconsciously seeking death. Thanatos may be present in the would-be or actual suicide. The ego carries on a continuing battle with the id. The biological urges of the id for sex in the form of rape, seduction, and promiscuity are opposed to the custom-observing motivations of the ego.

Love fights to overcome hate; this is shown in the drive to please, serve, and contribute to the welfare of others. On the other hand, people are viewed with suspicion and fear. We seek to belittle them or do them harm. Freud postulates that a young boy is ambivalent toward his father. He respects father's power and appreciates the protection he is given, but he hates his father because father can have sex relations with mother and such are taboo for the son.

Man, to Freud, was no simple being whose behavior could be explained by success, reinforcement, or satisfaction. Deep-seated inner drives must also be taken into account. Satisfaction or pleasure provides an example of man's complexity because it is opposed by pain as a goal or motivation. Freud perceived that some persons enjoyed either psychic or physical pain. These are called masochists and for them, masochism appears to be a way of life. For example, a woman lives a life of degradation and misery for years trying to rehabilitate her alcoholic husband. She finally gets a divorce. After a period of readjustment she gets married again—to another alcoholic. She needs, apparently, to hurt herself. Sometimes the pain itself becomes a polarity. Instead of seeking pain for oneself, the person enjoys inflicting it on others—he is a sadist.

The basic polarity of psychoanalysis is the battle between the ego and the id. The ego is the part of personality sharply in contact with reality. It is fully cognizant of personal responsibility, the need for doing one's work, the value of observing laws and moral codes, and of facing drudgery and discomfort. The id is the part of personality that lies deep in the unconscious (see Figure 7.1), seeks pleasure, and is unconcerned about self-indulgence. It seeks to express itself despite the alertness of the ego as the ego performs police duty. During states of drowsiness or sleep the id sneaks by the censorship of the ego and comes to the level of recognition by means of dreams.

Dreams are a significant part of psychoanalytic therapy because they provide clues to the drives that the id is striving to express. But the ego is alert. Even during sleep, dreams are disguised by the id and transformed into symbolism. Identification of the real libidinal drive is hard to recognize. Thus, a girl desiring intercourse cannot consciously acknowledge the fact in terms of her childhood conditioning. Hence, she dreams of standing holding open a door as deliverymen bring in a stiff roll of carpet. On awakening she recalls the satisfaction of the beauty the carpet could bring into her home. A psychoanalyst would interpret the open door as her vagina and the carpet as the male phallus. A man would not acknowledge his deeply disguised fear of losing his high executive position. He will dream instead of hanging tenaciously to a shaky scaffolding, as he paints his house during a strong wind. The skilled analyst would see such a dream in terms of the symbolic drive to power. He thus gets clues to an understanding of the conflicts a neurotic person is experiencing.

Slips of the tongue are another device used by the libido to slip something over on the ego. For example, a person who is somewhat resentful of the manner in which the boss treats him, might introduce him to someone with the words, "This is Mr. Jones, my officious boss." What he had intended to say was, "This is Mr. Jones, my efficient boss."

There is polarity between conscious and unconscious. It is not, however, a simple contrast like north and south. In addition to these polarities there is the preconscious and the subconscious. The preconscious is that misty area between conscious and unconscious where one remembers bits and snatches of a life episode. One cannot recall it clearly—perhaps, one thinks, he dreamed it. It is neither repressed and completely forgotten nor is it accurately remembered. On encountering an acquaintance his name is kept from the tip of one's tongue by the preconscious barrier or censorship. When the embarrassing moment of not recalling the name has passed, as the victim is walking home, he recalls the name.

At a still lower level is the subconscious. This is the part of the personality that has never been conscious. Whereas the unconscious was at one time a part of conscious experience, the subconscious never was in the realm of awareness. We need never have been aware of the fact that heart pulsation and breathing occur. We can never recall the events of the operating room when we're completely anesthetized.

Implicit in some of the polarities mentioned above is the polarity of self—others. It is necessary to live constantly with the idea that one is primarily concerned with self and self-satisfaction—**narcissism.** However, the nature of man as a social being creates a counterthrust of being aware of the needs and desires of others. A continuing challenge of personality growth is to be able to perceive when ego interest becomes self-defeating in terms of long-range satisfaction. The dichotomy and/or unity of the self—others may be illustrated in marital relations. The spouse who is aware of the wants and needs of the partner tends to beget a response that redounds to his own increased satisfaction. The spouse who vents his hostilities, anxieties, and unhappiness generates similar affective tones in his mate. The mate sooner or later withdraws or attacks and thus compounds the misery of the initiator.

Stages
of development

Much of Freud's theory focuses on the matter of sex. He included in his concept of sex that which is more broadly referred to as love (*e.g.*, love of mother for children, filial love, and ultimately compassion). Sexual love was not ignored. In fact, Freud believed that sex problems and sexual anxiety were the source of neurotic behavior.

Initially, the child loves only himself. Such maternal love as he later reveals is there solely because the child *needs* his mother. His first feelings toward siblings are ones of hostility and aggression. Siblings compete with him for his mother's love and for his father's protection. However, as he matures his hostility toward siblings is replaced, or overlain, by tenderness. He learns that it is to his own disadvantage to act out his aggression and to reveal his jealousy. Freud contends that it is sound psychology to face and accept the truth that underlying much of man's behavior are such destructive forces as hatred, jealousy, and rivalry.

Freud (1943, p. 285) acknowledges that people find his emphasis on infantile sexuality somewhat repulsive. Infantile sexuality means that the infant derives pleasure from manipulation of the penis or vulva. Freud contends that the seeds of lust are there. Denying that sexuality is present in the infant is similar to denying that a bean plant is a bean plant because it is so much like a seedling that will become an apple. Sexuality is sexuality even in the infant. It will, however, have a much different appearance in adulthood. The stages of sexual development are:

> Oral stage—The infant derives satisfaction from the lips and mouth by sucking. Early stages of development leave strong and lasting impressions. It is therefore hypothesized that smoking and drinking rank high among most cultures as a residue of the oral stage.
>
> Anal stage—Pleasure derives from the areas adjacent to the erogenous areas. The child, up to about two years of age, is interested in the feces.
>
> Phallic stage—From the age of two up to about age six the child derives pleasure from stroking the penis or putting fingers into the vagina or stroking the vulva. Sometimes, as a substitute, the child may probe his nose, ears, or eyes to compensate for the pleasures denied him by parents who punish exploration of the genitals. Nose-picking in adults is thus seen as a sexual substitute.
>
> Genital stage—As adulthood is achieved, a fusion of the preceding stages occurs and the sexual force is redirected from self to others.

This stage, as an overt activity, is often proscribed by culture, and normal (male-female) consummation is prohibited. The conflict between sex drive and social adaptation becomes a major source of neuroticism. Contrary to widespread misinterpretations of Freud's teaching, he did not condone extramarital sex relations (Bischof, 1970, p. 46).

Love also evolves through developmental stages. Initially, the infant is characterized only by *self-love*. The idea of the egocentrism of the child pervades the literature of children's personalities. Not being able to develop abstractions, there is nothing more concrete to the child than himself, his body, his wants. Again, initial development is persistent. We begin and end life with self-love being paramount.

The next developmental stage is *parental love*. Parents supply one's needs and provide comfort. The child reciprocates by smiling and by trying to do those things that will gratify his parents. This stage is complicated by polarities. The male child may come to be envious of his father (a phenomenon that Freud called the **oedipus complex**). The female child may be jealous of her mother (which Freud referred to as the **electra complex**).

During the normal course of events, the child grows in his perceptual skills. He begins to consider things at a higher cognitive level. He comes to see that his love for parents may not be all there is in his affective life. Parents command, demand, thwart his selfish desires. His expanding horizons reveal that some persons are more powerful and exciting than his parents. These persons are famous singers, wise teachers, actors, athletes, acrobats, or military heroes. His love expands toward these remote characters. This era is called the stage of *fictional love*. It is just a stage, however, and the child of early school age soon begins to tire of it. It is too one-sided an affair, with his expending so much devotion and the fictional love providing no feedback whatever.

Freud believed that all persons are to some degree bisexual. Males have some female characteristics and females have some male characteristics and tendencies. (His belief has since been confirmed by endocrine and biochemical evidence; the dominant male hormone, androgen, is found in women and the dominant female hormone, estrogen, is present in men.) Hence, Freud considers it to be natural and normal for growing boys and girls to be attracted to companions of the same sex. Boys prefer to be with and play with boys. Girls are deeply devoted and loyal to girls. Each sex swears undying fealty to others of their own sex. Pairs may even vow to carry on ceaseless competition with the other sex. Overt sex activities—examination and manipulation—may accompany this *like-sex devotion*. Freud, however, regards it as a passing phase of development. To treat it as a perversion might just be the thing that makes it difficult to outgrow the stage.

Heterosexual love is the culminating level of the developmental sequence. As puberty occurs the attractiveness of like-sex companions finds a strong competitor in the beauty, grace, strength, and bloom of the other sex. Girls cast glances at boys, push them, and make excuses to meet or brush against them. Boys tease, snatch books, pull hair, laugh loudly at secret jokes. They are ambivalently attracted and repelled by those beautiful female "witches." Such crude attempts to get attention are quickly outgrown and boys and girls pair off—at least to the extent of selecting one as a secret love. In contemporary United States there may be some junior high school girls and boys who are overt enough to hold hands, have long conversations in the hallways, sit together on the bus, and walk each other home. Such attachment becomes progressively deeper. After a normal five or six serious love affairs a couple "really finds" the ideal partner. Three times out of about four the idyllic partnership turns out, in marriage, to be at least tolerable.

There is practical wisdom contained in the Freudian postulations of the developmental stages of love. The really matured adult will have experienced, on the individual schedule of his own growth rate, all of these stages. Parents would do well to encourage their offspring to live through the stages. Too often they condemn or make sarcastic or humorous remarks about the stages. Should parents permit themselves to be alarmed by adult interpretations of normal and passing stages of development, they may introduce the trauma that fixes behavior at a less than mature level.

Ego defense mechanisms

Freud's naming and descriptions of ego defense mechanisms have become so much a part of psychology and personality theory that the terms are used without reference to their origin. They are words that are used with considerable accuracy by the man on the street because they are so well known. The words are not only a part of psychology, they are now a part of our culture. The various defensive techniques are dealt with by name in Chapter 13. In this context it will suffice to describe the dynamics of the mechanisms in accordance with Freudian theory.

The ego is a major component in the structure of personality (Figure 7.1). It has been shown that the ego is subjected to a constant barrage from social, or reality, demands for conformity. It is also subject to the onslaughts of the libido to ignore society and yield to the pleasure of self-indulgence. The dynamics of personality stability demand that the ego be defended against the trials of life.

The "defense" aspect refers to the fact that protection is needed for the preservation of identity and ego strength. One needs refuge from the conflicts, pressures, and dilemmas that one faces daily. A few such protective devices are deliberately planned. For example, one might consciously plan to assemble a wardrobe, actually somewhat beyond his means, in order to create the impression of success. He does this quite aware of his own lack of competence and feelings of insecurity. Most defense mechanisms are the result of unconscious processes. The individual is cognizant of neither his chronic emotional turmoil nor of the behaviors he had adopted to disguise the emotions. For example, one's loud and strident voice and positive assertions may be symptoms of anxieties and doubt. Many therapeutic approaches to personality improvement, including psychoanalysis, are designed to help the individual become aware of the reasons for his behaviors. It is assumed that such awareness is a first step toward dealing effectively with the symptom. A few outside observers may be aware of what the behaviors mean. Most are likely to perceive the loud-voiced, positive speaker as an opinionated braggart whom they prefer to avoid. It is thus a handicapping behavior to the person himself. He does not "come across" as the self-assured person he would like to appear to be. Defense mechanisms are sometimes referred to as adjustive mechanisms—and they may reduce tensions temporarily. It would be more accurate to refer to them as nonadjustive.

> One of the chief characteristics of an ego defense mechanism is that it does not enter the conscious state of reasoning but operates in the unconscious. Hence, the personality is not aware that it is defending its ego. Somewhere in the past it learned this defense technique. Now the personality utilizes the technique even though at times it in no way solves the problem of supporting the ego.
>
> Another chief characteristic of an ego defense mechanism is that it may distort, or even deny, reality. It is not outside the realm of possibility that man may lie to himself in order to protect himself from unhappiness. He may also so twist reality without realizing it that any resemblance to what actually happened and how he interprets what happened has disappeared. He may also be so disturbed by an incident which causes him great emotional discomfort as simply to pretend that it did not happen and do such a good job of pretending that he eventually comes to deny what truly existed. The outside world, his friends, and others stand confused.[1]

Freud was educated as a physician. His theories have permeated child, adolescent, business, educational, and counseling psychology, and many other of the 29 divisions of psychology (as listed by the American Psychological Association). It is, however, in the treatment of personality deviations that his most significant contributions and challenges have been noted. Even in therapeutic approaches that are distinctly different from psychoanalysis, his influence is noted. His theories help in diagnosing and identifying the nature of a particular individual's difficulties. Some of his vocabulary, and ideas such as the nature of conflict, defense mechanisms, and his emphasis on the vital

Treatment of personality disorders: Psychoanalysis

[1]Ledford J. Bischof, *Interpreting Personality Theories*, Second Edition (New York: Harper and Row, Publishers, 1970), pp. 52–53.

importance of the early years of life are simply an accepted part of psychological theory and literature.

Freud's therapy began with **hypnosis.** This is an externally induced state of relaxation and hence, because barriers were let down, of heightened suggestibility. Hypnosis was effective in enabling patients to recall experiences that in a waking state were entirely forgotten. One of Freud's colleagues, Joseph Breuer, had worked with **hysterical** patients until, on one occasion, a female patient fell in love with him. After that, he lost interest in therapy and went into the field of research. This phenomenon of the patient's falling in love with the therapist also occurred to Freud. With his curiosity about the eccentricities of behavior, he stayed with it and formulated the concept of **transference.** This means the patient's shifting of her thwarted love impulses to the therapist. Freud simply continued his therapy until the transference phenomenon could be assimilated by the patient.

Transference did present problems so Freud sought other methods. One of these was free association. Relaxed on a couch—the proverbial posture of the client in therapy—the patient was directed to express freely anything that fleetingly and sporadically came to mind. The expressions were deemed to be clues to that which was repressed.

Frequently the patient cited things that had occurred in dreams. Freud came to believe that dreams might contain keys to unlocking the unconscious. He undertook a self-analysis, depending largely on clues from dreams. As a result he developed an elaborate theory of dreams and published his book *The Interpretation of Dreams* (1900, 1955). Initially Freud thought that the repressed origins of dreams resided in some traumatic incident during childhood (a sexual attack or seduction by a father, uncle, or older brother), because such was so frequently reported. The frequency with which this happened puzzled him until he realized that such reports were often the result of some daydream or fantasy of childhood. Revival of the memory of such an actual trauma, or of the imagined one, taught the client the normality, and lack of danger, involved in these severely repressed and crippling anxieties.

The phenomenon of resistance looms large in psychoanalytic theory. Enculturated man is taught that many things—dislike for one's father or mother, covetousness, jealousy—and especially free expression of the sex drive, are shameful. The continued existence of such feelings, in contrast to societal taboos, gives rise to anxieties and conflicts. The feeling creates guilt in the person who wants to be seen as an upright, moral citizen. It is the task of the analyst to penetrate the disguises the patient assumes in order to hide his supposed depravity. The analyst aids the client in assessing the disguises. He gives the client status by letting him know that his impulses are much like those of others.

"Nondirective therapy," revived and expanded by Rogers (1942) and later called client-centered therapy (Rogers, 1951), had its origins in a method tried by Freud. The client, instead of being on a couch with the therapist out of his line of vision, faces the psychoanalyst and talks things out. This is known as **catharsis**—cleansing oneself by verbally purging oneself of guilt. It is not always necessary to probe deeply into the unconscious. It may suffice to deal as objectively as possible with the reality of behavior in terms of dialogue.

In addition to some of the psychoanalytic terms used in the foregoing discussion there are other concepts which can briefly be explained by reflecting on the processes already described. **"Regression,"** which has not previously been mentioned, means going backward to an earlier stage of life. Regression may occur, actually, when a hysterical adult behaves like a child or adolescent after having achieved some degree of adult functioning. Senility is the classical example, when, in old age, the person again becomes dependent and has to be fed, cleaned, and given attention as he did during childhood. The young wife's returning home to mother in order to avoid facing the reality of budgets, cooking, and housekeeping, is a common regression. The phenomenon may be noted in therapy when the client regresses only during the clinical session. As he probes his memories for the crucial events of childhood he may regress and relive the joy, hate, sorrow, or excitement of earlier moments. During counseling many clients regress to a little girl or a little boy voice.

Freud and psychological terminology

During his later years Freud placed increasing emphasis on the concepts of hostility and aggression. The roots of aggression are seen in some of the ideas mentioned previously. Aggression is shown in Oedipus and Electra complexes, jealousy of siblings, the polarity of love-hate, and the sadistic and masochistic tendencies that are a twisted functioning of the Eros-Thanatos polarity. During Freud's time the concept of human instincts was a fading one. This waning began after L. L. Bernard (1924) counted over a thousand behaviors that scientists, novelists, and philosophers had attributed to "instinct." Bernard's assessment was that anything that explains so much really explains nothing. Freud, nevertheless, used instinct as deep-seated drives that man had to learn to control and direct. It seemed that the instinct for aggression was as basic as that for love. It is manifested in jealousy, sadism, and in mankind's persistent plague—war.[2] Aggres-

---

[2]In order to avoid consolidating the already strongly established notion that war and aggression are the inevitable lot of mankind, let it be observed that this chapter is about psychoanalysis. There are other views of personality that perceive man as having no instincts—either cooperative or aggressive. Man is the product of a potential for development, plus experiences, plus a vision of what he might become. Such theorists oppose the notion that a complex being such as a human can be reduced to concepts such as love-hate, cooperation-aggression, life-death, etc. Murphy (1971), for example, says that it is foolish to extrapolate from what man has been to what he might become.

sion is regarded by Freud as the big problem in the "domestication" of man and, as such, is one cause of neuroses.

"Psyche" is the word Freud used to indicate the total person. It consists of the ego, id, and the super ego (Figure 7-1) and most of the psyche is below the level of contact with reality. Interpreters of Freud conceptualized the psyche as being somewhat similar to an iceberg. Seven-eighths of it is submerged below the water-line of consciousness and awareness of reality.

"Psyche," "Eros," "Thanatos," "Oedipus" are names derived from Greek drama and mythology. The author, on first encountering Freudian psychology, found these characters to be a humorous commentary on the theory. They seemed to be spirits or entities that resided within one's personality. Gradually it became apparent that these terms are used merely as convenient terminology to describe behavior or as potentials for development.

Limitations of psychoanalytic theory

We are still within the century of Freud's life. Whether he will be important in coming decades cannot now be said. Certainly, his theory has stimulated investigations of many varieties and is therefore good theory (see the criteria in Chapter 1). One of the alleged shortcomings of his theory is that it was rooted in the upper class of Viennese culture. His lack of contact with the lower class may have led him to conclusions that are not pertinent throughout a stratified society. Perhaps lower class people are not so emotionally devastated by adolescent sex experiences that the participants suffer psychological trauma. It seems that he was not acquainted with cultural anthropology. Many of the things he called sexual perversions are regarded as being acceptable in some other cultures (see Chapter 5). It is probable that Freudian theory overemphasized the role of sex as the source of personality problems.

> Having been exposed to Freudian postulations on the pivotal importance of sex and sex adjustments as a source of neuroses, the author, as a student in a psychiatric clinic, was prepared to hear about many sex trauma. This did not turn out to be the case. In fact, sex seemed to be a rather minor problem. One man, in the first six months of my clinical experience, was losing weight, was sleepless, made many errors at work, and so on. He was having an affair with an older woman but did not want a divorce. He was willing to take any course except to stop the affair. The other clients in those first months were having an unwanted child (I guess this could be sex), academic failure, child beating, pyromania, hypochondria, lonesomeness, running away from home, and extreme withdrawal as a result of lack of social practice (not trauma).

In a way, Freudian theory is a closed system—it focused on the workings of the psyche (Enelow, 1973). In a way, it is open because

Freud kept constantly adding to it. However, the additions constantly confirm or expand earlier postulations. It was closed in the sense that one could not argue against it. If one argued, for instance, that one felt no hatred for his mother or did not covet his neighbor's wife, it merely showed that one was resistant to the truth. The urges were so severely repressed that they could not even be examined. So you are damned if you do and you are damned if you don't—polarity.

To those theorists who believe that man is not doomed to failure and futility, who believe that man is capable of a more socially productive and personally fulfilling life, Freud seems to be unduly pessimistic. His biographer made the following assessment of Freud's orientation toward life:

> In *Civilization and Its Discontents* (1930, 1962), Freud gave the fullest account of his views in the field of sociology, one which, as he said elsewhere, "can be nothing other than applied psychology." The book begins with the widest possible problem: man's relation to the universe. His friend Romain Rolland had described to him a mystical emotion of identification with the universe, which Freud called an "oceanic" feeling. Freud could not, however, bring himself to believe that this was a primary constituent of the mind, and he traced it back to the earliest stage of infancy, to a time when no distinction is made between the self and the outer world. He then raised the question of the purpose of life. In his opinion the question has, strictly speaking, no meaning, being founded on unjustifiable premises; as he pointed out, it is one that is seldom raised in respect to the animal world. So he turned to the more modest question of what human behavior reveals as its aim. This seemed to him to be indisputably the search for happiness, not only happiness in its narrower sense but also bliss, pleasure, peace of mind, and contentedness—the satisfaction of all desires. Life is dominated by the pleasure-pain principle. In its most intense form this occurs only as a temporary episode; any continuation of the pleasure principle is experienced only as a mild contentedness. Human happiness, therefore, does not seem to be the purpose of the universe, and the possibilities of unhappiness lie more readily at hand. These have three sources: bodily suffering, dangers from the outer world, and disturbances in our relations with our fellow man—perhaps the most painful of all.[3]

The person who has optimism about man's future would prefer to believe that man is born neither good nor bad. Man's enormous potential for varied development permits freedom, and at least some choice, to become either. The idea that a great portion of the psyche is ruled by primitive instincts that must be conquered in everlasting battle is unattractive. The concept of heterostasis is consistent with what is known of all growing things—not just of man—and it provides a basis for hope and optimism.

[3]Ernest Jones, *The Life and Work of Sigmund Freud*, (edited and abridged) (New York: Basic Books, Inc., 1961), p. 477.

*Contributions
of Freudian
theory*

Probably the most significant contribution of Freudian theory is the part it played in making sex an openly acknowledged and normal aspect of life. In Western cultures, during Freud's time, sex relations or sexual organs were not discussed in mixed company. Bold adolescents, lower class men, and brazen women could refer to sex parts and sex relations. Others blushed, stammered, and psychologically turned their backs on the discussion of such subjects. Many had the notion that intercourse, except when pregnancy was planned or at least acceptable, was simply yielding to one's carnal and lustful nature. The consequence was much shame, emotional conflict, and neuroticism that had its origins in the opposition of social convention to a strong physiological drive.

It was Freud's belief that the roots of neuroticism were invariably in sexual conflict. "Always, always" the repression of sex interests and drives were the causes of neuroticism. Those persons who successfully resolved the conflict between their drives and activities were regarded as normal. Those within whom the conflicts were unresolved were neurotic—of course, in widely varying degrees. Other authorities believe that the reduction of neuroses to sex conflict is too simplistic. In some cases it seems that neuroses give rise to the sexual problems rather than vice-versa. Poverty, child mistreatment, psychological imbalance, unfortunate marriage, and many other pressures must also be considered as contributing to neuroses. Freud's finding sex so focal might have been due to (1) his questioning neurotics about sex and the feedback unintentionally given by his interest when sex was mentioned. (2) It may have been the mood of his time that suppressed sex expression and its discussion. Such repression has, in recent years, been greatly reduced but neuroses still occur.

A few parents still scream loudly if they hear that their children are being taught about sex in school. "They'll learn about the nasty subject of sex soon enough when they get older." Most parents today, and in increasing numbers, have profited from Freud's teaching. They are able to teach casually about sex, instead of making a big to-do about it and saying, "Now you have touched on an important question. Let's sit down and discuss it formally, systematically, and thoroughly." Such an approach adds mystery and tinges the subject of sex with emotion. It blows it up to an importance that outweighs the importance it has in the child's life.

A misinterpretation of Freud's teaching is that discussion and recognition are equivalent to expression. He did not say that expression of libidinal urges was a necessity for achieving emotional balance. Discussion allows for some catharsis. However, limitations and expectations of one's society—whatever they may be—are still a part of reality. Man's problem is not sex expression. The problem is direction, recognition, and control. Self-denial regarding sex is a part of the function of conscience (super ego) and consciousness.

Another substantial contribution of Freud was his emphasis on the importance of early childhood experiences. The data gathered in the 1960's and 1970's on the crucial role of the early years in children's learning (Gordon, 1972) confirms Freud's hypotheses.

> This state of things [the extremes of inhibited development and regression] has a certain interest for those looking to pedagogy for the prevention of neuroses by early intervention in the matter of the child's sexual development. As long as attention is directed mainly to the infantile sexual experiences one would think everything in the way of prophylaxis of later neuroses could be done by ensuring that this development should be retarded and the child secured against this kind of experience. But we know that the conditions causing neurosis are more complicated than this and that they cannot be influenced in a general way by attending to one factor only. Strict supervision in childhood loses value because it is helpless against the constitutional factor; more than this, it is less easy to carry out than specialists in education imagine; and it entails two new risks, which are not to be lightly disregarded. It may accomplish too much; in that it favors an exaggerated degree of sexual repression which is harmful in its effects, and it sends the child into life without power to resist the urgent demands of his sexuality that must be expected at puberty. It therefore remains most doubtful how far prophylaxis in childhood can go with advantage, and whether *a changed attitude to actuality would not constitute a better point of departure for attempts to forestall the neuroses.*[4]

Freud's theory was never static. Perhaps because of this predisposition to change, perhaps because of the dynamic and pervasive nature of his subject matter, especially sex, his theory is still dynamic. Thirty years after his death and 60 years after his first publications, current periodicals are still carrying articles discussing the pertinency of his theory for learning, adjustment, and personality formation.

ADLER'S EMPHASES

Alfred Adler (1870–1937), about 14 years younger than Freud, was also medically trained, and graduated from the same school as Freud. He became interested in the treatment of neuroses, and for a period of time was associated with Freud in the psychoanalytic movement.

Points of distinction

Adler became convinced that infantile sexuality was an overinterpretation of early behavior. He proposed that the motivation to grow stemmed from the child's lack of power. The child's helplessness during infancy initiated a lifelong struggle to overcome the actual physical inferiority of infancy and childhood. There is a struggle to

---

[4]Sigmund Freud, *A General Introduction to Psychoanalysis* (Garden City, New York: Garden City Publishing Company, Inc., 1920, 1943), pp. 318–319. Italics not in original.

deal with feelings of inferiority. Finally, there is a drive to power and for the establishment of superiority. Bischof (1970, p. 186) schematically pictures this life process as one of climbing a long staircase at the top of which are nebulous clouds of fictional goals. On the bottom steps are children with their actual physical weakness who are helped or neglected by parents. Help or neglect teaches them a style of life. Some find the struggle to climb the next step—maybe one-quarter, maybe three-quarters of the way up—too difficult. They develop neuroses or psychoses to disguise their inability to keep climbing. Some may even jump off the staircase by committing suicide. Others depend on help from others and develop a life style of dependence. Some recognize that helping others results in receiving help and they learn a cooperative life style. Others develop an aggressive, cut-throat style of fierce independence. Neglected children fail to develop psychological climbing ability. They too consistently encountered defeat in their early struggles. Spoiled, pampered children ride on the shoulders of parents and never develop the strength to climb by themselves.

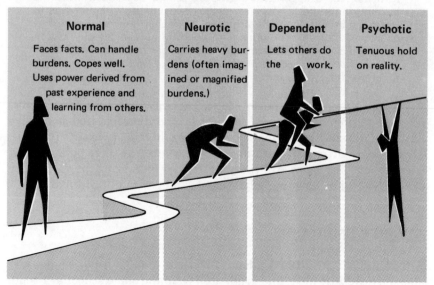

Figure 7.2   *Life styles.*

The way in which the "drive to power" reveals itself is determined by one's ordinal position of birth, according to Adler. The oldest child is presumably conservative, seeking to maintain that secure role which he had prior to the birth of a competing sibling. Because mothers can spend much time with the first (and for a time, only) child, they tend to place pressure on the child to speed his development. This pressure, added to the competition of later-born children, is thought to contribute to a greater incidence of anxiety in firstborns. The second child adopts the style available—the competitor. He becomes the "left-winger" who wants to change things so that power is more readily available to him. "Seconds" tend, presumably, to be less dependent and anxious than their older sibling. Mothers have become warmer and more relaxed through experience in child rearing. The second child develops a fun-loving, other-oriented, less introverted personality. Because they are helped by the older sibling, some later-borns continue to be dependent. Other later-borns compete vigorously to maintain "a place in the sun." They strive to surpass their older sibling. The younger child is often spoiled by relaxed or indulgent parents who have learned not to be so demanding of children. Their competitive striving may lead to defiance and aggressiveness.

The concept of **compensation** is one of Adler's enduring contributions. The classical example is that of Demosthenes who, as a boy, was a stutterer. In the Grecian era in which he lived, being an orator was an admired achievement. In order to compensate for his defective speech, Demosthenes ran and talked while holding pebbles in his mouth. He ultimately achieved fame as an orator. The legend does not tell how he developed the ideas about which he spoke.

Contributions of the Adlerian perspective

Glenn Cunningham, a famous distance runner, was crippled by severe burns as a child. By diligent practice he compensated for the weakness to become a champion.

Compensation may be either direct or indirect. Direct compensation (Demosthenes and Cunningham) means to concentrate on overcoming a weakness until it no longer constitutes a handicap. A poor scholastic record may be overcome by longer, more determined, more systematically scheduled study hours. However, it is possible that one's weakness is so pronounced that time and energy spent on direct compensation is not merely wasteful, it is destructive. The effort leads to failure to develop potential that might have been much more productive.

The frustrated effort could contribute to neuroses. If concentration is focused on developing a facet of personality other than that in which there is weakness, one uses indirect compensation. Thus a boy who is small, has slow reflexes, and lacks stamina and aggressiveness would do well to abandon the goal of being an athlete. He would be wise to devote time to some other aspect of possible potential—leadership, music, scholarship, creative art, or mechanical repair or invention. Menninger shows how indirect compensation might work:

> Among sixty prominent New Yorkers who are known to be deaf, I found thirteen physicians—most of them otologists! Eleven are lawyers, so that these two professions, in both of which hearing is so important, comprise forty per cent of the list. Of the others, seven are bankers and seven are business men, six are journalists, four are

novelists, three are manufacturers, two are in religious work, and there is one in each of the following vocations: architecture, cartooning, farming, politics, teaching, general science, and music.[5]

Compensation may result in anti-social behavior. Braggarts, bullies, and criminals provide examples of those who have chosen misguided avenues for atoning for their real or imagined deficiencies. Not all gangsters are the result of compensation. Remembering the case of the Dobuan (Chapter 5), gangsterism might just be the function of what one's culture and family milieu has taught. However, the Jungian emphasis of compensation and life style seems to have some contemporary implications.

According to Adler, the drive for power is almost universal.

The concepts of feelings of inferiority and feelings of superiority, widely accepted in personality theory, are contributions of Adler. These have their origins in the degree of success one has in achieving

[5]Karl A. Menninger, *The Human Mind*, Third Edition (New York: Alfred A. Knopf, Inc., 1953), p. 173.

that kind of power one perceives as being important. This perception, according to Adler, is a function of ordinal birth position. Thus, personality, or style of life, is pretty much determined by the age of five. Changes in this style of life thereafter are typically purchased at considerable psychic expense. Where one's feelings of superiority or inferiority are marked and crippling, the adaptation (not a real change in basic orientation) may be assisted by therapy. This therapy is, in Adlerian terms, typically much abbreviated in comparison to Freudian analysis. It consists of face-to-face dialogue with the therapist rather than the long processes of probing psychic depths with the client on a couch. The basic motivations may persist in large degree but the patient learns how to deal with them. He learns to compensate successfully.

Adler's theory of ordinal position has been productive of much continuing investigation. However, as shown in Chapter 3, research fails to confirm any reliable predictive capacity. Wise parents can be wise parents, whether through intuitive beliefs or systematic study, for their first as well as for their younger children.

JUNG'S EMPHASIS

Carl Gustav Jung (1875–1961) was a Swiss psychiatrist who wrote voluminously and convincingly about personality deviations. Freud's work on dreams interested Jung. A resulting correspondence grew into an association that lasted several years. Some biographers reported a strong dislike between Freud and Jung. Others attributed their interpersonal disaffection simply to differences in the ways in which they interpreted motivations and behaviors. Jung believed that man's driving motivation was an *élan vital* (a life force), an urge to grow, learn, and achieve. Freud attributed this urge to sex; Jung perceived it as an intrinsic and general drive to grow and be active.

Points of distinction

The psyche was, to Jung, a composite of (1) a subjective psyche—one's consciousness, (2) a personal unconscious that consists of repressed or forgotten material, and (3) a collective (or racial) unconscious. The latter is comprised of the common historical background of humanity. Out of this background the conscious and personal unconscious of an individual develops. The collective unconscious is the base of instinctual behaviors; it crops out in dreams or childhood fantasies.

Man's life, according to Jung, must consist in developing socially oriented values. Urges from the collective unconscious do not constitute any excuse for deviating from cultural values. No problem is created by the repression. The sources of neuroses reside in man's sense of futility, uselessness, and anonymity when he fails to discover, tap, and develop the latent potentialities he has. In contemporary society it is necessary for one to specialize in order to develop technical skills. This is a satisfactory way of life during one's first 40 years.

Thereafter the pressure to free one's *élan vital* and exercise a better balanced variety of capacities may become a problem.

Jung emphasized polarities, such as organic vs. cultural needs, self-orientation vs. other orientation, inferiority feelings vs. superiority feelings, progression vs. regression, and many others. Personality is healthy when there is a balance and reciprocity between these forces and needs. This balance he called self-actualization. This is a capacity to give expression to one's *élan vital* and keep it in harmony with moral and ethical values, Jung's orientation is an optimistic one. It is his conviction that man is always improving himself in contrast to his primitive ancestors. He believed that man is not just a product of the past. In addition, his dreams and hopes for the future constitute a dynamic part of man's being. Despite his being called a proponent of psychoanalytic psychology, Jung's conclusions about man's becoming, individual responsibility, and socially oriented behavior seem to be humanistic. His views have the flavor of current authors who are identified as humanistic psychologists (Chapter 9).

Jung's contributions

Jung contributed some concepts that are used, both with and without understanding, by many who have never studied any psychology—general or psychoanalytic. These concepts are extroversion and introversion. These are ways the individual has evolved for dealing with and using what Jung considers to be the four components of mental activity: thinking vs. feeling, and sense perception vs. intuition.

The extrovert is one whose energies are predominantly focused on the external social and physical environment. He may be either a perceiving, logically thinking extrovert or a feeling, intuitive extrovert. The introvert is one whose energies are, for the most part, directed toward his own feelings, behaviors, and perceptions. One orientation is not better than the others. A person is not exclusively one or the other. The introvert is psychologically set to deal with the inner world of ideas, feelings, and creativity. The extrovert finds it more interesting to be engaged with people and things. Life can be more meaningful when there is a balanced role for extrovertive and introvertive tendencies. Such balance may be facilitated by the cognitive processes that are encouraged in Jungian therapy.

The struggles of scientists to separate their work from the alleged mythology and superstitions of religion did not bother Jung. He was firmly convinced that religion, in the form of love and concern for fellow beings as well as belief in a higher being, was an essential of mental health:

> Among my patients in the second half of life—that is to say, over thirty-five—there has not been one whose problem in the last resort was not that of finding a religious outlook on life. It is safe to say that every one of them fell ill because he had lost that which the living religions of every age have given to their followers, and none of them

has been really healed who did not regain his religious outlook. This of course has nothing whatever to do with a particular creed or membership of a church.[6]

IMPLICATIONS OF PSYCHOANALYSIS

Neo-Freudians

As indicated previously, psychoanalysis is "good" theory. It has prompted continued investigation of the dynamics of personality. Except for some of the extreme behaviorists (see Chapter 10), most theorists acknowledge the existence of unconscious motivations. Whether the unconscious is "instinctive" urges or forgotten or repressed memories, both the scholar and the man-on-the-street must acknowledge that we do not always act rationally. We really do not know why we do certain things. While we may admit, or accede to the proposition, that all behavior is motivated or goal-seeking, it is necessary to hedge and say that some drives are purposive (unconscious strivings of the organism) and others are purposeful (consciously perceived). The scholars who conclude that reduction to sex, or power, or *élan vital* is too simplistic are known as the neo-Freudians.

Among the neo-Freudians are Abram Kardiner, who was one of the first to seek an integration of psychoanalysis with the emerging field of cultural anthropology. He postulated that there was a need to study the interaction between the individual's drives and the social and cultural institutions to which he was required to adapt.

Karen Horney, who worked with Freud in Europe and later as an analyst in New York, found the biological limitations of psychoanalytic theory too confining. She was dissatisfied with the role accorded to women. She believed there was neglect of the impact of the social environment (Woodworth, 1948, p. 205). Her contributions included balance between optimism and pessimism. She emphasized cultural interaction in personality formation, continuous evolving of character structure, and the importance of the self-concept. Her definition of personality orientation in terms of the tendencies of people to turn toward, against, and away from others finds application in occupational choice and adjustment theories. For example, some prefer to work with things or processes (mechanics, researchers) and others prefer to work with persons (teachers, lawyers, counselors) (Roe, 1964).

Erich Fromm is another neo-Freudian. Best known as a stimulating lecturer, provocative author, he is an optimistic analyst with strong sociological interests. He believes that man has, to a remarkable degree, created his own problems; and, although it will be a long and arduous process, he believes that man can solve the problems he has created. Man is an animal, but one capable of using rational processes.

[6]Carl G. Jung, *Modern Man in Search of a Soul* (New York: Harcourt, Brace and Company, Inc., 1933), p. 264.

Man is the only animal who finds his own existence a problem which he has to solve and from which he cannot escape. In the same sense man is the only animal who knows he must die.[7]

Man's needs to transcend himself, to establish a firm identity, and to relate to his fellow human beings are major considerations in Fromm's interpretation of personality.

Henry Stack Sullivan (1892–1949), in his relatively short lifetime, had a strong impact on personality theory, particularly on therapy and social psychology. His major emphasis was on the theme of anxiety. It is a prime motivator and is central in the self-concept. Anxiety has vital significance in what and how one learns. Sullivan developed an interpersonal theory of personality. He believed that man derives his significance, goals, and anxieties from the quality of human interaction. He, as many try to teach, perceived man's destiny as being dependent on the welfare of all people throughout the world.

Henry Murray may be best known for his construction of the "Thematic Apperception Test" (TAT). This is a device for assessing the direction and nature of one's personality. The theme of "personology," of which the TAT is but an aspect, is one which continues (after more than 30 years) to promote research and contemplation. Some of the persistent thoughts Murray initiated deal with such ideas as:

- The brain is central—without it there could be no personality.
- Man lives continuously with the need to reduce tension (an idea that would be debated by those who believe in the theory of heterostasis).
- The past cannot be dismissed as a factor in personality.
- Each person is unique (this postulation was discussed in Chapter 5 in reference to the "determinants" of personality).
- Each of us in a lifetime plays many roles, so that stereotyped descriptions of personality are misleading.

Limitations of psychoanalytic theory

Motivation and personality theory, as we now have it, developed a generation ago in large measure out of a psychoanalytic and early life experience framework with a corresponding emphasis on projective techniques to get at underlying motivations and on adjustment rather than on self-determination and competence as the evaluative ideals. Both this conceptual model and the psychometrics developed from it have been found wanting so that research in personality and motivation have in recent years failed to attract a sufficient number of good researchers into the field.[8]

In this quotation, Dragastin indicates the same limitation of psychoanalytic theory that led Horney to seek supplements to the

[7]Erich Fromm, *The Sane Society* (New York: Holt, Rinehart and Winston, 1955),
[8]Sigmund Dragastin, "Towards a Research Policy for Psychosocial Deprivation," in *Perspectives on Human Deprivation* (Washington, D. C.: U. S. Department of Health, Education, and Welfare, 1968), p. 329.

theory. Motivations residing within the individual do not constitute an adequate rationale. The id, life force, or the drive to overcome inferiority do not seem to be sufficient to explain varied personalities. This is especially apparent to those who recognize the tremendous, squeezing force of culture. Early life *plus* underlying drives are still inadequate for those who perceive man as having the ability to exercise logical processes (at least when he is intellectually mature). Many prefer to see man as being able to choose how he will respond to underlying forces.

Psychoanalytic theory is seen as being too "localized" in origins and application to have universal pertinence (Enelow, 1973). Freud's views on the debilitating effect of culture's inhibiting sexual impulses is seen as having no relevance in some cultures. It may have small pertinence in some socioeconomic strata. The same can be said about the drive to power. It just is not there in some cultures.

Miller (1972) perceives the value of psychoanalysis as residing in bringing to awareness the unconscious depths of man. Therapeutic analysis is so lengthy, and hence costly, that most people suffering from neuroses cannot afford treatment. Besides, there are not enough psychoanalysts to provide the service. Lengthy contacts may be just what some lonesome, isolated, alienated people need. Lengthy therapy provides that contact. Others, as Jung emphasized, can be aided by seeing, rationally, that one is often his own worst enemy.

Relaxed and open-minded attitudes about sex have been a contribution of the psychoanalytic movement. Carrying this attitude too far—no fault of the originators—may prove dangerous. Certainly, there are matters of biological sex drive and expression. There are also matters of control, goal seeking, and actualization of potentials other than sex that merit consideration. A possible limitation of psychoanalytic theory is lack of balanced perspective. Life is more than sex or power. This, however, is a limitation of all personality theories: Emphasis on any one factor has a great potential for obscuring the still existing force of a factor that may, in its turn, have been previously overemphasized.

SUMMARY

Freud, a creative thinker and prolific writer, developed a theory of personality and therapy based on the concept of polarity. No matter what aspect of life the concept is applied to, it works. At least it can be rationalized to make it appear to work. Such polarities can be perceived in life-death, love-hate, self-others, and, of course, ego-id.

Personality evolves through certain biologically determined stages: oral, anal, phallic, and genital. The latter is heterosexual love. In its highest state, love includes love and concern for all mankind. If early stages are interfered with by parental and social pressures or trauma, the achievement of full maturity may be hampered.

Personality, or psyche, consists, according to Freud, largely of the unconscious. Therein the id, with its libidinal forces, resides. The preconscious (that which is seeking expression or contact with reality) and the conscious (that which has contact with reality and therefore must have a socially accepted nature), and the super-ego or conscience are also parts of the psyche. Because the battle between the conscious and unconscious is so steady and in some persons so intense, some persons develop defense mechanisms to diminish its pressure. To treat the neuroses stemming from crippling pressure, Freud used many methods—hypnosis, free association, dialogue, and dream interpretation. Freud sought to have patients perceive and face the forces of the unconscious. Freud's contributions were to bring sex from the shadows of whispered indirections to being perceived as a normal and respectful aspect of life. He also emphasized the importance of early childhood experiences, especially those relating to love, as deeply formative personality influences.

Adler contributed to personality theory the idea that man's major driving force was a will to power. He perceived life as a long struggle to transform feelings of inferiority into actual or perceived power and superiority. His idea of compensation for weakness is a concept with which many are familiar.

Jung, despite being classified as a psychoanalyst, had many notions that would today be classed as humanistic. He stressed self-actualization, individual responsibility, and the need for balanced perspective between introvertive and extrovertive tendencies. He perceived religion as a powerful factor in preventing the extreme self-concern that could cripple personality function.

Neo-Freudians have demonstrated that Freud developed a "good" theory. It works in much therapy. It also provides a framework and stimulus for further study of the dynamics of personality.

SUGGESTED READINGS

ADLER, ALFRED, *The Science of Living*. Garden City, N. Y.: Doubleday and Company, Inc., Anchor Books, 1929, 1969 (paperback).
   In easy, journalistic style, the author proposes that the motivating force of life is to gain a goal, to exercise power. If one is inhibited he will be handicapped by feelings of inferiority. Adler expresses his ideas on marriage, sex, and child rearing.

FREUD, SIGMUND, *Civilization and Its Discontents*. New York: W. W. Norton and Company, Inc. 1930, 1962 (paperback).
   In explaining the pressures that culture places on the processes of domesticating the primitive instincts of man, Freud also provides insight into his basic theory.

ENELOW, ALLEN J., "Is Psychoanalysis Viable?" *American Journal of Ortho-psychiatry,* Vol. 43, 258–259, 1973.
   The perseverence of the psychoanalytic model is shown in this article.

Enelow says that the basic theory is not sufficiently open. The psycho-analyst must be receptive to new insights and new therapy techniques.

FROMM, ERICH, *The Art of Loving.* New York: Harper and Row, Publishers, 1956.

Brotherly love, mother love, erotic love, self love, and love of God are considered in hierarchical order. These loves are of different orders—while having some relationship, they are not mutually interdependent.

HORNEY, KAREN, *The Neurotic Personality of Our Time.* New York: W. W. Norton and Company, Inc., 1937.

Recognizing that neuroses often spring from childhood experiences should not exclude considering contemporary influences and a rational approach to solving current difficulties.

JUNG, CARL G., *Modern Man in Search of a Soul.* New York: Harcourt, Brace and Company, Inc., 1933.

As man matures the introverted, impulsive behavior of childhood must, if psychological health is to be maintained, shift to include larger concerns—spiritual, philosophical, and affiliative values.

MACCOBY, MICHAEL, "A Psychoanalytic View of Learning," *Change,* Vol. 3, No. 8, 32–39, 1972.

This article provides an example of how psychoanalytic theory is used to evaluate current problems. Greater recognition of individuality is needed from kindergarten to college and the ego needs are used to justify innovative approaches.

FOLLOW-UP LEARNING ACTIVITIES

What does polarity mean in psychoanalytic theory?

_____
_____
_____
_____

Why does the concept of defense mechanism have questionable merit?

_____
_____
_____
_____
_____

List what you consider to be the major contributions of Freud's theory.

_____
_____
_____
_____
_____

How does Bischof conceptualize Adler's hypothesis of a "drive for power"?

_____
_____
_____
_____
_____

What does Jung mean when he speaks of _élan vital_?

_____
_____
_____
_____

What changes, if any, would you now make in your response to the second and third items in the pre-reading learning activities?

_____
_____
_____
_____

Name three neo-Freudians and tell one emphasis of each.

1 _____
_____
2 _____
_____
3 _____
_____

8
Morphology and Physiology

You are what you eat. True or false?

LEARNING ACTIVITIES

Mark the following statements true (T), false (F), or neither true nor false (N).

_____ Fat men tend to be jolly.

_____ Strong back, weak mind.

_____ Beautiful but dumb.

_____ People with high intelligence tend to be small and to have defective vision.

_____ You are what you eat.

When you see a person, but have not yet really made his acquaintance, do his face and figure have any influence on what you think about him?

_____

_____

_____

_____

_____

_____

Would it surprise you if you saw a very fat man who was

president of a college   Yes_____ No_____

engaged in competitive athletics   Yes_____ No_____

a devotee of artistic paintings   Yes_____ No_____

Describe what you thought of your face and figure at any time before you reached the age of about fourteen.

_____

_____

_____

_____

_____

_____

Do any of those childhood thoughts still persist?

Yes _____ No _____ Comment _____

_____

_____

_____

Rank in order of importance (1 most . . . 5 least) the treatment you would recommend for an adult about to be placed in a mental institution.

_____ brain surgery   _____ therapeutic environment

_____ electric shock   _____ rest and solitude

_____ drug therapy

In what way, if any, do you think diet influences your personality?

_____

_____

_____

_____

The relationship between body and personality has intrigued man for as long as there has been a study of psychology. The early theories were so far from what are acceptable data today that the relationship between body and personality is far down the totem pole of psychological acceptability.

The overemphasis of popular clichés has probably been a factor in the discrediting of a positive correlation between body build and personality. For example, it is rather widely believed that fat men are jolly. Even Shakespeare stressed this fallacy with:

> Let me have men about me that are fat
> Sleek-headed men, and such as sleep o' nights.
> Yond Cassius has a lean and hungry look;
> He thinks too much: such men are dangerous.
>
> *Julius Caesar*, Act I

Therapy approaches by psychoanalysts and consulting psychologists have so dominated the field that they have contributed to an underemphasis on medication and surgery as a means of personality change. Yet there are **psychiatrists** who believe that the only real personality change is that accomplished by medical intervention. Drugs or surgery that alter the functioning of the brain or body are *the solid approach* to personality change.

Because psychological approaches do not explain all is not a reason for putting them aside. Because morphological and physiological considerations do not explain all, does not mean that they are not vitally functional. The functioning of a car cannot be explained by examining only the carburetor. This does not mean, however, that the carburetor can be excluded as a pivotal item.

This chapter will try to show that body build and physiological functioning help to shape personality. Proponents of the physiological approach to understanding personality are enthusiastic and convinced about constitutional determinants. They are as positive about personality as are the "early childhood experiences" devotees.

MORPHOLOGY

Body language   A young and newly introduced actor on the personality scene is body language. It is now the subject of systematic study both as a cause and as a result of personality manifestations. Nonverbal techniques and interpretations relating to interpersonal relations "have invaded the training field with a vengeance in recent years" (Birnbaum, 1972). One's body language is read by others (and it has been so read for centuries). It is also a matter of moving and acting in such ways as to induce predictable feelings. For example, if you want to know someone, move within the conventional space (18 inches), offer your hand, and, after proper acquaintance, touch him. Bend toward the person you want to contact psychologically. "Keep open" by revealing your palms. Body language can reveal a state of mind. It can also induce an inclination to behave in given ways.

Body language, it is believed, is read by children even before they are able to comprehend clearly what spoken words convey. Adults are often confused when the body language that they perceive in another conflicts with his spoken word. It is just such lack of consistent correspondence with what we see a person doing and what is inferred from body build and body movement that creates skepticism about the relationship between personality and **morphological** structure and function. Lack of a consistent relationship is not, however, equivalent to saying there is *no* relationship. There are many determinants of personality (see Chapter 5). Hence, as this chapter is studied, one must guard against the temptation of thinking that morphology is *the* determinant. Body language must be regarded as only a clue to personality, because other influences are also continuously operational.

Hippocrates (460–357 B.C.) claimed that personality was dependent upon the "four humors" of the body. His ideas persist at least to the extent of influencing current terminology. One occasionally hears reference to a *phlegmatic* personality. This is one who is sluggish, dull, imperturbable, hard to arouse to action. Hippocrates attributed this to an excess of phlegm. Another humor was blood. We still speak of a *sanguine* (bloody) personality. This is one whose **temperament** is warm, confident, optimistic, cheerful, passionate. The sanguine person is one in whom health abounds. Others are influenced by an excess of yellow bile, or choler. They are called *choleric* persons. These are people whose characteristic mood is anger and irritability. They are readily aroused to wrath. It is recognized that from the time of birth some babies may be characterized as irritable (Sontag, 1972). Current explanations are, however, not nearly so simplistic as being a matter of excessive yellow bile. The fourth humor is black bile. This leads to sad, depressed, pensive, and gloomy perspectives. The victims are *melancholic* personalities. Although the concept of humors is part of an obsolete physiology, the terminology persists: sanguine, phlegmatic, choleric, and melancholic personalities.

Centuries later Cesare Lombroso (1835–1909), an Italian criminologist, advanced a mind-body theory. He believed that criminal

Early hypotheses about body-personality relations

tendencies in a man could be identified by certain organic and physical characteristics. Overdevelopment of the lower jaw, projecting ears, ferocious facial characteristics, and defective teeth were supposed to describe the criminal type. A number of investigators have made careful studies that disproved Lombroso's theory. There are, nevertheless, many persons who permit their impressions of others to be influenced by facial characteristics. For example, "You can tell by looking at him that he will grow up to be a thug."

Kretschmer (1911) is given credit for stimulating interest in constitutional typology. He postulated that there were two broad types of body build and personality with a third in-between type. One extreme is those with short, fat bodies, described as *pyknic*. The other extreme is those with tall, thin bodies named *asthenic*. The in-between were those with balanced, muscular bodies called the *athletic*. Each type was presumed to predispose the possessor to a range of personality. Should life's pressures become too great, they were prone to a particular kind of disability. The pyknic types, with their overweight bodies, were extroverted, good-natured, matter-of-fact, and relaxed. When they did suffer emotional breakdown they were inclined to have **manic-depressive** psychoses. The asthenic types were humorless, introverted, and phlegmatic. When they broke down they tended to be **schizophrenic**—inclined to inconsistencies. Athletics were people of cool decision, systematic, and consistently thoughtful. When they suffered mental illness, it was likely to be of the paranoid type. Kretschmer himself had difficulty with this typology. He later added a "dysplastic" type. This consisted of those with upper bodies of the pyknic type and lower bodies of the asthenic type, or vice versa. Follow-up studies have found positive correlations (see Appendix I) in the range of .10 to .20. Such correlations are so small as to deny valid predictions, even though they are in the direction that Kretschmer postulated.

A theory of constitutional types

Sheldon (1943) has avoided the error of making sharp distinctions between types in a theory of body-personality. His theory is only about 30 years old and is still viewed with an open mind by some authorities. By providing for continuous variations between types he has avoided the criticism that makes types and classifications so vulnerable to logical attack. He saw the danger of drawing sharp lines between whites-blacks, boys-men, Swedes-Americans, young-old, rich-poor, and fat-lean. This avoidance of a tri-modal distribution, such as Kretschmer postulated (Figure 8.1), is accomplished by a numbering system. This system accounts for 17 aspects of morphological structure. Among items included are bone size, relative breadth of hips and shoulders, skin thickness, size of blood vessels, and size of internal organs (Sheldon, 1942, p. 7). The measurements are of the organs, limbs, and ratios of parts to other parts. They are measures of mass and ratio. Sheldon named three body types: endomorph, mesomorph, and ectomorph. Each would have variations within it that would show the continuous variation. The extreme within a type would have a seven as the major number. The figure one shows minimums of the other two classifications of morphological measurement. Thus, the most extreme type within a category would be:

Endomorph	Mesomorph	Ectomorph
7-1-1	1-7-1	1-1-7

Typically, though, there would be few such extremes in an experimental population; and, three persons, each within a type, might be:

Endomorph	Mesomorph	Ectomorph
4-2-2	3-5-1	1-2-4

In addition, there can be an average type whose body measurements are evenly balanced and his morphological index might be 4-4-4, 4-3-3, or 4-3-2, etc.

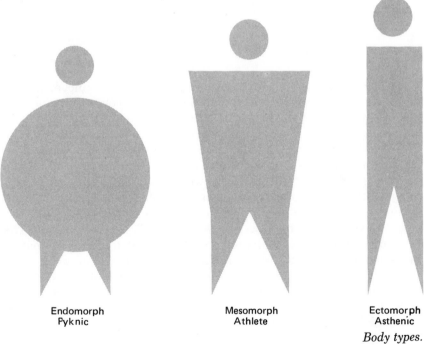

Endomorph
Pyknic

Mesomorph
Athlete

Ectomorph
Asthenic

Body types.   ***Figure 8.1***

With each type of morphological structure there goes a predominant temperamental predisposition. Initially, Sheldon (1942, p. 13) started with 650 alleged traits of temperament. He reduced the list for each personality type to 20 items. The relationships may be summarized as follows:

MORPHOLOGY

Endomorph—massive digestive organs, muscles weak, low specific gravity (floats easily in water), typically fat. Gut predominates. Softness and sphericity are noted.

Mesomorph—bone, muscle, connective tissue predominate. High specific gravity. Large blood vessels. Skin thick and tight. Hardness and uprightness prevail.

Ectomorph—fragile, linearity, flat chest, delicate. Slight development of both digestive organs and muscular structure. Pipestem bones. Relative to total body mass has large surface area. He is overly exposed or "thin-skinned."

TEMPERAMENT

Visceratonia—physically relaxed, slow action, loves eating, has good digestion. Enjoys company, wants affection and approval, even-tempered, tolerant, sleeps well, is complacent, "now" oriented, extrovertive.

Somatotonia—action oriented, loves adventure, needs exercise. Dominates, exercises power, is bold, has courage for combat, competitive, psychologically callous ("thick-skinned"), noisy, and overmature.

Cerebrotonia—physical restraint, poor appetite and digestion. Loves privacy, is apprehensive, emotionally restrained, self-conscious, socially inhibited, resists habit and routine, vocally restrained, poor sleeper, mentally active, future oriented, and introverted.[1]

Speculative implications of Sheldon's hypotheses

Visualize these three types, representing the rather distinct extremes, as they gather for a game of bridge. The endomorph (visceratonic) is pleased with the opportunity for fellowship. For him the game is a chance for fellowship and camaraderie. He opens the scene with the question, "What do we have for snacks?" The mesomorph (somatotonic), flexing his muscles, wants to "have at it" and cut out all the persiflage. He remarks that there are few words in the bridge language—"the numbers one through seven, clubs, diamonds, hearts, and spades, and pass and no-trump." He lets it be known that bridge is a competitive game. The object is to see who is the best player. The ectomorph (cerebrotonic) has reluctantly consented to make a fourth. Secretly, he would rather read or listen to his stereo. He plays his cards well. He has his own interpretations of bridge conventions. He plays not so much to win over others as he does to give his own skills and insights some exercise.

If body build and physiological constitution do have such implica-

---

[1]W. H. Sheldon and S. S. Stevens (collaborator), *The Varieties of Temperament* (New York: Harper & Row, Publishers, 1942), pp. 31–94.

tions as suggested, imagine, again, how the extreme types react at a junior high school party. The visceratonic boy is having a wonderful time conversing and waving. He sits comfortably in the easiest chair available. He has an ice cream bar in one hand and a hot dog in the other. The somatotonic PE teacher has heard somewhere that young people should be overtly participative. She finds one of her mesomorphic girl students. This girl has been bouncing about to the music. The teacher helps the girl pull the endomorphic boy out on the dance floor. There he stumbles about in misery. He wonders how soon they will bring out the main refreshments. The ectomorph was pressured in the first place to attend the party. He sits quietly in the corner gravely contemplating the odd ways in which people differ from each other. Wise teachers say "Hello" and leave him to his thoughts. There are, however, those teachers who mouth clichés about individual differences and then try to prompt "socialization for all." They try to find him some verbal or physical companion who can engage him in conversation or dancing. He makes the cerebrotonic wish, "Why don't they just leave me alone?" Sheldon may not have *the* key to individual differences, but at least he makes us aware of the reality of individuality. It just may be that some of the clues to understanding reside in constitution and body structure.

Occupation and body build

There is much concern in a technological and industrial culture about worker satisfaction and productivity. The school guidance movement started in 1908. The problem was one of finding young workers jobs that fit their personalities and preparations. It was assumed, on the basis of considerable pragmatic evidence, that personal preferences might run the gamut from working with people, things, or processes. Morphology suggests some theses for such preferences. The endomorph might be happiest and most productive as a YMCA executive secretary or host, or as a receptionist in a low-key office. The mesomorph might be most intrigued by door-to-door selling or being an executive in some corporation where pressure and competition are ever-present. The ectomorph might find his dream slot as a research scientist or as a professor in a university where publication takes precedence over contacts with students.

Of course, we know that, for the most part, one must take the job for which he is qualified at the time and place the job is available (see Chapter 11). Hence, there are mesomorphs in the YMCA job. They get the work done. They are, however, covertly hoping that they will find something that will represent more of a challenge. There are ectomorphs in executive positions because they understand the scope of the job and they have knowledge of people. There are also executives who have ulcers, high blood pressure, and heart attacks. It seems just possible that there are ectomorphs and endomorphs who do not thrive on the task of constantly having to meet challenge. Conversely, there are those who enjoy the executive pressure. Despite high status in their corporations, they seek a government post to test further their capacity to succeed. Perhaps they are predominantly somatotonic. It is quite possible that at least some worker dissatisfaction stems from having to do a job that is at variance with one's constitutional type.

There are productive workers in certain jobs who have body types that differ from what the jobs seem to demand. This does not disprove the personality-constitutional hypothesis. There are other, *many other*, factors that influence vocational choice and success: Family tradition, influence of a liked teacher, the wisdom and humanity of the supervisor, and what the culture and economy are currently calling for are typical factors in choice. Nursing for girls was much more popular in the 1920's than any other career. Today there is a healthy response to the call for secretaries. In addition, some jobs call for a variety of tasks that demand something of varied personality types. However, the process of self-actualizing might be facilitated in the rather pure types (1-2-7, 2-7-1, or 6-2-2) if the implications of Sheldon's theory were studied.

Delinquency and body build

Studies of delinquent boys have pursued just such an hypothesis. Glueck and Glueck (1950) have postulated body build as a predisposing factor to delinquency. They recognize that delinquency is not *caused* by body build. There are a number of factors that are predictive, at an early age, of the likelihood of a child's becoming delinquent. These are:

1. Stability of the home;
2. lack of affection of parents for the child;
3. restlessness in early childhood (unable to sit still in the classroom);
4. resistance to authority;
5. and the tendency to be destructive.

Body type has nothing to do with the above five items that improve the accuracy of prediction. However, when the child does become delinquent, the mesomorphic body type seems to be the most frequently associated with norm-violating behavior (Glueck and Glueck, 1970). The Gluecks state the perspective of the global problem as follows:

> The fruitful preoccupation with sociologic, psychologic, and cultural exploration of social problems in recent years has resulted in virtual neglect of, if not opposition to, the study of bodily constitution as related to behavior. Despite the recent development of psychosomatic medicine, even psychiatrists, psychoanalysts, and psychologists are too much inclined to take as their point of departure the instinctual-emotional or intellectual structure and function, forgetting that just as these aspects of human activity do not operate in a vacuum apart from socio-cultural milieu, so also they do not spring into being without some fundamental relationship to the body. Certainly, no analysis based on a comparison of delinquents and non-delinquents

can be said to be complete without some deep-probing exploration of the somatic as well as the psychic aspects.[2]

The Gluecks found that in gross body size and strength, delinquents were larger and stronger than nondelinquents, except that an ectomorph, when he was delinquent, was weaker than his ectomorphic peers. Delinquents tend to have wider bodies than the nondelinquents. The nondelinquents tend to be taller. Body disproportions are less frequent among the delinquents than among those who avoid trouble. Mesomorphics, relative to their numbers in the population and in absolute figures, contribute far more than their share to the delinquent population.

Learning about the physical superiority of the majority of delinquents is probably a surprise to those who have read research studies on late and early maturing boys and girls. It is generally found that boys and girls who are somewhat physically larger and more mature are the ones who are admired, are expected to be leaders, and who are self-confident (Jones, 1965). They would have little comparative need to resort to delinquency to achieve status. Such conflicting data should indicate to the student of personality the danger of extrapolating beyond the data. Specifically, home factors are the important factors in delinquency despite the consistency of the constitutional influence.

Body image and personality

It is easy for one to believe that if his physique and face are acceptable he is an acceptable person (Cavior and Lombardi, 1973). The belief is picked up, over the years, from glances, insults, compliments, and conversations. The mesomorphic boy and girl, at the present time in our society, have the physique that is most admired. Others tend to attribute to such persons desirable personality traits. Culture has its impact. Friends of the parents utter compliments for the baby who is big for his or her age. If the size does not consist of surplus fat, this admiration continues through adolescence. No longer does the tall girl stoop to hide her stature. She stands proudly "head and shoulders" above the crowd.

Size is not just of cultural importance, it also has clinical importance. Control over gross smallness or largeness is sought by glandular treatment (Garn, 1966). There are popular myths about the brightness of little children in school. Research data, however, indicate that the small coefficient of correlation that does exist between intelligence and size is positive. Bright children, as a group, are taller and heavier than those who are less bright (Terman and Oden, 1947). The misconception about the high intelligence of small children

---

[2]Sheldon and Eleanor Glueck, *Unraveling Juvenile Delinquency* (Published for the Commonwealth Fund) (Cambridge, Massachusetts: Harvard University Press, 1950), p. 183.

probably arises from the fact that the large bright child associates with companions and class mates who are older.

That which is most important relative to body size and personality is what the individual thinks about himself. People in general make little fuss about the color of one's hair. "My, your hair is black," or "How do you like having bright red hair?" are remarks seldom heard. This is not the case with body size and shape. These are the subject of greetings, conversation, and condemnation. "Fatty," "Slim," "High pockets," are common nicknames. The concept of one's stature becomes internalized in resentment or contentment. Staffieri (1972), basing his conclusions on the study of 90 boys from ages six to ten, concluded that how one perceived his body was the really significant item in the constitution-personality question. Most of the ultimate outcomes of body-personality correlates can be explained on the basis of expected behaviors. As children, the expectations are reinforced in many subtle and verbal ways. As an adult, one can decide that his responses and perceptions of body size are matters of personal choice. One can subscribe to the popular misconceptions, "Fat men are jolly," "lean men are dangerous," or he may say, "My behavior, my personality is as much a function of my choice as it is a dictate of my body."

A perspective on body image and personality has been provided by Berscheid and Walster (1972). They reported on their own, and surveyed other, studies relating to how good looks and physical attractiveness affect one's perception of the personality of others. We utter clichés about beauty being only skin deep. We assert that companions are picked in terms of their behaviors. Nevertheless, physical attractiveness by far scores the most points in creating favorable impressions. This is true from babyhood through college and the early adult years. The one exception was that the girls during the first kindergarten years did not consider attractiveness in choosing preferred playmates. Little boys did show preference for physical attractiveness from the time of entering kindergarten. Physically attractive youngsters received better grades. (This may be more than a matter of perception, because good looks and intelligence are positively correlated.) However, the coefficient of correlation is so small that individual predictions are hazardous. Teachers, when asked to select elementary pupils who are (1) likely to have gotten into trouble in the past and who are (2) likely to be problem children in the future, consistently select those judged to be unattractive. Children and teachers, when the performer of some misdeed is to be identified, pick those who are less attractive. When the wrong-doer is attractive, teachers state that "everyone has a bad day now and then." If the wrong-doer is not attractive it is a matter of "I told you so."

In college dating Berschied and Walster (1972) report being surprised by the consistency and overwhelming weight that physical attractiveness plays. Exceptional personality characteristics of intelligence made no discernable difference. It is physical attractiveness that scores in dating preferences. The investigators hypothesized that the less physically attractive college men and women would be less choosy than those who were physically attractive. The hypothesis was not confirmed. Questionnaire data showed that college students predicted that the attractive persons would get better jobs, create happier marriages, and live more fulfilling lives than would others. No follow-up data were sought in terms of business success. The authors did follow the lead on marriage and studied women now in their 40's and 50's. They concluded that there was a relationship—*slight* and in unexpected direction. The woman who was attractive in college was *less happy* in marriage. Possibly the woman who was attractive during her college years was spoiled. Perhaps she missed her waning beauty more. And so, considering all, the authors conclude, the cosmetics industry is likely to continue doing a booming business.

Kurtz and Hirt (1970) found confirmation of the hypothesis that physical health was related to one's body image. A group of 20 young women (ages 20–38 years) who were diagnosed as having asthma, heart disease, dermatitis, and arthritis was compared with normal healthy women **(controls).** Using a list of 30 items (color of skin or hair, size of hands or breasts, height-weight, etc.) they found that the ill women consistently had more negative perceptions of their bodies than did the healthy women.

Sontag (1963) became interested in the reverse of the problem of the influence of the body on personality. He studied the influence of personality on the body. He called this study "somatopsychics." The influence begins during the mother's pregnancy. If she were emotionally disturbed during the latter part of pregnancy the fetus became more active. Such fetuses, when they became nursery school children, especially boys, were less aggressive and more apprehensive in their activities than were those undisturbed during the prenatal period. Further follow-up studies have shown that this apprehensiveness at age two-and-a-half is predictive of apprehensiveness at 25. Sontag and his associates also found a great variation in heart rates. This phenomenon was called cardiac lability-stability. From childhood to adulthood those with great lability were independent. They were reluctant to depend on love objects. They showed more intense striving for achievement. As adults, the labiles were more anxious over erotic activities and showed more compulsive behavior.

The practice of psychosomatic medicine is predicated on the knowledge, that personality—at least as far as psychological stress is concerned—has tremendous influence on bodily functioning. It has been estimated that 50 per cent of general hospital beds are occupied by patients whose basic ailment is psychological. When the medical diseases are digestive, respiratory, or circulatory, the percentage may run as high as 80 or 90.

Psychosomatic diseases are those ailments in which the symptoms are primarily physical although there may be a large emotional component. This type of emotional illness is understandable to anyone who has ever suffered from a headache after arguing with his employer or has had diarrhea before taking an important examination. Included among the psychosomatic illnesses are asthma, peptic ulcer, colitis, hypertension, and certain types of arthritis.

The person suffering from a psychosomatic disorder may need psychological treatment, but he is also in need of medical treatment. He is very different from the hypochondriac who, although convinced that he is ill, actually has nothing organically wrong.[3]

PHYSIOLOGY AND PERSONALITY

Endocrine glands   The endocrine glands (thyroids, pituitary, parathyroids, adrenals, ovaries, testes, pineal, islands of Langerhans, and thymus) are known to have effects on behavior. These vary from profound to slight (or at least, little known) effects. Some authorities tend to create the impression that the glands of internal secretion regulate personality. Certainly, when cretins (with their defective thyroids that prevent adequate oxygen metabolism) are observed, one is tempted to conclude that the thyroid does regulate personality. An underactive thyroid causes one to be physically slow and lethargic. The victim, easily lulled into sleep, is lacking in mental alertness. When given suitable supplementary hormones the victims of slight thyroid deficiency may have their personalities literally changed overnight. They take a new interest in life. They have energy available to be "up and about." They may be somewhat tense because of sleeplessness.

Some children are a burden to parents and teachers because of their hyperkinetic energy. They seem to be on a rampage for much of the day. Some may be negativistic, inattentive, lacking in directed activity, and antisocial (Feshback and Feshback, 1973). As a sort of sad compensation for such harassed parents and teachers, another pupil may sit quietly, staring indifferently at the wall or his book. Like a piece of putty, he permits himself to be pushed obediently off to play. In a few minutes he resumes his rest. These conditions may be due to many physical factors. A hyperactive thyroid, a hypoactive thyroid, and accelerated or decelerated pituitary, or dysfunction of the pancreas may lie behind these conditions. Sometimes the behavior can be brought under control by administration of hormones. These are injected or taken by pill. Behavior change may result from surgically altering the function of the hormone-producing gland. Often, a sur-

---

[3] *What is Mental Illness?*, Public Health Service Publication No. 505 (Washington, D. C.: U. S. Department of Health, Education, and Welfare, 1965).

prisingly little amount of hormone makes a tremendous difference in behavior. It appears to be a possibility that a pinch of thyroxin is the difference between a feebleminded cretin and a genius. This, however, does not mean that the science of personality will be reduced to the test tube. The matter of personality change via drugs or surgery is really "not all that simple." The endocrines function as a highly coordinated system. What triggers a small reaction in one gland might greatly disturb the working of another glandular system. In addition, there is learning and choice with which to be concerned.

Eckstein (1970) has compared the workings of the endocrine system with the overall action of a circus. On most days the equipment, actors, animals, tents, master of ceremonies perform their functions. The result is an enjoyable show. Occasionally an actor is injured, an animal gets loose, a tent pole breaks, wind billows the canvas and fills the tent with dust. The whole thing falls into chaos. Similarly, the endocrine system is a coordinated one. What one gland does or does not do, affects the others. Digestion, circulation, breathing, moving, thinking are influenced by the hormones that are excreted from the glands of internal secretion. Gland secretions are poured directly into the blood stream. Following is a description of what it looks like in the case of defective functioning of the pancreas—a condition known as diabetes:

> Because the diabetic is not able properly to process glucose it rises in his blood, and spills over, as is said, into his urine, hence glucose in his urine, sugar in his urine, the energy tied up in that sugar lost to that man's cells. He feels weak. His brain lacks its principal fuel. His senses dull. Is not hearing as well as he used to. If he has the narrowed blood-vessels he probably has them in the brain also, therefore two excuses for forgetting that he knew you, like the woman forgetting then remembering the elderly gentleman in Mariemont Square. Anyway, misadventure follows misadventure. When the glucose spilled over into the urine, water spilled with it, so water was lost. Old Aretaeus these nineteen hundred years has been moaning across the sandlot that there is a "melting down of flesh and limbs to wine." Our physicians say simply "dehydrated." Thirsty diabetic, he drinks and drinks, and for that the elegant word is polydipsia, and for all the urination, polyuria, and for his hunger, polyphagia. Lacking sugar, his cells burn fat, so he loses sugar, water, fat. Lacking sugar and fat, his cells begin to feed on his own flesh, so he loses sugar, water, fat, protein. Round and round goes the merry-go-round. It squeaks.[4]

[4]Gustav Eckstein, *The Body Has a Head* (New York: Harper and Row, Publishers, 1970), p. 280.

In terms of Eckstein's circus simile, the pituitary could be called the master of ceremonies. It is the gland that coordinates the growth processes. It gives clues as to when some glands (the thymus, for example) should shut off. It indicates when others should get vigorously into the act (the sex glands). Little is known about the *pineal* gland, a tiny body located near the brain. It seems to function mainly during childhood and probably retards sexual development. The *thymus*, located in the chest, is relatively large during childhood. It atrophies in late childhood and adolescence. It, too, is presumed to function as an inhibitor of precocious sexual development. The *parathyroids*, located in the lower region of the throat, control the metabolism of calcium. The *thyroids*, also located in the lower region of the throat, control oxygen metabolism. The *islands of Langerhans*, located in the *pancreas*, control sugar metabolism. The *adrenal* glands, located near the pancreas, produce the hormone known as adrenin or adrenalin. The adrenals work with the nervous system to prepare the body for the emergence of violent emotions. Adrenalin functions less vigorously in the milder emotions. The *ovaries* produce the egg cells that, when fertilized by the products of the *testes*, the spermatozoa, become the embryo and fetus. Both the ovaries and testes produce the sex hormones—estrogen (the female hormone) and androgen (the male hormone).

In American culture we are concerned about sex role, sex identity, sex adequacy, and sex in entertainment, education, advertising, and moral survival. Hence, the functioning of the pituitary, ovaries, and testes are of theoretical but genuine concern. "Theoretical" because we do not know, with sufficient thoroughness, just how much or how far sex hormones effect male and female behavior. Both androgen and estrogen are produced in the ovaries and in the testes; androgens usually more abundantly produced in males and estrogens produced more abundantly by females. Estrogen inhibits activity of the pituitary. This causes deceleration, and finally, cessation, of overall physical growth processes. Estrogen stimulates growth of the breasts, mammary glands, uterus, Fallopian tubes, and vagina. In order to make room for the latter (all internal) organs, the girl's hips broaden and her abdomen protrudes during puberty. Androgen also causes the pituitary to decelerate. It stimulates growth of male sex organs—seminal vesicles, penis, and testes. Androgen stimulates growth of hair in the armpits, on the chest, and in the pubic area. It contributes also to the deepening of the voice.

The sex organs thus influence the chemistry of the body; they guide physiology; they contribute to behavior. The swashbuckling male, his shaving, his adventuresome questing, are in part a function of hormones. The seductiveness of the female, her swishing skirts, disconcerting glances, and her peevishness during menstrual cycles are, in part, attributed to the hormones that are circulating in the blood stream. However, the hormones alone cannot be held responsible for one's heterosexual behavior. One's choice of avenues for gaining recognition, or one's foci of energy are also involved. The brain intervenes. It shapes one's perception of his (or her) body and its drives, of the meaning of family tutelage, and of cultural demands (Eckstein, 1970, p. 296).

Inasmuch as a major part of this book deals with intelligence as an aspect of personality, its consideration here is omitted, except to observe the obvious: Intelligence does influence personality in predictable ways. For example, the behavior of a gifted person is markedly different from that of a cretin or mongoloid.

Brain and personality

It has been believed for centuries that the brain is a vital component of personality. Interest in the subject as a scientific investigation was aroused by a dramatic accident. In the mid-nineteenth century a Phineas Gage had a crowbar blown through his head by an explosion. The bar entered his left eye and emerged through the top of his skull. He was not killed. He was able to walk to a doctor's office for help. He lived for 12 years, but with marked personality changes (Langley and Cheraskin, 1954, p. 173). This accident, and discoveries that attended it, was the forerunner of the surgical technique known as prefrontal lobotomy. This surgery separates the prefrontal, or the primary associational area, from the motor areas of the brain. Some patients who suffer severe depression or antagonism are transformed into **euphoric** and amiable persons by such an operation.

The brain is an organ that functions by means of complicated interactions of chemical, biological, and electrical processes. The electrical aspects can be measured by means of an electroencephalograph. This is a machine that records on a moving drum the tracings emanating from brain waves. The resulting encephalogram (Figure 8.2) shows the intensity and duration of brain waves. These tracings, in normal persons, are rather regular and somewhat equal. In abnormal cases the waves are more differentiated and irregular. An abnormal EEG *might* indicate the presence of a brain tumor or injury. However, the results of encephalography have not, to date, been outstanding in the diagnosis of psychiatric disorders.

For reasons not clearly understood, electrical shocks applied to the brain surfaces have been used successfully in treating depressed persons and **schizophrenics.** This treatment fell into disrepute because of injuries resulting from the convulsions that the shocks induced. This hazard has been reduced by the administration of drugs that relax the muscles. Effectiveness of shock therapy is influenced by the nature and duration of the patient's illnesses. It has been found that drugs that induce less pain and fear are more effective than shock in some cases (Goldman, 1970, p. 382). Shock treatment is approached

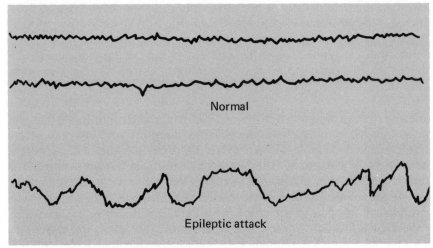

Normal

Epileptic attack

Figure 8.2   *Encephalograms of normal and abnormal brain waves.*

cautiously. There is danger that destruction of brain tissue might overbalance the good that is obtained.

In order to appreciate the scope, power, speed, and complexity of the human brain, it has been likened to a computer. If brain and machine were performing comparable functions, the machine taking the place of the brain would occupy the space of the Cow Palace in San Francisco. It would be as tall as the Rockefeller Center in New York. It would require the power of Niagara Falls to run it. The waters of Niagara would be needed to keep the tubes, units, filters, and resistors cool and clean. However, the machine would still come out second best because the brain is constantly repairing and replacing itself. Its billions and billions of cells are in a constant process of regeneration (Kubie, 1956). Viewed in this way, it is not really such a wonder that man uses such a small fraction of his brain power—5 to 10 per cent of the potential (Otto, 1972).

Centers and areas of the cortex of the brain are functionally designed for control of a particular part of the body. There are areas for (1) sensory input and (2) muscular output for various parts of the body. Specific areas control toes, trunk, shoulders, arms, fingers, head, eyes, and especially (the largest proportional area) the throat, tongue, lips, and larynx. Man's uniqueness, as revealed by proportional brain area, is speech. Personality and speech are interdependent functions (Brunelle, 1973).

The cortex is just the covering of the brain—a blanket. The rest of man's brain is, in comparison to the size of the brains of other animals, relatively massive and much more complex. There are parts of the brain, the cortex, that are responsible for perceiving and interpreting messages from the eyes, ears, sense of touch, pressure, and heat. Other areas take data from the internal organs. These areas indicate the position and placement of the body, arms, legs, head. The cortex is also responsible for associating ideas and messages. Hence, actions can be initiated, maintained, or stopped.

Another part of the brain, the *limbic system*, in cooperation with the cortex, is primarily responsible for the arousal, direction, expression, or inhibiting, of emotional states. The limbic system tells when to run for safety (psychologically or physically). It tells us when to pursue the object of love or lust. It tells us when to fight for the satisfaction of our needs. It dictates rest in anticipation of the next onslaught of sensory input.

Within the cortex and the various lobes of the brain are areas that seem to function with considerable independent freedom. One example is memory—although memory is influenced by emotions. We do not know how the network of fibers, axones, neurones, and globs of cells work to produce the phenomenon of memory. It was once explained on the basis of the closing of **synapses.** Most current theories of memory make reference to *DNA* (deoxyribonucleic acid). This substance has, as one function, the storage and retrieval of messages. DNA is also credited with being a sort of tape recorder that dictates what one inherits.

The major part of brain activity is that which deals with associating, interpreting, and creating new combinations. Brain activity deals with recalling old impressions, focusing on some things, and dampening the input of others. The diffuse network of cells concerned is called the *reticular activating system*. This system allows us to twist the car wheels from a rock on the pavement, focus eyes on the stride of a cute red-head, recall our disgust with an opinionated professor, crave a cigarette, and make us aware of an undigested cantaloupe. This does not occur all at once, but it does occur with amazing speed.

Not much is known about just how this system, the brain, works. More is known about how its work can be interfered with. Surgery can short-circuit the connection between logic and passion. One may be made to lose all interest in sex or to be constantly preoccupied with it. Drugs can jam the switchboard. They can cause gross errors in the input systems. Wild dreams and hallucinations may become a frightening reality. Each drink of alcohol destroys, according to one theory, millions of brain cells. In heavy drinkers or in those with not too many cells to begin with, behavior is reduced to that of a stumblebum— staggering and cluttering (Chapter 17). The brain requires a rich and constant source of oxygen to keep it going. Prolonged birth processes or birth injury may briefly deprive the neonate of oxygen and permanent damage may be suffered. Being knocked unconscious or being unconscious from disease slows breathing and circulation. Such may, when the period is extensive, result in marked personality change. As one grows older, calcification of blood vessels occurs, the availability of oxygen is reduced, and one becomes senile. Recent events are readily forgotten and regression to earlier, childish behaviors are noted.

The brain acts in paradoxical ways. At one time it sorts out sensory impressions and puts them into integrated patterns. At another time it allows, indeed seems to encourage, man to experiment with ways to alter its own functioning. Drugs, ranging from coffee and aspirin to LSD, alcohol, and heroin are taken (see Chapter 17). This is done even when one is warned repeatedly that drugs alter personality. These effects vary from slight to profound, known to unknown, helpful or harmful. The alterations may be temporary dysfunctions or permanent lesions. It is known that changing the brain changes personality.

Nutrition   A difficulty with clichés is that they are not entirely true or accurate. However, they do contain an element of the truth. Such is the case with the words, "You are what you eat." However, after basic food requirements are met no further influence is felt—except obesity. For example, in cases of certain vitamin deficiency, marked deterioration of personality may, and often does result. A competent, happy mother grew tired, slovenly, and irascible. Finally, when her tongue became cracked and fissured, she sought medical aid. She was given vitamin therapy in a Texas hospital. Salutary results were obtained almost overnight; tongue lesions healed, and she returned home a happy, calm, but more dietary conscious, mother.[5]

Vitamins differ in their action, function, and effect. Some are stored in the body in generous amounts, and some must be ingested daily. In some instances the person may be unable to synthesize the required amount and may need to have periodic injections of the vitamin. Effects of vitamin deficiencies that have received much attention are: night vision, skin health, amount of bleeding, bone structure (in early childhood), resistance to disease, hair and nail growth. Personality effects of vitamin deficiency include irritability, lowering of **inhibitions,** forgetfulness, lowered vitality, and inability to focus attention (Langley *et al.*, 1969).

Dieting is a popular custom in the United States. Health authorities have warned about the dangers of overeating and overweight, which include the shortening of life span, increased burden on the heart, and curtailing of energy for activity. The person becomes less attractive (see above on body image) and lonesome. Lonesomeness contributes to a "vicious cycle." Be lonesome, get hungry, eat, get fat, get repugnant, get more lonesome, and so on. For various reasons people go on sporadic diet binges. One may diet on a doctor's advice, on a friend's recommendation, to adopt current fads (a write-up in some

---

[5]This statement does not constitute an endorsement of patent medicines that encourage self-medication. These may, due to high alcoholic content, result in some temporary *feelings* of euphoria without correcting a basic deficiency.

popular magazine), or to meet contemporary concepts of the ideal figure. Diet may not have much effect on personality. That little effect, added to other factors, however, may make a noticeable difference in personality manifestations.

> A somewhat obese high school basketball coach, aware of the significance of overweight, passed on some of his knowledge about overeating to his players. One boy, on the second squad, took the advice somewhat too seriously and cut down on eating. Growth needs, plus basketball practice, plus walking to and from school, plus week-end skiing added up to considerable caloric needs for the boy. He became irritable at home and sassy to his mother. His father, a man of few words, said, "No more basketball until you eat normally and become civil."

It has been noted that when very young children (first postnatal year) have been deprived of warm mothering they become withdrawn, lose their appetite, and may become weak and emaciated. Recently it has been discovered that the physical wasting may be prevented by simply making more food readily available. This can be done without changing the amount or quality of human contact (Whitten, 1969). Undernutrition, seen extensively in developing nations of the world (Africa, Central and South America), is accompanied by restriction of the child's head size, visual retardation, and kinesthetic handicap. Beneficial results, in terms of IQ increase (up to 18 points), have been found in some malnourished children who have been given "nutritional therapy." Important vitamins in cell and brain development are thiamine, B-complex vitamins, and vitamin C. The relationship of poverty and nutrition is another of those "vicious cycles." Poverty leads to inadequate nutrition, inadequate nutrition lowers the level of performance, ineffective behavior contributes to poverty, and so on. However, nutrition is not equivalent to ample food supply. The matter of balanced diet containing all essential nutrients (vitamins, protein, sugars, etc.) is a concern for all (Bakan, 1970). Diet is particularly important in early childhood because of rapid growth processes. That which is lost is lost for good. Deprivation during the prenatal and early postnatal period cannot be remedied (Mead, 1970).

Thus far, mention has been made of differences in body build, physiological structure, and functioning of the brain in relation to personality. The influence of the glands of internal secretion as they affect personality have been cited. Williams (1956; 1972) has proposed that a grossly neglected aspect of the study of personality is the possible impact of organs of the body. He reports that there are marked differences in the size of normal sinuses, hearts, lungs, arteries and veins, stomachs, as well as the endocrine glands. These differences must account for some differences in behavior. If these were understood, Williams claims, it would go a long way toward explaining the

Biochemical individuality

unique drives, interests, and energies of individuals. Normal lungs in one individual, for instance, may inhale in one breath six or seven times the volume of air taken in by another's normal lungs. A normal heart may pump five or six times the amount of blood as another normal human's heart in one beat. In addition, one heart may have two branches in the aortic arch while another has four such branches. The arteries also vary in diameter. This ultimately makes for differences in the oxygenation of the blood. Hence, oxygen supply to the brain may be adequate or inadequate (Williams, 1956, pp. 28–32).

> Biologically, each member of the human family possesses inborn differences based on his brain structure and on his vast mosaic of endocrine glands—in fact, on every aspect of his physical being. Each of us has a distinctive set of drives—for physical activity, for food, for sexual expression, for power. Each one has his own mind qualities: abilities, ways of thinking, and patterns of mental conditions. Each one has his own emotional setup and his leanings toward music and art in its various forms, including literature. All these leanings are subject to change and development, but there is certainly no mass movement toward uniformity. No one ever "recovers" from the fact that he was born an individual.
>
> When a husband and wife disagree on the temperature of the soup or on the amount of bed coverings, or if their sleep patterns do not jibe, this is evidence of inborn differences in physiology. If one child loves to read or is interested in science and another has strong likings for sports or for art, this is probably due to inborn differences in makeup. If two people disagree about food or drink, they should not disregard the fact that taste and smell reactions often widely differ and are inherited. If we see a person wearing loud clothing without apparent taste, we need to remember . . . that each individual has a color vision all his own; some may deviate markedly from the pack.[6]

Individuals just are not carbon copies of one another. Generalizations, such as must be used in this and similar books, indicate trends and probabilities. Those generalizations must be subjected to individual interpretations for a given person. Nonconformity in academic activities, interpersonal relationships, marriage, and occupations are a natural and normal manifestation of biochemical individuality. Morphology and physiology make it clear that there are multitudinous reasons for the nature of personality.

SUMMARY

Body language is one evidence that personality is revealed, and read, as a function of what one is biologically. A theory dating from ancient

---

[6]Roger J. Williams, "The Biology of Behavior," *Saturday Review*, Vol. 54, No. 5, January 30, 1971, p. 17.

Grecian times is that men were sanguine, phlegmatic, choleric, or melancholic personalities due to body humors. The terminology persists but current explanations differ. Sheldon has a body-personality theory that has not been repudiated. His theory provides for continuous variations between ectomorphs, mesomorphs, and endomorphs. There are accompanying inclinations toward responsive feelings and actions. It may be conjectured that personality, influenced by body build, has bearing on occupational satisfaction or dissatisfaction. Body type has an influence on tendencies toward delinquency.

Body image—how one views his physical structure—has a discernable effect on behavior. This view is influenced by how others perceive body build and attractiveness. Research shows that attractiveness is even more important in favorable perception than is commonly admitted. Whether body image contributes to personality or personality contributes to body image is the sort of dilemma that leads to psychosomatic medicine.

Physiology has a number of personality influences that have been and are being studied. The endocrine glands are known to have profound impact on personality—particularly in their dysfunction. The endocrines work in a highly coordinated system. If one gland is thrown off balance the others have difficulty performing their specific function with efficiency. As powerful and persuasive as the glands are, it should be kept in mind that morphology, external reality, and one's problem-solving potential are also part of the totality.

The brain as an organ, rather than as a function, conditions personality. This fact is confirmed by prefrontal lobotomy. Electrical movements within the brain can be detected by means of an electroencephalograph. However, the interpretation of those movements is only dimly understood at present. Specific parts of the brain have specific functions. The function occupying the largest area is speech and speech-related activities. Actually, rather little is known about how the brain works in emotions, thinking, memorizing, and perceiving. It is unfortunate that we know more about how to keep the brain from working in a normal way (*e.g.*, drugs) than we do about increasing its effectiveness.

Diet affects body composition, endocrine activity, and physiological processes. Diet is, therefore, a factor in personality. This factor, however, may be so small as to be at times unnoticeable. Dieting should be under the supervision of a physician rather than the following of a current fad.

Much of what is known of, and postulated about, morphology and physiology in relation to personality is considered in Williams' theory of biological individuality. It is his conclusion that the study of personality cannot be complete without studying morphology and physiology.

SUGGESTED READINGS

BARDWICK, JUDITH M., "Her Body the Battleground," *Psychology Today*, Vol. 5, No. 9, 50–54, February, 1972.

The author addresses the question, "How much destiny does anatomy contribute?" Among other considerations, contraceptive medicines and the menstrual cycle have effects on hormones that have effects on mood, that have. . . .

FESHBACK, SEYMOUR, and NORMA FESHBACK, "The Young Aggressors," *Psychology Today*, Vol. 6 No. 11, 90–95, 1973.

Body chemistry and physique, along with many social factors, play a part in the aggressive personality. Aggression is present in girls as well as in boys. Girls, especially, learn from culture, to disguise their hostility.

KAGAN, JEROME, "The Emergence of Sex Differences," *School Review*, Vol. 80, 217–227, 1972.

Some differences in the behavior of boys and girls can be attributed to mothering and culture. Some differences must also be attributed to the biological fact of sex. There are differences between the sexes in cognitive functioning, emotional states, and temperament that are, in part, due to physiological makeup.

SONTAG, LESTER W., "Somatopsychics of Personality and Body Functions," *Vita Humana*, Vol. 6, 1–10, 1963.

Much has been written about the effect of emotions on bodily function. The author reverses the approach and presents data to show that the body influences emotions.

WILLIAMS, ROGER J., "The Biology of Behavior," eds. H. W. Bernard and W. C. Huckins, *Exploring Human Development*. Boston: Allyn and Bacon, Inc. From *Saturday Review*, Vol. 54, No. 5, 17–19, January 30, 1971.

It is time to bring about a closer liaison between the natural and life sciences and those that are called the behavioral sciences. The fences that are built around each are impeding progress in the study of personality.

FOLLOW-UP LEARNING ACTIVITIES

What is your reaction to Sheldon's theory of physical types in relation to personality?

_____ Rejection	because _____
_____ Tentative acceptance	_____
_____ Open mind	_____
_____ Positive belief	_____
_____ Other _____	

Discuss with four or five classmates or long-time acquaintances the matter of gestures, postures, and movements that have been noted in others. What, if anything, have others noted about you?

_____

_____

_____

_____

Do you believe the postulations of Berscheid and Walster; (*i.e.,* good looking people are more readily accepted, blamed less readily, etc.)?

_____. Because _____

_____

_____

_____

_____

Is there any conflict with your response to the above item and the way you checked the first "pre-reading" learning activity? How about other of the "pre-reading" activities?

_____

_____

_____

_____

What personal implications do you perceive in the statement that speech and personality are interdependent functions?

_____

_____

_____

_____

Compare and discuss your response to the above item with a couple of classmates. Can you add any further implications?

_____

_____

_____

_____

9
Humanistic Orientation

Children, too, have the power of choice.

LEARNING ACTIVITIES

I believe that man is

_____ a highly plastic organism, shaped largely by his environment

_____ mostly shaped by his instincts and inheritance

_____ quite capable of exerting force in the shaping of his life

I believe that man's basic drives or motives to action are (Examples: food, desire for power, etc.):

_____	_____
_____	_____
_____	_____
_____	_____

(Do this activity before reading further.)

I believe that

_____ You are only a child once. You should live freely with
only minimum interference from parents

_____ Children (ages 2–6 years) should obey their parents
without question

_____ Parents should be firm without being autocratic

_____ Other: _____

_____

_____

_____

I believe the motive most influential in my life now is to

_____ satisfy physiological needs   _____ be respected

_____ exercise my abilities   _____ be safe

_____ experience beauty   _____ be loved

I believe that

_____ My instructors know what learnings are best for me

_____ There is far too much prescription in college work

_____ I could make use of more independence in learning

_____ I have as much freedom to choose as I need

I believe that my best learning style is

_____ listening   _____ reading

_____ observing   _____ talking

_____ doing   _____ repeating

_____ understanding   _____ failing

(Compare and discuss your responses with two classmates.)

Psychology is a young science. It began as a distinct discipline about 1890. In comparison, medicine is hundreds of years old and physics is thousands of years old. There are still differences in opinion both in physics and medicine. Hence, the brawling and quarreling that goes on in the field of psychology, a science in its childhood, may be understandable and forgiveable. In fact, differences of opinion may be commendable. They stimulate study, encourage research, and the pursuit of more convincing theories. Each new school of psychology, as shown in Chapter 1, was a protest against, supplement to, or a call for an emphasis that seemed to be neglected in prior psychological theory.

Humanistic psychology is the most recently evolved perception of what the "true" psychology should be. Its adherents believe in freedom, self-determination, choice, and individual responsibility. In this chapter some of the major emphases of the humanistic orientation are presented. An effort is made to be objective. The reader should be warned, however, that the author has humanistic leanings. If it were necessary to make a choice that did not include **eclecticism,** then humanism would be selected.

ISSUES IN HUMANISTIC PSYCHOLOGY

Origins of humanism

Some of the emphases that constitute the humanistic orientation in psychology have been in evidence a long time. William James (1899) emphasized self-determination, responsibility, and vision of the future. Man to him was no machine, pushed inertly here and there by various combinations of forces. Man had a mind so that he could choose, learn, and make decisions. Carl Jung (1933) emphasized faith and conscience, neither of which can be reduced to quantifiable scientific terms.

The recency of humanism is suggested by the fact that neither Woodworth (1948) nor Hilgard (1956), in discussing viewpoints of psychology, mention it by name. Suddenly, large numbers of psychologists seemed to be thinking and publishing and stimulating one another with various statements about humanism. Man is an enactor as well as a reactor. Man in part creates his unique environment, through his unique perception, and his unique and deliberated response. Some dynamics of brain processes cannot be explained in terms of heredity or environment, or chemistry and physics. There is also an organismic, humanistic transaction.

Among those who have contributed to the shaping of humanistic psychology are Bonner, Bugenthal, Combs, Jourard, Earl Kelley, Maslow, Moustakas, Otto, Rogers, and Snygg. The binding theme is that each regards man as a being who has an active part in, and some responsibility for, the formation of his own personality. Man has the power to influence the conduct of his own life.

This robust, attention-getting infant in the kindergarten of psychology has not yet officially, or acceptably, been named. It is referred to by Maslow as *third force* psychology. In one of his latest publications he said that most of his academic work in psychology had no bearing on life. It was of no consequence in solving problems of love, ambition, or peak experience (Maslow, 1972).

Bonner (1965) calls the viewpoint *proactive* psychology. This is because of the natural tendency, revealed in a healthy man's growth processes, to move forward. The term "existentialism," borrowed from philosophy, is a term used by many. This emphasizes the contention that significant aspects of personality and behavior stem from the inner man. This inner man notion is opposed by many contemporary psychologists because it is indefinable; whereas past and present stimuli are tangible and quantifiable.

May (1969), who has been called "Mr. Humanist," asserts that man lives with purpose and intent. This is especially true when the man has a clear and healthy concept of identity. Without love of self and others, man is forced to turn inward with apathy or despair (to be sick). With identity his life is infused with a feeling of significance and influence.

Combs and Snygg (1959) call their interpretation of the phenomena of behavior "perceptual psychology." They particularly emphasize the processes of learning. They highlight the idea of the phenomenological field; that is, what an individual person uniquely perceives as the environment constitutes the fruitful approach to psychology and personality. Out of such views stems the name *phenomenology*.

The term that seems to be most indicative of this third force is *humanistic* psychology—meaning that man himself is the true subject of psychology; the emphases are not stimuli and reinforcement contingencies. However, these do influence man's responses and proaction. In between stimuli and responses is man with his potential for thinking or interpreting.

The focal issue in any viewpoint of psychology is the concept that is held of man. A focal concern relates to man's instinctive nature (as seen in Chapter 7 on psychoanalysis). For example, man may be seen as basically aggressive and warlike. He needs war as an outlet for this basic drive. Proof cited for this aggressive nature is the fact that war has been, inevitably, a part of man's history. Humanists take a different view. They admit that war is an historical fact, but they contend that man is also potentially capable of cooperative and

Prominent emphases

constructive activities—another historical fact. The difference between "instinctive" nature (if one wishes to call it that) and man in action are the experiences he has had plus the values he holds.

The instinct theory is largely discarded. It is replaced with the view that man is born neutral. He is ready to be shaped by the time and circumstances of life's happenings. One is neither good nor bad. He is only responsive to the stimuli that act upon him. Another theory sees man as a passively receptive organism ready to be molded by environment. This view is called mechanistic by those who see humans as exercising power and discretion over life. It seems to reduce man to principles of physics and chemistry. The protest against mechanistic conceptions was voiced long before humanistic psychology became identifiable as a distinctive orientation.

One source of dissatisfaction with conventional psychology, expressed especially by Maslow, Jourard, and Rogers, is its focal concern with the abnormal and deficient person. Presumably, clues to more effective living for the normal person can be gained from the study of the defectives and the psychologically ill. Their errors can then be avoided. But Maslow disagreed. He stated firmly that the way to find clues to psychological health is to study the life styles of those who are in unusually good health—self-actualizing persons. The following passage describes Maslow's concern for studying healthy persons:

> My investigations on self-actualization were not planned to be research and did not start out as research. They started out as the effort of a young intellectual to try to understand two of his teachers whom he loved, adored, and admired and who were very, very wonderful people. It was a kind of high-IQ devotion. I could not be content simply to adore, but sought to understand why these two people were so different from the run-of-the-mill people in the world. These two people were Ruth Benedict [see Chapter 5, "Culture"] and Max Wertheimer. They were my teachers after I came with a Ph.D. from the West to New York City, and they were most remarkable human beings. My training in psychology equipped me not at all for understanding them. It was as if they were not quite people but something more than people. My own investigation began as a prescientific or nonscientific activity. I made descriptions and notes on Max Wertheimer, and I made notes on Ruth Benedict. When I tried to understand them, think about them, and write about them in my journal and my notes, I realized in one wonderful moment that their two patterns could be generalized. I was talking about a kind of person, not about two noncomparable individuals. There was wonderful excitement in that. I tried to see whether this pattern could be found elsewhere, and I did find it elsewhere, in one person after another.
>
> By ordinary standards of laboratory research, that is of rigorous and controlled research, this simply was not research at all.[1]

[1] Abraham H. Maslow, "Self-Actualization and Beyond," ed. J. F. T. Bugenthal, *Challenges of Humanistic Psychology* (New York: McGraw-Hill Book Company, 1967), p. 279.

A part of the basic nature of a human being is a need to sense his own self-constancy. He needs to feel that he is a determining participant in repeatable experience (Cantril, 1967). If one's participation is confirmed—through approval and acceptance by others—then he has his identity confirmed. He is a piece of the human community. If one's participation is not confirmed, if the values by which he has been guided are denied, then one's self-constancy is shaken. He is a foreigner. He develops a feeling of alienation rather than identity. If one seeks social acceptance by superficially assuming the values of others, but not really internalizing them, he is still an alien.

Erikson (1959) focused on identity as a major theme in personality. He has continued to see it as a unifying concept in personality (1968; 1970). Erikson stated that his growing awareness of the psychosocial aspects of personality led him to believe strongly in the basic role of group and ego identity (1959, pp. 19, 101). The establishment and maintenance of health-giving identity is a lifelong struggle. It is particularly active during the years of youth. At that time there is a marked effort to be an individual and also to be a member of the group. One needs to act in accordance with the expectations of one's peers (Erikson, 1970). This is what is frequently referred to as the "identity crisis."

Emphasis on the centrality of the person pervades humanistic psychotherapy. In the behavioristic, psychoanalytic, rational, and reality models of therapy the therapist acts as mentor for the uninitiated and lost individual. Skinner (1955–56) asserts that the fact of control must be admitted. Good sense in human affairs will not be used unless someone designs and constructs a proper environment for learning and relearning. And the point may be underlined: *Behaviorism works.* The humanistic orientation is that growth (including therapy) comes from within. Rogers (1961) promotes the proposition that people have within them the power—the directional thrust—for growth and becoming. The role of the therapist is to help the person see himself clearly. One must learn to acknowledge his self-limiting defenses, to appreciate his strengths, and to choose his own goals accordingly. The therapist is nondirective. Counseling is client-centered in that the client defines his problem. He describes his conditions. He discusses himself. The therapist accepts and supports the client and gives him the companionship and comfort of a fellow human being.

Jourard emphasizes the centrality of the person in the following words:

> Psychotherapy and counseling have evolved as rational methods for helping people whose despair over seemingly insurmountable impasses in life, growth, or relations with others has led to sickness of some sort. What is psychotherapy? Among other things, it entails granting a patient freedom to be himself, in the presence of another;

it entails seeking to discover a man's individuality, his true self, and letting him be. Operationally, *letting someone be* means letting them disclose their unique being to another, and having this confirmed, received, acknowledged, heard—and spontaneously, unpredictably responded to. These responses in the spirit of good will from the therapist help the patient discover and confirm his own uniqueness, to regain contact with the ongoing flow of his actual self. This somehow aids self-integration, growth, healing and optimum function.

Being oneself thus seems to be a factor in wellness, in full functioning. Being oneself in the presence of others means operationally to disclose oneself to another person, spontaneously in dialogue. But self-disclosure sometimes yields consequences of a painful nature, which is likely one reason why many dread it so, therapists as much as patients. People hide themselves behind masks of their roles, for example, the bedside manner, the office manner, the couchside manner, the pulpit manner, the behind the counter manner, etc.—all unreal relationships. The French existentialist, Marcel, referred in this connection to a conflict between "being" and "having." To *be* something means to lose what you *have*. But to cling to possessions and people may mean loss of being, and ultimately, this is a more serious loss.

Existentialists, phenomenologists, and psychotherapists are rediscovering the importance of man's self and of relation, and are drawing large inferences about the role of the self, and "inter-self relations" with others in illness and health.[2]

Methods of humanistic psychology

The fundamental method of humanistic psychology is that of observation and description *of the whole man*. It is a protest against the laboratory and analytical method that has sought to dominate scientific psychological method. Reliance solely on science has left many students of psychology bored and dissatisfied (Cantril, 1967). The humanistic method does not require pretentious techniques of measurement. It does not ignore such data provided that the data do not compartmentalize the subject being studied—man. Method is regarded as being scientific even when the results are not readily quantifiable. It is scientific when the description of the action and outcome of needs, appetites, values, and temperament lead numerous observers to a point of consensus (Tompkins, 1967).

Humanistic psychology deals with the whole—the live and functioning—man in his total milieu. Hence, science must concentrate on that live and functioning man. Descriptive phenomenology, self-perception, and interpretation of cognitive experience is scientific when it is integrated by a skillful psychologist (Cantril, 1967). Man and method are inseparable. The humanistic orientation does not ignore data from the analytical and statistical approaches. It does, however, object to not fitting these parts back into the entire life

[2]Sidney Jourard, "Some Implications of Self-disclosure Research for Counseling and Psychotherapy," *Personality Theory and Counseling Practice.* Paper presented at the First Annual Conference on Personality Theory and Counseling Practice (Gainesville, Florida, 1961), p. 30.

pattern. Hence, there is no objection to reflexes, conditioning, reinforcement, morphology, the unconscious, glandular, and organic functioning. In addition, it seeks to have recognition given to values. Philosophy, social orientation, uniqueness of the experiencing person, creativity, transcendence of self, and future-seeking goals must also be studied (Sargent, 1967).

Humanistic method embraces more than the data usually viewed as being psychologically respectable. Literature, philosophy, religion, and art constitute a great storehouse of man's interpretation of life and effective living. Hence, these disciplines cannot be ignored as a source of inspirational and instructive data. Furthermore, the growth-producing experiences of individual psychotherapy and basic encounter groups have relevance for effective living (Bugenthal, 1967, p. viii). At one time examination of inner experience was *the method* of psychology (Titchener, 1898). However, introspection was ousted from the arena of reputable psychology by behavioristic demands for quantification. Humanism revives the emphasis on inner thoughts, feelings, aspirations, and self-appraisal. Humanists are not content with methods that reduce man to the status of larger white laboratory rats or to mechanical computers (Bugenthal, 1967, p. vii).

Personality: The humanistic view

Personality, in humanistic terms, considers man as a being who, in addition to his biological equipment and experiential background, is a forward-looking, future-making individual. Hence, values, aspirations, and dreams as well as prior conditioning must be considered. Man seeks first the satisfaction of his deficiency motivations and then lives and moves in terms of becoming more of what he, and his culture, think he is capable of becoming. While there is no known organic base for heterostatic motivation, the fact of its existence seems to be undeniable. It may spring from unusually good physical and mental health or it may be the power generated by a desire to escape unpleasantness or pain.

Learning is, in part, due to conditioning and reinforcement; but, in addition, it springs from that which does not yet exist—realization of ideals, new combinations of old data, the desire to be autonomous, to be involved, to be free and responsible. Learning springs in part from the urge of creativity, the desire for new experiences, and the desire to be a cause.

Humanism rejects the idea of determinism, and replaces that idea with belief in man's ability to transcend himself.

MOTIVATION: HUMANISTIC INTERPRETATION

Drives and motives

The thesis that all behavior is motivated is widely accepted by psychologists of all schools. All behavior is either purposive or purposeful. Behavior results from either tissue needs (purposive) or from social and individual goals (purposeful). Some of the basic wants stipulated by psychologists over a number of years include such things as the desire or need for:

Organic balance—(homeostasis)
Activity when rested or rest when tired
Security—physical and psychological
Companionship—to be gregarious
Independence—freedom, autonomy
New experiences—exercising one's capacities (heterostasis)
Significance and recognition
Accomplishment—to be a cause, to grow
Affection—love and respect.

These motives have been described in detailed lists. Some name a dozen or more items and other lists are as short as four items. Such lists frequently seem not to be functional in some persons; *e.g.*, some persons seem not to need companionship or achievement. Maslow, (1954, 1970) resolved the puzzling question of why people have differing motivations with his theory regarding the hierarchical nature of needs. His postulation is that needs have varying priorities or levels depending on the totality of life circumstances. Higher level needs such as significance (or esteem) and self-actualization do not become functional until the lower level needs have been satisfied. If low level needs are not satisfied they at least have to be well on the way to being satisfied. When lower level needs, such as physiological and safety needs, have been satisfied, they disappear as motivating forces. When one is not hungry or when he feels safe he no longer is primarily motivated by the lower level needs. Needs, from low to high, as postulated by Maslow, are described in the following subsections.

Physiological   The lowest level needs, those demanding satisfaction first, are the physiological needs. These are the demands of body tissues for food, water, air, warmth, and during the years of adulthood, sex. Until one has had his hunger and thirst cared for, nothing else seems to be of much importance. Hence, we hear stories of shipwrecked sailors or lost travelers who ate those of their companions who died. They even plotted and executed their deaths. The "veneer of civilization" can, it appears, be stripped off by the denial of physiological need satisfaction.

Most people in the United States have enough food and water, and, as adults, sufficient sex satisfaction. Hence, the physiological needs are rather much a topic for academic discussion. However, there are a considerable number of people who do not get enough food. These have little inclination to move on to the pursuit of higher level needs. Children may not rummage through garbage cans, as has happened in severely war-torn countries, but some are in no condition to be learning the alphabet or their "7" tables because they are just plain hungry. Many, because the cupboard is bare, come to school without breakfast. It is not surprising that beneficial learning results have been reported to result in those educational programs that admit food to the curriculum. School starts with fruit and toast. Soon afterward there is a mid-morning snack. Soon after lunch another physiological need—sleep—is considered.

One of our chief executives has described our nation as being, for a third of the population, ill-fed, ill-housed, and ill-clothed. For this third it cannot be assumed that much progress will be made toward higher level needs until basic physiological needs are given high priority. Achievement in school, adherence to law, affiliation in family and community will not be strong personality motivators until children are fed. It cannot be assumed that holes in one's shoes during the winter months, or thin clothes when insulated jackets are needed against the cold, can be the concomitants of school learning.

Safety needs

For most people, physiological needs are readily and regularly met. These may never seem to function as motivators. The individual is next impelled to seek satisfaction of his safety needs. These are the ones having to do with freedom from physical harm. These include the need to be protected from injury, illness, and physical abuse. Children are frightened by a bleeding finger or vomiting. Adults fear a gush of blood or the diagnosis of cancer. They are apprehensive about that which is totally unfamiliar. Safety needs are revealed in the cuddling of babies and the huddling of adults at the scene of disaster.

Safety needs are psychological as well as physical. One of the more pervasive personality traits of insecure persons is their alertness to the possible undercutting of their ego concepts. There is a sensitivity to possible insult that is widely typical. Safety needs, for the child, are met by parents who provide loving arms, accepting laps and chests. Parents are needed who, when the child reaches various ages, provide him with rules, regulations, and routines. This prevents their having to cope with continuously strange situations. An example is the hazard of a succession of foster homes. Unfortunately, far too many parents are unacquainted with the developmental, sequential nature of needs. They seek a panacea. They want *a solution* for child-rearing practices. A set method just does not work because safety needs change as the child matures. The young baby needs to be picked up, cuddled, talked to, and comforted when tired, hungry, or ill. He needs similar care when he is rested, stuffed, and healthy. Safety is not quite so physical in early childhood as during babyhood. Safety does mean increased adherence to family routines. "You eat [aside from a reasonable snack] when we eat. You go to bed when it is time to go to bed. You wait for me to hold your hand when crossing the street." This is not cold or arbitrary. Rather, it takes the burdens of decisions from him that, in his immaturity, would otherwise be too heavy.

Too many parents, misled by permissive child-rearing advice, misinterpretation of such advice, or in ignorance of Maslow's theory think they should not "impose their will" on the child. Actually, there is no alternative. Before the child is intellectually mature and experientially sophisticated, to force him to be autonomous is to impose a threat to his safety needs. It is frightening. Parents who acknowledge the existence of safety needs will be firm with young children. They may say "Because I said so" without violating humanistic principles. The child wants and needs to know that his father, mother, teachers are strong and wise people who can protect him from harm and the unknown. And so too, the adolescent. True, there should be a reduction of arbitrariness but not an abdication of authority. Parents are not peers. They are inescapably parents (Cottle, 1969).

College students, despite their bravado, are not exempt from the nature of safety needs. Hopefully, they will have outgrown the need for autocratic parents. Parents should have progressively loosened routines, regulations, and requirements. However, young people are not ready—in terms of their safety needs—to take over the administrative offices of a college or university. To the extent that they are permitted to do so, they are learning some misconceptions about their importance. They deny the limitations of safety needs. As adults, those who have not matured sufficiently through observance of regulations and conventions, will still be seeking external controls to satisfy their safety needs. Ideally, as adults, they will have internalized laws and regulations. They may then move toward higher level motivations.

Need for acceptance, to be loved, and to love

Selection processes occur constantly. Some unfortunate people will never be able to rise above the level of seeking satisfaction of physiological needs. Others will remain at the safety level and become chronic searchers for security. They seek safety either by pathological withdrawal or excessive dependence on others. Those who have had parents who know they are parents, will move toward the higher level of seeking love needs.

As a child, one must be accepted for what he is. He might be accepted as a mature person would accept a foreigner. A child might be viewed as one who is unacquainted with the customs and conventions of a strange world. He should not be condemned because he errs in the ways of mankind. Rather, the child needs to be loved because he *is*. Love should not be limited to when he does only those things that are approved.

The healthy child is egocentric. When his needs to be accepted and loved are adequately met, he can take another step within this level. He can move toward loving others. He must feel—at all ages—that he is wanted and appreciated for himself, not for what he can do for others. Many data regarding characteristics, developmental tasks, and human needs point to the need to be accepted as *unique individuals*.

People cannot grow at the same rates and perform with equal degrees of skill. It is necessary that they be accepted despite their differences. If children are rejected for being of the unwanted sex, because diet produces indigestion and petulance, or because of slowness in learning, then feelings of insecurity and of being unloved begin to be generated. The psychological care of the child is important to his personality development. It is as vital as proper feeding and nutrition are to his physical functioning. Women who reject their children cannot properly mother them, and regressive and negativistic behaviors are likely to develop.

> A counselor trainee, after working with several boys and girls, aged 16–19, in the Portland Residential Manpower Center (attended predominantly by school dropouts) remarked, "I am impressed by the consistency with which these youngsters report literally no home life. Some are orphans. Some do not know their father. The rest are torn by concern about [and this might be either affection or rejection] their mother or father who are living away from each other; either divorced or separated. Very few have both mother and father. Then their parents often live in a chronic state of dissension."

The sad part, especially for the girls, is that their search for love leads them to grasp for the love of an equally immature man—be he 17 or 47. Their search for their own love needs renders them incapable of bestowing love on their own babies. Their babies frequently are put out for adoption. Babies may be shunted from one parent to another, to an aunt, grandmother, or foster parents. A vicious cycle is perpetuated. The victims seek that which they are incapable of grasping.

Esteem needs

As one moves from the search for low level needs to higher ones the nature of the striving differs. There is less desperateness, all-or-none, exclusiveness. There is less specificity about the pursuit of higher level needs. The hungry person talks about food, thinks about food, reminisces about food, and fantasizes about food. At the level of higher needs, deprivation is not so noticeable and loss is less disconcerting. The higher the level of needs the more amenable one is to psychotherapy. Food, for instance, cannot be substituted for by discussing one's concern with a psychiatrist. At the esteem level, one may be helped, through individual or group therapy, to see that he is not so deprived of love as he imagines. He can learn that love exists among all cultures and socioeconomic strata.

Esteem needs become functional after one has come to know that he is a sufficiently capable, good looking, friendly, and acceptable person that others can care for him. When one has matured sufficiently that his own well being is a part of the well being of others, he may begin the pursuit of esteem needs. It is a matter of shifting from a jealous, possessive type of love to an outgoing love in which the wishes

Man does not live by bread alone

and welfare of the other brings satisfaction to the bestower of love. A glow resides in the giving.

Initially, esteem needs are met in terms of self-esteem. One feels confident, strong, adequate, and useful. If esteem needs are thwarted, one has feelings of inferiority, alienation, and **anomie.** One needs next to know that others share the view that one is competent and distinctive. Acceptance needs mean that one must be appreciated simply because he exists. At the esteem level, the appreciation of others must be based on developed abilities. Mother is admired not because she is a mother biologically. She is esteemed because she is proud of herself, her well-behaved children, and her role. Esteem needs are met on the basis of deserved respect.

> Two men received promotions to managers of State Employment local offices at about the same time. The cities were the same size. Their qualifications, time served, and prior positions were comparable.
>
> One manager seemed to change after his promotion. He had the manager's office moved to a position where he could see more of the office at one time. His former friends had to make an appointment with his secretary to see him. All letters from the office had to be signed by him. Memos were published and posted frequently: Memo from: R. M. Crank, Mgr. etc. His name and picture appeared frequently in the local newspaper and the State Employment Bulletin: "Employment Manager, R. M. Crank, announced today . . ."
>
> Top level managers in the state central office noticed two changes. (1) Complaints from members of minority groups were greatly increased over previous months. (2) Personnel from the office were quitting or requesting transfer to another office with markedly increased frequency.
>
> The other manager also moved his office where he could see more of the office. When personnel walked by he would wave them in, "got a minute or two?" He would then discuss a problem he had or would merely ask how things were going. He found little use for memos on parking priorities, coffee room litter, or tardiness regarding opening one's station. Newspaper articles cited the names of the personnel who had charge of special programs.
>
> Officials in the central office noted (1) a high incidence of personnel taking supplementary training, (2) that the local office had the largest number, comparing like-sized cities, of disadvantaged people in special programs.

The first manager functioned at the safety level of self-preservation. The second was above the level of safety needs. He could function in terms of the comfort of his colleagues and the welfare of clients.

Maslow makes it clear that self-actualization occurs only rarely and usually in older persons. His observations lead him to conclude that he can identify only a dozen or two contemporaries and some long-dead historical characters as being self-actualized. Self-actualization, like the needs preliminary to its becoming operative, is a style of living. It is a process rather than an achievement or status. It means that the

Self-actualization

individual is actualizing his potential. He is bringing into being those things that he is capable of becoming. It is not a concomitant of great achievement. It is not restricted to great statesmen, scholars, or creative geniuses. It may be revealed in a relatively uneducated workman. It may be seen in a woman whose concern has been with being the best mother she possibly can be. It is not a state of happiness. Ecstatic moments are temporary and transient. Self-actualization is, like other motivational levels, not a guarantee of contentment. Achieving any of the criteria (see below) of self-actualization leads to another step. After the excitement and fulfillment, the inevitable takes place. The thrill is taken for granted. One becomes restless again for more. Heterostasis is persistent.

Maslow (1970, p. 162) makes a distinction between deficiency motivation—the search for fulfillment of basic needs—and growth motivation, the outward thrust. The urge to grow is prominent in the person who is in unusually good psychological health. Self-actualizers need less of the confirmation that is part of the deficiency-motivated individual's style of life.

The criteria (see below) by which the self-actualizer can be identified may (1) serve the reader as descriptions of the meaning of the term. The criteria may serve as (2) identifiable goals for the individual's steering of his own personality development. The fewer criteria that one may identify within himself, the greater is the likelihood that he is functioning at one of the lower levels of needs fulfillment. Items in Maslow's (1970, pp. 153–180) description of unusually healthy persons, the self-actualizers, include the following considerations:

They are able to define accurately the true meaning of reality.

They are able to feel comfortable with both the harsh and the enjoyable aspects of reality.

They are able to accept themselves and the realities of life. They are also able to accept people despite their lack of manners, selfishness, and defensiveness. They are not so much satisfied with themselves as they are able to reduce the feelings of guilt and anxiety that plague the person who is less self-confident.

Their behavior is natural and spontaneous. Conventions can be observed for the sake of others but they are not ruled by custom. They are well aware of their own impulses, desires, and opinions.

They live problem-centered rather than ego-centered lives. Responsibility, choice, obligation are aspects of their own choosing. They do not feel that problems are impositions and infringements on their freedom and autonomy.

While they are not estranged from others, they can exercise the mode of detachment. They are comfortable by and with themselves. It is estimated that this condition of self-decision and self-determination is achieved by 5 to 30 per cent of the adult population (McClelland, 1961).

Because they are impelled by growth motivation, self-actualizers are relatively free from cultural and physical pressures. They are able to maintain serenity in the face of conditions that keep others in a state of constant turmoil.

They possess a continuing freshness of appreciation. Beauty, the glow of marriage, the thrill of seeing children learn and grow are felt repeatedly. Peak experiences occur frequently in their lives. Ennui, boredom, and "dull repetition" are overshadowed by a large capacity to count one's blessings—spontaneously.

Most, not all, of the actualizers Maslow studied report what have been called mystic, or peak, experiences. These feelings are difficult to describe because those who have not had them cannot grasp the message. One cannot really verbalize the feelings he has while walking through a grove of giant, golden-boled pines. It is hard to describe the thrill one gets from the warm, moist grasp of an infant's hand. It is hard to convey the flight of fancy experienced from a certain musical passage. At these times one feels in tune. All is right with the world and with oneself. He orchestrates with reality and the scheme of things. For the moment, needs, pressures, and doubts are lost in the rightness of self and of situation. One feels a harmony and a relationship which transcends communication and interaction to become what Kaplan (1969, p. 78) calls "communion."

Parallel to peak experiences is what Adler (1927) has called *Gemeinschaftsgefühl*. It is the feeling of deep identification with one's fellow beings. Self-actualizers can feel affection even for those who are weak, foolish, and spiteful.

They have weak ego boundaries. They must, consequently, establish deep interpersonal ties with only a *few* individuals. Although they are at ease with others, their circle of friends is small. This is because it takes much time to develop richly meaningful relationships. There are other, many other, things to do. They tend to be kind but see little reason, in terms of reality, to tolerate hypocrisy, pomposity, and pretentiousness.

They have a ready, philosophical, and unhostile sense of humor. They do not laugh at little moron, race, or smutty jokes. However, their own *faux pas* or those of mankind in general are amusing. They would be regarded by the generality as being sober and humorless.

They are universally, says Maslow (1970, p. 170), creative. This does not mean that they write challenging books, compose music, or paint pictures. Indeed, such creators are often far from living self-actualizing lives. It does mean that their routine, daily work is seen as a creative task. They are creative in that they are spontaneous and see perceptively. They share with children a freshness of appreciation.

It seems from the above listed criteria that the self-actualizing way of life is a demanding one. It is—and with no pot of gold at the end of the rainbow. Nevertheless, the criteria do provide a check list. The list is a standard for those who are high enough on the hierarchical scale of needs that they are approximating some of the items. The list does not promise bliss. It does, however, give a direction to those who are cultivating their occasional urges of heterostasis.

HUMANISTIC VIEW OF LEARNING

Motivation is a basic consideration as one views the nature and formation of personality. Equally important is the question of how humans learn when, as, and after they are motivated.

Frankly, we do not know just how learning takes place. Precisely what chemical, electrical, and biological changes occur are still matters of some conjecture. Despite this gap in knowledge the reader can be reassured: Much is known about the conditions under which learning best occurs. Rather firm theories are available for one's guidance.

Humanistic theory as protest

The psychology of learning has long been dominated by what has been called the connectionist view. That is, some kind of connection was made in the learner between a stimulus and a response. Thorndike (1924, 1932) postulated three primary laws of learning: exercise, readiness, and effect (see Chapter 1). This point of view works well for many pupils. They "learn" productively for the "effect" of teacher and parental praise, high grades, gold stars, diplomas, and degrees. While the incidence of success is noted, the humanists ask some aggravating questions.

What happens when the reinforcements are no longer bestowed? It seems that many pupils abandon any efforts toward planned, systematic learning. They continue to learn that which is required in life. There is, however, no pursuit of organized, recorded knowledge (Allport, 1968, p. 167).

Another disturbing question is: What about those learnings about which knowledge does not yet exist? We live in a world of cataclysmically rapid change. The connectionistic-reinforcement theory lacks some validity in this century because it constitutes a model for teaching only that which is already known (Snygg, 1966). Connectionistic psychology is satisfactory for teaching existing information but something also needs to be done about creativity, imagination, and inventiveness.

What about readiness for learning? It is agreed that it is important. It is more than a degree of intellectual and emotional maturity. Readiness is an individual, organismic, global thing, that must include the wars presently being fought, the shifting values of youth and their parents, socioeconomic status, and the financial tempo of the current year.

Where does the burden of learning rest? Behaviorists focus on the reinforcement and reinforcer. The reinforcer is the one who rewards the pressing of the correct lever or the speaking of the right number in response to 9×7. The humanist insists that the burden of learning be shifted from the teacher to the individual (Berrill, 1967).

Does exercise really consolidate learning? Some humanists are unwilling to accept the evidence. Boys do learn the capitols of states and faithfully record them on an examination. Then when traveling in Montana with dad and mom, they do not recognize Helena. Practice does not guarantee perfection. It may do much to consolidate what one is already doing, be it helpful or harmful. Pupils may be practicing a strong dislike for school.

Where is the impetus for learning centered? Is it located in the external conditions? Is it in the perception of the individual? The behaviorists seem to place the focus on the stimuli and on the reinforcing circumstances. The humanists contend that external events—stimuli and reinforcements—have meaning largely in the uniqueness of individual perceptions. The focus for learning must reside in the student.

Closely related questions are: What is really learned? Is learning to be judged solely in terms of subject matter outcome? If a boy learns to read but learns also that he is inadequate, he learns to dislike disciplined study. His learning is harmful. A psychological storm was generated by Jensen when he charged that compensatory education was a failure. He reported that compensatory education resulted in virtually no persistent advancement in subject matter mastery or IQ. Jensen did admit in a footnote to a 123-page article, that positive claims could be made regarding pupils' self-confidence, motivation, and attitudes toward school (Jensen, 1969, p. 3). His challengers responded, in effect, that ego-concepts and attitudes might very well be the crucial factors in establishing a predisposition toward systematic learning throughout a lifetime (Hunt, 1969; Kagan, 1969).

Humanistic views of learning are more than matters of protest and argument. Some alternative and positive statements have been evolving constantly since Thorndike, in the early 1920's, stated, clarified, and modified the connectionistic orientation. The following postulations include the major emphases of the humanistic point of view.[3]

Positive statements of humanistic orientation to learning

[3]The author and a former colleague, Wesley C. Huckins, now of Wright State University, Ohio, formulated the postulations. The ideas came from a study that allowed us to visit a score or more of innovative schools and colleges throughout the United States. The postulations were submitted to various authorities in education, counseling, anthropology, and psychology. The main criticism was neglect of the behavioristic-reinforcement point of view. Hence, let the reader beware. In a chapter on the "Humanistic Orientation" the bias may be pardonable.

- *Learners are more affected by the process of learning than by its verbal products.* Students learn what they do as contrasted to learning what they are told. So, too, do adults. Much talk to teachers-to-be about effective teaching methods does not counter their inclination to teach as they were taught. Much talk about effective child-rearing techniques does little to obliterate the tendency of young parents to behave pretty much like their parents did. Discussions of how to get along with others at work do not easily counter the tendency to behave with others in much the same manner that one behaves outside the discussion (Wassermann, 1973).

  Implication: Let the learner practice those behaviors, rather than verbalizations, that are seen to be desirable.

- *Learners gain more from some experiences than they do from others.* Increasingly, teachers are attempting to devise curriculum in terms of what pupils want to do. If they want to study the local dairy instead of about early American Indians, so be it. Goodman (1968) asserts that anything the child, up to age 12, wants to do can be educative. Others (including the author) are not quite so ready to abandon guidance. Providing guidance is akin to the idea that parents should be parents. With some teacher effort, studying the local dairy can involve reading, writing, and arithmetic.

  Implications: College students might consider that some curricula are irrelevant. They might also entertain the idea that not all prescribed curricula, especially theory, lack pertinence.

- *Learners have a natural desire to learn, to know, and to become more of what they can become.* School practices that rely on grades, passing, the threat of failure, and the promise of honor rolls ignore the heterostatic urges. Grades and threats suppress the directional impulse of growing. Greater reliance might be put on knowledge of progress. Less reliance might be placed on having pupils learn at a prescribed pace. Interpersonal comparisons are likely to suppress heterostatic movement. Curiosity about things other than the lesson plan might be rewarded by discussing and pursuing the object of curiosity.

  Implication: Students might take time *now* to read those books and articles that interest them. They might take an evaluative look at the relative importance of doing the assignment or pursuing a tangential lead.

- *The learner's whole being is involved in the learning process.* Learning, particularly in school and college classrooms, seems to be regarded solely as an intellectual process. Teachers in the lower grades are sometimes forced to deal with the angry, resistant mood of the child or to excuse pupils for their frequent illnesses. The more successful college teachers recognize the fact that different cultural backgrounds, varying levels of health and well being, and diverse ambitions affect learning.

The orientation of many teachers is, "If he can't keep up, he should get out of the class," or, "Let's admit it—only those in the upper reaches of mentality are college material." The mastery of subject matter is the concern of such teachers. Certainly the emphasis is not without some justifiable reason. None of us would put our lives in the hands of a surgeon or airplane pilot who had not met appropriate qualifying criteria. Neither would we want a surgeon or pilot whose emotional life was disturbed to the extent that he hated his wife and (at the moment) women in general, or was taking drugs as an escape. The humanist places the learner first. After the teacher understands his pupil's goals, style of learning, and level of present competence he becomes concerned about subject matter. In the humanist's eyes there is a vast difference between an educational technician and a teacher who guides the learning process.

Implication: The student who is experiencing some learning difficulty usually attacks the problem in terms of class load, more study, greater determination, sticking to a time-place schedule. Greater dividends might be derived from examining how varying courses fit one's goals. One might examine his *own* deeply desired goals. Effective study demands examination of self. It means evaluating one's attitudes toward the instructor. It means questioning one's attitudes toward the course. One must ask, "Do I really believe this course is significant?"

- *Pupils have varied learning styles and recognition of them facilitates learning.* The fact is that little is known about varied learning styles. Still less is *done* about the styles. This is indicative of the tendency to ignore the human aspects of the teaching-learning transaction. Some pupils are deliberate, step-by-step, methodical learners. Others are impetuous and intuitive learners. They make big logical (or illogical) jumps. Some learn best by reading. Another is a quiet and efficient listener. Still others learn by talking. Some learners rely on extrinsic rewards, immediate feedback, and teacher-determined structure. Some enjoy drill. Others want to pursue their own interests. Their reward is the gratification they gain from having learned something. They do not have to do a dozen problems after they get the idea of how to multiply with a two place number or work a problem on the slide rule.

The content-oriented teacher expects 30 pupils in a class to "turn to page 137 and get to work." If there is any difficulty he will place the slow learner in a remedial class. He will give the fast learner an *A*—but keep him in class so that he can show the student with pride. The humanist emphasis is that pupils are different. There is really no alternative to having them doing different things at the same time.

Implication: Assess yourself as a reader, talker, listener, observer, experimenter, plodder, intuitive-jumper-to-conclusions, convergent or divergent thinker. Without neglecting the development of weaknesses (perhaps reading or writing) plot a course to make better use of your preferred learning style.

- *Drill, recitation, practice, and repetition have their place in effective learning.* The conventional view is that learning is a difficult, time-consuming, often dully unpleasant task. It needs some reasonable discipline from the teacher. The humanist accepts the fact that learning is often difficult and unpleasant. Hence, it must be faced with resolve. However, instead of discipline there should be discussion. One admits the reality of work and unpleasantness. The behaviorists say that following the right course will result in reward. The humanist promises a temporary glow of achievement. Facing reality also demands that the learner accept the idea that he will achieve, not happiness, but the challenge of still more work. There is always the next task (Krill, 1971). The humanist, as teacher, wants to share with students, through dialogue, through demonstration, that life and learning will continue to be accompanied by the necessity for drill, repetition, and, if one permits its entry—boredom.

  Implication: If one could face the reality that school involves work, marriage involves work, and efficiency on the job involves work he might avoid the feeling of **anomie** and **alienation** that are so often the lot of the happiness-oriented person. He might, therefore, be a more receptive learner.

- *Continuous feedback rather than end-of-the-course grading or marking is a key to the full exploitation of one's learning potential.* Behaviorist Skinner (1954) is in agreement with this postulation; however, he places the responsibility on the teacher. The humanist hopes that the feedback will come in large part from the learner's recognizing his own progress, exercising his capacities, and fulfilling his own expectancies. The humanistic teacher capitalizes on the proposition by a word of praise. He gives a pat on the back. Sometimes he gives feedback just by letting the student know that he knows what the student is doing. Behind the teacher's providing occasional, incidental feedback (instead of scheduling it at six- or nine-week grading intervals) is the idea that soon the student will need to know how to supply his own feedback.

  Implication: Discuss with your current classmates ways in which you might come closer to the achievement of **functional autonomy.**

- *Students learn by listening, talking, doing, and from emulating models.* Conventionally, and verbally, teachers recognize the validity of this proposition and they give lip-service to "varied activities." They then proceed to do approximately 85 per cent of the talking that is done in class (Flanders, 1965). College professors may achieve an even higher percentage. Humanistic teachers practice the postulation by working in small groups. They trust students to work independently without the teacher's hovering over them to maintain silence and order. Such teachers have developed the rare skill of active listening; *i.e.*, trying to understand the feelings behind the students' words as well as the words themselves. Because pupils are going off "in a dozen different directions" the teacher becomes an active learner himself—he does not want to lose track of his students. In addition, he knows that students, from the beginning pupil to the college student, emulate the liked and competent teacher. His minimum professional obligation is to provide a model by being a learner himself.

Implication: Talk it over.

• *Learning may be facilitated by developing an appreciation of the verbal-linguistic approach to problem solving.* Man's brain specialty is that of having a large portion of its area and volume devoted to speech-related functions. In order to capitalize on this uniqueness the potential should be exercised. True, the input is emphasized—teachers' lecturing, telling, demonstrating, and books presenting their messages. Audiovisual aids are popular devices to vary the stimuli. The humanist says that communication is a two-way street. The value of verbal bombardment during early childhood is appreciated *but* the child should be throwing some of the bombs. The preponderance of "teacher talk" should be lessened and the percentage of "pupil talk" be increased. Krill (1971) says that one of the essential steps in existential therapy is communication—dialogue is a necessary ingredient of creative growth. It gives feedback that helps to validate one's feelings about self. Talk allows one to test without having to act out. Bruner (1968) has asserted that the fundamental ingredient of education may well be the dialogue between the novitiate and the sophisticate. A panel, reporting to the U. S. Commissioner of Education, stated that a promising innovation in American education was a new method in mathematics, science, and social studies that related to student-teacher interaction:

. . . The ideal form of such a relation is probably the dialogue between a learner and a wise and informed tutor. But it is encouraging to see the extent to which improvement in performance can be achieved by organizing class discussion into a generalized form of dialogue, using texts and documents as resources to be tapped when needed.[4]

Implication: Students have at least three avenues for improving use of the verbal-symbolic transaction in education. (1) Cut down on the number of hours spent passively receiving the messages of television. (2) Use the time, plus still more, to engage in dialogue with parents, peers, and passing acquaintances. (3) Put pressure on instructors to engage in dia-

---

[4]*Innovation and Experiment in Education,* A progress report of the Panel on Educational Research and Development to the U. S. Commissioner of Education (Washington, D. C.: U. S. Government Printing Office, 1964), p. 13.

logue. At the very least, one can supplement his preferred learning styles with planned dialogue with classmates.

- *Experiencing success is conducive to the continued pursuit of formal learning. Encountering failure inhibits the desire for continued pursuit of an activity.* Despite the great amount of phenomenological data available, plus the evidence from one's own experience, some teachers cling to the notion that the experience of failure is educative. "One must learn," they say, "to take failure in stride." The humanist replies that one does just that. He strides away from the failure-inducing situation. If one cannot hit a golf ball straight, get the message of a bridge game, or as a clerk, face a customer in a store, he goes to something else. Adults simply avoid those areas of activity where they may be identified as failures. One learns from failure to fail. The person who experiences much success can take an occasional failure in stride. He can give the thing another try. The chronic failure expects to fail at the next venture (if he tries). He incorporates into his self-concept that of being a loser (Gottlieb, 1971).

  Implication: Select those areas in which one's strengths are most apparent. Count these successes even at those times when failure is immanent. This is not advice to run away from that which is difficult. It avoids making failure the focus of one's attention.

- *Learning is facilitated when the student is involved in the planning, conducting, and evaluating of learning activities.* Involvement means that the student's voice is heard and that his vote counts. One of the hypotheses of student unrest in colleges is that as children they were treated as things rather than as persons. As they grew older, their broadened perceptions led them to believe that they had a voice in their own destinies. Autocratic discipline, rigid curricula, achievement of uniform standards, and being treated in the manner of a punch-card made it difficult to develop a sense of personal significance (Halleck, 1971; Keniston, 1971). When teachers see students as being different, meriting respect, needing to feel autonomous, and revealing heterostatic striving, then creativity is encouraged. When one is seen as having some wisdom, then setting up conditions for student involvement becomes a creative matter.

  Personnel from elementary and secondary schools and colleges are recognizing the need the individual has for feeling that he has some power. One must be seen as having the sense to direct at least some of his own affairs. Students so regarded respond by more quickly learning the essential lessons of responsibility and choice. One interpretation of the Women's Liberation movement is that women have not had a voice, commensurate with their potential, in the direction of their own lives and affairs of the world (Baumrind, 1972).

Implication: Many instructors, even in colleges that can justly be called authoritarian, would accept this postulation. In addition, many instructors will enjoy having students engage them in mature conversation regarding how this postulation might be implemented in individual cases.

- *Students learn more readily when their aims and interests are in accord with those of their peers.* This postulation probably has more significance for parents and teachers than it does for the learner (Lipton, 1971). Peer pressure is accepted because it is a way of, and part of, the process of growing up. It is a phase of the interaction that is called **enculturation.** Conformity in dress, hair style, attitudes toward authority, toward one's role in school and the world are all influenced by peer pressure. Such pressure is, however, responsive to current cultural pressure. For example, students shifted away from science during the depression years. They came back to it after the Russians (with Sputnik) showed some technological superiority to the U. S. Peer pressure encouraged students to lead the way in civil rights movements. Students led the protests of U. S. participation in an undeclared war. The postulation might justifiably be extended from learning as a result of peer pressure to including personality formation as a function of peer pressure.

  Implication: There is no avoiding the impact of this proposition. Even leaving the peer group would be a factor supporting its accuracy. Each individual does, however, need, during a process of self-examination, to ask himself what part of his behavior and learning is a function of peer pressure. One needs to ask whether or not this accords with what one intrinsically wants and is "good" socially; *i.e.*, promises positive long-range results.

- *Many factors must be taken into consideration when the products of learning are evaluated.* This postulation has been ignored for so long that the word "evaluation" in connection with schools means only grades. In spite of much criticism, the move away from grades is impeded by a considerable number of rationalizations: Grades motivate students; they are needed to inform parents; they are required by college registrars; they are needed by prospective employers. Because the real essence of learning resides in behavior, attitudes, and continued learning, Simon (1970) argues that "Grades Must Go." He claims that grades estrange teacher and student. They debase the student's feelings of self worth. They "squeeze a student's identity and self-image within the narrow confines of his transcript" (Simon, 1970, p. 400). Evaluation should consist in the continuous feedback the teacher gives the learner in daily transaction. Next steps, points needing further study, some interesting sidelights, and how learning can be pursued in terms of the student's particular learning style are the needed emphases in evaluation. If mass education prevents such interpersonal evaluation, then at least the student must know what is going on in grading. It then becomes his responsibility to decide what should be done.

A junior in engineering was required to fill out his curriculum with three more credit hours in social studies. He chose a course in Psychology of Childhood. He was also taking a course in advanced calculus that required many hours of work. The mid-term examinations told him that he could, by spending a couple of hours a week, get an *A* or *B* in Child Psychology. He chose to scan the text and spend the hours available to get a *C* in the calculus course.

No doubt another student would have chosen the time for Child Psychology in order to enhance his GPA, and for him that might have been the wise choice.

Implication: Students are advised to examine the evaluation system used in their respective schools. They should decide the extent to which the system should govern their behavior—now and in terms of the future.

- *Learning for a lifetime of coping with rapid change will be facilitated when values, ideals, and socially-oriented personality traits are part of planned curricular content.* Values, ideals, aspirations are the essence of learning to the humanist. They cannot be seen. They must be inferred (Kaplan, 1972). Some studies show that direct teaching did not have much effect on the incidence of stealing, deceit, and cheating. Empirical studies show that certain teachers have had an effect which lasts a lifetime according to students' reports (Fairbank, 1933; Hamachek, 1969). Rather than to abandon the teaching of character because it did not, in the past, change behavior, humanists want to know more details about *just how* the results seen by Fairbank and Hamachek happened to occur.

  Implication: Even if one's required curriculum does not include courses on values, one might consider taking a course in philosophy when such is available. Reading, especially biographies of famous persons, will show that values rank high in terms of an effective personality.

- *Learning is facilitated when it is recognized that one's self-concept is the central point of educative transaction.* To the humanist, one's self-concept is a central issue in life. It certainly functions in formal education. Such considerations as success and failure, praise or ridicule, freedom vs. control, authority vs. involvement, creativity or doing the assignment are vital issues (Rist, 1970). To the extent that a teacher must defend his unassailable knowledge, maintain his dignity, and establish his authority, he is unlikely to be able to do much for the ego concept of pupils. To the extent that the teacher knows who he is and what his function is, his role is creative. Whatever a teacher does, his basic concern should be with its impact on the student's ego concept.

  The college student, having matured sufficiently to recognize the phenomenon of teacher insecurity and its impact on students' personalities, has a responsibility. He can (1) avoid teachers who have the reputation for down-grading students, (2) make such a teacher the object of personality study, or (3) watch the processes of self-conceptions as they occur within himself. In any event, the academic gain from any course will have difficulty outweighing, plus or minus, what the study does for one's self-concept.

Implication: If the self-concept does not appear to be recognized by one's instructors, one might ask himself what input a particular course has now, and for the future. If the course and instructor belittle the self-concept, the student needs to face the impact of that belittling. Is it worth it?

SUMMARY

A psychological orientation, newly appearing, is one called by various names—proactive, humanistic, perceptual, phenomenological, or existential psychology. One name, "third force," implies that in addition to (1) man's biological equipment and (2) his environmental experience, there is (3) an active interpretation by the organism of what man *is* and *has.* What one does is significant. Purpose, intent, forward growth, love, identity, values, although presently not quantifiable, are powerfully present.

Healthy persons have a heterostatic drive to grow more; unhealthy persons are perceived as having some residual strength which the therapist helps them to discover and reveal. This is contrasted to other therapies in which the therapist is all-wise.

The methods of humanistic psychology are scientific in that they are observable, repeatable, descriptive, develop theory, and require trained observers. While measurement is acknowledged, it is viewed skeptically.

The perplexing puzzle of man's varied motivations is partly resolved by Maslow's hierarchy of needs theory. He postulates that lower level needs (deficiency needs) must be satisfied before the individual is motivated by higher level needs (growth needs). The needs are, from low to high: physiological, safety, love and acceptance, esteem, and self-actualization.

Learning is regarded in a distinctly different light from that of the prevalent—behavioristic and connectionistic—view. The learner is the focus rather than the stimulus or curriculum. Items ranking high in humanistic observations regarding effective learning are: Process outweighs product; perceptual uniqueness causes learning experiences to have different values for different students; students intrinsically want to learn; autonomy and exercise of one's strengths are more important than externally granted incentives; learning effectively means involvement; styles of learning are varied and call for individualized teacher-student interaction; drill has its place in the routines of life; feedback and dialogue are educational imperatives; success is essential to the development of the continuous learning habit; peer pressures influence learning; personal purposes are a part of the evaluation of learning; values are an integral part of humanistic education; and at all times the self-concept of the learner is the vital focus.

Personality, from the standpoint of the humanist, involves self-determination, values, aspirations, uniqueness, and the ever-present challenge of self-transcendance.

SUGGESTED READINGS

COLES, ROBERT, "God and the Rural Poor," *Psychology Today*, Vol. 5, No. 8, 31–40, January, 1972.

> *Humanists emphasize that life does not promise happiness but that personal perspectives determine, in some degree, how the satisfactions and dissatisfactions of life will be viewed. Coles, in this article, shows how religious faith bears on the life of economically poor people.*

"Ethical Forum: Psychology and Humanism," *The Humanist*, Vol. 31, No. 2, 7–23, March–April, 1971.

> *Six contributors focus on the meaning and distinctiveness of humanistic psychology. Brinckerhoff contrasts it with behaviorism and Freudianism. Matson discusses it as the third revolution in psychology.*

EYSENCK, H. J., "Definitions of Humanism—Reason with Compassion," *The Humanist*, Vol. 31, No. 2, 24–25, March–April, 1971.

> *This noted English psychologist perceives humanism as striving to maintain balance between reason and faith, between compassion and realism.*

LAMONT, CORLISS, and SIDNEY HOOK, "Definitions of Humanism," *The Humanist*, Vol. 31, No. 5, 9–11, September–October, 1971.

> *This reference is to two short articles. Lamont cites 12 points of a humanistic perspective. Hook warns against encapsulating a dynamic point of view in a definition; but a definition should be distinctive enough not to include everything.*

MASLOW, ABRAHAM, "Self-Actualization and Beyond," ed., J. F. T. Bugenthal, *Challenges of Humanistic Psychology*, pp. 279–286. New York: McGraw-Hill Book Company, 1967.

> *The steps taken by self-actualizing people are described. The goal of life and learning is to become more of what one is potentially capable of becoming.*

WASSERMANN, SELMA, "The Open Classroom in Teacher Education, or Putting Your Money Where Your Mouth Is," *Childhood Education*, Vol. 49, 295–301, 1973.

> *At Simon Frazier University in British Columbia, concern developed about practicing humanistic education via the old lecture system. Independence, different student programs, self-disclosure marked the attempt to change. Freedom to choose was the biggest obstacle and also the most productive of growth.*

FOLLOW-UP LEARNING ACTIVITIES

Who, of the following, *is not* considered to be a proponent of humanistic psychology?

_____ A. Maslow   _____ S. Jourard   _____ H. Bonner

_____ B.F. Skinner   _____ C. Rogers   _____ R. May

Which two of the following are prominent humanistic emphases?

____ choice   ____ conditioning   ____ drill

____ listening   ____ adult leadership   ____ responsibility

The central concern of humanistic psychology is

_____ responsibility _____ identity _____ choice

(Compare and discuss this item with several classmates—one at a time.)

I operate, predominantly, at the present time, at the

_____ physiologial _____ safety _____ love

_____ esteem _____ self-actualization level

In order to move to a higher motivation level, I will have to

_____

_____

_____

_____

_____

Match the following:

a mutual respect   _____ anomie

b directional thrust   _____ alienation

c foreign   _____ identity

d humanism   _____ eclectic

e belonging   _____ proactive

f lacking power   _____ self-actualization

                    _____ dialogue

                    _____ heterostasis

Review the postulations on learning. With which two are you most in agreement?

1 _____

2 _____

With which two do you most disagree?

1 _____

2 _____

10
Personality: Behavioristic View

Man, too, may be only a special kind of machine.

LEARNING ACTIVITIES

If training is the important way to achieve desirable behavior in children and youth, how would you account for children "going wrong" when parents have consistently called attention to their mistakes?

_____
_____
_____
_____
_____
_____

   (Compare your response with that of others and discuss.)
Can you think of a teacher, in the grades or high school, who might be accountable for your liking or disliking school, or a particular subject in school? Explain.

_____
_____
_____
_____
_____
_____

Is a child more or less responsible for his behavior than a person in the late adolescent years?
_____ More _____ Less _____ About the same
Because_____
_____
_____
_____

Would you be satisfied to live in a community in which wise parents, teachers, and other adults had prearranged ways for you to meet all your basic needs?
Yes _____ No _____ because _____
_____
_____
_____
_____

Each year, as we learn more about the origins of behavior, our potential for increasing control of man enlarges. Do you think you would like to live in such a controlled world?
Yes _____ No _____ because _____
_____
_____
_____
_____

Any school of psychology—behavioristic, humanistic, dynamic, psychoanalytic, or field theory—is a perspective on what its spokesmen believe to be the most important considerations in the study of behavior. Behavioristic psychologists, for instance, led the movement away from introspection. Introspection—subjective analyses of mental states—was the method used in the "structural" school of psychology. Behaviorists tried to get rid of such abstractions as mind, will, consciousness, sensations, and mental images. Both the early and contemporary spokesmen of behavioristic views (John B. Watson and Burrus F. Skinner) emphasize that vaguely defined mental states must go. The proper study of psychology, they maintain, must be behavior.

This chapter describes the discernable behaviors that constitute personality from the behaviorist point of view. It shows how behaviorists view man's reactions and how these actions are generated. It shows how daily behaviors are built into personality. The reader should be assured that behaviorism is not simply an historical point of view now outmoded. Its ramifications penetrate deeply into daily issues. Child-rearing, teaching-learning transactions, advertising, political campaigns, and personality theory are influenced by behaviorism.

MEANING OF BEHAVIORISM

Origins of behaviorism

The essence of behaviorism is that the organism adapts to environmental demands by virtue of a relationship between stimuli and responses. The stylized model of the *S-R* (stimulus-response) relationship is conditioning animals to respond to certain stimuli. A dog can be conditioned to salivate at the sound of a bell. A sheep can be conditioned to jump a barrier upon the flashing of a light. Such experimental conditioning is, however, only the beginning of the behavioristic orientation.

When human beings are conditioned—when they learn—to behave in a certain manner, the process is an exceedingly involved one. The contemporary spokesman for behaviorism, Skinner (1953, p. 15), states that behavior is a difficult subject matter. This is not because it is inaccessible but because it is so extremely complex. To illustrate, one may compare the behavior of a five-year-old boy with the sheep's jumping at a flash of light. The boy's house had been shaken by a sharp earth tremor and the mother called, "Billy! Where are you?" Billy's reply was, "Mommy, I didn't do it." One can make many guesses about the kinds of stimuli that caused the boy to respond in this defensive manner. But the idea can readily be accepted, as do the behaviorists, that the boy's response was learned. It was not the pull of the future. It was not an instinctive response. It was the result of some combination of conditioning processes—processes that had caused a specific perception of, and response to, "Billy!"

Watson (1914), who started the behavioristic perspective, emphasized that behavior was the proper, and only, subject for psychological concern. Personality is to be considered as one's accumulated responses to environmental conditions. There must be no such vague explanations as pleasure, pain, or satisfaction. The simple basic fact is that the behavior that becomes incorporated into personality is a response to the conditioning circumstances. Environment is the prime determiner of personality. Watson regarded man as an animal organism whose behavior can be predicted. It can be controlled by analyzing and living in a precisely defined environment. Much of what was said in Chapter 5, on culture, attests to the validity of the behavioristic point of view. Pupils' behaviors and personalities are shaped by a wide variety of palpable, observable, environmental conditions and conditioning processes.

Concept of man

Watson's book (1914) stirred controversy and debate in academic circles when it appeared. A recent book by Skinner, *Beyond Freedom and Dignity* (1971), has evoked similar vehement criticism. The protest stems from what is called the "mechanistic concept of man." Man is regarded by Watson and Skinner as an animal who is the product of his past experiences. Man's personality is conditioned.

Watson (1930, p. 82) claimed that if he were given a dozen healthy infants he would guarantee, if permitted to raise them in an environment that he designed, that he could make them into whatever kind of person that was desired. They could become doctors, lawyers, artists, merchants, or beggars or thieves. This could be done regardless of their talents, tendencies, race, or heredity. Let the assertion not be dismissed lightly. This seems to be, in part, what certain anthropologists are telling us. Alland (1972) denies the concept of human instincts—as do the behaviorists. He asserts that the so-called "territorial imperative" (man's desire for private space) does not exist among some primitive people in Africa. They live in peace with other tribes in the same territory. The human animal—the naked ape—does not show the aggressiveness and pugnacity, that are claimed by some to be universal traits, in the peaceful Senai or Malaya tribes. In short, Alland says that the *human* environment is the determiner of personality.

Skinner (1971) takes much the same position as Watson. He believes that the inefficient personalities of our society can be attributed to conditioning. Too few desirable reactions are consistently reinforced. Aggressiveness, possessiveness, and delinquency can be traced back to attention-getting behaviors. These traits are confirmed and consolidated by adults who reward the misbehavior by giving attention. Skinner, in his novel *Walden Two* (1960), describes a Utopian community in which peace and harmony prevailed. Children were reinforced for their commendable, imitative, and trial-and-error activities. There was no call for punishment and it was not used. Errors were ignored. Children learned to carry on approved activities. This was not because of prestige and power but because of environmental reinforcement. While such congenial behaviors are commendable, some critics are skeptical. They note that drive, ambition, and striving for self-transcendance are also lacking in the passively contented children and adults in *Walden Two*.

Humanists in particular prefer, and the dynamic and field psychologists somewhat less vigorously choose, to think of man as a thinking, willing, forward-looking creature. Creative man, with his large and complicated brain, not only can store memories but can *rearrange* them mentally. He can plan what will be made to happen in the future. Watson claimed that behavior, call it thinking or acting, must be and could be reckoned in terms of *S-R* situations. Inability to understand why different persons react in different ways means that we are not sufficiently aware of some of the minute details that comprise a complex environment. The task of the psychologist, if he would understand man, is to learn how to observe the crucial minutiae that have previously escaped attention. The contention seems to be valid. Many of the recent discoveries about children's personality and pupils' learning in school have consisted in pinpointing previously ignored contributing factors. For example, the harmony or lack of harmony between parents is a crucial factor in children's behavior and learning. Attention has usually focused on the manner in which the child was treated at home or instructed in school.

Skinner (1971) asserts that psychologists' reluctance to rule out such abstractions as states of mind, feelings, human nature, freedom, responsibility, and dignity retards the development of a science of behavior. A technology of behavior is needed. This technology must be based on observable facts. It is necessary, as was the case of moving physics and chemistry from magic to science, to stop explaining things in terms of essences, spirits, and gods. When we stop thinking of personality in terms of temperament, traits, feelings, intentions, and alienations and move toward observable explanations, we will be advancing toward a technology of behavior. The explanation for alienation resides in defective home environments. Probable causes of aggression are in accidents, crimes, wars, economic deprivation, and critical, punitive parents and teachers.

Thinking: A behavioristic view   If man is the product of his past conditioning, one wonders how thinking or problem solving with reference to the future can be accounted for. The source of novel solutions to daily dilemmas is a puzzle for all psychologists. Maltzman (1967) offers a behavioristic interpretation in terms of habit family hierarchies. Simple **habits** are organized into complex patterns. The underlying principle remains the simple *S-R* pattern. A schematization of the process involves many possibilities and combinations and recombinations of the simple *S-R*. For example, a child may have a temper tantrum that *apparently* defeats his purpose. However, the attention he gets—even though it may entail some pain—warrants the continuance of the behavior pattern. Without involving abstractions of logic and planning, the habit hierarchy of the temper tantrum is continued because it involves the "success" of a behavior pattern. It results as a solution of a problem as far as the child is concerned.

Watson was able to keep thinking on the behavioristic scheme by referring to overt and covert reactions. Overt reactions are those that are observable in movement and action. Covert, implicit, subvocal, reactions are so slight as to be unobservable by ordinary means. Thinking, he theorized, is a matter of implicit speech. It is a matter of talking to oneself. There are slight tongue, lip, and laryngal movements that are a part of thought. These, if there were sufficiently delicate instruments, could be detected as an accompaniment of thought. Evidence in support of his theory of thought is supplied in the fact that children often, and adults sometimes, think aloud. A child frequently talks about what he is doing as he does it. He names the objects with which he is playing. Watson was not dismayed when it was pointed out that deaf mutes and persons who had had their larnyx surgically removed were still able to think. He merely transferred the locus of activity to the mouth and tongue or to the gestures of the mute.

The validity of Watson's postulations receives some confirmation, and possibly an expansion, from current knowledge about the action of the cerebral cortex. The cortex stores up memories and its actions result in thought (Wilson, 1969, p. 19). The delicate instruments for measuring slight movement and neural impulses are now available (see Figure 8.2). However, brain activity is so complicated that separating thought, perception, motivation, and muscular coordination are problems yet to be solved. Indeed, if the hypothesis that the organism acts as a whole is valid, it may never be possible to trace the brain or muscular activity of thought without also involving emotions. The most that can be said at present is that Watson's theory of thinking has neither been proved nor disproved.

Respondent conditioning

Respondent conditioning, a so-called adequate (or normal) stimulus (presentation of meat to a hungry dog) results in a given response (salivation). If simultaneously with, or just before, the presentation of meat a bell is rung (substitute stimulus) a number of times, the sound of the bell will result in the dog's salivating. The salivating response has been conditioned. Such an experiment makes a neat, quantifiable, scientific approach. It can be determined that the best subjects (dogs, for example) should not be fed for six, ten, etc., hours before the trial. The number of repetitions (meat preceded by bell ringing) can be counted that are required to cause the bell alone to result in salivation. The amount of saliva can be measured through tubes inserted into the dog's cheek. It is possible to determine how many unrewarded responses (salivation) will persist with bell-ringing and no reinforcement with food. When the bell ringing is no longer stimulating the flow of any saliva, the conditioned response has suffered extinction. It can then be determined how many repetitions of the stimulus (bell plus meat) are needed to reestablish the conditioned response.

Operant conditioning

Operant conditioning can be subjected to quantification in much the same way as respondent conditioning. The behaviorist's emphasis on behavior as the source of scientific data is satisfied. Operant conditioning differs from respondent conditioning in that a natural response is the thing that is rewarded. Through operant conditioning animals and fowls can be conditioned to do amazing things. Dogs play basketball and chickens play ping-pong. Monkeys can be conditioned to play a few notes of a tune on a piano.

These impressive acts are produced by rewarding the subject for approximating in his natural behavior some action that approaches what the experimenter has in mind. For example, let the conditioning of a chicken to play ping-pong be the goal. The chicken is placed in a cage where a pellet of food is dropped periodically into a small cup. When the hungry chicken learns where the food is located, she checks the cup now and then as she moves about within the cage. On the first trials food appears (reinforcement) when she moves toward a ping-pong ball. Her actions focus about the area of the ball. She pecks the ball and is rewarded; but not every time. It has been found that periodic reinforcement is sometimes more effective in producing persistent behavior than is consistent reward.[1] Next, she must peck the ball in a certain direction before receiving her grain of food. Next she must knock the ball over a net before being reinforced. She is then rewarded for attacking only a moving ball. Finally, another chicken, similarly conditioned is put in the cage and reinforcement occurs when the ball crosses the net. Then reinforcement is withheld until the ball crosses the net three successive times, etc. One may notice that the

[1]This may be why slot machines in Las Vegas cause widowed dowagers to pull the handles of the machine by the hour. They would not be so fascinated by cutting the coupons on bonds that produced, less immediately, money every time. They would not play the slot machines if they were never paid. This is why hubby deserts wife and kids periodically to pull a piece of line, on which there is a bright piece of metal or a worm, through the water hour after hour. If a fish never hit he would quit. If a fish hit every time he would get bored and send the kids to the lake to get the fish. Periodic reinforcement is a powerful stimulus to bizarre action.

dogs who have high IQ's and perform so amazingly on theater and night club stages frequently come back to their master. He scratches their heads, pats them, and deftly slips a dog M & M into the performer's mouth. Reward does not have to occur every time. It should at first occur immediately and frequently for successful performance, and periodically thereafter.

Gradually, teachers are coming to see that children can be made into star performers by operant conditioning. However, it takes much time to watch children as closely as a dog or chicken needs to be watched—and rewarded—if we want results that could be as spectacular in the school world. In a few schoolrooms, teachers use rewards for small approved acts. A word of praise for giving attention, raising one pupil's neat paper for others to see, displaying another's creative product, patting one's shoulder, smiling at another, noting another's prompt performance of an errand. The teacher is careful not to imply derogatory comparisons by praising a well-done piece of work. By reinforcing each pupil's effort the emphasis is on individual progress from there to here—from yesterday to today. Praise, pat, praise, notice, show, praise, smile, etc. etc. Thus, children love to learn. They also learn to love the process of learning. Positive reinforcement works at home, in school, and in life (Sherman, 1973).

In contrast, some teachers in conventional classrooms reinforce failure. They give attention when the pupil makes mistakes or does not do his assignment. He is placed in a special class for slow learners where his ego is undermined. He is called some derogatory name such as a "dyslexic" or "child with mixed dominance." This provides an additional negative reinforcement by providing a reason for neglecting him until a specialist appears to remedy the ego damage. The behaviorists are telling teachers that approved action needs to be positively reinforced. Reinforcement need not be continuous. It should be on some sort of periodic (regular or irregular) schedule. Individual recognition is a reinforcement that begets approved behaviors and facilitates learnings (Kinkade, 1973).

Pressey (1927) devised a drill machine that had five buttons. Pressing the right button for answers to questions caused a new problem to appear. Thus, the pupil was immediately reinforced—he had to try again for failure, but got to move forward for success. Skinner (1954) advanced the concept of teaching machines and programmed learning by demonstrating that learning could be facilitated by making such easy, step-by-step, progressions that failure was improbable and by reinforcing success.[2] He described some of the

[2]Skinner and a colleague have devised a programmed book for introductory psychology that illustrates this step-by-step progression that is reinforced by immediate knowledge of success:
   J. E. Holland and B. F. Skinner, *The Analysis of Behavior* (New York: McGraw-Hill Book Company, 1961). (Note the title, "Behavior" rather than "psychology.")

astonishing results with animals and pigeons obtained through operant conditioning. His analysis of effects of reinforcement then continues:

> From this exciting prospect of an advancing science of learning, it is a great shock to turn to that branch of technology which is most directly concerned with the learning process—education. Let us consider, for example, the teaching of arithmetic in the lower grades. The school is concerned with imparting to the child a large number of responses of a special sort. The responses are all verbal. They consist of speaking and writing certain words, figures, and signs which, to put it roughly, refer to numbers and to arithmetic operations. The first task is to shape up these responses—to get the child to pronounce and to write responses correctly, but the principal task is to bring this behavior under many sorts of stimulus control. This is what happens when the child learns to count, to recite tables, to count while ticking off the items in an assemblage of objects, to respond to spoken or written numbers by saying "odd," "even," "prime," and so on. Over and above this elaborate repertoire of numerical behavior, most of which is often dismissed as the product of rote learning, the teaching of arithmetic looks forward to those complex serial arrangements of responses involved in original mathematical thinking. The child must acquire responses of transposing, clearing fractions, and so on, which modify the order or pattern of the original material so that the response called a solution is eventually made possible.[3]

Skinner stated that 50 years ago learning such skills involved much drill and considerable negative reinforcement. The pupil learned the arithmetic tables, formulas, and operations in order to escape the application of a birch rod. Today the situation has not greatly improved. Behavior control is now sought through criticism by teachers, ridicule by classmates, teacher's displeasure for slow learning, low marks, a special report to parents, and so on. Then, says Skinner, we wonder why we have so many aggressive personalities.

Teachers can provide positive reinforcement by moving about the classroom giving praise, a nod, a pat, and help when necessary. They can score papers, but that is often 24 hours late as reinforcement. Fortunately, better means of positive reinforcement are available. Machine teaching or programmed books can be used. Class members can be positively and immediately reinforced for each of the correct responses to the 25,000 contingencies that are required in addition, subtraction, division, and multiplication. The machine does not just provide positive reinforcement for each successful step. It does not laugh at, ridicule, or punish an error when it is made. It simply waits while the student tries again and wins success *and* reinforcement.

---

[3]B. F. Skinner, "The Science of Learning and the Art of Teaching," *Harvard Educational Review*, Vol. 24, 1954, p. 90.

Success may be only a mild reinforcer but it can be supplemented by others. Commendation for finishing a day's program, privileges granted for completion, name checked on a list (though comparisons must be avoided).

Skinner continued in the same article with the same confidence that was expressed by Watson in the possibility of making an infant into what one preselected. It is the same confidence that is contained in his recent book, *Beyond Freedom and Dignity* (1971):

> There is a simple job to be done. The task can be stated in concrete terms. The necessary techniques are known. The equipment needed can easily be provided. Nothing stands in the way but cultural inertia. But what is more characteristic of America than an unwillingness to accept the traditional as inevitable? We are on the threshold of an exciting and revolutionary period, in which the scientific study of man will be put to work in man's best interests. Education must play its part. It must accept the fact that a sweeping revision of educational practices is possible and inevitable. When it has done this, we may look forward with confidence to a school system which is aware of the nature of its tasks, secure in its methods, and generously supported by the informed and effective citizens whom education itself will create.[4]

BEHAVIORISM AT WORK

The principle of conditioning is recognized in the business and political world as well as in the classroom. Conditioning is often effectively used in advertising, political campaigning, traffic law enforcement, and wife's control of spouse. If one hears a brand name often enough, he comes to think simultaneously of the brand name and the product, "Have a Pepsi!" Some words come to have special meaning through processes of conditioning. Mothers are revered and spoken of respectfully even though some mothers neglect or even batter their babies. Norman Thomas, a socialist of yesteryear, ran for president a number of times, expressing his socialistic ideas. He received a negligible number of votes. A few years later the ideas he expressed were implemented. His ideas took the form of unemployment insurance, social security, legal aid, educational assistance, housing improvement, and medicare but this time under the name "democracy." He could not win as a "socialist." However, socialistic ideas, when called democracy, may be approved.

Man is controlled by words, repetition, and reinforcement (samples in the mail, "free" trials, approval of fellowmen). During World

The control of man

---

[4]B. F. Skinner, "The Science of Learning and the Art of Teaching," *Harvard Educational Review*, Vol. 24, 1954, p. 97.

War II, by means of repetition, drill, exclusion of competing stimuli (*e.g.*, school and family), and reinforcement by Nazi leaders, a generation of fanatic[5] Nazis was raised in youth camps (Mann, 1938). As foreign observers of this conditioning of German children and youth, we give it the name indoctrination. Nazis called it youth development. In short, words are conditioners.

The conditioning of Nazi youth shows one of the possibilities of behaviorism applied in daily living. *Walden Two*, in the form of a novel, shows it in a more acceptable form. Peaceful, benevolent, hard-working, noncomplaining people go about the processes of marriage, child-rearing, education, work, play, and art happily and effectively because from infancy their lives have been conditioned (controlled) by wise and competent adults. Bruce summarizes the problem presented to the student of personality in the following passage:

> Thus, when addressing themselves to the problems and issues of our times, these psychologists [behaviorists], believing people's behavior to be a result of the forces exerted upon them, find their answers in terms of the manipulation of these forces. The ethical problem implicit in this system, of course, is that somebody, other than the persons affected, must decide the desired direction the behavior is to take. This necessarily calls for a "great man" philosophy of dealing with people—somebody who knows where the people should go. This system calls for leaders who are supermen of a sort, skilled in the manipulation of forces to get people to behave in the ways desired by the knowing few.
>
> As you can see, Skinner's projection of his system is garbed in benevolence; however, the technical question still remains as to who is to determine the desired direction behavior should take. And presumably this molding of human behavior would be the function of the schools, and we ask if this is the function we want education to perform.[6]

The questions for the reader are, "Are we conditioned by our past experiences (stimuli) to respond to the problem in a certain way? Are we capable of drawing from the past, looking into the future, and living with ambiguity now?"

Learning: behavioristic interpretation   Watson's psychology was a reaction not only to structuralism (introspection) but also to Thorndike's connectionistic theory. Thorndike had postulated three laws of learning based, as was behaviorism, on the *S-R* bond hypothesis. These laws were:

- *Effect*—A stimulus response bond is strengthened when it leads to satisfaction and is weakened (this aspect he later modified) when it leads to annoyance.

[5]They were "fanatic" because they were Nazi Germans. If they had been American youth they would have been called "dedicated" Americans.

[6]Paul Bruce, "Three Forces in Psychology and Their Ethical and Educational Implications," *Educational Forum*, Vol. 30, 1966, pp. 278, 279.

- *Exercise*—The more frequently a stimulus-response bond is exercised the stronger it becomes. Other things being equal, when a modifiable *S-R* connection is not used, it is weakened.
- *Readiness*—When a modifiable *S-R* bond is ready to act, to do so is satisfying; when the modifiable connection is not ready to act, to do so leads to annoyance.[7]

Watson proposed some modifications of Thorndike's postulations. He did not like the term "satisfaction" because satisfaction was a feeling or state of mind. This was one of those vague ideas that was not quantifiable. Hence, the law of effect was eliminated and (1) exercise, (2) recency, and (3) frequency were emphasized by Watson. The conditioned response was facilitated by its leading to a goal, or success in achieving the learner's purpose. He argued that successful responses were reinforced because, ultimately, the proper course (*e.g.*, a rat's running a maze) was the behavior most frequently and recently used.

In such terms, successful school learning is facilitated by drill, review, discussion, recitation, and practice. Certainly, much of current teaching practice seems to be based on these postulations. Exercise of correct responses is very much a part of machine teaching and programmed textbooks. These approaches work. Elam (1970), describing innovations being used in Texarkana, reports pupils who made reading gains of 2.7 grade years in six months. The average pupil gained 1.4 grade years in the same period. In addition, there was less vandalism. There were fewer dropouts when pupils used programmed texts and teaching machines and were thus immediately reinforced. Material reinforcements were liberally used—including green stamps and transistor radios as prizes.

Critics are ever-present in education, and despite the academic gains of pupils, they are asking questions about autonomy, freedom, and creativity. Most of the questions bear clearly on what effect the behavioristic orientation has on pupil personality:

How is **functional autonomy** to be achieved? What happens to the pupil as a self-starting and autonomous learner after the reinforcements bestowed by machines and teachers are removed?

Can pupils realistically be treated as animal organisms or as machine-like beings without regard for varying potentials and motivations?

How are problem solving and creative production to be encouraged if so much emphasis is placed on preplanned input? Why is there so little emphasis on self-concepts and uniqueness of perception?

Let it be admitted that drill, review, practice, and programmed

---

[7]In addition to these primary laws, Thorndike also postulated five supplementary principles. For further explanation see Harold W. Bernard, *The Psychology of Learning and Teaching*, third edition (New York: McGraw-Hill Book Company, 1972), pp. 126–142.

learning work well with pupils whose learning style is convergent—what about the pupils whose learning styles are creative-divergent?

Is concern about motivation, ambition, insight, freedom, and other abstract states of mind really just a reluctance to change (Skinner, 1971); or do these really constitute the essence of education?

Is it not possible that the human transaction, rather than drill, subject matter mastery, or success on a learning program, is the factor that counts most in the processes of personality formation?

Behavior modification: behavioristic therapy

Personality is composed of the results of the conditionings that one has experienced. Learning is the product of conditioning. So too are thinking, emotions, and socialization the products of conditioning—from the behavioristic point of view. When one has learned ineffective behaviors, or failed to acquire productive ones, he can be conditioned or reconditioned to modify his behavior by means of planned stimuli and reinforcements (Sherman, 1973). There is no need to probe the client's subconscious, no need to recount his unproductive and miserable past. The therapist decides what a better mode of living will be and plans a program of experiences. He devises a schedule of reinforcements that will produce more effective behavior.

> Phillip was a seriously withdrawn, psychologically isolated young man of eighteen years who was taken to a hospital where he sat on the floor, face to wall, head bowed, and arms around knees. He would not respond to greetings, demands, or adhere to routines. He refused to go to the dining room but would take food from others.
>
> Operant conditioning, with the help of high school aides, was initiated. Every time he moved he was given a piece of candy, cookie, or some fruit. Then reward was less frequently given. Larger movements were rewarded more frequently. Standing resulted in a bit of food plus a pat on the back and some praise. He still would not respond to the dinner bell. When, during the few minutes other patients were moving toward the dining room, he moved toward the dining room door he was rewarded with a bit of food. Soon he was moving steadily toward the dining room at meal hours. When he would take food in his hand or pick up a bit with fork or spoon he was praised. He was then able to feed himself. Operant conditioning was then begun on social behaviors, using praise and acceptance as reinforcers.

A seven-year-old boy, who had a school phobia, was treated by means of operant conditioning. The therapist arranged a doll-play milieu. For each 30-second interval that the boy, in his "separation anxiety," did not look at his mother, he was given material reinforcement in the form of an M & M. Social reinforcement in the form of praise was given. For each move forward—leaving his doll, getting on his bike, saying good-bye to his mother—he was reinforced. Parents were encouraged to reinforce for such progressive steps. After a few weeks and ten periods of 15 minutes, plus 20 bags of M & M's, the boy readily entered school (Patterson, 1965).

Respondent conditioning can also be used as a therapeutic approach. One used by therapists, who do not necessarily rely only on behavior modification for all types of problems, is that employed in the treatment of enuretic (bedwetting) children. The child lies on a blanket containing a grid of wires that, when wet, gives the child a mild shock or rings a bell that awakens him. After being wakened a number of times, the distended bladder, rather than the urination itself, awakens the subject and the apparatus can be set aside (Goldenson, 1970, p. 151).

Aversive conditioning has been used successfully with some alcoholics. The idea is to provide so much pain or discomfort in connection with taking a drink that that behavior is abandoned. The alcoholic is given a drug (antabuse, for example) that produces nausea if the person then takes a drink. The illness more than overbalances the glow of warmth, the feelings of conviviality, and the escape from burdens that were formerly the reinforcers for the drinker. Such therapy is usually supplemented by other therapeutic approaches—group therapy, catharsis, or work therapy, because alcoholics are notoriously sly in avoiding the taking of their prescribed dosage of antabuse.

Much talk and writing in education have centered about the matter of accenting the positive and eliminating the negative. Skinner has consistently pleaded for a reduction in aversive controls. He admits that there are occasions when reinforcement of "counter controls" are feasible. Neale (1969), basing his tentative judgments on the efficacy of treating some children's behaviors rather harshly—slapping the thighs, mild electric shocks—advises that we not too wholeheartedly endorse love and acceptance and positive reinforcement as the only approaches. Schizophrenic children have been reached through aversive techniques where a positive approach has failed. It seems that some withdrawn children are not at all anxious and some anxiety needs to be induced. This is not an all-out endorsement for cruelty. The long-range good of aversive techniques may, however, overbalance the temporary repugnance the methods evoke.

Behavior modification therapy had its origins in one of Watson's experiments. He succeeded in producing a conditioned fear of rats in babies by striking an iron triangle with a bar behind the subject's back to produce a startle response. As the baby touched the rat, the triangle was banged. The clang was sounded when the rat was three feet from the child. Then the noise came when the child saw the rat enter or being brought into the room. Automatically, the fear spread until not only rats, but dogs, cats, rabbits, and even mother's fur coat became fear-producing stimuli. Then the process of reconditioning was begun.

The baby was reassured, patted, or given a bite of cookie as pictures of rabbits were shown. Then toy rabbits were introduced, bringing them closer and closer as the baby was being fed and reassured. Finally, he was able again to handle a spoon with one hand and fondle a rabbit with the other.

Wolpe (1958) has described a case very similar to Watson's experiment. He concluded that the anxious states experienced by disturbed persons were incompatible with states of relaxation. He then induced relaxation by direct instruction or hypnosis. Relaxation was induced by providing the pleasant association of congenial company. The method is based on Wolpe's theory that neurotic-anxiety states are the results of prior conditionings. These conditionings have been built into habit patterns. If a response inconsistent with anxiety can be induced in the presence of the anxiety-provoking situation, it reduces the strength of the bond between stimulus and response. The process of doing this is called "reciprocal inhibition." Patient and therapist discuss the nature and origins of the disorder. Talking is one kind of contact with a fear or anxiety-arousing situation. One woman, afraid of cats, was little disturbed by seeing a picture of a kitten in the arms of a small child. She was reminded to keep relaxed. When kitten and child no longer produced any feeling of anxiety, therapist and client discussed a kitten's playing with a ball. Then a kitten with a ball was really presented. Next the process was continued with a big black tomcat. The principle involved is that of introducing an anxiety-producing stimulus concurrently with a state of relaxation and acceptance (Eysenck, 1967).

Krumboltz (1969) endorses the use of behavior modification in elementary and secondary school counseling. Respondent conditioning and operant conditioning can be used for treatment of behavior problems. It can prompt the counselee to make choices. It can be used to build habits of persistent application to school tasks. He does not recommend that behavior modification be used for all cases. The technique used must be adapted to the life style of the individual. He does, however, say to counselors (who are dedicated to nondirective or client-centered techniques) that there are some individuals who want, and need, counselors who will give advice and direction. Counselors who "have been there" can help a less sophisticated person avoid some of the pitfalls of life. Krumboltz admits that people perceive things differently and have varied needs. He thus departs from the Watsonian behaviorism that sees individuals, not as unique entities, but as mere products of conditioning environments.

The success of behavior modification, in its various forms, has been such in recent years as to elicit many hearty endorsements. It works—despite the skepticism of those who are somewhat horrified to think that the therapist makes decisions and plots courses (schedule of reinforcement) for others. In one study, a comparison was made of psychiatric patients before, immediately after, and ten months after treatment. Twenty per cent of patients experienced spontaneous recovery (no treatment) after ten months. About 40 per cent of those treated by approaches other than behavioral theory were cured but about 3 to 4 per cent regressed during the ten-month follow-up period. Seventy-five per cent of those helped through behavior therapy were cured. After treatment, the number kept rising so that about 85 per cent were reported cured at the time of follow-up. Thus, it was concluded that behavior therapy was more effective, faster, and more permanent than other therapies (Eysenck, 1967). Behavior modification has been increasingly used in the full range of personality dysfunctions. Thumb sucking, stuttering, and smoking have been successfully treated. Personality disorders such as homosexuality, transvestism, alcoholism, and drug addiction cases have responded positively. Hysterias, phobias, hypertension, asthma, and ulcers have also been responsive to such approaches (Goldenson, 1970, p. 153). Behavior modification is making rapid inroads into children's learning. It is used in the treatment of vomiting, mutism, prolonged crying, timidity, tantrums, and reading problems (White, 1970).

PROS AND CONS OF BEHAVIORISM

The basic idea of behaviorism—that behavior is shaped by experience —is widely accepted by psychologists in general. It should be noted, too, that behaviorism, as is the case with other psychological doctrines, is not just one clear-cut, "this and only this," view. Many behaviorists can find, along with their respect for conditioning and the formation of neural bonds, room for the purpose, drive, creativeness, and disparate perceptions of individuals. Many, however, find behaviorism unacceptable as *the* explanation for what one is and becomes. Allport (1965), for example, observed that although people seem to be busy preparing for their futures, psychology is engaged in tracing people's lives into the past. Bonner (1965) has noted that there are many violent criminal acts committed by persons whose lives contain no suggestion of violence, or whose gentle past behavior gave no indications of such predispositions. He gives priority to man's creative thrust into the future.

Critics dislike what is called the deterministic dogma of behaviorism. The mechanistic orientation means that causation precedes in a straight line, cumulative fashion. Many do not believe that adding all input results in a predictable sum. Murphy (1971) is emphatic in saying that psychology will not get very far if it depends on extrapolation from the past. As soon as we decide that we can think, choose, and determine the course that we will follow, rather than that we are

Criticisms of behaviorism

victims of an inscrutable nature, we will be using the findings of science to plot a better course.

Maslow (1972) was one of the more openly critical spokesmen for an orientation that went beyond behaviorism. He said that much that he learned about psychology as an undergraduate was pretty useless. It is possible to learn to salivate at the sound of a bell. It is possible to have the response extinguished through lack of reinforcement. However, nothing important was changed in the whole quantifiable, scientific process. What was gained or lost was of no significance whatever. Maslow was dissatisfied with the notion that man is conceptualized as an organism striving to maintain balance in the face of constantly varying stimuli. His **empirical** data led him to believe that very healthy individuals were not governed by the past, or by the present, any more than they were pulled toward the future. The heterostatic drive, in the healthy person, transcends the homeostatic one.

Argyris (1971), in reviewing Skinner's *Beyond Freedom and Dignity*, says that there is much to agree with in Skinner's presentation. We do need a science of behavior. Behavior is amenable to study. Operant conditioning does work in daily life and in therapeutic milieus. Argyris pays respect to the scholarly nature of Skinner's work—it is the most systematic known. However, he, like so many other critics, finds Skinner's behavioristic conception of man unacceptable. Man cannot be regarded in the same way in which physical scientists regard the world. The nature of man must be defined in terms of what he moves toward as well as in terms of what he moves from. Man is not just responsive to the environment—he selects *and* shapes that environment.

Emphasis on the processes of conditioning in experimental milieus leads Kaplan (1972) to refer to the kind of technology of behavior that Skinner endorses as "life in the cage." Kaplan's concern is not so much with the nature of man as it is with the manipulator. Kaplan is not satisfied with the criteria by which the controllers of a technology of behavior would be developed, selected, and (in their turn) be controlled.

> The primary purpose of Skinner's book is not to set up a model for the future so much as to eliminate the psychological obstacles in its path. He has unlimited confidence in the capacity of behavioral science to solve human problems; what he doubts is our will to use it. The chief obstacles are generated from what he calls the "literature of freedom and dignity." He is not specific, in fact he is surprisingly vague in his references to this literature, but we gather what he means easily enough. The reference could of course include the whole Western religious and literary tradition. Briefly, the troublesome postulate is the concept of individual autonomy in the ethical sphere, the responsibility and the right to choose behavior.[8]

[8]Harold Kaplan, "Life in the Cage," (A review of B. F. Skinner's *Beyond Freedom and Dignity*), *Commentary*, Vol. 53, No. 2, 1972, p. 82.

Most critics are harsh in their condemnation of Skinner for his conception of man. They dislike his assumption that we know what the "good life" should be for all people. They do not like elimination of thought, decisions, feelings, and values. Kateb (1971) is not just harsh in his criticism. He expresses fear that if the society that Skinner endorses in *Walden Two* and *Beyond Freedom and Dignity* were to become a reality, the sentiments of civilized life would be extinguished. While freedom and dignity would, indeed, go, so too would purpose—except to go on living. Life would be painless; it would be a "wordless world." While Kateb perceived *Walden Two* as having a self-confident but conciliatory author, he sees no such humility in the author of *Beyond.* Beyond freedom and dignity is the image of a person who is not responsible for anything he does. Being a good or bad person, a good or bad worker, is of no value consequence. One is blameless because he is a creation, and a creature of his environment. Praise and blame are meaningless. The expression of thanks to a person conditioned to be polite is puzzling—why should one be thanked for something when there is no alternative?

> I know that it could be said that using the language of manners is just more behavior, learned like any other, and often automatic. If that is the case, why does Skinner exclude the language of manners from his Utopia instead of conditioning people in its use? The large point, I fear, is that *language itself* is incompatible with his Utopia of environmental determinism. That is really what *Beyond Freedom and Dignity* shows. Not only does he find the language of manners inappropriate, unnecessary, philosophically untenable, but by trying to undermine the practice of praise and blame, in the fullest senses of these words, he is casting out the language of judgment altogether. And by doing that he is stripping life of much of its recognizable content. Much of life is talk; much of talk is taken up with judgment—moral, aesthetic, social, emotional, erotic. Let us be clear: It is not the sublime dumbness of mysticism toward which Skinner's idealism moves. It is rather closer to the societies of *1984* and their Newspeak—the atrophy of consciousness through the shriveling of language. Skinner's Utopia approaches the wordless.[9]

At this time in the history of psychology and the study of personality, it is easy to focus on the flood of criticism that followed the latest behavioristic publication. However, the criticism of early behaviorism with personality being considered as an outcome of conditioning ("give me any healthy, well-formed babies . . .") was equally bitter. Watson was, even more than Skinner, *persona non grata* in psychological society. Mothers followed his advice not to spoil the infant with some regret. Picking him up, cuddling him, talking to him when he was in misery was proscribed. Simply feed him, keep him clean and dry and let him bawl—if you do not want to spoil him and reinforce

---

[9]George Kateb, "Toward a Wordless World," (A review of B. F. Skinner's *Beyond Freedom and Dignity*), *Atlantic*, Vol. 228, No. 4, October, 1971, p. 124.

objectionable behavior. This mechanistic execution of maternal functions is now regarded as having disastrous consequences. It tends to produce adults who have little feeling for others. Despite efforts to guide, persuade, and educate young people to behave in certain ways and to develop kind, loyal, flexible, and creative personality traits, we tend to be abhorred by compulsion used on others—brain-washing and indoctrination. Not all feel this way. There are those who would keep sex education, communism, and "controversial" subjects from being taught in schools.

If there are some who want their children not to be "conditioned" on some subjects there are some, equally dangerous, parents who do not want their children conditioned at all. They have gone so far with freedom and dignity that the growing child is left without values, and boundaries, and directional orientation. It seems to be a possibility that criticism of behaviorism is so vehement because it is one of the realities of life.

Contributions of behaviorism

Many of the contributions of behaviorism have been so sound that they have been thoroughly incorporated into the "mainstream" of psychology. The insistence on measurement and objectivity, on behavior rather than attitudes and will, is reflected in psychological experimentation today. It is true that some psychological conditions are not now amenable to such quantification. However, researchers aver that when adequate instrumentation is discovered or devised, our scientific psychology will be improved. The weakness of behaviorism, in this respect, is that insistence on measurement and objectivity as the only acceptable approach makes it necessary to overlook or avoid certain dynamic aspects of personality. Maslow (1972), for instance, insists that measuring the number of trials it takes a pupil to learn certain facts is of much less consequence than the empirical observation of how and why that pupil approaches self-actualization.

Intelligence testing is not a creation of behaviorism; but the way intelligence is assessed fits the behavioristic orientation: Intelligence is evaluated in terms of what one knows and does under stipulated conditions. It should be noted, however, that despite rather general acceptance over a number of years, there is currently a strong and growing protest regarding the validity of the widely used approaches ("Ethical Forum . . . ," 1972; Herrnstein, 1971). (This subject receives extensive treatment in Chapter 15.)

Behaviorism must be given credit for extending the use of psychology from the university classroom and psychological laboratory to the realm of business, industry, and child-rearing. It extended the scope of psychology beyond mind and consciousness to body, behavior, and concrete matter. One of the contributions of behaviorism was the emphasis on early conditioning. Fraiberg (1971) has traced certain defective personalities (persons without normal feelings and sentiments) to lack of warm mothering in the first 12 critical months of life. Harlow (1972), deriving his postulations from the study of infant monkeys, confirms the behavioristic position by proposing that today's inadequate mothering had its origin in inadequate mothers of yester-year. Only by prolonged therapy administered by patient monkey therapists can the damage of early maternal deprivation be counter-balanced.

There is plenty of evidence that behaviorism has had, and continues to have, great impact on classrooms. The prevailing doctrine is behavioristic: Control the environment to control behavior. Environment is the prime determinant of the academic personality. If pupils do not learn, it is because they do not have competent teachers who provide feedback and reinforcement. Poor learning occurs because the materials are not suitably programmed (organized) and presented. With this, many persons, including the author, tend largely to agree. There is a place for drill, practice, reinforcement, and discipline. Facts of arithmetic, for instance, must not only be understood (Gestalt orientation), they must also be automatic when the processes of computation are put into action. However, in addition, the pupil has some input. He has some intrinsic talents and interests—that may not be entirely shaped by prior conditioning. Furthermore (beware the author's opinion), as the pupil grows older, in the secondary and college years, it becomes possible to lengthen the time gap between *S-R.* The gap can be used to think and choose—*to become responsible.* In short, as positive, objective, and undeniable as are behavioristic interpretations, something more seems to be needed in personality theory.

Delgado (1972), a specialist in brain physiology and the relation-ship of brain manipulation to behavior, states that he agrees with and admires Skinner's recent book. The conditioning of which Skinner speaks begets results similar to those obtained through psychoactive drugs, psychosurgery, and direct chemical and electrical stimulation of the brain. Operant conditioning has been used

> . . . for educating normal and mentally deficient students and also as therapy for different types of deviant behavior, from homosexuality to phobias. Professor Skinner's recent book, *Beyond Freedom and Dignity*, represents a significant contribution to science and philoso-phy. I admire and agree with a good part of Skinner's ideas, including the necessity to design cultures and establish intelligent purpose in the behavioral shaping of the individual.[10]

Delgado continues with the support of a strong behavioristic orienta-tion in stating that hate and destruction are not functional properties

---

[10]José M. R. Delgado, "Brain Manipulation: Psychocivilized Direction of Behavior," *Humanist*, Vol. 32, No. 2, March/April, 1972, p. 13.

of the brain. They are the result of sensory input. They do not originate in the person but derive from environment. This becomes a debatable question when one considers that violent psychotic actions, accompanied by abnormal brain waves, have been controlled by surgery or drugs. Not all abnormal brain waves can be blamed on illness, injury, or stress.

The contributions of behaviorism might well be considered from the perspective of the current leading exponent of operant conditioning. Skinner, in response to one of his critics, states that

> A science of behavior does not, Floyd Matson notwithstanding (1971), dehumanize man; it dehomunculizes him. It rejects explanations of human behavior in terms of feelings, states of mind, and mental processes, and seeks alternatives in genetic and environmental histories. It treats a person as an object, but as an object of extraordinary subtlety and complexity, and by doing so it comes to understand him in the sense in which other sciences understand their subject matters.[11]

In Skinner's view, behaviorism is humanistic. It is humanistic because it has the distinction of facing the facts and being effective.

SUMMARY

Behaviorism originated as a protest against introspection as constituting a valid scientific method. It survives on the basis of using only behavior—covert or overt—as productive scientific evidence. Thinking, for example, is a process of mind, but it becomes explicable as a language behavior, (*i.e.*, talking to oneself). Conditioning, either classical or operant, is regarded by behaviorists as the source of man's personality, learning, and behavior.

In respondent conditioning, the simultaneous presentation of adequate and substitute stimuli, together with reward, results in making the substitute stimulus sufficient to produce a given response.

Operant conditioning means that a self-originated, on-going action is reinforced in order to ensure its persistence. Reward is withheld to promote the extinction of undesirable ongoing actions. Operant conditioning works effectively in animal laboratories and also in classrooms for children. Unwittingly, teachers sometimes reinforce undesirable behaviors. They tend to withhold reinforcement for the behaviors they are trying to obtain. School approaches to systematic reinforcement are programmed texts and teaching machines. Immediate feedback and reinforcement constitute the basic rationale for these approaches.

[11]B. F. Skinner, "Humanistic Behaviorism," *Humanist*, Vol. 31, No. 3, May/June, 1971, p. 35.

Behaviorism can be, and has been, applied to daily living. Skinner proposed the conditioning of people to become peaceful, benevolent, hard-working, noncomplaining members of society. Critics are shocked by the idea that some men should assume the role of conditioners, or controllers, of the destinies of others.

Behaviorism can be, and is, used effectively in school learning. Drill, review, recitation, practice, and programmed and machine teaching are applications of behaviorism. The use of immediate and positive reinforcement do result in academic gain. Critics challenge with questions about ego concepts, learning autonomously, and learning creativity. The critics want to know what is going to happen to human personality as a result of applied behaviorism.

Operant conditioning can be applied in the remediation of ineffective, or maladaptive, behaviors. Classical conditioning is also used in the treatment of some behaviors. Aversive conditioning is used effectively in the treatment of drug abuse and alcoholism, as well as with schizophrenic children.

The critics of behaviorism focus on the mechanistic conception of man. They dislike the idea of determinism. They question who is to be the controller. The elimination of choice and responsibility is an unwelcome thought.

The contributions of behaviorism are undeniable. Emphasis on early childhood, conditioning environments, drill and reinforcement in school learning and in therapy prove the validity of behaviorism. This point of view highlights the need for a science of behavior. The question raised is, "Is it the only avenue to the scientific study of personality?"

SUGGESTED READINGS

ARGYRIS, CHRIS, "Essay Review: Beyond Freedom and Dignity," *Harvard Educational Review*, Vol. 41, 550–561, 1971.
> *This review condenses the basic tenets of behaviorism and summarizes the competing existential theory. In so doing, a balanced presentation is given that allows the student room to make his own decision and choice.*

DELGADO, JOSÉ M. R., "Brain Manipulation: Psychocivilized Direction of Behavior," *Humanist*, Vol. 32, No. 2, 10–15, March/April, 1972.
> *A brain physiologist indicates that drugs, electrical stimulation, and surgery, in addition to conditioning techniques, are ways to direct brain action and, consequently, behavior and personality.*

EYSENCK, HANS J., "New Ways in Psychotherapy," *Psychology Today*, Vol. 1, No. 2, 39–47, June, 1967.
> *Various forms of behavior modification—simple conditioning, aversive control, reciprocal inhibition, instrumental conditioning—are showing high rates of recovery for disturbed personalities. Eysenck believes that these approaches hold promise for rehabilitation that are somewhat lacking in other therapeutic approaches.*

KAPLAN, HAROLD, "Life in the Cage—Beyond Freedom and Dignity," *Commentary*, Vol. 53, No. 2, 82–86, February, 1972.

   The author is harshly critical of Skinner's behaviorism on the grounds that it would dispense with the values that civilized culture has laboriously cultivated through the centuries.

KINKADE, KATHLEEN, "Commune: A Walden Two Experiment," *Psychology Today*, Vol. 6, No. 8, 35–42, 1973.

   Some of the trials and triumphs of a community run on Skinner's Walden Two *principles are described. Since 1967, a community in Twin Oaks, Virginia, has been testing behavioristic teachings.*

SKINNER, B. F., "Beyond Freedom and Dignity," *Psychology Today*, Vol. 5, No. 3, 37–80, August, 1971.

   This article is a condensation of his book that has stirred much protest in psychological circles. The facts are not strongly questioned but the philosophy and the implications arouse much concern.

FOLLOW-UP LEARNING ACTIVITIES

Read the article by Kinkade (Suggested Readings) and tell whether or not you think the experiment will, in the long run, be successful.

Yes _____ No _____ because _____

_____

_____

_____

_____

_____

If a Walden Two community were possible, who do you think should design it?

____ philosophers   ____ physicians   ____ educators
____ anthropologists   ____ clergymen   other _____

Comment: _____

_____

_____

_____

_____

Why do critics claim that behaviorism makes it impossible to blame a person for misconduct?

_____

_____

_____

_____

_____

Define, or give a concept of the following:

Aversive conditioning _____

_____

Respondent conditioning _____

_____

Operant conditioning _____

_____

Reinforcement _____

_____

Functional autonomy _____

_____

Stimulus-response gap _____

_____

Behavior modification _____

_____

/three/
Applying Personality Theory

11
Personality and Occupations

Does occupation shape personality or does personality dictate the choice?

LEARNING ACTIVITIES

Check the statement that you believe to be most accurate:

_____ One must have a job that fits his personality if he is to be happy and efficient.

_____ Aptitude and interest inventories can tell one what job fits his personality.

_____ If one is to be happy and efficient he must make his personality fit the job available.

_____ Most job dissatisfaction is caused by low income and long hours of work.

Check the most important factor of the following in job satisfaction.

____ intelligence   ____ prestige   ____ interest

____ motivation   ____ social demand   ____ education

(Compare and discuss with three or four classmates. The author's choice is listed below.)

Check the following as being true (T), false (F), or questionable (Q).

_____ One should select an occupation and stick to it for life.

_____ I agree with the author and have checked motivation in the second item.

_____ Today's worker seems to be most concerned with involvement in, and meaning of, the job.

_____ The most important factor in job satisfaction is security and amount of income.

_____ On today's labor market one would be wise to take the job available and assume responsibility for developing an interest in it.

_____ Twenty-five per cent, or more, of the population does not have the intelligence to become a doctor or an engineer.

_____ Level of intelligence is more important than social personality in job success.

_____ A worker tends to be involved when his voice is listened to.

Motivation—includes prestige, interest, and social demand.

One typically spends more of his adult years as a worker than he does in marriage. However, much more is researched and written relating to personality and marriage than on personality in occupations. Two problems regarding personality and occupational satisfaction and production seem to predominate: (1) occupational guidance and the choosing of a career, and (2) personal satisfaction and occupational productiveness. In each of these areas there are confident conclusions regarding the problem (choosing a career and job satisfaction) when personality and job are matched. Unfortunately, time and circumstance do not always (perhaps not even often) allow for such matching.

This chapter should promise the reader that the facts regarding personality in occupations will be separated from widespread fantasies. The actual promise is much less confident. The chapter does assure the reader that he will be exposed to the biases of the author. Those biases are little altered by a recent decade of team teaching experience in counselor education. There is an attempt to present the opposing points of view with some degree of fairness.

The discussion unveils a leaning toward the postulations of culture theory and the theory of perceptual psychology. One bias is that hereditary and intellectual limitations in occupational choice are played down. A second bias is that personal choice is not a very helpful guide in one's work life. More emphasis is placed on the adaptability of workers. There must be more emphasis placed on how one sees himself and his vocation, than on personality-job fit. The reader may recall that it is good theory (see Chapter 1) if it stimulates questioning and further search and if the theory fits current data.

PERSONALITY IN OCCUPATIONS

Need satisfaction

What one believes to be the nature of man (see Chapter 1) is intimately related to how the relationship of work and personality is perceived. One perspective seems to be that humans have an aversion for work: Man is naturally a lazy creature, and so is woman. People work to satisfy basic needs and, as soon as possible, turn to things that bring greater satisfaction. This seems to be the orientation that dictates much of current business and industrial practice. Another perspective is that work is a means of self-fulfillment. It is an avenue to self-actualization. The latter concept would assert that work is a way of life rather than a means of making a living.

Probably most workers the world over find that work is merely a means of making a living. It is so difficult for them to satisfy physiological and safety needs that it is difficult to perceive work as an avenue to satisfaction of higher level needs. Some miners and factory workers are able to see beyond the execution of their jobs. They are able to see work as a means of self-expression and the fulfillment of purpose. In part, whether the job is a task or a triumph is a matter of perception. A clue may be obtained from poetry:

> So live, that when thy summons comes to join
> The innumerable caravan which moves
> To that mysterious realm,
>   where each shall take
> His chamber in the silent halls of death,
> Thou go not, like the quarry-slave at night,
> Scourged to his dungeon, but,
>   sustained and soothed . . .

> William Cullen Bryant,
>
> *Thanatopsis.*

Bryant appears to assume that man has a choice in how he lives. Man has a responsibility for developing a perspective. The quarry-slave seems not to have such choice. But somewhere on the scale between the quarry-slave and the creative freelancer, the dictates of the job may be made to mesh with how the job is viewed. In part, how they are paired depends on the perspective one develops (phenomenology).

It is easy to see how work tends to fulfill physiological needs of food and shelter. It is not difficult to see work as a source of acceptance and esteem needs (Borow, 1964, p. XV). The dilemma, in the esteem needs, is that those occupations that are difficult, or take much time to prepare for, or that yield comparatively high income are the ones that beget social esteem. We do not, in our culture, typically perceive the carpenter, mechanic, waste disposal worker, or laborer as being prestigious. This occurs despite the fact that the work itself is highly significant. The needed correction is not about to be made by society. Schools and citizens are not likely to pronounce the wage earner in ecological conservation as being more prestigious than teachers, physicians, or investment brokers. It then becomes a matter of "boot-strap" lifting, or levitation. Each worker must find and verbalize the purpose and importance of his work if job satisfaction is to be achieved.

The really fortunate worker is the one who reaches the higher level need of self-actualization in both his working life and daily living. There is, to such a person, the challenge to become the highest quality workman he possibly can be. Maslow (1970) makes it clear that this is not entirely a matter of cultural prestige. It can appear in a "mere housewife." It can be seen in a "lowly clerk" who does his task efficiently, cheerfully, and with an air that enhances the good feelings (oneness with life processes) of those about him. The sometimes unpleasant fact is that when this is not done, the work tends to become monotonous, drudgery-laden, and onerous. A popular slogan a number of years ago concerned a boy who was carrying his smaller brother to Boys' Town who said, "He's not heavy. He's my brother." The saying has pertinence for all workers.

Work is not intrinsically satisfying, or dissatisfying. Some work conventionally, or culturally, begets respect. Other work is satisfying in terms of what the worker perceives as his contribution. The person who opens his eye to the reality that life entails some drudgery and obligation makes tedium more tolerable. Thus, the student, who is required by school regulations to take a required course, can complain about relevance. He can seek the satisfaction of doing that which is required as a challenge to his own sound performance. Work can thus be the avenue for maintaining self-respect (Samler, 1964, p. 418).

Values of work   In addition to need satisfaction, there are other psychological values of work. It may be used to provide some "spice in life." It provides varied avenues for exercising some of the major facets of personality—mental, physical, social, and emotional. It has been postulated that the higher an organism is on the phylogenetic scale, the greater is the need for the arousal of cortical activity. A cat or sloth can move and live at a slow pace, but man needs to engage in activity. If man is to survive he must satisfy his need for cortical stimulation (Herzberg, 1966, p. 32). This can be done, even in physical labor jobs, in trying to devise more efficient methods. Some types of work provide more intellectual, physical, or social challenge than do others. The emotional challenge, however, resides largely in how one regards his tasks.

Bartley (1971), analyzing the phenomenon of tiredness, found that

1. Tiredness may occur during the day and disappear in the evening.
2. We may wake in the morning feeling tired.
3. Tiredness occurs more frequently than otherwise when we are performing an unwelcome task.
4. We can be tired at one task but immediately tackle another with freshness.
5. The mere thought of an unwelcome task may make us tired.
6. We can work long at a pleasant task without rest.
7. When fatigued, we are unenthusiastic but rarely fatigued when enthusiastic.
8. More mistakes are made when we are tired.
9. Tiredness on a given job persists into the next session of that same job.
10. We are not able always to analyze what makes us tired.

Bartley does make an analysis: A common belief and conventional theory indicates that tiredness results from depletion of bodily energy and accumulation of metabolic waste. Bartley explains tiredness in terms of psychological processes. His interpretation of his research is that fatigue is a concomitant of aversion for, or feeling of inadequacy in, a particular field of activity.

We can translate Bartley's theory from tiredness to work in that it appears that the values of work depend to a considerable extent on how the worker views his role. Behavioristic theory would indicate that the values of work are inherent in the environmental condition. *In part*, we must agree. Perceptual theory suggests that the values of work inhere in large measure in how one's tasks are perceived. That view, too, appears to be plausible.

Work provides release from tensions. Providing meaningful work for inmates of prisons is considered to be a major problem in their rehabilitation. Finding a job for the ex-offender is a concern in progressive custodial institutions ("Prison Jaycees . . . ," 1972). A similar challenge is presented to those concerned with the lives of mentally handicapped and psychologically disturbed persons. In the more commonplace worlds of life, the person who has suffered the loss of a loved one finds the bereavement easier to cope with if he gets back on the job as soon as possible. Unfortunately, members of society sometimes unthinkingly criticize the bereaved one who does so as a penny-pincher.

One explanation of the alienation of so many of today's youth is that they are so largely denied a role in the work world (Figure 11.1). Tension is created by their willingness to work and denial of the opportunity (Barinbaum, 1972). Schools and communities that have sought to give youth a work role, even though it be unpaid and volunteer, have found that tensions are less likely to be noted. Goodman (1971), commenting on a tutoring program in which high school students were involved, says,

> The program is not limited to bright students but is open to all as an elective. Those who want to participate are selected more on the basis of attitude and sense of responsibility than on grade standing. Poorer students who show an interest are, in fact, encouraged to take part. Predictably, they generally complete the term having made significant gains themselves in addition to helping the tutored child.
>
> "Our experience with the George Washington program has contributed to a new conception of the potential contribution of volunteers," she says. "Obviously, we will continue our established program of recruiting adult volunteers as classroom aides and tutors. But if we are to fulfill our role as a catalyst for change, then we must draw upon all the resources the community has to offer. The young people at George Washington have taught us that such resources are more plentiful than we might otherwise have imagined."[1]

[1]Lillian Goodman, "Citizen Power: Tutoring for Credit," *American Education*, Vol. 7, No. 3, April, 1971, p. 27.

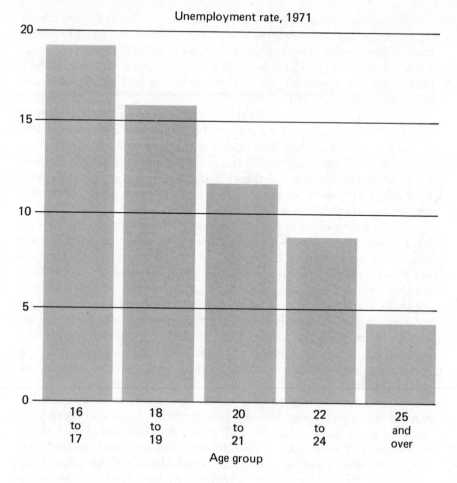

Unemployment rate, 1971

Age group

Unemployment rates for workers 20 to 24 are much lower than teenage rates but still far above the rate for adults 25 and over.

Source: Manpower Report of the President, 1972, Washington, D. C.: U. S. Department of Labor, p. 91.

Figure 11.1   *Teenager and youth unemployment.*

Depending upon how he views himself and the job he is currently doing, the worker becomes more knowledgeable. Some persons stick closely to a certain kind of work. Some loggers, for instance, may not seek other employment during off seasons. Others add to their logging experiences commercial fishing, road construction work, or operation of heavy equipment on various jobs. Some use a particular skill as a means of geographical mobility. For example, long-haul diesel truck drivers may operate from bases in various cities. Teachers may follow a similar course. They teach the same subject in the same school, or teach various subjects in different localities. A doctor may move his practice from one community to another; he may shift his affiliation from one hospital or clinic to another. Thus, there is truth in the contrast that school board members encounter, expressed or implied in the following: "This teacher has had one year of experience repeated twenty times," or "This teacher has had twenty years of experience."

The optimistic worker generates energy in himself and others. This is the clear implication of Bartley's research. Because optimism causes one to focus on the pleasant and fortunate things that happen during work, one is less likely to become tired, error-prone, and disgruntled about himself and others. The optimistic worker tends to see opportunity. His role is one of involvement, as contrasted to the worker who does his work in the oppressive atmosphere of obligatory functioning.

THEORIES OF OCCUPATIONAL CHOICE AND PERSONALITY

Concern about matching job and personality started with Frank Parsons, a Boston settlement house worker, who sought to help young men find jobs where they could perform well. The aim was to help them find enough personal satisfaction to become and remain productive. Parsons began his work in 1908 and it soon caught on in schools. Then "moral" and personal guidance were added. Between 1908 and 1970 guidance shifted more and more to personal matters of social adjustment, attitudes, and perception of self and others. Educational as well as occupational choice became concerns.

Genesis of the need for theory in vocational choice

In 1970 a school concept called "Career Development" received federal support. Many schools, indeed many school systems, are attempting to orient pupils toward thinking about "career clusters." This means that a pupil, in his thinking about a vocational life plan, would be encouraged to narrow his choice to a field such as health services. Therein he could think about work as a custodian or maintenance engineer. He might plan to be a technical aide, practical nurse, licensed nurse, equipment operator, clerk, medical records keeper, diagnostician, general practitioner, surgeon, or hospital administrator. Thus, there seems to be a "swing of the pendulum" back to Parson's days and the attempt to match man and job.

The psychological cupboard in Parson's day was bare in terms of personality assessment. Today many instruments are available for the assessment of intelligence. There are many questionnaires, inventories, and schedules used in the assessment of personality. In addition, there are a number of theories relating worker to job. In short, the guidance worker of the 1970's has something in the psychological cupboard to use in his work. Some skeptics (perhaps overly cautious persons), including the author, doubt that what is in the cupboard amounts to much more than cotton candy—a sweet taste but a very minute amount of substance. There will be more about this later in the chapter.

Roe: Choice as a function of life processes

Roe (1964) perceives occupational choice as a lifelong process. Occupational behavior is conditioned by the personality of the worker and personality is conditioned by the occupation. In addition, she says that there are a number of other factors that condition occupational choice: the socioeconomic position of the family, the state of the culture (depression, recession, or booming war-time economy), and the stage of technology in relation to the labor market.

Interpersonal relations are an important facet of Roe's hypothesis. She conceptualizes persons as warm or cold. The warm person tends to accept persons while the cold person tends to avoid them. The warm person is casual, loving, and protective. The cold person is neglecting, rejecting, and demanding. The warm person is oriented toward persons and the cold person is oriented toward things. Thus, occupational preference has its origins in the early life of the individual.[2] Roe focused more on parental attitudes than on child-rearing techniques. Parental emotional concentration on the child predisposes him to a preference of occupations oriented toward persons (social work, teaching, sales). Parental neglect or indifference predisposes the child toward ideas or things (research, mechanics, technical work). Her own follow-up studies did not disprove the hypothesis. However, there were many exceptions. The reference she made to culture, prosperity-depression, and technological influences must be kept in mind.

Super: Choice as a reflection of personality

Super (1963) postulates that in making a vocational choice one is expressing his idea of the kind of person one is.

> The implementation or actualizing of self concepts is the result of these processes [stages in the development of self concepts] as professional training is entered or as education is completed and the young man or woman moves from school or college into the world of work. In an early phase, the premedical student enters medical school, proud of his developing sense of professional identity. In a later phase, the young engineering graduate gets his first job as an engineer, and rejoices in his new title, symbol of his having converted a self concept into a reality; the young executive trainee who finishes his rotations through the planned sequence of training

[2]Note the similarity to psychoanalytic theory, wherein the seeds of emotional well-being or neuroticism are sown in child-parent relationships and ordinal position in the family (Chapter 7).

positions and settles at his own desk, with his own name-plate in front of him, feels that he has finally achieved success. At the other extreme, the high school dropout who never did well in his studies, who was never accepted by his classmates, and who is fired from the job that he finally got only after a number of rejections, finds the occupational translation of his self concept as ne'er-do-well confirmed and implemented. After a series of negative experiences, it takes a great deal of re-education to help him develop more positive self concepts, to find a suitable occupational translation of this favorable picture of himself, and to turn it into a reality. With the population explosion in the labor market which we shall now have every summer for years to come, the unfortunates who enter the market with poor self concepts and inadequate vocational translations of these self concepts will have all too many opportunities to confirm them.

These appear to be the elements of a self concept theory of vocational development. They are still not formulated as testable hypotheses, but, judging by the research results so far, they do suggest and permit the formulation of hypotheses which tend to stand up when tested, and they can be helpful to counselors in dealing with the vocational decision making of students.[3]

The role of the self-concept is reflected in another aspect of Super's (1957) theoretical formulation. Life and vocational choice evolve through stages. In adolescence exploration is the task, while stabilization is the adult task. The process may be divided into substages as follows: tentative, transition, trial-exploratory, establishment-trial, and stabilization. Super sees no need for a definitive choice during adolescence, aside from the matter of giving choice some consideration. The stages of trial-exploratory and establishment-trial may occur between the ages of 25-35; and typically one then does settle down. It should be noted that early choice is not considered to be a handicap. However, early choice is no more highly correlated with success and satisfaction than is later choice. It appears, to the author, that the most significant *and* applicable aspect of Super's theory is the idea that both career selection and satisfaction are functions of one's total personality and life style.

Havighurst (1964) perceives all of life as a succession of developmental tasks. These tasks are unique for early childhood, middle childhood, early adolescence, adolescence, youth, early adulthood, middle age, and for the senior citizen. Tasks are rooted in one's chronological age, level of physical and mental development, socioeconomic status, and the broader culture. Successful completion of the tasks at each age prepare one for his next developmental tasks. Success predisposes one to satisfactions and the earning of esteem from others. Failure to

Havighurst: Successive developmental tasks

[3]D. E. Super *et al.*, *Career Development: Self-Concept Theory* (New York: College Entrance Examination Board, 1963), pp. 13–14.

achieve one's age-appropriate tasks makes one unhappy, lacking in esteem, and leaves one unprepared for tackling the next developmental tasks. Life is, in short, just one _____ developmental task after another.[4]

Occupational choice and activity also follow a similar developmental sequence. From age five to ten the child identifies with a worker and develops a concept of work which becomes part of his ego ideal. From age ten to 15, one acquires basic work habits such as learning to organize one's time and energy and to get one's work done. From age 15 to 20, one acquires his identity as a worker. He chooses his job and prepares, through education and work experience, for the job that gives him some assurance of monetary autonomy. From age 25 to 40, he becomes a productive worker. He progressively masters the skills of his career and moves up the scale of responsibility. From age 40 to 70 one shifts from the personal aspects of work to maintaining a productive society and perceives himself as a contributing citizen who assumes some share of the welfare of others. Beyond age 70 one looks back to contemplate a productive and responsible career.

Ginzberg: Ages and stages

Ginzberg *et al.* (1951) also regard occupational choice as a developmental process. Early choice, up to about age 11, is a stage of fantasy. Choice is highly personal, subjective, and imitative. Whatever is emphasized on radio and television, or in stories he reads, may be reflected in his fantasies—cowboys, pilots, baseball players, and circus performers seem to be roles to challenge a boy's prowess. The next stage, lasting until about age 17, is the tentative period. It consists in the assessment of several alternatives in terms of interests, capacities, values, and readiness. The third stage, subsequent to the age of about 17, is called the realistic choice period. This embraces not only thinking about one's personality traits but also the matter of availability of opportunity. There may be, in this stage, an element of frustration when one finds that his psychological motives and subjective desires are not in harmony with the demands and restrictions of the world of work.

A SKEPTICAL VIEW OF OCCUPATIONAL CHOICE THEORY

The pertinence of personality

Earlier chapters have shown that personality originates in part from family, socioeconomic status, and culture (*e.g.*, Samoans—Americans). If the culture and personality of a seaman are different from that of a

[4]A condensed version of developmental tasks from middle childhood through youth is presented in H. W. Bernard, *Psychology of Learning and Teaching*, third edition (New York: McGraw-Hill Book Company, 1972), pp. 260–266.

business executive, then it seems that it would be possible to say that occupation shapes personality as much as it attracts a given type. Super (1963, p. 14) suggests that whether one is employed as a laborer or young doctor, one's initial success or failure, and the pattern of success or failure thereafter, is a consideration that has much bearing on job performance and satisfaction from it.

A twenty-eight year old glazier sought help from a counseling service to determine a kind of job that would yield greater satisfaction than his present one. He had heard, he said, of some tests that could be taken to determine aptitudes and interests. The counselor assured him that there were tests that purported to do just that. However, the counselor preferred to get acquainted with the client before giving the battery of tests. Such a procedure was agreeable to the client.

A miserable story of failure and frustration was related. As a high school student the boy was frequently absent and reported several episodes of conflict with teachers. He had been expelled once for fighting. Indians and blacks were especially vulnerable to his displeasure. He dropped out of school in his sophomore year. Shortly thereafter was "kicked out" of the home by his father, with whom he had had many arguments and two physical fights. He was "kicked out" on the occasion of his calling his mother names when he came home drunk. He left Arizona by box-car and drifted from town to town, working at odd jobs for short periods. He consistently got "canned" for argumentativeness and failure to show up for work when nursing a hang-over. He served a short prison term in Idaho for assault with a deadly weapon. He had been drunk and had attacked a fellow traveler with a knife.

Arriving in Portland, he got a job as a glazier. Shortly after starting to work, he was sent to another city for a brief training session. He responded to the recognition and settled down to doing a good job. He got married, had a son and then seemed to relapse into his old life style. He argued with his bosses, missed work days, but was kept on because his work was fast and competent. His bosses recognized his incompatability with others and, as much as possible, assigned him to jobs that required only one man. His life style was showing itself at home. He and his wife had many arguments and once in a while he "pushed her around." She left him after five years when he severely beat their four-year-old son.

He left Portland but came back after a year of wandering and two arrests and was hired by another glass company. His hostilities resulted in his being fired. He then got back his job with his former employer. Now, after being threatened with dismissal, he sought vocational counseling.

During the fourth counseling session, after the foregoing had been revealed and reiterated in several sessions, the client sat for 30–45 seconds, then looked at the counselor and said, "_____ ! I'm a mean bastard." By questioning and probing the counselor had been hoping for just such an admission. This was discussed and a plan was made. For one week he was to avoid argument and try to see why others might want their way. When the counselor said, "I guess we could take those tests now," the client said, "I don't want them. I'm a good glazier even though I'm a hell of a man."

Four years later the counselor was stopped by a workman who was putting some of the finishing touches on a university building that was just being occupied. The glazier reported that he had remarried. Now he had his own crew of eight glaziers, and they drew the prestige jobs of glaziers—installing swinging plate glass doors.

To the extent that the glazier's story is duplicated by other workers on other jobs—and it is repeated—finding the right job for that person is a fantasy. One takes his personality—abrasive and contentious or optimistic and congenial—to whatever work he performs. The onus is on the person. A highly pertinent question is "Am I the right person for the job?" as contrasted to "Is this the right job for me?"

Choosing a job   The whole matter of choosing a career and gaining satisfaction from a job appears to be based on the assumption that choice is an ever-present possibility. Davis (1948, p. 273) stated a quarter of a century ago, *a truth that is still more evident today*, that the question is not whether youth will be placed on a job appropriately and according to his interests, but whether or not he will find a job at all (Figure 11.1).

The author served four years as a classification officer in the U. S. Navy. This work called for testing and interviewing all recruits. Each was then designated as ship's company (shore duty for some job calling for his knowledge and ability), to school for special training, immediate advancement to rating, or to sea duty as a striker for a rating. Every two weeks a training station would receive what was known as a BuPers Letter. The Bureau of Naval Personnel in Washington, D. C. sent an order of ratings in which there were shortages or anticipated shortages and *the order was to be filled.* In a given two weeks, the orders might call for Great Lakes Training Station to send school selectees as follows:

Motor machinist mates	20	Great Lakes
Aviation mechanic	14	Norman
Radioman	25	Farragut
Signalman	35	Farragut
Quartermaster	12	San Diego
Aviation metalsmith	15	Norman
Storekeeper	7	San Diego
Submarine	12	Norfolk
Cook and Baker	10	Peary
Hospital Corps	150	Farragut
Hospital Corps	150	San Diego

There were other ratings with varying numbers of men being called for. It was the function of classification officers to fill the quotas every two weeks. No such things as, "if the men are interested," "if they are trained," or "if they have promise of being trainable" were mentioned. The mechanical ratings (metalsmith, mechanics) were easy to fill. American boys had training and experience with their own cars and mechanical hobbies. There were enough bright and eager candidates for radioman and signalman. However, there were not nearly enough men interested in, or even having desirable qualifications for training, to fill the total quota of 300 in Hospital Corps. Anyone who has been close to a military base knows what happened. The quotas were filled. There were dozens of well-qualified men left after selection for the mechanical and store-keeper ratings were filled. If, after a "sales talk" on hospital corps, we were still short, we "selected" volunteers and filled quotas. One hears terrible tales of military injustice and how one's interests and civilian experiences were ignored. However, after twenty MoMM's had been selected, a man, if he wanted to go to school at all, had better choose hospital corps school. Many volunteered and liked it. This was especially true when they took the attitude, "There's a job to be done—let's have at it" and on board ship or on shore the HC rating drew esteem.

The reader may say, "That's all well for the military. I already knew it." It is proposed here that, in the matter of job choice, the military and civilian life are very much alike. The big difference is that the Navy published its quota letter prior to the occurrence of the need. In civilian life, the quota letter is published *after the fact* in the form of the Bureau of Labor Statistics (Figure 11.2). In either case the moral is the same: If one wants a job he had better choose one that society (including the military establishment) wants done.

Much is confidently written about the intelligence needed on certain jobs. Presumably physicians, lawyers, engineers, professors, and entrepreneurs need to be high on the intellectual scale in order to qualify and be successful. Actually, it appears that we know relatively little about the function of intelligence in occupational adjustment. Stewart (1947) studied the occupations of men in relation to their scores on the Army General Classification Test. She plotted the results as shown in Figure 11.3. Note that 15–20 per cent of the top ranking miners exceed the scores of the lower scoring accountants.

Careers and intelligence

In another study, Strauss (1969) examined the high school IQ's of 89 men who earned Ph.D. degrees in physics, chemistry, and engineering. They earned degrees at the Ohio State University, University of California at Berkeley, and Cornell University. He found that 3 per cent had scored 96–100, 6 per cent scored from 101–110, and 29 per cent scored from 111–120—while in high school. Typically, it is thought that the chances of success as a college undergraduate are small if one scores below 120 IQ. Yet only 62 per cent of this group of Ph.D.'s had made scores higher than what is often deemed to be minimum IQ for college (not graduate degree programs) success. Strauss concludes that care must be exercised not to exclude potential scholars on the basis of IQ alone. Individual motivation and concern of caring teachers and parents are factors in job and college success that are all too often overlooked.

Table E – 10. Employment by Occupation Group, 1960, 1970, and Projected 1980 Requirements

(Number in thousands)

Occupation group	Actual				Projected 1980[1] requirements		Number change		Annual rate of change	
	1960		1970							
	Number	Percent distribution	Number	Percent distribution	Number	Percent distribution	1960–70	1970–80	1960–70	1970–80
Total employment[2]	65,778	100.0	78,627	100.0	95,100	100.0	12,849	16,473	1.8	1.9
Professional and technical workers	7,469	11.4	11,140	14.2	15,500	16.3	3,671	4,360	4.1	3.4
Managers, officials, and proprietors	7,067	10.7	8,289	10.5	9,500	10.0	1,222	1,211	1.6	1.4
Clerical workers	9,762	14.8	13,714	17.4	17,300	18.2	3,952	3,586	3.5	2.4
Sales workers	4,224	6.4	4,854	6.2	6,000	6.3	630	1,146	1.4	2.1
Craftsmen and foremen	8,554	13.0	10,158	12.9	12,200	12.8	1,604	2,042	1.7	1.8
Operatives	11,950	18.2	13,909	17.7	15,400	16.2	1,959	1,491	1.5	1.0
Service workers	8,023	12.2	9,712	12.4	13,100	13.8	1,689	3,388	1.9	3.0
Nonfarm laborers	3,553	5.4	3,724	4.7	3,500	3.7	171	-224	.5	-.6
Farmers and farm laborers	5,176	7.9	3,126	4.0	2,600	2.7	-2,050	-526	-5.2	-1.8

[1] These projections assume 3-percent unemployment and a services economy in 1980, as described in *The U.S. Economy in 1980* (Washington: Department of Labor, Bureau of Labor Statistics, 1970), Bulletin 1673.

[2] Represents total employment as covered by the Current Population Survey.

Figure 11.2   Occupations chart.

Adjusting to the World of Work

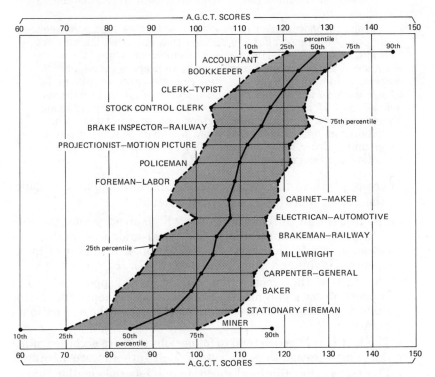

Approximately every fifteenth occupation from a list of 227 is represented above. The range plotted is from the 25th to 75th percentile, except that the 10th and 90th percentile is shown for accountants and miners.

Source: Naomi Stewart, "A. G. C. T. Scores of Army Personnel Grouped by Occupations," *Occupations*, 26:5–41, 1947. Reprinted by permission of the copyright holder and publisher, the American Personnel and Guidance Association.

Army General Classification Test Scores grouped by occupation of enlisted men.   **Figure 11.3**

Pang (1971) provides additional perspective on intelligence as related to career success in a study he titled, "Undistinguished School Experience of Distinguished Persons." Eminent persons whose school performance was poor include many highly noteworthy individuals: Isaac Newton, Winston Churchill, Albert Einstein, Pablo Picasso, Charles Darwin, Paul Ehrlich, Dwight Eisenhower, Franklin Roosevelt, Ernest Hemingway, and many others are included among those whose teachers perceived them as having poor intellectual promise. Pang summarizes as follows:

> Although our focus here had been on distinguished persons with mediocre or below-average school records, there are many individuals with brilliant records of scholastic achievement. There is even diversity within occupations. For instance, Robert Oppenheimer was always brilliant from early childhood, yet Albert Einstein appeared

to be rather slow and a failure. However, both were outstanding physicists.

Today the slow starter faces greater odds in gaining admission to college. We cannot afford to assume that only the ignorant are kept out, or that only the incapable are flunked out. One of the major purposes of an educational institution is to prepare individuals for creative achievement, yet the standard measures of fitness for college work do not measure potential creativity. It is an extremely difficult task. Our country, and all countries, need creative individuals of all types. Slow and late starters, and poor test takers have contributed significantly, and will continue to do so when given the opportunity. Truly it is sometimes difficult to distinguish between the idiots and the geniuses.[5]

There are several facts about careers and intelligence contradictory to the notion that they are casually related:

- The fact is that the chances to select high prestige jobs are more a function of membership in the upper-middle or high socioeconomic strata than that such selection is a matter of intelligence (Havighurst and Neugarten, 1967).
- The fact is that motivation, particularly rapport with and support of one's parents, is, more than intelligence, the factor that is more likely to determine one's rung on the occupational ladder.
- The fact is that youth tend to follow jobs that are accorded much the same prestige that the jobs of their fathers were accorded.
- The fact is that the less education one has the smaller chance one has of "choosing" anything (*Manpower . . .* , 1972, p. 79).
- The cruel fact is that the determination of one's career status begins in the early school years and the feedback the pupil receives regarding his intelligence (Kagan, 1972).
- And while distasteful facts are being cited, let a hypothesis be cited: The more one asserts his "independence and freedom" during the preparatory years, the smaller will be his autonomy during his working years—despite the exceptions noted above by Pang (1968).
- The inclusive fact is that, except for dullness or feeblemindedness, intelligence is not a very reliable criterion for vocational choice. IQ does not provide an excuse for evading one's responsibility for the exercise of choice.
- Choice of career is a function of a total pattern of living—not a decision of the moment.

We simply do not know how much intelligence is required to do a good job in various fields of endeavor. No career has been more frequently, intensively, and continuously researched than teaching.

---

[5]Henry Pang, "Undistinguished School Experiences of Distinguished Persons," *Adolescence*, Vol. 3, 1968, p. 326.

We assume that a minimum IQ level is necessary. A minimum is needed to pass the tests and courses that constitute the pathway to certification. However, the success of children as teachers, and the amount that children learn from their peers outside of school, suggest that human rapport, more than intelligence, is the key factor (Cicirelli, 1972). This notion may be supported by Bruner (1968). He has noted that the crucial factor in learning is dialogue between the sophisticate and the novitiate. Success on the job may be more a function of communication between supervisor and worker—whichever position one may occupy—than it is a function of intelligence (Figure 11.3). The theme of career and intelligence may be argued with considerable heat and little light; but then, it is personality theory.

Much of what has been previously said about involvement rather clearly suggests that the worker should be interested in what he is doing. However, some perplexing questions arise in the mind of the skeptic.

Careers and interest

How are interests to be assessed? There are instruments that purport to assess intelligence. However, despite rather widespread acceptance of these devices, they are skeptically viewed by some authorities. Guilford (1967) postulates that there are at least 120 different kinds of intelligences. The majority of these are not probed in conventional tests. Taylor (1972) asserts that the greater the number of intelligence tests that are given, the greater (up to a point) is the chance that various persons will appear in some "top 10 per cent." Wesman (1968) emphatically states that until psychometrists take a sample of all kinds of intelligences, we would do well to be cautious, very cautious, in the interpretation of what they mean in life and work. Kagan (1972) says that an IQ score has a poor relation to one's ability to think logically and coherently. McClelland (1972) suggests that the "virtue" of intelligence tests is that they can be used, as they were in ancient China (and contemporary United States), to exclude people from certain activities if they were unacquainted with the "pure" knowledge cultivated by the intelligentsia.

If the assessment of intelligence is questioned, the evaluation of interest presents an even more perplexing dilemma. Using their results is akin to a trip in Disneyland. Two devices dominate the interest assessment scene—the Strong Vocational Interest Blank and the Kuder Preference Record. Despite much research on construction and validation, some researchers find that stated interests are as valid in some situations as are inventory scores (Brown, 1970, p. 387). Gronlund (1971, p. 456) suggests that these instruments be used with caution because they can be easily faked. Moreover, interests change, especially during, and prior to, adolescence. Much research has been done on the relevance of interest inventories to career selection and success. The results are positive but the relationship is so low that predictions for an individual become extremely questionable. Ahmann and Glock (1967, p. 454) also suggest caution in the use of interest inventories. They advise the use of supplementary data in the process of vocational selection. Rothney and others (1959, p. 282ff.) are emphatic in their condemnation of interest inventories. They assert that it is psychological naïveté and the desperate need for better understanding that lead psychologists and counselors to grasp for the help of such dubious instruments. It is akin to a drowning man grasping at straws.

The author is on the same side of the fence as Rothney and his colleagues, but the reasons reside in the conditions of the work world rather than on the condemnation of inventories in terms of their equivocal validity.

- Society demands and will use workers in certain areas regardless of the interests of the worker. For example, a consuming interest in harness making for very many people would be a source of frustration today (Russo, 1969).
- Interest inventories may sow the seeds of discontent. As in marriage, one thinks he is inappropriately wed at the first quarrel. At work, when one encounters the first, and inevitable, difficulty of learning the job, he blames lack of interest, corroborated by inventory results. He may seek something more suitable to his interests. The inventory thus becomes an excuse for failure.
- Interests do not come fully into bloom as the result of some genetic predisposition. Interests are an outgrowth of aptitude, success, acquaintanceship, and familiarity. In short, interests develop. An inventory which shows a lack in some area may become a reason for not developing the acquaintanceship that is a source of interest.
- Let it be conceded that some interests are intrinsic (Mozart's interest in music—although interests and aptitudes are not the same thing). It must also be conceded that some are **extrinsic.** Interests may be a matter of a carrot before or a stick behind—if one cannot develop a taste for the job that society wants done, he may feel the stick behind: unemployment, frustration, scorn for indolence.
- Belief that success or failure on the job or that worker satisfaction depends on intrinsic interests is in the same logical category as love at first sight. It is akin to the romantic notion of a glance across a crowded room resulting in emotional ecstasy. Interests are quickened, much as love is, by acquaintanceship, touching, and experience over the years.
- Practical questions might be: Who's in charge of what? Are my interests to control me or am I to control the direction and intensity of my interests?
- Failure on the job may be attributed to low interest, confirmed

by the inventory score. The person is thus allowed to bypass examining his social skills—which will function on all jobs—and his developing job competency. Like the child failure in school, he can say, "I'm not interested in arithmetic."

Most of the foregoing adds up to saying, "The person who is characterized as having a stable personality had better have, or develop, an interest for the job available, at the place where he is, and at the time the workman wants a job."

PERSONALITY ON THE JOB MARKET

There should be no objection, even by the skeptic, about the merit of seeking a career in which one is interested. However, if the person must work at something other than his stated interest, he should not believe that he is doomed to unhappiness and mediocrity. He can set out to develop an interest if he understands the meaning of the word: *Inter*, between, and *esse*, the spirit, the substance. Q. E. D.: that feeling existing *between person and job*. It is a two-way thing. In fact, some place the responsibility on the person. "There is no such thing as an uninteresting job—just disinterested, naïve, discontented workers.

Interest

Again reference is made to the most intensively researched career—teaching. Ninety percent of teachers who fail do so because of their inability to work congenially with others—parents, peers, principals, or pupils. Generalizations should probably not be drawn from the case of the glazier cited above. However, the author has acted as consultant to the Division of Employment in several states and found considerable emphasis on the "person as worker" in employment and employability programs. In a recent employment program called MDTA (Manpower Development and Training Act, enacted 1962), the national and local employment agencies perceived the necessity of making the chronically unemployed person "job ready." This called not only for job skill training but also for a wide range of supportive services.

Social personality

> Among the many lessons learned in the administration of the Manpower Development and Training Act is the fact that some clients, particularly among the disadvantaged, may need intensive, wide-ranging supportive services. These may include orientation to work, day care [for young children], transportation, skill training, job development, referral to jobs, and even some assistance with medical and other problems in the initial stages of employment.[6]

[6]Eli Ginzberg, "A Critical Look at Career Guidance," *Manpower*, Vol. 4: February, 1972, p. 6.

Another reason why selecting a career in terms of personality characteristics seems to be theoretically hazardous is the phenomenon of rapid change. It has been predicted that 70 per cent of the pupils who are now in junior high school will work at jobs that do not as yet exist. The Department of Labor estimates that the 20-year-old man of today can look forward to six or seven separate job changes during his working life (McCully, 1969, p. 65). Some of these will be voluntary changes. Some will be the result of promotions. Some changes will stem from technological progress that makes the current job obsolete. Whatever the cause of job shifting, the attitudes of responsibility and flexibility will be factors in successful career change. Change, it seems, is an integral part of the contemporary worker's challenge.

Much the same thing can be said about other personality attributes that promote job success: getting along with fellow workers, taking pride in doing a good job on schedule, being on the job regularly and on time. These are habits that one can predict with disappointing accuracy. There are those who will be late, be on time, be present, be absent, do the work for pay, do the work for pride, in job after job. Such habits are among the determiners of job interest and success.

Studies of worker satisfaction, of workers' mental health, of industrial plant, or business firm success show that involvement of the worker is the key item in worker satisfaction. Involvement is also the key item in work efficiency. Retirement plans, medical benefits, unemployment insurance, paid vacations, counseling services, and high rates of pay are factors that are conducive to worker satisfaction. However, without involvement, other worker benefits are of doubtful value.

The priority of the worker benefit seems to be a reflection of the spirit of the times. In the 1930's having a job was itself a source of personality gratification. As jobs became more plentiful and the memories of unemployment caused only slight concern, job tenure, sick leave, and retirement plans were used as worker incentives. In the 1960's the young worker was often more concerned about the matters of employee benefits than he was about the nature of the work or identifying his interest in it. In the 1970's involvement ranks high. Even though the source of job satisfaction is, in part, a reflection of the spirit of the times, involvement has been a consistent and persistent factor in job selection and success. That is, when a worker feels that he is important, when his voice is listened to, when he feels that he is a part of the decision-making process, he is a happier, more efficient, and more reliable worker.

In spite of high wages and growing employee benefits, turnover rates and worker apathy seem to be at an all-time high. Absenteeism has doubled in the past ten years in the auto industry. Workers no longer put up with authoritarian bosses. A University of Michigan survey found that the leading factors in worker satisfaction, in order of rank, were (Herrick, 1972):

1. Interesting work.
2. Help and equipment to get the job done.
3. Enough information to get the job done.
4. Enough authority to do the job.
5. Pay [fifth place].
6. Opportunity to develop skills.
7. Job security.
8. Seeing the results of one's work.

Note that No. 5 and No. 7 are the only items that have conventionally been sought in labor union demands. The other items are those that are typically cited in studies of personality.

The studies of the Western Electrical Company, results of which are widely known as the "Hawthorne Effect," demonstrate that involvement is a durable factor in job satisfaction. At Western's Hawthorne plant, experiments indicated that any of a number of things conveyed to the worker that he was getting attention. Such attention tended to improve his efficiency. Better lighting, poorer lighting, more coffee-breaks, fewer coffee-breaks, looser inspection, closer inspection—all resulted in improved production—as long as the worker knew that the studies were designed to enhance his ultimate welfare. Enhancement of his feeling of belonging, his acceptance in the work group, his being a concern of the employer are more important factors than is the amount of economic gain (Herzberg, 1966, p. 38).

> This need for job satisfaction can best be met through the humanization of work: Through restructuring the work situation so that jobs provide autonomy, interesting work, and the opportunity to be active, to grow, and to achieve. Widely varying rates of dissatisfaction in various industries suggest a targeting of efforts to improve the quality of work. Just as society gives particular attention to industries with exceptionally high accident rates, perhaps special assistance might be tendered by the Government—and special concern shown by employers and unions—in industries with particularly high dissatisfaction rates. Similarly, special efforts might be made to alleviate the causes of unusually high job discontent among particular groups of workers such as women, blacks, and younger people.
>
> Work or life dissatisfaction were seldom reported by the self-employed. This supports the theory that independence of action is an important ingredient in satisfaction.[7]

[7]Neal Q. Herrick, "Who's Unhappy at Work and Why," *Manpower*, Vol. 4, January, 1972, p. 7.

Man's need to be responsible, flexible, and involved may be traced to his basic nature as a human being! Examples are his need to exercise his intellectual potential and his need to grow and change (Kleitman, 1963). Man's need to be involved, to have his input considered, is a factor that has been almost ignored since the beginning of the industrial revolution. Herzberg (1966), in studies involving engineers, factory workers, utilities workers, women workers, managers, supervisors, and so on, consistently found that the more important "worker satisfiers" were achievement, recognition, and responsibility. Oddly, in comparison to studies in schools and colleges, the matter of interest was cited, by Herzberg, only infrequently.

WORK, CULTURE, PERSONALITY

Work: A basic satisfaction

A long-standing Judeo-Christian ethic relates to the personality-enhancing value of work. It was well expressed in a quotation, cited by one of the author's professors, "In the working life alone is to be found lasting satisfaction for the soul and the hope of salvation for mankind." As the years passed, there seemed to be more and better reasons for respecting the statement. Recently, however, there are some indications that the work ethic might have to be changed. Increasingly, with the advance of technology, machines are doing the work—especially the manual labor, unskilled jobs—and each man-hour produces more goods and/or services (*Manpower . . .* , 1973). The number of chronically unemployed (or technologically unemployed) grows larger each year, and not just because the population is expanding.

Childs (1972) and Theobald (1965) are among those who forecast that if man is to have a purpose—and he must have purpose for psychological health—it may be necessary to identify that purpose outside the area of goods-producing work. Wages (or income) without work and more attention to the constructive use of leisure time are suggested alternatives. Such an orientation, challenging the time-honored ethic of work, has historical precedent. In ancient Greece the arts, literature, and philosophy were respected concerns. Slaves did the productive work without the deterioration of personality, on the part of the nonworker, that would be expected today. In England, in more recent times, "the gentleman and scholar" did not soil his hands in productive labor. Work, again, was considered beneath the dignity of those in the upper classes.

The author, steeped in the work ethic, finds it difficult to accept the notion that nonwork can be made to fill personality needs. Nevertheless, the idea can be accepted that goods-producing work is not the only avenue to personality fulfillment. Services (as contrasted to goods-production) designed to enhance the quality of life can supplement the production perspective. In short, more people engaged in teaching with smaller ratios of children to adults, more inclusive mental and physical health services, more artists and musicians to enhance the quality of life, and more persons engaged in the life sciences would provide wider access to work opportunities *of a kind.* Such an orientation is a society-wide concern, and demands the reconstruction of our value system. Although this is a society rife with problems, Gardner (1964, p. 115) contends that society is renewed by people who believe in, care about, and stand for the continuous reconstruction of values. Perhaps non-goods-producing work can be perceived as a new value.

Throughout this book, especially in Chapter 5, culture has been regarded as a nurturer of inherent potential. That work which is accorded respect in a given society is an outcome of local values. However, an aspect of culture and personality has not yet been emphasized. **Culture** not only shapes personality; but man, by definition shapes culture. Man is not just a product of culture; he is a producer of culture. The challenge is to shape, by conscious intent, our culture to fit current needs as contrasted to clinging to work values that technology is rendering obsolete.

Culture: A basic molder of personality

In this chapter it is proposed that instead of continuing the search for a career that fits one's intelligence and interest, the worker become more concerned about shaping his personality to fit the need. It is akin to the challenge of creating a satisfactory marriage. The emphasis needs to be shifted from that of finding the right mate to that of being the right mate. This entails the matter of involvement. It means seeking ways to make one's voice worth hearing. It entails doing what has to be done in such a manner that one can achieve worker satisfaction from achievement. It requires a shift to being a cause rather than a mere cog in an impersonal machine. It entails perceiving that life inevitably consists of doing some things as a matter of personal responsibility as contrasted to the goal of enjoyment. Because work involves one's fellow workers, it means developing respect and acceptance for, and communicating with, others.

Personality

SUMMARY

Work is a producer and molder of personality needs and satisfactions. Rather than being regarded as an onerous chore and obligation, work can be, and is, a way of life. In addition to being a satisfier of physiological and safety needs, it can be used as a source of esteem and self-fulfillment. It can be made to add "spice" to life, provide relief from tensions, and help one become more knowledgeable. Work gives exercise to various facets of personality.

Does physique, skill, or personality make the winner?

There are several theories of vocational choice and worker satisfaction. These are used in attempts to fit the right man to the right job and to explain worker satisfaction or dissatisfaction. Roe regards vocational choice as a function of one's style of life which is rooted in childhood. Super perceives one's job choice as a reflection of his ego concept. Havighurst sees career selection and competence as one of a series of developmental tasks of humans. Ginzberg also regards choice of work as a developmental process. Work involves an increasingly accurate perception of reality and self as one matures emotionally and intellectually.

Some persons regard the matter of choice as being limited by culture and technology. The question today is not one of matching man and job so much as it is of finding any job. Reality requires fitting one's personality to societal demands. Such choice as exists comes into being in terms of one's education and training rather than as a result of test taking. Much is written about the relationship of intelligence and job success but the conclusions are equivocal. It seems that education, socioeconomic status, and the spirit of the times are more pertinent factors in career placement than is measured intelligence. The situation with regard to interest and career selection is also equivocal. Interest inventories are an inadequate guide to career choice—indeed, the results, taken at face value, may impose some hazards.

The author takes the biased position of contending that intelligence can be used and developed on any job, if the worker can develop the needed perspective. The position is taken that interests can be developed, if one must work at that which was initially uninteresting. Further, it is postulated that achievement, co-worker congeniality, involvement, and experiences of success are sources of interest as much as work's being attractive or displeasing to the person. In brief, vocational choice and success are functions of one's total personality and perspective; and the task is to be the right personality rather than finding the right job.

SUGGESTED READINGS

GINZBERG, ELI, "A Critical Look at Career Guidance," *Manpower*, Vol. 4, 3–6, February, 1972.
> *The chairman of the National Manpower Advisory Committee of the Department of Labor recommends that school guidance services be upgraded by providing better trained counselors and by more honestly facing the facts of the job market. Guidance will not, however, compensate for inadequate homes and schools or for lack of community involvement in the lives of young people.*

HERRICK, NEAL Q., "Who's Unhappy at Work and Why," *Manpower*, Vol. 4, 2–7, January, 1972.
> *Both pay level and worker dissatisfaction are at an all-time high. Hence, worker satisfaction is not just a matter of income. Involvement, recognition, autonomy are among the many factors that merit attention in worker satisfaction.*

Manpower Report of the President, United States Department of Labor (Washington, D.C., 1973).
> *This annual report describes manpower requirements, resources, and labor trends. The 1973 issue devotes a section to the impact of population changes. Personality factors in employment are vital in discussion of employment of persons from minority populations.*

MENNINGER, WILLIAM C., "The Meaning of Work in Western Society," ed., H. Borow, *Man in World at Work*. Boston: Houghton Mifflin Company, 1964.
> *Many psychological needs can be met at work. Many workers fail to satisfy their needs. Personality traits developed since childhood, the capacity to get along with people, and self-concepts are factors that determine why needs are met or denied.*

SCHRAG, PETER, "The Forgotten American," *Harper's*, Vol. 239, 27–34, August, 1969.

America's hard-working, lower-middle class, the so-called backbone of society, is becoming disenchanted with inflation, welfare programs, vocational rehabilitation, and so on, when the honest man must often take a second job to pay his taxes, send his kids to college, and then put up with violence on the streets.

TODD, RICHARD, "Notes on Corporate Man," *Atlantic*, Vol. 228, 83–94, October, 1971.
Some of the realities of work at high level executive jobs in big (and small) corporations show how deeply one's vocational career affects one's life and values.

FOLLOW-UP LEARNING ACTIVITIES

Work provides many satisfactions. Do you think it possible that many people *could* find those same satisfactions in nonwork?
  Yes _____   No _____   because _____
_____
_____
_____
_____
_____
_____

Bartley found that fatigue, or "tiredness," was most likely to be caused by
  _____ poor health   _____ too many friends   _____ challenge
  _____ long hours   _____ boredom   _____ heavy work
Write the name of the person whose occupational choice theory emphasized each of the following:
_____ a series of developmental tasks
_____ a reflection of one's acquired life style
_____ a reflection of personality type; *e.g.*, warm-
                          cold; things-people
_____ a function of ages and stages
Stewart found that there were clear-cut levels of intelligence that separated the prestige levels of occupations.
  True _____   False _____   Questionable _____
Pang found that very few famous men failed to show their budding eminence by superior school performance.
  True _____   False _____   Questionable _____
Strauss found that successful post-graduate level performance was mostly a matter of rather high IQ.
  True _____   False _____   Questionable _____
Herrick found that six of the highest eight factors in job satisfaction were related to personality attributes rather than income and security.
  True _____   False _____   Questionable _____

12
Personality and Communication

The faceless child—is this communication?

LEARNING ACTIVITIES

Check the statement most closely in accord with your opinion of
the value of television.

_____ It helps keep one informed

_____ It exposes one to a variety of experiences

_____ It represents a kind of mental blank in one's life

_____ It tends to teach one to be callous and violent

Do you think you are one who

_____ Discloses himself readily to others—is open

_____ Is about average in the ability to communicate personal
feeling

_____ Is below average in the tendency to be self-disclosing

_____ Is far too self-disclosing but is unable to stop being so

What do you mean when you refer to "the generation gap?"

_____

_____

_____

_____

_____

_____

How large was the generation gap between you and your parents?
I think it was small _____ about average _____ large _____
because_____

_____

_____

_____

What responsibility do you think you had or should have for the
gap which did or did not exist?

_____

_____

_____

Were your parents permissive _____ demanding _____ or
indecisive _____? What effect do you think this now has on you?

_____

_____

_____

(Check this item five years from now; or, if you are over 25
years old, compare your response with how you felt when you
were 18.)

How do you react to criticism? (openly, angrily, etc.)

_____

_____

Man's superiority over other animals, it may be recalled, has been attributed to his large and complex brain, his ability to oppose thumb and fingers, and the ability to use language. Although it is easy to realize that communication is an avenue to the facilitation of human relations, it may be difficult to accept the idea that communication is *the* thing that makes us human. It does, to a large extent, however, mold basic personality. It is small wonder that scholars in varied fields are beginning to perceive improved communication as a focal consideration in human affairs. It functions in marriage, child-rearing, teaching-learning transactions, and business, as well as in local and international politics.

It may seem somewhat odd that something as important as communication is not a more familiar topic in psychology and sociology. It is possible that such neglect is a matter of taking communication for granted—as we regard being parents, becoming voters, or breathing. Almost anyone can be a parent. We reach a certain age and our accumulated schooling and life presumably give us the wisdom to vote wisely.

Taking communication for granted may be at least one explanation of why it has not served its ideal, and heavy burden, any better than it has. Young people seem to have grasped the idea that it is a highly significant human function and are now devoting more time to its study. However, just more time devoted to rapping and "telling it like it is" will not, alone, do the job. Also needed is **metacommunication,** (*e.g.*, mutual appreciation and discussion of just what message is being sent and how it is being received). Metacommunication is the burden of this chapter.

MEANING AND IMPORTANCE OF COMMUNICATION

Life and time   The process of communication begins almost at the time of birth. As typical adults, about 73 per cent of our waking time is devoted to various communication activities (Samovar *et al*, 1969). Talking, listening, reading, and watching television were included in Samovar's study but writing was not. Excluding writing seems like a scorning of authors. However, it does indicate that communication is more important in some life styles than in others. Administrators, salesmen, students, teachers, and professionals rank high as communicators. Farmers, housewives (really?), clerical workers, craftsmen, and retired people score low as communicators.

One deludes himself if he thinks that all communication is designed to send or exchange ideas and arrive at a common understanding. Much of communication is designed to control the behavior and attitudes of others. It does serve the purpose of exchanging ideas; but sometimes the function of speech, dialogue, or the printed word is deliberately to mislead or dissimulate. At other times the purpose of verbal interaction is merely to acknowledge another person's presence. Neither person perceives the encounter as having any significance. One of the author's colleagues, John Butler, psychiatrist, has schematized the various levels of communication as five concentric circles (Figure 12.1).

Level 5 communication is designed to pass the time and ease the pressure of meeting a stranger. One wishes to hide his prejudices and weaknesses and to present only the idea that he is aware of social amenities. One wonders just exactly what the other is saying. Is he friend or foe? Can the words be taken at face value or does the speaker have some hidden agenda?

> Although many misunderstandings and psychological problems probably would be eliminated if some stroke of magic could abolish level five discourse, we would find it extremely difficult to function without it. For we use it to feel our way into relationships. Like the ego defense mechanisms, it is a necessary part of interaction systems. We save face and cushion the impact of our confrontations with this type of discourse. In a sense, it permits the ice-breaking and warming up which we have to do with strangers before we can relate on more meaningful levels. So it is not this type of discourse but the manner in which it is used which determines whether our transactions will be useful, innocuous, or disruptive. Like all human behaviors, level five discourse has impact and power for influencing and managing relationships. Like our other behaviors, it helps to determine what we get back from our interpersonal transactions and what we may become as a result. Also like our other ways of acting, our use of this manner of discourse tends to be thoroughly engrained and habitual and to function below our level of awareness.[1]

Level 4 communication is straightforward, factual, honest, and without hidden agendas. One is as clear as he can be. He means what he says. The listener knows it and tries to understand the verbal message. He discerns no double message. If all communication were level 4 there would be none of the dissembling that characterizes level 5. Behind communication on level 4 is the ability to act on reason, to be logical, and to be calm. The major difficulty is that humans are emotional. They do have hidden agendas. Moreover, we would probably not really want to deny ourselves the luxury of emotions—the excitement, anger, and challenge—of vigorous interpersonal transac-

[1]Harold W. Bernard and Wesley C. Huckins, *Dynamics of Personal Adjustment* (Boston: Holbrook Press, Inc., 1971), pp. 282–283.

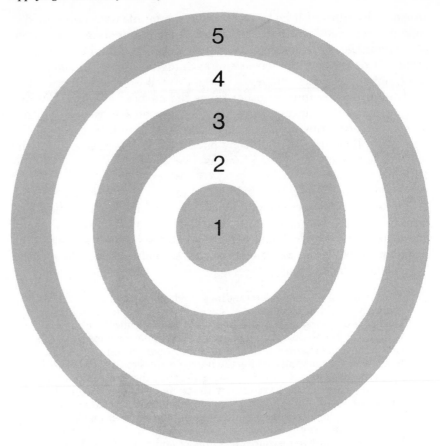

Level 5   Not really intended as communication -- defensive tactics, self-preservation; e.g., "How are you?" "I'm fine"-- and actually one feels depressed, would like to choke someone, almost anyone.

Level 4   No emotional load. Meaning is clear. No DOUBLE MESSAGES. People act as rational human beings; e.g., "Pi R² is the area of a circle," "Washington was the first U. S. president."

Level 3   Not only the ideas but other persons are described. There may be an emotional factor. Talk is about meaning and significance of things and people, but mainly the discourse is about what others are doing.

Level 2   Similar to level 3 but the emotional concern is more personal and significant. Feeling is as much or more, about how one feels than about the idea. One describes how and why he is angry, pleased, elated, or frustrated.

Level 1   Deeply personal, secrets are shared with one or two selected others--feelings at times, as in peak experiences, may be mutually felt without verbalization.

Figure 12.1   *Levels of communication.*

tions that add zest to living. Hence, the problem is to try to use level 4 more frequently when it is appropriate. It is good to attempt to understand the situation and its background that prompts level 5 discourse.

Level 3 communication, as contrasted to level 5, is adjustive and

integrative. Level 5 is often disruptive and isolating. At leve.
are describing how they see things and people and how they
their perceptions. For example, "I have met many long-haired
know them as admirable persons; but, each time I face a new l
I think 'What a clod.'" Such an admission tends to decrease psy
cal distance—perhaps even for the long-hair, because he pe
honesty—and invites sharing. An emotional component is p
However, it is light. It could quickly become heavier and jump l
level 5 to defensiveness, or more tentatively into level 2. The pu
of the communicants at level 3 is the mutual sharing both of fee
and factual information. Hence, it is highly personal and unic
perceptual. There is a continuous effort to test reality with c
fellows. It is an attempt to adjust one's values and standards to wnat
appear to be the different standards of other reputable humans. Level
3 communication is an important factor in the adjustive personality. It
is vital in productive interpersonal transactions.

Level 2 communication is the kind that psychotherapists (Rogers,
1961) aim at and hope for. It differs from level 3 in that 2 is deeply
personal and individualistic. Level 3 may concern feelings about
things, processes, and people that are outside of one's own skin. Level 2
and 3 are complementary—3 concerns things and others, while 2
concerns self. Level 2 is based upon the concept of openness (Maslow,
1970; Rogers, 1971). There is a readiness to identify one's innermost
feelings. There is a readiness to accept them, whether hostile and
punitive or loving and sentimental. It is an admission that one is a
member of the human race. It does not use the admission as an excuse
for unsocialized behavior. It takes practice to converse at level 2 for a
long period of time (10 to 15 minutes). Typically, in therapy the client
alludes to occasions when these deep feelings exist. Examples might be
contempt for one's mother, jealousy of one's sister, the wish to seduce
the minister's wife, or simply expressing one's liking for another. Then
in a split second, one jumps defensively back to level 5 or to the safety
of level 4. The therapist attempts to lure the client back to level 2 and
stay a few seconds longer when he gets there. Level 2 communication
is a key factor in dealing with anomie, alienation, and isolation in the
contemporary world. Level 2 is needed where crowding seems to be in
inverse ratio to feelings of belonging and acceptance. Level 2 communication is a commonplace habit for self-actualizing people. It is a
painful, if not impossible (except with the aid of therapeutic intervention), mode of communication for the chronologically defensive personality.

Level 1 communication is what has been called a Minerva, peak,
or mystic experience (Otto, 1967; Maslow, 1971; Rogers, 1961). It is
difficult to verbalize, but to those who have the psychological capabili-
ty, it is easy to the point of being automatic. A healthy mother and
father can feel the "vibes" of each other when they see their baby
sleeping. They smile together when their child takes his first steps or

first rides his two-wheel bike. Words are not needed. Words do not communicate, adequately, the feeling of oneness with mankind. Silence may say, "All's right with the world," but the communication with one's intimate and respected companion or one's loved one is there. For example, the flashing glance and crinkle at the corner of the eyes just before fishing partners are sucked into the rapids of a river they are running in a boat. Communication has to be brief because the turbulence is upriver in another five seconds and work has been done in those seconds. At the moment, one is "in harmony." The needs, pressures, and doubts of the fang and claw world are amusing. All in all, level 1 communication is rarely achieved and is felt emotionally rather than talked about. [Can you get a level 1 feeling from reading the above? Of course not. We were communicating at level 4. It may be level 5 if the reader is skeptical about the existence of level 1. Discuss the matter with classmates to use level 3 and with a therapist to reach level 2].

Humanization and communication

The newborn infant communicates his needs and wants with apparently mature lungs and vocal cords. From his initiation of communication he gets feedback. If he interprets it as positive (and he can) because his mother is proud and pleased with the manifest health reflected in the bellow, he gets the feeling that the world is a friendly place and he has a place in it. The feedback may be negative because his mother feels but does not necessarily say, "He's a messy, squalling brat." He then gets the feeling that the world is austere or even hostile. He feels that he is not quite smart enough to deal with the world. He is not good enough to have a place in it. These feelings produce a foundation on which to build. Though subject to continuous modification, depending on what is communicated to him in succeeding years, the initial messages tend to persist through a lifetime.

> . . . Our main point is that interpersonal systems—stranger groups, marital couples, families, psychotherapeutic, or even international relationships, etc.—may be viewed as feedback loops, since the behavior of each person affects and is affected by the behavior of each other person. Input into such a system may be amplified into change or may counteract to maintain stability, depending on whether the feedback mechanisms are positive or negative. From studies of families containing a schizophrenic member there can be little doubt that the existence of the patient is essential for the stability of the family system and that the system will react quickly and effectively to any internal or external attempts to change its organization. Clearly this is an undesirable type of stability. Since the manifestations of life are evidently distinguished by both stability and change, negative and positive feedback mechanisms must occur in them in specific forms of interdependence or complementarity.[2]

[2]Paul Watzlawick, Janet H. Beavin, and Don D. Jackson, *Pragmatics of Human Communication* (New York: W. W. Norton & Company, Inc., 1967), p. 31.

Feedback is an essential component of communication. It is needed not only in individual growth but in families, communities, and governments. Feedback may be negative, positive, or equivocal but it is essential to normal functioning.

The role of communicative feedback is reflected in Fraiberg's (1971) studies of personalities. She reported some so deviant that as adults they are called a-human. That is, they are without feelings or conscience. They experience no joy, no grief, no guilt. When one attempts to communicate with them it is as though nothing were there. Fraiberg calls them "hollow persons." One might note the frequency with which these feelingless, a-human creatures seem to be mentioned in connection with shocking crimes. Such were the assassins of President Kennedy and Robert Kennedy. When caught they expressed no guilt, no fear, no feeling.

> Several years ago in Portland, a young man, strong, good looking, and having a record of being an acceptable workman, kidnapped a teen-age girl. He took her under the St. Johns Bridge. He kept her there for several days without sexually molesting her, then beat her to death with a piece of pipe. When apprehended [I forget whether he was caught or gave himself up] he told what had happened *without show of emotion.*

The description of this a-human personality is similar to that of others who shock the nation with their deeds and their unbelievable calm. Fraiberg says that it is as though they knew something were lacking in their feelings and attachments and chose violence in their search to spark some missing feelings. The childhood of such persons typically had something in common, usually lacking the warmth of mothering and human communication. These a-human personalities received their discharge from the human race in their first few months of life—three to nine months is the particularly critical period. Their mothers, or some substitute mothers, did not communicate with them. They were not talked to. They were set aside. They were not touched, cuddled, chin-chucked, or petted. Human bonds are communication bonds. The baby deprived of stable communication partners is a baby who is being denied his humanity.

Fraiberg believes that communication is basic to the process of becoming human. Hunt (1968) and Krech (1972) postulate that communication is essential for the exercise of the baby's potential for developing intelligence. Hayakawa (1968a) asserts that good communication is at the heart of good sexuality. Sex for sweethearts, lovers, and spouses is conditioned by voice and verbal transaction as well as by erotic desire. Sexual union is a profound person-to-person communication, culminating all the communication that is antecedent to the union. Hayakawa is not speaking of mutual masturbation. He writes of the fullness of communication capable of being achieved by training for responsiveness from infancy onward. Politicians and historians see the possibilities of resolving world conflict through genuine communication. Communication between nations is not just a matter of a common language but also of respecting differences in value systems. People the world over are much the same in needs and social personality. Their value systems, however, do differ. History itself is an example of communication and there are lessons to be learned from it (Durant and Durant, 1968). Consequently, it is not surprising to find that some semanticists think that social problems are largely an outcome of ineffective communication.

COMMUNICATION AND ADULT PERSONALITY

The generation gap

The **"generation gap"** is an obstacle to communication between the "older and wiser" generation and their "younger and smarter" off-spring. It has been noted since the time of Plato. He complained that the younger generation no longer showed respect for their elders by rising when an elder entered the room. The generation gap has grown from a mild disease to what some regard as a devastating plague. The huge generation gap that exists today[3] is attributed to many things. Many persons would equate the gap with defective communication:

Rapid change—Change is taking place at such a rapid pace that youngsters and elders do not experience the same things. They do not have a common ground on which to base verbal transactions. Even the language is different. The jargon of youth is different from the patois of adults. In the days when change was paced more slowly the generations shared common experiences.

The NOW generation—role versus goal—An example of the impact of rapid change on communication is the differing value systems of adults and youth. The differences are culturally oriented. The adult generation planned and worked for the future. It was necessary for them to provide for illness, unemployment, and the infirmities of old age. Their lives were goal oriented. Times have changed. Health plans, clinics, and Medicare have promised that they will be cared for. Unemployment insurance takes care of the exigencies that occur during technological change and periods of economic depression. Social security and public welfare promise that retirement with pay is

---

[3]Some authorities say that the so-called gap is a myth: Robert C. Bealer, Fern K. Willits, and Peter Maida, *Rural Youth in Crisis: Facts, Myths, and Social Change*, U. S. Department of Health, Education, and Welfare (Washington, D.C., 1965), pp. 54–61. Others say that it is not sensible to think that it does not exist: John Parry, *The Psychology of Human Communication* (New York: American Elsevier Publishing Company, 1968).

possible even for the indigent. Hence, the challenge to youth is in terms of identity—role (Erikson, 1968; Glasser, 1970). Communication is made difficult because of these different value systems. The young perceive no struggle for existence. What they want, they want now. Deferred gratification is a good example of dad's lack of relevance when he speaks of "Now when *I* was a boy." It must, however, be observed that communication is not blocked by the value system. It is blocked by the would-be communicants who cannot, or will not, hear what others are saying.

Television—That generation reaching the age of 18 in the late 1960's was the first in history to have been exposed to more viewing of the box than present adults and prior generations spent in school. The 22,000 hours the typical American 18-year-old has spent watching television have given him some superb noncommunicative skills. Because television provides no feedback (does not engage in two-way communication) the young person has developed high skill in mentally "turning it off" and "tuning it out." Should an adult say something that the young person does not want to hear, the turn-off button is automatically pressed and communication is effectively blocked. Hayakawa (1968b) expresses the opinion that television is not dangerous in the messages it sends. The hazard is the fact that the child, while spending time in front of the television, is being deprived of communication with parents, adults, relatives, siblings, and peers.

Confused parental role—Quite properly the day is passing when a child obeyed when the parent said, "Because I said so." Unfortunately, the pendulum swung too far. Many parents confused the abolition of authoritarianism with the repudiation of authority. Most child-rearing authorities, sociologists, and cultural anthropologists would agree that children need parents who know that they are parents. Parents must take the responsibility for making decisions and giving directions (Cottle, 1969). *However,* as children move into adolescence and youth, they need less direction. Authoritarianism becomes an irritant that contributes to animosity and alienation. The parents' role is one demanding continuous change in the pattern of authority.

COMMUNICATION AND PERSONALITY PROBLEMS

The self has been defined as consisting in part of the internalized perception of how one sees himself reflected in the eyes of others. The child identifies with and imitates his parents in creating his perception of self (Allport, 1955, p. 45). In adulthood not only parents but significant others are involved in the feedback that conditions the self. What one is called makes a difference.

> A Jew, who had been incarcerated in a Nazi concentration camp, remarked that after a period of time, one, even a Jew, began believing the propaganda that was all around. German children were taught, radio emphasized, Hitler and his cohorts shouted and reiterated, and youth sang about Jewish avariciousness, their moral decadence, their inferior mentality. Those Jews in camps—treated like animals, cut off from news and literature, and from contact with those outside the camps—began themselves to believe it. It took deliberate effort to retain one's faith in self. Conversely, those who heard the other message (that Germans were the "Gott mit Uns," superior race) also, at least temporarily, believed it.

The self begins with and continues largely to be a matter of verbal transaction. The self is a verbal-symbolic process. Communication is the means by which we measure, validate, create, and facilitate our interaction with others. In the process of communication we develop our self image and identity.

> O [others] can accept (confirm) P's [person's] definition of self. As far as we can see, this confirmation of P's view of himself by O is probably the greatest single factor ensuring mental development and stability that has so far emerged from our study of communication. Surprising as it may seem, without this self-confirming effect human communication would hardly have evolved beyond the very limited boundaries of the interchanges indispensable for protection and survival; there would be no reason for communication for the mere sake of communication. Yet everyday experience leaves no doubt that a large portion of our communications are devoted precisely to this purpose. The vast gamut of emotions that individuals feel for each other—from love to hate—would probably hardly exist, and we would live in a world devoid of anything except the most utilitarian endeavors, a world devoid of beauty, poetry, play, and humor. It seems that, quite apart from the mere exchange of information, man *has* to communicate with others for the sake of his own awareness of self, and experimental verification of this intuitive assumption is increasingly being supplied by research on sensory deprivation, showing that man is unable to maintain his emotional stability for prolonged periods in communication with himself only . . .[4]

Mental health and communication

Mental illness is, to some extent, (because organic factors cannot entirely be ruled out) a matter of blocked communication. It is such an important consideration that communication is rivaling the self-concept as being the focal point of mental illness. Johnson (1946, p. 15) asserts that the one thing that mentally disturbed people have in common is their inability to communicate. They simply are unable to tell others what is bothering them. Johnson demonstrates throughout

[4]Paul Watzlawick, Janet H. Beavin, and Don D. Jackson, *Pragmatics of Human Communication* (New York: W. W. Norton & Company, 1967), pp. 84–85.

his book that mental illness is largely a matter of semantics and communication. Ellis (1966; 1972) bases his rational therapy on the thesis that emotional disturbances are an outcome of thought disturbances. The task of the therapist is to communicate to the patient the illogical nature of his thinking and behavior. The therapist is, in Ellis' words, "a frank propagandist."

Berne (1964) makes it clear that those of us (indeed, most of us) who want to fool people about who and what we are, play life games with comic seriousness. An example is the game he calls IWFY. This is the "If it were not for you . . ." syndrome. One doubts his ability to make a go of it in the professions but he says to his wife, "If it were not for you and the kids I could have. . . ." A man who wants to stay home and watch the ball game and drink beer says, "If it were not for you, I could have bought the down jacket and have been warm enough to go fishing." IFWY has many versions and starts at an early age. A four-year-old girl said to her mother, "Yes, I heard someone call my name but I did not know the voice." The odd part of the communication games people play is that one person often knows what the other player is *really* saying. Moreover, he allows the illusion to remain. It is a confusing game because, at other times, one cannot really "psych" it out. He then attributes the worst possible motives to the other— malice, avarice, jealousy.

Those people who have unusually good mental health are superior communicators. They feel secure enough that they can listen accurately. They do not need to be thinking of defenses, devising a way to be "one-up," or how the pieces can be moved so that they can win the game. Self-actualizers have closer relationships, tighter identification, and clearer communication with others than do the generality. Often this unusually healthy person is so sensitive and aware of others that feelings can be sent and received without words. There is an intuitive understanding that transcends the necessity of reducing the message to words (Maslow, 1967).

An **autistic** child has been so shattered by the absence of communication that he attempts to assert that he really does not need friendship. He withdraws. In extreme cases he withdraws so completely that he dies. Lonely, isolated, alienated adults are, like the autistic child, cut off from communication. Psychotherapists today are seeking to get the message across that isolated, anxious, and suspicious people would be wise to seek professional help. Fortunately, many people do know this. There is, for every emotionally disturbed person, an irreducible minimum requirement for recovery: "the provision of a therapeutic relationship with an accepting, understanding, and helping other" (Schofield, 1964, p. 89). He, literally, buys friendship from a psychologist, psychiatrist, or psychoanalyst.

Adolescents whose communication is blocked, or who feel it to be

The purchase of friendship

blocked in some degree, may try to purchase friendship by following the "gang." The use of drugs, beverage alcohol, or gang stealing may be the price they pay. Sexually promiscuous girls, far from being "oversexed," may offer their bodies, coolly and deliberately, in a rather contemptuous attempt to establish communication.

BARRIERS TO COMMUNICATION

Different language systems

The process of communication may be schematized by a sort of "systems analysis." Each step is influenced by many factors that may magnify the difference between the message sent and the one received. Figure 12.2 may be used to explain how communication may be impeded. It also explains how control may be exercised over potential message garblers.

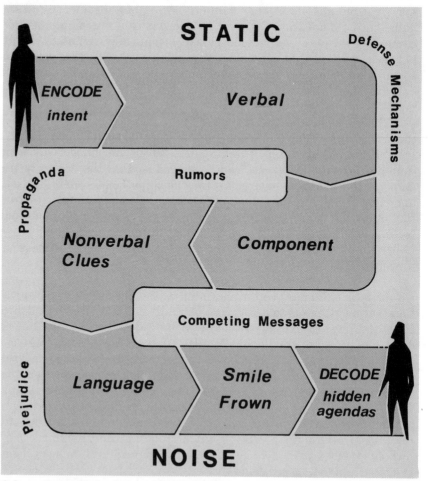

Figure 12.2   *Schematic analysis of communication*

The sender of the message must be using the same language as the potential receiver. The need for a common language system is obvious to anyone who has traveled in a foreign country. However, messages are garbled by the varied languages that exist within a nation or community (Szasz, 1973). Billy may be bewildered by the answer he gets, expressed in scientific, adult language, from his mother when he asks, "Where did I come from?" When mother finally runs down and says, "Now is that clear?" Billy says, "Not really. Jimmy came from Chicago and I just wondered where I came from." Mother, after carefully grooming herself to attend a dinner where her adolescent son is being honored as "scientist of the month," may be taken aback when he says, "You look tough."

The language used by a neophyte classroom teacher is often different from that of the pupil's home. In fact, one of the criticisms of education is that the answers to everyday problems are couched in academic terms. These terms have no relationship to the language used at home and in the community: "Chuck reveals reluctance to adhere to classroom protocol and persists in transgressing the property rights of others." To those who speak pedagese this means, "Chuck steals his classmates' pencils."

The language of the board room of the bank or business is different from the language used during the coffee break or at the drinking fountain. Intelligence tests are undergoing serious current criticism on similar grounds. The middle class language in which the test items are expressed differs from the language used by that 30 to 50 per cent of the population called the upper-lower and lower-lower classes. The latter are, nevertheless, required to take the tests in order to comply with "exclusion rituals" (McClelland, 1972).

Billy's questions about where he came from did not communicate because his mother used a false assumption. A white teacher in a Hopi Indian school asked four boys to go to the blackboard to work a multiplication problem. Each was to turn around when finished to see who could get through first. None turned around, despite the teacher's knowing that all had done similar problems previously. The teacher had falsely assumed that Hopi were as inter-personally competitive as were boys in his home town of Akron.

False assumptions

> Some years ago a young lady in one of my classes who did well in discussions did poorly in an examination. Not wishing to discourage her, I gave her a *C*. Her excellent work in class contradicted another low examination score. Again I gave a *C* and the girl stopped coming to class. I asked one of her housemates about the girl and was told that she was mad at me. When I asked "Why" I was told, "Her parents are forcing her to go to college. As soon as she flunks out she can go back home and marry the butcher boy. You keep passing her." Communication was clarified and her goal pursuit was simplified by my altering a false assumption I had made.

Double messages

Communication may be garbled by a lack of congruence between the verbal meaning and the vocal tone. For example, the words, "I trust you" may conflict with the intonation or the facial expression of the speaker. The receiver of the message may have difficulty determining the relative importance of the verbal, the vocal, and the facial message. Mehrabian (1972) analyzed these components of communication and found that the total impact of a message is 7 per cent verbal, 38 per cent vocal, and 55 per cent facial. Seeing is believing and we tend to rely much less on what we hear. Mehrabian suggests that when disturbed children are encountered the therapist might well examine the parent-child communication system. It may be that something in the child's behavior elicits a negative response from parents. There may be some action not really intending to irritate (*e.g.*, not looking up when spoken to but not intending to be inattentive). It may be that some negative parental attitude preceded the child's disturbing behavior. In either case, the difficulty is in determining which part of the double message to believe.

There is some tendency, perhaps a predominant tendency, to attribute the worst motive to the person who utters the double message. If there is any doubt about the words, "You're a hardworking bunch," the listeners will take it as an insult. They seek to confirm their own interpretation. In short, the "bunch" will show the speaker that they are not a hardworking group. It is small wonder that sarcasm is regarded as an impediment to clear communication.

Criticism

One of the major issues in mental health is the matter of a sturdy ego concept. One of our basic human needs is that for safety—the preservation of self. Communication, it has been shown, is a means of building and preserving self. Hence, it is logical that criticism would impede communication. Criticism prompts one to assume immediately a defensive psychological posture that filters words and nonverbal clues through a screen. The tendency is to contradict the criticism. One does not really listen to what the critic has to say.

It is only with considerable help and warnings against defensiveness that logic and criticism can be helpful to personality formation. Such a condition is known as openness. This openness can be taken only by a person who is unusually healthy. Most people are not so healthy as to be open to criticism. The result is blocked communication. The screen is too fine. The emotional overburden overbalances the logical load.

Child psychologists have for a long time endorsed the use of praise. Recently, the endorsement has come to be based on experimental verification. Positive reinforcement can more quickly gain a desirable mode of conduct than can criticism of undesirable behaviors (White, 1970, p. 682). Criticism may team with false assumptions as communication blockers. It is assumed (often falsely) that criticism is designed to belittle rather than to improve one's person or effectiveness.

Noise

One theory used to explain the linguistic inferiority of the lower class child in school, in comparison to the middle class child, is related to the concept of noise. Kagan (1968) postulates that it is not linguistic deprivation—a more popular theory—but a lack of *specificity* in verbal transactions that accounts for the lower class child's slower language development. It is not the lower class child's comparative lack of vocalization. It is the paucity of *distinctive* vocalization that accounts for his retardation. The middle class child awakens, cries or coos, and his mother, perhaps as she enters the baby's room, answers his call. The lower class child is surrounded by voices and noise—brothers, sisters, aunts, mother, and father may all be close by. Any one may answer his call. However, it is constancy, reliability, dependability, and safety that elicits baby's response. He is not ready to handle variety and unpredictability. In addition, street noises, radio, television, and others' speaking and yelling (perhaps heard through a wall from the next apartment) constitute a cacophony of sound that prompts the urge to tune out. The lower class child defends himself from the assault of noise.

Noise is more than loud and discordant sounds. One definition of noise (see Figure 12.2) is that it is any sound that interferes with communication. Bad reports, rumors, scandals, gossip, and chatter are noises that keep the lines of communication blurred. The grapevine, in office or plant, has been found to be amazingly fast but also distressingly inaccurate.

Sometimes noise is deliberately used in order to mislead the receiver of the communication. Messages are so placed that communication is diverted. Propaganda, advertising, and brain-washing are often deliberate attempts to slant the message. For years the tobacco industry fought the idea of stating that "Cigarette smoking may be dangerous to your health." Much pressure and varied research reports finally resulted in a statement, "Warning: The Surgeon General has determined that cigarette smoking is dangerous to your health." This is presented as inconspicuously as possible, and taste, flavor, country, and springtime freshness are made the prominent parts of the message. The clear-cut messages suffer the disadvantage of being stated in "scientific" language:

1. Epidemiological studies have demonstrated an association of cigarette smoking with cancer of the urinary bladder among men. The association of tobacco usage and cancer is less clear-cut.

2. Clinical and pathological studies have suggested that tobacco

smoking may be related to alterations in the metabolism of tryp-
thphan and may in this way contribute to the development of urinary
tract cancer.[5]

Maternal smoking during pregnancy exerts a retarding influence on fetal growth as manifested by decreased birthweight and
an increased incidence of prematurity, defined by weight alone.
There is strong evidence to support the view that smoking mothers
have a significantly greater number of unsuccessful pregnancies due
to still-birth and neonatal death as compared to non-smoking
mothers. There is insufficient evidence to support a comparable
statement for abortions.[6]

Analyses of the noises that are deliberately used to distort the
message are part of the study of propaganda. There are carefully
designed techniques that are designed to focus attention on a peripher-
al part of the transaction. Hence, the real message is obscured or
obliterated. Such techniques are:

Name calling—*Jews, Communists, scabs, hippies,* and *pater-
nalism* are words designed to have a negative connotation while
American (in the United States), *mother, loyalty,* and *relevance*
are words with positive connotations.

Glittering generalities—These words say little but imply much.
"Ask the man who owns one." "A chicken in every pot." "Tax
reduction, now." and "Rock of Gibraltar" are terms that leave
much to the imagination of the listener.

Transfer—The picture of a pretty girl is shown beside a car, bottle
of bourbon, or a U-Bank card.

Testimonial—A famed athlete's, motion picture star's, or television hero's endorsement of a given product or action (buying U. S.
Savings Bonds) shows that the product or action is "good."

Plain folks—The politician wears a western hat, farmer's overalls,
or kisses the baby to prove that he is just one of us.

Card stacking—One is dealt all the aces, (*i.e.,* the satisfied owners
of a certain make of car or golf ball are listed).

Band wagon—All the people (particularly those with good sense)
are doing it.

Repetition—Repetition tends to emphasize because if one hears it
often enough he tends to believe it; however, the technique must
be carefully controlled or it may be a case of Shakespeare's "The
lady doth protest too much, methinks" in *Hamlet,* Act III.

FACILITATING COMMUNICATION

Analysis of some of the barriers to communication implicitly calls
attention to some of the ways in which communication might be

[5]*The Health Consequences of Smoking* (A Report of the Surgeon General), U. S.
Department of Health, Education, and Welfare, Washington, D.C., 1971), p. 199.

[6]*Ibid.,* p. 415.

improved. Desirably, the same language must be used by sender and receiver; but lovers do seem to understand one another despite language barriers. Occasionally one must test assumptions. When there are double messages one tends to believe the facial component. Criticism must be used with strict respect for the self-assurance of the criticized person. There are some additional clues to the facilitation of communication.

Paul recognized the key to effective communication when he wrote, "If I speak in the tongues of men and angels, but have not love, I am as sounding brass or a clanging cymbal" (I Corinthians, 13: 1). In some translations the word love is charity, which is more apropos in this context. The receiver or sender must have respect, positive regard, and charity for the other. The desire to understand or to be understood is a basic attitude for clear communication. In fact, the golden rule of communication is about the same as the golden rule in ethics: Communicate with others as you would have them communicate with you.   *Attitude*

In counselor education we emphasize the concept of active listening. This is far, far beyond the level of waiting to break into dialogue with one's own comments. It is a matter of really trying to feel what the other person is saying. It is a matter of saying, "Check me out—this is what I'm hearing . . . ," "This is how I understand it . . . ," "My feeling is . . . ," and testing what one thinks he is hearing. Teachers have a difficult time listening because they mistake telling and teaching for communication. The attitude, implicit or inferred, "I'm older, wiser, better informed, and this is the way it is!"—No communication.

Teaching may be a legitimate function of communication but the one being taught must be ready and willing to learn. Another purpose is understanding—this is more than getting a descriptive chronology of events. It is a matter of comprehending the emotions that accompany the event. Communication serves the function of defining personal relationships and simultaneously helping the participants to define, and to verify and validate, themselves.   *Purpose*

The importance of defining the purpose of communication may be illustrated by reflecting on how the definition of self may function in parent-child communication. Trust and safety are issues at stake. The child can be rejected and belittled, or he can be accepted and made to feel important and wanted. He can be ignored as an incompetent dolt, or he can be placed in the key role of bringing joy to the family by his mere presence. Rejection is painful but it is preferable to being ignored. Children at home and school are known to misbehave rather than be ignored. They do not know how to contribute to the group (family, friends, church). Rather than be ignored, they act out their frustrations. Even adults are known to interject quite inappropriate comments rather than remain silent and be ignored. Verbally we accept the notion that "It's better to keep quiet and let people think you are ignorant than to speak up and prove it." Operationally, we would just about as soon prove it. As one gains skills he "scans" the field. He assesses the risks involved, and studies others to see what kind of contribution will be most relevant (Beier, 1967, p. 39). Many parents' and teachers' actions defeat their instructional purposes. Their actions are habitual, customary, imitative, or spontaneous. However, if considered logically in terms of purpose (raising children to be confident, autonomous persons) they would readily modify their mode of communication. Snubs, slights, loud statements, criticism, and sarcasm would also be minimized by adults who looked at the long-range purposes of their communication activities.

Adaptation to person and circumstance

Communication is manipulative (Shostrom, 1967). A basic human need is to belong, to be included, and to be a part of the human community. Words are major means of showing how we are accepted and how we accept others. Words set the tone for action. Words manipulate the situation. Words set the stage so that others can perform some complementary, or complimentary action. "I'm sorry about this hasty meal, but . . . ," or "I almost said 'No' because I didn't have a thing to wear." Becker (1962, p. 104) remarks that by properly delivering our lines we fulfill our role in the social milieu and we force others, by those same words, to fulfill their roles.

How one wants to exert his influence determines the tone, quality, and inflection, as well as the words selected; and care must be exercised to see that the role of one function does not conflict with that of another function. For example, a teacher endangers his role of parent if he is instructor in both. He endangers his marital status by being instructor to his wife. He weakens his social role by being instructor at the bridge table or on the golf course. Parents sometimes have difficulty shifting their role from the protective role of parents of children to the confidante role during their offsprings' adolescence. Parents often have difficulty shifting to a peer role when their offspring marry and are maintaining their own homes. Again—communication must be suited to person and circumstance.

There are many languages in the United States for indicating one's purpose. In some "primitive" cultures there are special words for indicating the chief's food and wives. The words differ from those used to indicate the braves' food and wives. There is, in the United States, variation in the words, pronunciations, and inflections when one speaks at home, at church, to children, to adults, to friends, to employee, to employer, to men, and to women.

Adaptation of communication to purpose is also dependent on physical arrangement. Note the difference in a lecture hall, a conference room, and one's home as related to the facilitation of communication. Note how the lecturer arouses hostility when he speaks in our home.

It is obvious that preparation must be made for a lecture on some scientific subject. Presumably, teachers prepare for their classroom presentations. Even in the day when lecturing is viewed skeptically, the effective instructor structures the situation so that certain things will happen. It is not so obvious, but nonetheless significant, that preparation for everyday transactions can be made. The adolescent plans just how and when he can most effectively approach dad regarding the trip or a job he wants to take. The young lady plans her strategy so that her sweetheart will say the words she wants to hear. Just as probably, the young man plans how he can avoid saying the words he is not yet ready to utter.

Preparation

At one time in ancient Greece, oratory was a highly respected activity. One cannot but wonder if this might not have been a factor in the phenomenon of the "Golden Age." Preparation for oratory concomitantly involved thinking and exchange of ideas on politics, science, literature, and art. It is to be hoped that an antidote to the one-way message of television, with which children are intellectually malnourished, is the growing popularity of rap sessions. Family counseling sessions, sensitivity groups, management seminars, etc. are today's communication media. The reader is advised to examine the potential of such groups in terms of his preparing for more effective communication.

There is a rather clear-cut difference of opinion on the matter of level of language that should be used in communication. One view is that the style and vocabulary should be suited to the audience. The other is that the audience should be "brought up to the level of" the expert. Would-be communicators will have to judge which direction to swerve in terms of the total situation. Factors in the decision are his own attitude, the receptiveness of the audience, the purpose of the confrontation, the age of the participants, and the role of the participants. There exists in such a milieu some risky terrain for assumptions. One factor is that one can go too far in assuming that others will not understand. The consequence is a feeling of "talking down." At the other extreme, overestimating the sophistication of the listeners could make it appear that one is talking in some foreign language.

Language

It is possible to be somewhat more definitive about language in terms of overall personality development. One is judged by his language. The more precise and accurate he can be the greater respect he tends to be accorded. Winston Churchill was an outstanding example of the use of linguistic precision. Each reader will be able to select his own examples of persons who were capable of using precisely the correct word and inflection at the appropriate time.

It is probably no fortuitous happenstance that vocabulary is such an important factor in conventional intelligence tests. Vocabulary items are the tools with which one (1) gets hold of ideas, (2) classifies them, and (3) expresses them. The assumption, with considerable justification, is that one is intelligent when his vocabulary enables him to grasp more ideas, to formulate them more precisely, and to express the nuances of closely related concepts. Hence, language broadens experiences and conserves them. It aids perception and conservation of ideas. It aids in the refinement of differentiations and distinctiveness.

Organization and delivery

Effective communication is aided by organization, but organization is not essential. If there are step-by-step processes involved in communication, one can be led to a given kind of conclusion. It would seem that, logically, one should be able to assemble a carburetor, fishing reel, or puzzle in a number of sequential moves. We are not at all sure that the carburetor, reel, or puzzle was initially created in that logical way. In fact, John Dewey's (1910) five steps in thinking (defining the problem, gathering data, formulating hypotheses, testing hypotheses, making a generalization) have been criticized because in actual problem solving, the steps seem to be all jumbled together. A baby learns a very complicated language structure with no formal presentation, logic, or stylized grammar (Brown and Bellugi, 1964).

Delivery, as implied in the foregoing discussion of verbal, vocal, and facial components, makes a difference in the way a message is received. A hesitant, halting manner of speech suggests that the speaker is not sure of himself. It is hard to place trust in him. One theory of stuttering is that it is an indication of psychological insecurity. Conversely, we tend to trust the speaker who is fluent, speaks calmly and confidently, and enunciates clearly. Trust is heightened by his giving to each listener a sort of personal attention. Mode of delivery is subject to training and practice. Unfortunately, in some cases, the confidence man and the con artist have practiced the art of delivery. Our trust in them is ill-placed. Typically though, we trust the person who has a smooth delivery style. Nevertheless, there are no conclusive studies indicating that delivery is any more of a clue to personality than is handwriting. Neither is a reliable clue.

LIMITATIONS IN COMMUNICATION

Politics

In the "good old days" of small communities and town meetings the effective speaker probably enjoyed an advantage over his opponent for office. As population increased the message was printed and could be edited. When radio came into existence the impact of the spoken word again became important to the politician. Today oral skills must be combined with the skills of the make-up man in order for the politician to make his maximum impact on the voter.

In presidential election years it becomes apparent that the meaning of communication must be carefully analyzed if we are to elect the leadership that can steer the "great ship of state." It is much easier to listen to the grammar, rhetoric, and delivery style than it is to look at the candidate's record. Rather than depending too much on the verbal content, the citizen needs to remember the consistency of personality from year to year. This is true whether the concern is for self or for the president. We need to recall the roles of language system, the double messages, the false assumptions, and the noise that are parts of what we know about communication.

Many problems have been solved by open communication. However, not all problems will be so solved. Who is talking, the communication milieu, and the purposes must be taken into account.

When dissension arises between working-class husband and wife, it is likely to be suppressed or fought out, often leaving a smoldering residue. Middle-class couples also inhibit anger or exhibit it by open quarrels; but if this becomes frequent, they have some faith that their talking things over between themselves or with friends or professional helpers will enable them to work their problems out. Far more than lower-class couples, they believe in the efficacy of confession, catharsis, and understanding to modify their impulses and behaviors. Far more, too, they are concerned with analyzing and weighing their personal "happiness" and what they are "getting out" of marriage. Communication has become the current key word among middle-class couples and their professional helpers today, almost as if some powers of magic are attached to being able to say out loud to the other what one feels and thinks (I am reminded of E. B. White's gentle plaint that it isn't silence you can cut with a knife any more, but the exchange of ideas, that intelligent discussion of practically everything is what is breaking up modern marriages.) The lower-class marriage is neither plagued nor blessed with this interchange of confidence or self-other appraisal. Most lower-class women seem to miss it, though many, schooled by adversity, as are their husbands, to taciturnity and suppression because "it's no good talking about it—you've just got to *take* it," push down and deny even to themselves the recognition of feelings or unfulfillable desires. But for the middle-class couple there perhaps needs to be some further thought about *what* is useful and constructive to communicate— certainly not everything, particularly if it is destructive to "other" or even to the self.[7]

[7]Helen Harris Perlman, *Persona: Social Role and Personality* (Chicago: University of Chicago Press, 1968), pp. 108–109.

Personal reserve

Not all persons are ready to share themselves freely and openly with others. They get along efficiently and happily without revealing their souls to others. They may hide themselves from their best friends and spouses. This is not to say that communication and sharing are not an essential part of being human and healthy. It is saying that there is also some room for private reserve.

Several authorities in that realm of communication called sensitivity groups or interpersonal process groups warn that there are dangers of tearing down the defensive-protective reserves that people have built up and successfully maintained for years. Rogers (no date) says that those persons who struggle along on the border of neuroticism need to have an expert available to stop the "communication process" when one is on thin ice. Birnbaum (1972) says that teachers in a school system may come to know each other too well. They may become suspicious and paranoid following sensitivity sessions that are too enthusiastic. Blacks and whites, he says, may confront each other but it takes more than letting the other know how he feels to reduce social tensions. Shostrom (1969) cites instances in which there is too frank an admission of feelings. Remarks about one's mate, attractive neighbors, or former sweethearts cause a break-up of the marriage. He says that both the advantages and disadvantages from communication must be weighed.

SUMMARY

The process of becoming fully human requires communication with fellow beings. Facile, accepting, mutually respectful communication enhances one's social personality. Blocked communication leads to distortion of personality and to feelings of inadequacy. There are various levels of communication. These range from casual acknowledgement of the other's presence, or the desire actually to hide, to that kind of communication which is deeply meaningful, revealing, and also positively developmental.

Communication, although important, is often taken for granted. It may be neglected as a systematic approach to personality development. Factors which render communication difficult and that are exemplified in the "Generation Gap" are rapid change, the changed roles of the parent generation and young people (specifically the shift from goal to role), the pervasiveness of television, and parental indecisiveness on how to act as parents.

Communication is a factor in how one's self is defined. Stereotypes such as Jew, Chink, hick, dude, and hippie, have a tendency to make the named person fashion his personality after the verbalized stereotype. It is not, therefore, surprising that mental health is to a marked extent a verbal-linguistic problem. One antidote to alienation and social withdrawal is the purchase of friendship in dialogue. This implies paying a psychotherapist for time, attention, and conversation.

Barriers to communication are different language systems, erroneous assumptions on either the senders' or receivers' parts, double messages (contrast between verbal content and facial or bodily message), and criticism. Noise in the form of rumors, malice, criticism, hidden agendas, and contrasts in status also tend to block clear communication.

Improved communication involves, first of all, an attitude. It involves mutual respect for, and concern about, the fellow communicator's well being. In the form of sensitivity groups and interpersonal process groups, metacommunication has some admirable developmental potentials. Metacommunication is not a cure-all. In order for it to yield maximum benefit such communication groups should be guided by competent professionals.

SUGGESTED READINGS

ELLIS, ALBERT, "Humanistic Psychotherapy: A Revolutionary Approach," *The Humanist*, Vol. 32, No. 1, 24–27, January/February, 1972.

The rational-cognitive approach to therapy depends on communication that may be logical, frankly propagandist, or simply didactic and authoritarian. It consists in the therapist's getting across the idea that past behaviors do not justify or dictate current and future behaviors.

FARBER, LESLIE H., "He Said, She Said," *Commentary*, Vol. 53, No. 3, 53–59, March, 1972.

The author believes that the easy intimacy that can be achieved in man to man talk is not obtainable in man/woman talk because of differences in biological and cultural motivation.

JENSEN, BENT, "Human Reciprocity: An Arctic Exemplification," *American Journal of Orthopsychiatry*, Vol. 43, 447–458, 1973.

The author postulates that sharing has become a vital part of man's make-up and survival. He uses hunters of Greenland as his example. Sharing and reciprocity involves many media of communication.

KURTZ, PAUL, "Imperatives for the 1970's," *The Humanist*, Vol. 30, No. 1, 3–4, January/February, 1970.

U Thant has asserted that if we do not resolve our ancient animosities and launch a global partnership within the decade, our problems may grow beyond control. The way to resolve these problems and initiate the partnership is through communication.

SHOSTROM, EVERETT L., "Group Therapy: Let the Buyer Beware," *Psychology Today*, Vol. 2, No. 12, 36–40, May, 1969.

The wave of popularity for group therapy, a contemporary approach to improved communication, may be self-defeating if not competently guided. A potentially important avenue of communication may lose its usefulness if not kept out of the hands of inept and overly enthusiastic endorsers.

STEWIG, JOHN WARREN, "Creative Drama and Language Growth," *Elementary School Journal*, Vol. 72, 176–188, 1972.

Ostensibly this article might seem to be of interest only to prospective elementary teachers. It does, however, show the role of practice, positive reinforcement, and encouragement of individuality in personality development.

FOLLOW-UP LEARNING ACTIVITIES

Next time you get together with a group of four or five others, note the level of communication that was most predominant and tell what you think this means.

It was level _____ This suggests that _____

_____

_____

_____

_____

Try to think of someone you know who seems to be without any noticeable fluctuation in feeling level. Engage him in conversation and record how he describes his parents—particularly his mother.

_____

_____

_____

_____

_____

Does your observation seem to confirm Fraiberg's theory about "hollow persons?" Yes _____ No _____ because _____

_____

_____

_____

_____

What do you think you might do *as a parent* to reduce the generation gap?

_____

_____

_____

Suppose you have very few close friends, tend to be anxious when in a crowd, talk little in groups. Would you think it worthwhile to "buy friendship" from a psychotherapist?

Yes _____ No _____ because _____

_____

_____

Cite an example of a double message you have received recently.

_____

_____

_____

(Compare and discuss your responses on the last two items with a classmate.)

13
Life Styles and Defense Mechanisms

Defense by hiding. You can't fall down if you don't get out of bed.

LEARNING ACTIVITIES

List a number of key words that you think describe your life style (friendly, optimistic, lazy, etc.):

_____

_____

_____

_____

_____

What or who do you think are the factors or persons responsible for the life style you have developed?

_____

_____

_____

_____

_____

Why do you think mankind has so universally and consistently used drugs and alcoholic drinks?

_____

_____

_____

_____

_____

(Compare and discuss your response with several classmates.) Write a definition of rationalization. Use your past studies, if they have covered the term, but do not now consult a text or dictionary.

_____

_____

_____

_____

_____

What behaviors, if any, do you have that could be classed as techniques for escaping or evading reality?

_____

_____

_____

_____

What behaviors, if any, do you have that could be classed as attacking techniques?

_____

_____

_____

_____

(If you have difficulty with this [or the previous item] discuss it with a classmate or two and then try it again.)

The reader's attention is called to the placement of this chapter—next to the one on communication. It should be noted—though communication will not be repetitiously mentioned in the various sections—how often a defense mechanism is an outcome of faulty communication. A defense mechanism is often a chronically hostile message.

Probably the most noticeable thing about human personality is the consistency with which any one person behaves. This consistency has been called one's style of life. Others quickly, but often unconsciously, identify this style of life. They are either attracted or repulsed by it. However, in a great many instances, life style probably just makes no difference. One is, either correctly or incorrectly, almost immediately identified as a grouch or a cheerful person. One is seen as an aggressive or as a retiring personality, a confident or an anxious individual.

It might be better to title this chapter, "Styles of Life." It would be correct to do so; however, not all lifestyles are defensive. Some people are so bold, confident, and heterostatically inclined that they simply do not permit a noticeable degree of defensiveness to pervade their style. Such persons, defined as self-actualizers (Chapter 6) are rare. The majority do have at least an element of defensiveness in their make-ups. The title "Defense Mechanisms" was chosen because so much of the research done in personality has focused upon how people cope, rather than how they grow. The reader gets a conventional approach by using the concept of defense. He can, therefore, more readily transfer his knowledge to other related readings and discussions. In addition, one of the major approaches to the study of personality (Chapter 7, "Psychoanalysis") depends largely on what were called the "ego defense mechanisms." Many of the defenses discussed in this chapter were initially identified and defined by various psychoanalytic authorities.

PERSONALITY AND ADJUSTMENT

Defense mechanisms

Freud's idea, as shown earlier, was that there was a conflict between the drive of the ego and the urges of the id. The ego seeks to perform socially approved, culturally sanctioned actions. The ego is opposed to the blind drive of the id to satisfy its wants and urges. As a compromise measure, defense mechanisms were developed. These behaviors, kept in balance, can satisfy our social and personal needs.

They can also avoid the frustration of completely blocked "instinctual" or physiological needs.

The problem, in terms of personality balance, is to avoid permitting the adjustive mechanism to become so marked that it is called into action when it is unnecessary. When this occurs, as it frequently does, it is fitting to say that the defense mechanism no longer defends. The adjustive mode becomes nonadjustive because the tension and frustration avoided in one circumstance are aggravated in another. For example, a lie may help one avoid embarrassment or punishment in one situation. It may weaken one's disposition to assume responsibility in another dilemma. It does this weakening by virtue of the liar's beginning to believe what he initially knew was not so. Perlman (1968, p. 109) says that there is a phenomenon worth noting—when something is said aloud and believed by listeners, it seems to be true to the sayer. It is this self-defeating, snowballing, aspect of defense mechanisms that makes them a hazard. This occurs despite their being a possible source of temporary relief from pressure.

Sheldon (1942, 1954), Williams (1972), Lombroso (1918), and others have tried to show that there are certain life styles that are characteristic of given body types and glandular compositions (see Chapter 8). Sheldon and Williams have some data to support their views. There are also exceptions to the predicted trends. For example, there is the effective and satisfied athletic type who accommodates to the life and style of a college professor. As a professor he is supposedly cerebrotonic rather than somatotonic. Of course, the explanation is that, in addition to constitutional predispositions, learnings also shape one's personality. The big question, at present unanswered, is "At what cost, in terms of pressure and tension, does the athletic type adjust to the logical, contemplative life of the professor?" In other words, the question concerns the kinds of defense mechanisms he must use to resolve the conflict between role expectation and bodily inclination.

Constitutional factors in life styles

There is no doubt that babies are born with different kinds of dispositions (Sontag, 1966). Some are smiling, contented, easily fed, sound-sleepers while others are sober, cry frequently, regurgitate their food, and sleep fitfully. Furthermore, there are mothers who want and need each of these different kinds of personalities in their babies. Not all mothers want the smiling, "easy" baby. It may be that they enjoy the martyr role that the child imposes on them. Most mothers would enjoy the happy, easy baby. Such a baby may unwittingly seem to confirm the fact that the mother is a capable and cheerful person. And herein a question arises about the mother's constitutional predisposition—does she react in terms of her own being or does the baby elicit her response?

Brain weight and cellular composition of the cortex have an

influence on the speed and quality of thought (Sullivan, 1972). Endocrine glands act in an intricate interaction pattern. Some normal glands differ by as much as seven times in size from other normal glands. Each of us has a distinctive set of drives (Williams, 1972). Some need much physical activity. Others need a comparatively great amount of rest. Some want power. Others are content to follow. Some find it easy to control their sex drives. Others have a continuous and turbulent struggle to control their sexual impulses. Many believe that there is an inborn tendency for some people to overeat—providing that there is the opportunity.

There are constitutional predispositions to the development of life styles. It is also true that experience, conditioning, and learning are needed to implement or impede realization of the predisposition.

Learning a life style

It is widely taken for granted that the way a baby is accepted when he appears in this world determines his personality. This creates a tendency to overlook morphological and physiological inclinations. If he is welcomed, patted, admired, kept warm and dry, fed when he is hungry (rather than on a prescribed schedule) it is generally believed that this shapes his perception. He begins to trust people and to feel that the world is a friendly, gratifying place. His perceptions may be shaped when he is neglected, left to suffer deprivation, filth, and noise, and is the helpless butt of adult resentments and frustrations. It is likely that he will judge the world to be austere, forbidding, and needing to be endured or conquered. The baby meeting a friendly world can be curious, confident, and heterostatic. The baby encountering the depressive environment is more likely to be defensive, withdrawn, and alienated. Much of this view is expressed in a number of statements that have been circulated as wall placards:

> If a child lives with criticism,
>   He learns to condemn.
> If a child lives with hostility,
>   He learns to fight.
> If a child lives with approval,
>   He learns to like himself.

One could say to these statements, "Well, pretty much so" and "Yes. Other things being equal." It may also be that the child who lives with hostility learns to retreat; or the child who lives with encouragement may learn, not confidence, but the habit of depending on support from others.

It was shown earlier (Chapter 5) that, although there are variations within a culture, certain life styles are learned as a matter of social heritage. Some isolated tribes, for instance, tend to respect and develop hostility and bellicose behaviors while others regard highly such things as peace and friendliness.

Learning, however, is not simply a matter of stimulus input—whether formal instruction within a classroom or tribal conditioning. For reasons we do not yet understand—enzymes within the brain, speed and the course of tracking of electrical impulses, memory traces—different people learn different things from what ostensibly is the same material milieu (Sullivan, 1972). The psychological dilemma is contained in the cliché, "The optimist sees the doughnut and the pessimist sees the hole."

We do not know exactly how and why a baby learns a life style. We know that early in life a life style is developed and that that style tends to persist. Unfortunately, the preceding sentence would be characterized, in terms of the previous chapter on communication, as a glittering generality filled with noise. "Early in life" could mean two years. It has meant six years. In the United States our compulsory education laws would seem to say that we think personality modification is possible up to age 16 or 18. Some psychotherapists refuse to deal with children. Some are reluctant to work with those over 40 years old. The statement contains "noise" because we do not know how persistent the "tends" part is. It may be that each person is born with a tendency to be friendly, optimistic, or curious. He may be born aloof, forlorn, and placid and it may be that the tendency never changes. Nevertheless, the degree to which it is manifested may be subject to cultural conditioning and to conscious and intentional control. The author's belief is that throughout life, perhaps in continuously diminishing degree, one can change the manifestation of his life style. One can, through conscious intent, decide to reduce certain of his hampering defense mechanisms. One can hasten the process of change by enlisting the aid of a competent teacher or therapist. Tendencies are, in short, tendencies, not life sentences. It may be that it is not age but motivation that determines one's susceptibility to learning new life styles.

Tension and conflict

Life styles have their constitutional, cultural, and learning components. In addition, it is pertinent to consider tension and conflict. **Tension** is an inescapable part of motivation insofar as it makes the organism alert to certain kinds of stimuli. Tension is generated by **conflict** of opposing drives. For example, the feeling of hunger and the wish to avoid obesity.

Tension and conflict are parts of normal living. To avoid conflict or to be without it would be to live a life in which one was a nonentity—a cipher. If, for instance, there is no conflict in marriage, it would mean that one partner has given up any claim to a life of his/her own. If there is no conflict between instructor and student, one of two things may be happening. The student is not learning in terms of his unique perspective, or the instructor is working over thoroughly plowed ground.

It is unresolved and continuous unrelieved tension and conflict that are the concerns of those who wish to live productive lives. Persistent conflict is the concern of the psychotherapists who are supposed to help disturbed persons. How people seek to avoid tensions and conflicts is the concern of the remainder of the chapter. The reader should be warned that often the defenses are against a normal amount of tension. Such normal tension might be regarded as an incentive to grow rather than as a condition to be avoided.

DEFENSES BY ESCAPE

Withdrawal   Withdrawal can be either physical or psychological. The young divorcee showed a perspective on withdrawal when she said, "I had heard so much about 'married and lived happily ever after' that on the first experience of conflict, I thought I was miserable." It is wise to withdraw when one is facing insurmountable odds. It is, however, difficult to determine when those odds are insurmountable. Sometimes it takes years for the wife of an alcoholic to realize that she may be impeding the progress of her husband to the "bottom of the pit" by forgiving and by being patient. Only after he reaches the bottom can he see that it is his own decision, not the support of his wife, that can cause a change of direction.[1] Often it is wise for the discouraged student not to drop school. However, it may be wise for him to change courses or to avoid certain teachers. An example of this is when a black child is subjected to a prejudiced white teacher.

Withdrawal may be a sound method of dealing with some dilemmas. There are two implicit hazards. One is that it may be a habitual response to a slight difficulty. When there are repeated instances of withdrawal, it is wise to suspect that the precipitating factors are within the person. Too often we blame the situation. Two, if after one has withdrawn, quit trying, changed his goal, he continues to regret his decision or ineptitude, then the withdrawal is nonadjustive.

Daydreaming   When the tasks of life are too strenuous, when one defeat is followed by another, some people defend themselves by daydreaming, or reverie. The extreme cases are the autistic child, the person under the influence of those drugs called hallucinogens (*Use and Misuse . . . ,* 1968), and the psychotic who has lost contact with reality and lives in a dream world. As is the case with many other defense mechanisms, it is the extent and persistence of the daydream that may render it adjustive or nonadjustive. If one can temporarily fantasize about his former sweetheart (who has found another love) returning *but also*

[1]The conclusion that a woman abets her husband's drinking by repeatedly forgiving him is by no means a universally accepted view.

go on about the business of finding another for himself, then the daydream may have merit. Daydreaming to the extent of no action is not helpful. An example is the boy who dreamed of being a big league baseball player but did not even try out for his high school team. Such daydreaming is nonadjustive.

All persons may need to daydream to some extent. One must dream of distant goals and of future accomplishments. Then, he needs to put some element of a plan to reach those dreamed of goals into action. The chronic dreamer is often referred to as one who listens to, and keeps step with, a different drum. "Normal" people—those who conform to the expectations of society—have a difficult time understanding dreamers. There are people who focus on their distant goals and who, in so dreaming, have less intimate contact with the reality of the here and now.

Lying

Some lying may simply be a matter of excluding some persons from a particular area of concern. It is simply none of their business. There are many social lies that are told, not as a matter of defense, but as a matter of avoiding a pointless injury. "My! It's good to see you," may cover the feeling that the two have little in common. It would be easier not to have to appear courteous and friendly. It may be better to say to the open-house hostess, "I'm late because we had a soft tire" than to admit that attendance is compulsory and that you really wanted to minimize the time spent at the get-together.

Lying as a characteristic defense mechanism starts in childhood. (1) Lying begins when the pressures imposed by parents are too heavy for the immature and inexperienced child. (2) It begins when the child, in his naiveté, really cannot distinguish clearly between reality and what the child hopes for, has nocturnal dreams about, or sees but cannot identify. An example of the latter is the child who was told that he must not lie when he reported seeing a lion in the back yard. When the mother did check, she saw a huge St. Bernard.

Lying is one of the more common defense mechanisms. It is used to escape the consequences of one's weaknesses or to avoid shouldering responsibility. The motive is to conceal the perceived facts. Lying may cover some error, neglect of duty, be used to save face, or to win approval by deluding another into thinking one has done his job.

The hazards of lying hardly compensate for the temporary gains. Facing one's weaknesses and shortcomings is, in the long run, a step toward overcoming them. Often the lie is discovered with a consequent losing of face—or the necessity of telling more lies. Then there is the persistent danger that one may come to believe in the lie himself. One's lying may be so successful that he becomes a pathological liar. This is a person who cannot tell the truth when to do so would be clearly advantageous. The pathological liar lies even when it would be better to be truthful.

Regression   Another way to withdraw is through the defense of regression. This means going back to a former immature behavior after having once established a degree of maturity. This defense is frowned upon in little boys. They are supposed not to cry when hurt or disappointed. Crying like a baby is an acceptable behavior for little girls, big girls, and women. There are some who believe that this social disapproval of regression for men is disadvantageous. The cultural prescription of regression is a partial explanation of cases of high blood pressure, heart attacks, and gastrointestinal disorders. Maybe, it is proposed, men should let down their defenses, cry more readily. They should play freely without feeling guilt for neglected responsibilities. They should more readily "vent" their emotions.

Regression also has its questionable side. When the newly married woman finds that all is not "sunshine and flowers" and runs back to be "mama's and papa's little girl," she solves no problems. When the devoted mother is unable to release her son to his wife, the mother neglects her own developmental tasks. She also adds burdens to what is, at best, a difficult time for newly married persons (Roy and Roy, 1970). When an old man, no longer able to compete vigorously with young and middle aged persons, resorts to the behaviors that were successful when he was "in the saddle," his regression makes life more difficult for all. Overholser summarizes regression succinctly:

> Just as there are decreases in the elasticity and resilience of the skin and muscles [in old age], so there tends to be a decrease in the resilience as to habits of thinking and acting and feeling. These rigidities are sometimes very conspicuous. If careful study of the preexisting personality is made it is found that "senile" peculiarities are really exaggerations of traits concealed earlier in life. Mental hygiene is not something which should be put on suddenly at one's sixtieth birthday. The degree to which the individual has been well-adjusted in his earlier life will have much to do with his ability to maintain a reasonably equable and happy old age. The man who in his twenties and thirties was a bully, a boaster, a whiner or a hypochondriac will show these traits in an exaggerated form when he becomes seventy. The characteristics will be more marked and his ability to conceal them will be less.[2]

Introversion   Introversion is a word originally employed by Jung (1928) to indicate one polarity of personality types. It refers to the tendency of one to direct his attention and energy inward. This contrasts to attention directed outward to the external world of people and things. Unfortunately, introversion is often thought to be maladjustive and as a condition to be corrected. Of course, in its extreme manifestation of being unable to mingle and deal with others, it is maladjustive. Many

[2]Winfred Overholser, "The Mental Maturity of Later Maturity," ed. W. B. Terhune. *Living Wisely and Well* (New York: E. P. Dutton and Company, Inc., 1949), p. 90.

schizophrenics and criminals have been noted for their extreme introversion. In Jung's concept, introversion meant that one was a thinking, sensing, and intuitively oriented person. To the extent that adjustments are made by withdrawing and fantasy, introversion may be an ineffective adjustment mechanism. To the extent that the introvert needs to be independent, self-reliant, and logical, then introversion has its advantages. It is worth considering that many of us could be somewhat more introverted and less the crowd-follower.

In the final analysis, the evaluation of introversion cannot be achieved by subjecting it to scrutiny in isolation. The ultimate tests must be in terms of the adjustive or nonadjustive nature of the other behaviors. It is the person's *total* reaction pattern that counts.

Identification

Identification refers to the increase of one's feelings of worth and power by allying oneself with certain prestigious persons or groups. It is closely related to fantasy in that no action on the individual's part is necessary. It should be made clear that identification, as a defense mechanism, is not synonymous with the phenomenon of identity. One's identity with a group or institution may be established through having a role or function to perform in that group. It requires work and service to achieve and maintain that identity.

Identification as a defense mechanism means that one simply pays his dues as a Kiwanian, Sigma Nu, Republican, member of the Smith family, or student at Algae College. He lets others know he is so identified. However, he makes no effort to enhance the power and prestige of the group concerned. Identification may also be with things—ownership of the most expensive automobile or home. Identification, typically an unconscious process, begins with the quite normal belief in dad's omnipotence. It is a retreat mechanism for those with exaggerated feelings of inferiority.

Drugs and drink

There are many reasons why people resort to drugs or the excessive use of beverage alcohol.[3] Each reason may, in itself, be a manifestation of personality. Many users have resulting changes—or revelations—of personality. A few of the reasons that drugs or alcohol may be used are:

- As a part of participation in ceremonials;
- Proof that one is growing up and can engage in an "adult" activity;
- To follow the crowd;
- To distinguish oneself from the crowd;
- To lessen the tension of a challenge or disappointment.

[3]This entire subject is of such current concern and importance in the study of personality that an entire chapter is devoted to it later in the book—Chapter 17.

Drinkers separate themselves into not very clear-cut categories: casual drinkers, social drinkers, problem drinkers, and alcoholics.

It is postulated that the cause and manifestation of some drinkers and drug users is the need to evade reality. For example, it is believed that the incidence of drug usage in slums and ghettos is high because of the pervasiveness of frustrations and the predominance of hopelessness (Yahraes, 1965). One explanation of the high incidence of alcoholism is the desire to escape by blotting out the sharp realization of frustrating conditions—boredom, grief, challenge beyond one's ability, a nagging spouse, a domineering boss. It is not safe to say that all drug addiction and alcoholism are reducible to escape. Williams (1972), for instance, proposes the theory that some people are alcoholics from the time of their very first drink. The chemical composition of their bodies is such that there is an affinity that literally causes one's body to say, "Alcohol, you wonderful thing, where have you been all my life?" However, certainly for some, drugs and alcohol are escape mechanisms.

DEFENSE BY ATTACK

The attack syndrome   Whether one will attack or seek to escape in the face of frustration seems to be, in part, an innate predisposition. A cornered rabbit cowers and will fight only on contact. Certain breeds of dogs advance to meet the challenge. Similarly, some people are spontaneously aggressive or retiring. The tendency is shown in infants, some of whom bawl lustily, readily have temper tantrums, throw toys, or bat the spoon or cup away. In many other ways they show a distinctly aggressive orientation. Others are distinctly different. They whimper quietly when displeased. They seem patiently to wait the indulgence of their mothers. They permit other children to monopolize their toys.

Although these tendencies *seem to be* innate, we cannot be sure. It may be that the aggressive child learned, very early in life, that the way to get service was to make a lot of noise. The way to get what one wanted was to demand and seize. The retiring child, encountering different parents and siblings, may have learned that he was ignored when he demanded. He was admired when he was quiet and courteous (if a baby can be courteous).

Negativism   The attacking nature of negativism is most readily seen in the small child who after a series of "No" answers regarding what he might want would then say "No" when asked if he would like to have an ice cream cone. Negativism is noted in the adult who is silent during the discussion of a proposed project. Then, as the stage for considering details is reached, he comes forth with the idea that the whole thing is

worthless. Rebellion against authority, stubbornness, and argumentativeness are common manifestations of negativism.

The self-defeating nature of negativism is so evident that it is
difficult to understand how it could get started. One explanation is that
it is better to be actively rejected than to be ignored. Inciting
resentment is better than to have one's presence simply not be noticed.
Another explanation is that expectations are beyond the individual's
capacity to perform, or are beyond what the individual believes is his
capacity. Negativism might hide one's inadequacy by making others
think one could perform if he just wanted to. It is a case of "You can't
fall down if you don't get out of bed."

It may be difficult for parents to endure the negativism of their
adolescent offspring. Typically and normally, it is a passing phase of
conduct. Furthermore, negativism may be a healthy sign if it is a
phase of growing up and wanting to be independent. Parents might,
despite needing the patience of Job, be thankful that their adolescent
sons and daughters have enough self-assertiveness to rebel against
parental dominance. It is a first step toward avoiding the life style of a
Mr. Milquetoast.

Displacement means that hostile and aggressive inclinations, generated by one set of interpersonal transaction, are transferred to
another, innocent, person or situation. Thus, the meek employee in the
office who is too insecure to respond to his boss's criticism—just or
unjust—takes his hostilities out on his wife or children. They, he
knows, are too weak to retaliate for his attack.

Phobias and **psychosomatic illnesses** are explained in terms of
the defense mechanism of displacement. In the case of claustrophobia,
for instance, fear of a harmless enclosed space is presumed to be the
displaced or symbolized fear of something deeper. It represents being
hemmed in by social protocol or a demanding father. The displacement
of the emotion into fear protects the individual from acknowledging
his hatred of his father. Eysenck (1961, p. 752) states that the
phenomenon of functional neuroses is an example of displacement; for
example, the person who focuses his dislike for his job onto his
gastrointestinal system may find one day that he has ulcers.

Displacement

Irradiation is a generalized form of displacement. Instead of the
employee's taking out his resentments on his wife and children (in the
case cited in the foregoing section), he permits the emotion to pervade
his whole living pattern. He is irritable and angry with anyone whom
he encounters. The store clerk, other drivers, the gas station at-
tendant, his secretary, the barber, and the telephone operator may be
the butt of one's resentment of one's boss.

An often cited case of irradiation is that described in Watson's

Irradiation

(1924) experiments. He conditioned a child to fear a rabbit by making a sudden loud noise behind the child's head every time a rabbit was brought close. The fear irradiated to other furry animals and even to the mother's fur coat.

Compensation

Compensation may be either direct or indirect. In direct compensation one attempts to make up for a weakness, or imagined weakness, by concentrating more time and energy on overcoming the deficiency. A number of athletes have so successfully used compensation that they have become champions. Glenn Cunningham, a famed distance runner a few years ago, began running in order to keep his legs from stiffening after they had been severely burned. Such compensation is a rather successful attacking defense. Compensation is self-defeating when the activity demands so much time and energy that other normal activities (social, occupational, esthetic) are cut out of one's living regimen.

Indirect compensation means counter-balancing one's lack, or imagined lack, in one area by developing some other talent and skill. The new skill obscures the deficiency. The socially unpopular girl may devote herself so assiduously to her studies that she becomes noted as a scholar. The young person who is ashamed of his inadequacy as a scholar may, on the other hand, make social recognition a planned goal. The success of indirect compensation depends more on attitude than it does on accomplishment. If the socially successful person continues to let his academic deficiency pervade his thought, the gain is not compensatory.

Projection

Projection is the habit of blaming others for our own shortcomings. It means attributing to others the deficiencies that we covertly feel to be our own.[4] The person takes his own inner emotional state and blames it on the outer world. Thus he denies any connection or responsibility with himself (Stagner, 1961, p. 125). Refusing to acknowledge any role of one's inner state, one looks for the slightest clue that will indicate some indecent or ulterior motive in another. Projection is at work in the conditions that give rise to the stories about old maids and the threats to their chastity that they so readily perceive.

Projection is all too common in the day-to-day lives of ourselves and those about us. Students project their academic boredom or difficulty onto the instructor; the instructor is to blame for not making the course more interesting. The instructor blames his inadequate preparation on assignments that are outside his field of concentration; he excuses himself by citing the hours spent on committees. House-

[4]Further information regarding the nature of projection is contained in Chapter 15, in which the device called "Projective Techniques" is described as an approach to personality evaluation.

wives project their sloppiness on the carelessness of their children; and husbands blame the uncut grass on their slave-driving supervisors; their hard work leaves them exhausted at the end of the week.

It should be noted that projection (as an attack mechanism) is functionally related to introjection (as an escape mechanism). This means attributing to others one's own negative emotions. In both projection and introjection, selective attention is given to certain stimuli.

Rationalization

As popular as projection is, **rationalization** is more frequently used. This is perhaps because projection can be classified as one manifestation of rationalization. Despite the roots of the word "rationalization," it means just the opposite of rational or logical. Rationalization consists in making excuses for incompetence or neglect so that one will be forgiven by others. In psychoanalytic terms, rationalization refers to protecting the ego. The process denies acknowledgment of the elements of repressed love or hostility that are really behind the behaviors being rationalized. It would be easy to think of rationalization as belonging to the retreat type of defense mechanism. It is included in the attack category because others do not consistently ask for the reasons why we are not perfect. Rationalization seems to be an implementation of the cliché, "The best defense is a strong offense."

Rationalization may be of the "sour grapes" variety. This type stems from Aesop's fable about the fox who was unable to reach the grapes. He then said he really did not want them because they were probably sour anyway. The boy whose girl friend tells him to "flake off" proceeds to find numerous condemning faults that she had. This is actually a pretty effective defense mechanism in such a case. The "sweet lemon" variety of rationalization means that one accepts the inevitable. One can say that his failure to achieve the honor roll or to close the deal on a Mercedes-Benz was a good character-building experience.

DEFENSE BY AILMENT

Illness or injury is regarded somewhat differently in various families, socioeconomic strata, cultures, and by different individuals. Generally, one who is sick or injured is given just a little more attention than usual. He is excused from most of his responsibilities and someone else takes over his duties. The expression of fussiness and impatience by the ill person is indulged or forgiven. Only occasionally is the sick person shunted aside, made to take care of himself, and ignored as a functioning member of the group. One consequence of this conventional indulgence of the ill person is that some discover that illness is a way to place a burden on someone he dislikes. It is a way to get even with someone, or a way to escape onerous tasks.

Pyschosomatic illness

In popular thinking there is a distinction between what is called "real" illness and a "mental" illness or psychosomatic ailment. There is a difference between organic and psychosomatic illness *but* both are quite real. Both are quite disabling, and quite painful. The main difference is in how the disorder was initially contracted. There is a difference in how it might be successfully treated.

Organic diseases are caused by the body's being invaded by germs, bacteria, or viruses. Some trauma or prolonged overburden may result in broken bones, twisted skeletons, or skin lesions. Such diseases and trauma are treated by means of medicine and surgery. However, it has been found that kindly treatment, the rekindling of hope, and the discovery that one is loved can aid the healing and recovery process in organic disease.

Psychosomatic illnesses are caused by psychological and social pressures that wear away hope, love, and aspirations. One's defenses are lowered. The reality of these disorders is attested to by the statistic that half the beds in general hospitals are filled with patients whose ailments are psychosomatic. When it comes to diseases of the circulatory system, respiratory system, and gastrointestinal system the proportion of illnesses that are psychosomatic may run as high as 90 per cent.

> . . . The fact of the matter is, however, that we do not know how many people are mentally ill—partly because the boundaries between mental health and illness are as yet only dimly defined, and partly because many people with emotional disorders do not seek treatment.[5]

It may be that our perception of the nature of mental illness as being not real—"It's all in your mind"—is reflected in the statistic that in 1966 there were 21 state hospitals for the mentally ill that were without a psychiatrist (Figure 13.1). The mind and its distress, however, are real. The attempt to escape the harshness of reality is a very real problem for the individual and society.

Distinguishing between organic and psychosomatic disease is much more easily achieved on paper than it is in practice (McConville and Purohit, 1973). An ulcer is a "frank" disease. It can be seen by X-ray, during surgery, and in a post-mortem examination. It is, nevertheless, a psychosomatic disorder. It is evident that something (in the mind) is gnawing away at the stomach (Eckstein, 1970, p. 673). Medical doctors on occasion have tried for years to cure some disease in a given person. They were either baffled by their lack of success or irritated by the fact that their patient would, at the moment of cure,

[5]*What is Mental Illness?* Public Health Service Publication 505, Series No. 88 (Washington, D. C.: U. S. Government Printing Office, 1965). Not paged.

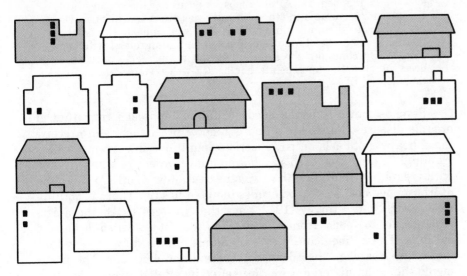

Source: What Are the Facts about Mental Illness in the United States? 1966, Washington, D.C.: National Committee Against Mental Illness, Inc., p. 48.

Twenty-one state hospitals for the mentally ill do not have a staff psychiatrist.   **Figure 13.1**

get another equally persistent and disabling disease. A psychosomatic disorder does not yield to medical intervention.[6]

On the other hand, one of the reasons for preferring a psychiatrist over a psychoanalyst or psychologist is that the organic factors will not be slighted in diagnosis and treatment. Presumably, the medically trained psychiatrist would be less likely to continue a psychotherapeutic approach when the case was actually a medical one.

A mother of five children, whose husband earned just enough money that they could be considered above the poverty level, became ill. She was listless, irritable, grew pale, and developed deep and painful fissures in her tongue. Medical examination did not yield any helpful clues. She was sent to a hospital for further observation and examination. Almost immediately she seemed to recover and was sent home where the dysfunction soon developed again. It was suspected that she was depressed or overburdened by her large family and the discouraging financial struggle. She was sent to a rest home where she immediately recovered. This seemed to confirm the suspicion of psychological pressure. Counseling was of no avail as soon as she went home. When she got back with her family the

---

[6] Certain drugs are used in psychosomatic conditions to tranquilize or stimulate the extremely disturbed person so that he may be amenable to psychotherapeutic approaches (Laufer, 1970).

symptoms reappeared. After almost a year one of the medical consultants postulated that her difficulty was vitamin deficiency. He prescribed a "shot-gun" dosage. Recovery was immediate and the mother resumed her former efficient and optimum role of wife and mother. By changing the family diet and taking some prescribed doses of vitamin supplements her health was restored and maintained.

Psychosomatic illnesses need a different approach from that of organic diseases. Fortunately, more general practitioners are receiving a heavy emphasis on psychiatric orientations in current medical training. The patient with psychosomatic disorders is being treated with greater consideration than was the case a few years ago. Then the overburdened doctor was sometimes tempted to say, "There is nothing wrong with you." Torrey (1972) says that western psychotherapists have much to learn from the witchdoctors of so-called primitive cultures. These "medicine men," shamans, and mediums knew that many diseases were disorders of the mind and emotions. The treatments they administered were quite effective. Belief, even in the face of organic disease, is a healing factor and combines effectively with what is called spontaneous recovery. When the disorder is psychogenic in nature the factors of faith, love, concern, and feelings of worth, are of vital significance.

Neuroses and psychoses

Neuroses is a term rather than a disease. The word covers so many psychosomatic disorders that it denotes nothing specific. Neuroses can indicate headaches, a stiff neck, painful feet, a dislike for crowds, anxiety about school, feelings of inferiority, feelings of persecution, and allergies. The term is used in contrast, or in complement to, psychoses—another rather elusive term. Some authorities regard neuroses as being psychogenic in nature. In contrast, psychoses have a heavy component of organogenic factors. Separating intrinsic from extrinsic factors is so difficult, plus the fact that psychological factors can induce organic changes, that this distinction has no clarifying influence.

The common distinction between neuroses and psychoses emphasizes the severity of the disorder. Neuroses are discomforting and burdensome but they are not totally disabling. Psychoses are so severe that the victim has lost contact with reality. He is unable to function competently in life. Severity seems to be a generally accepted distinction (Chaplin, 1968; Dever, 1952; Goldenson, 1970). However, the point at which a neurosis becomes severe enough to be disabling is not clearly demarcated. Actually, there is a way to sharpen one's perception of psychological mechanisms and of personality in general. It is profitable to think in terms of specific causes, contributing factors, individual responses, and of *specific* steps toward alleviation or remediation. A poor way to kill a bear is to shoot at a bear in general. A poor way to diagnose a personality or pain is to define it in general as a neurosis or psychosis. Hence, some specific neuroses and psychoses are described in the following examples of escape by ailment.

Hypochondria is making the most of an ailment. It is the enjoyment of an illness. Hypochondria is the exaggeration of minor indispositions. The idea may be clarified by defining a hypochondriac as a person who, when greeted with "How are you?" tells you. One gets so much attention from hubby (breakfast in bed, first rumpling of the newspaper, freedom from dishpan hands, etc.) that one enjoys a mild headache or a seizure of cramps. The children stop screaming, get their own breakfast, and miraculously get to church on time so that the illness pays. It does not always continue to pay. The helpers get bored in time and the sick person is ignored. Sometimes, however, especially if the sick person is a sensitive actress, the devotion becomes habitual and mother becomes a confirmed neurotic. However, the symptoms in various mothers and the treatment in various families are richly varied. In one case mother becomes a martyr. The youngsters shrug it off with, "Oh, you know mother." In other instances, every time adolescent Mary has a date mother suffers a disabling attack of asthma and Mary ultimately gives up having a date because she might cause her mother's complete asphyxiation.

Hypochondria

It may take an expert to distinguish between malingering and hypochondria (if the distinction were to serve some valid purpose). On paper the distinction is simple. Malingering is pretending illness where there is actually no organic upset, however slight. Malingering is a common disorder in military camps. It is used to avoid unpleasant training or cleanup duties. It is effective because the too hasty decision that the illness is feigned may lead to actual maltreatment or medical malpractice. A way to sift the sick from the "goldbrickers" was hit upon by a navy doctor.

Malingering

> Those who, because of frequent appearance at sick call, were suspected of malingering caused the doctor to be greatly alarmed. He ordered the man into sick bay immediately. There was not even time for him to return to his quarters to get shaving gear. Curtains were drawn around his bed because until a diagnosis was made no excitement could be allowed. The strain of listening to radio, watching television, or reading might be too much for the undiagnosed ailment so these were forbidden. Of course, no company! The disease might be contagious. The bowels were flushed with a dose of castor oil. Diet was liquid because solids might aggravate the mysterious ailment. Exercise might be dangerous so the patient had to relieve himself by using the bed pan. Sometimes this might not effect a cure but it was the man's own decision if he returned to duty.

Hysteria refers to a condition in which one takes on the symptoms and behavior of a person who has a physical illness. In the hysteric, however, there is no organic lesion or impairment. Thus, one may have a "functional" illness of ulcers. He may have the pain and disablement

Hysteria

of ulcers; but, the usual medical examinations do not reveal the physical eroding of ulcers. If the worry, anxiety, and hostilities pervading one's job did cause an ulcer it would be a psychosomatic disorder. Hysteria is also psychosomatic. It is amenable to psychotherapeutic treatment. It is as disabling as psychologically induced illness, but there is no physical destruction. If the doctor explains the condition, the hysteric goes on feeling the distress. He either develops another functional disorder—painful headaches, asthma, paralysis of a hand—or goes to another physician. The patient is sure he will find a doctor more discerning and skilled than the "incompetent" who discounts the reality of his complaint.

Hippocrates believed that hysteria was due to the loosening of the womb (the word has the same root as the Greek word for womb). It was, therefore, a woman's disease. It was discovered that hysteria had many varied guises and that it was not related to the womb. It then also became a man's disease (Eckstein, 1970, p. 678). Hysteria is also called a conversion neurosis—one's animosities or feelings of inferiority are transferred (converted) into an ailment. One pretends he has a headache to avoid going to school. He is malingering. Then he begins to believe in his own duplicity and feels the headache. Carried far enough, one may become functionally blind. Hysteria has kept men from having to appear on the battlefield. It has kept women from conceiving.

Hysteria may be precipitated by a given incident. It may be caused by an automobile accident and getting a bruised arm, or having one's head bumped in dormitory play. The *causes* are likely to be found in *successful* illness during childhood. The child was fussed over, pampered, read to more than usual so that sickness became a reward. As an adult, evading the pressures of life is made excusable by developing hysteria.

An extreme degree of hysteria is what is known as a fugue. This is the case in which an individual denies his identity to the extent that he forgets who he is. It is the kind of process that is referred to in the newspapers as amnesia. Closely related is the double personality—the Dr. Jekyll, and Mr. Hyde. This is a dual role in which one is a "good guy" part of the time, then, forgetting that personality completely, is, for another period, a jealous, vindictive, and cruel person.

Fears and phobias   There are various ways of classifying defense mechanisms. Some authorities make fear and repression a separate category. Others would class fear as a runaway or escape reaction (Jenkins, 1969). Inasmuch as the fear may be disguised as an illness, there is some justification for including its discussion in this section.

> Paula P. was a 14-year-old girl who was brought to the counseling office to see what might be done about her school phobia. She was an

attractive but only average pupil who proved to be more ambitious than her talents seemed to merit. Initially she had called her mother because she became very nervous while the cast for a play was being selected. She was allowed to rest at home for the remainder of the day. Within a couple of months she was calling for her mother once or twice a week. By the end of the third month after the casting incident she had to be brought to school. Within a week or two she was so nervous that she could not enter the school building at all.

Phobias are both highly unusual and highly specific fears of ordinary things, situations, and events. One may be afraid of eyes, running water, closed spaces, open spaces, round vegetables, dogs, men with beards.

Phobias, or abnormal fears of some things, may lead to compulsions. For example, the fear of germs may lead the victim to a compulsive act of wiping off door knobs, tableware, cups. Typically, phobias tend to spread. It is possible, however, that the person who is compulsive about wiping off his silverware feels no anxiety about eating a sandwich without first washing his hands.

NORMAL AND NEUROTIC PERSONALITIES

It is frequently claimed that each and all of us is a little abnormal or abnormal in a few limited situations. Using the reference of Maslow, (1970) to the rarity of the self-actualizing person, it would seem to be statistically normal for persons to defend their ego and their social status on everyday occasions. In fact, it might be healthful to defend one's ego status and social prestige by the planned use of defense mechanisms.

Normality of adjustive mechanisms

The danger point in defensive behavior occurs at the time one ceases to, or is unable to, recognize that certain behaviors are defensive. There is no way that this point can be identified uniformly because people differ in their tolerance for stress. Some are more open to new and difficult situations than are others. It may also be postulated that tolerance can be strengthened by enduring some ego stress. As a corollary thought, that intolerance for stress can be magnified by a too ready resort to such behaviors as withdrawal, attack, or illness. Adjustive mechanisms become nonadjustive when they intensify one's problem of ultimate adjustment. For example, the girl's distress during the play casting might have been endured to preclude her ultimate inability to attend school at all.

Neurotic personalities are those who are rather consistently tense, apprehensive, overly cautious, and view life as a heavy burden. They may function adequately in life but there is the danger that (1) a sudden change in one's situation, (2) a traumatic experience (*e.g.*,

Neurotic personalities

death of a loved one), or (3) a slow accumulation of life's minor but persistent tensions finally makes one incapable of further adequate life performance (Goldenson, 1970, p. 872). Such a person then moves from being a neurotic personality to a person who is suffering acute neurosis. Such a person is clearly in need of help. His suffering is just as real as though he had a severe burn or had been in a bone-crushing accident. Most desirably, (1) preventive steps will be taken while one is at the stage of revealing only occasional neurotic tendencies. Better yet, (2) positive steps will be taken to enhance one's already healthy behaviors.

> There are many psychiatrists today who are convinced that the treatment and control of mental illness must be accompanied by intervention prior to the times of crisis, and that if these interventions are based on sound social and clinical knowledge, the conditions and quality of living can be improved for individuals, families, groups, communities, and entire populations. These are the premises upon which the practice of community psychiatry is based.
>
> To modern psychiatrists, this hardly seems a revolutionary notion, but it has been a long time coming. While we like to think of psychiatry as a modern discipline, its roots stretch back to antiquity. And it is to the dawn of antiquity that we must look to find a period in history where the "mental sufferer" was not looked upon with scorn, fear, and derision.[7]

SUMMARY

For the great majority of people, life styles are almost synonymous with the defense mechanisms that they chronically use. Defense mechanisms serve the valid purpose of protecting the ego from injury or deflation. Too often the mechanism is so thoroughly learned that it becomes a handicap when defense is not requisite. There is some evidence that the kind of defense mechanisms one develops is evidence of a congenital predisposition. That predisposition, however, is certainly influenced by learning.

Some persons seek to avoid tension and conflict and become, or show themselves to be, shy retiring personalities. Some of the common techniques of escape and psychological and/or physical withdrawal include daydreaming that is not accompanied by any overt action and lying. One may escape criticism or the performance of duty by regressing to prior and immature behavior. It is possible to retreat within oneself—be an introvert. One can retreat by identifying with another person or group without making a positive contribution. Drugs and excessive use of beverage alcohol are used as escape devices

---

[7]Stanley F. Yolles, *From Witchcraft and Sorcery to Head Shrinking*, Public Health Service Publication 1864 (Washington, D. C.: National Institute of Mental Health, 1969), p. 2.

by many people. Both these excesses are regarded as serious national problems.

Many people defend themselves by making an early and vigorous attack. Again, the defense style is influenced by congenital factors and cultural expectations. Defenses are shaped by what one has learned to be successful. Negativism is an early attack style and parents must run the narrow gauntlet between permitting attack to become too vigorous and stamping out individuality. One may displace his hostilities on specific innocent people. Hostilities may irradiate on anyone who is weak and available. Compensation, either direct or indirect, is in the attack category. One can mount an attack by projecting his own faults or motives onto others. Rationalizations may be either an escape or an attack mechanism. Rationalization is here called an attack because few people really care about the reasons for defeat.

Defenses by ailments are truly dubious escape mechanisms. This is because the delusion is about as successful with the performer as it is with the beholder. Specific escapes by illness include psychosomatic ailments, including neurosis, hypochondria, malingering, and hysteria. Such ailments are caused by psychological and cultural pressures. Fears and phobias are classed here as ailments, although they are psychological rather than physiological dysfunctions.

Most people have neurotic tendencies. Most people are neurotic on occasion. Those whose neuroticism is pervasive and uninterrupted are referred to as neurotic personalities. One meets them daily on the street. They function painfully and at part-power rather than heterostatically and confidently.

SUGGESTED READINGS

BERSCHEID, ELLEN, and ELAINE WALSTER, "Beauty and the Best," *Psychology Today*, Vol. 5, No. 10, 42–46, March, 1972.
> *Despite the cliché that beauty is only skin-deep and the conviction that those of us who are not beautiful have the superiority of character over appearance, the fact is that we are judged by our looks and that judgment becomes a part of our personality.*

DENGERINK, H. A., "Anxiety, Aggression, and Physiological Arousal," *Journal of Experimental Research in Personality*, Vol. 5, 223–232, 1971.
> *This article is of value more in terms of showing one method by which more knowledge is sought about varied personality functioning than in terms of knowing the effect that anxiety has on aggression.*

KENISTON, KENNETH, "Youth, Change, and Violence," *The American Scholar*, Vol. 37, 227–245, 1968.
> *The effect of frustration, hostility, and lack of identity on today's youth is described. Some postulations on the effect of rapid change and social disorganization on personality are offered.*

MCCONVILLE, BRIAN J., and ARJUN P. PUROHIT, "Classifying Confusion: A Study of the Results of Inpatient Treatment in a Multidisciplinary

Children's Center," *American Journal of Orthopsychiatry*, Vol. 43, No. 3, 411–417, 1973.

> *The chaotic state of terminology in child psychiatry makes it difficult for psychotherapists to communicate with one another. The authors suggest a way that the confusion might be lessened.*

MINDE, KLAUS K., *et al.*, "How They Grow Up: 41 Physically Handicapped Children and Their Families," *American Journal of Psychiatry*, Vol. 128, No. 12, 1554–1560, 1972.

> *The personality development of persons with handicaps has taken a big step forward with the discovery that attitudes toward handicaps by parents of the handicapped is more important than is the handicap, per se.*

SULLIVAN, EDWARD A., "Medical, Biological, and Chemical Methods of Shaping the Mind," *Phi Delta Kappan*, Vol. 53, No. 8, 483–486, April, 1972.

> *There are many ways that chemical, medical, and physical science can help one defend against or cope with the world; BUT powerful discoveries can be dangerous if misused. The author sees both threat and promise in available and immanent ways of controlling personality.*

FOLLOW-UP LEARNING ACTIVITIES

Match the following words and clues:
- a rationalization
- b compensation
- c reverie
- d phobia
- e conflict
- f regression
- g introversion
- h identification

_____ continuous unresolved tension
_____ gaining satisfaction from belonging
_____ saying "No" to every request or suggestion
_____ making false excuses
_____ an adolescent acting like a child
_____ unusual concern with self
_____ fear of insects or open spaces
_____ gaining satisfaction from developing previously unused talents
_____ making the most of a minor illness

Describe someone you know who has some form of psychosomatic illness.

_____
_____
_____

What ailments have you had that you suspected might be psychosomatic?

_____
_____
_____

What are some features of a life style that you would like to have but do not now have?

_____
_____
_____

What keeps you from developing those features?

_____
_____
_____

Do you agree or disagree with the idea that "everyone is a little neurotic?"

I agree _____ disagree _____ because _____
_____
_____

14
Conformity and Divergence

Is there conformity in divergence?

LEARNING ACTIVITIES

Do you consider yourself *generally* to be creative _____ or conformist _____ ?

In regard to conformity or divergent tendencies, would you like to be

more conformist _____ because _____

_____

more divergent _____ because _____

_____

What are some conformist attitudes or behaviors in our society that you think need change urgently?

_____

_____

_____

_____

What are some social practices, almost ignored in our society, that you believe need to be initiated?

_____

_____

_____

_____

Have you yourself experienced, or witnessed, a school incident in which the teacher seemed to show a dislike for creative divergence? Describe it.

_____

_____

_____

_____

Have you had a teacher who actively encouraged creativity in pupils? If yes, tell how he (she) revealed this encouragement.

_____

_____

_____

_____

Some of the above items may seem vague. Talk to some classmates about their responses. Then add any pertinent conclusions below.

_____

_____

_____

The previous chapter on Defense Mechanisms indicates one way in which personality variations may be categorized. That chapter, however, dealt with differences in personality that might easily turn into the abnormal. Such marked divergence from the normal is usually handicapping and undesirable. In this chapter the emphasis is on desirable and enhancing aspects of personality variations.

People the world over live in groups. This is not just for social companionship and protection from dangers. It also is because the specialization that can be developed in groups is a part of an efficient economy. Unique patterns of interests, aptitudes, and learnings that enhance man's productiveness and significance can be encouraged. The smaller the living group the more likely it is that it would be accurate to say of its citizens, "Jack of all trades; master of none."

Conformity and divergence are not personality types that the student will ordinarily see listed in books on personality. Nevertheless, one way to perceive some of the nuances of the study of personality is to examine these contrasts. Conformity and divergence have been the subject of many popular books relating to personality. Society does need some people who find it easy to abide by the protocol of culture. We need those who are able to fill social demand. There is also a need for the person who finds it uncomfortable to abide by some of society's dictates. The need for divergence is not widely recognized. Society should admit that those who find personal satisfaction in being different are needed. Even a rebel helps society by being different. Those who upset the apple-cart help society be creative.

CONVERGENT PERSONALITIES

The meaning of conformity and divergency

In this chapter, conformity and divergency are used to indicate two different life styles. Conformity refers to the person who feels comfortable doing about the same things that are done by others. He dresses and grooms himself much like his peers. He attends school about the same length of time as do his age mates. He works at the things for which the community is noted. He marries at the typical age. There is, in much of the conformist's action, a tendency to be shaped by community mores. His behaviors are governed by home-town attitudes. Generally, the conformist does what is expected.

The divergent person is usually not totally so. However, in a few behaviors he is notably different. He may dress differently. He may keep what are regarded as odd hours. He may not work regularly. He may take art when others are taking mechanics or agriculture. He may work at a job that others regard as off-beat. An example would be the young woman who works as a crane operator or as a lineman for an electric company.

Conformity and divergence may be regarded as intellectual traits. The conformist accepts typical data. He wants clear-cut, routine conclusions. He is secure with convention. He wants rules and restrictions. The divergent person combines what appear to be unrelated data. He makes off-beat choices. He does not need final solutions. He finds rules are too binding. He can feel secure with that which is novel.

We would have no culture if each person had to learn anew, and independently, how to dress, feed, house, and protect himself. Much time and energy can be saved in these essential life activities if one can just copy his parents' and neighbors' ways of doing things. Much of a young person's life is spent in learning how his parents and community associates conduct their lives. Schools are, for the most part, designed to teach the young how to conform. Schools demonstrate to the young the advantages of conformity. Only recently has the term "Master" fallen into disuse when referring to teachers. In fact, in "underdeveloped" countries, the teacher is still regarded as the master who knows the answers. Much of the recent criticism of American schools has stemmed from the belief that in a world of rapid change, the school has been too authoritarian. Schools are said to be too little concerned about the fostering of individuality and creativity. They are too little concerned with the encouragement of divergence (Bruner, 1970; Dennison, 1969; Lieberman, 1972).

The need for conformists

The need for conformity is well demonstrated in military organizations. There it is necessary to have a team of specialists perform prescribed functions. There is no room for a collection of independent thinkers. The same is true in some business and industrial firms. Even the innovators must be specialists. They feed their ideas into the ongoing organization in stated ways, at stated times, and to stated groups. The more cars that appear on highways, the clearer it becomes that conformity is a necessity of life. Coming across the prairies and mountains 125 years ago from Independence, Missouri, to Portland, Oregon, the bodies of those who died were disposed of in any convenient manner. Today in view of ecology, property rights, disease, and the sheer press of numbers, conformity to protocol (perhaps not so much protocol, as to what morticians have established) is much more necessary than in the wagon train days. Similar arguments may be advanced with regard to the selling of groceries, financing automobiles, buying a home, or disposing of waste.

Conformity contributes to ease and satisfaction of living. However, as is the case with defense mechanisms, too much conformity may be a self-defeating style of life.

Hazards of conformity

Darwin, in his theory of evolution, rather convincingly documented the idea that conformity—to the degree that it limited adaptability to changed and changing conditions—was a threat to the survival of a species. Durant and Durant (1968, p. 34) indicate that custom and tradition within a group make for ready adjustments to "typical and frequently repeated situations." However, new situations do arise. They require novel, unstereotyped solutions. Gardner (1964) contends that there is no such thing as a static society. Change is constant and inevitable. There are, however, static individuals who do not see the need for constant renewal. They resist change in themselves and in the institutions of society.

The individual who lives his life within the bounds of job requirements and cultural expectations has been referred to as "encapsulated" man (Royce, 1969; Wrenn, 1962). This is an individual who believes that his approach, or his firm's approach, or his educational institution's approach is *the* approach. He is a captive of the past. He denies his human capacity for change and ignores the challenge to transcend himself.

The bases of conformity

Guilford (1967, pp. 138ff.), in his postulation on the structure of human intelligence, uses the concepts of divergent-production and convergent-production as major aspects of mental organization. Divergent-production refers to the tendency to derive new conclusions from given information. Such a person tends to emphasize variety and originality and to transfer one idea or bit of information into a new context. The convergent thinker tends to confine the limits of a problem by defining it precisely. He seeks closure, or definable conclusions, for given concepts and dilemmas. Clear-cut answers provide him assurance and satisfaction, while ambiguity or uncertainty leave him anxious, or at least restive.

Endocrines *may* have some influence on the degree to which conformity is an innate tendency. Some children are slow and placid and need much rest and sleep. This has been noticed particularly in hypothyroid cases. Their activity level and conforming tendencies have been altered by the medical administration of thyroxin. Some youngsters, who, in extreme cases, we call hyperactive or hyperkinetic, have so much drive to be active that in schools they have to be controlled by drugs. They cannot conform to rules for remaining seated. It is hard for them to stick to a task until it is completed. They cannot refrain from bothering others (Laufer, 1970). Teachers say of these extremely nonconforming youngsters, "They drive me up the wall!"

What one learns constitutes another of the bases of conformity. Some children have authoritarian parents. They soon learn to adhere to the dicta, "Jump when you are told to do something" and "Listen when you are spoken to." To do anything else than conform to adult expectations would result in being slapped, spanked, going hungry, or being sent from the room.

> A principal in a large city school system reported that he dreaded being called into the office of the superintendent. He stood at attention and was uneasy when he was asked to sit down. Even though he knew that the superintendent was genuinely seeking to find the principal's view on a given matter, the principal evaded an answer. He would ask questions designed to find out first how the superintendent was inclined to think. He would then express a view that confirmed what the superintendent *seemed* to prefer.
>
> The principal said of himself, "I know the superintendent honestly wants my view from my experiences in my local community; but it petrifies me to give it. I know where the feeling comes from. My father told—never asked—what should be done. And if compliance were not complete he would beat me and my brother. When we were older, he would rave until no deviance seemed to be worth while. Knowing this does not make me change my servile character. I am immobilized in the face of authority.

Not all persons learn the same thing, even from the same circumstances. As might be concluded from the previous chapter on defense mechanisms, another son might have irradiated the hostilities he felt toward his father. Another son might have felt the desire to do and be himself so strongly that he learned to defy even his father. As one boy said, "Go ahead and beat me now. I'm going camping this week end."

Sherif and Sherif (1964, pp. 6, 184ff.) use the term **reference groups** to emphasize the idea that one learns, especially during adolescence, to adopt the values of his age group. Reference groups explain the differences in values and behaviors in different cultures (Chapter 5). These groups, especially in cities where housing tends to be somewhat alike in various sections, form along socioeconomic class lines. Hence, there are certain patterns of recreation. For example, cars are much more frequently owned by upper and upper-middle class boys and girls than by lower SES young people. Reference groups shape varied dating patterns, different occupational aspirations, different attitudes toward school attendance, and different rationales for attending college.

Reference groups

Reference groups do not dictate the values or goals of boys and girls. They are *one* factor. Their most powerful influence is exerted when there is lack of congruity or lack of convergence in other immediate influences. For instance, if a mother and father have different ideas about the importance of schooling, then the reference group attitude on this matter is likely to prevail. If teachers (or parents) and the reference group frown upon early marriage, then the reference groups might seem to have the deciding influence.

There are some who believe that adolescent peer groups are more powerful than parents in shaping the behavior of adolescents.

Certainly it is true that the peer culture takes precedence over the parental culture in the adolescent years and the advice of one's contemporaries, whether overtly or covertly communicated, sets the standard in almost every aspect of conduct. We should not assume, therefore, that the socialization process is completed by the time the teen ages are reached. On the contrary, this is the time when the pressures for conformity are perhaps at their height, when deviance in the ordinary affairs of life is punished most severely by one's associates, when conformity is required with a daily and almost hourly insistence. The American high school might be described, in fact, as a hotbed of conformity. No one who suffers it is competent to write about it and those who write about it can no longer remember it with precision.[1]

There are others who are not so sure about the power of adolescent reference groups in contrast to parental influence (Bernard, 1971, p. 206). Herriott (1963) reports that in terms of academic motivation, both in terms of staying in school and level of achievement, parents and teachers are predominant over the peer group *when parents and teachers are in agreement* against the opinion of the group. Smith and Kleine (1966) found that peers have more influence on conformity to clothing and grooming of adolescents. Parents are dominant in terms of the acceptance of ethical values. Colemen (1961), reporting intensive studies of variously located societies, found much variation between communities and individuals. Some youth groups as a whole conform to adult mores. Some youngsters within a group will not conform to the group, while others do.

The organization man

The industrial revolution, with its accompanying assembly-line production, has evoked much comment on the suppression of individuality. "In the good old days" a cobbler made shoes. A cabinet-maker made cabinets. A doctor dealt with patients. Each could see the end product. Today one fits into the organization and has little feel for the end product. Even the cardiologist or anesthetist may get little more than a glimpse of the patient. He does not really know him as a person. In such regimes, it is necessary for one to seek satisfaction of those human needs related to being a unique person. There is a struggle for recognition, to be a cause, for esteem—in something other than his work.

The decline in the importance of the individual has led some scholars and novelists to express concern about the impact of conformity. They wonder about the future of mankind when there is such a loss of identity through the impersonalization of production.

Riesman (1950), in his influential book, *The Lonely Crowd*, indicates that many persons are anxiety-ridden. Their natural inclinations

---

[1]Robert Bierstedt, *The Social Order*, Third Edition (New York: McGraw-Hill Book Company, 1970), pp. 200–201.

are at odds with economic and cultural demands for conformity. He postulates that there are three broad categories of personality types. There are those who are tradition-directed. Another group is other-directed. These two categories would find conformity to be convenient and comfortable. Another group, the inner-directed, find their own drives and interests more powerful than the need to conform. Depending on how emphatically others demand conformity and how odd they view the "odd ball" as being, the inner-directed person would function under varying degrees of stress in contemporary society.

Riesman perceives, for contemporary man, widespread danger of developing psychotic behavior. In our current culture, in which there are high levels of health, industrial production, wealth, scientific curiosity, mobility, and rapid, worldwide communication, there is a lessening of accepted customs. Such conditions give little comfort to the tradition-directed person. In contrast, the inner-directed person cannot find the comfort, security, and identity that the narrow circle of home and community might give. The outer-directed person is bewildered by the many modes of expression in art, music, and literature that can be seen. Hence, he too lacks a point of reference.

Horney (1937) does not make specific mention of conformity or reference groups. She does, however, employ in her book, *The Neurotic Personality of Our Time*, the concepts of conformity and reference groups. The problem of conformity may be perceived constantly in her description of the dilemmas and behaviors of neurotics. Those who cope successfully appear to be those for whom conformity is not a pervasive, or compulsive, issue. Horney questions Freud's heavy emphasis on biological factors in producing neuroses. She does agree, however, with his emphasis on the impact of early childhood experiences. Not all persons arrive at adulthood with the same predispositions to react to the situations they encounter. Some take in stride the challenge that fills another with disabling anxiety. Hence, different persons meet the problems of life with varied levels of readiness to deal with them.

The problems met by persons are, in contemporary culture, much the same for all. The five major areas of difficulty that Horney (1937, p. 35) identified can readily be related to problems of conformity.

1. There are problems related to giving and receiving affection. Some persons are excessively dependent. Receiving reassurance of being approved and being liked by others is a pressing need. All of us have this desire but the neurotic is indiscriminately hungry for such assurance.

2. There are attitudes concerning self-evaluation. In the neurotic, feelings of inferiority and inadequacy prevail in all situations. Hence, he may develop a tendency to show off. Whatever the culture values, the neurotic values more highly. Money, travel, old pictures, knowledge, furniture, and automobiles are

among our varied values. One sees little room "to be oneself" in this aspect of Horney's description of the "neurotic personality of our time."

3. The tendencies one has toward self-assertion also involve inhibitions. There is a reluctance to assert oneself even in conversation. Even resisting a salesman who pushes his product is a crushing experience.

4. Aggression involves some form of hostility in going against someone—attacking, disparaging, encroaching. Aggression is distinct from self-assertion.

5. There are problems related to sexual activities and inhibitions. All phases of sexual matters are involved—the presence of someone of the other sex, wooing, the manner of sexual expression, and the degree to which one enjoys sexual activities can be sources of anxiety.

The positive role of conformity

Much of the foregoing material seems to present conformity as some kind of loathsome disease. Let the essence of the first subsection of this chapter be repeated. It is not conformity but the causal reason that is significant in personality structure. Without conformity there could be no society. There could be no culture—none of the assurance that gives one the ego strength to be himself. It is culture that allows one to be somewhat different. It is when conformity becomes compulsive, a dreaded responsibility, is combined with paranoid feelings, and is blind (without occasional logical examination) that it is referred to disparagingly. It is when we teach children and youth to be conformists when the situation to be conformed to has changed that conformity becomes a major issue in the study of personality.

DIVERGENT PERSONALITIES

As is the case with conformist personalities, there are times when to be divergent is advantageous. At other times divergence is a handicap and is socially disapproved. The undesirable divergencies were discussed, on a sampling basis, in Chapter 13, Defense Mechanisms. Here a look will be taken at divergence as a positive personality orientation.

Creative-divergent personalities

Society needs to have persons who can do and are content to do the routine, repetitive tasks that comprise stable, dependable patterns of living. It also needs those who take joy in thinking differently. We need those who are discomfited by routine. We need those who constantly seek "new worlds to conquer." Otherwise we would sink into a culture that would continue to deny many people freedom from want, freedom of worship, freedom from fear, and freedom of speech.

Intellectually, there are few people who disagree with the idea of the foregoing paragraph. Practically, conventionally, daily, we act as though divergence should be stamped out. Parents want, for the most part, their children to obey and conform. Teachers want—unless they have been specially prepared for creative teaching—their pupils to be orderly, systematic, and obedient. Teachers want pupils to do their lessons on time and in accord with a prescribed standard of performance. Employers want, except in isolated departments and on scheduled times, their workers to fit the mold. They want them to fill their slots and refrain from "rocking the boat."

Duality in the make-up of personality has been noted from time to time in this book. One instance of duality is the excitement we get from watching the strange and unusual phenomenon, as contrasted to the security and identity we derive from ordinary and accustomed situations. Occasionally, as individuals, we are intrigued by the deviant individual. However, he makes us feel uncomfortable. More likely we will have a feeling of comfort when people believe, and appear, about as we do.

In a classroom, for example, there may be an occasional teacher who enjoys the deviant individual. The majority of teachers are likely to feel some degree of irritation with the pupil who breaks the train of thought. They resist those who interrupt the smooth routine with off-beat questions. Getzels and Jackson (1962) and Torrance (1962) give us a word picture of creative-divergent individuals about as follows: They have an odd sense of humor. They will put together some concepts that are, to the convergent thinker, logically unrelated. They ask questions that seem to be unrelated to the subject matter. They think up some twist of the assignment. They pursue some tangential aspect of it to the exclusion of the purpose the teacher had in mind. They have rather strong ego concepts and are more ready to argue with the teacher. They take issue with the textbook more often than is the case with the conventional thinkers. They are susceptible to fantasy. Their wild and silly ideas cause them to laugh at what we—the generality—think are odd and inappropriate times. They are less interested in grades and the teachers' opinions. They have a wider variety of out-of-school interests than do the comfort-giving conformists. Altogether, they do not allow the teacher the ease of slipping into a smooth, self-assured classroom routine. Anderson (1961, p. 37) describes such individuals as being ". . . unconventional and as resisting the drives toward conformity and convergent thinking often found in the schools." Divergent pupils are, he says, more original, less suggestible, and more tolerant of structural disorderliness and ambiguity than are typical students.

There are, of course, instructors who are creative-divergents themselves. They may enjoy the presence of others of their kind. Some who by nature are conformists, may, through special instruction, have come to perceive the value of the nonconformist. They have learned to tolerate and even to encourage them. Many, like the manufacturers and businessmen referred to earlier, would prefer to designate certain periods for creative activities. The rest of the time the student should, we tend to think, be reasonably able to get at the job of learning.

The resistance to change, innovation, and the innovative person is indicated by Lieberman in the following passage. He is concerned about the results of the population explosion and the creation of brand new cities. He thinks the chance to do some innovative thinking about persistent problems is unusually great in these new cities.

> In view of all the rhetoric about the vested interests and the bureaucracies which allegedly stifle educational creativity and innovation, one might suppose that the foundations and federal agencies and academicians who play the innovation game would have at least made an effort to capitalize upon the enormous possibilities for innovations where the traditional roadblocks do not even exist, or exist in much weaker form. In fact, not a single educational agency or organization in the United States, governmental or nongovernmental, seems to recognize the existence, let alone the potential of the new communities movement.[2]

Test data on creative persons

There has been an upsurge of interest in creative persons since 1959. The National Defense Education Act has been especially helpful in building this interest. The value of the creative person in a dynamic society has been acknowledged. Hence, attempts have been made to assess creativity by devising new types of tests (see Chapter 15). Some clues have been obtained from tests already in existence. For one thing, barring scores that are considered to be abnormally low, high intelligence is not positively **correlated** with measures and judgments of creativity. Beyond the level of being a moron, or low-normal, we would not expect high IQ persons to be any more, or any less, creative than those with IQ's in the range say of 95–115. We would, in terms of current knowledge, be just as likely to find a person with an IQ of 140 to be convergent-conformist as one who had an IQ of 100.

The Minnesota Multiphasic Personality Inventory (MMPI) is an instrument designed to evaluate tendencies toward such psychological states as depression, hysteria, paranoia, or schizophrenia. Creative persons tend to make somewhat higher scores on these measures than do the generality. Creative persons score 5 to 10 points higher than do typical persons. These higher scores are not considered to be an indication of **pathology** or psychopathology. They indicate, rather, flexible intellect, richness and complexity of personality, and a general lack of defensiveness (MacKinnon, 1971b). Creative men make higher scores on the femininity scores of the *California Psychological Inventory* and *Strong Vocational Interest Blank.* These scores, says MacKinnon, indicate that the more creative one is, the more one reveals

[2]Myron Lieberman, "Education in New Cities," *Phi Delta Kappan*, Vol. 53, March, 1972, p. 411.

openness to feelings and emotions, a sensitive intellect, selfawareness, and a wide variety of interests. In short, the creative man does not deny the feminine characteristics of awareness of self and others. The creative male accepts such emotions as sympathy, sorrow, and sentimentality. Tests also indicate a tolerance for ambiguity. Creative persons can see beauty in asymmetry, imbalance, and contrast.

Creative persons are more open to experience. They are ready to be intuitive and to experience feeling They react with *élan* and excitement somewhat more than we think the solid citizen should. However, such things—or tendencies toward such things—as paranoia, depression, hysteria, or femininity do not endear the creative-divergent person to the man-on-the-street. It is entirely possible that the level of accomplishment and the consequent working of jealousy and projection, on the part of the generality, contribute to some of the characteristics that are revealed in the inventory scores of the creative individual. Society just is not highly tolerant, let alone encouraging, with the creative-divergent personality.

It is the creative person who accounts for, and is responsible for, technological and cultural progress. While the world needs "hewers of wood and drawers of water," it also needs those who wonder if there are not easier ways to do the routine tasks. After describing the meaning of what it is to have ordinary and conformist intelligence, Hollingworth wrote ". . . it is the contribution of the superior endowment that determines the course, although perhaps not the pace of social development" (Hollingworth, 1928, p. 279). Today a distinction is made between high test intelligence and creativity; but, the need for creativity is succinctly expressed in his words.

The role of creativity

We need to recognize not only the need for creativity but also how to encourage it. Terman, who pioneered studies of the intellectually gifted, discovered that there was a wide range of achievement (Terman and Oden, 1947). We know, of course that this is also true in the range of average intelligences. The differences could be accounted for in terms of drive for achievement. Research has given us some clues regarding how the motivation to achieve might be fostered.

Those who achieve less than intelligence test scores indicate that they should or could achieve are called underachievers. Havighurst (1961) summarized many studies that have been made of achievement in relation to intelligence. These have yielded surprisingly consistent results regarding the dynamics of underachievement. The traits of underachievers are:

Encouragement of creativity

- They do not think of themselves as being adequate persons.
- Compared to achievers, their goals are low.

- They do not like school or books.
- They are unpopular and are not leaders.
- Their personal adjustment is poorer than that of their achieving peers.
- Their range of interests is narrow.

We would expect that such traits as the foregoing might have some biological base. They might have something to do with metabolism and health. In part, they might be a reflection of cultural expectation. In the main, however, we would look to conditions in the home. Sibling relations and especially child-rearing patterns adopted by parents are key explanatory factors. This is the area in which most of the work has been done. Moreover, this is the area most amenable to intentional modification.

It has been said, probably with a high degree of accuracy, that a child never repeats a behavior that *for him* was not successful (Hohman, 1947). This may be doubted by parents who punish their child for a given act and find him repeating the act. However, Hohman and Skinner (1971) would reply that the adult does not necessarily know the child's goal. The child may be more concerned about being overlooked than about the discomfort of a spanking. He gets what he wants or he does not repeat the act. In short, it is postulated that the underachiever, or the achiever, learns (within the limits set by his congenital endowment) to behave the way he does because of the type of negative or positive reinforcement he receives.

Socioeconomic status is not something amenable to facile modification. It is one of the explanations of learned patterns of motivation. It is hard, authorities maintain, to be highly motivated about school work when one is cold, wet, hungry, or otherwise uncomfortable. Nonachievers come, more frequently than not, from unstable or broken homes. Those in the lower SES have no corner on unstable homes. However, unstable homes occur more frequently under conditions of economic stress. Grades in school are awarded along socioeconomic lines, with higher grades more frequently given to pupils from high SES, and lower grades to lower SES pupils (Havighurst and Neugarten, 1967, pp. 82ff.).

The kind of discipline exercised in home and school is related to the incidence of creativity. Severely disciplined children and those who literally have no discipline are not likely to be creative. Apparently, a balance must be found between a harsh discipline that inhibits autonomy and curiosity and the lack of discipline that leaves the child seeking some anchors to offset his feelings of insecurity.

Parents who are interested in a variety of things and who are interested in their children but encourage them to set their own goals are establishing a climate for creativity. There is mothering without smothering. The mother of creative children does not dominate her children's interests. This may be because she has interests of her own. Hence, there is a lack of intense closeness. While there is a relative lack of discipline and a lack of formal religious training, there are expectations of some kind of accomplishment. There is freedom to roam. Both mother and father have artistic interests, but there is no pressure for the child to have such artistic inclinations. There is no pressure to choose a career (MacKinnon (1971b).

It has been found that creative children come from homes in which there is a high incidence of mother dominance. This may be because the mother has a need to express her own creative urges. Thus, creative persons have permissive, friendly, cooperative homes, even though mother dominated with higher incidence than in the typical home. Creative children are less insistent upon independence from their parents. Apparently they feel that they are treated as people instead of as babies or children. Affectional support rather than child submission leads to integrative and creative human relationships (Foster, 1968). Easy communication, shared interests, and acceptance by parents of childish behavior are typical in creative homes. There is tolerance for **ambiguity** in things and in persons. Such items are indicative of the flexibility in the homes of creative young persons. Creative persons ". . . need recognition and rewards in order to continue producing their best work. Similarly, they tend to learn most from those who are demanding yet fair. A typical creative scientist comes from a home where parental authority, although somewhat impersonal, was consistent, predictable, fair, and psychologically supportive."[3]

Encouraging creativity in school

It would be paradoxical to set a format for encouraging creativity. There is, however, a conviction on the part of those who have studied creativity that we cannot generate it. However, it can be encouraged when it does appear. Conditions that characterize a creative climate focus mainly around the personality of the teacher. Hallman (1967) describes such a teacher in terms such as the following:

- He is one who recognizes that it takes knowledge to generate creativity and to combine and recombine information into novel patterns and contexts.
- He encourages learning, especially self-initiated learning.
- He is nonauthoritarian but he does believe in the discipline of work.
- He encourages creative thought. He does not laugh at pupils' assertions that appear to be ridiculous. He defers judgment—his need for closure is not overpowering.
- He encourages pupils to change their minds and to conduct their own evaluations of their work.

[3]Harold K. Hughes, "The Enhancement of Creativity," *Journal of Creative Behavior*, Vol. 3, 1969, p. 76–77.

- He points out instances in which recognition of the moods and feelings of people are significant. This helps pupils become more sensitive persons.
- He knows how to question—this is no simple art in which one elicits predetermined answers. It is one in which open-ended questions leave the pupil free to range and to wonder.
- The creative teacher constructs situations in which materials, ideas, concepts, and tools are manipulated and arranged.
- He teaches that one does not fail when he finds that something does not work. Rather, one discovers that there is something he cannot do. He is thus teaching that important lesson of coping with frustration and ambiguity.
- The creative teacher deals with problems as a whole rather than dealing with the piece-meal additive parts. (Note the similarity of this to the frustration generated by the worker in technological industry where the assembly line prevails and the end-product is not seen).

The teacher's creative role is to encourage the student to be himself. This would not, of course, call for the sanction of anti-social acts. It does mean, beyond the acquisition of the tools of learning, that considerable autonomy is given in terms of what and how one exercises his thrust to grow and become.

THE CONFORMITY-CREATIVE DILEMMA

Experimental evidence

Crutchfield (1955) developed a research technique in which subjects were deliberately misled in order to determine the extent to which one would follow the crowd. He found that there was a strong and consistent tendency, even among prominent men and women, and among college students, not to trust their own judgment when it conflicted with that of others. After several trials in judging the similarity of geometrical figures, the subjects were asked to compare two lines of different length. If a subject saw clearly that one line was shorter but that this impression conflicted with the judgment of others in the experiment he would change his vote (but not necessarily his mind). In short, the typical subject will accept group consensus despite its conflicting with his own perception. For instance, Crutchfield found that in a control group over 19 per cent agreed with the idea that free speech was a right but that it is proper for a society to suppress it when it feels threatened. Under experimental conditions, when subjects thought others were agreeing, the number in agreement was 58 per cent. The number of people who thought that subversive activities were the nation's greatest threat was 12 per cent. When subjects were led to believe that their co-workers in the experiment were voting for subversive activities, the number in agreement rose to 48 per cent.

There are some who feel that all persons are creative in some degree. Some are highly creative and some are low-creative. In a sense, everything we learn is creative because we add our own perceptions and interpretations. The purpose of this chapter is to encourage the development of a climate that will enhance whatever amount of creative potential one has. This may be done, in part, by examining the dynamics of conformity. Conformity is studied not so much to see how others behave but to encourage our respect and support of persons who make experimental thrusts toward getting off the beaten path.

The continuum of creativity

There are, of course, some whose drive to be different is so great that society's disapproval makes them neurotic, seclusive, or aggressive. Others can cope with the suppression of their differences. Gradually, however, the urge to be unique and creative atrophies. One then becomes the "man in the grey flannel suit" and the "organization man."

SUMMARY

One of the ways in which personalities may vary is on the continuum between convergent-conformity and divergent-creativity. Our democratic society professes to admire and value divergent-creativity activity. Social and technological progress is dependent on it. Nevertheless, there is much evidence that convergent-conforming behavior is the kind really endorsed.

One of the functions of a society is to teach conformity. This is done formally in school and informally in reference groups. Adolescent peer groups are a powerful factor for conformity among youth. However, it is clear that home and school are also influential—either for conformity or divergence. Young people have their feet, literally, in two or more reference groups. Conformity may be very discomforting or reassuring, depending in some measure on whether one's personality is tradition-directed, inner-directed, or outer-directed.

Divergency, especially in the excessive use of defense mechanisms, can be disadvantageous. As a source of new ideas, inventions, and progressive change, divergency is as much a requisite as is food and water to the individual. Creativity demands, more than high intelligence, a high level of motivation to do, to struggle, and to become. In order for this motivation to function the person needs the kind of feedback that tells him he is an adequate person. He needs reinforcement in establishing high goals. He needs to know that failure can be a valued learning experience. Varied interests can be sanctioned by sharing the interests of different people. Tolerance for divergence is increased by remembering that people are, generally, egocentric and have their own interests. To them your unique interests are "peculiar."

Homes that provide a climate for creativity are characterized by mother dominance, interest in children, but not smothering relationships. There is expectation of learning and for achievement but no pressures. There is interest in a variety of things. There is firm but not harsh discipline. There is freedom without license.

Schools can foster or suppress creativity. Teachers are the key factor. To encourage creativity they must, first of all, be open to experience. Teachers should be tolerant of the deviant, use open-ended questions, not seek closure on all issues, and manifest interest in varied activities. They should, typically, place a high value on knowing and seeking.

SUGGESTED READINGS

ASHTON-WARNER, SYLVIA, "Getting the Hang of Equality and the Evil of Authority," *Saturday Review*, Vol. 55, No. 26, 33–39, June 24, 1972.
> *The article provides a glimpse of creative behavior in action. The author describes her own dilemmas and the dilemmas of teachers as she considers structure vs. direction, discipline vs. license, overstimulation vs. imagination.*

BARRON, FRANK, "The Creative Personality: Akin to Madness," *Psychology Today*, Vol. 6, No. 2, 42–44, July, 1972.
> *The author of several standard references on the personality of creative persons gives a brief summary of his discoveries of the past 20 years.*

CHRISTIE, T., "Environmental Factors in Creativity," *Journal of Creative Behavior*, Vol. 4, No. 1, 3–31, Winter, 1970.
> *This scholarly article deals with such subtopics of creativity as the concept of creativity, and the home, parental, discipline, education, and cultural climate for creativity. It is thoroughly documented but is clearly and convincingly written.*

GUILFORD, J. P., "Creativity: Retrospect and Prospect," *Journal of Creative Behavior*, Vol. 4, No. 3, 149–168, Summer, 1970.
> *The man who postulated the convergent-divergent hypothesis as an aspect of intellectual structure, describes the history and future of the emphasis on creativity. He is optimistic about the indications that schools and colleges are becoming less authoritarian and dogmatic.*

PARNES, SIDNEY J., and RUTH B. NOLLER, "Applied Creativity: The Creative Studies Project," *Journal of Creative Behavior*, Vol. 7, No. 1, 15–36, 1973.
> *The article concludes with more questions than answers. The first part of the article, however, deals with traits of creative persons and how they can be encouraged.*

FOLLOW-UP LEARNING ACTIVITIES

Make a notation of several things you would do to encourage creativity in your own children.

_____

_____

_____

_____

Do you think creativity or conformity is primarily environmental _____ or congenital _____? Why?

_____

_____

_____

How would you class yourself?

crowd follower _____   divergent _____

loner _____   friendly divergent _____

other_____

_____

_____

_____

Would you care to change your behavior so you did not have to check the foregoing item as you did?

Yes _____   No _____   because _____

_____

_____

_____

Does the career that you intend to follow call for conforming _____ or creative _____ individuals?

Comment _____

_____

_____

_____

Does the above accord with your personality orientation?

Yes _____   No _____   because _____

_____

_____

_____

Do you believe that a characteristic of creativity is neuroticism?

Yes _____   No _____   because _____

_____

_____

_____

What is your reaction to the proposition that males who are creative tend to have some feminine characteristics?

_____

_____

_____

349

15
Personality Assessment

How much can be learned about personality in half an hour?

LEARNING ACTIVITIES

Have you ever taken a personality inventory?
Yes _____ No _____
If "Yes" what did you find out about yourself?
If "No" talk to someone who has taken one and make some notes about his impressions of the inventory.

_____
_____
_____
_____
_____

Do you make judgments about people (try to guess what they will be like) before you really get to know them?
Yes _____ No _____
If "Yes" what clues do you use?
If "No" why do you avoid doing so?

_____
_____
_____
_____
_____

Do you consider intelligence to be a part of personality?
Yes, a major part _____
Yes, a minor part _____
It is not part of personality _____
Have you ever studied cloud formations to see what kinds of things you could see in them? Yes _____ No _____
If "Yes" what kinds, and classes, of things did you see most frequently?

_____
_____
_____
_____
_____

Do you think the theme of the things you saw most often tells you anything about your personality?
Yes _____ No _____ because _____
_____
_____
_____
_____

There are many situations in which it would be good to have precise, objective data about personality. There might be more happy marriages if we could know in advance what traits of prospective spouses were most outstanding. A physically attractive, curvaceous girl might also be patient, dependable, and tenacious. The strong, skilled, disciplined athlete might not have patience with the physically weak. He might have an inflated idea of his worth. He might, in short, be a disaster as a husband and father. Test data could aid in making wise choices.

Employers could save money if they knew which workers would be most dependable and honest. They would gain from knowing which people would add most to company harmony. By the same token, employees would be more productive if they could select their jobs in terms of a fit between their basic traits and job demands. School personnel and pupils would profit from knowing about the personality traits, including functional intelligence, that make for academic success.

Psychologists have done much research on personality assessment. There is, in fact, a division in the American Psychological Association in which members are primarily interested in personality assessment. There are similar divisions in the American Personnel and Guidance Association and the American Educational Research Association. The results, thus far, are not highly gratifying. It does appear that some negative traits—neuroticism, anxiety, **paranoia**—can be screened, roughly. Positive traits—honesty, ambition, leadership—appear to be more elusive in terms of assessment.

The reader can appreciate some of the difficulties involved in personality assessment. This book, even thus far, suggests the many aspects of personality that must be probed. Personality is a growing, dynamic entity. That which is found today may not be true in years to come. Personality involves the reaction of other people. Personality is revealed in action and crisis situations, which are hard to simulate in a test situation. One has a different personality at home, in school, while working, when entertaining. The result is that personality assessment, while moving forward, leaves much to be desired. The conclusion must be: Personality assessment is tentative. It provides clues, not answers. It must be supported and corroborated by whatever other data are available. Such corroborative data might be observation, action-under-fire, anecdotal reports, or personal history.

INTELLIGENCE TESTING

It is assumed, herein, that intelligence is a basic factor in personality (Tyler, 1963). Much behavior is reflexive, and much of it is "blindly" emotional. It also seems to be true that some of it—and that which is most readily responsive to control—is intellectual. Presumably, too, the greater the intelligence one has the greater is the possibility that it (rather than reflexes, conditioning, or emotions) will be reflected in personality. Insofar as we accurately assess intelligence, we have important clues to the understanding of personality.

The underlying idea of intelligence testing is that observing samples, or representative bits of behavior, yields clues regarding the totality of intellectual functioning. If one took just one sample, the test would not be adequate. If enough samples are taken there can be more confidence that the sum of the samples will rather accurately reflect the whole. Instruments can be used to measure height, weight, blood pressure, and blood content. These clues, incidentally, have been used in various assessments. However, to date, the weight of the brain, the speed and size of brain waves, the number of folds per square inch of the cortex do not yield **reliable** data regarding mental functioning. There is no way to assess intelligence *directly*. Mental testing is approached indirectly. Samples of the products or processes of intellectual functioning are taken. The pieces are added. The summation is presumed to assess intelligence as it will be or behave in future intellect-using milieus. We *infer* from the samples probed, by the particular test given, what the total or "global" intellectual level will be.

Rationale for intelligence testing

There are many definitions of intelligence. Good's (1959) *Dictionary of Education*, lists two columns (a full page) of 25 definitions. Chaplin's (1968) *Dictionary of Psychology* uses just one definition (one column), but it includes the postulations of several authorities. Someone once remarked that "Intelligence is what intelligence tests measure." The remark is often regarded as being witty but it is, in fact, quite accurate. Whatever an intelligence test is, it is designed to sample those aspects of intelligence that the maker of the test postulates as being the prominent manifestations of intelligence.

Intelligence testing started in the early part of the century with the work of Alfred Binet and Theodore Simon. They sought to assess the intellectual ability of French school children and children in institutions for the mentally retarded. Terman adapted, altered, and developed the idea in the United States. He devised a test that is still used (Terman and Merrill, 1960). This test is used not only in schools and clinics, but also in assessing the **validity** of new tests that are being constructed, **standardized,** and published. Mental testing re-

Meaning of intelligence

ceived a big boost in World War I when it became desirable to assess the potential of thousands of men to do a variety of jobs in the armed forces. It was presumed that these jobs required varied levels of intellectual ability. The Army General Classification Tests (AGCT, see Figure 11.3) worked. Possibly it was because of the tests. Possibly it was because of man's adaptability and his tendency to live up to expectations.

Intelligence testing today   The initial enthusiasm and hope for intelligence testing have lasted for half a century. Today there is considerable skepticism about the adequacy, validity, and reliability of these tests. Initially, the tests did pretty well what they were designed to do—they predicted the future school performance of pupils. Skepticism grew as predictions failed when test results were used to forecast marital, social, vocational, and professional success. Even the success of tests for school children, adolescents, and youth began to be doubted. As the drive for education for *all* children and youth really got underway in the 1960's, tests were viewed skeptically. Disadvantaged, culturally deprived, or simply culturally *different* children did not show up well on mental tests. However, under the guidance and encouragement of accepting and confident teachers, such children often seemed to perform well. They did as well as those middle class children who consistently had scored higher on the conventional intelligence tests.

This finding, repeated in various studies, supplemented another insight that has been sharpening for years: Intelligence tests do a pretty good job of forecasting for certain pupils. Those pupils are ones who have the kind of intelligence that has led to school success in the past. They also tend to succeed in school work. However, there is accumulating evidence that successful, test-based, predictions cannot be made regarding vocational success and successful living (Nash and Agne, 1973).

Skepticism about the merits of intelligence testing has risen to such a level that some people and some organizations, even entire school systems, have formed a "let's abolish tests" movement. Hopefully, the reader will not join the panic-stricken mob. Tests have much merit when used to forecast what the designers originally sought to achieve—prediction of school success. Tests have merit when they are regarded as being *clues* to the assessment of intelligence. They are not a "measure" of intelligence. They have merit when used to locate strengths of pupils. They can help identify talents that merit cultivation. That merit becomes a liability, and a reason for skepticism, when they are used to categorize and exclude the subject from opportunities to develop his potentials. Other personality factors must also be considered.

Intelligence is assessed (actually not measured) by **sampling** what the test subject does, or knows, in various realms of life. We then infer, from adding the many samples, what the total is. A big question today is whether enough samples of intelligent behavior are **sampled.**

It is postulated that adding many facets of intelligence together leads to erroneous conclusions about how one might perform—even in school (Guilford, 1971). Let it be assumed that two eighth grade boys of the same age have taken a "differential" mental aptitude test that led to an IQ score for both of 115. However, the subscores on the test were added and expressed as an IQ (see glossary) of 115:

	A	B
Numerical	2	12
Verbal	12	2
Form perception	10	10
Logical reasoning	7	9
Memory	9	7
	40	40 = 115 IQ

One boy turns out to be a "dummy" in arithmetic and appears not to be living up to expectations. He is branded as an underachiever. He is sent to a counselor with his problem of motivation. He is given special classes. He is turned over to a remedial teacher. There he develops such a depressed ego concept that his social studies achievement, once high, declines. The other boy breezes through his arithmetic. He neglects his reading assignments and depends on his logic and memory to hide from his teachers the fact that he is virtually a nonreader. The moral is that one cannot get a valid total out of the addition of different things. We get something—like adding four ounces of coffee and four ounces of tea. It is eight ounces of something, we can agree, but it is neither tea nor coffee. Because it is pretty difficult to add vocabulary and the ability to interpret geometrical shapes, a number of skeptics have raised the question as to precisely what is being measured. Hence, the relevance of defining intelligence as being "that which intelligence tests measure."

The tests used to assess the intelligence of babies are different from those used for testing adults. There are even different instruments for use at given age levels. It might be likened to using the metric system to measure in childhood. We then use inches, feet, and yards to measure in adulthood.

Since 1950 there has been a growing practice of using what are known as multifactor tests. These instruments do not vary substantially from the "old reliables," the Stanford-Binet and the Wechsler-Bellevue. The long-used Otis and Kuhlman-Anderson tests also broke down the total scores into sub-tests. Multifactor tests attempt to assess more of the various aspects of intelligence—mathematics, vocabulary, memory, and logical processes, form perception, artistic perception, etc. This is regarded by some as a step in the right direction. To others it is a matter of "No matter how thin you slice it, it's still bologna." Careful statistical treatment of intelligence test scores does not mean that all of the various facets of intelligence have been probed adequately.

At the present time multifactor intelligence tests sample about 12 to 17 facets of behavior. Guilford (1967) postulates that there are at least, and perhaps even more than, 120 kinds of intelligences (Figure 15.1). Taylor (1972), basing his recommendations on Guilford's hypothesis, suggests that more tests be given—not that their use be shunned or abandoned. Taylor says that the more tests that are given the greater is the likelihood that any one person will appear in some top 10 per cent in some measured category. He believes that if more facets of intelligence were tested, half of the people could be in the top 10 per cent in something. All people would be average or above in some area. He believes that the resulting self-concept is as important in personality as is the intellectual component.

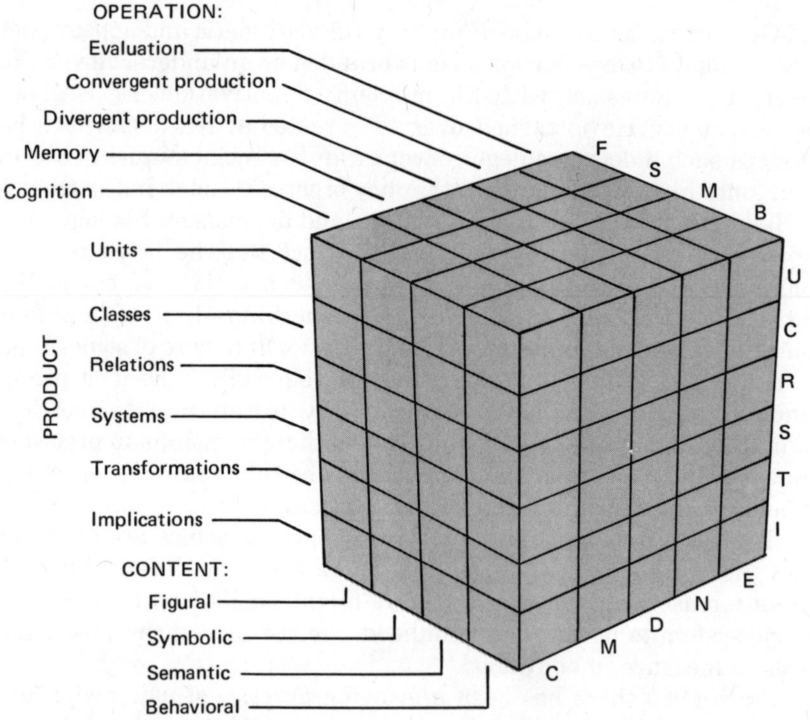

Note that the three parameters—operation, product and content—contain 5, 6, and 4 subcategories, which when multiplied yield 120 intelligences.

Source: J. P. Guilford, 1967, The Nature of Human Intelligence, New York: McGraw-Hill Book Company, p. 63.

Figure 15.1   *The structure of intellect model.*

At the time this is being written there is a heated controversy taking place about exactly what is being assessed by such intelligence tests as are available. Jensen (1972) is prominent among those who contend that intelligence can be assessed with enough accuracy to avoid gross misplacement of children in school activities. In addition, Jensen (1969) maintains that intelligence is about 80 per cent determined by hereditary factors and about 20 per cent by environmental influences. Others strongly oppose this view (because it is likely to result in premature categorization and classification) and they contend that intelligence—whatever it is—is modified by other personality factors.

Those aspects of personality that are evaluated by means of mental tests are subject to continuous modification by the environment. Most important of all, in this conception, is the belief that we will never be able to assess this potential. This is because the potential itself is subject to environmental influences. Rats in a good rat environment develop healthier brain cells than those in a milieu in which their opportunity to explore is limited. Krech (1972) suggests that babies who are given exercise in the unique potential of humans, verbal transactions, would also develop healthier brain cells. Some data on early childhood environment (Wellman, 1940; Hunt, 1969) also suggest that the nature of intellectual development in the first few years of life creates potential, or fosters its atrophy.

Research effort is continuously directed toward the development of intelligence tests that will improve the accuracy of the instruments used. A pervasive obstacle to assessment is that of distinguishing intellectual potential from what is learned. This problem was focused upon in the early 1930's, presumably well settled by the 1950's, and is now aggressively reasserted in the 1970's. Prior to 1930 it was assumed that intelligence was inherited. In the 1950's it was agreed that heredity and environment were inseparable facets of a total process. It was agreed that arguing which was the more important was an exercise in futility. In the 1970's the argument has become part of a national dilemma. We do not know whether or not to give special attention to those whose early environment leaves much to be desired. An inseparable partner of concern about heredity-environment is just how much different milieus contribute to different tested, developed, and utilized intelligence. There is doubt about whether or not tests of intelligence yield valid clues to providing differentiated teaching-learning milieus.

One thrust in testing is the attempt to assess intellectual potential by direct assessment of the strength and nature of brain waves by means of an encephalograph. This, presumably, will separate genetic struc-

Prospects for intellectual assessment

ture from environmental externals. However, data already at hand will disqualify such direct measurement. The kind of food a baby eats has some influence on the genetic potential—even prenatally.

In view of the complexities involved in mental assessment, the conclusion of Sigel (1972), addressed to another aspect of personality, seems apropos: We need to continue to seek simplification of the problem. We need to seek to eliminate some things (perhaps the effort to separate the inseparable—heredity and environment).[1] We need to tie some things together (perhaps motivation and intelligence). We need to raise some questions about categories (perhaps belief in relationships of intelligence to job and life success). We need to determine some priorities (perhaps the testing of more facets of intelligence) before we reach the point of "hardening of the categories."

It would seem that the purpose of testing is better to understand people. It is to provide them appropriate opportunities for development. If tests are used for purposes of exclusion and categorization (as they have been), it really is not the fault of the test. The fault is a human misuse and overuse of a technical instrument. It is especially questionable to use intelligence tests to make critical decisions in one's life when the instruments themselves are, quite properly, subject to criticism. However, to abolish their use, either because of misuse or current lack of scientific sophistication, would be to deprive ourselves of a resource that might become highly valuable. Their use in research merits continued study.

PROJECTIVE TECHNIQUES

Intelligence testing is, as has been seen, an area of great complexity. When other aspects of personality assessment are considered, the questions of validity and reliability are even more perplexing. One of the older approaches to the assessment of typical behavior is that of **projective techniques.**

Merits of projective techniques

Several of the criticisms of personality evaluation are avoided by means of projective techniques. These include a number of devices— ink blots, interpretation of pictures, match-stick figures—that permit and encourage the subject to put himself (to project himself) into the assessment situation. In this approach, there are no rights and wrongs about what the subject says about the stimulus situation. What he does with the objects he manipulates or interprets is not correct or incorrect. An example may clarify. The Rorschach (1942) *Psychodiagnostik* is a series of meaningless blots of ink. One might make such

---

[1]It is suggested that the reader insert his own thoughts in the several parentheses.

blots by dropping some ink on a piece of paper from a height of 12–20 inches. The paper is folded while the ink is wet to spread it as far as possible. Because the paper is folded it will reveal a balanced "whatever-it-is." The blot is amorphous. It is without shape and without meaning. The blot is then shown to the subject and he is given some standard direction, "Tell me about it." "What do you see in the blot?" There is nothing there. (No story is being told in the picture.) What the subject sees or says is really a revelation of himself. He is telling what he sees (projects) in a meaningless, amorphous, ambiguous situation.

Most of the readers have taken a projective test—in a manner of speaking. When one lies on his back and gazes up at a bank of fluffy, rolling, curly, cumulus clouds and tells what he sees in them, he is projecting himself. Because there is nothing there, he is putting into the clouds, and describing, his hopes, dreams, topics of interest, or his mood of the moment. For example, early teen age girls often see dogs and horses. Late teen age girls see young ladies in beautiful gowns, surrounded by panting young men, with one who is particularly handsome. He, with tunnel vision, sees only one girl. Bass, trout, salmon, sailfish, crappie, and sturgeon swim through the author's clouds, as rowboats, runabouts, cruisers, and yachts sail among them.

> The task of assessing the human personality is beset with many obstacles. As even the layman "knows," personality is highly complex. The psychologist has learned, moreover, from research and from clinical experience, that the personality may be conceptualized in many different ways. Personality is a variable phenomenon in respect to both time and situation; and, the meaning of any component in the make-up of personality is highly dependent on other components and their organization. Any method of assessing "the personality" or aspects of personality has serious limitations as well as possible virtues. The projective approach to assessment is, as we shall see, even more hazardous than many of the so-called objective methods of measurement; at the same time, the projective method has many advantages, chief among which, according to the present writer, is that it examines the personality "in process," *i.e.*, while it is functioning.[2]

Rorschach ink blots

The Rorschach "test" consists of ten basic $7 \times 9^{1}/_{2}$ inch cards, most of which are black, two have some red with the black, and three are pastel colors. These present no great problem to the taker of the test, because any response he gives is correct. The test requires a trained administrator. It is used in clinics and research much more often than in school or personnel offices. According to one group of Rorschach authorities (Klopfer *et al.*, 1954), the subject is evaluated in terms of various items. (1) The nature of the response (*e.g.*, humans, sexual connotations, animals, artistic concepts); (2) location of the response

[2]Max L. Hutt, "Psychopathology, Assessment, and Psychotherapy," ed. A. I. Rabin, *Projective Techniques* (New York, Springer Publishing Company, Inc., 1968), p. 64.

—whether the subject responds to specific parts or to the blot as a whole; (3) determinants, that is, whether the subject discusses form or movement; (4) shading responses—whether the subject concentrates on light or dark shadings in the blots or sees them as smooth or rough textures; and (5) how he responds to color—the difference in his reaction to all black or colored blots (sometimes the subject suffers "color shock" and is unable to respond at all to the pastel cards).

Although the Rorschach is not designed or perceived as an intelligence test, a standard part of the technique is to estimate the intellectual capacity and efficiency of the subject (Klopfer *et al.*, 1954, p. 352). This is derived from the speed, quality, quantity, variety, and orderliness of successive responses. The presumed advantage of the Rorschach as an intelligence test is that intellectual processes are seen in action.

A great deal of research has been done on the uses, variations, and potentials of the Rorschach. To date, the outcomes have been of limited benefit. It has some merit as a supplementary diagnostic instrument. It may lead to insights into the "inner life" of the individual. Presumably, it yields clues to the way people feel about their bodies (Goldenson, 1970, p. 1135). Among the many critics of the Rorschach is Cronbach (1960). He discredits the theory on which it is based as well as the statistical procedures used in its validation. He estimates that 90 per cent of the conclusions derived from Rorschach findings are unsubstantiated. It has not proved to be a valid instrument for vocational guidance or predicting vocational success. Many claims are made for the Rorschach, however, and probably many of them are well founded. Whether or not a therapist can get to the nature of the client's problems any faster by means of Rorschach techniques than by face-to-face sessions probably depends more on the client's mood and the therapists's techniques than upon the Rorschach *per se.*

Thematic Apperception Test

Murray's Thematic Apperception Test (TAT) has been a rival to the Rorschach as a clinical device. The test consists of a set of 30 black and white pictures that show men, women, and children in various situations. For example, a woman is shown tucking a cover over something, there is a suitcase and window in the background. The picture is **ambiguous** so what is seen by the subject is presumably a projection of *his* past, *his* perception of people, and *his* hopes for the future.

The pictures are introduced to the subject as a "test of imagination." He is asked to tell the story portrayed in the picture. The story should describe what led up to the scene shown, how the characters are acting, and feeling, and how the story will end. The specific pictures that are used in the set shown to man, woman, or child are somewhat different. After the story, or protocol, for each picture is recorded, the examiner seeks to find some persistent theme. Because people do develop a style or pattern of life, they can, typically, be depended upon to reveal that pattern in daily behavior.

The reader might, for a period of time, study the way people he knows dress, talk, or behave. It may be that without deliberate intent you have already done this. One of the secretaries in an office, despite having a varied wardrobe, always dresses in blacks, white, greys, and browns in the office. The cut is straight, maybe mannish, and the skirts are on the long side of the current mode. One knows men will not make passes at her. If they did she probably would not recognize it. On the other hand, she might frequently interpret male politeness as a proposition. The other secretary also has a varied wardrobe but reds, pinks, and pastels completely exclude the black or brown outfits. Blouses are fluffy and low cut and skirts consistently are on the short side of the mode.

Males also project themselves in behavior. Some consistently turn the subject of water fountain conversation to sex, fishing, unfair working conditions, or the Dow-Jones Average. Some consistently appear on the job a few minutes (perhaps a couple of hours) early, some arrive precisely on time, and others punch in late a couple of times a week. Can one learn about personality from such observations?

Whatever the observations, TAT protocols, or Rorschach responses mean *they need corroborative data.* The girl who dresses in a "provocative" manner may not be setting out to provoke at all. She is proud of herself and knows how she looks her best. She likes to be seen as being attractive. She is, however, as virtuous as we expect grandma to be. The other girl just might be willing to have an affair but does not want it known about the office or with a fellow worker. The man who consistently turns the conversation to sex or the stock market may have much of the product concerned or little of the product concerned. It may be almost entirely a matter of imagination.

Rosenwald (1968), in considering the merits of the TAT, has found what he calls a "wideband" component. It yields data on a variety of personality processes. It may include one's daydreams, creative insights, logical processes, aspirations, past experiences, and outlook for the future. He asserts that the test is still not completely understood. Hence, it does not rest on "solid scientific ground." He considers that the value of the results to the therapist is "indifferent." However, the strides toward its continued and growing usefulness are large ones. The future of the TAT will probably be more illustrious than its history.

Doll play

Diagnosis and therapy in children's problems is sometimes approached by means of doll play. Haworth (1968, p. 327) considers doll play and puppetry as having limited clinical usefulness. Axline (1964), on the other hand, has shown that play (not necessarily restricted to dolls) can be used not only to understand but also to provide therapy for a child. She does this through presenting a case history of Dibs.

> Dibs' story starts in his preschool days where he was seen as an **autistic** child by some of his teachers and by others as being feeble-minded. Dibs passively permitted himself to be drawn by Dr. Axline into a room containing various toys, dolls, a sandbox, and a chair. Axline talked to Dibs but initially he did not respond verbally though he would react physically. He smashed the male doll and buried it in the sand. Gradually, he began to talk to the dolls and then to Dr. Axline. He came early to the scheduled sessions and tried to prolong them. He began to talk with his teachers and to his mother when she came to get him after school and after the sessions with Axline.
>
> Ultimately, it became known that Dibs was not feeble-minded but actually bright. Later it was discovered that his IQ score would place him in the gifted category. By the time he was a teenager he was doing well in college and having serious thoughts about man's place in the world. Dibs not only had been rehabilitated by play therapy (helped, of course, by a supportive but reality-facing Dr. Axline) but, through the open style of life he developed, he was a therapist to his father and mother.[3]

Haworth (1968) judges the merit of doll play in about the same way that the Rorschach and TAT were evaluated above. Doll play has been much studied but it has dubious value in terms of yielding *informative* data. It must be questioned regarding the extent to which it reveals drives, defenses, conflicts, and anxieties. For instance, one is led to ask, "Is it necessary for a therapist to know what caused Dibs to be withdrawn and to mask his intelligence?" Dibs gained "normality" in functioning by learning that there was someone who would take time for him alone. He learned that his ideas were acceptable, and that he was admired and accepted. He was well on the way to recovery before it was discovered that his mother felt that Dibs' birth had interrupted a promising professional career. It seems that one of the author's biases might be confirmed by projective techniques: It is not what they tell but the process of using them that yields results.

Projection in everyday life   Projection of personality takes place constantly in daily life without the use of formal techniques. However, as in the case of structured projective techniques, the processes are overlain with such things as SES, cultural learnings, and habits. There are conscious or unconscious attempts to mislead. Imitation of parents or other key people are

---

[3]Many of the students who have read the 220-page paperback, Virginia Axline, *Dibs: In Search of Self* (Boston: Houghton Mifflin Company 1964), say that once started, they were unable to put the book down until it had been read completely.

such that strict interpretations may be misleading. Thus, the way one dresses and grooms himself yields some clues. Hypotheses formed will, however, bear "checking out" with some other evaluative approaches. The neat, clean person is one, we say, who is proud of himself and thinks of himself as meriting an attractive package. Conversely, the slovenly, unkept person may be so sure of himself that grooming really does not matter. He may be so insecure that he knows that nothing he does will change the low status he thinks others give to him.

The language one uses may provide some sort of clue. The four-letter words of the man's card or pool room when used by a college instructor may be indicative of a bid for attention. They may be an indication that he has no regard for those who are offended by such language. The man's card-room words may be utterly inappropriate for women. Such words may suggest that they want attention and are hoping the invitation will come soon. At least, that is what *some* perceive as being projected!

The quality of one's voice—high pitched and tense or low, clear, and firm—are projecting clues that others read or misread. The way one sits or walks is seen as a manifestation of the projecting process. Upright, shoulders back, equals confident and open personality. Slouched shoulders, pulled toward chest, suggest low ego concept and a closed social stance. Sitting with only buttocks and shoulders touching the chair suggests that what is going on bores this sophisticated person. He has "already heard it a dozen times." Upright posture sends the message: "What you say is important" or "I've heard this before but you are important enough to merit my attention."

In short, it is being said that all we do, or say, or wear are projections of our personality. Moreover, those around us are reading the clues. They read them differently, depending on how well they know the other person. Accuracy depends on how much they have revised their assessments in terms of other projective clues. The clues are also read in terms of the apperceptive set of the perceiver.

These paragraphs will probably not do much to change the clues one sends. They should warn the reader, however, not to permit first impressions (that come from just such clues as cited) to close the doors to adequate sampling. It takes many data to render an accurate interpretation of the personality of others.

INVENTORIES AND QUESTIONNAIRES

Personality means so many things that there is a wide variety of approaches to its assessment. Rating scales, self-reporting devices, projective techniques, and situational evaluations are used to provide clues. The device used depends on the test makers' perceptions of what aspects of personality appear to be most worthy of assessment.

Inventories   An inventory consists of lists of questions focusing around given areas of conduct. For instance, one of the better known, and extensively researched, inventories is the Minnesota Multiphasic Personality Inventory. This 500-item device consists of nine scoring scales. Each scale is comprised of items to which the respondent responds as being true or false. The areas covered are:

Hypochondriasis—questions center about the subject's concern about health (not health itself but concern regarding it).

Depression—items deal with one's tendency to feel useless or helpless.

Hysteria—items deal with the extent to which one uses physical illness to solve, or avoid solving, personal problems.

Psychopathic deviation—scale items deal with the extent and frequency of one's tendency to disregard others and to avoid emotional involvement with others.

Masculinity-feminity—items are used to determine whether one's interests follow the "conventional" pattern of male-female preferences.

Paranoia—items are designed to detect feelings of suspiciousness and persecution.

Psychasthenia—items seek to probe the extent to which one feels **compulsions** or experiences excessive fears.

Schizophrenia—this scale seeks clues that might reveal the accuracy of the subject's perception of reality.

Hypomania—items are designed to reveal the extent to which one is overactive either mentally or physically.

By stating T-F items in different ways and at various points, but on the same specific behavior, a check on the honesty and consistency of the subject is also obtainable. It is possible to use selected items, distributed throughout the test, to score for the tendency to be socially withdrawn or to participate socially. Altogether, the nine scales may be scored to yield 14 different scores or tendencies. That is, there are 14 *possible* combinations of test items. The inventory is a popular one, probably as frequently used in research as in decision-assisting processes. In part, the popularity is because the designers have built into it the notion that persons in different nations, cultures, and SES have varied perceptions that limit the wide applicability of results. In part, the popularity is because there is a built-in check against deliberate falsification.

There are many other inventories, each designed in accordance with what the authors deem to be the more significant facets of personality.[4]

[4]Many books on educational or psychological tests and measurements will have detailed descriptions of several such instruments. The *Mental Measurements Yearbook*, published periodically rather than yearly, by Gryphon Press, Highland Park, New Jersey, contains an encyclopedic listing of such inventories, together with remarks concerning their validity and reliability.

Except in unusual circumstances, one wants to "put his best foot forward." One exception is when one wants an excuse to be discharged from the armed services. A high school boy deliberately did poor work in his junior year so that he would not qualify for West Point. His father, a career officer, had the way all cleared but the boy could not talk him out of the idea. Failing his courses won out for the boy. In most situations, however, one wants to appear to be good in the eyes of others.

Only the very young and the very naïve do not know that their personality is being evaluated. Hence, they often deliberately disguise the motives they recognize and substitute motives that they know are socially commendable. This disguise is rationalized with "It's nobody's business but my own—how I got along with mother." Perhaps we do not want our prospective employer to be aware of our hypochondriacal tendencies.

It is often hard to be honest, even if we want to be. We may not, because of unconscious motivations, know ourselves. Thus, we may feel that we are confident and ambitious. The facts may be that we feel inferior and fear failure. It may be that we think we are socially oriented because we teach, consult, or lead church classes. It may be that the real reason is fear of being ignored. Or, we may want a higher income than our peers.

Even when we wish to be candid and objective there may be difficulties in responding to a questionnaire. We may confuse what we report with what we would, ideally, like to be. We may have difficulty seeing ourselves as we really are. Comparative scores are misleading because different respondents have different perceptions.

The distinction between a questionnaire and an inventory is not sharp. Questionnaires consist of a set of questions focusing on some area of behavior. They are designed to probe interests, personal problems, opinions, or memories. Questionnaires are, as is the case with inventories, difficult to interpret because they are inevitably subject to varied interpretations. Some respondents deliberately try to hide some of their prejudices and weaknesses, while others are much less defensive. However, their unique perceptions lead them to view the questions differently. Others have basic difficulty in perceiving a difference between their current self and their ideal self.

> A young man responded to one such questionnaire, and the results caused the administrator to look on him with some concern, if not outright apprehension. On several key items his combined responses were so atypical that it seemed that he might be headed for an immediate psychotic break. He had been knocked unconscious. He had been a bed-wetter. He walked in his sleep. He had been arrested several times. He was accident prone. He had frequent headaches. He had difficulty getting along with people. All-in-all his score was such that psychiatric evaluation and help seemed to be imperative.

His behavior in the office, however, was such that he was seen, by those who did not know the questionnaire results, as a respectable and competent worker. A face-to-face confrontation dispelled the concern of the questionnaire administrator. The subject had not really been unconscious. He had had his breath knocked out by a fall from a tree that left him breathless and dizzy for a few moments. He did not remember when he stopped wetting the bed (and bed-wetters do remember). He had, his parents told him, walked in his sleep when he was visiting his grandparents after a two-day-long train trip. His "arrests" consisted of tickets for illegal or overtime parking. He had had a bone broken only once but he had burned himself a time or two, cut or pounded his fingers many times, and had fallen a few times. His headaches were a result of overindulgence in alcohol on festive occasions, reading for too long at a time, and from driving in glaring sunlight. His idea of not getting along with people was that he remembered two age mates and a teacher whom he disliked. In short, his excessive candidness about himself led to a misreading of the kind of person he really was.

Most authorities are not so outspoken as the following in their skepticism about the merits of personality inventories. The statement may be too harsh, especially in view of the potential research value of the instruments concerned. It is, however, a statement with which the author heartily agrees when it comes to diagnosing personality.

> There is a great deal of evidence that personality questionnaires, controlled interviews, and interest inventories are widely used in counseling. Just why this should be so in view of the demonstrated inadequacies of these devices is difficult to understand. It seems that it must be a combination of amazing, psychometric innocence on the part of the users, naïveté in considering the counseling job as a "quickie" affair rather than a complex longitudinal problem, mistaken faith in statistics on the part of inventory producers and consumers, expediency, and a desire to keep up with the other fellow who uses them for any of the above reasons. Perhaps another reason for their popularity can be found in the seeming exactness they give to the counselor's work. Counseling interviews may seem not scientifically respectable enough to impress one's colleagues or clients, but an array of scores seemingly supported by pedantic jargon might possibly do so. The popularity of the instruments may be due in part, then, to the psychological support that counselors, working in a relatively new area, and without adequate evidence of their effectiveness, may feel that they need; and the round-the-clock hucksterism in the sales of the instruments must account in large measure for their widespread use. Certainly it cannot be justified on the basis of logical reasoning or experimental evidence.[5]

Not all authorities are quite as enthusiastic in their repudiation of personality assessment devices as the above. Consistently we are warned that caution must be exerted in interpreting the results of

[5]John W. M. Rothney, Paul J. Danielson, and Robert A. Heimann, *Measurement for Guidance* (New York: Harper & Row, Publishers, 1959), pp. 283–284.

questionnaires, rating scales, and projective techniques (Brown, 1970, p. 424; Ahmann and Glock, 1967, p. 448; Tyler, 1963, p. 88). Many would agree with the following statement:

> The limitations of personality inventories are such that their use should be severely restricted in school situations. They are probably most useful as a general screening instrument for identifying pupils *who should be* studied more closely by the school counselor. If scored at all, only the total score should be used. From a counseling standpoint, it may be most helpful to ignore the scoring and use the pupils' responses to individual items as a basis for counseling interviews. Although teachers may assist in the administration of personality inventories, the interpretation and use of the results should be left to the psychologically trained counselor.[6]

OBSERVATION

One's hope for the future of personality assessment is contingent on the question raised in the first chapter, "What is one's conception of the nature of man?" If one believes that personality is formed by the age of three or six or ten, then assessment has much merit in terms of predicting future personality orientations. If personality is relatively static it may be susceptible to capture in some assessment device. If one believes that man is a flexible, uniquely perceptive, and creative being, then personality assessment will be regarded as a tentative, transient process that yields *clues* about the present situation. If one thinks of man as a problem-solving creature who copes with the present by varying his responsive *and* proactive behavior to fit the current situation, then assessment must be situational. The latter perception makes observation an important technique in assessment.

A wide variety of ways of revealing the "real me" in group situations has been reported throughout the country. These revelations of personality (or the "real me")[7] are called by a variety of names: Sensitivity groups, T-groups, group dynamics, basic encounter groups, and heuristic training. The success of such groups in helping people assess their strengths and weaknesses has been notable. There are, unfortunately, a number of rather "way out" groups that have been devised by self-designated, professionally unprepared, opportunistic persons (Birnbaum, 1969). These supposedly reveal the "real me" in terms of

Interpersonal process groups

[6]Norman E. Gronlund, *Measurement and Evaluation in Teaching*, second edition, (New York: The Macmillan Company, 1971).

[7]The "real me" is an elusive concept for the author. I think it is the real me when I choose to behave differently as a father than I behave as a professor. It is really me when I permit my love or anger to show, just as it is still me when it is conventional to mask such feelings. See, for example, James W. Felt, "How To Be Yourself," *America*, Vol. 705, May 25, 1968. Reprinted in *Psychosocial Dynamics of Effective Behavior*, eds. H. W. Bernard and W. C. Huckins, (Boston: Holbrook Press, Inc., 1971).

encouraged anger, meetings in which members are naked, and group sexual encounters. With such variety it is difficult to convey just what degree of encounter one means. It is difficult for the reader not to project into what he reads and hears any experiences he may have had in them.

Herein, reference is made to interpersonal process groups led by trained facilitators of communication. These leaders recognize the hazards of allowing the "real me" to mean expressing one's feelings without regard for conventions. Such controls have evolved from centuries of social experience. Interpersonal process groups are designed to present a milieu in which one tries to reduce defensiveness. Thus, he may understand how others perceive him as a social person. The merit of interpersonal process, or encounter, groups is that those who participate are not just talking about social transactions. They are engaged in a situational milieu in which the personality of each member is revealed in words and action.

> In a family counseling session a mother, father, nine-year-old son, and thirteen- and seventeen-year-old daughters were present with another family of similar membership. The boy was trying to call attention to himself by kicking the younger sister. He was snickering at a girl about his age in the other family. Mother was fluttering over him trying to keep him in order. Father was concentrating on the topic under consideration. Thirteen-year-old was contributing eagerly and pertinently. Seventeen-year-old was withdrawn—coat kept buttoned, somewhat slouched in her chair, and back half-turned to facilitator and father.
>
> The family was in action—in a different setting than at home but definitely not role playing. It was clearly a matter of "this is how I behave" and this is how you are seen by others.
>
> The concern of the first family was the seventeen-year-old daughter's staying out late, or on occasion, staying away from home all night. The father had been critical of his daughter, he described his shouting at her and told her during the session how self-centered she was. His voice suggested anger and hostility. However, at one point he said, with tears in his eyes, "I get so scared for _____ when I read about drugs, car thefts, high pregnancy rates out of wedlock, abortions that I'm almost insane." At this point, the daughter got up and put her arm over her father's shoulder, put her cheek to his, and said, "I didn't know you cared that way."

Interpersonal process groups are a slice of life. They provide an opportunity for all to see. They can verbalize what they see as the "real me." They can perceive what is seen (more accurately by others than by the self) in everyday behavior. The behavior is spontaneous and situational. Attitudes and behavior are not screened through a questionnaire or a series of ink blots or pictures. There is a dilemma of choice as one wonders whether to state what will describe, or disguise, himself. He may puzzle about what he now is as contrasted to what his ideal self should be. In group interaction, behavior is screened with just about the same degree of openness or defensiveness that characterizes one's life outside the group process milieu.

Interpersonal process groups at least potentially have promise as an evaluative technique which is particularly valuable because of the immediacy of feedback. In addition, the value is enhanced because evaluation is teamed with a teaching-learning function. This, in the final analysis, is the purpose of personality assessment and the aim of the facilitator.

Sociometry is a procedure by means of which the interpersonal likes and preferences of members of a group may be schematically diagrammed (Figure 15.2). The use of sociometry is restricted to classroom teachers. They are concerned about providing a comfortable social milieu in which pupils feel most secure. Pupils can then, presumably, be most productive in their learning activities. It begins with a *sociometric question*, "With whom would you like to work in daily assignments?" "Who do you want on the nomination committee with you?" "Who is your best friend?" This changes periodically, especially in the preadolescent years, and the groupings should be redone. The answers, even in beginning school pupils, will vary somewhat according to the activity concerned. Advantageous employment of a sociogram for structuring productive working relationships calls for application as follows:

> Mutual choices are placed together.
> Isolates are given their first choices.
> A minimum number of isolates are placed in a small group.
> Stars are placed wherever they may be needed—they are social experts and can get support from many peers.
> Natural groupings are maintained as far as possible.
> Groups are changed periodically to provide the new experiences that make for flexibility in social interaction.

The naturalness of sociometric grouping may be appreciated by noting the clusters that form spontaneously on the playground; for example, a sociogram may be read into a schoolground photograph taken from the roof of the school during recess. Advantages claimed for applied sociometry are:

> Reduction of anxiety in isolates;
> Improved pupil achievement;
> Diminished need for teacher-imposed discipline;
> Teacher's improved perception of who actually are the isolates and stars—pupils' values and perceptions often differ from those of the teacher;
> Heightened group responsibility;
> Teachers are helped to capitalize on group dynamics.

Thus, sociometry is simultaneously an evaluative record and a teaching approach. It is not proposed as a nostrum that will solve all the problems of a teacher. It appears quite certain, however, that some insight and assistance can be obtained from its use.

Recalling the role of interpersonal congeniality in worker satisfaction (Chapter 11), it might be advantageous for employers to compose work crews on the basis of sociometry. When committees are appointed in institutions, it might be useful to assess the "mutuality" of committee members. When sales personnel are assigned to depart-

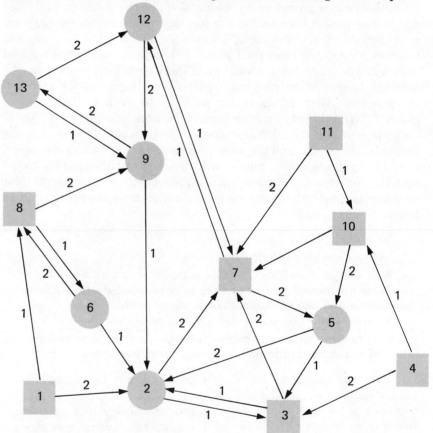

Squares represent boys and circles represent girls. The number by the line indicates first or second choices. Numbers 7 and 2 are "stars," or much–chosen individuals. Numbers 1, 4, 11 are "isolates" – not having been chosen by anyone so far as the particular sociometric question was concerned. Numbers 2, 3, 12 and 7, 13 and 9, and 6 and 8 are "mutual choices."

Source: Harold W. Bernard, 1972, *Psychology of Learning and Teaching,* 3/e, New York: McGraw-Hill Book Company, p. 246.

Figure 15.2   *Sociogram of an eighth grade class.*

ments it might be worth considering the living sociogram of who sits by whom at coffee break time.

An interview milieu is, of course, not the same as the working conditions that will prevail if the interviewee gets the job. Nevertheless, a trained and experienced interviewer can make some rather accurate assessments regarding the way one will perform on the job. He knows what questions to ask: Why did you leave your last job? How much school did you miss? What are your leisure-time activities (social or loner type)? Answers to these questions will assume a pattern that, to the interviewer, are much like the graphical representation in a sociogram. They indicate attitudes and preferences.

Interviews

The interviewee often knows very well how to present himself. The advice given by the Oregon Employment Service to job seekers who are to have an interview is:

Be on time.

Dress in clean clothes—avoid extremes in style.

Hair, nails, teeth, and hands should be clean. Men should be clean-shaven and hair should be combed neatly.

Make a thorough inventory of your skills and have something to sell. List skills that do not appear to be needed on the job. One woman got the bookkeeper job with a construction company because she had driven a cat and operated a power shovel for her father.

The real test of personality is how one lives from day to day. Courtship, presumably, functions as an assessment procedure for evaluating what kind of partner one would get if the couple married. Unfortunately, self-assessment is not used frequently enough in courtship. The crucial "test" item is "What kind of partner will I be?" Marriage counselors advise a long (six to 12 months) courtship so that an adequate sampling of habits, attitudes, and preferences can be evaluated.

Performance

The case is similar with respect to job success. The real test is daily performance. Past history provides only clues—albeit reliable ones. Recall the case of the glazier (Chapter 11) who decided that *he* was responsible and began systematically to change the way he regarded, and behaved toward, supervisors and fellow workers. His is the exceptional case. Life styles are, to a counselor and teacher, often discouragingly consistent. Changed motivation, however, is a possibility.

The *College Admissions Data Yearbook* provides data concerning the probabilities of success in given colleges—Yale, Harvard, Illinois, Missouri, North Dakota, Hamline, Rhode Island University, and so on. If one has aptitude scores in certain categories (high, medium, or low) his probable success in various colleges is indicated. However, it is made clear, and frequently reiterated, that the statistics are probabilities only. Students do make it at College X with low scores. Students do fail at the same college with top-ranking assessments. The real test is what is done with the opportunity—performance. The same is true in marriage, occupations, and social interaction. Prior assessments are indicators. They provide grounds for postulations. They yield clues. The real, adequate, and reliable test of personality is performance.

SUMMARY

The assessment of personality is a task of almost overwhelming size and complexity. The difficulties that continue to be encountered in that major aspect of personality called intelligence exemplify the hazards. Intelligence tests presently available are viewed skeptically. They do not sample adequately the many kinds of intelligences that are regarded as potentials in different persons. Another dilemma is whether intelligence is some kind of stable thing, or entity; or whether it is a process, or style of living, that is subject to continuous modification. At best, intelligence tests must be regarded as current and tentative clues to personality assessment. These clues must be supplemented by other data, especially observed behavior.

Personality assessment may also be approached by means of projective techniques. Rorschach blots, TAT, doll play, and interpretations of overt behavior are presumed to reveal unconscious, as well as consciously concealed motivations. They suggest life styles of the respondent. All these require a trained, well-informed, and objective administrator. Projective techniques are used daily by everyone. They are used to express basic motivations and to "read" the personality of others. However, the untrained observer may confuse the reading by projecting himself into his translations of the behavior of others.

Questionnaires, inventories, rating schedules, and self-rating devices are subject to much the same criticism as projective techniques. They have merit as rough screening in research projects. They can help locate general tendencies and inclinations. In individual personality assessment, their best use might be that of locating areas of concern that could be the subject of face-to-face counseling situations—a point of departure for dialogue.

Observation, subjective as it is, is one of the better personality assessment approaches. It is used constantly, with varying degrees of accuracy. It possesses the great advantage of viewing personality in action. Sociometry makes a record of observed behavior. Its use has not become so standardized as to discount flexibility of interpretation. Interviews also permit action, language, and grooming to be observed, but these are subject to deliberate misrepresentation by the interviewee.

Although personality assessment is a part of daily living it is not readily reduced to formal devices and quantification. Both formal and informal techniques are useful when regarded as providing tentative clues and corroborative hypotheses.

SUGGESTED READINGS

CROPLEY, A. J., "A Five-Year Longitudinal Study of the Validity of Creativity Tests," *Developmental Psychology*, Vol. 6, 119–124, 1972.
> *A five-year follow-up of creativity tests given to seventh grade pupils, of which 111 were tested five years later, indicates that creativity tests have reasonable and encouraging long-range predictive validity.*

EBEL, ROBERT L., "The Future of the Measurement of Abilities II," *Educational Researcher*, Vol. 2, No. 3, 5–12, 1973.
> *This article is a follow-up of one written 25 years ago by E. L. Thorndike. Ebel thinks we have made much progress in these years. However, the real concern is how to make intelligence tests reflect other personality factors—emotions, social class, creativity, social traits.*

"Ethical Forum: I. Q. and Race," *The Humanist*, Vol. 32, 4–18, January/February, 1972.
> *The case for and against testing, especially intelligence testing, is presented by such authorities as Arthur Jensen, Jerome Kagan, David McClelland, Richard Light, H. J. Eysenck, and Kenneth Clark. In the author's perception: the most interesting journal publication in the first half of the year.*

HERRNSTEIN, RICHARD, "I. Q." *Atlantic*, Vol. 228, No. 3, 43–64, September, 1971.
> *He puts it "all together." A difficult subject, with many ramifications, is clearly and concisely stated; and, the many ramifications (heredity, changing IQ, family influences, SES, cultural discrimination, etc.) are dealt with.*

MISCHEL, WALTER, *Personality and Assessment*, pp. 41–72. New York: John Wiley and Sons, Inc., 1968.
> *This chapter, "Traits and States of Constructs," will help the reader appreciate the difficulties involved in reducing such a global concept as personality to quantifiable results on assessment schedules.*

ROTHNEY, J. W. M., PAUL J. DANIELSON, and ROBERT A. HEIMANN, *Measurement for Guidance*, pp. 282–318. New York: Harper and Row, Publishers, 1959.
> *The authors forthrightly condemn the use of personality questionnaires, interest inventories, and projective techniques in terms of validity and reliability for guidance purposes. They believe that a skilled counselor can get useful information better than the formal instruments; and, if the counselor is not so skilled, he should not call himself a counselor.*

FOLLOW-UP LEARNING ACTIVITIES

What is your present evaluation of intelligence tests?
    highly valuable _____   dangerous _____
    of doubtful value _____   discriminating _____
    other_____

_____

_____

_____

Do you agree _____ or disagree _____ with the notion that projective techniques are superior to inventories as assessment devices? Why?

_____

_____

_____

_____

Do you think young children should be allowed to express their aggressions or hostilities on dolls?
    Yes _____   No _____   because _____

_____

_____

_____

Cite an instance in which you projected a feeling, shortcoming, or error on someone else when that feeling, etc. was actually your own.

_____

_____

_____

_____

The author is distinctly anti-inventory in attitude. Do you agree _____ or disagree _____ with him? Why?

_____

_____

_____

What do you think is the best way to assess the personality of others?
    first impressions _____   observation over time _____
    intuition _____   others' opinions _____
    other_____

_____

_____

16
Causes and Treatment of Personality Dysfunction

Some sleep, some drink, some use drugs, some act mechanically to avoid harsh reality.

LEARNING ACTIVITIES

Do you think personality disorders are caused primarily by organic or environmental factors? Why?

_____
_____
_____
_____

Do you believe that, for yourself, you should seek help when troubled or that you should be strong enough to resolve your difficulties by yourself?

_____
_____
_____
_____

If you had a friend or acquaintance who recently has talked occasionally of suicide what would you do, if anything?

_____
_____
_____
_____

If you had a friend or acquaintance who has talked with you about a pending break-up of his marriage and who wanted you to help him, what would you do or say?

_____
_____
_____
_____

(Compare and discuss the above items with two or three classmates.)

What role do you perceive your own self-image to have in your life?

_____
_____
_____

Has "mere talking" ever helped you in resolving some personal dilemma?

Yes _____ No _____ because _____
_____
_____
_____

Humans have for eons been of the opinion that theirs was a time of unprecedented strain, stress, and uncertainty. Some persons, whatever their circumstances, would find that the processes of coping and adjusting to current demands were too much for them. One has little chance of finding any book or periodical (that deals with personality) that does not somewhere state or imply that the human dilemma is now at an all time high level of complexity and frustration. Many state that if we do not, within a decade or two, find solutions to our problems of living we may progress to the point of no return. Perhaps we are already there.

Things may or may not be so bad comparatively as the current (and probably perspectively limited) critic says they are. However, there can be no doubt that personality dysfunction is a serious current problem. Some years ago Menninger (1930) stated that one out of every 20 of us is, has been, or would be hospitalized for mental illness—and that the other 19 of us did not feel any too good all of the time. This startling statistic has not been controverted in the 40 years since its publication. It is estimated that one out of ten persons has some form of mental illness or emotional disorder. One out of 20 is in need of hospitalization for such dysfunction ("Facts About . . . ," 1972).

One clear difference between today and four decades ago is that there is an open admission and discussion of deviant personalities. Great progress has been made in the last decade in the matter of helping people recover from personality breakdown. This chapter surveys some of the numerous approaches to therapeutic intervention. All of these, and others, have some degree of success. Those who need this intervention are the one in ten, one in 20, or the "other 19" who are functioning at a lower level than need be the case.

THE NATURE OF PERSONALITY DYSFUNCTION

Organic dysfunction

In most cases of personality disorder organic and environmental factors combine to provide a causal explanation. In other cases, it is difficult to perceive a precipitating or contributing environmental factor—the difficulty seems to be clearly organic.

> Lee J. was a 15-year-old high school sophomore. He had been referred to the school counselor because of his disruptive behavior in class. He talked loudly and made uncalled-for disrespectful remarks. During the interview the counselor noted that there were apparently

unconnected thoughts. Lee showed delayed reactions to something that had been said moments before. Lee offered no excuses for his unpredictable behavior. He indicated that things would get better. However, in a follow-up conversation with the referring teacher it was found that things did not get better. The counselor then talked with other of Lee's teachers, including one who had had Lee the year before. This teacher said that Lee was not at all like he was in his freshman year.

Checking intelligence test scores in Lee's cumulative record the counselor found that Lee had scores on various tests over the years ranging from 125–135. The score in his freshman year was 115. Another test was given on an equivalent form of the test taken the year before and Lee's score was below 100. This alarmed the counselor because he had recently heard that such a decline of test scores might be a symptom of brain injury. He talked with the parents. He found that they had been disturbed by Lee's unruly and, for Lee, unusual behavior. The counselor asked if Lee recently had complained of headaches or dizziness. The response was "Yes" plus the reporting of some nightmares. However, inquiry revealed no knowledge of head injuries at any time. On the suggestion of the counselor, Lee was taken to a brain specialist. The doctor discovered a small, operable tumor on the brain. After the ensuing operation Lee's behavior immediately reverted to his former reputation of cheerfulness, superior academic achievement. The headaches and nightmares disappeared.

Mental retardation and bizarre behavior can result from birth injury. Abnormal pressures in the birth canal or inexpert use of instruments may cause brain damage. The brain may be deprived of the necessary rich supply of oxygen during a prolonged birth. This causes a statistically significant amount of abnormal behavior. Behavior changes have been noted as the result of head injuries that were severe enough to cause periods of unconsciousness. One of the puzzling factors in relating personality to brain injury is that for years after the injury behavior may be normal. Then a sudden change is noted. It is not, therefore, possible to be sure that the behavior and the injury are related. Moreover, behavior modification experiments—or in other words, environmental factors—have shown that brain-injured children are amenable to behavior change under planned reinforcement regimes (Hall and Broden, 1967).

Certain diseases, such as sleeping sickness (encephalitis lethargica) or syphilitic infection, may cause brain lesions that are visible under a microscope. Imbalance in insulin or glucose are also associated with behavior change. These changes can be detected by sophisticated medical examination. However, little or nothing can be done to reverse the processes. Brain cells, unlike many other cells which can replace themselves, once dead cannot be regenerated. It has been reported that alcohol is particularly deadly to brain cells. Theoretically alcohol causes coagulation of the blood cells. It interferes with the capacity of the blood to carry an ample supply of oxygen to the brain. Each drink allegedly kills some cells. Over a period of years it causes the shuffling, stumbling mental and physical gait of the alcoholic. These conclusions are not universally accepted. Authorities are reluctant to say that the problems that preceded the heavy drinking were any more, or less, important in producing the alcoholic psychoses than was the drinking itself.

Chromosomal abnormality

The combination of organic and environmental factors in explaining personality orientations may be illustrated in what might be called the "Case of the Missing Chromosomes." The sex-determining chromosomes are known as X and Y. If the genetic combination is XX the organism will be female, if the union is XY the organism will be male. It has recently been discovered that some genetic anamoly may create an extra, a supernumerary, Y in the male cell (XYY, $XYYY$, or XY/XYY). Such human males, as adults, are often unusually tall, somewhat dull, and have acne-marked faces. The incidence of crime among such men is higher than among those having normal XY chromosomes. The incidence of abnormal XY chromosomes is higher among prison populations. Among 36 tall college basketball players examined none had chromosomal abnormality. Among a group of 34 prisoners 11.8 per cent had chromosomal abnormality (Montagu, 1968).

A survey of studies to date on personality and chromosomal abnormality emphasizes that genes do not determine anything. Chromosomal abnormality does not mean that the possessor will be subnormal in intelligence. One need not have an aggressive or depressed personality, or engage in criminal activities. However, supernumerary Y's in the sex chromosome may contribute to the development of abnormality. The gangliness of the boy's build, his slow mental processes, and his unsightly acne may make him the butt of childhood cruelty in teasing and taunting. This may drive him toward withdrawal or aggression. The genetic error probably does, in some individuals, predispose them to aggressive or extreme behavior.

Richard Speck, convicted of murdering eight nurses in Chicago over a period of time (1966), had an XYY chromosome. He wrote the plea in lipstick on a mirror, "Catch me before I kill." He had the tallness, the acne, the mental dullness of chromosomal abnormality. His character was indicated in his record of 40 arrests. Nevertheless, Montagu (1968) reflects the consensus of hereditarians when he says that in addition to the genetic constitution, there must be a debilitating social environment that would trigger the potential.

Biochemistry of anxiety

Typically, anxiety—a state in which one is generally apprehensive, hyperreactive to stimuli—is explained in terms of psychogenic factors. Vague fears and feelings of impending doom are symptoms of anxiety. They have no specific referent, and are thought to arise from environmental uncertainty and conflict. Pitts (1969), reporting on experiments at the Washington University School of Medicine, found that anxiety could be artificially induced by the injection of lactate. Lactate is a product of cell metabolism which is typically at high level during periods of strenuous exercise. Some patients report that their anxiety is at a high level when, or shortly after, they exercise vigorously. Anxiety does the same thing as exercise. It causes the system to produce an unusually large supply of lactate. All the questions are not yet answered: Why do some people not get anxious when their lactate level is high? Is it possible to reduce the incidence (5 per cent of the population so afflicted), or gravity, of anxiety by chemical intervention?

Schizophrenia is another personality disorder that entails chemical factors (Frohman and Domino, 1972). In a normal brain an enzyme acts to prevent an excess of DMT (dimethyltyptamine). DMT is chemically related to the hallucinogen drug LSD and has similar effects (see Chapter 17). In some persons there is retardation in the counteracting of DMT. Such a person is prone to schizophrenic episodes. The possibility exists that a chemical way can be found to control the excess of DMT.

The (1) success of lobotomies (severing certain cranial nerves through surgical operation), (2) electric shock treatment (which destroys or inhibits defective neural circuits), (3) obtaining predictable behaviors from electrical stimulation of the brain, and (4) the use of drugs for treating some personality disorders have led some enthusiasts to say that biochemistry is the way to personality rehabilitation and transformation of abnormal behavior. Others are not quite so sure—in fact, some are in emphatic disagreement. The latter claim that drugs only calm, or stimulate, the patient to the point that they can be worked with in terms of perceptual or environmental change.

Environmental stress

The experimental production of neuroses in laboratory animals suggests the belief that humans may, under conditions of environmental stress, become neurotic. Dogs, for instance, have been required to make increasingly fine discriminations of shades of color or be given an electrical shock. A point is reached where the task of discrimination is too great. The animal crouches unresponsively in a corner. He may become dangerous to his handlers. He may refuse to eat. He may chew his flesh raw.

Similarly, we are quite sure that burdens such as prolonged pain, solitary confinement, or uncertainty about one's being loved by his mother cause mental illness. Perhaps job insecurity, a rasping wife, or an alcoholic husband can produce so much strain that one becomes nonfunctional or dysfunctional. It is believed that the hazardous living of slum conditions is conducive to high rates of neurotic characteristics (Coles, 1967).

If personality function were solely due to organic factors then operations, drugs, and electrical shock or stimulation would have to be the means of remediation. There is too much evidence that children and adults can materially improve their behavior (1) under conditions of reduced environmental harshness, (2) by living in a "therapeutic regime," and (3) by enlisting the aid and advice of a counselor or psychiatrist, to allow the conclusion that environmental stress can be discounted. The techniques of helping, discussed in the next section, presume that most personality dysfunction is associated with some form of excessive environmental pressure.

VARIED THERAPEUTIC TECHNIQUES

Havemann (1969), in a popular article, discussed in some detail a half dozen of the more popular current models of therapy. He added a sort of glossary-addendum of 14 other alternatives to classical psychotherapeutic procedures. This section deals with seven approaches with the idea of showing some of the rather sharp contrasts that exist. The interesting part is that each of these methods is effective with some persons. One is led to speculate that it may be less the method and more the therapist that makes for success. Perhaps too, particular clients who determine that they will get well might do so with any method or any therapist. It must further be observed that some people do not respond to any therapist, any method, or any biochemical intervention.

Psychoanalysis

Psychoanalysis is not, by any means, any *one* thing. Freud used many techniques as he continued to develop his theory throughout a long lifetime of innovation. His so-called disciples, Jung and Adler, broke away from him and developed theories and techniques that varied somewhat from those of "the master." In turn, students of all three of these men also developed their own points of emphasis. In the case of Freudian theory, discussions of psychoanalytic techniques include a subtopic of "Neo-Freudianism."

The important feature of most psychoanalytic techniques is to trace the history of a disabling problem so that the client can have a full appreciation of its origins. Presumably, knowing the nature of the causal factor of the neurosis will free the individual from continuing to have to behave as though the disabling cause were still in existence. For example, a person who is aggressive, unfriendly, and lacking in close companions may discover that he is really afraid to get close to others or let them get close to him. His defense mechanisms are such that people realize or intuitively feel that he wants to be alone. The lonesomeness becomes sufficiently acute that he seeks help. The analyst seats himself and the client in such a position that the client cannot see the therapist. He will, theoretically, be less inhibited or embarrassed while revealing some of his secret deeds or thoughts if he does not have a face-to-face position. The analyst, having been psychoanalyzed himself (Freud (1935) psychoanalyzed himself over a period of months) is aware of areas that are tender or sensitive. He knows this either through experience, training, or by observing closely how the client breathes, stutters, hesitates, or uses vocal tones and inflection. By asking questions or saying "Tell me more," he gets the client to tell about his crucial and traumatic experiences. He may, in the case of the person who avoids close personal contacts, discover that he is afraid that others will abandon him. That is what his mother did when she died or ran off with a man other than his father. The patient unconsciously believes that such a painful experience will not recur if no further close contacts are permitted.

The process of talking about the problem provides the client with **catharsis**. His guilt and anxiety are relieved by the process of talking it out. Sometimes such talking is so painful that the client tries to avoid the topic. This reluctance to speak is called **resistance.** There are different ways to get the client to talk about the real problems of life despite **repression** and resistance. One is through **dream analysis**. The subject is led to talk about his dreams—the recurrent and persistent ones. It is postulated that dreams are a means by which the id gets by the censorship of the ego. The analyst, versed in the symbolism of dreams that the id uses to fool the ego, can interpret the real meaning of the dream. The dream may represent the wish to seduce the daughter of his best friend, the desire for power, or hate for one's mother when society dictates that she be loved. Dreams provide the analyst with clues to the realm of the unconscious or repressed wishes.

In order to focus on crucial items of life style, the analyst may use **free association**. This approach requires that the client relax and speak about the things that come freely to his mind. Sometimes this is varied with association-reaction, a process that consists of the analyst's pronouncing a list of words, some of which are "emotionally loaded." The client does not know which words are key items and which are there just to facilitate the response process. His task is simply to speak the first word that comes to his mind in response to the stimulus word. If he blocks or hesitates after hearing certain words, it is presumed that the word is related to a crucial area.

Some of Freud's students were concerned about **transference**. This involves the client's shifting his emerging love or debilitating hate to the analyst for a period of time. As treatment continues and rehabilitation advances, this transference may take the form of **ambivalence**. This is a state in which the analyst is alternately loved and hated. Gradually, as the client gains faith in himself and realizes that the therapist, despite all the probing personal questions, is being honest and objective, the feeling of **rapport** comes into existence. Having established rapport with one human, it becomes somewhat easier to do somewhat the same with the next.

Reality therapy

Quite a different approach to personality reconstruction is taken by those who are called, or call themselves, reality therapists. The approach may be represented by Glasser (1966, 1970) who takes the attitude that relating history and describing traumatic episodes in childhood is not just futile. It may be a means of perpetuating self-defeating behavior. The more one talks about the terrible things that happened to him during childhood and earlier life, the greater is the likelihood that he will find an excuse for continuing to be irresponsible. If one can blame his situation on a nagging mother, an incestuous father, incompetent teachers, an immoral gang, poverty, or frequent moving, then there is no need for one to assume any responsibility for his future. Glasser's conviction is that one must face up to the fact that regardless of life circumstances one can choose his goals and control his behaviors. Another dissimilarity from psychoanalysis is that a long period of therapy is not needed. The quicker one can get to the painful and irresponsible acts of his life the more quickly he will be able to deal with them on a reality basis.

Much of Glasser's work was done with girls who were judged to be delinquent. They were placed in the Ventura (California) School for Girls, where therapy consisted of trying to get girls to see that the past does not dictate the future. It consisted of accepting the notion of responsibility, (*i.e.*, no one forced the girl to take drugs, steal a car, neglect her schoolwork, or show disrespect for teachers). Glasser is saying that one must face the reality of creating his own perceptions and his own responses.

The key concept in reality therapy is responsibility. It is easy to see the irresponsibility of norm violators. However, depressed patients, persons who have ulcers, underachievers in school, and neurotics are also persons who evade responsibility. History cannot be rewritten. What is past is past. What counts is how much responsibility the individual will take for his own present and future. Glasser also emphasizes that the concept of happiness is a stumbling block. No one can promise happiness. No one promises luxury or wealth without the expenditure of effort. Tranquilizers or hallucinogens cannot assure happiness. Nor can the therapist assure that there will be no difficulties in the future. He can only indicate that any course not involving responsibility is futile and self-defeating.

Reality therapy consists of asking the individual what he is doing now and how he likes it. Then he is asked about the kind of results his present actions are getting. Is that what you really would like to have? What would you like? How might you get it? What behaviors would you have to change? Together the client and therapist make a plan. A time schedule is set for putting the plan into action and at the next session the therapist checks his progress. If the correct steps have been taken the client is commended. If excuses are offered the therapist is blunt. "No excuses! The sole and entire question is when are you going to get it done?" When progress is made the therapist shows his respect and asks the client to respect himself. They then move to further development of plans. They establish new goals and set a time schedule for the next check-up.

The essence of rational therapy is that the neuroticism of individuals resides in their illogical thought processes. Adjustive behavior consists of replacing these handicapping and persistent ideas with logical thoughts and ideas (Ellis, 1966). When one accepts the basic premise that emotional difficulty and turmoil are due to errors in thinking, it becomes difficult to sustain self-defeating behaviors for an extended period of time. It is the person's guilt and fear about a situation—rather than the situation itself—that leads him to develop and continue his neurotic behavior. For instance, Ellis does not deny the validity of an Oedipus complex (the desire of a preadolescent to have sex relations with his mother, or father in the case of a girl). It is when one feels guilty about such thoughts, and when he comes to feel he is abnormal, or a-human, to have such thoughts, that he develops the handicapping notion that he is depraved. When he sees himself as an unworthy person he becomes neurotic. Let's face it, says Ellis, many people have such thoughts. If they are logical and accept the facts that others also have them, then they feel no guilt. They can decide not to pursue the fantasy. They can seek gratification in other, socially approved manners.

Rational therapy

The job of the therapist is to point out, literally, the facts and the logic of life. Ultimately, this is what most therapeutic approaches strive to accomplish. Psychoanalysis tries to accomplish this by talking about the history of the neurosis. Reality therapy says "forget the history and get at the job of contriving a logical plan that will have long range advantages." Rational therapy may also do these same things. The whole process is generalized and brought to focus on what are rational, logical thought processes and how they pertain to multiple problems.

Rational therapy may be quite brutal in the therapist's letting the client know that some of his ideas are downright silly. It is silly, for instance, to let something in one's childhood continue to affect the way one perceives today's situations. Such confrontation is not necessarily just for everybody. If the client needs sympathy and support and acceptance and approval, then confrontation may just send him to another counselor whom he feels will be more sympathetic and understanding. It may lead him to feel that no one can really understand such an inept person as he is.

The rational therapist may point out that society as a whole may manifest neurotic symptoms (Horney, 1937; Ellis, 1966, p. 98). That does not mean that its members are rational and logical. Statistical normality does not mean behavior normality in the sense of coping adequately with life. At times, the rational therapist may listen to history, he may be patient with **rationalizations**. He may encourage, cajole, and entreat. Finally, however, he is a counter-propagandist of excuse-making and nonsense. He may be cautious, supportive, permissive, and emotionally warm. These are, however, preliminary steps toward getting the client to assess and accept his irrational behavior. The patient must look at the facts of life in a rational manner. For instance, the fact that one's mother was cruel, neglectful, and repudiating does not mean that everyone is like that. Her behavior does not mean that others will, or do, view the client as an unworthy person. The fact that a teacher or one's boss thinks that one is stupid does not mean that everyone shares that view. It may be necessary to point out, and emphasize, and repeat, and reiterate instances in which the patient did worthy things.

Gestalt therapy   The word *Gestalt* (capitalized because all nouns in German are capitalized) means shape, form, or configuration. The shape or configuration of a perception or situation necessarily entails an emphasis on the wholeness or totality of events—how things fit together. Hence, the function of Gestalt therapy, as described by Perls and others (1951), is to overcome the fragmentation of feeling, thinking, and behaving that characterizes our society. This fragmentation must be replaced by a unified, holistic Gestalt of life. This is sought by a therapist's pointing out the major *figures* in life and helping the client to put the unimportant aspects into the *ground* (background). Thus, the purpose of Gestalt therapy is to help the client achieve a unified, discernable figure-ground, in life. After all, the Gestalt therapist seems to be saying that one's difficulties are the result of the inability to perceive accurately. It is necessary to separate the wheat from the chaff. Concentrate on the important things and let the minor details take care of themselves.

These lessons—these more accurate separations of figure from ground—can be learned by living through experiences with the therapist. This occurs usually in the presence of others in a group. These living experiences are designed to explore one's unique perceptions of reality. One's perceptions are reflected in his behavior in the group. He begins to see what keeps him from gaining wholeness in his life. The group members combine efforts and help each other to achieve a more flexible perception and relationship. Others, who have their own distorted perceptions, can often see how another is inaccurate in his perception. They are quite willing to point out the errors of the group fellow. It is presumed that a disturbed, ineffective personality is one whose perception is so fixed and rigid that he is unable to meet the varied complexities of life.

Neurotics and psychotics (as was shown in Chapter 13) are ones in whom this rigidity has reached such an extreme degree that normal functioning is impeded. To the Gestalt therapist, neurotics and psychotics tend to be rigid and inflexible in the way they look at life. Their lives are dominated by Gestalts that are distorted by compulsions, anxieties, and confusions (Perls, 1947, p. 224). By means of the therapist's and other group members' seeing these in action and seeing the distortions reflected in words, they can help the client develop a new orientation. The encounters the client is faced with by the therapist, in the presence of group members, help him restore his fragmented integrity. It is hoped that he can be helped to unify his thinking, feeling, and behaving. The hope is that he will be able to see the relationships of the parts of his life to the wholeness of human existence.

Gestalt therapy does not, as do psychoanalytic approaches, probe for repressed feelings and conflicts rooted in one's childhood. It is not necessary to probe the unconscious to discover repressions and anxieties. It is unnecessary to explain blocks and resistances. The aim is to develop a perspective that is more creative, elastic, and flexible. The emphasis is on seeing how the individual perceives and misperceives his unique world. The counselor learns that myopic visions keep the client from perceiving accurately. By pointing out, and living through, numerous experiences, the therapist hopes that the client can establish contact with reality. The aim is to resume personality growth because a realistic, adaptable personality orientation has been initiated. Thus, Gestalt therapy is much like rational therapy. In both the emphasis is upon accurate perception of reality. Therapy is successfully completed when one learns to perceive more accurately. Therapy helps when the parts and subaspects of life fit comfortably and logically into their proper places. Thus, while the rationale of Gestalt therapy is somewhat different from other approaches, the procedures and methods seem to be similar to those used in at least some techniques.

Behavioral counseling

Beginning in the 1950's with the work of Wolpe (see p. 242), who published his theory recently (1969), there have been a number of therapeutic approaches based on learning, or conditioning theory. The basic idea is that learning theory and learning principles can be used to bring about improved patterns of living. Krumboltz (1966) calls learning theory approaches, or behavioral counseling, a revolution in counseling because it presents new answers to familiar questions: How does the counselee perceive his problems? What are his goals? How did he learn his present behaviors? Are they effective? What might be a better pattern of behavior?

People are regarded not so much as being sick as being victims of inappropriate and ineffective learnings. However, what one learns, one knows. One is not capable of a great deal of judgment about what he *might have learned*. One cannot compare until he learns something else. For example, one learns to be upper class, lower class, a Methodist, a boy, a clerk, a student, a husband, an American, to cover one's tracks, or to be honest. At this point, behavioral counseling becomes quite different from client-centered counseling (the next subsection), in that the counselor *teaches* the client what a better approach will be.

> The essence of behavioral counseling is that one is systematically rewarded by word, by token, or by material gain for each step that is taken in a desired direction. Thus, a teacher who was disturbed by an eleven-year-old boy's constantly volunteering, interrupting, and monopolizing class time with *his* answers, decided to see if she could cut down on his spontaneous verbalization and give others a chance. She told him her plans. She ignored him when he raised his hand and turned away from him in studied silence if he interrupted. When he kept quiet she asked him questions, praised his answers, and commented favorably on his good behaviors. There was no criticism for interruption—he was just ignored. In three weeks' time she had reduced his remarks from a recorded 38 times a day to six times a day. His reward was recognition when he waited to be called on and he did not receive recognition—negative or positive—when he behaved in the manner the teacher deemed not to be desirable.

Some people protest that this counseling is dangerous. The counselor must, in effect, set himself up as being an omniscient god. In many instances it would seem that we need not be alarmed. Critics, however, say, "Who has the right to decide that the high school boy should be academically successful? As long as he harms no one else, why not let him go his way?" Critics point out that the counselor should be there to help the boy decide what his goals are; counselors should not provide the goals for the boy. This is the point at which so many are disillusioned about Skinner's *Walden Two*. Someone else decides what the young should be. Through conditioning (behavioral counseling, if you will) they become the unthinking, unfeeling individuals who might as well have been automatons. An extreme example is that of Adolph Hitler who taught a generation of German youth to be egotistical, prejudiced, and chauvinistic soldiers by the consistent use of learning principles. Hitler was able to teach German young people that whatever action showed German superiority—however cruel, however devastating to non-Aryans, or to family and loved one, whatever it might do to humanity—should have precedence over mere people.

Some schools have programs called performance contracting. Pupils are rewarded for success in reading or for gains in arithmetic—

M & M candies, green stamps, transistor radios are given as prizes. It works. Pupils who had previously been slow made normal or better progress (Elam, 1970). Many school people are horrified. What happens when one is out of school and there is no one around to reward one for small steps in learning? No one rewards adults for reading books or seeking knowledge. It seems that they have been conditioned not to learn. Adults are just punished if they do not continue to learn. This is pretty much what has happened in many schools. Why learn if one is not to be rewarded with a grade, a credit, a certificate, or a diploma? Hence, behavior counseling is questioned because it takes a certain amount of autonomy away from the individual (Lindsey and Cunningham, 1973). Too much emphasis is placed on extrinsic rewards or rewards given by other people and personal responsibility is reduced to a minimum. But one must remember—it works. Behavioral counseling is effective in changing behavior. Much of that behavior is "good" for the individual and for society.

An experienced counselor or therapist uses different approaches with clients with different kinds of problems and different kinds of attitudes. If the client admits his difficulties and his own inability to deal with them effectively, advice may work. If he is frankly and eagerly seeking help a direct—perhaps "brutal"—approach might work. The rational therapy of Ellis, the reality therapy of Glasser, or the behavioral counseling by the learning theorists might be highly effective. There are persons who take the attitude, "Here I am, fix me." There are others who are shocked at the idea that there could be anything wrong with them. They take the attitude that "I'm all right. Fix the other people who are unable to straighten up and fly right." With the latter, a direct approach would serve merely to heighten their defenses. Bluntness might send them to another more outwardly sympathetic and understanding person. These might be fortunate enough to discover someone of the Carl Rogers persuasion. This is a counselor with the belief that *every person has within himself* the strength and wisdom to solve his own problems. As a unique person one must solve his problems in a way to fit him. The prescription of rational therapy or behavioral counseling might be inappropriate. A corollary to this persuasion is that the therapist does not have the wisdom to perceive the solution to another's unique problem.

Rogers (1942; 1961; 1969) has been evolving his theory for three decades. The changes made have been more in the ways of explaining his view than in his altered perception of the nature of man and the role of the therapist. Man, he believes, has strength and durability. Man needs, he believes, someone whom he trusts and who, reciprocally, trusts him. One is respected as a human being, regardless of his distorted behaviors and twisted perceptions. With this trusted confi-

Client-centered counseling

dante the client will be able to find a constructive way of life. He will not be a scoundrel when he does "his thing." There is within every man the desire to be socially right and socially approved.

Rogers' counseling technique was once called, by others, "nondirective." The counselor wished to keep in the background—his role was to encourage verbalization. Through verbalization the counselee was able to see himself and his problems more accurately. The counselor offers no advice. He does not judge. He does not indicate how he would do it. Actually, of course, a counselor cannot be nondirective. His very presence is at least mildly coercive. His "Hms" and "Uh-huhs" or silences are coercive in that they encourage or inhibit thinking and verbalization along some certain line or trend. The aim of client-centered counseling is to encourage individual freedom and responsibility. It is to reduce dependence on authority and a father figure.

Rogers (1966) has summarized much of what his theory is about in an article regarding the necessary conditions for effective personality change. In condensed form these conditions are:

1. It is necessary that two persons be in psychological contact. This means that there is rapport, mutual, positive, and unconditional positive regard. There is acceptance, and awareness of the needs and nature of each other.

2. The counselee must be searching for some help. He seeks to resolve some of the inconsistencies and difficulties he is experiencing in life. He wants to strengthen his self-concept. He is seeking to reduce anxieties.

3. The counselor must present himself as a genuine, real individual. If, for instance, he feels bored or angry with the client he can say so. He must be congruent (share) with the feelings of the client. Although the counselor is not the focus of the counseling relationship, it is appropriate for him to express his feelings.

4. It stimulates personality growth if the counselor has unconditional positive regard for the counselee. No conditions are attached to his acceptance of the client. A child, for instance, is accepted when his feelings cause him to behave in an offensive manner. When a client's good intentions exceed his ability to put them into action, the counselor can understand and accept.

5. The counselor possesses an empathic understanding of the counselee's problems. He is able to understand and to share the counselee's feelings. His actions are in accord with the mood and content of the counselee's remarks.

6. The counselee perceives that the counselor does accept and therefore has empathy for the one who is helping him.

One of the major contributions of the Rogerian approach is the technique of reflecting feelings and clarifying difficulties through careful listening. It is *active listening*, rather than passive listening. One is trying to hear the feeling behind and beyond the words. The technique of reflecting, or providing feedback, through recognition of what the client has said, is a focal emphasis. The counselee's statements may be paraphrased. Elaborations may be requested. Asking for clarification may be an excuse for the counselee to run through his problems again. All the way (and this is Rogers' great contribution), there is an emphasis on the merit, worth, and strength of the individual. One's ego concept is strengthened in Rogerian counseling.

In the majority of well-staffed clinics, group therapy is an established method of treating personality dysfunction. It is also used in the treatment of alcoholics, with couples having marital difficulties, and with students in schools and colleges. In some churches, businesses, and clubs personnel engage in group counseling. These groups have names such as basic encounter groups, interpersonal process groups, and sensitivity training. They are regarded not as therapy but as a means of promoting self and social enhancement. The use and misuse of group counseling was discussed in Chapter 12. In this survey of treating personality disorders, groups need not be elaborated on further.

Group counseling

PRINCIPLES OF PSYCHOTHERAPY

Including group counseling, seven different psychotherapeutic approaches were discussed in the foregoing section. All of these, it can be repeated, are successful insofar as they work for some therapists and with some clients. There are many experimental therapeutic thrusts being made at the present time. Other techniques will be developed that will supplement or even overshadow those that are now effective and popular. If they do achieve such prominence, it is likely that they will contain many of the features listed below. The following are elements that are contained in some form in most of the successful therapies.

Principle: Successful therapy and personality enhancement are dependent upon a sturdy and confident concept of self.

The importance of the self-image, or ego concept, has been a helpful concept for many years. It was not, however, until Allport voiced the idea that the self-concept had pervasive importance in therapy that it assumed primacy in the treatment of personality dysfunction. Present-day therapy, almost but not quite uniformly, is largely devoted to helping the client "examine, correct, or expand this self image" (Allport, 1965, p. 47). Examining the self-image consists of asking the person to look at and evaluate his abilities and his status. Self-image shows in various roles in which one functions as student,

Self-image

spouse, parent, worker, citizen, etc. It also involves what Horney (1950) calls the idealized self-image. This means what one might become as he seeks to actualize his potentials.

Therapeutic assistance, or developmental counseling, is quite typically helpful because it is difficult to be objective about oneself. The self-concept is *rather* stable from childhood on. If one's parents were accepting, admiring, and gave positive feedback for efforts and support during time of trial, then one would be likely to have a secure self-concept. If parents were overindulgent and effusive one might be overconfident and overbearing. If parents were insecure, rejecting, or held too high expectations for the growing youngster, then he might tend to underestimate himself. He would exaggerate the size of challenges and obstacles. Whether one is too harsh or too lenient in judging himself, the help of an outsider might prove to be of crucial importance. In short, while the self-image is rather stable, it is not, by any means, static and unalterable.

Dialogue

Principle: As a social, gregarious creature, man's self-concept and his group affiliation are conditioned by dialogue.

There are many people who agree with Johnson (1946) that personality disorientation is, in large degree, a semantic problem. Lines of communication with other persons are sound, filled with static, or completely severed. The neurotic is one in whom communication is impeded. The psychotic—and particularly the autistic child—is one for whom communication is totally blocked. Bruner (1968) asserts that the very essence of education may prove to be the process of dialogue between the learner and the learned.

Dialogue, let it be understood, is not telling or being told, nor is it a matter of "mere conversation." It is a personal, emotional process in which both participants or members of a group listen actively to the words and feelings of the speaker. The listener, in his turn, becomes the speaker who is accepted and respected. Dialogue repudiates one-upmanship. It repudiates lecturing, demanding, and it denies an autocratic and authoritarian stance.

Defined in such a manner, dialogue does several things.

1. It provides an avenue for catharsis. It helps to get rid of pent-up negative feelings by verbal expression. This, it may be remembered, is a part of the process of psychoanalytic therapy.

2. Dialogue provides a means of testing reality. One can test one's status in a social group. As such it eliminates to some extent the costly process of having to try out in action one's ideas, hostilities, or what one believes to be his group status.

3. Dialogue is a means of defining self. Becker (1962, p. 103) asserts that the self is primarily a verbal-linguistic device.

4. A skilled therapist is an expert in conducting dialogue. He listens actively and checks his interpretations. He encourages

verbalization and seeks understanding of feelings. His own responses are fed in mentally digestible doses. He does not show shock at what he hears; rather, he is nonjudgmental of the opinions and actions described. He respects the worth and good intentions of the client.

Roy C was obviously under considerable tension as he sat in the sixth grade counselor's office. Slowly the story began to take shape. On the way home from school, between the bus stop and his home there was a tree-sheltered cemetery. Roy decided it might be fun to push over a headstone. When he did, he was now reporting, "It made me feel real good so I pushed over some more. All at once I seemed to come to and I said, "What am I doing?"

The counselor thought of his professional training—unconditional positive regard, acceptance, avoidance of moralizing, etc. His dialogue got to what happened at school before the headstone incident. Roy was seething because the teacher had yelled at him. The teacher had blamed him for creating a disturbance for which Roy was not responsible and in which he had not been involved.

Such an action has been called a defense mechanism of kicking the cat or, in psychological terminology, projection. It can also be called an absence of dialogue between teacher and Roy. There was expression of feeling on the boy's part. Getting at the feelings was a case of dialogue between Roy and counselor.

Principle: The client's personality development is facilitated when there is mutual acceptance between counselor and counselee.

Mutual acceptance

The malady of our time is said to be alienation. The feeling that one is cut off from a caring, accepting relationship with other humans is alienating. Those who work with seriously disturbed children have noted that after a period of time, when progress is hoped for, the children become still more obnoxious and increasingly trying. This phenomenon has been explained in terms of the children's skepticism about there really being anyone who can care for them. Before they will trust the adult they try him still further by becoming increasingly antagonistic. If the counselor can continue to accept these children, they shift gears and make gratifying progress (Bettelheim, 1960).

Compulsions, obsessions, sexual fantasies and acts, and hostilities can be more easily handled if they can be described and discussed. Discussing them, however, means opening one's private life. It means revealing "abnormality" and running the risk of shocking and alienating still another person (Strom, 1969, p. 372). Hence, in order to open up one must trust the counselor. The counselor, in turn, must never show shock. He must show that he feels *with* the person even though he perceives the action as self-defeating. He can regard one as being sick, having difficulties, and bearing heavy burdens. He does not feel that it is just some kind of depraved individual revealing his traits.

This mutual acceptance is called empathy, unconditional positive regard, respect for person, charity, love, and compassion. While acceptance of the client is a professional responsibility, it is not an easy task. Redlich and Hollingshead (1958) have shown, for instance, that in psychiatric clinics the senior psychiatrists take the upper-middle and upper class patients. The younger and new psychiatrists are assigned the lower class clients.

Clients do not always accept the therapist. They do not consistently admit the need for help. This is called resistance, projection, repression, and transference. Until the client does accept the counselor, growth is slow. When trust, acceptance, and mutual positive regard are developed, then therapy has already taken place.

Changed perception

Principle: Personality enhancement and rehabilitation are dependent on changed perceptions. They change in the direction of increased accuracy and the objective appreciation of reality.

Therapy can be achieved through (1) changing the person. This may be done by means of drugs in the case of a hyperactive thyroid or with one who has a too high energy level. Or, the person may be changed by developing skills. These permit him to cope with the realities that were previously so frustrating. Therapy can also be achieved by (2) changing the milieu. Children can be removed from a classroom where a teacher has neither the understanding nor the professional competence to deal with the deviant child. The pupil can be placed in another classroom. A child may be taken from incompetent or cruel parents and put into a healthful foster home. An adolescent can be taken from a delinquency predisposing environment and placed in more salutary conditions. Finally, therapy may be achieved through (3) altering perceptions. It is a valid belief that problems are frequently not as serious as the attitude that is taken toward them.

Maslow (1970) says that a major distinction between the self-actualizing person and the neurotic is accuracy of perception. The disturbed person is highly inaccurate. We call these misperceptions illusions, delusions, hallucinations, obsessions, and the like. Therapists can, in various ways, help the client be more accurate in his perceptions. In fact, this is the emphasis in reality, rational, and Gestalt therapy.

Responsibility

Principle: Planned personality growth is contingent upon the individual's assumption of responsibility for the way he sees things, for what he says, and for what he does.

It is true, especially during childhood and in totalitarian societies, that one is largely the product of environmental conditioning. As one grows, matures, and learns, he becomes capable of making choices. He can assume responsibility. In the final analysis, many authorities

Therapy can also be achieved in work, plastic arts, athletics . . .

believe that one is not sick or disabled as much as he is unwilling or unable to assume responsibility for his own actions and future. Many theories emphasize this indirectly and implicitly. Many approaches— behavioral counseling, rational therapy, client-centered therapy, reality therapy—make specific mention of responsibility. Responsibility is the major avenue toward personality rehabilitation. It is a major step toward self-actualizing.

Principle: The success of a counseling relationship is more dependent on the skills and personality of the counselor than it is upon the nature of techniques employed.

    If the various approaches to personality therapy need to be

***Therapist
as a person***

reconciled, it might well be done in terms of the personality of the counselor. As one counselor educator put it, "We have no proof that hanging a person by his thumbs will not serve as therapy." In fact, some of the techniques used by witchdoctors seem somewhat cruel, but in the days of Clifford Beers (1917), who is given credit by some for founding the mental health movement, therapy was not far removed from hanging by the thumbs. The patient was, however, given attention by a significant person. Various methods work because they all involve human contact. Such a contact has been broken in the case of personality dysfunction. One can be a psychoanalyst and sit behind the client so he cannot be seen. He can sit across the desk from the patient, or across the room in a group situation. He can sit knee-to-knee with him. If the counselor can show acceptance, regard, friendship, and respect, then therapy will be facilitated. The counselor can be reflective, directive, or demanding. If the client knows he has care and concern, the method probably will work.

Nonverbal communication (discussed in Chapter 12) develops in children before verbal communication is mastered. In the counseling situation this communication of feelings is revived. The counselor can say, "That's a damn fool way to act" or he can say "Mmm," and if he feels with, and for, and by the client, communication remains in effect. Therapy is not, in short, a matter of what one does or says. It is more a case of who one is and the nature of the human relationship that exists.

SUMMARY

Some personality disorders are rather clearly a result of organic dysfunction; glandular imbalance, brain injury, oxygen deprivation, nutritional deficiency, and chromosomal abnormality are some examples. These can be treated by means of chemical or surgical intervention. Other personality disorders are the result of disorders of perception, psychological deprivation, or trauma. Consequently, these demand a psychotherapeutic approach. To some extent this may mean teaching the client skills. It may mean changing the environment. By far the greatest amount of psychotherapy consists in trying to alter the client's perception of self and his world.

There are a score or more of psychotherapeutic techniques. These involve varied conceptions of the nature of man as well as contrasting methods of treatment. The seven approaches discussed in the chapter were:

Psychoanalysis considers man to be the victim of instinctive drives that conflict with social demands. In order to control these drives in a socially acceptable manner it is necessary to bring them from the subconscious to the conscious level. The client can then deal objectively with social-instinctive conflict.

Reality therapy postulates that one is not sick, rather, he is irresponsible. Therapy consists in making a plan and carrying that plan into action. Revelation of past history is futile because it provides excuses for not assuming responsibility.

Rational therapy assumes that personality dysfunction is a result of illogical thinking. Therapy consists of showing how the client is illogical. Therapy shows how one might be more rational and reality oriented.

Gestalt therapy assumes that the bits and parts of a disturbed person's life do not fit harmoniously. There is a distortion in the perception of the nature of reality. Rehabilitation consists in fitting the parts of one's life into a symmetrical entity.

Behavioral counseling assumes that one has learned ineffective and irresponsible behaviors. These can be replaced by learning new behaviors. Desirable actions are reinforced by material or social rewards or by the experience of what the individual perceives to be success. Goals are set by the therapist, not by the client.

Client-centered therapy assumes that the individual has the strength and intelligence to solve his own problems. The role of the counselor is to encourage dialogue by reflecting, showing interest, rephrasing, and asking questions but not providing answers.

Group counseling takes many forms. In some degree it is assumed that group members can help one another learn more effective behaviors. The role of the professional leader is to protect the weak. He provides fruitful direction to the discussions.

The various theories have some common themes. These core thoughts include: the importance of strengthening the client's self-image, participation in dialogue, mutual acceptance between counselor and client, altering perceptions, and the assumption of responsibility. It is postulated that the therapist as a person is more important than the techniques he uses.

SUGGESTED READINGS

ARD, BEN N., JR., *Counseling and Psychotherapy: Classics on Theories and Issues*, Palo Alto, Calif.: Science and Behavior Books, 1966.
  Six therapeutic approaches are discussed in Part II. Among those who are presented in this book are Ellis, Glasser, Maslow, and Rogers. In addition, some other theories are presented by Leona Tyler, O. H. Mowrer, and Frederick Thorne.

BRINCKERHOFF, ROBERT, "Freudianism, Behaviorism, and Humanism," *The Humanist*, Vol. 31, No. 2, 16–17, March/April, 1971.

The author believes that humanists tend to overlook some of the darker aspects of man's life and being as they look at what man might become.

FULLMER, DANIEL W., and HAROLD W. BERNARD, *The School Counselor-Consultant*, Boston: Houghton Mifflin Company, 1972.
Chapter 6, "Varieties of Counseling Orientation," shows how various theories may be used by professional counselors in working with both pupils and teachers.

"A *Kappan* Pro/Con Series," *Phi Delta Kappan*, Vol. 54, No. 9, 593–601, 1973.
These pages contain four articles on behavior modification as techniques used in schools. Some of the authors are for and some are against the use of such techniques. The reader, says editor Stanley Elam, must beware of bias and must make his own decisions.

TORREY, E. FULLER, "What Western Psychotherapists Can Learn from Witch-doctors," *American Journal of Orthopsychiatry*, Vol. 42, 69–76, 1972.
The same qualities that make for success in contemporary psychiatrists—accurate empathy, nonpossessive warmth, and genuineness—are the traits that characterize what we sanctimoniously refer to as witchdoctors, but who call themselves wise men and shamans. Faith and trust of the client are also essential factors in therapy for both psychiatrists and witchdoctors.

FOLLOW-UP LEARNING ACTIVITIES

The cause of personality disturbances can never be entirely organic. The statement is true _____ false _____ because

_____

_____

_____

_____

The heavily contributing factor to chronic anxiety is
    chromosomal abnormality _____ excess lactate _____
    brain injury _____ parental strictness _____
A heavily contributing factor to schizophrenia is
    deficient lactate _____ deficient DMT _____
    hallucinogenic drugs _____ parental pressure _____
Describe any of several therapeutic processes that you would recommend for personality dysfunction caused by environmental stress.

_____

_____

_____

_____

What is the essence of reality therapy?

_____

_____

_____

What is the essence of rational therapy?

_____

_____

_____

What is the essence of behavior modification?

_____

_____

_____

Name several characteristics of any sound counseling relationship. (Review the text if necessary.)

_____

_____

_____

_____

What are several ways dialogue might be of value in the development of personality or in therapy in personality dysfunction.

_____

_____

_____

17
Instant Therapy

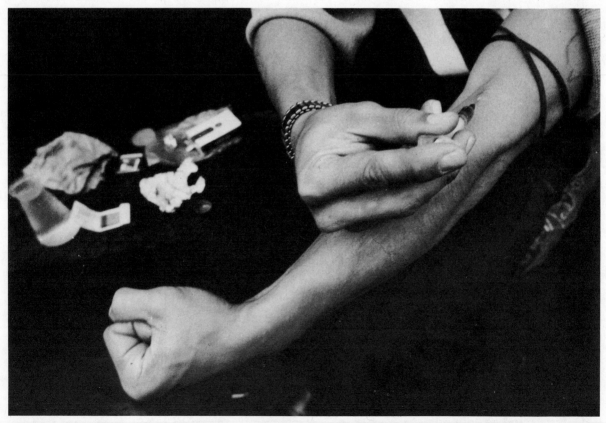

Drugs can be the servant of man—or the roles can be switched.

LEARNING ACTIVITIES

Make an actual count of the pill boxes and medicine bottles you have in your bathroom cabinet—or wherever you keep your medicines.

There are _____ varieties of pills, liquids, and powders.

What number of these have been prescribed by a physician?

Almost none _____ about 1/4 _____ about 1/3 _____ about 1/2 _____ about 2/3 _____ about 3/4 _____ almost all _____

What do you think your responses to the above items indicate about your personality?

_____
_____
_____
_____
_____

Do you smoke at the present time?

Yes _____ No _____ Occasionally _____

What is your rationale for smoking or not smoking?

_____
_____
_____
_____

(Check these two items a year and five years from now. The date now is _____.)

What is your attitude toward the use of marijuana?

_____
_____
_____
_____

What is your attitude toward the use of LSD?

_____
_____
_____
_____

What is your attitude toward the use of beverage alcohol?

_____
_____
_____
_____

This chapter deals with a particular approach to personality change that has captured the rapt devotion of the American public. We refer to the taking of drugs to bring about instant change in personality. It is a difficult subject to deal with for several reasons. (1) The presenter has a bias. An attempt is made, however, to depend on research and survey findings. (2) The bias of the reader is such that he tends to believe those things that accord with his former learnings, biases, and convictions. (3) Drugs, are, of course, no *one* thing. The arguments that hold for one are not necessarily appropriate in discussing another. Nevertheless, there is a temptation, in presenting and in reading, to group and to categorize. (4) The effects of drugs are paradoxical. That is, they have one kind of effect on the same person at one time, and another effect at another time. They have different effects on different persons. (5) The intentional bias of "the establishment" makes it difficult to get at the facts and to deal with them objectively. For example, governmental agencies and schools oppose some conclusions and intentionally encourage the presentation of official positions (biases).

The bias of the author is that (1) personality development is the outcome of the interaction of the individual with his environment. (2) Constructive personality changes are the result of a long and continuous application of energy and effort toward specified goals. (3) The instant therapy of drugs may do no harm to this developmental process; but there is a hazard in glandular and physiological imbalance. (4) Drug usage does such little positive good that the alleged gains must be viewed with skepticism.

THE LAW OF MINIMUM EFFORT

Wheeler's organismic law

Wheeler (1940, p. 40) formulated a law of behavior called "Least Action." This means that "When action is defined as units of energy multiplied by units of time, movement occurs from one position to the other over the shortest possible path." In short, men and women are lazy creatures. They will *take what they perceive to be the shortest route to a goal.* It is a laudable trait. It would be foolish to spend more time and energy getting a job done than is necessary. However, there is a danger. Our perceptions, as to what the shortest route is, may be inaccurate. When sweethearts take the long road home it is because the primary objective is not home. The hazard of perception was illustrated in Chapter 13, where it was shown that self-defeating defense mechanisms develop because one does not clearly perceive the long-range goal. The relative importance of immediate and ultimate results is not clear-cut.

Americans have been called the pill-taking society. This, that, or the other pill has been recommended as the alleged, or the hoped for, rapid solution of some problem or minor discomfort. The average middle class medicine cabinet contains approximately 40 drugs. Many of these are mind-altering substances (Fort, 1969, p. 195). When aspirin and the caffeine in tea and coffee are included, virtually the entire population of the United States takes some form of drugs to alter feeling states. A few religious sects frown on coffee and aspirin as well as on other drugs and beverages, but the number of such persons is statistically negligible. The fact that ours is a pill-taking society suggests that drugs are very much tied to family life, education, community mores, business, industry, values, government, personal philosophy, and other personality-influencing factors.

The pill-popping society

> We must begin our answer [to the question, "Why do people use drugs?"] with the understanding that we live in a drug-ridden, drug-saturated society, in which from infancy onward we have been taught to accept and live the industrial slogan of "Better Living Through Chemistry." We are taught that there is a pill, a drink, or a cigarette for every real or imagined pain, trouble, or problem, and that the more of these substances we use, the better off we will be. Both the alcoholic-beverage industry and the tobacco industry spend between one and two million dollars every single day in the United States alone to promote and encourage the earliest possible use of their drugs by the greatest possible number of people, and hopefully in large quantities. The imagery which is used to disseminate these drugs, and which is beamed particularly to young people by the use of space or time in publications or programs of special interest to them, *e.g.*, sports events on TV, stresses (eternal) youthfulness, sexual pleasure, and happiness to be obtained, supposedly, from the drug. Sex is, of course, used to sell everything from deodorants to automobiles to the over-the-counter pseudosedative, such as Compoz, which has been advertised in multimillion-dollar campaigns as the "little gentle blue pill" which makes women presidents of their clubs and men successful executives. The company marketing this substance and its advertising agency go one step further, by featuring on their packages as an ingredient of the substance extract of passion flower, thereby communicating that, in addition to all the other imagined benefits to be obtained by using it, there will also be an aphrodisiac effect. A typical Scotch whisky, vodka, or cigarette ad will show an attractive miniskirted woman standing with her legs spread seductively apart holding the drug in her hand with such lines of print as "The first thing about a holiday bash is don't be bashful." "Wade in, straight on," "Don't stand there, get with them." Another one says, "Must a Girl Really Prove Herself to Earn Her [a particular brand of whiskey]," showing a partially clad man and woman facing each other in a manner having obvious sexual overtones. According to Madison Avenue you can't be a man, a

woman, or have fun without these substances being a prominent part of the setting. With alcohol and tobacco, even though their use is illegal for most people under twenty-one, the advertising is beamed equally to teen agers and "grown-ups."[1]

Least effort and the generation gap

In a way, the law of least effort seems to be applied to the generation gap. Instead of trying to understand drugs and drug abuse and trying to pursue communication about them, the whole thing is dismissed with "Don't trust anyone over the age of thirty." In regard to drugs the statement is still more extreme, "Don't trust anyone." (Fort, 1972). Instead of attempting to unravel the legal, commercial, ethical, and emotional dilemmas associated with an evaluation of drugs, there is resort to implausible non-sequiturs. For example, "Why should we trust adults when they so freely use the destructive product, tobacco, and when adults so widely use the dangerous drug, alcohol?" The fact that adults are duplicitous and ignorant hardly seems to be justification for continued ignorance and self-delusion.

It must be borne in mind that adults have no more ready access to accurate information than the young. Perhaps in some positions there is a sincere search for objectivity. Oregon, for instance, has a professorship in higher education, supported by the State Division of Alcohol and Narcotics, the responsibility of which is to assemble and disseminate information to teachers and other interested groups. There is, however, some doubt that, even in such positions, credibility is on a high level. In some instances, if one does not support "the party line" he may be discharged.

> In 1966 James L. Goddard, the then U. S. Commissioner of the Food and Drug Administration, wrote an article published in the magazine of the U. S. Department of Health, Education, and Welfare. He condemned the illegal use of three classes of drugs—stimulants, depressants, and hallucinogens. No mention was made of tobacco, alcohol, or marijuana (Goddard, 1966).
>
> Later Goddard, speaking at a major U. S. university, was questioned by students and he admitted that current knowledge [and the data are still in accord] indicated that marijuana was not addictive, led to no known physiological effect, and should be legalized. The statements led to public furor. Marijuana was illegal and therefore must be bad and dangerous! Such tentative truths, coming from a high ranking official, constituted a grave danger to youth. Shortly after his remarks—an interval long enough so the action could not be labeled punitive—Goddard left his post as Commissioner of the Food and Drug Administration.
>
> . . . . .
>
> In California, in the early 1970's, John Kaplan was given a contract to study and report on the use and abuse of drugs. Some

---

[1]Joel Fort, *The Pleasure Seekers: The Drug Crisis, Youth and Society* (Indianapolis: The Bobbs-Merrill Company, 1969), pp. 194–195.

preliminary reports were issued that suggested that available evidence was such that the use of marijuana should be legalized. The contract was immediately terminated because the conclusions did not fit the official position.[2]

THE SANCTIONED DRUGS

Alcohol has been referred to as the "Servant of Man." This is because it is an antidote for tension, serves to facilitate social communication, and is alleged to kill unhealthy sperm, thus decreasing the likelihood of genetic defects. It enhances festive occasions. Furthermore, it must not be "too bad" because it is used in some form in virtually all cultures. It is legal. It is used by 70–90 per cent of all American adults. It is presented as wine, beer, or distilled beverages. Immense volumes of information and misinformation have been assembled to show the superiority of one or the other of these forms. Choice of beverage is a national prejudice. Distilled liquors are the favorite in the United States, beer is the favorite in central Europe, and wine is the favorite in France.

Alcohol

Little can be logically said in defense of alcohol as a beverage. An exception is some emergency, in the jungle or on the desert, when it is necessary to amputate a man's leg with no other anesthetic. The known results of excessive use of beverage alcohol are impairment of work efficiency. It creates a dependency that strains social interaction. It lowers inhibitions so that illegal or immoral acts are more readily committed by an otherwise upright citizen. Physiologically it is a depressant. While sexual inhibitions are lowered, so too is sexual potency. Speech and fine motor acts are immediately impaired in proportion to the amount of alcohol imbibed per unit of time and body weight. (Some increase in accuracy may be experienced by a nervous rifle marksman or tense competitive typist who uses a very small amount of alcohol.)

All kinds of superstitions are constructed about offsetting the effects of alcohol by drinking milk, coffee, or eating food. Effects allegedly vary with one's psychological state. What really counts is how much alcohol in proportion to body weight is present at a given time. One does not learn to "handle" alcohol. One can control the symptoms. However, an experienced drinker is just as dangerous behind the wheel of a car as is the first timer. A particularly damaging aspect is that confidence is raised as one's physical efficiency is lowered. One thing that is not a superstition is the admonition, "If you *need* a drink, don't take it."

[2]See John Kaplan, *Marijuana—The New Prohibition* (Cleveland: The World Publishing Company, 1970).

There is widespread agreement that a dangerous combination is alcohol and gasoline. The U. S. Department of Transportation reported that there are approximately 55,000 highway fatalities and nearly two million persons disabled annually in vehicle accidents in which alcohol is the major contributor (*Alcohol . . .*, 1968). There are other ways in which alcohol is a costly burden. In 1965 it cost the federal government 20 billion dollars to enforce liquor laws. Over two billion was used to enforce laws against intoxicated drivers and laws governing the sale and use of alcohol (*Encyclopedic Almanac*, 1970, p. 236). Half the people in jails and prisons committed their crimes after excessive drinking.

***Tobacco— nicotine,* et al.**

What drugs adults use, employed as an excuse for not trusting what they have to say, reaches a low of relevance when it comes to tobacco. Adults do use it, they advise against its use, and it is nothing short of a suicidal practice. One would be hard pressed to prove that it performs any psychological or physiological benefit. Smoking is not initially a pleasurable experience. However, the body, being a tough, durable mechanism, can become habituated to it despite the inescapable physical erosion that accompanies its use.

The alleged culprit in tobacco is nicotine. This substance when concentrated, even in small amounts, can kill cells and cause death to small animals. Actually, nicotine is only one of the dozens of damaging substances found in tobacco and tobacco smoke. Gases, acids, and other dangerous chemicals must share the scene with the super-criminal, nicotine. Twenty damaging vapors, including cyanic acid, nitric oxide, carbon monoxide, nitrogen dioxide, acetone, and ammonia are contained in tobacco smoke. Every part of the body, from cortical cells to circulation in the toes, may be affected. It is less than comforting to know that quitting the habit is more difficult than kicking narcotics. Damage is not just the result of years of devoted smoking. Damage occurs in about three seconds (Ross, 1972). Smoking accounts for six times as many fatalities per year as do highway accidents. Heart attacks, cancer, respiratory disease associated with smoking, plus fires and automobile accidents caused by lighting a smoke, ·bring the mortality figure to about 300,000 per year.

Tobacco smoking indicates the nearly universal desire of man to change whatever he has. If we feel good, smoking can change the feeling. If we feel bad, smoking can make one feel worse—but it is change. Boredom, monotony, and tedium, tobacco smoking seems to tell us, are more unpalatable and intolerable than is physical deterioration, headaches, blistered lips, sore throat, and cancer operations.

A frank statement finally has been made possible despite the prejudice of people and the power of profits. "The Surgeon General Has Determined That Cigarette Smoking Is Dangerous to Your Health" is really mild. Numerous studies show that smoking increases the incidence of cancer, emphysema, high blood pressure, and heart dysfunction, as well as premature and small babies borne by smoking mothers. There is fetal damage and impairment of brain cells. Nevertheless, people are still loath to accept the evidence (*Health Consequences . . .* , 1971). Not all smokers, mothers, and allergic persons suffer the same and immediate damage. Hence, there has been a tendency to disregard the higher statistical frequency of the disorders named above as being *caused* by smoking. "Predisposition" and "contributing factors" constitute some of the semantics used to avoid facing the frightening facts.

The scare technique is criticized as an approach to teaching about drugs. Such techniques have some efficacy in keeping children from playing on the double center stripe on highways. Scare techniques reduce the number of youths who shoot the Grand Canyon in a birch bark canoe. It is difficult, in the case of tobacco, to distinguish between what is a statement of reality and what is scare psychology. The use of tobacco is suicidal. If this be scare psychology, let us make the most of it. The comforting antidote is to cite one's knowing a man who lived to be 100 years old. "He was never sick a day in his life and he smoked since he was fourteen." With this we can set aside the scientific, prolonged, repetitive statistical data that try to teach us what we do not want to know.

Aspirin

A favorite pill in the scientific laboratory is the *placebo*. It is a harmless sugar pill with no medical effects which is used in laboratories to study the suggestibility effects of other drugs. For example, if benzedrine sulfate if given to a group of overactive fifth grade boys to see if it decreases diffuse physical activity or increased mental alertness, then a placebo would be given to a control group to compare effects.

Society's favorite placebo is aspirin. It is used to wake one up, induce sleepiness, clear the nasal passages, to relieve headaches, and arthritis in the feet, to comfort one's hangover and to prevent its onset. As long as one's faith is strong, its placebo effect is such that it does correct or allay the pain of such disorders. Its effects are, however, more than psychological. On the negative side, this freely used, omnipresent pill—found in medicine cabinets that children can reach, in car glove compartments, women's handbags, school desks, and fishing tackle boxes—is not the harmless pill we wish to believe it is. It has effects on virtually every system in the body.

> In statistics reporting hospital admissions classified as resulting from drug-induced disturbances, aspirin is often the most frequent cause. "Salicylate poisoning can result in death and the drug should not be viewed as a harmless household remedy. The toxicity of the salicylates is underestimated by both the laity and physicians." There were 5700 poison cases in Florida in 1966, of which 418 were

reported by the four hospitals in Pinellas County. Of these 418, 199 were cases of poisoning from internal medicine and 92 were from aspirin.

At excessively high dosage levels or as result of individual idiosyncrasy, acute poisoning may occur. Headache, dizziness, ringing in the ears, difficulty in hearing, dimness of vision, mental confusion, lassitude, drowsiness, sweating, thirst, nausea, vomiting, and occasionally diarrhea may occur. As poisoning progresses, central stimulation is replaced by depressions, stupor, and coma, followed by respiratory collapse and convulsions. Salicylate poisoning is considered an acute medical emergency and death may result even when all recommended procedures are followed. In persons with hypersensitivity to aspirin, skin rashes, asthma, swelling of the eyelids, tongue, lips, face, and intestinal tract are not uncommon. Asthma constitutes the chief manifestation and may result in death. Aspirin may cause mild hemolytic anemia in individuals with certain blood deficiencies.[3]

Aspirin also has an effect on personality. The conclusions must be theoretical and speculative because it is impossible to separate and isolate the impact of one influence. There are many influences simultaneously interworking. It may be speculated that from aspirin children learn that one should tolerate no discomfort—take a pill! They learn that lack of self-discipline, for example, overeating, can be counterbalanced by taking a pill. They learn that controlling the symptom (illness) can help one avoid admitting the cause (gluttony). In order to insure that children are not misled about the dangers of aspirin, the pills are sugar-coated. Aspirin will not be mistaken for bad-tasting medicine. It might be that the really serious danger (despite the foregoing quotation from Nowlis) is the psychological one relating to facing the reality of some discomfort in living.

Caffeine   It seems a little facetious to include coffee in a discussion of drugs. However, it is a mild stimulant. It helps to keep some people awake. It irritates the stomach lining of some people, especially when used in copious (eight to ten cups per day) amounts. Caffeine is included in this discussion because some investigators have noted a progression in the use of drugs. The progression is in the order of coffee, tobacco, wine or beer, distilled alcohol, amphetamines, depressants, and narcotics. The succession is by no means inevitable or predictive. It is a factor to be considered, however, because it does occur in some cases.

Caffeine is the active drug in tea, colas, cocoa, coffee, and No-doze. It is one of the very few that, in moderate amounts, has a stimulating effect without the typical, negative-depressive after-effect of most drugs. The highly usual after-effect of stimulating drugs is to be still more tired, depressed, or tense when the effect wears off than one was

[3]Helen H. Nowlis, *Drugs on the College Campus* (Garden City, New York: Doubleday and Company, Inc., 1969), p. 108.

before the drug was taken. Caffeine stimulates respiratory, circulatory, and cortical activity. It thus stimulates thought and counteracts drowsiness. No known fatalities from caffeine usage have occurred. Its use is habit forming—a gram or more (six cups of coffee) per day may have toxic results and produce restlessness and insomnia. In some people who are hypersensitive, caffeine may cause stomach upset, nausea, and skin rashes. There may be withdrawal symptoms in the form of headaches when coffee drinking is stopped.

Some reports have been issued on the dangers of marijuana smoking in terms of chromosomal damage. What effects such damage have on growth and development of the fetus, embryo, and neonate are not yet known. This item is mentioned here because caffeine and aspirin also effect chromosomal damage.

THE CONTROVERSIAL DRUGS

Amphetamine, a synthesized drug (that is, not produced in nature), has the stimulating, exciting effect of caffeine. It is, however, more powerful in its effects. There are many amphetamines, commonly known as benzedrine, dexedrine, methedone, or "bennies" and "speed." Classing beverages and aspirin as mild drugs, amphetamines are the most widely used potent, mind-altering drugs in the United States. They are used both legally and illicitly. This distinction is a fine one because a prescribed drug can so easily be reissued beyond the intended period of use.

Amphetamines

Amphetamines are used by college students to stay awake when cramming for examinations or to endure boring classes. People of many categories use them to counteract depression or grief, to treat mild mental disorders, Parkinson's disease (a paralytic, trembling disorder), or narcolepsy (a pathological need for sleep). They are used to control appetite and hence excessive weight. Legally used amphetamines, in typical doses of a 5-milligram tablet, prescribed by a physician, have medical benefits. However, psychological habituation is easy and rates are high. Illicit doses may cumulate to 20–50 milligrams per day. They produce restlessness, cluttered speech, irritability, insomnia, stomach disorders, convulsions, delusions, hallucinations, and psychoses. Hazards as summarized by the U. S. Food and Drug Administration are:

1. The false feeling of alertness is deceptive. A person may feel wide-awake one minute and collapse from exhaustion the next.
2. Vision is limited and distorted because of dilated pupils. The abuser may wear dark glasses to protect his eyes against bright light, thereby further limiting vision.
3. Automobile drivers have difficulty in driving normally and may use poor judgment in passing, stopping, and reacting to traffic

situations. Frequently the driver will swerve to avoid "ghosts" or multiple headlights (objects they imagine they see in front of them). These delusions and hallucinations may be both visual and auditory.

4. Mental depression and extreme fatigue may follow when amphetamines are withdrawn from the abuser.

5. Organic brain damage and serious psychiatric disorders may occur after a long period of abuse.

6. Psychological dependence on this drug may lead the abuser to seek more potent drugs to replace the decreasing "kick" given by the amphetamines. Or to come down from the "highs" of amphetamines, he may turn to barbiturates to bring relaxation and sleep. A cycle of "high" to "low" to "high" (or stimulation to depression to stimulation) may follow.[4]

Cocaine   This drug, and narcotics with which it is classed for some purposes, is a stimulant with a marked depressing after-effect. Initially it was used medically as a pain killer. Its use has been declining because of the availability of equally effective but less rapidly habit-forming alternate drugs. It is still used as a local anesthetic. Its short-term effects in large amounts are irritability, depression, and psychoses. Its physical effects are damage to nasal passages and blood vessels.

Cocaine, caffeine, nicotine, antidepressants, and amphetamines are classed together as stimulants. With the exception of nicotine, which is not illegal, each of these has some medical use. The disorders that they seek to counteract are obesity, depression, fatigue, narcolepsy, and children's behavior disorders.[5]

Marijuana   Marijuana is one of several drugs classed as a hallucinogen. It produces illusions, delusions, and hallucinations. In short, it is productive of distorted perceptions. It is used in several cultures and is called by various names—hashish, marijuana, grass, hemp, hay, pot, reefers. Initially, it was harshly condemned in association with tales about trained troops of assassins who were seduced into their bloody work by eating, drinking, or smoking hashish. Objectively viewed evidence is that such reports are fabrications. Rarely does marijuana lead to violent aggressive behavior. Its physical effects in large doses are bloodshot eyes, increased pulse rate, urinary frequency, dryness of the mouth and throat, nausea, and vomiting.[6] Its psychological effects are drowsiness and a sense of well being, altered perceptions, and in-

[4]Food and Drug Administration, *The Use and Misuse of Drugs* (Washington, D. C.: U. S. Department of Health, Education, and Welfare, 1968), p. 11.

[5]It may be pertinent to note that behavior modification regimes have been, in the last year or two, quite successful in treating children's behavior disorders, including hyperactivity, without drugs.

[6]One of the arguments for legalizing marijuana is that legal packages could be accurately labelled in terms of purity and amount, and overdosage could more easily be avoided.

creased appetite. Its effects are often **paradoxical.** It may produce hilarity on one occasion and depression on another with the same person—or with varying amounts. Hence, mood alterations are dependent on both person and the drug. There is some danger of emotional dependence. It is not addictive and tolerance for increased amounts does not develop. There are no known withdrawal symptoms. However, there are no recorded, long-term, benefits.

If these statements are compared with the statements about alcohol and nicotine (and the accompaniments of nicotine) marijuana comes out ahead. However, emotions—including fear, prejudice, and superstition—are powerful behavioral influences. Marijuana is illegal. A maximum fine of $5000 and one year in prison for possession at the federal level is the present penalty. Most drug arrests are, however, made at the state level. State laws vary. Many are more strict than the federal law.

Many authorities endorse the legalization of marijuana. The premise is that its known negative effects are less damaging than alcohol, caffeine, amphetamines, barbiturates, and narcotics. It is believed that one's attitude toward the law are endangered. Contempt for unjust laws, and the practice of breaking them to gain a crowd pleasure, are not sound reasons for legalizing it. The most serious indictment of marijuana is that it leads to identification with the "drug culture." (This could mean virtually the entire population in our pill-taking society.) Hence, marijuana is a step in the progression leading to hard drugs—heroin, morphine, opium. This allegation is fallacious. Such progression is neither typical nor statistically alarming. Most marijuana users do not take this route. Many hard drug users have not used marijuana.

These statements do not constitute an endorsement of the use of marijuana. Neither did the repeal of prohibition constitute a recommendation that people use alcohol. The whole thesis of this book is that personality development is a slow process of the accretions of growth and developmental experiences. One cultivates his mind at the cost of some investment of time and energy. The recommended procedure is to learn to relate to others, to develop the habit of happiness, to work and achieve without drugs. Alcohol, tobacco, marijuana, stimulants, depressants, or any other of the mind-altering drugs do not ease the task of personality growth.

LSD

LSD, or d-lysergic acid diethylamide, is one of many drugs classed under the heading of hallucinogens. Others in this class are mescaline, peyote, psilocybin (psychotropic mushrooms), and DOM—a synthetic hallucinogen. These differ in their potential for emotional dependence and physical dependence. All, as far as is known, do develop tolerance. That is, there develops a need for larger doses to produce the same intensity of effect.

LSD has attracted some attention in the United States. It was temporarily a fad on campuses after its use was endorsed by no less a figure than a professor at Harvard. Since that time the indictment of LSD seems none too severe. It results, when swallowed mixed with sugar, even in small amounts, in marked perceptual changes. The results are unpredictable alterations of sensory perception. There is an intensification of sound and smell. Tactile sensations are altered and brilliant flashing colors may be seen. The faces and bodies of one's companions, or of self, are so distorted that panic and suicidal moves may occur. The suicide motive may occur because of unawareness of the dangers that are involved.

The author has, of course, read many biographical accounts of the agony of narcotics users. The characters of users change to the extent that absolutely nothing has any merit except getting another fix. The horrors are no more stark than the descriptions given by several girls who have taken "LSD trips."

Some of these girls, in regular high schools, special learning centers, and in homes for delinquents, said that given the opportunity they would again use alcohol, narcotics, or marijuana. None who had used LSD enough times to experience a bad trip would, they said, do it again. The bad trip was a horrible experience. It was one during which some of the girls had been helped by others from committing suicide. However, the unpredictable possibility, and even probability, of a flashback [a recurrence of a trip without taking more of the drug which may occur up to a year after taking the drug] was a dynamic deterrent.

There is some evidence that LSD can cause chromosomal damage in laboratory animals. Potential danger to the human fetus remains to be verified (Western Institute . . . , 1972).

Sedatives and tranquilizers

Along with alcohol and narcotics are barbiturates and tranquilizers. The latter two synthetic drugs serve as depressants. They produce relaxation, decreased alertness, drowsiness, and impaired coordination. Because tranquilizers relieve anxiety and tension and suppress aggressive tendencies, they are known as "don't give a damn" pills. Tranquilizers are moderately habit forming in terms of psychological dependence, but they do not build tolerance. Commonly known tranquilizers are Thorozine, Compazine, and Stellazine. Medical and psychiatric journals advertise these pills somewhat like various brands of cigarettes are advertised in popular magazines. Each, in some way, is alleged to be superior to all competitors. In the hands of a psychiatrist, tranquilizers may predispose a patient to a reduction of tension and anxiety. The client may relax to the point where psychological treatment becomes more effective.

The barbiturates (amobarbitol, pentobarbitol, phenobarbitol, and secobarbitol) have all the characteristics of dangerous drugs. They are psychologically habit forming. They create physical dependence. The taker's development of tolerance demands heavier and heavier dosage for like results. The major dangers are individual rather than social. However, accidents due to impaired judgment and fires due to smoker's carelessness may involve others. Withdrawal hazards include pneumonia, convulsions, and death caused by cardiovascular collapse. Withdrawal from barbiturates is more likely to cause death than is withdrawal from heroin (A Summary . . . , 1971). Overdosage has resulted in numerous deaths that are reported to be accidental or due to suicidal intent. In terms of fatalities and the "hardness" of a drug, alcohol leads. Barbiturates come next. Heroin is far behind. With hardness defined as habit-forming, heroin leads and is followed by alcohol and barbiturates (Fort, 1969, p. 99).

THE INDIVIDUAL, SOCIETY, AND DRUGS

The use and abuse of drugs typically, as in the foregoing, centers on the nature of the drug, its effects, and the extent of its use. In recent years, especially, an increasing amount of attention has been devoted to the personality of the user and potential abuser of drugs. This focus is the real reason for including drugs in this book on personality.

Personality factors in drug use

Some drugs, wine and peyote, for instance, are used for ritualistic purposes. Our real concern is for the personal use of drugs to alter thought, sensation, and behavior. In some instances, users are innocent people who are unaware of the fact that they are using mind-altering drugs. This might include children who begin drinking wine or coffee because it is served with meals. To them it is no more a drug than are carbohydrates, proteins, and vitamins. It could include little old ladies who "never touched a drop in their life." They do, however, get physical and psychological comfort from tonics containing alcohol and opiates. In other instances the drug is initially and openly used in search of changed feelings and perceptions.

Considerable attention has been devoted to the effects of drugs on personality. It also has been known for a long time that personality influences the effect of drugs. Psychiatrists are less likely to prescribe sedatives for the person who is chronically disturbed than for the typically stable person who is undergoing some marked but temporary stress. Some persons respond markedly to drugs, others react mildly. Some are quickly habituated, others resist habituation.

> Juvenile addicts in general—even before they take drugs—are easily frustrated and made anxious, and they find both states intolerable. They cannot enter into prolonged, close, friendly relations with others; they have difficulties assuming a masculine role. Such troubles can be traced to their family experiences. For example: Relations between parents were often seriously disturbed, as evi-

denced by divorce, separation, hostility; the parents often gave the children no clear standards of behavior to follow, so the boy who eventually took drugs had no strong incentive to suppress impulse and develop discipline; since the father was absent, or cool or hostile, the child had relatively little chance to identify with and model himself after a male figure; most of the parents had unrealistically low ambitions for their boys, reflecting their own pessimistic attitude toward life, and they were distrustful of teachers, social workers, and other representatives of society.[7]

The worried person uses drugs to reduce guilt, insecurity, anxiety, and regret. The tense person seeks for anesthesia from feelings of concern, sensitivity, and unpleasantness. The bored person seeks to magnify the intensity of his feelings. He may develop curiosity, rebellion, or nonconformity. The alienated person may yield to group pressure. He desires to achieve belongingness and daring by using drugs. He may recognize his own faults and take the short route to their modification by magnifying his conviviality by taking a stimulant. He may use a depressant to lower his typical inhibitions. These various motivations and predispositions are neither distinct nor mutually exclusive.

Except for those who are innocent or very young, the approach to drug use might be to ask the question, "What is it that I wish to accomplish?" An alternative to this query is, "What are the probable long-range eventualities?" Answers to these questions should leave room for drugs, under medical prescription, used to relieve temporary pain. It should leave room for psychiatrically prescribed drugs used to render one amenable to psychological therapy.

Physiological factors in drug use

It was mentioned earlier (Chapter 13) that individuals have different degrees of tolerance for drugs or different predispositions toward habituation. Williams (1971), it may be recalled, suggested that there may be something in the body chemistry of an individual that makes him an alcoholic from the first drink. Others can drink regularly in moderation with no increase in amount. Some drink only on occasion and then in moderation. Some persons are sensitive to aspirin or coffee and have to avoid their use. A routine question for doctors is to inquire about allergies a patient might have before using an antibiotic.

Suffice it to say that generalizations about the effects of drugs, either in terms of altered behavior or habituation, must take into account the physiological constitution and condition of the person. There are paradoxical effects of drugs; for example, alcohol makes some people friendly and congenial. It appears to bring out the meanness of others. This may be due to physiological factors, to the social setting, or to psychological expectation. Certainly, many drugs

[7]Narcotic Drug Addiction, 1969, Mental Health Monograph No. 2, Washington, D. C.: U. S. Department of Health, Education, and Welfare, p. 6

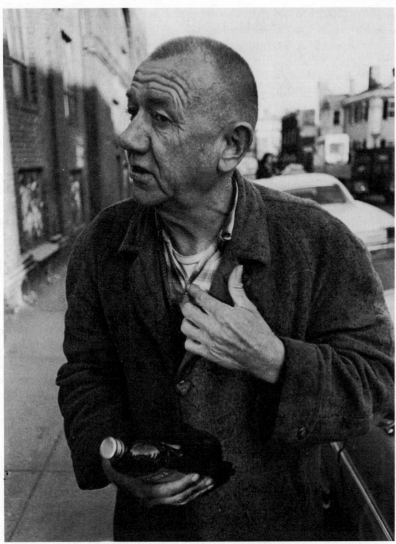

Does the potion shape personality?

have been found to have their influence affected by how relatively tired or rested the taker is. This rested-tiredness influence is, in part, now being attributed to the amount of the self-generated drug, lactate, in one's system.

As was shown in Chapter 3, family influences do much to shape personality. This is especially true in view of the fact that culture makes itself first felt by the growing individual through the family. Studies of drug users indicate that the pathological family is a statistically reliable factor in the abuse of drugs. Blum and his

Family

associates (1972) found that the drug-risk score—that is, the extent to which individual youth tended to use drugs abusively—had a direct relationship to professional judgments of the soundness-sickness score of the family. Those homes that were judged to be good or superior homes had youth whose drug-risk scores were low. Those from pathological homes produced youth whose drug-risk scores were high.

Factors that constitute a good home include the following: Parents love their children and are able to show it without pampering indulgence. The sound family is characterized by unity. Unity not only between parents but also in terms of the **extended family.** Parents in superior families take notice of their children. They accept their limitations and praise their achievements and potentials. Children can be frank with parents and parents with children without arousing hostilities. Families of low drug-risk youth did not depend on education, police, and law to teach about drugs. It was assumed that teaching in the home and the intelligence of the young people would constitute proper preparation. Mutual confidence and charity permit parents and children a variety of self-expression and pardonable errors. Children feel that they can lean on their parents in case of need. All family members know that the parents can be firm leaders without being autocratic. Mistakes are made, by parents and children, in superior families. For example, children do use drugs but much less frequently and with much less chance for dependency and habituation than in the case of pathological families. "Love, charity, tolerance, respect, self-confidence, trust, humor, clear communication, and an ability to create a joyous atmosphere are some of the ingredients that lead to excellent parenthood." (Blum and associates, 1972, p. 283).

Choice and responsibility

It was once thought that blacks and people of low socioeconomic status were particularly predisposed to abusing drugs. The data confirming or controverting such a belief are difficult to assemble. The legal transgressions of blacks and poverty level persons are more likely to show on police records than are those of people in the upper-middle class. Certainly, drugs on campus have received as much recent attention as have drugs in the ghetto. Some black organizations are successfully militant against the use of drugs by their members. Good families are no guarantee that children and youth in them will not try drugs (though drug-risk is smaller than in disturbed families). All these factors make it pertinent to conclude that the element of choice and individual responsibility is a factor in drug use and abuse.

Pregnant women can and do choose to bear their babies without the use of drugs. Sometimes this is despite the preference and convenience of their attending pediatrician. They are willing to endure the temporary pain and discomfort of parturition on the premise that anesthetics do depress breathing rates. Drugs affect oxygenation of the blood stream. Hence, a rich and continuing supply of oxygen to the neonate's brain cells is endangered. Some youth have resisted the use of tobacco, alcohol, marijuana, and LSD on the assumption that if their popularity and acceptance were dependent on drug usage, they could do without the peer affiliation. Those who tested this premise have, for the most part, found that they suffered no loss of popularity by abstinence. However, the majority lack the strength to assert themselves. They follow what they think is the crowd consensus. Many report taking drugs when actually they have not done so (Riesman, 1969).

There are a number of conditions and contingencies that influence the use of drugs. Kline (1971) has summarized the factors that determine how drugs may produce alterations of life patterns:

> Some laboratory rabbits can eat belladonna leaves while to rabbits of another strain the leaves are fatal. Heredity is an influence on drug effect.
>
> Environment influences effect. For example, barbiturates and alcohol are depressants and if taken in a quiet room they induce sleep. In a noisy room they stimulate.
>
> Anxiety prone persons, introverts, and extroverts are affected differently by drugs. Effects vary with intellectual capacity.
>
> The effect of drugs varies with expectations.
>
> Hunger, being tired or rested, oxygen supply, nutritional state, and emotional state influence the impact of drugs.
>
> Timing has an influence—time of day and time of life, whether one is tiring or resting are factors in effect.

Kline (1971) has also summarized a number of specific and advantageous ways (in addition to those cited here and there throughout the chapter) in which personality changes can be effected by drug usage. He asserts that the drugs to do these things may have been discovered. However, dosage and conditions of administration have not yet been determined. Some of the needed drugs have not yet been discovered. He believes that as the need is specified the discovery, or creation, of the drug will follow closely. Drug usages that may play a part in man's future personality development include:

> Prolonging or shortening childhood and adolescence
>
> Reducing the need for sleep
>
> Providing safe, short-acting intoxicants to relieve pressure. Contemporary drugs do not do this safely and ideally.
>
> Regulating sexual responses and thus reducing some of the many problems that man experiences in this area.
>
> Controlling affection and aggression
>
> Mediating nutrition and metabolism
>
> Altering alertness or relaxation
>
> Prolonging or dimming memories
>
> Encouraging or discouraging learning
>
> Provoking or relieving guilt

Fostering or shortening mothering behavior

Altering the perception of time

Creating feelings of wonder and newness for routine experiences (marriage, school, and business)

Deepening one's sense of awe and beauty

Examination of the foregoing list will show that many of the effects already have been discussed. Reduction of the need for sleep was not mentioned. It is known that bored people use more sleep. People who create adventure in life use less. Only recently have experiments been conducted to show that people can control digestion, metabolism, and blood pressure by means of intentional, mental concentration. The perception of time may be dependent in part on how much one is involved in life at the moment. As for the other items, many of the effects are matters that have been discussed earlier where the concern was with processes of self-actualizing.

In a study of drug usage in high schools on the west coast, Moskowitz (1970) found that experience was teaching young people that meaningful experiences were more readily available through work than through drugs. Boys and girls were saying with conviction, "Discard rationalizations and clarify your concepts of life and self." "Latch on to life and let loose of drugs." "Tune in to involvement in personal meanings." Alcoholics Anonymous, and some drug-withdrawal programs, have experienced considerable success when determination and self-concern were shifted to concern for others. When the alcoholic is involved in helping another who is in the same, or worse, shape as he, he is less compulsive about his own drinking.

Moskowitz (1970) tells of a youth who made his way through college on speed. He determined to go straight when he entered Hastings College of Law. He went, instead, to heroin. He was able to master drugs when he dropped law and got involved in helping high school youngsters deal with their drug dilemmas.

If the implications were in any areas other than sex, alcohol, or drugs, it would be permissible to indicate them. When implications are stated regarding sex, alcohol, or drugs, one is moralizing or being "preachy" to designate implications. So be it: Choice not only involves responsibility; but the action is reversible. Responsibility makes choice possible.

SUMMARY

Drug use and abuse is a difficult subject to handle because of prejudices on the part of presenters and receivers. "Official" positions, some known to be based on errors, and paradoxical effects combine with the temptation to oversimplify to make factual presentation difficult.

Man takes the shortest route to a goal. However, what is seen as the shortest route may not, in the long run, prove to be so. American people rather typically take the short route to popularity, power, security, ego inflation, pain-avoidance, and reality facing. They take pills, inhale a gas, or swallow a drink as the easy route to personality growth.

There are a number of sanctioned drugs that range from dangerous to helpful. Although legal, alcohol is one of the most dangerous of drugs in terms of habituation with many people. It decreases mental and physical efficiency. Home and work difficulties are imposed. Nicotine, and several gases generated by smoking tobacco, is the most dangerous of drugs. The danger is in terms of tissue and cell damage and the number of people involved. Because the results are not immediate and invariably fatal, its effects are often rationalized and its use continued. Aspirin is widely used. It typically has minor side-effects and does produce some pain-allaying results. Some people are sensitive to it. Overindulgence does occur and it is thought to be responsible, in part, for the pill-taking tendency of the young. Caffeine, used by virtually all—old and young—in the United States, only rarely has marked allergenic and toxic effects. It is stimulating without subsequent depressing results.

The controversial drugs are so classed for various reasons. The amphetamines may be medically prescribed. However, they are dangerous because of their illicit use and the tendency to develop tolerance and overdosage. Cocaine is the scare drug and rightly so in terms of painfulness. However, it is not widely used. Marijuana is a dangerous drug, not so much because of its known physical effects but because lies and propaganda against it have contributed to a "generation gap." LSD had brief popularity but its users reported "bad trips" with enough consistency that it is currently little used. Sedatives and tranquilizers are used widely—legally and illegally. Barbiturates, are dangerous and habit forming. Withdrawal is painful and can be fatal.

Major attention in current studies of drugs is focused on the personality of the users and abusers. Those with personality defects, weak egos, and poor family backgrounds "need" drugs more than others. However, they are also more quickly and seriously damaged by them. Drug abuse may be statistically related to family pathology. To the mature person statistics is a means of evading the real personality issues. The real issue is one of assuming choice and responsibility for personality development.

SUGGESTED READINGS

AVORN, JERRY, "Beyond Dying," *Harper's*, Vol. 246, No. 1474, 56–64, 1973.
Experiments suggest that psychedelic experiences induced by LSD may have a practical use. These experiments indicate that some of the

anxiety, fear, and pain of death, for those who are terminally ill, may be transformed into quite different feelings by LSD.

BLUM, RICHARD H., *Horatio Alger's Children*. San Francisco, Calif.: Jossey-Bass, Inc., Publishers, 1972.

The Horatio Alger stories of the early part of the century emphasized hard, honest, regular work as the key to success and winning the boss' daughter in marriage. Why so many of today's youth turn to drugs, dropping out, and tuning out is examined in terms of the health or pathology of the family.

FORT, JOEL, *The Pleasure Seekers: The Drug Crisis, Youth and Society*. Indianapolis: The Bobbs-Merrill Company, 1969.

This is a factual presentation of the effects of the mind altering drugs. The author applies his medical knowledge to the interpretation of psychological investigations and sociological surveys.

KAPLAN, JOHN, *Marijuana—the New Prohibition*. Cleveland: The World Publishing Company, 1970.

Kaplan uses the story of marijuana to illustrate the generation gap. The elder generation sees long-hairs and pot-smokers as representative of a style of life that is different and should therefore be repressed and outlawed. To marijuana users the outlawing of marijuana is a manifestation of hypocrisy on the part of those who use alcohol, tobacco, and amphetamines to wake up and barbiturates to relax and to sleep.

KLINE, NATHAN S., "The Future of Drugs and Drugs of the Future," *Journal of Social Issues*, Vol. 27, No. 3, 73–87, 1971.

The tendency in discussing drugs is to focus on the drug itself. This author shifts the emphasis to the person using the drug. There are good and bad, licit and illicit uses of drugs. How they will be used and by whom ultimately is dependent on the individual.

NOWLIS, HELEN H., *Drugs on the College Campus*, (with introduction by Kenneth Keniston, Anchor Books Edition). Garden City, New York: Doubleday and Company, Inc., 1969.

The complexities of the drug problem, even at the level of definition, are explained. This is a factual presentation about drugs on campus rather than a sensational "scare piece" about what can happen to an abuser.

FOLLOW-UP LEARNING ACTIVITIES

Reviewers have said this chapter contains only conventional material and conventional conclusions. Nothing will be new to the college reader.

Do you agree _____ or disagree _____? Why?

_____
_____
_____
_____

What material would you include or exclude?

_____
_____
_____

(Discuss the above items with some classmates. The author is interested in your conclusions. Please send your responses to H. W. Bernard, care of Holbrook Press, Inc., 470 Atlantic Avenue, Boston, Mass. 02210.)

To what extent do you think your personality accounts for such use of drugs as you make? Name the drug(s) and record your response.

_____
_____
_____
_____

What is your reaction to Williams' postulation that constitutional factors may account for alcoholism?

_____
_____
_____

"Choice and responsibility" have been referred to often in the text. What is your reaction to these references, especially as the concept refers to drug usage?

_____
_____
_____

Do you fall asleep readily when you go to bed?
Yes _____ No _____ Remarks _____
Do you ever take drugs to help you sleep?
Yes _____ No _____ Remarks _____
Do you ever take drugs to keep you awake?
Yes _____ No _____ Remarks _____

18
The Maturing Personality

The dignity of work.

LEARNING ACTIVITIES

What do you mean when you use the word mature or maturing?

_____

_____

_____

_____

Do you consider yourself to be mature?

Yes _____ No _____ because _____

_____

_____

_____

Can a child of twelve years be mature?

Yes _____ No _____ because _____

_____

_____

_____

What aspects of personality would you like to know more about?

_____

_____

_____

Has this text or course given you any clues regarding how to find better answers?

Yes _____ No _____ because _____

_____

_____

_____

(Discuss the above two items with classmates.)
In what ways have you shown an eagerness to face change?

_____

_____

_____

In what ways have you shown a reluctance to face change?

_____

_____

_____

Do you think that the search for happiness is a valid goal in life?

Yes _____ No _____ because _____

_____

_____

_____

Do you think play and recreation have a proper place in your life?

Too little _____ Too much _____ Not the right kind _____

Kind is OK _____ Time is about right _____

This final chapter is viewed as a summary with a twist (or bias). The theories and postulations that were presented in the foregoing chapters will not be condensed and reiterated. That was done in the summary for each chapter. The purpose here is that of selecting some of the emphases of earlier presentations and relating them to the reader's life. Possibly he can use them in constructing his own, personally applicable, theory of personality. If, however, such a theory is to be personally applicable, it must be individually designed. One will probably not find the author's or instructor's theory acceptable. It is hoped, however, that the text and the instructor's observations will serve as a stimulus. They can be a sounding board for one's own interpretation of his life experiences—including the recent one of studying this book.

It is suggested that the student review Chapter 1 as an initial reminder of the emphases and contents of this book. If there is not time to do this, at least peruse the section on "Directing Personality Development." The idea of this review and the purpose of this chapter are to help the student integrate various perspectives into a unified orientation. This, hopefully, will enable him to take a step toward better understanding the personalities of other people. It will be a step toward developing goals that merit immediate and long-term pursuit. It is an involvement in the process of maturing.

While we are reiterating and emphasizing, let it be repeated (as per "Preface") that personality theory is not, and probably never can be complete or final. The various authors cited in the text inescapably reflect the tenor of their times. Because the times will change, the nature of such an all-inclusive concept as personality must also change. Because the individual changes, matures, and (hopefully) learns, one's individually applicable theory of personality must change to fit his evolving needs. This is why periodic reviews of the text and learning exercises can have great merit.

APPLICATIONS FROM VIEWPOINTS

Personality perspectives

The various theories of personality were devised by scholars who perceived emphases that they thought had been neglected previously. Freud, for instance, believed that our unconscious and instinctive nature was so frequently ignored that conflict resulted. That is, ignoring the power of our sexual, aggressive, egotistical needs led to suppression, repression, and neuroses. It led to eventual outbreaks of an explosive nature or in a slowly seeping, draining away of energy. Watson and Skinner, as behaviorists, believed that good intentions, dependence on will and determination, and emphasis on affect or emotions led us to neglect careful, *detailed*, analysis of the conditioning factors—repetition and reward. Conditioning really accounted for personality formation. They therefore emphasized the environmental factors that shaped personality. Erikson and Fromm, as contemporary psychoanalysts, perceived other problems of personality—identity and affiliation or belongingness—as being focal.

Varied viewpoints are not right or wrong, correct or incorrect, as much as they are simply, viewpoints. Viewpoints consist of emphases that some think have been neglected. It is like the old legend of the blind men and the elephant: Each touched a different part of the elephant and reported that the animal was much like a rope, a wall, or a trunk of a tree. The very purpose of reading a book about personality is to open our eyes to details that had previously been obscure or overlooked. Reading a book may be likened to seeing a little part of the world through the author's eyes. He need be neither right on nor wrong—he just has his 20/20 or his 20/200 vision or his astigmatism altered by the lenses through which he sees. "Friends, Romans, countrymen, lend me your ears . . ." (Shakespeare, *Julius Caesar*)— and your eyes, and your other sensory equipment.

In conventional terms, maturing means coming of age, ripening. Maturation, strictly speaking, means the stage at which growth and development have reached a maximum. Maturing, by implication, means that one accepts with graceful resignation and dignity the fading of abilities and the involution of concerns. However, in this text more is meant. In Chapter 6, self-actualization was postulated as the goal of personality study. That concept is also included in maturing.

The maturing personality

Maturing as used in the present chapter title refers to matters of transcending oneself. It is more than simply drawing comforting comparisons with some statistical average. It means self-actualizing in the sense of an attempt to make better use of one's potential than has heretofore been made. In addition, maturing means that we agree with the many theorists who believe that we really do not know what our potential really is. Maturing also means that one uses logical processes. We evaluate past experiences. We use rational means to assess what is and might become reality. As such, mental maturity recognizes the value of affective states. These include acceptance by society, love from one's intimates, and temporary gratification from exercising the need for accomplishment. Finally, the word "maturity," in this context, means a process—an unrelenting challenge. Maturing is not being gracefully resigned to fate or being gratified at any comfortable level.

**Unfinished
business**

In various ways the idea has been expressed that the ability to get a quarter of an inch into man's cortex would pay far greater dividends than traveling thousands of miles into space. Space has a long running start on psychology. Astronomy, physics, and mathematics have histories reaching back five or six thousand years. Medical science, by contrast, is still an adolescent with its history of about two thousand years. Psychology, born as a science about 1890, is still in its infancy—perhaps in its fetal stage. What we do *not* know about personality is immense.

It seems highly probable that personality theory will be replaced shortly with much more tenable and fruitful hypotheses than we now have. Moreover, it is also highly probable that some reader of this book (or one of his contemporaries) will formulate this new and more respectable theory. This is a probability because of the increasing rate at which new knowledge is accumulating. Better theory is possible because of faster feedback, and because of the accelerating interdisciplinary nature of scientific study. Note, for instance, the references to sociology, cultural anthropology, biology and genetics, medicine and drugs, and to psychology and philosophy.

The study of personality is unfinished business.

**Psychoanalytic
theory
in action**

Psychoanalysts have contributed numerous applicable ideas to personality theory. One contribution was inadvertent. It taught us that theory derives in part from the then contemporary scene. Freud, writing at a time when sex was a whispered word and "Victorian prudery" contributed to neuroses, worries, conflicts, and repressions, initiated the message that sex was normal and natural. He paved the way to current thinking that sex can be pleasurable and beautiful. He did, however, recognize social restraints and taboos. This thought has been missed by some who rationalize promiscuous sex activities by the partial quotation of Freudian postulations. Freud emphasized the importance of childhood, especially in terms of the child's being loved, accepted, and having a childish sexuality. The importance of childhood is a concept that is still gaining momentum. However, Freud also believed in therapy, rehabilitation, and personality change. He was also saying, as this entire book is saying, "Childhood is important, but even more important is the way we live, and act, and think today." It is not too late (according to Longfellow) until ". . . the tired heart shall cease to palpitate ("Commemorative Ode"). The really important time is today.

Horney also indicated that personality theory was a reflection of the time. Living and working in the depression days, she indicated that society contributed to neuroses by virtue of the unceasing pressures and demands that pervaded man's existence. The emphases continue to change. The neo-Freudians, Erich Fromm and Erik Erikson—writing at a time when discipline was relaxed, financial security has been enhanced, and when society shows some concern for all its citizens—indicate that the contemporary psychological needs are identity, love, communication, and affiliation.

One need not be a behaviorist in order to recognize that stimulus, repetition, reward, habits, and teaching-learning, conditioning are factors that mold personality. The emphasis on the cultural formation of beliefs, behaviors, and biases is but another way of saying that behavioristic theory is solidly rooted in the facts of life.

Behavioristic theory in action

Anyone who sets out to mold his personality in a planned direction will be well-advised to recognize that there is inertia from the past. Former habits can be either an asset or a liability.

> Tim O was a somewhat typical student in that he seemed to think that harder work would immediately improve his scholastic grades. He made his plan, developed a time schedule (which was realistic in terms of providing time for recreation and personal duties, as well as for planned study time). He followed the schedule for five weeks and then began occasionally to find excuses to delay or avoid the study periods. His old habits caught up with him. Some progress had been made. He raised one D to a C and slipped from a B to C in one subject and went from C to B in another. Another term another try, and he stuck to his resolve for seven weeks. It took four quarters to make the plan work for the full 11 weeks of the quarter.

One of the major themes of humanism is that we ourselves are a part of the Gestalt that produces personality. We can think, and choose, and determine our goals. We can assume responsibility for planned personality development. A statistical concept of normality is not very helpful to the humanist. He would like to see man undertake the unachievable task of transcending himself. He should ever be seeking to do better or ascend to a higher level of achievement. Maslow has criticized the whole field of psychology, including his own early work in the field of abnormal psychology, for not giving more attention to the unusually good, the unusually dedicated, the unusually persistent individual. Such studies might provide clues for the individual who wants to go beyond statistical normality.

Humanistic theory in action

Humanistic theory recognizes that shedding the burden of one's childhood memories—including those so faint as to exist only in the subconscious—is not an easy task. Therapists of many persuasions, be they psychoanalysts, rational therapists, behavioral counselors, or reality-facing adherents, can help one place his past into a fitting context. Therapists, regardless of persuasion, can see the validity of the psychoanalytic concept of polarity. They can, for instance, understand that man may do self-destructive things, such as taking dangerous drugs or driving too fast, and also keep a regime of diet and exercise to maintain health. Humanists accept polarity when they acknowledge the reality of a man's being kind to his children and wife yet gladly accepting the lures of a street-walker. Humanists cannot deny the power of learning and conditioning theory. One's environment and culture are inescapably factors in shaping one's ideals and, consequently, one's personality.

The positive emphases that make the humanistic orientation attractive and useful are the notions that:

1. Man can transcend himself by making use of his capacities. He can be less concerned about his limitations and traumas.
2. Man is an organized entity that includes past, present, and future. Man's entity must include self and others.
3. Man is responsible. He is responsible for involvement and fulfillment, for making the frustrating past lead into a productive future.

There is much similarity in the concerns about transcending self, living an organized life, and assessing responsibility for self-others and for now-future.

PERSONAL PHILOSOPHY

One's personality is reflected in his personal **philosophy.** Philosophy is, in its turn, a matter of how one views such things as, for example, the concerns cited in the previous paragraph. Throughout history, various persons, no doubt reflecting the temperament of their times, have condensed their beliefs into tenable and durable philosophical orientations. Four sample philosophies are presented for the reader's consideration. There may be some concepts in these historical systems that have merit in one's personal philosophy.

Epicurean philosophy

The Epicurean philosophy advises that one should take as many simple pleasures from life as possible. These simple pleasures include such things as good food, eaten leisurely and in the presence of congenial company. It means the exercise of one's physical body in the open air. It means the exercise of one's mentality in the indulgence of one's curiosity. Exercise includes using one's affective potential in the enjoyment of art, music, drama, and companionship. Epicureans would tell us that one cannot enjoy his work consistently and continuously. We need variety to titillate some of the great range of our capacities. Leisure-time activities are, therefore, a serious concern of the Epicurean.

But—and herein lies the practical use of the definition of philosophy as a well-thought-out system of values—the Epicurean philosophy need not, indeed must not, exclude the need for balance. In everyday life there must be balance between work and play. There must be balance between diet and overindulgence, between obligation and sensory enjoyment.

Epicureanism emphasizes happiness. This is, quite frankly, a low level goal in the eyes of many people. Because it is low level, it is all the more blameworthy that we should fail to take advantage of opportunities for fun that are available. Nevertheless, happiness as *the* goal in life must share some of the blame for the feelings of frustration, deprivation, and anonymity that happiness-oriented people feel. We also must meet the routine, petty, ordinary obstacles and challenges of a vigorous life (more on this later in the chapter).

The Platonist advises man to lift his soul and vision above the petty and imperfect things of life. He should move toward the refined atmosphere of the good, the true, and the beautiful. This counsel seems to be in accord with the personality precept that problems are frequently no more serious than the attitude that is taken toward them. Certainly, there is sound wisdom in the admonition, "Don't sweat the little things." Too many of us, too often, allow minor irritations—noisy children, tardy students, horn–tooting motorists, discourteous co-workers—to color our perceptions of the many good things that occur daily.

Platonic philosophy

Let the reader neither heartily endorse nor summarily dismiss the Platonic message of maintaining serenity in a not-so-serene world. Religion has been referred to as the opiate of the masses. Karl Marx said religion was the "opium of the people." This was because it so often asks people to endure the distress of the present for the promise of glory in the future. The religious devotion of slaves made their conditions somewhat tolerable. Religious devotion can help make discrimination against blacks tolerable today, for example. Fortunately, the future and the now are joining hands. The practical person must see his living today as being continuous with the future. One can rise above the petty irritations but the major irritations cannot be dismissed with a Platonic air.

The philosophy of Aristotle endorses a concept that, in a way, is the polar opposite of Platonism. Reality, Aristotle says, is in the here and now rather than in some perfect hereafter. Goodness or badness are dependent upon the way people and things are used. There is a need for balance and proportion in our lives. This means different things to different people. Hence, each must formulate his own philosophy in terms of what things merit priority and what things should be placed in the background.

Aristotelian philosophy

A forty-five-year-old man suffered a heart attack while watching television one evening after work. It was a serious case and for several days the prognosis in the hospital was "uncertain." While there, the man began to think of what things were really important to him. He had worked long hours at his job. He often took work home in the evening or stacked it up to be done on week-ends. He liked his work; however, he decided that the tension he felt about doing a good and complete job could be called pressure. He looked at his rationalizations—maintaining a financially respectable home, providing his wife a standard of living to which he hoped she would become accustomed, establishing monetary assurance of their children's college education, etc.

He decided that love, time, and attention for his family now were better than the hurried, part-time, and occasionally postponed vacations of the past. He decided that his job could be done adequately with a normal and planned regime. Many of the details he had cared for could be executed by junior executives and secretaries.

The shift was not easy. He found himself tempted to stay at work on certain occasions. It was not always easy to answer his children's questions or play with them when they wanted to play. Often there was some professional literature inviting his attention. Initially it took some concentration to share his wife's interests in bridge and concerts. However, the choice for balance was made.

One can wait for misfortune to strike himself or his family before deciding that the Aristotelian formula of proportion is worthwhile. One might also, by contemplating relative and enduring advantages of balance, make some decisions now. He can be stimulated by self-actualizing motivation as contrasted to crisis motivation.

Christian philosophy It is not really the Christian philosophy that constitutes the subject matter of this subsection. The philosophical concern is with the religion of the New Testament with its emphasis on love, concern for one's fellowmen, and compassion in daily action. This Christian philosophy is shared with other great religions of the world— Confucianism, Mohammedanism, and Buddhism, also teach concern for fellowmen. The Golden Rule, "Do unto others as you would have them do unto you," is expressed in all major religions.

Christ's teaching, "Inasmuch as ye do it unto one of the least of these, ye do it unto me," is a practical bit of worldly philosophy. It is a thought expressed in various ways by some of the "far out" young of the present generation. The Christian philosophy does not place emphasis on fear of God but on love of man. It promises not a hell for sinfulness but love, despite human frailty.

The Christian philosophy may be considered to be a matter of divine revelation. It may also be an accumulation of wisdom over the ages. Man has discovered, and each generation must discover anew, that self-concern as a primary activity is self-defeating. As one's vision and action embrace his fellowmen he moves in the direction of self-actualizing. Many psychologists have said, explicitly or implicitly,

"Christ's teaching that you should love one another is the world's most profound insight into human personality."

FACING THE FACTS

"One man's meat is another man's poison" might be said in regard to mental as well as physical diet. What are listed as facts in this section may be mere postulations to another. Let the following constitute the starting point for some solitary deliberations or some cooperative dialogue.

"There's nothing new under the sun" is one concept. There was never before an individual with the unique set of genes and chromosomes that you possess. It seems that change might be an inevitable fact because perceptions are different. Varied views lead to new ideas, new combinations of things, and to new descriptions of people.

Change

In our technological society change is taking place at such a rapid rate that adjusting to new circumstances is, in the eyes of some authorities, man's greatest problem. Man does so many things routinely and automatically that changing conditions impose a burden. Deciding whether living in accordance with a routine is an essential or merely a comfort is an unresolved dilemma. We know that babies are disturbed by interruption of routines. This is especially the case if that interruption relates to removal or inconsistencies on the part of a key adult—mother, nurse, or whoever takes primary care of him. We know that old people, bearing the habits of years, are disturbed by changes in the patterns of their life. In general, insecure people, those with weak or unstable self-concepts, are upset by abrupt and rapid alterations in the conditions of their lives.

On the other hand, people who are emotionally healthy, who enjoy the exercise and challenge of their capacities, who have accepted the task of transcending themselves, look upon change as a chance to prove their worth. Some people are "bored to death" by routine. If, then, our postulations have merit, it is not so much the impact of change that really counts. It is the person who must change that constitutes the pivotal point in how change will influence personality. To a degree, this will depend on the home, community, and school experiences that influence personality development. Whether one is recessive, defensive or aggressive, creative or confident will also be concerns. To a degree, it will depend on how one's peers react to change—and here the merits of inter-personal process groups may be brought to bear. To a degree, one's flexibility will depend on his personal philosophy. If he will value process more than possessions, if he values people more than things, then material change will have less than devastating impact.

Personality theorists have, as was shown earlier, postulated their ideas in terms of their then contemporary world. Change in personality theory is itself a proof of man's flexibility. Concentration on robust ego concepts, prizing differences and deviations, and valuing group discussions are personality assets. A "well thought-out system of values" can transform the phenomenon of change from a threat to an opportunity for actualizing potential.

Happiness syndrome

Suicide rates are higher in some countries than in the United States— but the U.S. rate is high. Divorce rates in the United States are about as high as any place in the world. Institutional help for the mentally ill is needed in increasing amounts in the U.S.

The above data are presented to suggest that happiness is not a characteristic of American life. Statistical data, such as the foregoing, reflect many things; perhaps the happiness syndrome is of some importance. In terms of such evidence as we have, it is postulated that our national belief that we should be happy is one factor contributing to suicide, divorces, and unusual emotional turmoil.

Happiness in marriage (or success in business or building a sturdy ego concept) is a day-to-day, step-by-step achievement. The first sentence in the second paragraph of the Declaration of Independence has been misunderstood. It says, in part, ". . . the *pursuit* of Happiness." Immigrants have come to the United States with great hopes and found many disappointments along with many new-found advantages. Child psychology has been dominated in recent years by the idea that children are young only once and should be guaranteed happiness and freedom.

Winston Churchill, with forthright honesty and down-to-earth philosophy, offered a key to reality, as well as to winning a war, when he said in a famous statement, "I have nothing to offer but blood, toil, tears, and sweat." This is a far cry from the happiness syndrome that seems to grip our nation. Churchill's statement seems to be in line with what the signers of the Declaration of Independence had in mind: ". . . the pursuit of Happiness." The goal of happiness is defeated by its direct pursuit. Accumulation of wealth, leisure that is not compensated for by work, or instant happiness through drugs, the right mouthwash, or alluring cosmetics, do not make fulfilled lives. Identification with people, difficult goals, and high ideals can provide the glow of happiness. These give more assurance than do pills, diet, perfumes, six easy lessons in mysticism, deodorants, the right wheels, and adornment in mod style.

Churchill and philosophers throughout history seem to be saying that happiness is an inadvertent result, a concomitant, of work. The feeling of satisfaction of completing a task and demonstrating to self and to fellows one's worth is the key to fulfillment. Happiness is a concomitant of giving vigorous exercise to one's capacities and potentials. Happiness is a concomitant of feeling at one with the world and its citizens of every status, color, and country.

All of man's behavior is either purposeful or purposive. Purposeful behavior is that which is consciously, cognitively planned to achieve certain goals. Purposive behavior is the striving of the organism toward goals that may not be intellectually, objectively identified. For example, being irritable because one is tired or hungry—or as the psychoanalysts might emphasize, being generally aggressive because one's mother was rejecting.

Purpose

When one's purposes are not recognized, or when recognized purposes conflict with one another, the basis for personality deterioration, frustration, and confusion is established. Horney asserts that such conflict is the basis of neurosis. Psychoanalysts in general emphasize the concept of polarity—another way of saying that purposes (life-death, love-hate) conflict. Reality and rational therapists are advising that the parts of life be put together—determining what goals are most worthwhile. Humanists are saying that man's personal purposes must be in accord with the welfare of one's fellowmen.

That respected philosopher (only he was called a playwright), Shakespeare, writes the lines in *Hamlet*,

> This above all: to thine own self be true,
> And it must follow, as the night the day,
> Thou canst not then be false to any man.
>
> *Hamlet*, Act I, iii

The passage may cause perplexity and debate but it seems to be saying what psychologists and religionists are saying: One's purposes must coincide with the purposes of fellow beings. Otherwise, in the long run, one finds himself alienated and ostracized. And John Donne also said it in the words "No man is an Iland, intire in itselfe; every man is a peece of the Continent, a part of the maine." As one thoughtfully plans the purposes in his individual philosophy, he must take into account what his actions and goals do to those about him.

The pursuit of purposes must, in addition to being socially oriented, consider which of multiple purposes are to have priority. Often this means a choice between two goods rather than between good and dubious. If one has chosen one goal over another in terms of long-time dividends, he must also (for the purpose of avoiding conflict) be able to stop thinking about how nice it would have been if another choice had been made. The words of Whittier are a sound bit of philosophy, "For of all sad words of tongue or pen, The saddest are these: 'It might have been!'"

Freedom and responsibility

Parallel to the illusion of happiness as a freely given right, parallel to the concept of self as isolated from others, and parallel to the fallacy of drifting through life without purpose is the illusion that one can have freedom without responsibility.

There is much in our society that points to the fallacy that one can have freedom to grow and to become without the responsibility of effort, devotion, toil, and just plain drudgery. The guidance movement in schools and the removal of responsibility of the pupil for expending effort is one example. Teachers are made responsible for the pupil's unhappiness, boredom, lack of motivation, anxiety, and misconduct. Sociologists, psychologists, and educators look for excuses in the pupil's environment. The fact is that the pupil may have been tempted, but he was not forced. In this failure to distinguish between developmental atmosphere and the learner's responsibility, there has been bred a category of students who feel that learning must be interesting, effortless, and immediately rewarding. Adolescents talk of freedom to destroy their bodies without the responsibility of respect for parents, cost of maintenance, and the price of rehabilitation. The free-load, no-responsibility promises made by a government seem to flourish despite the economic tradition of centuries. Abundance without effort existed only in the Garden of Eden. It may be that a guaranteed minimum wage of $6000 (or whatever is a "nice round figure") is a practical aspiration in view of technology and automation. History, confirmed in the increasing size of the national debt, continues to demonstrate that freedom entails responsibility.

It is altogether proper that Wheeler's organismic law—an organism always takes what it perceives to be the shortest route to a goal—should be observed. Minimum effort to achieve a given goal is logical and meritorious. It is impractical to lift water in a bucket when it can be done better by means of a pump. No effort and no responsibility is an orientation that is continuously alluring. However, this is contrary to the teachings of all those personality theorists who have talked and written about goals, self-transcendance, and actualization of potential.

The lesson of freedom and responsibility is a hard one to learn, as is attested to in our becoming the "Ugly Americans." Doles, gifts, subsidies, and loans to foreign countries have repeatedly made us enemies who bite the hand that feeds them. On the other hand, when technical advice and teaching assistance are given so that developing nations can be free and responsible, the efforts have given the recipients strength. We have won appreciation. Paul Elmer More, literary critic and theologian in the early part of the century, summarized the historical thought as follows: ". . . the simple and tyrannical fact [is] that whether in the world physical, or in the world intellectual, or in the world spiritual, we can get nothing without paying an exacted price." One's personal philosophy must, it seems, acknowledge that personality growth and satisfaction derive from the freedom to be responsible.

Otto Rank referred to the process of being born as the "birth trauma." One was thrust from the warm, all-providing, plushy atmosphere of the mother's womb into a cold, noisy atmosphere. There one had to strive and struggle for oxygen, warmth, and food. Others viewed birth as release from a confining space no longer adequate to comfortably accommodate one's growing body or to challenge one's encompassing mind. Life continuously is filled with a perplexing mixture of danger and opportunity.

Hazards must be faced

There are hazards in life—including many at birth. Inadequate parents, incompetent teachers, selfish businessmen, dishonest politicians, disease, accidents, deaths, all constitute hazards. In part, these are points of view. One can also find competent parents, inspiring teachers, sincere politicians, and businessmen who say, "I'm going to be here for the next ten years." Health, challenge, and demanding goals are also pleasant realities.

It would be foolish to think that all hazards can be surmounted, avoided, or ignored. It is equally foolish to allow these hazards of life to so dominate the scene that the beautiful and gratifying aspects of life are obscured. How seriously in your life might you regard the following words?

> Be still, sad heart, and cease repining;
> Behind the clouds, the sun is shining;
> Thy fate is the common fate of all.
> Into each life some rain must fall.
> Some days must be dark and dreary.
>
> Longfellow, *A Rainy Day*

The representative philosophies cited in the foregoing—Epicurean, Platonic, Aristotelian, and Christian—can be reconsidered in terms of dealing with the inevitable hazards that a free and responsible life entail. How they are considered is part of both personal philosophy and personality.

There is no way of knowing what ultimate truth might be. This may be an excuse for failure to adopt, with conviction, any value. However, "valueless" logic is a vicious trap. It is no excuse for failure, at least tentatively, to devise and cling to values today. If it be true that man today is more dominated by meaninglessness (and its accompaniment of *laissez-faire*), despair, pleasure seeking, and freedom without responsibility than ever before, it is in part due to failure to respect the

Self and the worth of others

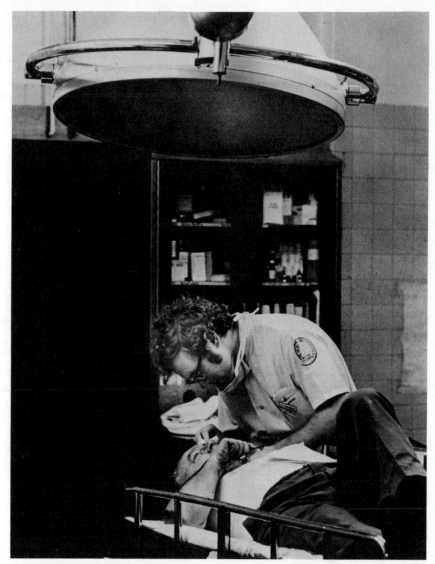

Other concern is a symptom of maturity.

merit of transient values and goals. One value that has yet to be scientifically disproved relates to the worth of others in a personal philosophy.

Self-concern and self-interest may be likened to circumscribing the orbit of one's life with a piece of chalk on a string. The circle is limited by focus on self; life is confining and is ultimately arrested. Let the chalk get off the string and it leads to ever new, and ever expanding interests. When, for example, one's children reach the age of two, ten, or 20 years only the naïve person can say, "Now they will begin to be interesting." They were, in fact, interesting at the age two, ten, 15, 20, and will continue to be interesting to the interested parent. Their careers in business, family, and self-actualization continue to unfold and to be of interest.

> A man who had been moderately successful in his moonlighting career in real estate decided at age 48 to retire after 20 years of service in the FBI. He moved to another community and, deciding that fishing, boating, and golfing were not quite enough, he did some volunteer work in community projects with and for youth. He got interested in drugs, attended several city and state-wide conferences on drugs, and became an authority. He was invited as a consultant to the city council. He was elected to the city council and by age 58 was elected mayor. His days, he says, are not long enough. He asserts, "I'm having the time of my life."

Losing our life in the life of others, as perceived by William James, Maslow, Rogers, and a host of others, is the key to a rich philosophy of life. It is an avenue to the facilitation of self-actualization.

Man is a social animal. Lacking fang, claws, great size, or speed, and destined to a long period of childhood dependency, his existence is dependent on the care, nurture, and teaching of others. Man "learns" his intelligence, his personality, and humanity from his family, peers, and neighbors. When communication with these human associates is blocked or blurred, one tends to become alienated, disinherited, and neurotic. Hence, one's personal philosophy must include strategies for establishing and maintaining intimate and durable contact with one's fellow beings.

One is already sick, one is already neurotic if he is so defensive that he recalls all insults and traumas of past experiences. He is sick when he places the burden on others for proving their worth. The responsibility must reside in the individual for taking friendly initiative. Even after atypical samplings of the hostilities and defensiveness of others he must assume responsibility. One may, if unfortunate, have to search for the friendliness, empathy, and compassion of others. However, if one is open and if one is discerning, these favorable traits can be discerned. Though it is easy to focus on the unkind, cruel, selfish, and sick, these are not the prevailing personality traits. Friendliness, empathy, and compassion are the prevalent values of mankind. They are dominant trends in mature personality.

SUMMARY

One culmination of the study of personality is that of sorting from many data some key ideas. These must be worthy of being included in the goals one wants in his own personality development. Each must formulate his own philosophy; hence, the intent of this chapter is to present some items for the reader's consideration. These ideas are gleaned from the earlier chapters of this book but constitute more than a summary.

It is suggested that one be flexible enough to consider various viewpoints. One can strive toward maturity by learning from others; one need not experience everything directly. One can, in short, use rational processes. Psychoanalysis recommends open-minded consideration of sexuality, recognition of the power of, but not binding restrictions of childhood. There is wisdom in seeking professional help in reducing self-defeating behavior. Behaviorism suggests that one consider the culture and physical environment as factors that condition life. Humanism suggests that in addition to instinct (psychoanalysis) and environment (behaviorism) that personal aspirations and goals are also part of the psychological milieu. Humanism makes self-transcendance, responsibility, and human contact key concerns in philosophy.

Additional clues to a personal philosophy are contained in certain historical views. Epicureanism advises taking advantage of routine opportunities for small pleasures. Platonism advises rising above petty daily irritations and focusing on ultimate goals. Aristotelian philosophy recommends avoiding extremes—maintaining balance in living. Christianity and other major world religions endorse the idea that brotherhood, compassion, and love for fellowmen are the enduring and focal values.

Some of the highlighted data of personality study indicate that certain facts must be faced by the maturing personality. Change is inevitable and, while not always welcome, it is often a challenging opportunity. The concept of happiness as a human right constitutes a hazard. Clearly defined purposes help one maximize his time and opportunity. Freedom and responsibility might well become one, hyphenated, word in the maturing person's philosophy. Unpleasant facts in life are inevitable and can be taken in stride when viewed with a reality-facing perspective. The maturing personality regards others as an inseparable part of self.

SUGGESTED READINGS

Committee on the Student in Higher Education (Joseph F. Kaufman, Chairman), "The New Students," a chapter in *The Student in Higher Education*, pp. 16–27. New Haven: The Hazen Foundation, 1968.
Many descriptions have been written of today's college student. This is said by some to be one of the more accurate portrayals. The eight summary statements may provide the reader some suggestions in formulating his own goals.

INGOLD, JEANETTE, "Where Handicaps are Forgotten," *American Education*, Vol. 8, No. 2, 25–28, March, 1972.
> *A number of students at Missoula (Montana) technical center demonstrate that your problems are not so serious as the attitude taken toward them—or perhaps they are saying, "It is not what you don't have but what you have left, and use, that is important."*

KENISTON, KENNETH, "College Students and Children in Developmental Institutions," *Children*, Vol. 14, No. 1, 3–7, January–February, 1967.
> *Keniston likens some of the restrictions imposed on college students to the requirements placed on children living in custodial homes and orphanages.*

LEVINE, SAUL V., "Draft Dodgers: Coping with Stress, Adapting to Exile," *American Journal of Orthopsychiatry*, Vol. 42, 431–440, April, 1972.
> *The 60,000 to 100,000 young Americans who have left the United States for Canada, presumably to avoid being drafted into an unjust war, actually have many reasons for their actions and many degrees of success. The fact that one carries his personality and problems with him is one fact that is illustrated.*

MARTIN, MALACHI, "The Scientist as Shaman," *Harper's*, Vol. 244, No. 1462, 54–61, March, 1972.
> *As one seeks to develop his own philosophy and goals this article should prove timely. The author warns against our taking the advice of scientists who are counseling outside the field of their speciality or who are extrapolating beyond their data. He makes some observations about B. F. Skinner and about the individual's need to assume responsibility for his own thinking.*

TAVRIS, CAROL, "Harry, You are Going to Go Down in History as the Father of the Cloth Mother," *Psychology Today*, Vol. 6, No. 11, 64–77, 1973.
> *Harry Harlow, the famous monkey psychologist, in an interview with Tavris describes some of the things that we could learn from monkeys. Proponents of Women's Liberation may encounter some disturbing thoughts.*

FOLLOW-UP LEARNING ACTIVITIES

At the present time, which of the personality viewpoints do you find most acceptable?

_____ because_____

_____

_____

_____

State your personal philosophy. (What values or aspirations do you rate as being most important?)

_____

_____

_____

_____

Why do you agree _____ or disagree _____ with the author's postulation of the "happiness syndrome?"

_____

_____

_____

_____

Why do you agree _____ or disagree _____ with the author's postulation on the relation of freedom and responsibility?

_____

_____

_____

Cite some specific ways in which the importance of others might be more of an emphasis in your life.

_____

_____

_____

_____

Take now fewer than ten minutes to reflect on and review this course as a whole. Then list the items that you consider to be most prominent in what you have learned.

_____

_____

_____

_____

_____

GLOSSARY

Achievement Motivation The drive, or need to strive for high levels of performance in various fields, especially in schoolwork and occupation.

Affective Referring to feelings and emotions; frequently used in conjunction with, and in contrast to, cognitive or intellectual aspects of behavior.

Ambiguous Having amorphous, shapeless, meaningless structure or outline. Something susceptible to varied interpretations.

Ambivalence A state in which one simultaneously has opposing wishes or contrasting feelings about a thing or person.

Anomie A feeling of being a nobody; having no affiliation, roots, or attachments. Feeling faceless, powerless, and isolated.

Autism Tending to withdraw from external reality. A rather severe personality disorder of withdrawal from people and situations.

Basic Encounter Group A group of about six to ten people who meet for the specific purpose of learning how each comes across to others; the group members seek understanding and control of the affective phases of their lives. Also called sensitivity groups, T-groups, inter-personal process groups.

Catharsis A psychoanalytic approach in which the client gets emotional relief, or cleansing, from tension or conflict by verbally describing his feelings.

Charismatic Having qualities of prestige and leadership that make it easy for others to follow and to have devotion and admiration for the person possessing such charisma.

Client-Centered Counseling A helping relationship in which the therapist reflects the feelings, attitudes, and expressions of the counselee, assuming that the resources for growth and change reside within the one being helped. The process consists in helping one to see his strengths and to perceive alternate and fulfilling ways of behavior.

Cognitive Related to the mental aspects of personality; intelligence, knowledge. Often contrasted to **affective.**

Compensation Making up for a weakness or a frustration by emphasizing more desirable traits, or allowing for substitute gratification in an area other than that of the weakness.

Compulsion A stereotyped, mechanical behavior. One may have a compulsion to win, to be defeated, to wash his hands frequently, to lie, to disparage others, even when such action is inappropriate. The external situation does less to dictate the act than the compulsive person's inner state.

Concept The mental image of a thing or class of things formed by generalizations from specifics. As used here, the broad idea of processes and relationships that extend beyond definitions. Combination of several ideas into a single notion.

Concomitant Occurring with; a correlate of an action; something simultaneously learned with a purposeful learning.

Conflict   A state in which one is under stress because of ambiguous or ambivalent feelings about some thing or some person. Conflict is normal when it is temporary and is resolved; it becomes abnormal when it remains unresolved and results in disablement.

Congenital   Present in an individual at birth; born with. Acquired during prenatal development or during the birth process, but not a product of heredity.

Construct   An idea, or concept, indicating the relationship between empirically observable data or processes.

Control Group   A group used to evaluate the reliability of a variable experimental factor when the factor is held constant in the control group and varied in the experimental group; *e.g.,* in studying the effect of hunger on ability to concentrate on arithmetic problems, the control group does the problems but is fed on a normal schedule. In studying the effect of illness on some phenomenon, the control group is the healthy comparison group.

Correlation   In psychological terminology, correlation refers to the extent to which one phenomenon occurs in relationship to another; or the more of one thing the more (or less) of another; *e. g.,* size of foot and size of shoe would be highly positively correlated—the bigger the foot, the bigger the shoe. Correlations between personality and parental discipline, between intelligence and school marks, between body build and personality traits all have been investigated.

Cultural Discontinuity   Contrasts between cultures; normal expectations in one culture are regarded as abnormalities in another. Differential societal expectations that contrast with what one is accustomed to and that therefore arouse anxieties.

Culture   The man-made aspects of one's environment. The language, laws, customs, and institutions that one finds in a given segment of society.

Cybernation   The stage of technological development in which machines regulate and correct themselves or other machines.

Defense Mechanism   Any of several kinds of evasive behavior in which the individual seeks to avoid, or deny the existence of, conditions that make adjustment difficult.

Delusion   Believing something that is not based on sound evidence; a false belief; an idea that cannot be modified by logical processes.

Dialogue   Conversation between two persons in which both are listened to and both are heard.

Displacement   The shifting and discharge of emotion, usually hostility but sometimes affection, on a person or object thought to be more vulnerable or amenable than the one who generated the initial feeling.

Double Message   A situation in which one simultaneously gets opposing messages. One's words may express courtesy and affection while one's tone and countenance may express contempt and dislike.

Dream Analysis   A psychoanalytic approach in which the content of a subject's reported dreams are interpreted by the analyst in terms of the client's motives or unconscious wishes.

Eclectic A selection and organization into a unified system of compatible findings from a variety of sources. Often used disparagingly as a hodge-podge; but often of ideas that are fundamentally reconcilable.

Electra Complex The female counterpart of the Oedipus Complex, in which the girl has incestuous thoughts and wishes for her father.

Empathic Being able, or having the capacity, to experience with another person his affective states.

Empirical Data based on naturalistic and systematic observation.

Enculturation The process and condition in which one has internalized and made a part of his own personality the values, beliefs, and actions endorsed by his culture.

Euphoric Characterized by an extremely high level of good feeling; extremely optimistic outlook, and having a high energy level.

Extended Family A family unit consisting not only of parents and children (the nuclear family) but also including grandparents, uncles, aunts, and cousins.

Extrinsic From the outside. Extrinsic motivation is not for self or to win a personal goal, but to gain the reward or recognition given by others. Extrinsic is in contrast to **functional autonomy.**

Extrovert One who is socially outgoing; one who is concerned with others as contrasted to being self-centered.

Free Association An unconstrained sequence and relationship of words and ideas. In psychoanalysis, the client is asked to speak freely of whatever comes to his mind, with the idea that sources of unconscious conflict may be identified.

Functional Autonomy A condition in which an act is carried on because of its own motivating power—outside incentives are no longer needed. For example, having learned to read well (perhaps under some pressure) one's reading is kept alive by the skill and satisfaction derived from reading.

Generation Gap The differences between parents and children in terms of values and outlooks, magnified by the accelerating rate of social and technological change. The gap is essential in terms of authority and responsibility. The gap is simultaneously normal and potentially tragic.

Genotype Characteristics shared in common by a biological group; traits that can be transmitted by individuals.

Habit An automatic response to a specific situation. Habits may include not only motor responses but attitudes, language, and thoughts.

Heterostasis The tendency of the individual to grow, learn, satisfy curiosity, and to become. The thrust of directional growth.

Heuristic Leading to the discovery of new thoughts or insights. A teaching-learning situation in which the student is led to discover things for himself.

Hyperactive Excessive activity. The prefix is used with many other words indicating excessive, too much, beyond the ordinary.

Hypoactive Excessively small activity. The prefix is used with many other words to indicate too little, insufficient, deficient.

Hypnosis An approach to therapy in which the practitioner induces a sleeplike condition in the subject, who then shows extreme responsiveness to directions and suggestions given by the hypnotist. The method has been used in therapy, dentistry, surgery, and childbirth.

Hysteria A neurotic reaction pattern in which one feels organic dysfunction in spite of biological normality. A **psychosomatic disorder.**

Identification The process of receiving personal satisfactions or tension reduction through association with the achievement or renown of others.

Idiosyncratic Possessing unique and specific identifying characteristics. The temperament or mental constitution specific to a particular individual or group.

Inhibitions A hesitance to behave or permit feelings to be expressed. A mental blockage or area of resistance.

Inter-personal Process Group See **basic encounter group.**

Introvert A person whose interests are directed primarily toward self. One who shuns the company of others in his excessive self-concern.

IQ Abbreviation for intelligence quotient. The numerical ratio of mental age to chronological age, multiplied by 100 to avoid decimal points; for example, a pupil has a chronological age of 90 months and on a test scores a mental age of 100 months; mental age divided by chronological age is 1.11, multiplied by 100, the IQ is 111.

Longitudinal Study Tracing the development of an individual, group, or situation over a long period of time; contrasted to cross-sectional investigations in which passage of time is not a factor; it is a study of present status, whereas longitudinal studies trace change over time.

Manic-Depressive An emotional disorder characterized by extreme states of elation and hope (mania) and then plunging into extreme states of discouragement and despair.

Maturity A relative term meaning "appropriate ripeness or development" of physical or intellectual behavior. A child of six may be mature for his age. A 20-year-old who acts like an adolescent is immature.

Metacommunication Communication about communication. Discussing what is *really* being said and heard at the time the verbal transaction and interaction is taking place.

Mobility Transition from one socioeconomic strata to another, usually refers to upward movement in social status.

Morphology The study of body types and the manner and results of studying personality in terms of body build.

Multiple Causation A principle of psychology emphasizing that explanations of behavior or growth are based on a number of interacting factors; repudiation of the notion that one causative factor is adequate to explain behavior and personality.

Narcissism Excessive self-love. Regarded by psychoanalysts as an early stage of psychosocial development.

Neurotic An individual characterized by a number of behavioral traits that exaggerate threat, distort reality, and give rise to rigidity or a restricted range of behavior. Anxiety, guilt, ambivalence, and sexual abnormality are among the neurotic's many handicapping traits.

Oedipus Complex A child's repressed desire to have sex relations with his mother. Oedipus was a character in the Greek play, *Oedipus Rex*, by Sophocles, who through a series of events won and married his own mother. When he discovered the truth he put out his eyes.

Paradoxical A contradictory situation or result. One may have a sensation of heat from plunging his arm in an icy tub. A drug may produce euphoria on one occasion and extreme despair on another. A mother may be kind to her child one day and be extremely punitive on another.

Paranoia A mental disorder characterized by the persistent feeling that one is being persecuted. One feels that others are his enemies—they are out to "get" him.

Parturition The process of giving birth. Delivery of the baby.

Pathology The study of disease. A condition of defectiveness, disease, or disorder.

Peak Experience Happy, ecstatic moments of life in which one's sensations are heightened and simultaneously appreciated. Experiences having strong affective components that play a positive role in further personality development.

Philosophy A well-thought-out system of values that guide one in making decisions and establishing goals.

Phobia Abnormal fears of some harmless object or situation. Fears stemming from the illogical connection of some neutral object or situation to a potentially dangerous event.

Polarity The pull of forces in opposite directions; *e. g.,* feelings of pleasure vs. sorrow; contrasting emotions of joy and pain.

Projective Technique An assessment device in which one is asked to interpret ambiguous stimuli such as inkblots, incomplete stories, and neutral pictures, or to draw pictures and act roles so that one's motives and tendencies toward action can be evaluated. One's personality is presumed to be "projected" in what he sees or reports.

Psychiatrist A medically trained specialist in the treatment of emotional difficulties. One qualified to use drugs in therapy, as contrasted to a consulting psychologist, who uses psychological approaches only.

Psychoanalyst One who is prepared to treat patients in the Freudian, Jungian, Adlerian, or neo-Freudian approaches.

Psychosomatic Disorders Various conditions in which symptoms of physical illness are generated by psychological stress.

Rapport A feeling of oneness between two or more persons. Unusual congeniality, mutual respect, and understanding.

Rationalization The use of irrational defenses or excuses for inappropriate behaviors. Thinking up socially approvable reasons for inadequate behavior.

Reference Group The set of individuals with whom a person identifies and from whom he derives his values; and by means of which he tests his behaviors and goals.

Regression Returning to a younger level of behavior after once having reached a more mature and appropriate mode of conduct.

Reliability A criterion of a good test. A test is reliable when it consistently gives the same results, on the same person, under similar circumstances in which an earlier, equivalent form of the test was used.

Repression Prevention of painful or dangerous thoughts from entering consciousness; refusing to think about unpleasant things.

Resistance The opposition of a client in therapy to revealing his inner self, to describing his conflicts; the effort to prevent suppressed thoughts from coming to the surface of consciousness.

Rut A period of high sexual drive on the part of a male animal; the female counterpart is "heat."

Sampling A characteristic of a test which requires that a sufficient number of examples or instances be assessed so that one has a representative view of the entirety.

Schizophrenia A general name for a number of serious emotional disturbances characterized by withdrawal, inappropriate emotional response, or lack of it; hallucinations, delusions. Actually, the word has fallen into psychological disrepute because it is so loosely used that it is really minimally descriptive.

Self-Actualization The process of becoming all or most of what one wishes to be and is capable of achieving; living at a level in which lower level needs are no longer dominant; the process of bringing into accord one's concept of self, one's ideal self, and one's potentialities.

Self-Fulfilling Prophecy The tendency for an individual to be, or behave, as others expect him to be or act; or, the inclination to become what one believes he can become.

SES A standard sociological abbreviation for socioeconomic status.

Sociometry The study of inter-personal likes and preferences of members of a group by means of columnar or graphical plotting of attractions or isolations. The graphs or columns are called **sociograms.**

Standardized A criterion of a good test. It is standardized when it has been given to a sufficiently large number of subjects that reliable norms, or standards, have been established.

Standardizing The process of establishing norms by collecting data on a large number of cases. Frequently used in connection with establishing norms for a test so that the scores have some measurable consistency and meaning.

Stereotype A conventional or typically consistent way of thinking or action—but not in a logical, data-based manner; "canned" thinking. Jews, blacks, New Yorkers, westerners are erroneously alleged to have certain traits by which they can be identified—according to legendary stereotypes.

Suggestibility A state of mind in which one is readily open to accept uncritically the ideas of another; or to behave according to a model or instruction provided by others, with little or no self-determination.

Synapse The functional, not necessarily physiological, connection between two neuroses. The point of resistance when a message, or nervous impulse, has to jump a gap between two neurons.

Syndrome A variety of typical behaviors or attitudes that are combined as a defense from, or response to, a given situation.

TAT Abbreviation for Thematic Apperception Test.

Temperament The characteristic mood of an individual; *e. g.,* phlegmatic, optimistic, grouchy, outgoing, etc.

Tension A feeling of disequilibrium. A condition of discomfort that may range from the organic irritation that is a part of motivation to a stage of distress that inhibits or distorts action; "uptight."

Theory A statement of general principles designed to explain the interacting relationship of a group of phenomena.

Therapeutic Having healing qualities. Those factors, and that help, which enhance the mental health of the individual.

Transference A condition in which the patient of a psychoanalyst falls in love with the analyst or transfers his hate or love for some key person in his life to the analyst.

Trauma Wound or injury. In psychology, the conditions that precipitate an emotional illness or disturbance.

Validity A criterion of a test characterized by items that really probe what is purported to be tested. A valid test is a *good* test in that it gets at the thing being assessed.

Vectors In a certain psychological orientation (field psychology), vectors refer to the representation of converging, conflicting, and diverging forces acting upon a unique individual who responds in terms of his current personality status.

BIBLIOGRAPHY

ADLER, ALFRED, *Understanding Human Nature*. New York: Greenburg Press, 1927, (New York: Premier Books, 1957).

AHMANN, J. STANLEY, and MARVIN D. GLOCK, *Evaluating Pupil Growth*, Third Edition. Boston: Allyn and Bacon, Inc., 1967.

Alcohol and Highway Safety: A Report to Congress. Washington, D. C.: U. S. Department of Transportation, 1968.

ALDRIDGE, JOHN W., *In the Country of the Young*. New York: Harper and Row, Publishers, 1969.

ALLAND, ALEXANDER, JR., *The Human Imperative*. New York: Columbia University Press, 1972.

ALLPORT, GORDON, *The Person in Psychology, Selected Essays*. Boston: Beacon Press, 1968.

ALLPORT, GORDON W., quoted in Hubert Bonner, *On Being Mindful of Man*. Boston: Houghton Mifflin Company, 1965.

Almanac and Yearbook. Pleasantville, New York: Reader's Digest Association, Inc., 1972.

AMOS, WILLIAM E., and CHARLES F. WELLFORD, eds., *Delinquency Prevention Theory and Practice*. Englewood Cliffs, N. J.: Prentice-Hall, Inc., 1967.

ANASTASI, ANNE, "Heredity, Environment, and the Question 'How?'" *Psychological Review*, 65, pp. 197–208, 1958.

ANDERSON, KENNETH E., ed., *Research on the Academically Talented Student*. Washington, D. C.: National Education Association, 1961.

ARGYRIS, CHRIS, "Essay Reviews: Beyond Freedom and Dignity," *Harvard Educational Review*, 41, pp. 550–567, 1971.

ASIMOV, ISAAC, "The Fantastic If," in H. W. Bernard and W. C. Huckins, eds., *Exploring Human Development*. Boston: Allyn and Bacon, Inc., 1972. From *Long Island News*, April 15, 1967.

AXLINE, VIRGINIA, *Dibs: In Search of Self*. Boston: Houghton Mifflin Company, 1964.

BAKAN, RITA, "Malnutrition and Learning," *Phi Delta Kappan*, 51, pp. 527–530, 1970.

BANE, MARY JO, and CHRISTOPHER JENCKS, "Five Myths About Your IQ," *Harper's*, Vol. 246, No. 1473, 28–40, 1973.

BANFIELD, EDWARD C., *The Unheavenly City*. Boston: Little, Brown and Company, 1970.

BARINBAUM, LEA, "Role Confusion in Adolescence," *Adolescence*, Vol. 6, No. 25, 121–127, 1972.

BARTLEY, S. HOWARD, "What Do You Mean 'Tired'?" in H. W. Bernard and W. C. Huckins, eds., *Psychosocial Dynamics of Effective Behavior*. Boston: Holbrook Press, Inc., 1971. From *Today's Education*, 58: 40–41, February, 1969.

BAUMRIND, DIANA, "From Each According to Her Ability," *School Review*, 80, pp. 161–197, 1972.

BECKER, ERNEST, *The Birth and Death of Meaning*. New York: The Free Press of Glencoe, 1962.

BEERS, CLIFFORD, *A Mind That Found Itself*. New York: Longmans, Green and Company, Inc., 1917.

BEIER, ERNST G., *The Silent Language of Psychotherapy*. Chicago: Aldine Publishing Company, 1967.

BENEDICT, RUTH, *Patterns of Culture*. New York: New American Library, (A Mentor Book), 1934.

BERNARD, HAROLD W., *Adolescent Development.* Scranton, Pa.: Intext Educational Publishers, 1971.

BERNARD, HAROLD W., *Psychology of Learning and Teaching,* Third Edition. New York: McGraw-Hill Book Company, 1972.

BERNARD, L. L., *Instinct, A Study of Social Psychology.* New York: Holt, Rinehart, and Winston, Inc., 1924.

BERNE, ERIC, *Games People Play.* New York: Grove Press, Inc., 1964.

BERRILL, N. J., "Human Potential," in D. W. Vermilye, ed., *Man in Perspective.* Washington, D. C.: American Personnel and Guidance Association, 1967.

BERSCHEID, ELLEN, and ELAINE WALSTER, "Beauty and the Best," *Psychology Today*, Vol. 5, No. 10, 42–46, 74, 1972.

BETTELHEIM, BRUNO, *The Informed Heart.* New York: The Macmillan Company, 1960.

BIERSTEDT, ROBERT, *The Social Order*, Third Edition. New York: McGraw-Hill Book Company, 1970.

BILLER, HENRY B., "Father Absence and the Personality Development of the Male Child," *Developmental Psychology*, 2, pp. 181–201, 1970.

BILLER, HENRY B., and L. J. BORSTELMANN, "Masculine Development: An Integrative Review," *Merrill-Palmer Quarterly*, 13, pp. 253–294, 1967.

BIRNBAUM, MAX, "Sense about Sensitivity Training," in H. W. Bernard and W. C. Huckins, eds., *Exploring Human Development.* Boston: Allyn and Bacon, Inc., 1972. From *Saturday Review*, Vol. 52, No. 46, 82–83ff., November, 1969.

BISCHOF, LEDFORD J., *Interpreting Personality Theories*, Second Edition. New York: Harper and Row, Publishers, 1964.

BLUM, RICHARD H., and associates, *Horatio Alger's Children.* San Francisco: Jossey-Bass, Inc., Publishers, 1972.

BONNER, HUBERT, *On Being Mindful of Man.* Boston: Houghton Mifflin Company, 1965.

BONNER, HUBERT, "The Proactive Personality," in J. F. T. Bugenthal, ed., *Challenges of Humanistic Psychology.* New York: McGraw-Hill Book Company, 1967.

BOROW, HENRY, ed., *Man in a World At Work.* Boston: Houghton Mifflin Company, 1964.

BOYER, WILLIAM H., and PAUL WALSH, "Are Children Born Unequal?" *Saturday Review*, Vol. 51, No. 42, 61–63, October 19, 1968.

BRONFENBRENNER, URIE, "The Changing American Child—A Speculative Analysis," in H. W. Bernard and W. C. Huckins, eds., *Exploring Human Development.* Boston: Allyn and Bacon, Inc., 1972. From *Journal of Social Issues*, 17, pp. 6–18, 1961.

BROWN, FREDERICK G., *Principles of Educational and Psychological Testing.* Hinsdale, Illinois: The Dryden Press, Inc., 1970.

BROWN, ROGER, and URSULA BELLUGI, "Three Processes in The Child's Acquisition of Syntax," *Harvard Educational Review*, 34, pp. 133–151, 1964.

BRUCE, PAUL, "Three Forces in Psychology and Their Ethical and Educational Implications," *Educational Forum*, 30, pp. 277–285, 1966.

BRUNELLE, EUGENE A., "The Biology of Meaning," *Journal of Creative Behavior*, Vol. 7, No. 1, 1–14, 1973.

BRUNER, JEROME, "Culture, Politics, and Pedagogy," *Saturday Review*, Vol. 51, No. 20, 69–72, May 18, 1968.

BRUNER, JEROME S., "The Skill of Relevance or the Relevance of Skills," *Saturday Review*, Vol. 53, No. 14, 66–68, April 18, 1970.

BUGENTHAL, JAMES F. T., ed., *Challenges of Humanistic Psychology.* New York: McGraw-Hill Book Company, 1967.

CANTRIL, HADLEY, "A Fresh Look at the Human Design," in J. F. T. Bugenthal, ed., *Challenges of Humanistic Psychology.* New York: McGraw-Hill Book Company, 1967.

CARROLL, HERBERT, *Genius in the Making.* New York: McGraw-Hill Book Company, 1940.

CATTELL, R. B., D. B. BLEWETT, and J. R. BELOFF, "The Inheritance of Personality," *American Journal of Human Genetics,* 7, pp. 122–146, 1955.

CERVANTES, LUCIUS F., "Family Background, Primary Relationships, and the High School Dropout," in H. W. Bernard and W. C. Huckins, eds., *Exploring Human Development.* Boston: Allyn and Bacon, Inc., 1972. From *Journal of Marriage and the Family.* 27, pp. 218–223, 1965.

CHABON, IRWIN, *Awake and Aware: Participation in Childbirth through Psychoprophylaxis.* New York: Delacorte Press, 1966. (Available as a Dell paperback.)

CHAPLIN, J. P., *Dictionary of Psychology.* New York: Dell Publishing Company, Inc., 1968.

CAVIOR, NORMAN, and DAVID W. LOMBARDI, "Developmental Aspects of Judgment of Physical Attractiveness in Children," *Developmental Psychology,* 8, pp. 67–91, 1973.

CHILDS, G. B., "Is the Work Ethic Realistic in an Age of Automation?" in H. W. Bernard and W. C. Huckins, eds., *Psychosocial Dynamics of Effective Behavior.* Boston: Holbrook Press, Inc., 1971. From *Phi Delta Kappan,* 46, pp. 370–375, 1965.

CICIRELLI, VICTOR G., "The Effect of Sibling Relationship on Concept Learning of Young Children Taught by Child-Teachers," *Child Development,* 43, pp. 283–287, 1972.

CLAUSEN, JOHN A., "Family Structure, Socialization, and Personality," in L. W. Hoffman and M. L. Hoffman, eds., *Review of Child Development Research,* V. 2. New York: Russell Sage Foundation, 1966.

COHEN, DAVID K., "Does IQ Matter?" *Commentary,* Vol. 53, No. 4, 51–59, April, 1972.

COLEMAN, JAMES S., *The Adolescent Society.* New York: The Free Press of Glencoe, 1961.

COLES, ROBERT, "Violence in Ghetto Children," *Children,* 14, p. 102, May/June, 1967.

COMBS, ARTHUR W., and DONALD SNYGG, *Individual Behavior, A Perceptual Approach to Behavior,* rev. ed. New York: Harper and Row, Publishers, 1959.

COTTLE, THOMAS J., "Parent and Child—The Hazards of Equality," *Saturday Review,* Vol. 52, No. 5, 16–19, February 1, 1969.

CRISWELL, ELEANOR, and SEVERIN PETERSON, "The Whole Soul Catalog," *Psychology Today,* Vol. 5, No. 11, 57–64, April, 1972.

CRONBACH, LEE J., *Essentials of Psychological Testing.* New York: Harper and Row, Publishers, 1960.

CRUTCHFIELD, RICHARD S., "Conformity and Character," *American Psychologist,* 10, pp. 191–198, 1955.

DAVIS, FRANK G., *Pupil Personnel Service.* Scranton, Penna.: International Textbook Company, 1948.

DAVIS, JOHN M., "Biological Psychiatry," *American Journal of Psychiatry,* Vol. 130, No. 1, 87–88, 1973.

DAYTON, DELBERT H., "Early Malnutrition and Human Development," *Children,* Vol. 16, No. 6, 210–217, November–December, 1969.

DELGADO, JOSÉ M. R., "Brain Manipulation: Psychocivilized Direction of Behavior," *Humanist,* Vol. 32, No. 2, 10–15, March/April, 1972.

DENNISON, GEORGE, *The Lives of Children.* New York: Random House, 1969.

DEVER, JAMES, *A Dictionary of Psychology.* Harmondsworth, Middlesex, England: Penguin Books, Ltd., 1952.

DEWEY, JOHN, *How We Think.* Boston: D. C. Heath and Company, 1910.

DICK-READ, GRANTLEY, *Childbirth Without Fear: The Principles and Practices of Natural Childbirth*, Second Edition, rev. New York: Harper and Row, Publishers, Inc., 1958.

DURANT, WILL, and ARIEL DURANT, *The Lessons of History.* New York: Simon and Schuster, 1968.

ECKSTEIN, GUSTAV, *The Body Has a Head.* New York: Harper and Row, Publishers, 1970.

EISELEY, LOREN, "An Evolutionist Looks at Modern Man," in H. W. Bernard and W. C. Huckins, eds., *Psychosocial Dynamics of Effective Behavior.* Boston: Holbrook Press, Inc., 1971. From Thruelson and Kobler, *Adventures of the Mind.* Alfred A. Knopf, 1961.

EISENBERG, LEON, "A Developmental Approach to Adolescence," in H. W. Bernard, ed., *Readings in Adolescent Development.* Scranton, Pa.: International Textbook Company, 1969. From *Children*, Vol. 12, No. 4, 131–135, 1965.

ELAM, STANLEY M., "Heredity, Race, Intelligence, and Environment," *Phi Delta Kappan*, 51, pp. 509–514; 53: p. 297, 1972.

ELAM, STANLEY M., "The Age of Accountability Dawns in Texarkana," *Phi Delta Kappan*, 51, pp. 509–514, 1970.

ELLIS, ALBERT, "The Essence of Rational Therapy," in B. N. Ard, Jr., ed., *Counseling and Psychotherapy.* Palo Alto, Calif., Science and Behavior Books, 1966.

ELLIS, ALBERT, "Humanistic Psychotherapy: A Revolutionary Approach," *The Humanist*, Vol. 32, No. 1, 24–27, 1972.

Encyclopedia Almanac. New York: The New York Times, 1970.

ENELOW, ALLEN J., "Is Psychoanalysis Viable?" *American Journal of Orthopsychiatry*, 43, pp. 258–259, 1973.

ERICKSON, DONALD A., "The Persecution of LeRoy Garber," *School Review*, 78, pp. 81–90, 1969.

ERIKSON, ERIK H., "Identity and the Life Cycle," *Psychological Issues*, Vol. 1, No. 1, monograph 1, 1959.

ERIKSON, ERIK H., *Identity, Youth and Crisis.* New York: W. W. Norton and Company, Inc., 1968.

ERIKSON, ERIK H., *Insight and Responsibility.* New York: W. W. Norton and Company, Inc., 1964.

ERIKSON, ERIK H., "Reflections on the Dissent of Contemporary Youth," *Daedalus*, 99, pp. 154–176, 1970.

"Ethical Forum: IQ and Race," *The Humanist*, Vol. 32, No. 1, 4–18, January–February, 1972.

EVANS, RICHARD I., *Dialogue with Erik Erikson.* New York: Harper and Row, Publishers, 1967.

EYSENCK, H. J., *Handbook of Abnormal Psychology.* New York: Basic Books, Inc., 1961.

EYSENCK, HANS J., "New Ways in Psychotherapy," *Psychology Today*, Vol. 1, No. 2, 39–47, June, 1967.

"Facts About Mental Illness," *Almanac and Yearbook.* Pleasantville, New York: Reader's Digest Association, 1972.

FAIRBANK, RUTH E., "The Subnormal Child—Seventeen Years After," *Mental Hygiene*, 17, pp. 177–208, 1933.

FEHR, ALEX J., "Automation—A Challenge to America's Social Wisdom," in *Preserving the Individual in an Age of Automation*. Hartford, Conn: Connecticut Mutual Life Insurance Company, 1963.

FERGUSON-SMITH, M. A., "Sex Chronation, Klinefelters' Syndrome and Mental Deficiency," in K. L. Moore, ed., *The Sex Chromatin*. Philadelphia: W. B. Saunders, 1966.

FESHBACK, SEYMOUR, and NORMA FESHBACK, "The Young Aggressor," *Psychology Today*, Vol. 6, No. 11, 90–95, 1973.

FLANDERS, NED A., *Teacher Influence, Pupil Attitudes, and Achievement*. Washington, D. C.: Office of Education, U. S. Department of Health, Education, and Welfare, 1965.

FORT, JOEL, "The Drug Explosion," *Playboy*, Vol. 19, No. 9, 139–142, September, 1972.

FORT, JOEL, *The Pleasure Seekers: The Drug Crisis, Youth and Society*. Indianapolis: The Bobbs-Merrill Company, 1969.

FOSTER, FLORENCE P., "The Human Relationships of Creative Individuals," *Journal of Creative Behavior*, 2, pp. 111–118, 1968.

FRAIBERG, SELMA, "The Origin of Human Bonds," in H. W. Bernard and W. C. Huckins, eds., *Psychosocial Dynamics of Effective Behavior*. Boston: Holbrook Press, Inc., 1971. From *Commentary*, Vol. 44, No. 6, 51–57, 1967.

FRANK, LAWRENCE K., "The Adolescent and the Family," in National Society for the Study of Education, 43rd Yearbook, *Adolescence*. Chicago: University of Chicago Press, 1944.

FRANK, PHILLIP, *Modern Science and Its Philosophy*. Cambridge, Mass.: Harvard University Press, 1949.

FRANKEL, CHARLES, "The Awful Idea of Being an Individual," in H. W. Bernard and W. C. Huckins, eds., *Psychosocial Dynamics of Effective Behavior*. Boston: Holbrook Press, Inc., 1971. From *The Love of Anxiety and Other Essays*. New York: Harper and Row, Publishers, 1965.

FREEDMAN, D. G., "An Ethological Approach to the Genetical Study of Human Behavior," in S. G. Vandenberg, ed., *Methods and Goals in Human Behavior Genetics*. New York: Academic Press, 1965.

FREUD, SIGMUND, *An Autobiographical Study*. London: Hogarth Press, 1935.

FREUD, SIGMUND, *Civilization and Its Discontents*. London: Hogarth Press, 1930. (Also in paperback, W. W. Norton and Company, 1962.)

FREUD, SIGMUND, *A General Introduction to Psychoanalysis*. New York: Garden City Publishing Company, Inc., 1943.

FREUD, SIGMUND, *The Interpretation of Dreams*. New York: Basic Books, Inc., 1900, 1955.

FREUD, SIGMUND, *The Standard Edition of the Complete Psychological Works*, 24 Vols., Translated by James Strachey. London: Hogarth Press, 1953–55.

FROHMAN, CHARLES, and EDWARD DOMINO, "Schizophrenia Laid to Chemical Cause," reported in *Portland Oregonian*, February 24, 1972.

FULLMER, DANIEL W., and HAROLD W. BERNARD, *Counseling: Content and Process*. Chicago: Science Research Associates, 1964.

FULLMER, DANIEL W., and HAROLD W. BERNARD, *Family Consultation*. Boston: Houghton Mifflin Company, 1968.

GALLAGHER, JAMES J., *Teaching the Gifted Child*. Boston: Allyn and Bacon, Inc., 1964.

GARDNER, JOHN W., *Self-Renewal: The Individual and the Innovative Society*. New York: Harper and Row, Publishers, 1964.

GARN, STANLEY M., "Body Size and Its Implications," in L. W. Hoffman and M. L. Hoffman, eds., *Review of Child Development Research*, Vol. 2. New York: Russell Sage Foundation, 1966.

"A General Classification of Drugs and Volatile Chemicals of Potential Abuse," Western Institute of Drug Problems Publication. Corvallis, Oregon: Continuing Education Books, 1972.

GETZELS, JACOB W., and PHILIP W. JACKSON, *Creativity and Intelligence.* New York: John Wiley and Sons, Inc., 1962.

GETZELS, J. W., and P. W. JACKSON, "The Highly Intelligent and the Highly Creative Adolescent: A Summary of Some Research Findings," in R. G. Kuhlen and G. G. Thompson, eds., *Psychological Studies of Human Development.* New York: Appleton-Century-Crofts, 1963.

GILMORE, JAMES V., "Parental Influences on Academic Achievement," *Normline*, Vol. 2, No. 2, 1–4, (Published by Test Department, Harcourt, Brace and Jovanovich, Inc.) 1969.

GINZBERG, E., S. W. GINZBERG, S. ALEXRAD, and J. L. HERMA, *Occupational Choice: An Approach to a General Theory.* New York: Columbia University Press, 1951.

GLASS, BENTLY, "Evolution in Human Hands," *Phi Delta Kappan*, 50, pp. 506–510, May, 1969.

GLASSER, WILLIAM, "Reality Therapy: A Realistic Approach to the Young Offender," in B. N. Ard, Jr., ed., *Counseling and Psychotherapy.* Palo Alto, California: Science and Behavior Books, 1966.

GLASSER, WILLIAM, "Understanding the Adolescent," Lecture, Providence Hospital, Portland, Oregon, January 14, 1970.

GLUECK, SHELDON, and ELEANOR GLUECK, *Toward a Typology of Juvenile Offenders: Implications for Therapy and Prevention.* New York: Grune and Stratton, 1970.

GLUECK, SHELDON, and ELEANOR GLUECK, *Unraveling Juvenile Delinquency.* (Published for the Commonwealth Fund) Cambridge, Mass.: Harvard University Press, 1950.

GODDARD, JAMES L., "The Menace of Drug Abuse," *American Education*, Vol. 2, No. 5, 4–7, May, 1966.

GOLDENSON, ROBERT M., *The Encyclopedia of Human Behavior.* Garden City, New York: Doubleday and Company, Inc., 1970.

GOLDSCHMIDT, WALTER, "A Word in Your Ear," a record of a radio series broadcast, *The Ways of Mankind*, prepared by the Center for the Study of Liberal Education for Adults, University of Chicago, 1953.

GOOD, CARTER V., ed., *Dictionary of Education.* New York: McGraw-Hill Book Company, 1959.

GOODENOUGH, FLORENCE L., and LEONA E. TYLER, *Developmental Psychology*, Third Edition. New York: Appleton-Century-Crofts, 1959.

GOODMAN, LILLIAN, "Citizen Power: Tutoring for Credit," *American Education*, Vol. 7, No. 3, 27, April, 1971.

GOODMAN, PAUL, "Freedom and Learning: The Need for Choice," *Saturday Review*, Vol. 51, No. 20, 73–75, May 18, 1968.

GORDON, IRA J., ed., *Early Childhood Education*, 71st Yearbook of the National Society for the Study of Education, Part II. Chicago: University of Chicago Press, 1972.

GOTTESMAN, I. I., "Genetic Variance in Adaptive Personality," *Journal of Child Psychology and Psychiatry*, 7, pp. 199–208, 1966.

GOTTLIEB, DAVID, "Poor Youth: A Study in Forced Alienation," in H. W. Bernard and W. C. Huckins, eds., *Psychosocial Dynamics of Effective Behavior.* Boston: Holbrook Press, Inc., 1971. From *Journal of Social Issues*, Vol. 25, No. 2, 91–120, 1969.

GRONLUND, NORMAN E., *Measurement and Evaluation in Teaching.* New York: The Macmillan Company, 1971.

GUILFORD, J. P., *The Nature of Human Intelligence.* New York: McGraw-Hill Book Company, 1967.

GUILFORD, J. P., *Personality.* New York: McGraw-Hill Book Company, 1959.

GUILFORD, J. P., "Some Misconceptions Regarding Measurement of Creative Talents," *Journal of Creative Behavior*, Vol. 5, No. 2, 77–87, 1971.

HALL, R. V., and M. BRODEN, "Behavior Changes in Brain-injured Children through Social Reinforcement," *Journal of Experimental Child Psychology*, 5, pp. 463–479, 1967.

HALLECK, SEYMOUR L., "Hypotheses of Student Unrest," in H. W. Bernard and W. C. Huckins, eds., *Psychosocial Dynamics of Effective Behavior.* Boston: Holbrook Press, Inc., 1971. From *Phi Delta Kappan*, Vol. 50, No. 1, 2–9, 1968.

HALLMAN, RALPH J., "Techniques of Creative Teaching," *Journal of Creative Behavior*, 11, pp. 325–330, 1967.

HAMACHEK, DON E., "Characteristics of Good Teachers and Implications for Teacher Education," *Phi Delta Kappan*, 50, pp. 341–345, 1969.

HARLOW, HARRY F., "The Nature of Love," in H. W. Bernard and W. C. Huckins, eds., *Exploring Human Development.* Boston: Allyn and Bacon, Inc., 1972. From *The American Psychologist*, 13, pp. 673–685, 1958.

HAVEMANN, ERNEST, "Alternatives to Analysis," *Playboy*, 16, pp. 133–134+.

HAVIGHURST, ROBERT J., "Conditions Productive of Superior Children," *Teachers College Record*, 62, pp. 524–531, 1961.

HAVIGHURST, ROBERT J., "Youth in Exploration and Man Emergent," in H. Borow, ed., *Man in a World at Work.* Boston: Houghton Mifflin Company, 1964.

HAVIGHURST, ROBERT J., and BERNICE L. NEUGARTEN, *Society and Education*, Third Edition. Boston: Allyn and Bacon, Inc., 1967.

HAWORTH, MARY R., "Doll Play and Puppetry," in A. I. Rabin, ed., *Projective Techniques in Personality Assessment.* New York: Springer Publishing Company, Inc., 1968.

HAYAKAWA, S. I., "Semantics and Sexuality," *ETC.: A Review of General Semantics*, Vol. 25, No. 2, 135–153, 1968a.

HAYAKAWA, S. I., "Who's Bringing Up Your Children?" *ETC.: A Review of General Semantics*, Vol. 25, No. 3, 299–308, 1968b.

The Health Consequences of Smoking—A Report to the Surgeon General: 1971. Washington, D. C.: U. S. Department of Health, Education, and Welfare, 1971.

HEBB, D. O., "Cognition and Physiological Effects of Perceptual Isolation," in P. Solomon, *et al.*, eds., *Sensory Deprivation.* Cambridge, Mass.: Harvard University Press, 1961.

HEFFERNAN, HELEN, "Challenge or Pressure?" in R. C. Doll and R. S. Fleming, eds., *Children Under Pressure.* Columbus, Ohio: Charles E. Merrill Books, Inc., 1966.

HERRICK, NEAL Q., "Who's Unhappy at Work and Why," *Manpower*, Vol. 4, No. 1, 2–7, 1972.

HERRIOTT, ROBERT E., "Some Social Determinants of Educational Aspirations," *Harvard Educational Review*, 33, pp. 157–177, 1963.

HERRNSTEIN, RICHARD, "I. Q." *Atlantic*, Vol. 228, No. 3, 43–64, September, 1971.

HERZBERG, FREDERICK, *Work and the Nature of Man.* Cleveland: The World Publishing Company, 1966.

HETHERINGTON, E. MAVIS, "Girls Without Fathers," *Psychology Today*, Vol. 6, No. 9, 46–52, 1973.

HIGHET, GILBERT, *Man's Unconquerable Mind.* New York: Columbia University Press, 1954. (Condensed and Reprinted in *Reader's Digest*, Vol. 100, No. 598, 274–287, February, 1972.)

HILGARD, ERNEST R., *Theories of Learning*, Second Edition. New York: Appleton-Century-Crofts, Inc., 1956.

HOHMAN, LESLIE B., *As the Twig is Bent.* New York: The Macmillan Company, 1947.

HOLLINGWORTH, H. L., *Mental Growth and Decline.* New York: Appleton-Century-Crofts, Inc., 1928.

HORNEY, KAREN, *Neurosis and Human Growth: The Struggle toward Self-realization.* New York: W. W. Norton and Company, 1950.

HORNEY, KAREN, *The Neurotic Personality of Our Time.* New York: W. W. Norton and Company, Inc., 1937.

HUNT, J. MCVICKER, "Has Compensatory Education Failed? Has It Been Attempted?" *Harvard Educational Review*, 39, pp. 278–300, 1969.

HUNT, J. MCVICKER, Interviewed by Patricia Pine, "Where Education Begins," *American Education*, Vol. 4, No. 9, 15–19, October, 1968.

HURLEY, RODGER L., *Poverty and Mental Retardation: A Causal Relationship.* New York: Random House, 1969, (Vintage Books).

HUXLEY, ALDOUS, "Can We Be Well Educated?" *Esquire*, 47, 112ff., December, 1956.

HYMES, DELL H., "The Functions of Speech," in J. P. DeCecco, ed., *The Psychology of Language, Thought, and Instruction.* New York: Holt, Rinehart and Winston, Inc., 1967.

JAHODA, MARIE, *Current Concepts of Positive Mental Health.* New York: Basic Books, Inc., 1958.

JAMES, WILLIAM, *Talks to Teachers on Psychology.* New York: Henry Holt and Company 1899, (New Edition, 1939).

JANIS, IRVING L., GEORGE F. MAHL, JEROME KAGAN, and ROBERT R. HOLT, *Personality: Dynamics, Development, and Assessment.* New York: Harcourt, Brace and World, Inc., 1969.

JEFFERY, C. RAY, and INA A. JEFFERY, "Prevention through the Family," in W. E. Amos and C. F. Wellford, eds., *Delinquency Prevention Theory and Practice.* Englewood Cliffs, N. J.: Prentice-Hall, Inc., 1967.

JENKINS, RICHARD L., "Classification of Behavior Problems of Children," *American Journal of Psychiatry*, Vol. 125, No. 8, 1032–1039, 1969.

JENSEN, ARTHUR R., "The Case for I. Q. Tests: Reply to McClelland," *The Humanist*, Vol. 32, No. 1, 14, January–February, 1972.

JENSEN, ARTHUR R., "How Much Can We Boost IQ and Scholastic Achievement?" *Harvard Educational Review*, 39, pp. 1–123, 1969.

JOHNSON, WENDELL, *People in Quandaries: The Semantics of Personal Adjustment.* New York: Harper and Row, Publishers, 1946.

JONES, ERNEST, *The Life and Work of Sigmund Freud.* New York: Basic Books, Inc., 1961.

JONES, MARY C., "Psychological Correlates of Somatic Development," *Child Development*, 36, pp. 899–911, 1965.

JUNG, CARL G., *Contributions to Analytical Psychology.* New York: Harcourt, Brace and World, 1928.

JUNG, CARL G., *Modern Man in Search of a Soul.* New York: Harcourt, Brace and World, 1933.

KAGAN, JEROME, "The Child: His Struggle for Identity," *Saturday Review*, Vol. 51, No. 49, 80–82, December, 1968.

KAGAN, JEROME, "The Concept of Intelligence," *The Humanist*, Vol. 32, No. 1, 7–8, 1972.

KAGAN, JEROME, "Inadequate Evidence and Illogical Conclusions," *Harvard Educational Review*, 39, pp. 274–277, 1969.

KALLMANN, FRANZ J., and GERHARD SANDER, "Twin Studies on Senescence," in

R. G. Kuhlen and G. G. Thompson, eds., *Psychological Studies of Human Development*. New York: Appleton-Century-Crofts, 1963.

KAPLAN, ABRAHAM, "The Life of Dialogue," Lecture, Nobel Conference, Gustavus Adolphus College, St. Peter, Minnesota, 1969.

KAPLAN, HAROLD, "Life in the Cage—Beyond Freedom and Dignity," *Commentary*, Vol. 53, No. 2, 82–86, 1972.

KATEB, GEORGE, "Toward a Wordless World," (A review of B. F. Skinner, *Beyond Freedom and Dignity*), *Atlantic*, Vol. 228, No. 4, 122–125, October, 1971.

KEMP, BARBARA H., *The Youth We Haven't Served*. Washington, D. C.: U. S. Department of Health, Education, and Welfare, 1966.

KENISTON, KENNETH, "College Students and Children in Developmental Institutions," in H. W. Bernard and W. C. Huckins, eds., *Psychosocial Dynamics of Effective Behavior*. Boston: Holbrook Press, Inc., 1971.

KINKADE, KATHLEEN, "Commune: A Walden Two Experiment," *Psychology Today*, Vol. 6, No. 8, 35–42, 1973.

KLEITMAN, NORMAN, *Sleep and Wakefulness*, rev. ed. Chicago: University of Chicago Press, 1963.

KLINE, NATHAN S., "The Future of Drugs and Drugs of the Future," *Journal of Social Issues*, Vol. 27, No. 3, 73–87, 1971.

KLOPFER, BRUNO, MARY D. AINSWORTH, WALTER G. KLOPFER, and ROBERT R. HOLT, *Developments in the Rorschach Technique*. Yonkers-on-Hudson, New York: World Book Company, 1954.

KLUCKHOHN, CLYDE, and HENRY A. MURRAY with the collaboration of DAVID M. SCHNEIDER, *Personality in Nature, Society, and Culture*. New York: Alfred A. Knopf, Inc., 1948, 1953.

KONOPKA, GISELA, "Formation of Values in the Developing Person," *American Journal of Orthopsychiatry*, 43, pp. 86–96, 1973.

KORNER, ANNELIESE F., "Individual Differences at Birth: Implications for Early Experience and Later Development," *American Journal of Orthopsychiatry*, Vol. 41, No. 4, 608–619, 1971.

KRECH, DAVID, "Psychoneurobiochemeducation," in H. W. Bernard and W. C. Huckins, eds., *Exploring Human Development*. Boston: Allyn and Bacon, Inc., 1972. From *Phi Delta Kappan*, 50, pp. 370–375, 1969.

KRILL, DONALD F., "Existential Psychotherapy and the Problem of Anomie," in H. W. Bernard and W. C. Huckins, eds., *Psychosocial Dynamics of Effective Behavior*. Boston: Holbrook Press, Inc., 1971. From *Social Work*, Vol. 14, No. 2, 33–49, April, 1969.

KRUMBOLTZ, JOHN D., *Behavioral Counseling*. New York: Holt, Rinehart and Winston, Inc., 1969.

KRUMBOLTZ, JOHN D., Panel discussion, American Personnel and Guidance Association, Annual Convention, Chicago, March 27, 1972.

KRUMBOLTZ, JOHN D., ed., *Revolution in Counseling*. Boston: Houghton Mifflin Company, 1966.

KUBIE, LAWRENCE S., "Hidden Brain Power," *Saturday Review*, 39, p. 26, October 13, 1956.

KURTZ, RICHARD, and MICHAEL HIRT, "Body Attitude and Physical Health," *Clinical Psychology*, 26, pp. 149–151, 1970.

LAUFER, MAURICE W., "Medications, Learning, and Behavior," *Phi Delta Kappan*, 52, pp. 169–170, November, 1970.

LEAR, JOHN, "Spinning the Thread of Life," *Saturday Review*, Vol. 52, No. 14, 63–66, April 5, 1969.

LEDERBERG, JOSHUA, "Humanics and Genetic Engineering," in H. W. Bernard and W. C. Huckins, eds., *Exploring Human Development*. Boston: Allyn and Bacon, Inc., 1972. From *1970 Yearbook of Science and the Future*, (Copyright, 1969, by Encyclopaedia Britannica, Inc.)

LEWIN, KURT, RONALD LIPPITT, and RALPH K. WHITE, "Patterns of Aggressive Behavior in Experimentally Created Social Climates," *Journal of Social Psychology*, 10, pp. 271–299, 1939.

LIEBERMAN, MYRON, "Education in New Cities," *Phi Delta Kappan*, 53, pp. 407–411, March, 1972.

LINDSEY, BRYAN L., and JAMES W. CUNNINGHAM, "Behavior Modification: Some Doubts and Dangers," *Phi Delta Kappan*, Vol. 54, No. 9, 596–597, 1973.

LIN-FU, JANE S., "New Hope for Babies of Rh Negative Mothers," *Children*, Vol. 16, No. 1, 23–27, 1969.

LIPTON, AARON, "Classroom Behavior: Messages from Children," *Elementary School Journal*, 71, pp. 254–261, 1971.

LOMBROSO, CESARE, *Crime: Its Causes and Remedies.* Boston: Little, Brown and Company, 1918.

"LSD Some Questions and Answers," *Public Health Service Publication No. 1828.* Washington, D. C.: U. S. Department of Health, Education, and Welfare, 1968.

McCLELLAND, DAVID, *The Achieving Society.* New York: Van Nostrand Reinhold, 1961.

McCLELLAND, DAVID, "IQ Tests and Assessing Competence," *The Humanist*, Vol. 32, No. 1, 9–12, January–February, 1972.

McCONVILLE, BRIAN J., and ARJUN P. PURHIT, "Classifying Confusion: A Study of the Results of Inpatient Treatment in a Multidisciplinary Children's Center," *American Journal of Orthopsychiatry*, Vol. 43, No. 3, 411–417, 1973.

McCORD, WILLIAM, and JOAN McCORD, *Origins of Crime.* New York: Columbia University Press, 1959.

McCREARY, EUGENE, "Some Positive Characteristics of Disadvantaged Learners and Their Implications for Education," in S. W. Webster, ed., *The Disadvantaged Learner.* San Francisco: Chandler Publishing Company, 1966.

McCULLY, C. HAROLD, *Challenge for Change in Counselor Education*, (Compiled by Lyle L. Miller). Minneapolis: Burgess Publishing Company, 1969.

McDONALD, FREDERICK J., "The Influence of Learning Theories on Education," *Theories of Learning and Instruction*, in National Society for the Study of Education, 63rd Yearbook, Part I. Chicago: University of Chicago Press, 1964.

MacKINNON, DONALD W., "Conditions for Effective Personality Change," in H. W. Bernard and W. C. Huckins, eds., *Psychosocial Dynamics of Effective Behavior.* Boston: Holbrook Press, Inc., 1971b. From *Nurturing Individual Potential.* Washington, D. C.: Association for Supervision and Curriculum Development, 1964.

MacKINNON, DONALD W., "Creativity and Transliminal Experience," *Journal of Creative Behavior*, Vol. 5, No. 4, 227–241, Fourth Quarter, 1971.

MALTZMAN, IRVING, "Thinking: From a Behavioristic Point of View," in J. P. DeCecco, ed., *The Psychology of Language, Thought, and Instruction.* New York: Holt, Rinehart and Winston, Inc., 1967. From *Psychological Review*, 62, pp. 275–286, 1955.

MANN, ERIKA, *School for Barbarians.* New York: Modern Age Books, 1938.

Manpower Report of the President, Washington, D. C.: U. S. Department of Labor, 1970, 1972.

MARSHALL, DONALD S., "Sexuality—Too Much in Mangaia," *Psychology Today*, Vol. 4, No. 9, 43–44, February, 1971.

MASLOW, ABRAHAM H., *Motivation and Personality.* New York: Harper and Row, Publishers, 1954, 1970.

MASLOW, ABRAHAM H., "Music Education and Peak Experience," in H. W. Bernard and W. C. Huckins, eds., *Exploring Human Development.* Boston: Allyn and Bacon, Inc., 1971. From *Music Educators Journal*, Vol. 54, 6, 72–75, February, 1968.

MASLOW, ABRAHAM H., "Self-Actualization and Beyond," in J. F. T. Bugenthal, ed., *Challenges of Humanistic Psychology.* New York: McGraw-Hill Book Company, 1967.

MATHIS, B. CLAUDE, JOHN W. COTTON, LEE SECHREST, *Psychological Foundations of Education.* New York: Academic Press, 1970.

MATSON, FLOYD W., "Humanistic Theory: The Third Revolution in Psychology," *Humanist*, Vol. 31, No. 2, 7–11, March–April, 1971.

MAY, ROLLO, *Love and Will.* New York: W. W. Norton and Company, Inc., 1969.

MEAD, GEORGE H., *Mind, Self and Society.* Chicago: University of Chicago Press, 1934.

MEAD, MARGARET, "The Changing Significance of Food," *American Scientist*, 58, pp. 176–201, March–April, 1970.

MEAD, MARGARET, *Coming of Age in Samoa.* New York: William Morrow and Company, Inc., 1928.

MEAD, MARGARET, *Sex and Temperament.* New York: William Morrow and Company, Inc., 1935. (Also a Mentor Book.)

MEAD, MARGARET, "Youth Revolt: The Future is Now," *Saturday Review*, Vol. 53, No. 2, 23–25, January 10, 1970.

MEHRABIAN, ALBERT, "Communication without Words," mimeographed report, 1972.

MENNINGER, KARL, *The Human Mind.* New York: Garden City Publishing Company, Inc., 1930.

MENNINGER, KARL, WITH M. MAYMAN AND P. PRUYSER, *The Vital Balance.* New York: Viking Press, 1963.

MESSENGER, JOHN C., "Sexuality—The Lack of the Irish," *Psychology Today*, Vol. 4, No. 9, 41–42, February, 1971.

MEYER, JAMES A., "Suburbia: A Wasteland of Disadvantaged Youth and Negligent Schools?" in H. W. Bernard and W. C. Huckins, eds., *Exploring Human Development.* Boston: Allyn and Bacon, Inc., 1972. From *Phi Delta Kappan*, 50, pp. 575–578, 1969.

MILES, CATHERINE COX, "Gifted Children," in Leonard Carmichael, ed., *Manual of Child Psychology*, Second Edition. New York: John Wiley and Sons, Inc., 1954.

MILLER, GEORGE A., "Psychology as a Means of Promoting Human Welfare," in H. W. Bernard and W. C. Huckins, eds., *Exploring Human Development.* Boston: Allyn and Bacon, Inc., 1972. From *American Psychologist*, 24, pp. 1063–1075, 1969.

MINUCHIN, PATRICIA, "Correlates of Curiosity and Exploratory Behavior in Preschool Disadvantaged Children," *Child Development*, 42, pp. 939–950, 1971.

MONEY-KYRLE, R. E., "Towards a Common Aim—A Psycho-Analytical Contribution to Ethics," *British Journal of Medical Psychology*, 20, pp. 105–117, 1944.

MONTAGU, M. F. ASHLEY, "Chromosomes and Crime," *Psychology Today*, Vol. 2, No. 5, 42–49, October, 1968.

MONTAGU, M. F. ASHLEY, "Constitutional and Prenatal Factors in Infant and

Child Health," in W. E. Martin and C. B. Stendler, eds., *Readings in Child Development*. New York: Harcourt, Brace and Jovanovich, Inc., 1954.

MOSKOWITZ, RONALD, "Leaving the Drug World Behind," *American Education*, Vol. 6, No. 1, 3–6, January–February, 1970.

MOUSTAKAS, CLARK, *The Authentic Teacher*. Cambridge, Mass.: Howard A. Doyle Publishing Company, 1966.

MURPHY, GARDNER, "Parapsychology: New Neighbor or Unwelcome Guest," *Psychology Today*, Vol. 1, No. 12, 52–55, May, 1967.

MURPHY, GARDNER, "Where is the Human Race Going? in H. W. Bernard and W. C. Huckins, eds., *Psychosocial Dynamics of Effective Behavior*. Boston: Holbrook Press, Inc., 1971.

NASH, JOHN, *Developmental Psychology: A Psychobiological Approach*. Englewood Cliffs, N. J.: Prentice-Hall, Inc., 1970.

NASH, ROBERT J., and RUSSELL M. AGNE, "Career Education: Earning a Living or Living a Life?" *Phi Delta Kappan*, Vol. 54, No. 6, 373–378, 1973.

NEALE, DANIEL C., "Aversive Control of Behavior," *Phi Delta Kappan*, Vol. 50, No. 6, 335–338, February, 1969.

NEWTON, NILES, "Childbirth and Culture," *Psychology Today*, Vol. 4, No. 6, 74–75, November, 1970.

O'CONNOR, JOHNSON, "Redirecting Americans," *Atlantic*, 167, pp. 193–200, 1941.

OLSEN, JAMES, "Challenge of the Poor to the Schools," in H. W. Bernard and W. C. Huckins, eds., *Exploring Human Development*. Boston: Allyn and Bacon, Inc., 1972. From *Phi Delta Kappan*, Vol. 47, No. 2, 79–84, 1965.

OTTO, HERBERT A., "The Minerva Experience: Initial Report," in J. F. T. Bugenthal, ed., *Challenges of Humanistic Psychology*. New York: McGraw-Hill Book Company, 1967.

OTTO, HERBERT A., "New Light on Human Potential," in H. W. Bernard and W. C. Huckins, eds., *Exploring Human Development*. Boston: Allyn and Bacon, Inc., 1972. From *Saturday Review*, Vol. 52, No. 51, 14–17, December 20, 1969.

PANG, HENRY, "Undistinguished School Experiences of Distinguished Persons," in H. W. Bernard and W. C. Huckins, eds., *Psychosocial Dynamics of Effective Behavior*. Boston: Holbrook Press, Inc., 1971. From *Adolescence*, 3, pp. 319–326, 1968.

PARNES, SIDNEY J., "Creativity: Developing Human Potential," *Journal of Creative Behavior*, Vol. 5, No. 1, 19–36, 1971.

PATTERSON, G. R., "A Learning Theory Approach to the Treatment of a School Phobic Child," in L. P. Ullman and L. Krasner, eds., *Case Studies in Behavior Modification*. New York: Holt, Rinehart and Winston, Inc., 1965.

PAVAN, BARBARA N., "Good News: Research on the Nongraded Elementary School," *Elementary School Journal*, 73, pp. 333–342, 1973.

PELTIER, GARY L., "See Differences in the School: Problem and Proposed Solution," in H. W. Bernard and W. C. Huckins, eds., *Exploring Human Development*. Boston: Allyn and Bacon, Inc., 1972. From *Phi Delta Kappan*, 50, pp. 182–185, 1968.

PENFIELD, WILDER, "The Uncommitted Cortex, the Child's Changing Brain," in H. W. Bernard and W. C. Huckins, eds., *Exploring Human Development*. Boston: Allyn and Bacon, Inc., 1972. From *Atlantic*, Vol. 214, No. 1, 77–81, July, 1964.

PERLMAN, HELEN H., *Persona—Social Role and Personality*. Chicago: University of Chicago Press, 1968.

PERLS, FREDERICK, *Ego, Hunger and Aggression*. London, England: George Allen and Unwin, 1947.

PERLS, FREDERICK, R. HEFFERLINE, and P. GOODMAN, *Gestalt Therapy*. New York: Julian Press, 1951.

PIERSON, GEORGE A., *An Evaluation: Counselor Education in Regular Session Institutes*. Washington, D. C.: U. S. Office of Health, Education, and Welfare, 1965.

PILEGGI, NICHOLAS, "Revolutionaries Who Have to Be Home by 7:30," *Phi Delta Kappan*, 50, pp. 561–566, 1969.

PITTS, FERRIS N., JR., "The Biochemistry of Anxiety," *Scientific American*, Vol. 220, No. 2, 69–75, February, 1969.

PLANCK, M., *The New Science*. New York: Meridian Books, Inc., 1959.

PRESSEY, SIDNEY L., "A Machine for Automatic Teaching of Drill Material," *School and Society*, 25, pp. 549–552, 1927.

"Prison Jaycees: Forging the Missing Link," *Manpower*, Vol. 4, No. 3, 15–19, March, 1972.

RANK, OTTO, *Trauma of Birth*. New York: Harcourt, Brace and Jovanovich, Inc., 1924.

REDLICH, F. C., and A. B. HOLLINGSHEAD, *Social Class and Mental Illness*. New York: John Wiley and Sons, Inc., 1958.

RIESMAN, DAVID, *The Lonely Crowd*. New Haven, Conn.: Yale University Press, 1950.

RIESMAN, DAVID, interviewed by T. George Harris, "The Young Are Captives of Each Other," *Psychology Today*, Vol. 3, No. 5, 28–31, October, 1969.

RIESSMAN, FRANK, "The Lessons of Poverty," in H. W. Bernard and W. C. Huckins, eds., *Exploring Human Development*. Boston: Allyn and Bacon, Inc., 1972. From *American Education*, Vol. 1, No. 2, 21–23, February, 1965.

RIST, RAY C., "Student Social Class and Teacher Expectancy: The Self-Fulfilling Prophecy in Ghetto Education," *Harvard Educational Review*, 40, pp. 411–451, 1970.

ROE, ANN, "Personality Structure and Occupational Behavior," in H. Borow, ed., *Man in a World at Work*. Boston: Houghton Mifflin Company, 1964.

ROGERS, CARL R., *Client Centered Therapy*. Boston: Houghton Mifflin Company, 1951.

ROGERS, CARL R., *Counseling and Psychotherapy*. Boston: Houghton Mifflin Company, 1942.

ROGERS, CARL R., *Freedom to Learn*. Columbus, Ohio: Charles E. Merrill Publishing Company, 1969.

ROGERS, CARL R., "Interpersonal Relationships: U. S. A. 2000," in H. W. Bernard and W. C. Huckins, eds., *Psychosocial Dynamics of Effective Behavior*. Boston: Holbrook Press, Inc., 1971. From *Journal of Applied Behavioral Sciences*, Vol. 4, No. 3, 265–280, 1968.

ROGERS, CARL R., "The Necessary and Sufficient Conditions of Therapeutic Personality Change," in B. N. Ard, Jr., ed., *Counseling and Psychotherapy*. Palo Alto, Calif.: Science and Behavior Books, 1966.

ROGERS, CARL R., *On Becoming a Person*. Boston: Houghton Mifflin Company, 1961.

ROGERS, CARL R., "The Process of the Basic Encounter Group," LaJolla, Calif.: Western Behavioral Sciences Institute (mimeographed), no date.

RORSCHACH, HERMANN, *Psychodiagnostik*. Bern: Hans Huber, 1942.

ROSENTHAL, ROBERT, AND LENORE JACOBSON, *Pygmalion in the Classroom*. New York: Holt, Rinehart and Winston, Inc., 1968.

ROSENWALD, GEORGE C., "The Thematic Apperception Test," in A. I. Rabin, ed., *Projective Techniques in Personality Assessment.* New York: Springer Publishing Company, Inc., 1968.

ROSENZWEIG, MARK R., and ARNOLD L. LEIMAN, "Brain Functions," in P. R. Farnsworth and others, eds., *Annual Review of Psychology*, Vol. 19. Palo Alto, Calif.: Annual Reviews, Inc., 1968.

ROSS, WALTER S., "Do You Know What Happens When You Smoke?" *Reader's Digest*, Vol. 101, No. 603, 121–125, July, 1972.

ROTHNEY, JOHN W. M., PAUL J. DANIELSON, and ROBERT A. HEIMANN, *Measurement for Guidance.* New York: Harper and Row, Publishers, 1959.

ROY, RUSTUM, and DELLA ROY, "Is Monogamy Outdated?" *The Humanist*, Vol. 30, No. 2, pp. 19–26, 1970.

ROYCE, JOSEPH R., *The Encapsulated Man.* Princeton, New Jersey: D. Van Nostrand Company, Inc., 1964.

RUSSO, MICHAEL, "14 Million Vocational Students by 1975," *American Education*, Vol. 5, No. 3, 10–11, 1969.

SAMLER, JOSEPH, "Occupational Exploration in Counseling: A Proposed Re-orientation," in H. Borow, ed., *Man in a World at Work.* Boston: Houghton Mifflin Company, 1964.

SAMOVAR, LARRY A., *et al.*, "A Survey of Adult Communication Activities," *Journal of Communication*, 19, pp. 301–307, 1969.

SARGENT, S. STANSFELD, "Humanistic Methodology in Personality and Social Psychology," in J. F. T. Bugenthal, ed., *Challenges of Humanistic Psychology.* New York: McGraw-Hill Book Company, 1967.

SCARR, SANDRA, "The Inheritance of Sociability," *American Psychologist*, 20, p. 524 (abstract), 1965.

SCHOFIELD, WILLIAM, *Psychotherapy: The Purchase of Friendship.* Englewood Cliffs, N. J.: Prentice-Hall, Inc., 1964.

SCHRAG, PETER, "The Forgotten American," *Harper's Magazine*, Vol. 239, No. 1431, 27–34, 1969.

SEXTON, PATRICIA C., *Education and Income.* New York: The Viking Press, Inc., 1961.

SHELDON, W. H., C. W. DUPERTUIS, and E. McDERMOTT, *Atlas of Men: A Guide for Somatotyping the Adult Male of All Ages.* New York: Harper and Row, Publishers, 1954.

SHELDON, W. H., and S. S. STEVENS, *The Varieties of Temperament: A Psychology of Constitutional Differences.* New York: Harper and Row, Publishers, 1942.

SHERIF, MUZAFER, AND CAROLYN W. SHERIF, *Reference Groups: Explorations into Conformity and Deviation of Adolescents.* New York: Harper and Row, Publishers, 1964.

SHERMAN, A. ROBERT, *Behavior Modification: Theory and Practice.* Monterey, Calif.: Brooks/Cole Publishing Company, 1973.

SHOSTROM, EVERETT L., "Group Therapy: Let the Buyer Beware," *Psychology Today*, Vol. 2, No. 12, 36–40, May, 1969.

SHOSTROM, EVERETT L., *Man the Manipulator.* Nashville, Tenn.: Abingdon Press, 1967.

SIGEL, IRVING E., "Review of *Carmichael's Manual of Child Psychology* by Paul Mussen," *American Educational Research Journal*, 9, pp. 337–342, Spring, 1972.

SIMON, SIDNEY, "Grades Must Go," *School Review*, 78, pp. 397–402, 1970.

SKINNER, B. F., *Beyond Freedom and Dignity.* New York: Alfred A. Knopf, Inc., 1971.

SKINNER, B. F., "Freedom and the Control of Men," *American Scholar*, 25, pp. 47–65, Winter, 1955–56.

SKINNER, B. F., *Science and Human Behavior*. New York: The Macmillan Company, 1953.

SKINNER, B. F., "The Science of Learning and the Art of Teaching," *Harvard Educational Review*, 24, pp. 86–87, 1954.

SKINNER, B. F., *Walden Two*. New York: The Macmillan Company, 1948.

SMITH, LOUIS M., and PAUL F. KLEINE, "The Adolescent and His Society," *Review of Educational Research*, 36, pp. 424–436, 1966.

SNYGG, DONALD, "A Cognitive Field Theory of Learning," in W. B. Waetjen and R. R. Leeper, eds., *Learning and Mental Health in the School*. Washington, D. C.: Association for Supervision and Curriculum Development, NEA, 1966.

SONTAG, LESTER W., "Implications of Fetal Behavior and Environment for Adult Personalities," in H. W. Bernard and W. C. Huckins, eds., *Exploring Human Development*. Boston: Allyn and Bacon, Inc., 1972. From *Annals of the New York Academy of Science*, 134, pp. 782–786, 1966.

SONTAG, LESTER W., "Somatopsychics of Personality and Body Function," *Vita Humana*, 6, pp. 1–10, 1963.

SPITZ, R. A., and K. WOLF, "Anaclitic Depression," *Psychoanalytic Studies of the Child*, 2, pp. 313–342, 1946.

STAFFIERI, J. ROBERT, "A Study of Social Stereotype of Body Image in Children," in H. W. Bernard and W. C. Huckins, eds., *Exploring Human Development*. Boston: Allyn and Bacon, Inc., 1972.

STAGNER, ROSS, *Psychology of Personality*, Third Edition. New York: McGraw-Hill Book Company, 1961.

STENT, GUNTHER S., "DNA," *Daedalus*, Vol. 99, No. 4, 909–937, 1970.

STERN, CURT, "The Continuity of Genetics," *Daedalus*, Vol. 99, No. 4, 882–907, 1970.

STEWART, NAOMI, "A. G. C. T. Scores of Army Personnel Grouped by Occupations," *Occupations*, 26, pp. 5–41, 1947.

STRAUSS, SAMUEL, "Looking Backward at Future Scientists," in H. W. Bernard, ed., *Readings in Adolescent Development*. Scranton, Pa.: International Textbook Company, 1969. From *The Science Teacher*, 24, pp. 385–387, 1957.

STRIKE, KENNETH A., "Explaining and Understanding: The Impact of Science on Our Concept of Man," *Philosophical Redirection of Educational Research*, in 71st Yearbook, National Society for the Study of Education, Part I. Chicago: University of Chicago Press, 1972.

STROM, ROBERT D., *Psychology for the Classroom*. Englewood Cliffs, New Jersey: Prentice-Hall, Inc., 1969.

SULLIVAN, EDWARD A., "Medical, Biological, and Chemical Methods of Shaping the Mind," *Phi Delta Kappan*, Vol. 53, No. 8, 483–486, April, 1972.

"A Summary for Parents and Students on the Subject of Teenage Drug Abuse," Mundelein, Illinois: Americana Interstate Corporation, 1971.

SUPER, D. E., *The Psychology of Careers*. New York: Harper and Row, Publishers, 1957.

SUPER, D. E., R. STARISHEVSKY, N. MATLIN, J. P. JORDAAN, *Career Development: Self-Concept Theory*. New York: College Entrance Examination Board, 1963.

SZASZ, THOMAS S., "The Second Sin," *Harper's*, Vol. 246, No. 1474, 68–73, March, 1973.

TAYLOR, CALVIN W., "Cultivating New Talents: A Way to Reach the Educationally Deprived," in H. W. Bernard and W. C. Huckins, eds., *Exploring*

Human Development. Boston: Allyn and Bacon, Inc., 1972. From *The Journal of Creative Behavior*, Vol. 2, No. 2, 83–90, Spring, 1968.

TAYLOR, GORDON R., *The Biological Time Bomb.* Cleveland: The World Publishing Company, 1968.

TELFER, MARY A., D. BAKER, G. R. CLARK, and C. E. RICHARDSON, "Incidence of Gross Chromosomal Errors Among Tall Criminal American Males," *Science*, 159, pp. 1249–1250, 1968.

TERMAN, LEWIS M., *Genetic Studies of Genius*, Vol. I. Stanford, Calif.: Stanford University Press, 1926.

TERMAN, LEWIS M., and MAUD A. MERRILL, *Stanford-Binet Intelligence Scale*, Manual, Third Edition. Boston: Houghton Mifflin Company, 1960.

TERMAN, LEWIS M., and MELITA H. ODEN, *The Gifted Child Grows Up.* Stanford, Calif.: Stanford University Press, 1947.

THEOBALD, ROBERT, "Cybernation, Unemployment and Freedom," in R. M. Hutchins and M. J. Adler, eds., *The Great Ideas Today Work, Wealth, and Leisure.* Chicago: Encyclopaedia Britannica, Inc., 1965.

THOMPSON, WILLIAM R., "Genetics and Personality," in E. Norbeck, D. Price-Williams, and W. M. McCord, eds., *The Study of Personality: An Interdisciplinary Appraisal.* New York: Holt, Rinehart and Winston, Inc., 1968.

THORNDIKE, E. L., *Educational Psychology: Briefer Course.* New York: Bureau of Publications, Teachers College, Columbia University, 1924.

THORNDIKE, E. L., *Fundamentals of Learning.* New York: Bureau of Publications, Teachers College, Columbia University, 1932.

THORNDIKE, EDWARD L., *The Psychology of Learning.* New York: Teachers College, Columbia University, 1913.

THORNDIKE, ROBERT L., "Book Review: Pygmalion in the Classroom," *Teachers College Record*, 70, pp. 805–807, 1969.

TITCHENER, BRADFORD, *A Primer of Psychology.* New York: The Macmillan Company, 1898.

TOFFLER, ALVIN, *Future Shock.* New York: Random House, (A Bantam Book), 1970.

TOMPKINS, SYLVAN S., "Homo Patiens: A Reexamination of the Concept of Drive," in J. F. T. Bugenthal, ed., *Challenges of Humanistic Psychology.* New York: McGraw-Hill Book Company, 1967.

TORRANCE, E. PAUL, *Guiding Creative Talent.* Englewood Cliffs, N. J.: Prentice-Hall, Inc., 1967.

TORREY, E. FULLER, "What Western Psychotherapists Can Learn from Witchdoctors," *American Journal of Orthopsychiatry*, Vol. 42, No. 1, 69–76, January, 1972.

TYLER, LEONA E., *Tests and Measurements.* Englewood Cliffs, New Jersey: Prentice-Hall, Inc., 1963.

The Use and Misuse of Drugs, (Publication No. 46). Washington, D. C.: Food and Drug Administration, 1968.

VALENTI, CAROL, "The Child: His Right to be Normal," *Saturday Review*, Vol. 51, No. 49, 75–78, December 7, 1968.

VELLAY, P., *Childbirth Without Pain.* New York: E. P. Dutton and Company, 1960.

VERNON, J., *Inside the Black Room.* New York: C. N. Potter, 1963.

WASSERMAN, SELMA, "The Open Classroom in Teacher Education, or Putting Your Money Where Your Mouth Is," *Childhood Education*, 49, pp. 295–301, 1973.

WATSON, JOHN B., *Behavior: An Introduction to Comparative Psychology.* New York: Henry Holt and Company, Inc., 1914.

WATSON, JOHN B., *Behaviorism.* New York: W. W. Norton and Company, Inc., 1930.

WATSON, JOHN B., *Psychology from the Standpoint of the Behaviorist.* Philadelphia: J. B. Lippincott Company, 1924.

WAUGH, LYNNE, and JOHN WAUGH, "Subduing the Dragons of Reading," *American Education*, Vol. 8, No. 1, 13–15, January/February, 1972.

WEISS, D. A., "Central Language Imbalance (cluttering): A Basic Problem of the Pathology of Communication," *American Journal of Orthopsychiatry*, 37, pp. 369–370, 1967.

WELLMAN, BETH L., "Iowa Studies on the Effects of School," *Intelligence: Its Nature and Nurture*, in National Society for the Study of Education, 39th Yearbook, Part II. Chicago: University of Chicago Press, 1940.

WELLMAN, BETH L., and E. L. PEGRAM, "Binet I. Q. Changes of Orphanage Preschool Children: A Re-analysis," *Journal of Genetic Psychology*, 65, pp. 239–263, 1944.

WESMAN, ALEXANDER G., "Intelligent Testing," *American Psychologist*, 23, pp. 267–274, 1968.

WHEELER, RAYMOND H., *The Science of Psychology*, Second Edition. New York: Thomas Y. Crowell Company, 1940.

WHITE, SHELDON H., "The Learning Theory Tradition and Child Psychology," in P. H. Mussen, ed., *Carmichael's Manual of Child Psychology*, Third Edition. New York: John Wiley and Sons, 1970.

WHITTEN, CHARLES, *et al.*, "Evidence That Growth Failure from Maternal Deprivation Is Secondary to Undereating," *Journal of the American Medical Association*, 209, pp. 1675–1682, 1969.

WILLIAMS, ROGER J., *Biochemical Individuality.* New York: John Wiley and Sons, Inc., 1956.

WILLIAMS, ROGER J., "The Biology of Behavior," in H. W. Bernard and W. C. Huckins, eds., *Exploring Human Development.* Boston: Allyn and Bacon, Inc., 1972. From *Saturday Review*, Vol. 54, No. 5, 17–19, January 30, 1971.

WILSON, JOHN ROWAN, *The Mind.* New York: Time-Life Books, 1969.

WOLPE, JOSEPH, *The Practice of Behavior Therapy.* New York: Pergamon Press, 1969.

WOLPE, J., *Psychotherapy by Reciprocal Inhibition.* Stanford, Calif.: Stanford University Press, 1958.

WOODWORTH, ROBERT S., *Contemporary Schools of Psychology.* New York: The Ronald Press Company, 1948.

WOODWORTH, ROBERT S., *Dynamic Psychology.* New York: Columbia University Press, 1918.

WRENN, C. GILBERT, "The Culturally Encapsulated Counselor," *Harvard Educational Review*, 32, pp. 444–449, 1962.

YAHRAES, HERBERT, *Narcotic Drug Addiction*, Publication No. 1021. Washington, D. C.: U. S. Department of Health, Education, and Welfare, 1965.

YARROW, LEON J., "Separation from Parents During Early Childhood," in M. L. Hoffman and L. W. Hoffman, eds., *Review of Child Development Research*, Vol. I. New York: Russell Sage Foundation, 1964.

Name Index

Subject Index